The Experience
of Research

MARTIN BLOOM

VIRGINIA COMMONWEALTH UNIVERSITY

The Experience of Research

MACMILLAN PUBLISHING COMPANY

NEW YORK

Collier Macmillian Publishers

LONDON

PRINTED IN THE UNITED STATES OF AMERICA

Macmillan Publishing Company
866 Third Avenue, New York, New York 10022

Collier Macmillan Canada, Inc.

Library of Congress Cataloging in Publication Data
Bloom, Martin.
  The experience of research.

  Bibliography: p.
  Includes index.
  1. Social sciences—Research. I. Title.
H62.B5855 1986   300′.72   85–295
ISBN 0–02–311040–6

Printing: 1 2 3 4 5 6 7 8   Year: 6 7 8 9 0 1 2 3 4 5

ISBN 0-02-311040-6

Preface

Like many other recent graduates with a doctoral degree, I was afflicted with a touch of omniscience, which provided me with unmerited confidence in accepting my first solid job offer—research associate at a private social-work agency dealing exclusively with the aged. I knew practically nothing—or certainly, nothing practical—about the aged, although on paper I was reasonably well qualified, having minored in human development, possessing a certificate in social work, and bearing a newly written dissertation in social psychology from a respectable university. Being flown to my job interview, dined at a fancy hotel, and driven around an exclusive residential area in the back seat of the executive director's convertible (while she and my future boss, the director of research, were talking about old times they had known) was heady stuff to me, and I accepted the job with great expectations. Needless to say, I did not buy a house in that exclusive neighborhood; and I rode the bus to work carrying my brown-bag lunches for the next seven years. But the richness of that experience with my colleagues at this social agency was to more than fulfill my expectations—in ways unimagined at that time.

Recognizing my own ignorance about the aged, I asked my boss what I might read to obtain a background for doing research on the aged. Expecting a list of learned references, I was quite surprised when she took a long look at me and suggested that I might start with Muriel Spark's novel *Memento Mori* (1958). Ever the optimist, I read the book. It is a good quasi-mystery story that involves a set of very elderly people engaging in some very human activities, overtly or covertly. The mysterious element is an unknown telephone caller who speaks to each of the principal characters, saying only one thing: "Remember you must die."

I recall enjoying the book, but I didn't find the revelation that I expected, whatever it was that I did expect. These very elderly people seemed all too human, even in their various states of physical and mental infirmity. I was a

v

little surprised to find some characters driving cars in their late eighties, or holding philosophical conversations—literary license, I thought (then). I mused at the preoccupation of some in reading the obituaries, making wills (and changing them as threats to their caretakers), and bearing up well under the misfortunes of others.

But where is the truth about the aged? From my graduate education, I had come to expect nice clear answers or at least, research programs directed toward discovering them. Spark's fictionalized account was amorphous. I recognized the artistic skill that interrelated the lives of these aged characters, but I couldn't get beyond the story, or outside it, to the elderly with whom I would be working. And yet, as I started my job, I found *Memento Mori* turning up in a variety of experiences: little things like the way some very elderly talk (slowly, but often with great intensity); the way they deal with pain, as in holding or balancing a newspaper with arthritic hands; and the props that supported their memories (especially photographs or small knickknacks whose significance was far beyond the value of the object itself).

And so began my education in research, evolving from arrogant academic postures and jargon to the compromises and stratagems of the real world. This book is a personal attempt to come to terms with both of the worlds that have been so much a part of my life, the academic and the pragmatic. It is also an "introduction to social research," a double introduction—to what research ought to be as well as to what it really is. In order to convey this double sense of research, I have chosen to use a double format throughout most of the book. The beginning of each chapter presents a narrative of my research experiences on one major study; following this, I present technical notes of various types. These technical notes include definitions of the terms I have used in the narrative, and they describe specific points and methodological issues in greater detail so that students will be able to use these notes if and when they engage in their own research studies. In short, the technical notes provide a brief set of discussions and operationalized instructions on how to think about and do research, whereas the narrative provides a continuous story, from the perspective of one insider, about how one study was, in fact, conducted. These technical notes are an introduction to the conduct of research; there are ample references to sources of further instruction on the fine points for the interested student.

This double format seems to be one way of giving the learner a sense of the two necessary ingredients without slighting one or the other. It also permits an uninterrupted presentation of one research project, while describing the large number of ingredients for conducting research, in approximately the order in which they appear in the research process. However, because the technical notes are discrete topics, the student will be able to find them by means of the Index whenever a specific topic is needed.

The double format may seem confusing at first, but once the reader captures the spirit of this arrangement, he or she will very likely find it more useful than conventional arrangements, because the format reflects the reality of his or her educational needs. In addition, I have provided in Appendix B, a list of the technical materials, which makes it possible to read this book as if it were a conventional introductory text on research. But my hope is that students will first read the narrative and then, as needed or as assigned, read the technical notes. I believe that this organization will make research more understandable as well as more appealing. I regret not a moment of my own struggles through the labyrinths of the university research experience, nor the equally mysterious paths through the community—its hospitals, social agencies, political structures, and diverse neighborhoods—that we had to travel to conduct our studies. Academic and pragmatic research offer very different types of experiences, and both are fully necessary to the conduct of research that holds promise of informing the helping professions.

This is why I have entitled this book *The Experience of Research.* I try to present my own experience as vividly as possible, while explaining the technical steps as clearly as possible. I hope the autobiographical feature will make the text more comprehensible, especially in illustrating the spirit of research. I think that the specific technical notes on nearly one hundred research topics, definitions, and operations furnishes more clarity than if they were embedded in a longer text. Thus, by giving the reader more options on how to experience research, I seek to build the bridge between the academic and the pragmatic worlds of research for the helping professions.

I recognize that there is an unusually large proportion of "story" as compared with the technical details that most research books stress. This format is intentional. I believe that a thorough understanding of research can come only through a lengthy direct experience in the field or laboratory. This book attempts to simulate one type of research experience by conveying as many aspects of the big picture as of small details, of the research organization as of the human beings involved, of the provocative as of the esoteric. I frankly hope to make this experience of research enjoyable, perhaps exciting in places; learning research does not have to be painful. But make no mistake: The "story" contains a considerable number of the technical aspects of doing research, but these aspects appear in human guises.

Thus, short of actually doing research in a real-world setting for a substantial period of time under the guidance of a first-rate scientist like Margaret Blenkner, this type of presentation may be the closest approximation that I can share with my students and yours.

ACKNOWLEDGMENTS

It is easy to list names of persons who provided information or support that aided the writing of this book, but it is difficult to express the gratitude that I feel in thinking back to the many experiences of research that I shared with them. I offer this whole book as a testament to my deep appreciation:

To my colleagues on the Benjamin Rose Institute staff: Margaret Blenkner, Ruth Weber, Margaret Nielsen, Edna Wasser, Marcella Farrar, Elliot Markus, Rosalyn Hurwitz, Helen Cole, Gertrude Frires, Helen Hanson, Vivian South, Charlotte Grimm, Odelia Robinson, Helen Beggs, Jane Lenahan, Margaret McGuire, Melanie Olm, Patricia Bruce, Dorothy Schur, Gary Meek, and Margaret Lenahan.

To the 164 elderly participants in the Protective Services Project whose fight for life becomes increasingly meaningful and intelligible to me as my own extended family, friends, and I grow older.

To Barbara Silverstone, executive director of the Benjamin Rose Institute at the time of the writing of this book.

To the several generations of students who suffered through various versions of this story in my research classes. In particular, I would like to acknowledge some students from whom I learned more than usual: Pamela Darr, Andrea Levinson, Susan Connor, Carolyn Badila, Terry Davis, Alan Gross, and Nancy Vosler. To the deans who supported my explorations: (the late) Richard Lawrence, Shanti Khinduka, Elaine Rothenberg, and Grace Harris.

To the helpful critical readers of various drafts of the manuscript: Edward Mullins, Aaron Rosenblatt, Jacob Hurwitz, Joel Fischer, and Margaret Nielsen. They are, of course, blameless for the way the book finally emerged.

To my diligent editor, James D. Anker, and to the able production staff at Macmillan, particularly my production editor, Wendy Polhemus.

And to my family. I have always expressed my love and appreciation of my family in these public acknowledgments, but this time it is special. Much of this book was written on a personal computer at home, for which I owe my education and encouragement to my incomparable sons, Bard and Laird, and to my wife, Lynn, whose life time sharing arrangements with me have been a Glorious Experience.

M. B.

Contents

CONTENTS

Introduction
to the Reader

Do you recall seeing *The Wizard of Oz* for the first time? Dorothy (Judy Garland) is living a gray existence in Kansas, tormented by a nasty teacher, and wistfully seeking Something. Her aunt and uncle, with whom she (mysteriously) lives, and the kindly farm hands try to make her comfortable, but Something is missing. The first part of the film is in black and white, but mostly gray. Then comes the tornado, and everything is topsy-turvy; when it ends, Dorothy opens the door of her house and walks into a world of her dreams, in technicolor, complete with good friends and terrible enemies and a great Challenge. Through many adventures, Dorothy and her friends learn a fundamental lesson—that whether one is seeking courage or becoming aware of the importance of love even in dull surroundings, the important thing is that all learning and accomplishment require a personally involving experience.

Some people may see research as a gray, dull experience when they are forced to live with it for a semester or two. Perhaps they are right, as perceiving that way makes it so. However, I would like to offer this book as a small tornado to those people, to open the door to the beautiful and wondrous world of research, by personally involving readers in the experience.

The experience of research means many things. First, I present research as an experience from the perspective of a team of researchers on one large-scale project. I was a member of that team, and so, in part, this experience of research has an autobiographical element. I have made a number of modifications for the sake of confidentiality, and I have written portions of the book so as to capture some of the critical moments, the humorous turns of events, and a few of the dangers of doing research. (No teacher of research ever warned me that one of my interviewees would be a gun-carrying, spaced-out psychotic!) Thus, as you read the following chapters, you will be following the stages of development of a single real project from its inception to its conclusion—and its aftermath (a storm of critical reactions from other researchers and practitioners) as well. This one project was complicated enough so that almost all of the issues concerning classical research were raised along the way, but because it was one project, you will become familiar with it, as if it were your own . . . experience.

Second, in order to maintain the story line, I have organized this text in a different way. At the beginning of each chapter, I present the experience of research as I perceived it—one continuous story. Following this narrative portion, I present a number of technical notes that augment and explain some of the concepts and ideas that emerge from the story. Keeping these two aspects separate takes a bit of getting used to, but I think you can share the experience of this research project more fully without the interruption of the technical details. I suggest, therefore, that you read the narrative section first, and then go on to pick up whatever technical notes you need (or are assigned) afterward.

Each technical note is self-contained. Therefore, if you come across an unfamiliar concept, chances are that it is explained in a technical note somewhere in the book—most likely in the chapter where the concept first occurs. Simply check out the subject index, and read the technical note wherever it appears. (Terms that are discussed in technical notes are presented in italic type for easy recognition.)

As you move back and forth between the narrative and the technical notes, I hope that this personally involving experience will become your linguistic technicolor. I hope that this double format will produce a qualitatively new entity: your experience with the research study in vivid, living terms. That's the intention. Let's see whether it works for you.

CHAPTER 1

Dramatis Personae

Overview

This chapter introduces 5 participants in the focal study of this book whose situations and responses to questionnaires are used throughout the book to represent the 164 participants in the Benjamin Rose Institute (BRI) Protective Services Project. In addition, the research staff, the practice staff, and the agency itself are introduced because their unique characteristics colored the project and its findings, and because they represent an important part of what research is really like, as contrasted with the somewhat sterile academic formulas of typical "textbook" presentations. The format separates a narrative description of this one study from a series of technical notes that explain aspects of the research process in general, as indicated in the brief outline of the topics discussed that introduces each chapter.

Narrative Section

Introduction to Miss Eleanor Edel, an older person in need of protective services, and to her unexpected death, which raised a serious question for research and practice

Five participants in the Protective Services Project

The Project Staff: Researchers, Practitioners, and Support Staff

        The Director of Research, Margaret Blenkner

        The Structure of the Project

        The Practice Staff

        The Research Staff

        The Support Staff

The Agency and the Community

        The Benjamin Rose Institute, Cleveland, Ohio, a social work agency dealing exclusively with the aged, is described

Technical Notes Section

The Narrative

INTRODUCTION TO MISS ELEANOR EDEL

On a beautiful fall morning in 1963, Miss Edel finally responded to the insistent ringing of her door bell. She peered cautiously through a crack in the doorway and saw a well-dressed, smiling young man, who greeted her, told her he would like to take a few minutes of her time for a survey on how older people felt about their current life situation, their health, and their interests, so that social agencies might better provide relevant services. Miss Edel, all four feet ten inches of her, aged eighty-two, with snow white hair, opened the door a bit wider, stood back, paused only an instant before telling the interviewer to go to hell, and slammed the door shut.

Such was my first meeting with Miss Edel, a none-too-eager participant in the Benjamin Rose Institute (BRI) Protective Services Project. Undaunted, I persevered, rang the door bell many more times, and waited patiently. As I waited, I became aware of how dirty this portion of the hall in this old public-housing unit was, and of a distinctly unpleasant odor; I wondered whether it came from Miss Edel's apartment.

Again, she cautiously opened the door, and before she had time to reflect on my origins or could again suggest my future destination, I asked her a question about her health—one of the short-form items to be asked, if possible, when the entire long form of the interview could not be used for one reason or another. It was a long-shot question, but apparently it hit close to the mark because Miss Edel turned from casting aspersions on me and began instead to criticize her neighbors, who were making her ill. I asked for more details about her comments and was able to direct the conversation to a few other items on the short-form interview form (see Chapter 5). I tried to appear relaxed and motionless so as not to frighten her; I wondered whether she saw through my own tensions of that moment. I did not attempt to write down any of the answers in front of her, but they were so dramatic that I can still hear her responses to this day—some two decades later.

My interest in her comments was genuine: I was truly amazed at her story. (This interview came early in the project and I had a lot to learn about protective situations as well as about how to conduct a good interview.) My probes for additional details unleashed a flood of words and feelings. Miss Edel had outlived kith and kin and had of late become the victim of attack and abuse by her neighbors and by strangers. Even today, she told me, there were voices coming out of her stove. "What did they say?" I ingenuously, although unprofessionally, blurted out. Miss Edel looked me in the eye, squinted, and once again told me to go to hell as she slammed the door and locked it.

I stood there, looking at the closed door for a minute, trying to figure out what a Good Research Interviewer ought to do now. I didn't recall anything in my four years of research work prior to my present job that gave any clear indication of what to do. So I returned to my car, filled out the short form of the initial research interview in as much detail as I could recall, and returned to the office.

If fact, I saw Miss Edel two more times, at the three-month and the six-month interview intervals. She never recognized me from one time to the next, but I could detect some major changes in her behavior, as I will describe shortly. Miss Edel was a participant, possibly a somewhat unwilling one, in a demonstration study of older persons in need of protective services that was conducted in Cleveland between 1963 and 1968. By chance—literally, by random selection—she was chosen to be in the experimental group; therefore, after my initial, although foreshortened, interview with her, which provided some baseline information against which later events and behaviors could be compared, an experienced social worker visited Miss Edel and offered assistance, friendship, and tangible aid to her in her struggle against the world of foes, real and imagined.

The social worked managed, after some tries, to gain entry into Miss Edel's apartment and, to some degree, into Miss Edel's confidence. The worker provided some forms of assistance, although Miss Edel never said that she wanted any. And indeed, Miss Edel strongly resisted some of the services that the worker wanted to provide—a point to which I will return shortly.

We will meet Miss Edel again on these pages because she represents a number of older persons who participated in the BRI Protective Services Project. The names I use are fictitious, but the events described happened to a particular person. I have also disguised her identity by adding features from other participants in the study, so that no one individual may be identified in the composite portrait. I must emphasize that even though I use common traits in these illustrations, it is the diversity and the individuality of the participants in the study that stand out most in my mind. I know that science seeks uniformities among many diverse instances, but it is hard to forget these "diverse instances" when you have spent several minutes staring at a closed door in the hallway of a run-down public-housing project, having talked with a tiny ball of fire who hears voices from her oven.

But let me finish telling her story, so far as I know it from the interviews I had with her. Three months later, I again ran her door bell. She opened the door with the same caution as before but seemed less fearful and far less verbally abusive. The neighbors were still bothering her, but there was this woman who kept coming around, and maybe she was making the neighbors be less bothersome. (That must have been the social worker, although Miss Edel couldn't remember much about her.) There was no mention of voices from the stove.

The sixth-month interview was about like the third-month one, but the fire seemed to have gone out of Miss Edel. She was no longer at her apartment, having been relocated to an adult care facility that was privately run—a homey and carefully protected environment where Miss Edel got good food, plenty of TLC, and protection from some of the hazards in her life. But in spite of these pleasant surroundings, Miss Edel complained about being "hijacked" from her own apartment and was feeling depressed.

I never saw her again. She died several months later, amid clean, pleasant surroundings. There was a medical cause listed on her death certificate—she had some chronic ailments to be sure. But there didn't seem to be any reason for her death at that time. Everything seemed to be going along so well. She had almost given up her abusive language, I was told, and was eating enough, although not with any enthusiasm. And she had received all the medical and personal attention that any relocated eighty-two-year-old would need. But she had the audacity to die anyway. A death in delightful surroundings.

Sounds like the beginning of a mystery story. A fabulously wealthy old lady mysteriously dies of a minor ailment in a foreign country. Who did it? No one "did it" in that sense—a murder in cold blood for money, revenge, jealousy, or whatever. For one thing, Miss Edel was poor, and for another, there was precious little about her life situation that anyone might be jealous of. But the life tables that are used in predicting the life chances of persons with various demographic characteristics (age, sex, and the like) suggested that a person like Miss Edel might have lived at least several years longer on the average. Helping professionals familiar with the aged who knew about Miss Edel were also surprised by her death; everything seemed to be under control in this case. But she died anyway, and that death, combined with the equally puzzling deaths of other participants in the experimental program, led many to wonder about the mysteries of life and death among the aged who needed protective services— and who got them.

Among the most curious about this phenomenon were the staff of the Protective Project. It was like the story of a detective who, after a thorough examination of the evidence surrounding a mysterious death, found that the only clues to the identity of the murderer pointed to . . . himself. Don't take this analogy literally. Ours was not some television story that would all become clear in the twenty-five minutes allotted to the detective. This kind of death is real, and the events involved are extremely complex. It took nearly a million dollars and five years of work to sort out even some of the threads to this mystery. The major point I want to make at this moment is only that the staff of this research project were very much a part of the story that they were helping to write. I believe that this is true of any social research of significance, particularly research that studies the process and outcome of professional helping.*

FIVE PARTICIPANTS IN THE PROTECTIVE SERVICES PROJECT

We have literally caught only a glimpse of Miss Edel, one of 164 elderly residents of Cleveland who were in the BRI Protective Services Project.** It will be helpful to be able to refer also to some other participants in this study in order to provide a sense of what it was like to conduct a demonstration project with people in need of protective services—that is, to do research at the same time

---

* At this point in the narrative, I want to call your attention to Technical Note 1.1 (p. 19), on *scientific definitions.* This is an important topic that covers types of definitions and illustrates the process we went through to arrive at them. But because this discussion would distract attention from the narrative if it were inserted here, I've put it in the "Technical Notes" section—as I have other topics. Each time, I indicate, by means of a footnote, that there is a technical discussion that relates to a point in the narrative.

** Technical Note 1.2 (p. 22) discusses the *demographic characteristics* of the sample and their relationship to comparable national figures. Demographic information, like age, sex, and race, represents a shorthand way of indicating the salient common features of a group of persons. This information is very helpful, even if it doesn't tell us anything about the unique aspects of each of those persons.

that one is experimenting with treatment methods. However, do not take this description of five people as a description of older persons in general. Helping professionals, who largely see the most ill, dysfunctioning, or hopeless cases, inappropriately generalize these to the elderly as a group. For a more nearly accurate description of the strengths of older persons, as well as their limitations, see Butler and Lewis, (1983).*

In the following five sketches, I simply illustrate the complexity and pathos that must be multiplied more than thirty times to get a sense of the sample of people in this study. These five participants are composites of a number of people in the study. I am not exaggerating the problems; I am merely disguising the players in this life drama.

The first three persons to be introduced became participants in the experimental treatment group, and the last two people were in the control group that received only what they might ordinarily receive from the community. The Benjamin Rose Institute did not give any services to people in the control group for the duration of the project year during which any one case was involved.**

Miss Edel was eighty-two years old at the beginning of the project, a long-retired salesperson and a lifelong resident of this city. You have been introduced to her in the preceding pages.

Mrs. Edwards was an eighty-seven-year-old woman who lived with her sixty-seven-year-old son. She was very confused and in poor health, which was made worse by the home remedies that the son forced on her, such as giving her enemas using mouthwash as the solution. She was inconsistent: on the one hand, she asked strangers (such as the research interviewer) to get her to a hospital or nursing home, and later she denied this, especially if her son was near. There was a strong element of rational fear in this regard, as her son, Jonas, was mentally unstable, made hostile comments and gestures, and was said to carry a gun. Mrs. Edwards was the primary participant in this situation, but the social worker necessarily had to make plans in regard to Jonas as well. He was an unemployed day laborer who took occasional odd jobs, leaving his mother alone for long periods of time without adequate care. He occasionally talked in strings of words that were meaningless to others. There was a neighbor who helped with the shopping and visited Mrs. Edwards on occasion. She reported that Mrs. Edwards frequently cried, but that it was rarely clear what had provoked her tears.

Mr. Emery was a seventy-six-year-old retired lawyer who was unable to care for his food (his diet was inadequate and his meal preparations irregular and insufficient) or his home (his apartment was filthy, and insects roamed the floors as if they were holding a convention). Mr. Emery was exceedingly friendly and very verbose, as a way of trying to hold on to a visitor who might offer any source of help. He had written novels, four of them, in the indefinite past, all unpublished and sitting in boxes on his bookshelves. He was quite hard of hearing and communication was difficult between him and the interviewer, so he simply read long snatches of his novels and talked at length on

* Complete source data for citations in this text can be found in the Bibliography.

** Technical Note 1.3 (p. 23) discusses *experimental and control groups* and places them in the context of a *basic group-research design*. This research design tells us how we intend to get at valid information about our basic question: Does our experimental intervention produce the desired results? Because research designs involve many issues, I discuss them in other technical notes as well.

whatever he thought it was that the interviewer had asked him. His medical situation was serious and became further complicated because he forgot to take his medications. But it may also have been that he was living on such a small income that he was stretching the medications rather than taking them in the recommended doses. He had a very good friend living nearby, although the friend wasn't able to do much to help Mr. Emery.

Mrs. Caraway was a seventy-four-year-old widow who had three adult-aged children living in the city—but they would have nothing to do with her. She had abused and neglected them as infants, and they had been removed from her and placed in foster homes, where they had remained in touch with each other. They refused to talk with the interviewer about their mother. Mrs. Caraway had a serious medical problem (diabetes) that was completely out of control; she ate candy constantly, spending a significant portion of her limited budget on sweets. Her illness did not interfere with what appeared to have been a lifelong pattern of hostility toward others: she was in constant trouble in her neighborhood because of all sorts of annoying and threatening behavior (like shaking sticks and clubs at passersby).

Miss Colson was a classic hoarder. Her house was filled from wall to wall, and from floor to ceiling, with boxes and bags stuffed with items of clothing—some still in their original wrappers—and junk possibly taken out of refuse bins. Her several dogs were locked in the apartment and were never taken outside—with the inevitable olfactory consequences. She had no friends, although the local minister expressed some concern about her condition. He had tried to get some church volunteers to visit her, but they never achieved any sustained contact. Miss Colson was suspicious of everyone, but she was very intelligent; in fact, she had one of the highest scores on the brief intelligence test given to all participants. She was very assertive with regard to her legal rights, and so no one had been able to get her to do anything she didn't want to do. She was also forgetful; there was evidence of fire damage in the kitchen. She was eighty-one years old at the beginning of the project.

I refer to these participants throughout the book, not only to add a bit of flesh to the skeleton of research, but also to provide a basis for discussing the varieties of services that were provided in the Protective Project: medical, legal (including guardianship), financial, personal, interpersonal, and social.

Each of these people was referred to the project staff by one of thirteen participating agencies in the city. These agencies were selected because they frequently encountered people in need of protective services even though they were not able to provide such services. The participating agencies were in the fields of health, housing, counseling–referral–information services, and economic maintenance. For example, the metropolitan housing authority was a participating agency. It coordinated a number of public housing projects where many elderly lived. Some of their most difficult clients—people who caused trouble to others or appeared to be a danger to themselves—were clearly in need of protective services, but the housing-authority staff were in no way able to provide this type and extent of services. And so they were only too happy to cooperate with us in hopes that someone would help these difficult residents. I discuss later the constraints that were placed by the research staff on the participating agencies, such as the fact that a random selection process determined whether a person went into our experimental group or our control group. These constraints tended to dampen the enthusiasm of the participating agency personnel when they learned that some of their clients were not to be a part of the experimental service program.* But except for a few particularly obtuse agency workers who never understood the necessity and usefulness of random assignment of clients, most bore up remarkably well under the agony and ecstasy of research with protective service participants.

THE PROJECT STAFF: RESEARCHERS, PRACTITIONERS, AND SUPPORT STAFF

I believe that it is important to know something about the staff who were involved in this demonstration project because their personal styles, strengths, and limitations vitally affected the construction and the implementation of the research. Ordinarily one does not hear anything about the researchers. They are intentionally kept as anonymous ciphers who make Olympian choices with the best available knowledge and the most honorable judgments—in the service of society and science, never for reasons of personal interest or advancement. Having known some of these anonymous ciphers, I would suggest that they are no more and no less trustworthy than the average businessperson. But the content of research involves many pressures, from funding agencies and from colleagues who are "getting ahead," as well as from an understandable self-interest in seeing in research the results what one hopes to see. The context of research is often an isolated one; the researcher is on her or his own during the research project, even though its eventual presentation to the scientific community will make it possible for others to critique it and to repeat the study. (On rare occasions, studies are replicated.) The point is that there are many pressures to make something out of a study that may not be there, at least in the degree that it is claimed to be. It is very difficult to be clear in the presentation of the process and the results, to be fair in interpreting what is present and what is absent, and to be objective in one's analysis of the current study and its implications for other people in other contexts.

For these reasons, I think it is important to become acquainted with the researchers and the practitioners in this project, so that you can weigh the presentation of the results against your sense of their strengths and their limitations, their biases and their objectivity. This is a more subtle reason than the gross malfeasance that is reported on occasion. (As I was writing this chapter, I found an article in the *Washington Post* about an investigation by the U.S. Health and Human Services Department in which doctors were alleged to be getting kickbacks from certain manufacturers for using their heart pacemakers, as well as for performing thousands of unnecessary operations that might be costing the Medicare system as much as $200 million a year—(Philip J. Hilts, "Probe Finds Kickbacks on Pacemakers," *Washington Post,* September 5, 1982, p. A1, A18).

---

* Technical Note 1.4 (p. 26) describes the broad *types of research—laboratory/research field experiments,* and *field demonstrations*—and characterizes the strengths and limitations of each. This book focuses on one type, but the lessons we learn here are easily transferable to the other types of research as well, even though they do have unique problems and possibilities.

Researchers, like others, may come to have a vested interest in their own work so that the results come to bear on them as persons rather than as scientists, in which case they lose their perspective and become self-serving, rather than serving science and society. It is one thing to have faith in the goodwill and honesty of scientists; we have this almost all of the time when we read the dozens of papers appearing in our professional journals—because we do not and probably cannot assess their authors as persons. But what goes into producing a good and honest scientist? When we stop to think about this question in the context of the isolation in which most research is produced, we may recognize the human dimension of our social knowledge—and the associated frailties.

The Director of Research

As a case in point, I want to provide some introduction to the people who worked together for about seven years on the studies discussed in this book. The director of research, Margaret Blenkner, died a few years after the completion of the BRI studies. She completely dominated these studies, and so it is important to understand something of her style and interests in this research. Dr. Blenkner will be identified by name throughout this book. However, I have decided that, lest this book read like Tolstoy's *War and Peace,* in which it is necessary to have several pages at the beginning listing the characters and their principal roles, it will be sufficient to talk about "the social worker" and "the research interviewer," as the people in each of these categories shared some important attributes that were central to their roles. I do, on occasion, mention personal factors that produced some unintended differences among the social workers and among the researchers. Likewise, I refer to the secretarial staff and other service staff people in a general sense, as needed, with an occasional excursion into individual factors that may have had some important effect on part of the research process.

Dr. Margaret Blenkner, Director of Research at the Benjamin Rose Institute throughout the duration of the Protective Services Project (and also during some later research projects), was no pussycat, although she dearly loved cats and was devoted to her own two. She was a powerful and dominating woman who stood out at any meeting or forum by the sheer exercise of her personality. She was an extremely intelligent and witty individual who had devoted her life to social work and gerontology, and to research on which a valid and effective practice could be built.

However, Margaret Blenkner also had one of the most acerbic personalities in the profession, the sharpest tongue, the swiftest retort, and a highly critical disposition, coupled with a most scrupulous combination of scientific and humanitarian interests. I know some individuals in high professional circles who expressed their fear of having Dr. Blenkner come to their presentations at professional conferences because they knew she would tear their flimsy reports to shreds and castigate them for their weaseling manipulations and self-serving interpretations of their data. One researcher who knew her well described her as a cowboy with a gun on each hip and a belt of bullets, ready to shoot it out with anyone. She was "one tough hombre," as he put it.

But if Margaret Blenkner was hard on fellow scientists, she was perhaps even more strict with herself—and her staff. We were never allowed to skim

9

over anything; everything had to be in the open, double-checked for accuracy, and letter-perfect. We made our fair share of mistakes in the course of the study, as I discuss in due time, but it wasn't because there was any tolerance of error by the boss; some things just slipped by everyone, even Margaret Blenkner.

Dr. Blenkner, as she was known by most of the world, was a rugged empiricist. She had little trust in theories or concepts, although she contributed some insightful terms to the literature (for example, see her paper on "filial piety," Blenkner, 1965). Rather, her abiding love was for a pile of computer printouts on sensitive human attributes, health and illness, life and death. She would study the raw data for hours on end, playing first with one hunch on how to extract meaning from them, and then with another hunch. Galileo, among others of the first generation of modern scientists, understood fully that the meaning of the universe could be understood only in the language in which universal meanings were expressed, the language of mathematics. I believe that Margaret Blenkner fully understood this principle, at a time when social work had little interest in quantification, even in regard to the uniformities of complex human behavior. Some of her early papers grapple with the dilemmas of applying rigorous research methods to a soft and amorphous social-work practice in order to learn what, if anything, is effective. Thus, in personal style and professional orientation, she was on a collision course with her generation.

This description of Dr. Blenkner's personal style raises the interesting and unanswerable question about what directions the BRI Protective Services Project might have taken under another person's leadership. I want to speculate about this issue because it will help to make the point of the importance of the human factor in research on human behavior. I am certain that the Protective Project was a direct outgrowth of Dr. Blenkner's earlier research (as I will describe later), combined with some new questions that had emerged in the interim. The very choice of a complex, expensive, longitudinal study—in contrast to other possible ways of conducting research on this topic—also reflected her organizational ability and scope of mind, as well as her need to demonstrate to the world her abilities and perspective. A more modest person might have constructed a more modest proposal. She was a player of high stakes in a game whose stakes were intrinsically very high, and she knew it.

The Structure of the Project

The organizational structure of the research group is important to understand. With Dr. Blenkner at the top, there was an intentional split between the research and the practice divisions. She argued that good research calls for evaluation by people who are not themselves delivering the service, lest there be any bias in interpreting the results in favor of the practitioners. It was not possible to disguise the participants in the experimental group after the initial interview because the participants themselves often talked about "their social worker." Nor was it possible to disguise the variables under study, as the interviewers were continually pressed to ask certain kinds of questions repeatedly, and the practitioners likewise made periodic ratings on these same variables. But so far as it was possible, the research staff constructed the conceptual models and the instruments for testing them independently from the day-to-day actions of the practice staff. For their part, the social workers performed as best they could under the often bizarre circumstances surrounding each experimental participant, and at the conclusion of the study, they were asked to make retrospective judgments about their clients without knowing the specific issues under examination. All staff members had heard Dr. Blenkner discuss the possible hazards associated with relocating an aged person to an institution, but how this connection worked out in real life was unknown to the practitioners and the interviewers simply because no one knew for sure what the active ingredients were.

Ideally, it might have been better to conduct a completely "blind" study where neither the interviewers nor the practitioners knew what the purpose of the study was. This approach was clearly impossible in a field context, and perhaps it would have been undesirable in a demonstration project where part of the purpose was to test new ideas of practice so as to be able to demonstrate their effectiveness. Awareness of the issues was, to that extent, needed if both researchers and practitioners were to be sensitive to innovative practices and reasonably objective evaluations. In any case, the organizational structure reflected this compromise on awareness of the variables under study.

Moreover, to separate the function of evaluating practice from practice itself, Dr. Blenkner arranged to establish a separate research office, called Associates in Gerontology (AIG)—a purposely ambiguous name—so that people in the community, who easily recognized the name of the Benjamin Rose Institute and associated it with bountiful services, would not assume that participants in the research project (specifically the control participants) would inevitably receive services as well. Given the design of the project that Dr. Blenkner constructed, there were no feasible alternatives to having a no-experimental-service control group to allow comparisons with the experimental group, who were given innovative services.*

The Practice Staff

The practice staff for the Protective Project consisted of a highly experienced social-work supervisor (Helen Cole) and three social workers who had more than ten years' experience each, with either the aged or child protective services (Helen Beggs, Jane Lenahan, and Margaret McGuire). All had been trained in psychoanalytic or neoanalytic forms of social work, as was typical of that day. Two of these workers (Cole and McGuire) were borrowed from the regular staff of BRI for the duration of the project. I don't know their motivations for taking on what was acknowledged as a difficult, almost masochistic, activity, that of serving protective cases. It may have been the glamour of working with Margaret Blenkner, whose national reputation had already been established from her earlier research in New York; it may have been the curiosity of trying something new in the context of research. They were also assured of being able to return to the regular staff at the conclusion of the project, so it was a time-limited adventure.

---

* Technical Note 1.5 (p. 28) considers *research designs* again, especially *single-system evaluation designs.* This note also introduces the term *practice design* and compares such a design with various research designs. Although this book emphasizes group research designs, keep your eye on single-system designs (Chapter 13) because they may be more immediately useful to helping professionals.

The other two workers (Beggs and Lenahan) came to the project from a national search during which many talented persons applied. I think Dr. Blenkner was looking for a mix of practitioners, as the point was to generate innovative methods in dealing with this difficult clientele. To a degree, this objective was attained. There was some carryover from the traditions and lore of regular BRI work with the protective—more hearsay than systematic practices. And there was some application of ideas and methods related to children's protective work. But by and large, there was not much known about working effectively and humanely with elderly protectives. I cannot judge the degree of creativity among these social workers because the ethical and practical constraints in dealing with fragile though stubborn individuals were so omnipresent. I think it is clear that some workers more than others took advantage of the inherent possibilities of these difficult situations to try new approaches, so in that sense, some were more useful to the larger purpose of the study—the demonstration of new and effective methods—than were others.

I think it also fair to note that these social workers were not well versed in research tasks. Like most social workers, they had had a course or two in research, in contrast with the half dozen or more courses they had taken in fieldwork and practice methods, so there was no reason to expect much more. But "Professor Blenkner" gave them, in effect, a crash course in research that enabled them to be willing and reasonably able, if not knowledgeable, participants in their portion of the research process. There were some systematic differences in the ways in which they evaluated their clients, just as there were patterns in the ways in which they worked with their clients. But such individual differences were to be expected. Overall, I would say that these four social workers on the project not only were as able practitioners as anyone at that time but fulfilled their research tasks with reasonable skill. It is necessary to establish these facts because, after all, the project ultimately came down to a test of their skills in resolving some extremely difficult human-behavior problems in ways that were clear enough to be reported by independent observers.

There are inevitably some constraints on practice that are set within a research context. Practice by experienced workers at BRI was traditionally fairly autonomous. Each social worker practiced as he or she thought best, constrained only by writing detailed case records; holding discussions of the cases with an experienced supervisor; and, occasionally, presenting a sticky case for a psychiatric consultation. In the research context, practice had to conform to some additional guidelines. First, the cases were discussed with colleagues more frequently so that the social workers might brainstorm and come up with new approaches for dealing with difficult problems. This was a kind of experimentation on methods of practice, as the existing body of knowledge for working with elderly protectives was thin. Second, this innovative practice had to be specified in enough detail and studied with enough objectivity so that if it proved to be successful, others might learn how to use similar methods with similar effects. Both tasks proved to be very difficult, as I describe in greater detail in Chapter 9.

Training can help one to achieve a higher degree of rule-governed practice. The workers on the project held training sessions in which simulated cases were presented on which they could clarify their common definitions of targets (problems and goals*) and choices among the ways of responding. The function of the director of practice was, in part, to establish some consistency in the practice methods, as well as to stimulate innovative thinking that could be added to the fund of practice knowledge that the workers shared. The four social workers and Dr. Blenkner met frequently early in the project to consider practice strategies. In principle, the technical vocabulary of the service profession should have facilitated the accurate analysis and construction of a service program. But in fact, a technical vocabulary created in one context may not transfer easily to another, and so being trained in and bound to the psychoanalytic vocabulary dealing with unconscious conflict in the first five years of life may have been more of a burden than an aid in dealing with these elderly protectives (see Wasser, 1971, for a further consideration of this point).

On the other hand, one of the major objectives of the project was to demonstrate new strategies and techniques whose effectiveness could be verified. This objective required the freedom to be innovative. Consider what this requirement means. Innovation tends to require new methods that violate established principles to some degree in order to resolve problems that conventional methods appear unable to do. Innovation in the context of life-threatening conditions, such as those that the very elderly are always subject to, imposes great constraints on the practitioner. This complex topic is discussed in Chapter 9, on practice.

Thus, the social workers were poised uneasily on the horns of a dilemma: the necessity of being innovative while at the same time following a safe standardized treatment package. Any innovations had to be very carefully conceived and suitably protected against possible unintended consequences. Likewise, standard treatment methods were engaged in with an eye to preventing a routinization from which no new information might be forthcoming. On top of this dilemma were the ever-present demands of research for randomized assignment into experimental or control groups, and for objective statements of what services were provided and what effects occurred.** Many eyes were following the social workers in their everyday activities, and this scrutiny was bound to have some impact on their performance. Some performed very conservatively, doing what they thought would be least harmful to the clients; others appeared to perform in a more risky fashion to obtain what they thought best for the client. "Not doing what is harmful" and "doing what is best" may be two separate dimensions in work with the elderly protective or with any client. In any case, calling attention to these dimensions may help to clarify the service task.

Ultimately, Dr. Blenkner described the overall practice directive as follows: "Do, or get others to do, whatever is necessary to meet the needs of the situation" (Blenkner et al., 1971). This is clearly a directive that emphasizes innovation. But it must be understood in the context of a profession with a strong sense of ethical behavior toward clients. A wide array of supportive services was

* Technical Note 1.6 (p. 31) distinguishes among several classes of *goals of research:* those that are ultimate, intermediate, and immediate. These classifications played an important part in the BRI Project, as they do in any research, because the success of a project depends on what one intends to achieve. The tricky part is to state your predictions clearly and unambiguously in advance.

** Technical Note 1.7 (p. 32) introduces the topic of *randomization* in the research and practice contexts of a demonstration project. Randomization is perhaps the major step that distinguishes strong from weak research designs.

13

made available to the social workers, either from within the research agency itself (such as nursing evaluations by one of the staff who was a registered nurse) or by contract with the agency (such as the diagnostic services of physicians and psychiatrists). In addition, the workers constructed such relationships between themselves and their clients, or among relatives, friends, and community agents (like ministers and druggists) as they thought would best meet the unique needs of their protective clients. Understandably, it was hard to establish any rules for effective practice with elderly protectives beyond describing what patterns of helping services were provided. We will return to a detailed look at these services in Chapter 9.

The Research Staff

The research staff was heterogeneous. Some individuals were employed to do specific tasks, such as to survey the participating agencies to learn how many new cases of persons in need of protective services occurred in an average month (Weber, 1964). Others were involved in ongoing tasks, such as the development of measurement instruments and the training and monitoring of research interviewers. All of the research staff were new—new to the agency and to each other. Margaret Blenkner's leadership style was to set a task and leave the researcher alone to perform it until it was in late draft form. Then she and the researcher would analyze it closely for its utility for the purposes intended. (Then it would be back to the drawing boards to patch up or rework the problems that she had raised.) I'll discuss these activities in later chapters in connection with instrument construction and related matters.

Researchers came and went during the years of the Protective Project, and during the overlapping subsequent studies conducted by BRI. I was the first hired and about the last to leave the agency (when I was offered a university teaching position that I had long desired). With a brand-new Ph.D. and with a strong theoretical bent stemming from my training in social psychology and philosophy, I tried to serve as a counterbalance to Dr. Blenkner's empirical tendencies. (With minimal success, I should add, although we did try some miniexperiments in the course of the several BRI projects that stemmed from purely theoretical considerations.) But this was a very fertile time in my own development, under the stimulus (some might say the hammer) of Margaret Blenkner's influence. Others likewise flourished in this setting: one of the research interviewers returned to college to obtain her doctoral degree; the principal secretary eventually went on to get a master's degree in social work and to head a social agency; two other staff members also returned to academe to become professors of social work; and members of the practice staff went on to administrative positions in BRI. There was no question but that this was a highly stimulating environment for the staff of the research project.

I was coordinator of the research aspect of the project. My day-to-day tasks included developing research instruments, training and monitoring the research interviewers, and writing reports. (Dr. Blenkner, for all her skills, occasionally had a writing block. She labored over papers, often procastinated to the last moment, then worked in a flurry to finish barely on time—much to the discomfort of the secretarial staff. However, her papers were usually graceful as well as

14

clear and insightful; you would never have known how much agony went into their construction.)

I was a rank novice in each of my tasks and had to learn rapidly on the job. For whatever talents I may have had in conceptual areas, I was a third-rate empiricist, an even worse statistician, and less than interested in the minutiae of the flowcharts that kept track of four interviewers in their initial, three-month, six-month, and one-year interviews of 164 participants and 164 collaterals (friends or relatives of the participant). These flowcharts had to be done, like clockwork, on 88 of those experimental participants, in coordination with the comings and goings of the practice staff. That was not what I had learned at school.

The Support Staff

Fortunately, Dr. Blenkner built up a good secretarial crew that really managed these daily transactions, once I had figured out a flowchart system for the project. They also had enormous amounts of typing to do, keeping records for the social workers, who were doing elaborate recordings of their services, and producing the tons of varied-colored interview instruments—a different color for each time period, type of instrument, and research person involved—to say nothing of the many reports and papers that the staff wrote during these years. The principal secretary was the chief coordinator of these productions, as well as the personnel manager, the private secretary to Dr. Blenkner, and a mother figure for distraught practitioners, interviewers, and staff. She also was our operator of the card-punching and sorting equipment. These were in the good old days before micro-computers, and although an interesting part of the story of the BRI projects, I will modify my discussion of record keeping so that it covers the types of machines that the readers are likely to encounter in their own careers.

Dr. Blenkner devoured several secretaries before she got to a workable team. "Devoured" might be too strong a word because, although she was a "tough hombre," she was quite distressed when it came to firing any staff member. She simply couldn't abide incompetence, but for all her overpowering brusque-ness and drive, she delivered the *coup de grâce* with all the skill of the experienced and sensitive social worker that she was. (By the way, I learned about this aspect of her style only secondhand.)

The final team of four secretaries stayed throughout the seven years I was at BRI. Three were young women who, it seemed to me, labored far beyond the usual for such workers, I like to think because they were caught up in the excitement of the demonstration project. However, the lunch hours and coffee breaks were sacrosanct, and supervision was much freer in the research office than at BRI. Occasionally clients wandered into the office, and the secretaries had to "handle the case," which they did with reasonable aplomb. Frequently overburdened with deadlines for progress reports or new interview forms, they sometimes gave vent to their frustrations. One time, one of the secretaries who was particularly overburdened answered the phone, "Grand Central Station." Dr. Blenkner was on the other end, a surprised caller, but quick enough to respond, "This is the station master speaking." The camaraderie of the office was, for the most part, strong, and a necessary, if informal, element in the

15

workings of the project. Not that interpersonal problems didn't occur, but they were usually worked out with only a few tears and some short-lasting tensions.

There were also doctoral students from Case Western Reserve University who came to work at the BRI research department. These bright young people were a leavening agent at the office, working on projects of their own, or occasionally on an aspect of ours. I was amused at how academic their methods were, compared to the realities of what we were facing in the field—with just exactly the same amusement that Margaret Blenkner must have felt about my proposed solutions to methodological problems early in the project.

There you have it, a brief sketch of the people involved in the Protective Project. It may appear from my encomiums that Dr. Blenkner assembled the best and the brightest that ever there were for this one project. Not so. She definitely had some problems at first gathering an effective staff, as well as some problems in its ongoing maintenance. But why dwell on the fact that two of the four secretaries couldn't type a straight line, when they could do other research tasks very effectively? Why mention that the social workers were occasionally obnoxiously moody and snappish, when in general they adapted to their masochistic assignments with good cheer and determination? Why report that one interviewer left her brief case filled with completed questionnaires on top of her car and drove for several miles before discovering its absence, when she and her colleagues were willing to travel in strange and unpleasant settings to ask complicated questions of difficult participants. This also permits me to suppress my own stupidities, like leaving out of the final interview a set of questions that was used in the initial interview. I wrongly thought that the comparative questions on the same topic would suffice.

What emerges from my memory of this project is how well the staff did work together inspite of differences and difficult circumstances. Not every staff is as successful at working together, I later discovered. So I credit the success in the relatively harmonious relationships and the reasonably productive outcomes to the native talents of the staff members along with Margaret Blenkner's orchestrations. I don't know how she did it, except to have clear goals and tasks, as well as unit directors who were in close communication with the unit members. Maybe it was simply good luck—although I am inclined to think it was good planning and monitoring as well.

THE AGENCY AND THE COMMUNITY

The Benjamin Rose Institute, Cleveland, Ohio

Cleveland was the site of the Benjamin Rose Institute studies. This large, heavily industrial city on Lake Erie was surrounded by a string of suburbs and an "emerald necklace" of parks. In spite of the wealth generated by its industries and the pleasant environment, there were serious problems in Cleveland in the 1960s, including the accumulated effects of poor black-white relationships; uncontrolled pollution—a cause of the unfortunate label Cleveland received, the "mistake on the lake," an accusation fed by the nationally reported incident of the river that snakes through the downtown area catching on fire because of the industrial pollution; and the antagonism between the business community and the local political reformers that bursts out on occasion when the ethnic coalitions aren't in control. Cleveland is a marvelous collection of large and strong ethnic communities that maintain their individuality—and turf. If Cleveland was an "American melting pot," there were still large cohesive lumps in this churning kettle. Pluralism remained a goal to be attained.

The Benjamin Rose Institute, located in the heart of downtown Cleveland, was the creation of Mr. Rose's will, in which this early twentieth-century industrialist left part of his fortune to the establishment of an agency entirely devoted to serving the elderly. Reflecting his culture and times, Mr. Rose's will discriminated against various minority groups, but later contributions by other philanthropists have extended the scope of its coverage and its personnel.

This agency is unique in that Mr. Rose set up its governing board so as to be composed entirely of women from the upper echelons of Cleveland's society, whose moral sense was assumed to be especially keen and focused—perhaps in contrast with that of the businessmen of Mr. Rose's acquaintance. In any case, for more than seventy years, the governing boards have maintained an enviable record of humane services for the agency's aged clients, as well as some progressive and innovative leadership in services for the elderly that includes establishing a senior citizen center in the late 1930s, developing services and programs for the elderly nowhere else available in Cleveland, and spearheading such national innovations as an organized home-aid service.

Each board elects new members to replace those who leave or retire, thus perpetuating the character of the board as Mr. Rose intended. There have been some tensions between the professional staff's objectives, which reflect the scientific practice of the day, and the lay board's grand style of goodwill toward the elderly. The executive director has the delicate task of enlightening the board while leading the professional staff along the lines of what is feasible as well as what is desirable, a task familiar to many agencies with similiar structural arrangements.

At the time of the Protective Project, the executive director (Mary Hemmy) was effectively expanding the services of the agency to include the development of a nursing home, which was among the first to qualify under the Medicare definition as an extended-care facility. Likewise, BRI was responsible for developing a specialized rehabilitation hospital in cooperation with Case Western Reserve University, and it later turned over the hospital to the University for its administration. Like the classic model of a well-funded, private agency, BRI introduced many service innovations and turned them back to the community as it sought to adapt its programs to meet newly emerging needs. Perhaps its most unusual innovation was the development of the research department itself. Few private agencies around the country had one, perhaps because of the expense and the difficulty of seeing how such a department could possibly benefit practice. But also, research was mysterious and perhaps even dangerous for something as delicate as reputation. I will expand on this point in a later chapter, but I want to call attention here to the social and political environment in which research takes place. What were the reasons for inviting a nationally known researcher to an established practice agency? The early 1960s, you will recall, were a time of great ferment, when enlightened social action seemed possible and fundable. The many social problems were well known to frontline practitioners, and they were being discussed at many levels of society. However impressive were Margaret Blenkner's credentials in conducting strong research, it is nevertheless true that the agency's reputation was being put on the line, along with that of its leadership. Dr. Blenkner stated quite clearly that a research project is an unknown, a mystery, and it could have outcomes that had been unexpected at the time of its inception. Yet the research department was set up and the project was born.

I must conclude that the executive leadership and the board made some gutsy decisions in the early 1960s for which they must be given all due credit. (For a description of the recent developments at BRI, see Chapter 15.) The next chapter explores further the various contexts that influence the formation and handling of a research project such as the Protective Services study.

Technical Notes

1.1 SCIENTIFIC DEFINITIONS

The differences between Technical Notes and the Narrative are, in principle, quite clear. In these Technical Notes, I will provide not only (1) more elaborate definitions of terms and (2) some insight into scientific methods in general, but also (3) some methodological instructions for performing some operation in any research context. I will begin each of these Technical Notes by connecting with some point of departure from the Narrative section, so you can understand the context in which the Technical Note is discussed. Later in the book, there will be a convergence of the Narrative and of the Technical Notes needed to present it.

For example, we began by discussing the Benjamin Rose Institute Protective Services Project by introducing one participant in that project, Miss Edel. But we had to have some way of identifying her and the other 163 individuals eventually selected for participation in the project, and that required some clear definition of who was eligible for inclusion and who was not. I will describe not only what definition we eventually constructed, but I will also discuss the types of definitions that scientists use in moving from abstract ideas to the practical steps in engaging in a field demonstration project with citizens living in the community.

Let's begin with the *working definition* that was evolved by considering how protective services were described by others in the literature and what experiences the BRI social workers had had with these types of people. *A person in need of protective services* in this Project was defined as

> A non-institutionalized person 60 years of age or older living in the community whose behavior indicates that he is mentally incapable of adequately caring for himself and his interests without serious consequences to himself or others, and has no relative or other private individual able and willing to assume the kind and degree of support and supervision required to control the situation. (Blenkner, Bloom, and Weber, 1964, pp. 4–5)

This lengthy and complex definition was important in the conduct of the project because it gave relatively precise boundaries for persons who could or could not be included in the study. Moreover, when it comes time to generalize from the specific sample used in one study to other persons in need of protective services, then one can determine how applicable the first study is to people who are to be included in a second.

Let's examine this definition as an introduction to operational and nominal definitions as used in the social sciences. The *operational* approach provides a definition of some abstraction in terms of relatively simple procedures by which one can observe the manifestations of that abstraction. These arbitrary and observational procedures constitute the full meaning of the abstraction. For example, in the BRI project, the definition of a person in need of protective services is

19

mainly operational. This definition says that if you find a person who is sixty years old or older, living in the community, who indicates by means of his or her persistent patterns of behavior that he is mentally incapable of adequately caring for himself, etc.—if you follow these observational steps as given in the quoted definition, then you will have identified a person who qualifies as being in need of protective services.

Sometimes the observations involve more than simply looking. They may also include making measurements—which are systematic observations, possibly employing some device to aid in the accuracy and reliability of those observations. For example, temperature is generally measured by the use of a thermometer; the meaning of the term *temperature* is fully defined by reference to the operations of placing a thermometer in a given location and after one minute reading the number from it. In a social sense, we attempt to measure a given event by a device that approximates the accuracy and reliability of the thermometer. The steps or operations used in this measurement would be called an operational definition for social science terms.

It would be preferable if all definitions could be of this operational type because other researchers would know quite exactly what someone had done in a prior research study. But often we are obliged to use *nominal definitions,* in which we agree on using words with commonly accepted meanings to define a given concept. This is especially true when we come to the end of a series of operational definitions and still have to define the basic meanings of the terms used in our operations.

For example, take the phrase "mentally incapable," which appears in the definition of being in need of protective services. As used in the defining sentence, the phrase "mentally incapable" is assumed to be comprehensible to persons in the helping professions. But knowing that different helping professions might define the term differently, the BRI staff went further and tried to give it an operational definition: "The person is unable to maintain at least minimal social standards of self-care and conduct by reason of mental disorder or malfunction" (Weber, 1963, p. 2).

Now we have to define "mental disorder or malfunction," as these are not self-explanatory terms. Here is the next step in the definition:

> Mental disorder or malfunction refers to serious disturbances or abnormalities of thought, feeling, and behavior, which may be due to organic brain damage or deterioration, affective psychosis, psychoneurosis, toxemia, or life-long mental retardation. The mental disorder or malfunction may be manifested by confused thinking and poor judgment, by extremes in expressions of emotions, or by bizarre, asocial, or harmful behavior. (Weber, 1963, p. 2)

In attempting to define one phrase, "mentally incapable," we have ended up with a large collection of specific instances of mental incapacity and the ways it might be manifested. Clearly, each of these technical terms, such as *organic brain damage* or *affective psychosis,* requires further defintion, but there are limits beyond which a researcher need not define basic terms, lest all of one's time be given to an infinite regression of terms to be defined. Standard technical dictionaries or standard diagnostic terms (such as those in the third edition of the *Diagnostic and Statistical Manual,* see Technical Note 4.5, p. 120) are arbitrary but useful end points for such nominal definitions. However, remember that they are arbitrary. It has been pointed out, for example, that clinicians and researchers in England and America have quite different perspectives on how to apply such terms as *schizophrenia* or *depression* to clients (Albee, 1983). So cultural meanings or orientations make the use of nominal definitions risky—even though probably all terms, even those used in operational definitions, ultimately descend to a point where a consensus on the meaning of the words is assumed. Depending on our culture, our social stratum or ethnic background, our age, and our sex, we may interpret affective expressions differently and thus use the words defining them differently as well.

Some general characteristics of any scientific definition are worth noting. First, one does not seek to demonstrate the truth or falsity of definitions. They simply exist to be used and are to be judged only on their utility. Are they clear and distinct indicators of the referents of the definition? Do they provide ways in which the term defined can be linked with other terms in a network so as to form a theory? (This is a very important function, as we will discuss in Chapter 4.) The point is that concepts should have overlapping or shared definitional constitutents so they can be logically interrelated.

Scientific definitions are arbitrary constructions and depend on cultural and social forces for their evolution and use. Therefore they are value-laden. Think for a moment of the evolution of descriptions of the poor, including the "deserving poor" or the "culturally deprived," each implying some value posture of its day (cf. Zimbalist, 1977). The same scientific term may have several different operational definitions—such as the various ways of measuring (and therefore defining) intelligence. Possibly, the same measure may be used as indicating different concepts; for example, questions framed about one's view of oneself may be used in definitions of self-image, self-esteem, or identity. These cases suggest that we should consider our concepts carefully and the way in which we define them. Strictly speaking, each operational definition is of a unique term. And strictly speaking, if several different terms all use the very same definitional ingredients, these terms reduce to the same concept. But life isn't this simple; people go on using words and definitions in their own way, and the ultimate suggestion for readers of research is simply to be fully aware of how any given researcher or practitioner is using a term.

I spoke of the earlier definition of being in need of protective services as a *working definition*. The reason is that it emerged only after months of careful consideration and compromise. In looking at potential participants in such a project, we had to face such questions as these: Should people living in licensed boarding homes be viewed as being in noninstitutionalized community settings? (Answer: Yes.) What if a person were physically impaired to a high degree; would this constitute being in need of protective services? (Answer: No; physical disorder or infirmity by itself was not sufficient for admission to the Protective Services Project, as there were ample programs for such persons in contrast with services for those whose limitations were mental in nature.)

These and other distinctions did not come easily. No one told us what was right or wrong in defining the population at risk in the way we did. We simply tried to find what was typical of the experiences of social workers and others familiar with this type of client and to define terms in such a way as to include as many of these persons as possible while excluding others having only one

21

or two of the three needed characteristics: (1) living in the community; (2) being mentally incapable of caring for oneself and one's interests; and (3) having no relative or friend able and willing to provide the proper support.

In general, the efforts one puts into defining the core terms of one's research are amply repaid throughout the life of the project and its discussion among other scientists and practitioners thereafter. One should seek to include just those who are central to the task of the project and to exclude those who are not. This is not an easy task, but it is a necessary one. It is, however, an arbitrary decision that, once made, is difficult to undo.

1.2 DEMOGRAPHIC CHARACTERISTICS OF THE SAMPLE

In addition to getting a sense of the persons involved through the brief sketches in the Narrative section of this chapter, we can also gain some perspective on the whole group by describing them on essential characteristics, and then by comparing these with the population as a whole from which they were drawn. For example, the ages of this sample ranged from 60 to 102, with the median age being 78 years of age. About one third were between the ages of 60 and 74. One can note that this sample is older than the average older American of that time (when the life expectancy was about 68 years). But more than that, one can begin to make some comparisons between the older persons in the Cleveland Standard Metropolitan Statistical Area (SMSA)—an artificial geographical unit constructed by the U.S. Bureau of the Census in order to have a standard reference for general statistical purposes—and in the United States as a whole (Bloom and Chellam, 1963). Quite by chance, it turned out that the Cleveland SMSA was nearly 1 percent of the entire United States in 1960; to be exact, the figures were 1,796,595 for the SMSA and 179,323,175 for the United States. The proportion of persons between the ages of 60 and 74 among all persons 60 years and over was nearly 80 percent of the elderly in the Cleveland SMSA, and thus this is another indication that the BRI sample was older than the average elderly person because only one third of the participants in the project were in this 60- to 74-year-old range. These, and other detailed comparisons, permit one to describe the sample accurately and to compare it with corresponding characteristics in the SMSA and the country at large.

Having found differences between one's research sample and these larger populations, one must both call these differences to the attention of readers and also try to compensate for the differences statistically while making predictions or testing them. For example, it also turned out that the experimental participants who received the special treatment program were older than the control group participants, who did not. This difference required some statistical analyses to ensure it would not influence other factors. So all analyses were divided into the young old (60–74) and the old old (75 and over). In this way, the difference was controlled for because like age groupings were compared each time.

There were some other demographic characteristics used to describe the BRI sample. Indeed, these same characteristics are frequently used in any research study because they are the basic factors on which people's life experiences differ: sex, race, marital status, sources of income, education, and the like. What these different experiences are is a question beyond this research book, but it is the subject matter of sociology and social psychology. A brief description of the BRI sample includes the following: Over two thirds of the sample were women, and 91 percent were white. Nearly 30 percent were foreign-born, reflecting Cleveland's large ethnic population. Only 15 percent were currently married; the largest portion of the sample were widowed (59 percent). "Never-married" persons (that is how the idea of being "single" is expressed technically) composed 17 percent of the sample, and divorced or separated persons the remaining 9 percent.

The major source of income of these people was from social security (about 47 percent), and old age assistance (public welfare) was the second leading source (34 percent). Pensions, other income, and withdrawals from savings were the main sources of income for about 17 percent, and 3 percent had no income at all. The median monthly income was $102. A quarter of the sample survived on less than $75 a month, and 5 percent had an income of $200 or more a month. In terms of education, most participants had a grammar-school education, typical of persons of their age at that time.

Demographics are the largest brush stroke with which we can describe the characteristics of the sample we are studying. With these demographics, we can compare this sample with others, although we must be sensitive to these characteristics in relation to the era in which they occur. Living on $75 a month in the present time of inflation would seem to be impossible; the value of the dollar at the time of the project (1964–1965) made it merely very difficult.

1.3 EXPERIMENTAL AND CONTROL GROUPS

Logically, it would have been preferable to study every older person in need of protective services in order to describe that population of persons completely and accurately. But it would have been prohibitively expensive to do this, and so we selected a sample of this whole that was hopefully representative of it to a known degree. I say "hopefully" because although there were some procedures we could perform, such as random selection of persons from the project and random assignment to treatment and nontreatment groups, there were no easy ways to guarantee exactly representative and equivalent samples. (I'll discuss this point more fully in a later Technical Note, 1.7, p. 32).

In this Technical Note, I want to present a brief overview of how the treatment (or experimental) and nontreatment (or control) groups fit into the flow of research. Then I will discuss some of the implications of creating experimental and control groups in a demonstration project such as the BRI study. Figure 1.1 represents a simplified view of the research process, which begins in some sociocultural value context, in which literally millions of events are occurring simultaneously with the few factors that we are investigating in the project itself. Some population of persons, with the defined characteristics that we are seeking to understand, are identified; in the BRI study, that population was all older persons in need of protective services who were living in the community and lacked adequate social supports.

From this large population, we draw persons as participants into the project itself. Ordinarily one seeks to select persons at random from this population

23

Physical Context of Research

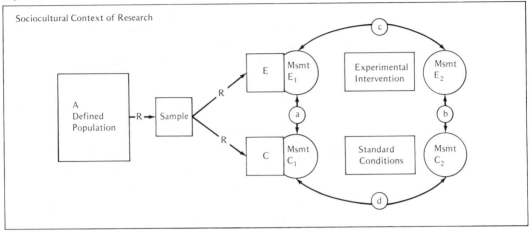

R = Randomized allocation, *from* a defined population (to a sample), or *to* experimental or control group status (from that sample).

E = The experimental (or treatment) group, i.e., the group that is to receive the experimental intervention, services, or treatment.

C = The control group, i.e., the group that is to receive whatever standard treatment or standard conditions exist in the sociocultural context.

Msmt = A measurement package given to E and C groups at specified times.

◯ = Comparisons made in order to determine the similarities between E and C at time (a) , and the differences between E and C at time (b) in relation to (c) , the predicted changes of E_1/E_2, and to (d), the predicted non-changes of C_1/C_2.

Figure 1.1 Experimental–control-group design: A basic model.

in order to form samples, but for our project, such a selection would have been expensive and difficult, so we first went to thirteen agencies that were known to have relatively high proportions of clients showing signs of need of protective services. From this agency population—that is, all older persons who were living in the community and lacking adequate social supports and who were known by thirteen cooperating social, health, and welfare agencies in Cleveland—we accepted all who met the entrance criteria. Then we randomly allocated these persons to either an experimental or a control group, as indicated in Figure 1.1.

The members of both groups were measured at the beginning of their entry into the project so that we had a baseline with which changes could later be compared. In addition, the demographic characteristics of the groups were compared so that we could see whether our random assignment had produced two groups with equivalent characteristics. One hopes that this will occur, but there is no guarantee that it will; in fact, we discovered differences in our treatment and nontreatment groups. Again, these differences required that we deal with the groups in a statistical manner that would in effect control for these random differences. Clearly, we did not intend that the treatment and nontreatment groups be different; and so statistical procedures were used so as to make comparisons with comparable subgroups. I'll discuss these details in Chapter 10, where the results are presented.

Once the groups are selected and beginning similarities and differences are noted, the intervention program can begin. The treatment group gets the experimental program that the researchers seek to test for its effectiveness. The non-treatment group acts as a control to suggest what would have been likely to happen to the experimental group had it not received the special treatment. Let's examine the logic of this procedure more closely.

In an ideal world, we would be able both to leave a group of subjects alone and to change that *same* group of subjects, so as to examine what differences the intervention has brought. But, of course, we must either leave a group alone or change it; we can't do both at once. As an approximation of this ideal, researchers locate a population at risk from which they draw samples so that each person has an equal chance of falling into the treatment group or the nontreatment group. (This procedure is part of the operational definition of *randomization of subjects,* as I will discuss in Technical Note 1.7, p. 32).

Then, the researchers give the treatment to one group (variously termed the *treatment, service,* or *experimental group*) while doing nothing to the other (called the *no-treatment, control,* or *standard condition group*). By re-measuring both groups on the same factors that were measured before the treatment began, the researchers are able to generate a "before" and "after" picture. The logic of this basic experimental design is that because the two groups were more-or-less equivalent to begin with (or were made to be roughly equivalent through statistical procedures), any change that occurs may be attributable to the experimental intervention that one group had and the other did not have.

In applied settings, such as the one that social agencies face, it is unethical to keep people from having services that they need. So, in practice, a research group cannot prevent people from obtaining needed services—if they are available and if the people can afford them. Many experimental services are new and thus unavailable; moreover, it is not objectively known whether the services are, in fact, beneficial—this is exactly what the research on effectiveness is all about. Moreover, there isn't enough money to provide the experimental program to all people in any case. Thus, from a scientific perspective, it is ethical to withhold experimental programs from control subjects under these conditions, especially when they can obtain standard treatment in the community that would be available to them whether or not the experimental project were present. This type of control group is called the *standard condition* or *standard treatment group.*

Clearly, such standard treatment groups are less tightly controlled than pure laboratory control groups because experimenters have more ability to select the subjects and the stimuli that they receive in the laboratory than do researchers in the community, where most applied social research takes place. But what the experimenters give up in control over the factors that make these subjects different from those in the experimental group is compensated for by the reality of the variables involved. The control group reflects the way people really live, and so what happens to the standard condition group would very likely have happened to the experimental subjects as well. The literally millions of external factors that are occurring simultaneously with the few experimental variables make it very challenging indeed to produce a demonstrable difference in the experimental and the control groups.

In the BRI Protective Project, it was relatively easy to show that the experimental participants received a greater range of services than did the control group because, except for financial supports coming from federal and state governments on an equal basis, there were few other places where persons could turn for the kinds of services that the BRI team provided, even if people had the funds to purchase them.

These definitions of experimental and control groups in applied settings have several important implications. First, in our project, the experimental program had to be quite strong to be demonstrably more effective than the best available services existing in the community. Second, it was necessary to describe quite clearly what the experimental program was so that, if it produced a statistically significant improvement over the standard conditions, we would be able to reproduce what had been done to obtain this effect. Obtaining this knowledge was complicated by the fact that we had little control over, or access to, the services that were given to the control participants. But if experimental and control (or standard condition) groups are to have any meaning, once a program effect is obtained one would need to be able to describe the program itself and how it exceeds the standard conditions found in the community. It is on the bases of such facts that decision makers can decide whether to adopt some portions of the experimental program for ongoing use in new settings.

1.4 TYPES OF RESEARCH: LABORATORY, FIELD STUDIES, FIELD EXPERIMENTS, AND FIELD DEMONSTRATIONS

When you think of the stereotypical researcher, you probably have in mind a person in a white coat mixing chemicals in test tubes in a laboratory. With good reason. Such laboratory scientists, from Dr. Faust to Dr. Frankenstein to the most recent Saturday-night thriller, have got very good press for the past several hundred years, whereas research conducted in field settings is more difficult to describe or portray on the TV screen.

The differences between laboratory and field experiments are real, but I will make the point that there are some important similarities as well. To begin with, consider the laboratory experiment. A laboratory is a planned environment in which the experimenter attempts to manipulate as many of the factors judged releevent to the issues at hand as possible, although this manipulation is usually done in stages, involving one or a small number of variables at any one time. The building in which the apparatus for the planned stimulation and measurement is housed is usually socially defined as a science building. People expect scientific work, teaching, and research to occur there. The experimenter, therefore, is given the license to rearrange specific laboratory rooms in particular ways so that they are not like ordinary rooms in a home or dormitory. Like the stage of a theater, the laboratory is a designed set that conveys nonverbal information to the subjects.

Perhaps in the middle of the laboratory stands a specially constructed table with partitions on it, and with some electronic apparatus at each of the segments of the table. The subjects come into the room and expect to sit at the strange table and do things with the apparatus; they also recognize that they would almost never expect to do such things at their own home. Such a stage sets up questions in the subjects: What is the experimenter really up to? Subjects who are not utterly naive recognize that the manifest content is not likely to be the real object of the research. This is frequently a game that subjects play with experimenters—and vice versa—to outguess or to disguise what the real purpose of the experiment is, even when the experimenter attempts to be fully honest in presenting the experiment. In such circumstances, some subjects try to give the experimenter what he or she wants—or does not want. It is hard to be "honest" in the sense of playing the game straight, without bias in one direction or the other, just because it *is* a type of game.

Well-controlled and well-designed laboratory experiments can go far toward reducing the temptation to outfox the experimenter—or even to want to. With the tidal wave of revulsion against dishonest and even harmful research perpetrated on unsuspecting subjects, there have been major safeguards imposed on research. (These will be discussed in Chapter 3.) The point at the moment is that laboratory design has become increasingly sophisticated so as to permit planned manipulation of variables at the same time that the subjects are informed about the nature and purpose of the experiments. There may still be an element of surprise—provided that the value of deceiving naive subjects greatly outweighs the risks to those subjects and would add significant information on the human condition. Many writers argue that we can learn all we need to know—perhaps even more than we can learn from deceived subjects—if we take these participants into our confidence in doing research (See Kelman, 1972, 1968, 1967; Schinke, 1981).

This brief discussion of laboratory research does have a bearing on the kinds of applied social research discussed in this book. Laboratory research sets the standard for objectivity and reliability and provides a testing place for methods that might be adapted to other circumstances. But there are other types of research that take a different approach to the question of obtaining valid, as well as objective and reliable, information. Instead of going into an artifically designed laboratory that exaggerates some aspects of real life while minimizing or possibly ignoring others, some researchers choose to use field experiments.

Field experiments take the research into settings where people actually live and where they perform their usual activities of daily living. This is life; this is how people are likely to behave under ordinary circumstances. And even though many extraneous factors may confound or drown out the variables under consideration, still the opportunity for measuring behaviors and events that are exactly the content that one seeks to understand is a powerful attraction for the applied researcher.

Let's distinguish field studies from field experiments. *Field studies* are essentially observations of naturally occurring events. (For example, a scientific *survey* asks people for their opinions and attitudes about certain topics; a *census* counts certain characteristics of people; a *needs assessment* in some section of a city seeks to understand the pattern and scope of unfulfilled needs.) Research tools and designs may vary from the simple to the highly sophisticated in such field studies, but the essential point is that these studies do not plan to change the events under study.

A *field experiment* does introduce some ingredients into a situation and then describes what happens, much as a laboratory scientist does, but without the degree of control possible in the laboratory. The variable introduced may be simple or complex, but it is intended to be clearly defined so that the outcome can be attributed to that variable and not to something else. For example, if someone (who is really part of the research team) pretends to get sick while riding a crowded subway, who will volunteer to help? Does it matter what the race or sex of the "ill person" is? By setting up this deception and then observing and categorizing the responses of riders, one can begin to answer these questions, which are part of the larger research issue regarding altruism (Piliavin, Rodin, and Pilivan, 1969). It would be difficult, but not impossible, to design an experiment of the same nature in a laboratory, so as to have more control over who the "riders" are. It would also be possible to travel the subways day in and day out waiting for people to get sick in order to see what true illness does to ordinary passengers in real-life settings. But the power of the field experiment is to bring these events together more rapidly and with more control by introducing some artificial (research) elements into the natural setting, and by carefully monitoring what occurs. There are ethical issues involved in all research, but they seem most potent when experiments are carried to the field because people don't expect research to be conducted there, and when it is, it may constitute an invasion of privacy.

The BRI Protective Services Project is an instance of a field experiment in which a planned intervention was introduced into the natural environment of the participants. However, there were some important differences between the BRI project and the study of altruism on the subways described briefly above. Whereas the study of samaritan behavior sought to *understand* the nature and conditions for this type of altruism, the BRI Protective Services Project attempted both to *evaluate* and to *transmit* the usefulness of practice knowledge gained in the study. Let us call this extended version of the field experiment a *field demonstration,* meaning that some planned intervention not only is measured for its effectiveness but is also studied so that practice knowledge of successful techniques can be transmitted to appropriate helping professionals. This dual focus of the field demonstration sometimes presents additional difficulties to the experimenter in the community setting. It is hard enough to do one of these tasks; to do both to a degree that adds to knowledge and advances the state of the practice arts is very difficult indeed.

1.5 RESEARCH DESIGNS AND PRACTICE DESIGNS

As mentioned in Technical Note 1.4, a field demonstration has two components: the evaluation of the effectiveness of the intervention and the transmission of the practice program to others. This means that the development of research designs and practice designs must be integrated, a point I would like to discuss in this Technical Note.

Let's discuss research designs first. (There will be additional discussions at several other points throughout the book, as befits a complex topic.) Any *research design* is a general plan for collecting, analyzing, and evaluating data related to the purposes of the study and to the practicalities of the context in which the research is to be conducted. Beginning with some classical models of research design (such as those reviewed by Campbell and Stanley, 1963, and by Cook and Campbell, 1979), the researcher evolves and constructs a plan for conducting research by considering the dual forces of what she or he would like to know and what she or he has to deal with in order to get any information.

There are two broad categories of research designs: those involving groups compared with one another in various arrangements and those involving a single individual or social unit (family, group, and so on) in which the comparison is between a "before" state with an "after" state. The former type is called *classical research* or *experimental–control-group design;* and the latter is called *single-system design* or the *single-case study.* This book focuses mainly on the former type; other books focus on the latter (Hersen and Barlow, 1974; Bloom and Fischer, 1982; see also Chapter 13 for a *practical* introduction to single-system designs.)

Figure 1.1 illustrated the minimal ingredients needed for one form of a classical research design. Later I will describe additions to this basic model in order to accomplish additional tasks in the research process (Table 13.8). It will be helpful to review the discussion of this basic experimental–control-group design (Technical Note 1.3) because it will be compared with practice designs to be discussed shortly.

Figure 1.2 illustrates the minimal ingredients for a single-system design. Let me discuss some of its features. First, the *dependent variable*—the variable that

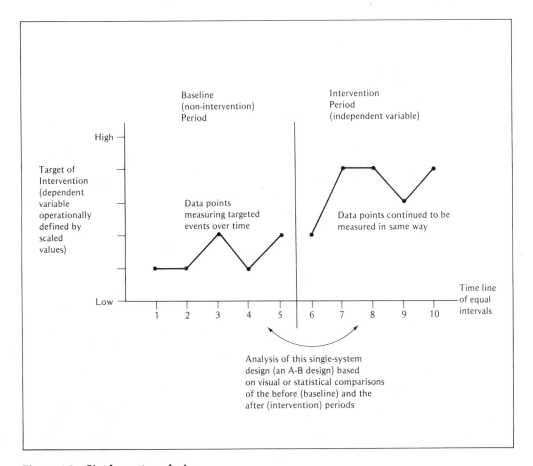

Figure 1.2 Single-system design.

29

we seek to influence through some experimental program—is operationally defined on the vertical axis by means of some scale or measurement tool. The control state, or the *baseline* condition of that targeted dependent variable, is ascertained during a preintervention period so that we know objectively what its nature is, that is, the magnitude and pattern of the occurrence of the targeted thoughts, feelings, or behaviors. Then an intervention period is begun that represents the *independent variable*—the variable that we manipulate in order to influence the *targeted dependent variable*. Measurement of the dependent variable continues as before. After approximately equivalent periods of time are used to gather data "before" and "after" the intervention, we can compare them to see whether there has been any significant change in the dependent variable. By using more complex single-system designs, we can also discover whether we were causally involved in producing that observed change.

The logic underlying the single-system design is very similar to that underlying the classical group designs. In each, some new events are compared with some original state of affairs. The single-system design compares the "after" state with the "before" state of an individual unit. The experimental–control-group design compares a randomly selected control group and an experimental group, which are presumed to be equivalent to the extent that what happened to the control group without any intervention would very likely have happened to the experimental group had it not had the intervention. There are strengths and weaknesses in each approach. The experimental–control-group designs are much stronger than single-system designs in nullifying alternative explanations of why results occurred as they did (see Technical Note 4.6, p. 123). On the other hand, single-system designs are much more adaptable to clinical research needs; they are closer to the immediate case situation; supply more rapid feedback, which can be incorporated into practice modifications; and are far more simple to perform. But the experimental–control-group designs are the standard of the social sciences and present the strongest information to date about causality.

I would like to introduce the term *practice design* to represent for the scientific practitioner what research design represents for the experimenter: a general plan for specifying, implementing, and monitoring preventive or interventive actions related to the purposes of one's professional helping and to the social-legal realities of the context in which one works. Such a practice design is a practice strategy that is translated from a practice theory into the specific steps that the helping professional uses to attain client objectives within the sociocultural value contexts.

Practice theories are conceptual entities that weave a network of logical relationships among abstract terms. When the constituents of these practice theories are translated into specific operational meanings, one develops a concrete practice strategy: "Under these conditions, do this with that in order to achieve a given objective."

The main point of this Technical Note is to interrelate research and practice designs in applied studies. Clearly the *experimental intervention* is a practice design, but surrounding considerations, such as how to select participants for a project and how to maintain the distinction between experimental and control groups, require an integration of research and practice considerations that may, at times, operate at cross-purposes to one another (cf. Thomas, 1978). Practice may call for meeting any need that arises with the best available tools, but research considerations may demand limits in order to study the impact of specified services.

More positively, the general structure of the practice design must be related to the equivalent structure of the research plan. For example, if a global practice directive is issued, such as the BRI directive "Do, or get others to do, whatever is needed to meet the needs of a situation," then the array of outcome measures must be equally broad so as to pick up gross movements on any of the many possible outcomes. Where specific practices are intended to have precise effects, the measurement program can focus on these in greater depth (assuming that the resources available are equal in both the broad and the narrow conditions).

In general, the operational definitions for what constitutes the experimental intervention should be directly linked with what constitutes the practice package. As the practice is derived from a practice theory, so the research variables should be connected with other behavioral and social theories. This linkage suggests that at the conceptual level, there must be a connection between the practice theory and the behavioral or social theories being employed. A practice theory may be derived from the broader social and behavioral models, or it may be separate. But the more the researcher-practitioner can link these conceptual models, the more precise the translations can be for both research and practice.

1.6 GOALS OF RESEARCH: ULTIMATE, INTERMEDIATE, AND IMMEDIATE

Because scientific work involves stating one's predictions in advance in order to test later whether the experimental intervention was successful, we have to consider the very difficult topic of goals. Just what do we want to achieve, for whom, and under what conditions? These kinds of questions took on poignancy in the context of the Protective Project because we were literally dealing with life-and-death matters.

Everyone will die at some time, but the older persons in the Protective Project were likely to die sooner than the average older person in the community for many reasons: advanced age and various mental and physical conditions. And yet Margaret Blenkner chose survival as a basic goal of this project. Although both were members of the same population to begin with, the experimental participants had to survive longer than the control participants, regardless of whatever else happened in order for the project to claim to be successful. Why should this have been so?

The rationale for this goal has to be reconstructed because Margaret Blenkner took it as a given from the beginning of the project. Critics have challenged the project on the choice of ultimate outcome measures, so I believe some rationale is needed on its behalf. Let's distinguish temporal and nontemporal goals. Temporal goals further divide into the immediate and the intermediate. *Immediate goals* involve the removal of crisis symptoms, whereas *intermediate* goals involve the replacement of the conditions that created the crisis with other conditions that maintain the person in safe, sanitary, and decent circumstances, or that promote desired changes. Seems straightforward.

Consider Miss Colson, the hoarder living with several dogs that were locked in her apartment and never taken out. Miss Colson was seen to have a wound on her leg that did not get better. This ulcerous condition was a crisis condition, and the immediate goal was to treat that wound. The intermediate goal was to change conditions that aggravate the wound and that perpetuate the unsanitary surroundings, that is, the presence of the dogs. Note that *intermediate* means only "after the immediate goal"; the time is not specified. Clearly, sooner than later was desirable here. But given the importance that these dogs had for Miss Colson, a worker might have been wise to move slowly, lest he or she upset the fragile helping relationship.

A worker could have forced a showdown, based on the conditions surrounding the keeping of the dogs, but this showdown might have had a negative effect on what was the *ultimate or underlying goal* in this situation: that which must be present no matter what else is occurring in the case. In the protective project, the ultimate or underlying condition is that the person involved remain alive. It didn't matter how "successful" the "social surgery" was if the client died. A social worker, as agent of the state, can bring enormous pressure to bear on a client to behave in a certain way, but the ultimate question is whether the price (a risk of premature mortality) is worth the cost in conformity. Dr. Blenkner came down very firmly on the point that professional helping must, in the first place, keep the person alive.

But not merely alive—the helping professional has a second and coequal responsibility to ensure that the client will live in a psychological, social, and physical state of reasonable contentment. In the immediate crisis situation, a person's state of discontent is often the impetus for getting treatment to a client. For each intermediate step in the removal of crisis-provoking conditions, the worker is equally concerned about the client's state of contentment. However, as the surgeon's knife does inflict pain, so, too, do some social treatments create pain—in the expectation that this pain will soon be followed by a more satisfying quality of life.

Social workers have been uneasy with the societal assignment that might involve inflicting pain so as to lead to more satisfying consequences and have found protective work particularly anxiety-producing because of the unclear legal directives. Dr. Blenkner recognized that intermediate interviews at 3 months and 6 months might reflect the participant's dissatisfaction with a worker's attempts to force changes—even though these changes might lead to desirable outcomes. Thus, she chose to make the ultimate basis of a successful outcome the joint occurrences of survival and contentment at the end of the year of service. These were difficult joint goals to achieve, but what were the alternatives? One might be tempted to add other ultimate goals, but I think no one could reasonably remove either of the two that Dr. Blenkner chose as the defining characteristics of a successful demonstration.

1.7 RANDOMIZATION AND MATCHING

You will read about randomization at many points in this book, first because it is a basic tenet in the experimental–control-group design, including that used in the BRI Protective Services Project, and second, because it is a controversial issue raised by some critics of this study. The major idea of randomization is clear: each person in the population should have an equal opportunity of being allotted to the experimental or the control group. This does not mean that each individual will be like every other individual, only that they have an equal chance of receiving the experimental intervention or the standard conditions of the control group.

Some of the controversy stems from the point at which one begins to use randomization. It can occur as one begins to select individuals *from* the total population for allotment to samples. Or it can occur after one has stratified the total population into more useful subgroups (for example, males and females), and then has allotted participants randomly from each subgroup *to* the actual samples (for instance, experimental males, control males, experimental females and control females). These stratifications may be disproportionate to the actual distributions of persons in the total population, such as when one chooses to overrepresent minority persons in order to get an adequate number with whom to conduct the study.

Once individuals are randomized into the samples, the research interviewers may know or may not know to what group a given individual belongs. Such knowledge may subtly influence how the questions are asked or how the responses are interpreted, and so "blind" interviewing is preferred. Over time, it is difficult to maintain this degree of secrecy from interviewers because there are many clues, such as the presence of service workers in the household when an interviewer visits at follow-up.

Double-blind experiments are those in which even the experimenter does not know to which group a given individual belongs during the course of the experiment. Only afterward, when it is impossible to give clues or to interpret responses differently, does the experimenter uncover the blind. This planned self-deception can be attained in a number of ways, including having a third party make the allocations and keep the identifications secret until the appropriate time. It is difficult to do double-blind studies in field experiments.

Randomization itself is relatively simple. One way to randomize is to list the persons to be admitted to a project in order and then to enter a table of random numbers blindly (such as by putting one's pencil on the page without looking—really highly sophisticated technology—and, starting with that number, deciding whether even numbers go to the experimental group and odds to the control, for example; then one simply goes down the list of numbers looking for odd or even and assigning the participants their designation accordingly.) Many statistics texts have pages from the tables of random numbers. (See Loether and McTavish, 1980; Blalock, 1972; Grinnell, 1981; Bailey, 1982.)

Matching is a different process entirely and is not favored by researchers who have a chance to randomize instead. *Matching* means identifying the major demographic variables or characteristics in the study and then finding two individuals in the population who are equivalent on these (within defined ranges). Then one can randomly assign one to the experimental group and the other to the control. (It helps at this point to use a random or chance assignment, such as flipping a coin to see who goes where.) Then one is assured that the participants are relatively equivalent on basic demographic characteristics at the beginning of the study.

Unfortunately, that is all that matching guarantees. It may also be that many unintended factors are brought in at the same time that are not known to be significant variables in the study—but that are. Not everyone has an equal chance of appearing in one of the two groups, and so it is hard to claim that the matched sample is representative of the whole population. Matched samples contain merely the first individuals who appeared who were relatively equivalent on a small number of factors out of an enormous number that are characteristic of the population from which they were drawn.

Stratification based on some category is an approximation of matching, but the bases for the stratification are more explicit. Moreover, by using stratification instead of matching, one can continue to use statistical procedures in order to make statements about generalizability. Thus there are good statistical and research reasons for using randomization and even stratified random sampling methods, rather than the matching procedures. It may seem to be easier and more certain to use matching, but in fact, this is not the case. Sometimes one runs out of good matches (because of a small population) and so has to change the ground rules for admitting some pairs that are less than perfectly matched. Each such modification weakens the basis for making interfences from the resulting data. (See Blalock, 1972.)

CHAPTER 2

In the Beginning: How Research Projects Start

Overview

Any research project begins in a configuration of interrelated events at many levels. For a project the scale of the Protective Services study, there was a need at the national level for information about the fiscal accountability of elderly persons unable to care for their social-security funds. At the state and community level, there were indications that some elderly persons were not managing to live decent and contented lives because of personal deficits or lack of social supports. There were questions and discussions circulating in the professional literature about the best ways to aid older persons in need of protective services. However, some spark had to occur that crystallized these separate beginnings into one entity. The specific Protective Services Project emerged at the intersection of these social forces, shaped and modified by the personalities of the researchers and practitioners involved.

Narrative Section

The Configurations of Action
The Beginnings of the Protective Services Project at the National Level
      Social Problems
      Social Policies
      Social Institutions
The Beginnings of the Protective Services Project at the State and Community Levels
The Beginnings of the Protective Services Project Among Relevant Helping Professional Groups
The Beginnings of the Protective Services Project as Representative of the Impulse to Do Research

Technical Notes Section

The Narrative

THE CONFIGURATIONS OF ACTION

Any given happening is the product of a configuration of the events that give it shape and continuity. When that happening is a large-scale social-research effort, its beginnings are likely to be correspondingly diverse. To reconstruct what social structures and forces were at work in the beginnings of the Protective Services Project is an exercise in imagination because I really don't know if the events happened exactly as I describe them. But something like this configuration of events probably occurred—and recurs each time a significant social happening emerges—so that it is a story worth telling.

Some of these beginnings are found in the events happening in the nation at large. Others may be discovered at the state and the community levels. These influenced the course of the investigation—but not necessarily in a straight line. The configuration of events pulls and pushes, and it is only the resultant, the average of compromises and balances among forces, that appears as "history" records the outcome. Another set of structures and forces involved is that of the professional groups and persons who are engaged in the study, for "helping," even among practitioners with the best interests of citizens in mind, is a compromise among scarce resources and talents.

Perhaps within any social configuration there must be one ingredient that crystallizes the others, forming the distinctive shape that the outcome eventually takes. In the case of research, I think this ingredient is the principal researcher, who selects which of the objectives, resources, and values he or she will respond to, in the process of implementing a given study. But even these choices have to be resubmitted, as it were, up the line to the people representing other decision-making structures so that final approval may be obtained for a given study.

Who takes the final responsibility for the final outcome? Look at the final written report: It bears the name of the principal researcher (and his or her associates directly involved in the research and writing). But it also indicates the affiliation with the immediately sponsoring agency. Inside the covers, these people acknowledge the cooperation of persons and agencies in the local community without whose assistance the project could never have been done. And in small print, there is a brief and jargony notation to the effect that this study was supported by a grant number XXXX from the department of something or other. Each of these statements provides a glimpse of the configuration involved. Each is necessary; none is sufficient by itself. Each has some resources and interests that have to be resolved, by compromise, so that it may work in coordination with the others. This is the social configuration of research. Let's look more closely at how these structures and forces interacted in the Protective Services Project.

THE BEGINNINGS OF THE PROTECTIVE SERVICES PROJECT AT THE NATIONAL LEVEL

You were introduced briefly to five participants in the Benjamin Rose Institute's Protective Services Project (in Chapter 1). Imagine about 1½ million people like these five individuals. This figure represents a rough epidemiological guess about the scope of the problem in the nation at large.* How did such an estimate emerge? From a variety of sources including broad censuses of persons with various kinds of mental and physical afflictions, as well as from some specific studies of noninstitutionalized older persons living in several different communities. Margaret Blenkner had studied one such sample of persons, a cross section of older people living in New York City (Blenkner, Jahn, and Wasser, 1964).** In that New York study, these investigators assessed the mental status and the possible supporting networks these older persons possessed, and they estimated that about 15 percent of these elderly were in such a mental state as would constitute a significant cognitive impairment. Of these 15 percent, about half had friends or relatives willing and able to provide the necessary support to maintain the older person-at-risk in the community. So one can take the remaining 7 to 8 percent as a rough estimate of the need for protective services in that community. (Note that the configuration in question here is the combination of mental impairment and lack of a supportive network.) Then, multiplying this 7 to 8 percent by the number of persons in the age range under consideration (about nineteen million over the age of sixty-five at the time of the project) gives the number of about 1½ million elderly persons estimated to be in need of protective services.†

It is risky to base such an estimate on one sample because no one place (like New York City) can be representative of a whole nation. But when Dr. Blenkner searched the literature for similar samples—there were very few at that time—she found a reasonable degree of agreement on the range of persons living in the community who had been determined as having significant cognitive impairment. And so we offer these estimates for whatever they are worth—as estimates of the scope of the problem.

Social Problems

The reason for making these kinds of estimates is to attempt to grasp the scope of a problem that appears in its concrete manifestations as particular individuals like a Miss Edel or a Mr. Emery. When sizable numbers of persons are involved

---

* Technical Note 2.1 (p. 48) reviews the topic of *epidemiology*—the distribution in time and space of specific kinds of health or illness events, which may lead to hunches about causal conditions. Epidemiologists work like detectives on matters of health and illness.

** Technical Note 2.2 (p. 49) describes *cross-sectional* and *longitudinal research studies*. The differences between these two broad classes of research are vital, and they are frequently confused. For example, a cross section of attitudes by persons in different age groups may make it look as if older people are more liberal (or more conservative) than younger people. In fact, one would need a longitudinal study following one group of persons over time to see if there really were changes during the aging process, or whether these differences in attitudes are due to the sociocultural environments in which younger and older persons grew up.

† Technical Note 2.3 (p. 51) reviews the topic of *needs assessment*, a term that is used frequently in research in the helping professions, but that has been used in different ways during its long and checkered history. Terms related to needs assessments are also described, such as *social indicators*.

in serious personal or social behaviors that threaten their own health and/or the health of others, we have the makings of a social problem. Another aspect of a social problem is its continuity. Taking the protective service population as an example, it is likely that some of these elderly people will die within a given year; but it is also likely that new persons will, as it were, take their place. That is, these new people will become mentally incompetent and will lack social supports during this same year. If the problem is one of a biological character—that is, if mental incompetence is caused primarily by a breakdown in the tissues of the brain due to the cumulative effects of aging—then the proportions of older persons so labeled should stay relatively constant. (The absolute number will change as the population of older persons increases.) On the other hand, if the cause of mental incompetence is sociological, reflecting the cumulative impacts of social stresses, poor nutrition, or whatever, then we might expect different proportions as social conditions change. For example, in difficult economic periods, people may pull back from supporting an aged relative in favor of holding their immediate family together.

Another indication of national concern for the older person in need of protective services is the fact that twenty-two states had submitted recommendations at the 1960 White House Conference on Aging with regard to the need of such services. There was a rapid increase in basic research in the gerontological area. For example, in 1948, one grant was awarded in the Extramural Studies on Aging (for about $6,000), whereas in 1962, 44 grants were made (in an amount of about $1.6 million; see Segal, Boomer, and Bouthilet, 1975). And the then newly-formed Gerontological Society was actively developing a series of books on what was known in this multidisciplinary area. For example, Birren, 1959; Tibbetts, 1957.

There are many problems that affect sizable numbers of persons, but not all of them become recognized as social problems. The reason is that recognition is itself an important part of the process of becoming a social problem. Investigative reporting, for example, is one way in which the private difficulties of a handful of individuals become recognized as involving common concerns for large numbers of unnamed persons. But our newspapers and magazines print many stories about people in need. Of these, only some continue to get the recognition required for further development as a large-scale collective need, a *social problem*. It is hard to determine the causal factors at this point. Perhaps it is just good luck that a wealthy industrialist took an interest in child abuse so as to aid in marshalling of the ideas, resources, and personnel that have resulted in an effective national committee devoted to its prevention and treatment. (This is the National Committee for Prevention of Child Abuse.) Or possibly the fact that a sister of a president of the United States was retarded personalized this condition to the point where it gained national attention. (This was President J. F. Kennedy.) Whatever the cause, it is surely the case that this national recognition is needed to make an aggregate of situations a focal problem so that it is placed on the social agenda for taking collective action.

These are the elements of a social problem: an undesired and usually continuous condition that affects a significant proportion of the population, and that is identified by community leaders as requiring collective action. All of these elements must be present for a given situation, like older persons needing protective services, to receive concerted remedial attention.

39

Social Policies

For any social problem, there is need for a collective response, a plan of dealing with these many separate people who manifest a similar kind of problem, each in his or her own idiosyncratic way. We can speak of a social policy as such a collective response, a systematic plan for various responsible persons to react in cooperative ways so that the combination of all their efforts constitutes an effective program that deals with the persisting social problem.

This is not the place to discuss the development of social policy; there are a number of books dealing with that topic (Gil, 1973; Meehaghan and Washington, 1980). The point at present is that a collective problem eventually generates some planned reactions that act as guides to people with authority to do things for others. Nationally, laws may be written that provide the funds, the personnel, and the objectives for the separate units that may be set up all around the country. For example, social security legislation created a new system of government offices and agents whose task was to administer this body of laws. The scope of the law was national because growing old happens to everyone who lives long enough, regardless of social class, ethnic background, sex, or whatever. So far as possible, each of these field units operates on the same guiding principles. For example, people over sixty-five (or some other arbitrarily chosen age) are entitled to receive certain amounts of social security funds because of their prior membership in work groups that made contributions to the society throughout their working careers. (This is an assumption of the social security system.) Spouses are to share the breadwinner's social security by getting an additional fraction. (Remember that the original legislation of 1935 was written at a time when the majority of white middle-class married women did not work for pay out of the home.)

The administrative process of qualifying has been made as simple as possible. A person comes to a social-security-field office and proves his or her age with the necessary documents (including records in old family Bibles if there are no available birth certificates). Then, after the information is processed, the individual is registered in the system and receives in the mail a monthly check made out to that person from the U.S. government.

The administrative organizations that are established to carry out social policies are probably always more nearly perfect on paper than they are in operation. Policies and programs assume more uniformity of conditions and people than really occur, so there is always a need to interpret the intention of the legislation, either by the agency handling it or in the courts, if need be. In the case of the social security laws, large amounts of money are being sent to older persons who have applied and have been accepted as eligible to receive these grants. Fine, that was the intention of Congress in setting up the legislation that provides people with an income when they retire. (There may be other intentions of the people who set up the legislation, such as "regulating the poor" in times of depression so as to forestall civil rebellions; see Piven and Cloward, 1971.)

Once the program was in place, field workers in social security offices, here and there, with increasing and perplexing frequency, were reporting instances of elderly people coming in who were obviously confused and bewildered about social security, and who were careless about how they were handling their money. Sometimes it seemed as if the friends or relatives who accompanied them were using these older persons to their own personal advantage, or so it seemed from fragmentary reports. A new social concern was emerging from a newly enacted social program.

Social Institutions

Society sets up social institutions that respond to persisting human needs. The family, the economic system, and the educational system are some of the common institutions of a modern society. Within this broad concept are specific agencies or units that carry out the mission of the institution. Social security was a product of both the economic and the family institutions; the underlying purposes strongly affect both of these structures.

The major focus of a given social-security office is to transfer money to eligible persons, but a secondary function is to observe how well this primary focus is being conducted. Thus, when there were instances in which confused older persons came to social-security offices around the country, it is probable that eventually official reports were made from the field unit to some national center. That is how bureaucratic units operate: they follow general rules and make reports, particularly when those rules appear not to be followed. You have, no doubt, run across bureaucratic rituals that have been annoyances, but these are one way in which large-scale organizations take cognizance of local problems and organize a systematic response affecting all local units.

Reports of troubles on money transfers must have been accumulating from around the country. The persons receiving these reports very likely identified common problems among them—issues that may not have been raised in any individual case but that appeared common to some set of them. What, for example, was happening to those older persons who were not cashing their own social-security checks, or who were not receiving the money intended for them? Social security rapidly became the mainstay of economic support for the majority of the elderly, so this question was serious. What about the confused older person in particular?*

Newspapers and the mass media around the country often supplied some lurid details that startled their audiences—at least for a short time, before being forgotten. Here, an elderly person left a stove burner on and subsequently caused a fire that took his life along with those of his neighbors in his rickety apartment house in the slums of a city. There, a story of violence, some elderly recluse mugged in a search for nonexistent wealth supposedly buried in her home. But these are stories that last only an instance in the public record. How does this continual flood of isolated bits of information get captured so as to create a concerted effort to contain the problem, if not to prevent it?

Let us now praise anonymous public servants, because I believe that many of the corrective reactions or adjustments to social programs come through the

---

* Technical Note 2.4 (p. 53) introduces some important distinctions in the purposes for doing research. Taking the questions related to social security checks and confused older persons, one could conduct *basic research* on what causes confusion, for example. Or one could *apply* existing information, for instance, on training confused people to minimize their problems in handling finances.

channels of people administering the system. Not all, by any means, but a significant portion. Who are these anonymous bureaucrats? I suspect they are people very much like us. They read the papers and are horrified by the occasional story of the fire victim or the recluse. But unlike us, these bureaucrats have the opportunity to take matters further. They can begin to frame questions like these: How many people are involved in these needless tragedies? What is the nature of the problems that cause them to act in this manner? What part do others play in aiding or not aiding these persons?

Governmental bureaucrats also have access to information or information-obtaining devices that most of us lack. They can find out whether any answers to their questions are available in the scientific literature; so can helping professionals. If not, it is possible that they can attempt to gather information or have others gather that information for them. For example, some social institutions are given funds to provide them with feedback on their service delivery. They may offer specific contracts for the conduct of a defined project that is, in effect, controlled by the funding organization. Or they may issue a call for proposals* from whoever is interested and able to do some research on the general topic or evaluation of an existing program.** Responders are likely to be people who have some experience with one or another aspect of the problem already, so that they can build on their past experiences in making intelligent proposals for future research. Such proposals are received, and a board of critical reviewers assesses which proposals, if any, are likely to be useful in obtaining the information desired. Thus, a process of information gathering begins at the national level.

THE BEGINNINGS OF THE PROTECTIVE PROJECT AT THE STATE AND COMMUNITY LEVELS

At the beginning of the 1960s, Ohio could not be said to be a leader in social welfare legislation. In fact, it took relatively little interest in some aspects of social welfare, as this quotation from a progress report from the BRI study indicated:

> In Ohio, the old age assistance program has until this year been state administered. The state has not participated in the Kerr-Mills program for medical assistance; budgetary standards are low and a ceiling of $180 per month is placed on nursing home care; worker caseloads are very high and the state has not chosen to take advantage of the 75% federal reimbursement of administrative costs for providing services other than establishment and review of financial eligibility; several months are required to process applications for emergency

---

* Technical Note 2.5 (p. 54) deals with *research proposals*, and Appendix A presents the forms currently being used for generic public-health-service grant applications. In this Technical Note, I present background for how certain "calls" (specific research topics) come to be made.

** Technical Note 2.6 (p. 57) distinguishes between *research* and *evaluation*, that is, contributions to the development of new information (research) and tests of the usefulness of existing knowledge applied to a specific situation (evaluation). Obviously, there are important links between research and evaluation.

assistance during the waiting period. (Blenkner, Bloom, and South, 1966, p. 20)

These various statements refer to welfare legislation of that era, but the point is strongly made that the aged of Ohio could not look forward to excessive kindness at the hands of state officials because there was no legislation to direct and to support such actions.

In hearing various officials speak at state or community meetings, I was aware that often they were most frustrated by these legislative restrictions, because these people knew best of all the scope of the problems and the human side of the demographic reports. But at that time, there was a split between the more progressive, urban-based legislators and the more conservative legislators from rural and semirural areas, and on balance, the state held to a conservative stance: individuals were responsible for themselves; it was not the business of the state to provide social welfare.

But times, they were a-changing, and Ohio changed with them. Slowly at first, and then in a flood of national legislation in the mid-1960s, concern about various vulnerable groups emerged center stage on the national agenda. Money became available for a large variety of social projects and evaluations, including some regarding the aged. Proposals had to be submitted, but the spirit of that time was to discover what could be supported, rather than the spirit of the early 1980s, which is to get government out of the business of supporting social welfare service programs, let alone studying them.

Cleveland was served by a network of social, health, welfare, and educational agencies, some of which had as their primary goals contact services to the elderly. The Welfare Federation of Cleveland was an agency that attempted to coordinate the efforts of its member agencies in defining and achieving objectives to serve the common good. It was a forum in which common problems and concerns could be discussed, even though it had no power other than persuasion over its constituent agencies. As a planning agency, it could collect information from diverse sources and attempt to combine them in ways that provided rational guidance for the network of helping agencies.

As is often the case, the Welfare Federation was influenced by some prominent personalities in the city, as well as by dramatic local events. For example, at the time of the beginning of the BRI studies, a study was made of the conditions in nursing homes in Cleveland and Ohio that showed some to be less safe than required and less effective and humane than desired. (Indeed, there were some fires at nursing homes at this time that supplied gruesome proof of the validity of these reports.) Moreover, the Benjamin Rose Institute, with its unique focus on, and experiences with, the aged, aided in drawing attention to other vulnerable portions of the older population, particularly those affected by a variety of the agencies in the Federation. The Federation urged BRI to undertake a study of protective services, and it provided the support to secure the cooperation of other agencies that had some contact with protective cases, whether or not that was a direct service function of the agency.*

* Technical Note 2.7 (p. 58) presents the background of the *BRI Protective Services proposal*. There are some surprises in this Technical Note. History is often presented as a smooth progression of events. This was definitely not the case in the BRI study, nor in any other case with which I am acquainted.

There were special meetings of agency representatives to discuss the problems and possibilities. In the end, BRI formed working relationships with thirteen agencies and organizations in the community that were known to have contact with protective cases. A look at their titles will reveal that a wide net was cast in seeking to identify protective service cases:

- A county office of the state old-age-assistance program.
- One of the local social-security offices.
- The public-health nursing division of the city health department.
- The Visiting Nurses Association.
- The Catholic Charities Bureau.
- The Cleveland Family Services Association.
- The Jewish Family Services Association.
- A chronic-illness information-and-referral center.
- A community information-service unit.
- The social services department of the city general hospital.
- The psychiatric unit of the probate court.
- One of the local public-housing-authority projects.
- The intake division of the county welfare department.

In retrospect, there were other agencies that had some contact with protective cases, such as the police, but the thirteen chosen agencies undoubtedly had most of the relatively frequent contact with the mentally confused elderly living in the community, excluding BRI itself, which was not to be used as a source of participants for the study.

Several important questions were raised at this point. Were the clients of these agencies representative of the protective cases known by helping agencies, let alone of the protective cases at large? There was no way of knowing because we had no knowledge of the specific population (of persons in need of protective care) of which ours was one kind of sample.* We could describe the participants in our sample and compare them with other known groups, such as older persons in general, but as to the specific question, we had to make some guesses about where we could find protective clients—they ordinarily do not come to agencies looking for services because of the very nature of their problems: mental confusion and lack of support. Thus, we were really dealing with a unique group of persons and were making some assumptions that they were, indeed, representative of the type of person we were seeking to learn about.

We did make one kind of check on the nature of our population that was important. In the course of working with the thirteen agencies, we asked them to give us a count of all protective clients on their rosters during a given month's time. This preliminary study (Weber, 1964) tested our working definition of a person in need of protective services and gave us information about the volume of persons in question, as well as about their major demographic characteristics. We were able to say that our research sample was generally like the people on the roles of the participating social, health, and welfare agencies during that

---

* Technical Note 2.8 (p. 60) contrasts *populations, samples, and cases.* These terms are reasonably clear in the abstract but may be confusing in particular instances. Sampling procedures that ensure a truly representative portion of a population can involve some rigorous methods.

preliminary study. So we were getting a representative sample of the people who were known to these agencies. Whether these, in turn, were representative of all persons in need of protective services is another question and, for now, an unanswerable one.

THE BEGINNINGS OF THE PROTECTIVE SERVICES PROJECT AMONG RELEVANT HELPING PROFESSIONAL GROUPS

In the winter of 1963, the National Council on Aging gathered together an unusual body of experts from medicine, law, nursing, psychiatry, and social work to meet at Arden House (Harriman, New York) for a week-long discussion on protective services for the aging. What was particularly significant about this meeting was that its cosponsors represented a broad spectrum of helping professions: the American Public Welfare Association, the Family Service Association of America, the Family Section of the American Bar Association, the National Institute of Mental Health, the Veterans Administration, the Bureau of State Services of the U.S. Public Health Service, the Social Security Administration, and the Office of Aging of the Welfare Administration in the Department of Health, Education, and Welfare (Epstein and Lindley, 1964).

Note that local representatives of these national organizations were also represented in the participating agencies of the BRI Protective Project. In these discussions, the state of protective care was reviewed. In recognition of the lack of information on effective interventions, one of the recommendations emanating from this conference was a call for a research and demonstration project to explore the services that the older protective needed—and how effective such services were.

Helping professionals at the national level were very much involved in creating a climate receptive to the inauguration of the Protective Services Project. By good fortune, Margaret Blenkner attended that conference, along with the executive director and several other consultants and social workers connected with the Rose Institute. The eventual plan of service for the BRI project was nurtured by the discussions at Arden House and was consonant with them.

As mentioned before, helping professionals in the Cleveland area were receptive to the BRI Protective Project and pledged cooperation, even though the experimental design (requiring that some of their clients be "control" subjects who received no service) was not always an easy pill to swallow. Moreover, some of the persons involved held some strong opinions on the best way to approach the problem and its solution, so that Dr. Blenkner established the position of registrar, a staff member who not only received the names of persons who were referred to the project in order to ascertain whether or not they fit the criteria of admission, but who also maintained liaison relationships with the participating agencies. In this role, the registrar had to interpret and reinterpret aspects of the research project to some agency personnel, particularly the need for a strict randomization of participants into an experimental and a control group.

45

Another feature that had to be reinforced continually with the participating agency personnel was the existence of the dummy research agency, Associates in Gerontology, rather than the parent agency, BRI. Helping professionals were used to referring to the institute by name and found it difficult to stop at times. There were occasional wounded egos when project staff kept reminding other personnel; I'll describe an instance in Chapter 9.

But overall, the professionals from the participating agencies cooperated very well, and the procedures for identifying and admitting protective cases went smoothly. In reflecting back on the success of that portion of the study, I suspect it was due in large measure to the advance preparation and the continual contact that the registrar maintained with the agencies.

THE BEGINNINGS OF THE PROTECTIVE SERVICES PROJECT AS REPRESENTATIVE OF THE IMPULSE TO DO RESEARCH

Now we have to bring all of these separate beginnings together to recognize the configuration that eventually took the form of the BRI Protective Services Project: the ideas, the organizations, the funding, the personnel, the time and place for concrete implementation—and one more ingredient, the impulse to do research. This is of particular interest, I think, to students studying research methods because all too often the discussion of this particular ingredient is lost.

I believe that the beginning impulse to do research can be best described by the use of a metaphor. Metaphors are not the usual vehicle for communicating scientific knowledge, and that is all the more reason to use a metaphor at this moment, because the information to be conveyed concerns something more inclusive than science. I wish to speak about the creative impulse. Let's bring on the metaphor:

I have discovered, over the years, that research—its processes and products—is like a combination of passion and love. The beginnings of the research process bear an uncanny similarity to the spark of intensely focused feelings of excitement, not located as specifically in the genitals as it is in moments of passion, but like the intensely pleasurable discoveries of curiosity, the wonderings about the what or why or wherefore of some aspect of our world. It takes this initial stimulus to get the machinery moving, to generate the energy, the direction, and the will to undertake an extensive research project whose rewards, after all, are some distance away, at the point where it reaches its final, climactic resolution. Curiosity, the great tempter, leads us on.

But raw passion dissipates as other bodily and social urges clamor for expression. So, too, with curiosity, for the world is full of curious things. It is only when passion develops into love, when curiosity grows into a fully sustaining interest and intimacy that gives nurturance as well as receives it, that research becomes a self-sustaining process. The daily routine of being in love is like the necessary routines that maintain a complex program of research, each piece reflecting a loving care of the whole in spite of the tediousness of some of the parts. In sickness (and there will be times when you are sick of the whole project) as in health (something always goes right, at least for a time) so long as you both shall live.

A corny metaphor?* Perhaps, but it is one with which most students can identify in the sense that if they don't experience that first spark of deep curiosity, there isn't a lot of hope for the second enduring phase of loving care bestowed on the mass of necessary detail. The metaphor also permits the student to look for (and look forward to) some aspects of research that are rarely discussed: its being an abiding pleasure mixed with moments of beautiful ecstasy. But loving someone also involves doing the housework, changing the diapers, and visiting the relatives. Likewise, in research, there are necessary chores that no one loves except that they are a part of loving research and the future results of that research. Passion and love—look for them in the research process. And like any sort of intense relationship, research involves your investing passion and love in order to receive it.

Not to belabor this metaphor, let me suggest that there are false passions and loves, when we get too much taken with a momentary dalliance for which there is little hope of development. But how does one know this in advance? Ah, yes, how does one ever know? I will try to present an answer by way of folk wisdom rather than science. But to young lovers I would in general recommend going forward with a passion to see if it has the stuff to become a love. Passion may spawn germinal ideas; love raises them to maturity. Passion may lead one to great exertions (as climbing the mountains of information in the library, or bending over a hot computer); love sustains these efforts. Passion leads one into strange and wondrous territories; love provides settlement and continuity. What is most important in the beginnings of research is that there be both passion and love for what you are about to undertake.**

* Long after writing this section, I read a quotation from Albert Einstein that expressed a similar thought: "The state of feeling which makes one capable of such [scientific] achievements is akin to that of the religious worshipper or of one who is in love." (Keller, 1983, p. 118.)

** Technical Note 2.9 (p. 63) discusses one passion common to most researchers, the passion for an orderly and systematic *research design* that provides the logical tools for teasing out secrets from nature. In this Technical Note, I dispassionately present an overview of the designs that animate a great deal of the research that we read in the current journals.

Technical Notes

2.1 EPIDEMIOLOGY

You would be correct if you inferred from the term itself that epidemiology is connected with the study of epidemics, but that is the original meaning dating back to the studies of Hippocrates (469–399 B.C.) on the relationship of medical problems to the airs, waters, and places in which people lived. We still use much of this same meaning—and, indeed, the same perspectives of analysis— today. (See, for example, the medical detective work of Fraser and McDade, 1979, on Legionnaires' disease, or the more recent work on AIDS.)

But the sense in which we used the term for the BRI Protective Services Project included a broader meaning that can be stated as follows: *Social epidemiology is the scientific study of the nature (that is, the description and the distribution) and of the causes of social, psychological, and physical health and illness.* Although a given researcher may study only the distribution of certain illnesses and the factors related to them, it is clearly possible to study the patterns of forms of health as well and, indeed, to relate the two studies. What patterns of health coexist with what patterns of illness or dysfunctioning that produce an overall configuration of healthy functioning?

MacMahon, Pugh, and Ipsen (1960) distinguished *descriptive epidemiology* from *analytic epidemiology*. The descriptive branch supplies vital statistics on the number of events occurring for certain people at certain times and places—and equally important, on the number of events not occurring for persons in other contexts. This information is basic knowledge about the practical nature of the events in question; this is the scope and depth of the problem in collective terms, so to speak. The analytic branch seeks to analyze the logical relationships among the events that could lead to causal inferences. This type of information is translated into action programs, including those that might be applied to individual persons.

For example, in the past decade, there has been a dramatic increase in the numbers of suicides among young black adults, particularly males. Descriptive epidemiology can provide a description of the locations where these suicides took place and the demographic characteristics of the persons involved. From these descriptive pieces of information, analytic epidemiology can attempt to find relationships among them that might not only account for the shift but also suggest causal mechanisms that provide leads for preventive efforts, even in individual cases. In this example, it turns out that a high proportion of these suicides occur among young unmarried black males who have recently moved to a large city and are not employed or are underemployed. Analysis of these facts suggests that the increased suicide rate reflects the lack of integration that these people feel with their community; the lack of close supportive networks may be the reason that these people commit suicide and that others, who are equally stressed but who have supportive networks, successfully resist suicidal pressures. Following this analytic hunch, it would make sense to try to link a given individual (who fits the epidemiological pattern—young black male, recently relocated to a large city, unable to find employment) with some supportive network while the larger employment question is pursued.

Margaret Blenkner wanted to do some basic epidemiological research on the characteristics and distribution of older persons in need of protective services in the Cleveland area, as she had in New York City, but the nature of her funding did not permit this research directly. The best we could do was to reconstruct a demographic profile of Cleveland's older population in 1963 (See Technical Note 1.2, p. 22) in terms of basic census characteristics and information on financial assistance, on the elderly in mental institutions, on older persons charged with offenses, and on suicides among the aged. This was essentially descriptive epidemiologic information. We did not have specific information on older persons in need of protective services within this larger population of the elderly from which to make analytic inferences about the causes of their problems or the strengths that they possessed in order to remain in the community on their own as long as they had.

2.2 LONGITUDINAL AND CROSS-SECTIONAL STUDIES

Blenkner, Jahn, and Wasser's New York study (1964) involved some elaborate sampling procedures that tried to obtain a cross section of the population in the geographic areas that they studied, but they interviewed these people on several occasions over a period of time. It is important to distinguish two general types of research, the cross-sectional and the longitudinal, because the inferences that can be drawn from them are very different. Let's examine the *cross-sectional* approach first. This type of study involves gathering data from subjects at one point in time. This "slice of life" is intended to represent the complexities of life by focusing in great detail on this one segment. For instance, the U.S. Census Bureau collects a vast amount of information at the beginning of each decade, but it is static information—a still photograph of the demographic characteristics of the people at that point in time. (The "point" in time may in fact be several months or several years, depending on the project, but it is treated as if it were one point in time—the decennial year in the case of the U.S. Census.)

For example, suppose that in 1980 the following groups were asked their opinion on changes in social security payments:

- Group *A* (persons aged 30 to 39 years)
- Group *B* (persons aged 40 to 49 years).
- Group *C* (persons aged 50 to 59 years).
- Group *D* (persons aged 60 to 69 years).
- Group *E* (persons aged 70 to 79 years).

If these five groups differ in their attitudes toward social security payments— say, the older the average age of the groups surveyed, the more favorable they are to increasing social security benefits—can we say that the older people get, the more liberal they are on increasing social security benefits, perhaps because such benefits would be more likely to influence their wallets? No, strictly speaking, we cannot say this because people in Group *E* may have started out with this more liberal attitude about social security benefits than did persons in Group *D*, and so on. Or persons in the younger age groups may have become opposed to increases in the withholding taxes that feed into the social security fund. We don't know the reasons for the differences, that is, the causal events that produced the different group averages. Cross-sectional data cannot, strictly speaking, yield longitudinal or developmental inferences. These cross-sectional data are essentially descriptive: This is what five different age groups believe, on the average, about changes in social security payments in 1980. The attitudes of the participating groups may differ. This descriptive finding may lead to new research—including longitudinal research—to discover why this difference exists and what dynamics may be operating over time.

In contrast, the *longitudinal study* follows some group of persons over time. Ordinarily, because of the costs and the complexity of following people over time and space, researchers doing longitudinal studies generally use smaller samples than in cross-sectional research. But they make up in depth what they lack in scope. The several sets of data on the same persons over time are something like demographic photographs of the group over time. One can begin to see some motion or change in the group. This metaphor of the motion picture is overdrawn because many longitudinal studies may have only a couple of time frames, and many assumptions must be made to connect the changes in group scores so as to infer causal patterns. The BRI Protective Services Project took four time samples of the older participants—four interviews over a year's time at prescribed intervals—but only two, the initial interview and the one-year interview, were used to provide information about changes on the major variables. The others were mainly checkups on the living situation and the health of the participants.

Several types of longitudinal study can be distinguished. *Trend studies* involve looking at the same type of data at different time periods, such as census data over a series of decennial periods. We can see the gross trends of large numbers of Americans whose data are averaged together. We do not have information on trends in subgroups unless specific questions are asked about the demographic characteristics that form these subgroups.

Another major type of longitudinal study involves the *cohort,* some specific subpopulation identified because of a given characteristic (like year of birth, or having a common experience such as being a Holocaust survivor). Different members of this cohort are then sampled to be studied at different periods of time. For example,

1. In 1975, *A, B, C, D,* and *E* are studied (members of Cohort *X*).
2. In 1980, *F, G, H, I,* and *J* are studied (Cohort *Y*), as are the surviving members of Cohort *X;* the same instruments are used as in 1975, plus others, if desired.
3. In 1985, *K, L, M, N,* and *O* are studied (Cohort *Z*), as are the surviving members of *X* and *Y* cohorts; the same instruments are used as in 1975 and 1980, and new ones if desired.

In this case, we have information on the cohorts, but not on individual differences over time.

Yet another basic form of longitudinal study is the *panel,* in which the same set of people is studied over time. These people may or may not belong to the same cohort. That is, the people may be randomly selected, or they may be chosen because of their membership in a given cohort. The essential ingredient is continued study of the same people over time. This approach is described as follows:

1. In 1975, persons *A, B, C, D,* and *E* are identified and interviewed with regard to a given study.
2. In 1980, persons *A, B, C,* and *D* are located and reinterviewed with the same instruments used in 1975. New instruments may also be introduced. Person *E* may have died or moved away, may refuse to be reinterviewed, or may simply not have been found.
3. In 1985, persons *A, B,* and *C* are again located and reinterviewed for the third time, with the same instruments as in 1975, plus whatever new instruments were introduced in 1980. Additional instruments may again be added in 1985. Person *D* has dropped out for some reason; presumably person *E* has not been found either.

With the panel, not only can we make some descriptive statements about the group averages over time, but we can also look at the patterns of changes in particular individuals. These patterns may indicate some common causal factors as well.

It is possible to conduct some intensive observational studies (such as Barker and Wright's *One Boy's Day,* 1951, in which a team of researchers follow one person in minute detail throughout a short period of time). Every word and gesture may be captured, along with the corresponding reactions or actions of others around this person. It would be possible, moreover, to record a person's actions by audiovisual techniques, which would provide an even finer look at the enormous details that make up a person's life experience.

But even such enormous detail does not directly reveal causality. The researchers still have to conceptualize what it is from their mass of data that constitutes what is happening within or outside the individual that causes him or her to respond as observed. Moreover, the more microscopic the detail and the more there is of it, the greater is the pressure on the researcher to provide a large framework to make sense of all of the data. Also, the greater is the likelihood that the researcher under these conditions will miss happenings in the larger social and cultural spheres that are having an impact, immediate or delayed, on that individual. Thus, all research is a compromise on ways of obtaining information as the basis for forming inferences on how and why people behave as they do, think as they do, and feel as they do. Whether we obtain a large amount of information on one person or a small amount on many people, at one time or over time, is a matter of logistics. Each approach has its benefits and its costs.

2.3 NEEDS ASSESSMENT

There were ample indicators of need for a study on protective services for older persons (as discussed in the Narrative part of this chapter) nationally, on the state and local scene, and in the helping professions. In this Technical Note, I would like to expand on the history of this approach to research because it has played such an important part in the helping professions. I will take Zimbalist's book (1977) on the history of research in social welfare as our guide in this discussion.

The term *needs assessment* refers generally to various methods for studying groups of people, as in whole communities or specified cohorts of persons, such as those sharing the characteristic of being sixty-five or older. In its early form as the *social survey* (such as in the Pittsburgh Survey of 1909), there was an attempt by experts to determine underlying needs in sanitary and civic areas. But as Zimbalist pointed out, the 1909 Pittsburgh Social Survey was predominantly motivated by a strong critical orientation in which the scientific worth of the investigation was diluted by the blatant criticisms presented through journalistic means.

Although the investigators were able to present many shocking problems related to the conditions of immigrant groups, blacks, children, factory workers generally, and the like, their methods of galvanizing popular reactions to remedy these situations had the long-term effect of creating more problems than they solved. Hypotheses were prejudged from the start; the investigators' social values colored the data that were found and the interpretations that were made, so that when contradictory data emerged in some cases, it was difficult to make a strong case for their empirical evidence. Thus, although the problems clearly existed, the method of communicating them in order to promote change had problems of its own and was not effective.

Zimbalist noted that the helping professions then turned to more focused assessments of specific needs. Local persons who were knowledgeable about the community were involved in these investigations, rather than outsiders, as in the early social surveys. Their more sensitive findings helped to improve some of the social conditions, and the need for the grosser forms of muckraking was reduced. For example, the Second Pittsburgh Study (1934–1938) dealt with a specific analysis of needs and available services in the major fields of social work. I'll return to some later developments in this area shortly.

There are many other ways in which the needs of people have been assessed. Some forms of social-welfare statistics have been gathered for centuries, but a critical turning point into the modern age came from the work of Charles Booth and his associates who published a seventeen-volume series called the *Life and Labour of the People in London* (1892–1897), a shocking view of the difficult life at the time. What was especially noteworthy was the fact that even the working poor shared this misery. Some leaders of the Fabian Socialist group had worked with Booth, such as Sidney and Beatrice Webb, and carried these experiences into their social programs.

Later surveys of this type that were conducted in America, such as the Consumer Purchases Study of 1935–1936, provided the basis for the official Consumer Price Index to which so many social-welfare programs would be linked to an accelerating or decelerating clause. Moreover, the Consumer Price Index was also used in the operational definitions of the poverty level, which played a major part in the political process in America as leaders of both parties tried to ameliorate these difficulties (Zimbalist, 1977).

A new form of social survey emerged as investigators tried to link empirical data with a conceptual scheme to indicate such abstract ideas as *social breakdown*. The empirical rates of mental diseases, crimes, divorces, and the like were combined to identify or index the breakdown of given social areas. These empirical facts were indicators of an abstract conception of social structures and forces operating in a given locale. Although a great deal depends on the variables selected and on how the rates are interpreted—compare, for example, Hill (1971) and Moynihan (1965)—this idea of *indexing* has been developed to the point where it has once again become very popular and widely—if indiscriminately— used. Zimbalist (1977, pp. 206–207) listed the limitations of this indexing approach: The selection and weighting of items to be included is largely arbitrary and subjective. The raw data are frequently of limited accuracy; for example, considerable amounts of crime and delinquency go unreported so that census tract figures may be misleading. Geographical areas (such as census tracts) are heterogeneous and changing, circumstances that make the average figures that are reported in the indexes of dubious meaning.

On the other hand, *epidemiological studies* (see Technical Note 2.1, p. 48) have proved to be extremely helpful in dealing with indicators of physical and mental health and illness, including the construction of apparent causal links that have provided directions for effective intervention. The major differences between the epidemiological study and the indexes of social breakdown include the precision in measurement of the variables under study and the conceptual networks in which these elements are placed, which subsequently serve as guides to practice. In both cases, precision and clarity favor the epidemiological study, probably because the size of the target concept is more circumscribed.

A more recent approach to the assessment of needs or social conditions is the *social indicator*, a "statistic of direct, normative interest which facilitates concise, comprehensive and balanced judgments about the conditions of major aspects of society" (*Toward a Social Report*, 1969, p. 97). Social indicators include the numbers and proportions of persons with various health, education, and welfare characteristics (viewed over a period of years), which are taken as indicating trends in the nation's health, education, and welfare systems. This approach sounds reminiscent of the early social survey, but at a national level. Although techniques of measurement have grown more sophisticated over the years, there are still many conceptual and practical—or political—problems to be overcome in their use. Statistical abstracts have been around for a long time; the question is essentially what use one makes of this information.

2.4 BASIC AND APPLIED RESEARCH

Research, in its most general sense, refers to any systematic and objective study of some portion of social reality, such as specified psychological and sociocultural events. The knowledge derived from this study may serve a variety of purposes, from understanding the nature and operation of that piece of reality to applying this knowledge in order to influence parts of that reality. This definition suggests a continuum of purposes that needs further clarification.

We can conceptualize the two ends of the continuum as having distinctive emphases. *Basic research* may be defined as seeking to develop principles to expand a portion of substantive knowledge or the methodological tools of a discipline. These purposes answer the questions: How do things work? and How can we know about how things work? The overall emphasis of basic research is to obtain knowledge for its own sake (Thomas, 1975). It was once thought that such research was value-free because "pure" knowledge was the result, with no implications for people implied (see the classic statement by Max Weber, 1949). However, time and again, researchers have pointed out that there are many points at which one's values direct the choice of one's topics and methods, as well as the interpretations of one's data, so that little in life is "pure," that is, untouched by human values.

The other end of the continuum is known as *applied research,* which seeks to develop principles that enable people to resolve problems or to obtain desired objectives. The question here is how to make things work for human betterment. The overall emphasis is on knowledge for use, with the implication that values are much involved in the entire process from beginning to end. After all, people are to be affected by the application of scientific knowledge to their lives and therefore have a natural interest in these applications.

In the middle of the continuum is what is known as *mission-guided research.* In these situations, the researchers are given direction on what type of outcomes are sought, but the means of exploration are much broader than in the usual applied setting. Some far-out ideas might be supported for study (as in basic research), even though the researchers are consciously looking for solutions for a given problem (applied research). This is the context where one might find a high proportion of serendipitous outcomes, that is, accidental findings valuable in their own right but not related to the study immediately at hand.

The real meaning of the basic, applied, and mission-guided research depends on the institutional auspices under which one is doing one's research. If one is being paid for finding a specific solution to a defined problem, then one is doing applied research regardless of the setting. If one is enabled to try out new ideas and methods related to a general goal, then this approach is most appropriately labeled *mission-guided research.* If one is left on one's own to a high degree, with only the expectation that some research results will be forthcoming at some time, than that is an idealized form of basic research. If one is working at home on the weekend at one's microcomputer, tinkering with some ideas that were stimulated by one's general experiences, one is—like the Benjamin Franklins of an earlier age—still doing research, the meaning of which depends on its eventual use. Franklin's work with electricity was basic research in his generation, but it has had enormous applied outcomes in ours.

Thus, the distinctions among basic, mission-guided, and applied research are probably overdrawn in the long-term sense, but they may be useful for categorizing current work. Moreover, these meanings are not fixed; one piece of work may shift into another category, depending on the context and the outcome itself.

2.5 RESEARCH PROPOSALS

Who pays for research? Even Galileo had his patron, someone who gave him money to pay the grocer and the landlord while he fiddled with his contraptions and thought new thoughts about the universe. Today, almost all research of any magnitude is funded by organizations, generally the federal government or major foundations (or branches of commercial organizations) set up specifically for this purpose. Because it is likely that the readers of this book will, at one time or another, have contact with research programs, it will be useful to describe the process through which research proposals are solicited and developed. Although the details have changed since Margaret Blenkner wrote the proposals for the BRI Protective Services Project, the major outlines remain the same. Let's begin with an extended illustration of a call for research by a branch of the federal government (see also, Appendix A).

Requests for proposals (RFPs) are issued from time to time by the federal government, as well as by foundations and other organizations. These RFPs are invitations to interested researchers to suggest ways in which they would propose to study some target problem so that a funder would be willing to negotiate supporting the researcher in this endeavor.

On December 7, 1982, the Office of Human Development Services (OHDS) in the U.S. Department of Health and Human Services (DHHS) issued a public statement in the *Federal Register* that contained four parts. First, there was a general announcement of monies available for research in certain broad areas. These monies were allocated to constituent programs of the OHDS, including the Administration for Children, Youth, and Families; the Administration on Aging; and agencies concerned with other special population groups.

The first part of the RFP explained the background of this announcement. In order to obtain information on priority problems, the OHDS initiated a Coordinated Discretionary Funds Program in which the constituent agencies sought *preapplications*—brief statements of proposed research that would encourage a large number of persons to consider doing research. In fact, some 5,620 preapplications had been received the year before, and 167 of these had received federal funds. Presumably the larger number of preapplications improved the pool from which selections were finally made, as well as stimulating many to think seriously about research questions.

These discretionary funds were intended to "expand the boundaries of human services knowledge by drawing on new ideas from a variety of fields . . . [so as] to respond more effectively to State and local needs" (p. 55112). The announcement also presented the philosophy that probably guides the selection of projects at the highest level of that agency:

> . . . The well-being of the public is primarily a responsibility of individuals, families, and the communities in which they live. . . . The role of the Federal Government in addressing social problems is:
>
> • To adopt and implement national policies or programs aimed at promoting economic growth and prosperity and thereby reducing the need for social services. . . .
>
> • To provide national leadership in (a) the development of effective methods of addressing social service needs; and (b) the development of State and local capacity to deliver social services appropriately targeted at local problems;
>
> • To foster the efficient and effective use of available resources through improved social service management. . . . (p. 55112)

In the fiscal year 1983, these discretionary funds were to be aimed at two major themes that support this federal role. First, there was to be increased

55

social and economic self-sufficiency through prevention, targeting of resources, and strategies for socioeconomic development. Second, there was to be more efficient and effective administration of programs, so that they would be responsive to local needs. As expected, these themes permeated the actual program priorities. The first part of this RFP announcement ends with a listing of the statutory authorities providing the actual funds, such as the Head Start Act of 1981 and the Child Abuse Prevention and Treatment Act, as amended.

Part Two presents the program priorities, which had been developed through a participatory process in which some national organizations, government agencies, and private individuals were invited to recommend major research issues that should be addressed. Specific topics were identified under the two major themes mentioned above: increased social and economic self-sufficiency and improved administrative effectiveness and efficiency. For example, under the first major theme were the following specific topics: employment and income generation, community and family-based care, prevention and early intervention, and so on. Under the second major theme were the topics of improved use of management information systems, evaluation assistance, and training.

Then each of these suggested topics is further illustrated by examples in order to be as specific as possible for readers of the announcement. For instance, under the topic of community and family-based care, the following illustration is provided:

> [Research is called for, regarding:]
>   Demonstrations of family and community-based techniques for the prevention of inappropriate placement of developmentally disabled children in foster care, as well as the reduction of risk of abuse and neglect of these children.
>   (p. 55114)

Each of these sections closes with a statement about the approximate level of funding for projects through given agencies; for example, the Administration on Developmental Disabilities was to get about $130,000 to fund acceptable projects. All projects independently competed for these discretionary funds. Competition was often very stiff.

Part Three describes in detail the preapplication process: Who was eligible to apply? (Any state, nonprofit organization, or agency.) How much money was available? (About $21 million, divided among the nine programs within the OHDS.) How much money had to be supplied by the organizations that received government grants? (At least 25 percent of the total cost of the proposed project had to come from sources other than the federal government.)

The preapplication was reviewed by federal officials and qualified persons outside the government, but the decision about who could submit a full-fledged proposal was made by the Assistant Secretary for Human Development Services, thus assuring that the decisions reflected the dominant philosophy of the granting agency. There were discussions with some of the applicants on the preapplications, and others were referred to more appropriate funding sources.

As you can see, developing an application can be complicated; the statements of purpose and goal are often general and depend on the interpretation of actual officials who decide whether a specific application is really what the agency is looking for. But these officials are human beings, in spite of their bureaucratic positions, and generally speaking, it is easy to communicate with them by letter or telephone as one is developing a preapplication. It is, moreover, advisable to do so, to clarify terms, procedures, and goals that never seem as clear to the responders as to the writers of RFPs.

Next in the announcement, there is an elaborate statement of the details of the process. Criteria for screening are presented, including procedural matters like having the exact number of application copies of the exact prescribed length, and so on. Substantive criteria are also given, such as being in conformance with the announced topics, being innovative, and having a solid research design. Points are indicated for each of these types of criteria; these points are very revealing. For example, innovativeness rates 30 possible points, whereas project design can earn 15 points.

Those who submitted the highest ranked preapplications were asked to submit final applications, which went through another review process, with other criteria for evaluation. These criteria focus on the more technical aspects of the applications (because they have been all screened as being substantively and philosophically appropriate): the technical approach used in the study rates up to 25 points, the predicted beneficial impact of the study may earn up to 25 points, and so forth.

Part Four provides further details: "Project narrative, no more than ten pages long, double-spaced and typewritten on one side only. . . . $8\frac{1}{2}$" x 11" plain white bond with 1" margins on both sides" (p. 55123). Such detail is necessary— although it seems overwhelming at first—in order to ensure that each proposal will receive an equal and fair hearing, both for the benefit of the applicant and for the society seeking understanding on vital issues of the day. (See also the set of grant application forms from a major source of funding for the social and behavioral sciences, reproduced in Appendix A.)

2.6 RESEARCH AND EVALUATION

"Research" is often distinguished from "evaluation." It will be useful to clarify this distinction because there are many implications in categorizing an investigation as being one or the other.

In a sense, one might link "evaluation" with applied research, whereas "research" would be more closely associated with basic research (see Technical Note 2.4, p. 53). Thus, evaluation is typically used as the method for supplying relatively short-term answers to specific questions, such as Did this program do what it set out to do? or Did this individual client achieve the objectives that he or she set out to reach? Research, on the other hand, is more often used in seeking long-range goals or underlying principles on how things operate.

With the results of an evaluation study, one can make decisions about continuing, modifying, or terminating a given project or case intervention (Weiss, 1972, p. 4). But with research results, which usually arrive after a long and involved effort, one may not be able to change or may not be interested in changing the events in a single situation. The knowledge obtained is aimed at a broader understanding that may affect many future studies, or it may be the building block on which future researchers continue a search for basic knowledge that need never be applied in any socially profitable way. If this sounds irresponsible,

I don't intend it to; rather, it is a statement of a fundamental scientific stance: knowledge, even on esoteric topics, may be a good in itself simply as knowledge about the universe or about how the constructed symbolic universe operates.

Further implications of the distinction between research and evaluation are that research is rigorous and follows specific procedures that can be exactly replicated, whereas evaluation is more adaptable to the particular context in which it is to be employed. That is, because evaluation is sensitive to the particular nuances of a given applied situation, it is not as rigid in observing strict procedures for the sake of replicability when the focus is on the uniqueness of the specific case at hand.

I believe that these distinctions are overdrawn. There is a germ of truth in the flexibility of evaluation in the face of the unique situation at hand, but research can be highly flexible even within the strict codes of its practice. Moreover, evaluation procedures are in no way less strict as to what steps an investigator must follow, although the evaluator may be more willing to accept approximations and shortcuts to get information than the researcher might be. However, these are matters of degree rather than type, and we can find casual researchers as well as rigorous evaluators. Moreover, some investigators blend both stances in one project. I think that the BRI Protective Services Project included some serious research work—including instrument development and rigorous attention to research design—while it also sought to evaluate the practices that evolved from this one project. However, because it was a research demonstration, the project could not take knowledge about its own practice effectiveness to modify that practice during the project year. That was a restriction derived from the research perspective. But flexibility in making modifications in the research and practice designs during the course of the study derives from the evaluation perspective, trying to find what it is that is working so as to be able to describe that final practice package. (See Technical Note 2.7, page 58.)

2.7 THE BRI PROTECTIVE SERVICES PROPOSALS

From the previous discussions about Margaret Blenkner's prowess as a nationally renowned researcher, it may come as a surprise to learn that her first proposal on protective services was rejected. The object lesson is that even good researchers can't win them all, but they do rebound and try again.

The several protective service proposals are instructive for another reason: they illustrate the pressure that can be brought to bear on the researcher by the funding organization and its panels of experts. Proposals are carefully constructed documents. They identify a significant social problem, summarize what research and practice knowledge is available that relates to this problem, and then indicate gaps in this knowledge or skill base that the proposal seeks to fill in. Although the details may be sketchy, the proposal indicates clearly the broad outlines of the planned demonstration or research project, as well as what results and benefits are foreseen from its results. Citations of current relevant materials are provided, as corroboration that this proposal is well grounded in the activities of the field.

Readers of such a proposal, either the full-time staff members of the funding organization or temporary appointees who come together periodically to review a batch of proposals, are generally very well qualified by virtue of their own successful research records in the broad area. For example, one might find sociologists, psychologists, physicians, and social workers who are in the field of gerontology as readers of proposals sent to agencies funding research on aging. However, no one would necessarily have specific experience with the topic of the proposed research. But their general background in gerontology, together with their experience with a specific aspect of research in this area, qualifies them as expert readers. Indeed, with their variety of experiences, they can often provide the proposal writer with a wider perspective on the given project than would content specialists in that exact topic.

So it was that Dr. Blenkner submitted a formal proposal (after the smaller "seeding grant" that permitted her the time and the resources to develop the larger proposal). Let me describe briefly the proposal that didn't get funded. It was vintage Blenkner, a very carefully conceived, grandiose scheme calling for four stages of research in which between thirty and fifty cases would be obtained from different sources, with enough time between the stages so that the service team could learn by doing, could record the essence of the successful methods, could offer empirical evidence of the superiority of these methods over other solutions or current practice, and then could report the demonstrated skills and strategies to the practice literature.

The specific stages are interesting because they offer a preview of what happened in the actual Protective Services Project—and the origin of some of the problems in the project. The first stage involved identifying participants from the member agencies of the Welfare Federation of Cleveland, because of whose expressed concern and instigation the project originated in the first place. A typical experimental–control-group design was planned for this first wave of participants. The second stage would obtain participants from agencies that typically referred clients to the first-stage agencies, such as the housing authority, social security, and the office on aging. Again, a typical experimental–control-group design was suggested.

The third stage was quite different. Dr. Blenkner recognized that protective cases emerge in a variety of contexts, and so she proposed that professional persons in private practice—particularly physicians, members of the clergy, lawyers, and trust officers—be involved in providing participants for the study. This decision raised a complicated question about sampling and securing the cooperation of professionals who were not very experienced in participating in community research, but Dr. Blenkner reasoned that by the time the third stage had come around, the reputation of the project would have been established and these private professionals might be more accepting of the challenge. One more point was expanded in the fourth stage, that clients of bankers, lawyers, and private physicians are probably very different from the clients of public assistance agencies, and so we would get an opportunity to look at protective care from differing economic vantage points.

The fourth stage makes this economic point explicit. At this time, the general public was to be invited to aid in identifying participants, older persons in need of protective care. Let's look at Dr. Blenkner's explicit statement on the economic issue:

> This will also be the logical time to try to arrive at some measure of the cost of the program should the community wish to incorporate it into its on-going services, either at a separate agency or as a specialized function of an existing agency. An epidemiological study of the incidence and prevalence of this type of case might also be carried out during this stage with particular attention to strategic points of early identification. (Blenkner, 1963)

Dr. Blenkner thought that such a project would take at least four years, and possibly even longer. The review committee apparently thought otherwise. It was too large a project and too expensive, and it had too many uncontrolled factors that could limit its usefulness as a demonstration project. But the basic ideas were sound: Would Dr. Blenkner please rewrite the proposal with only one stage, fewer participants, and less complexity in the design?

She did indeed rewrite the proposal and, regretfully, collapsed some of its ideas into a one-stage proposal, even though she thought that, logically and practically, one would need more time and more experience to identify and demonstrate effective practices. One of the compromises she made was to create two experimental conditions reflecting her concern about the cost factor. One experimental group was to get all the planned social work and ancillary services as well as money from an emergency fund to purchase small items as needed. The other experimental group was to have all of the services except access to the emergency financial fund.

How important was this distinction? It was an attempt to have two stages in one, except that the amount of money involved was relatively minimal (especially compared to the cost of the other services provided all experimental participants). The average expenditure was $225 per client per year, or less than $20 a month (Blenkner, Wasser, and Bloom, 1967, p. 18). However, she also noted that financial assistance was the top-ranking ancillary service rendered the experimental participants, with 75 percent receiving this aid. This was far more costly than the next most used ancillary service, medical evaluation, with 54 percent receiving this service. I was not a party to the handling of this service distinction, but it is my impression that the project workers found ways to get material goods to participants who needed them, whether there was a fund or not. In a word, I think that this variable of an emergency fund was not a strong variable in practice and that its compromise origin was reflected in the project itself. Dr. Blenkner at some stage collapsed the distinction of the two types of experimental participants (I do not know when this occurred) because it became a difference that didn't make a difference in practice. Critics were later to point out that this combining of experimental groups was a significant problem in handling the data (Dunkle, Poulshock, Silverstone, and Deimling, 1983). I don't think Dr. Blenkner would agree, but I am surprised that anything as inelegant as this deviation from the practice design occurred at all.

2.8 POPULATION, SAMPLE, AND CASE

In research, as in any aspect of life, the answers you get depend on whom you question, as well as on what you ask. Except in rare instances, researchers never ask all the potentially relevant people; they obtain samples instead, which are intended to represent all of the others. This sounds straightforward enough, but it becomes complex in the actual carrying out of the sampling procedures. In order to clarify this process, three major terms have to be distinguished, for all refer to persons involved in a research study.

The term *population* (or *universe*) is the largest unit of analysis; it includes all persons meeting the defined characteristics. However, researchers immediately begin to impose some boundaries on their population. For example, the BRI Protective Services Project studied "older persons." In fact, this category referred not only to an arbitrary beginning age of sixty-five or older but, practically speaking, was limited to older persons in a given country. We knew something about this portion of the population because the U.S. Census Bureau provides an analysis of this subset of the total population. Scientists recognize that there are errors in the census itself, such as the underrepresentation of minority persons, to say nothing of aliens who have entered the country unlawfully. But the census represents the most nearly complete picture of a population available.

A *sample* is some defined portion of a population. There are many ways to define and select that sample, but the general intention is to have some feasible way to obtain needed information at a price that the research organization can afford, so that we not only learn what this sample thinks but also can infer what the total population thinks on the topic under consideration. These three dimensions—the *information,* the *cost,* and the *degree of generalizability*—are the primary choices researchers face as they select a sample. Thus you may choose to take a purely *random sample* (selected by means of scientifically rigorous methods in which each individual has an equal chance of being included) or a *casually* chosen handful who happen to be walking by when you want to ask your questions. The latter sample is much less useful for purposes of later generalizing your results because it is representative of no known group of other persons (no population with defined characteristics). However, it is a fast way to get a sense of popular sentiment, and it is very inexpensive. In each case, the questions you ask may be almost identical, although you are likely to invest more care in developing the questions for the scientific sample than in developing those for the casual one because the generalizing opportunities are so much more powerful.

Between the purely random sampling from the entire population and the purely casual selecting of passersby are many other ways of identifying a group of persons with whom to conduct the research. Even popular pollsters employ techniques that are much closer to the scientific approach, and commercial or political pollsters also use scientific techniques because the quality of the resulting information is so much better. However, rather than taking pure random samples, it is more economical and efficient to *stratify* the larger population into *relevant subgroups* and to select randomly from these subgroups. Or it is more economical and efficient to stratify by the types of *locations* in which specific individuals will be studied. These ways of stratifying portions of the population (by subgroups or subareas) do not reduce the equal opportunities for admission into the study. Rather, these are some steps that filter out persons in larger groupings before the actual specific selections take place.

The sample for the BRI Protective Services Project was selected by means of such a compromise procedure within the limits of the situation. First, a geographic zone was selected for feasibility; it would have been difficult for workers to drive all around the state, and so far as we knew, the rural areas did not have as large a concentration of persons in need of protective services. Thus the practicalities demanded that the demonstration project be started in an urban area; adaptations would have to be made later for rural use (see Davenport and Davenport, 1982, for an example of the adaptation of a social services program to rural culture).

Dr. Blenkner did consider doing a random survey of persons in the Cleveland metropolitan area, but it would have been expensive to locate sufficient numbers of older persons meeting the criteria of need for protective services. And so as another expedient, she chose to go through existing social, health, and welfare channels by using thirteen agencies in Cleveland known to have large numbers of older clients. A preliminary survey of these agencies pointed out the wisdom of this choice, as they had in their caseloads in one month more than enough cases to supply the demonstration project for the several years of the study. However, not all older persons with protective problems were known to these agencies, and so not all such persons had an equal chance of appearing in the BRI Project. One might argue that all people had an equal opportunity to use the services of one or another of the thirteen agencies—including social security, welfare, housing, medical services at the city hospital, and family agencies—but this is a limitation of the sampling procedure that we recognized.

From the preliminary survey of agencies, we assigned a quota system of applicants to the BRI Project to reflect the proportions of persons in need of protective services then existing among the city's service organizations. This quota system simply reflected the reality of the situation as we knew it.

However, from this point onward, strict random procedures were used. There was no known bias in determining whether a person was admitted to the experimental or the control group. Thus we can say that this final BRI sample was representative of the older persons who were known to thirteen social and health agencies in Cleveland at that period of time. Whether this sample was truly representative of all older persons in need of protective services (in the United States at that time) cannot be discovered except by the use of some broad parameters using national census data or comparisons with similar clientele in other cities. Thus the compromises used in selecting the original sample also limited the generalizability to some degree. But there were few other ways of identifying comparable groups, let alone the comparable population, because so little was known about this kind of person, who stays invisible as part of his or her mental condition. Thus the reader takes some risk in trying to infer that what happened to the participants in the BRI study would be likely to happen to his or her client. There are points at which such generalizability breaks down because of the compromises required by the situation.

A *case* is usually one specific person within the sample, and is, ordinarily, no problem to identify. But cases can also be composed of units other than individuals. For example, families might be the sampling unit. Thus the terms *population, sample,* and *case* are relative terms. What is constant is the order among them. The actual content of these units may change in different circumstances. For example, a single nursing home may be the population or the universe for a given study, the sample for another, or the case instance in a third investigation. As long as you know the relative status of the persons involved, this distinction won't be a problem.

2.9 GROUP RESEARCH DESIGNS: AN OVERVIEW

This book presents the experience of research through an intensive exposure to one project because I believe that this presentation will give the most nearly adequate understanding of what it means to do research—short of doing some significant research yourself. However, the BRI study is only one project among thousands, and it is important to survey some of the other types of research designs that can be used in the study of human behavior. This Technical Note is in the form of a table that begins with some basic elements and then expands and varies these elements to form a wide range of designs, each of which has its own special strengths and limitations. I base this table on Campbell and Stanley's germinal work (1963).

The ingredients are (1) one or more groups, (2) which are randomly assigned to experimental and control conditions, or not, and (3) are tested either at the end or at the beginning of the study, or both. Campbell and Stanley pointed to a critical mass or combination among these ingredients as constituting true experimental designs. Others they politely called "preexperimental designs," and they pointed out how limited these are in providing sound empirical evidence. The *one-shot case study* is limited because it uses only one group, with no comparisons with what existed before the intervention. The *one-group pretest–posttest* design is better than the one-shot case study, but again only one group is used. A third preexperimental design, the *static-group comparison*, has two groups, but they are not randomly assigned, and so they are limited in preventing alternative explanations for the results that occcur. (See Technical Note 4.6, p. 123.)

The critical mass or combinations of ingredients occur in the first example of Figure 2.1; thus is is a true experimental design. As you study this figure, which begins on the following page, note how the ingredients are modified and combined to attain more thorough analyses of how some portion of nature works.

Figure 2.1 Group-research designs.

Design	Flow Diagram	Advantages	Disadvantages
Design #1: **Pre-test/Post-test,** **Experimental/Control Group Design** *Discussion:* The units to be studied, such as individuals or groups, are randomly selected *from* the population P to form a sample S from which units are randomly assigned *to* an experimental E or a control group C. The E group receives an experimental treatment or intervention X, while the C group receives either nothing at all, or else whatever is available in the community (standard treatment). Both groups are observed at time 1, in which a check of their comparability is made. At time 2, the experimental intervention is given only to E. Observations at time 3 are taken on both groups so that comparisons can be made between O_2-O_1, and O_4-O_3, as well as between O_2-O_4.	Time 1 2 3 E : O_1 X O_2 C : O_3 C O_4 P — (R) — S — R — R *Variations:* Only randomization *to* E and C groups is required by this design -- R; randomization *from* the population is desired where possible -- (R). One could also compare two different E groups with no C, obtaining information on the differences between them, but one would lack a frame of reference to interpret what the differences meant. The control group always supplies this frame of reference of what groups randomly selected from the population would be like without the experimental intervention.	1. This design presents information on the effect of X on E, as compared with a comparable C group. 2. This design eliminates many threats to internal validity—e.g., history, maturation, statistical regression, selection, etc. (See Campbell and Stanley, 1963.) 3. This design minimizes the probability of threats to external validity (i.e., generalization). (See Campbell and Stanley, 1963.)	1. Many research projects involving human subjects in the community would have difficulty making random assignments *from* the population, although it is possible to make random assignments *to* treatment conditions in many contexts. 2. Pre-testing may itself produce an effect, apart from the X, and this would not be detectable in Design #1. 3. Differential attrition rates may affect the comparability of the two groups.
Design #2: **Solomon Four Group Design**	Time 1 2 3 E_1 : O_1 X_1 O_2 C_1 : O_3 C_1 O_4 E_2 : — X_2 O_5 C_2 : — C_2 O_6 P — (R) — S — R — R	1. This design tests for the effect of the pre-testing itself on the outcome. 2. This design would be useful with studies of controversial topics (where mention of the subject may influence the client's attitudes), or when the participants are relatively sophisticated in responding to questions.	1. This design requires double the participants in the research and related costs and difficulties in organization of the project. 2. Interpretation may be difficult if some combinations of outcomes occur, e.g., $O_6 > O_5$ and $O_2 > O_4$. 3. With more participants, there is more chance of dropout occurring.

4. See disadvantages listed for Design #1.

Discussion: Design #2 adds to Design #1 a second $\boxed{E}$ group and a second $\boxed{C}$ group, both of which are not pre-tested, so as to be able to compare the effects of pre-testing per se on the outcomes. If O_2 and O_4 significantly differ from O_5 and O_6, then pre-testing is shown to have an effect. If O_2 and O_5 (the two experimental groups) significantly differ from O_4 and O_6, then the experimental intervention is shown to have an effect.

Variations: It would be possible to add only an additional no pre-test control group to study the effects of pre-testing at a reduced cost. If the subjects for a Solomon Four Group Design were all in a clinic setting, and thus automatically getting some treatment, it might be necessary to obtain additional comparable samples of those who were not in the treatment setting because being in a treatment setting may be just as influencial as a pre-test observation.

3. Likewise, this design is useful if the timing between pre- and post-testing is relatively short.

4. See the advantages listed in Design #1.

**Design #3:
Post-test Only,
Experimental/Control Group Design**

Discussion: Design #3 is like Design #1 up to the point of selecting $\boxed{E}$ and $\boxed{C}$ groups. Then, instead of observing each in a pre-test, the researcher goes directly into the experimental variable $\boxed{X}$ for the $\boxed{E}$ group, and the control conditions for the $\boxed{C}$ group, followed by post-test measurements on the effects of the intervention. Note that this is essentially the addition that Solomon Four Group Design (#2) makes over Design #1.

```
                     Time
                  1   2   3
           R    E ··  — X — O_1
P —(R)— S
           R    C ··  — C — O_2
```

1. When there is need to act (treat) immediately, but where randomization (at least to $\boxed{E}$ and $\boxed{C}$ groups) is possible, then this Design #3 offers the advantages of an experimental/control group design.

2. The risks and the demands of pre-testing are eliminated.

1. Since the comparability of the $\boxed{E}$ and the $\boxed{C}$ groups cannot be tested (as in time 1 of Design #1)—and hence cannot be corrected through statistical means—the random assignment procedure is crucial.

2. Biases due to attrition are difficult to assess due to lack of a pre-test on individuals (unless archival information is available).

**Design #4:
Factorially Organized,
Pre-test/Post-test,
Experimental/Control Group Design**

```
               Factor    Time
                       1   2   3
                 eg ♂   O_1  X  O_2
           R   E
                    ♀   O_3  X  O_4
P —(R)— S
                    ♂   O_5  C  O_6
           R   C
                    ♀   O_7  C  O_8
```

1. In Design #1, factors such as sex differences may be present, but may not be visible (e.g., if males score high and females score low, the average blurs this pattern), whereas in Design #4, these factors are directly observed.

2. See the advantages of Design #1.

1. Design #4 requires a clear conceptualization prior to data collection so that the most appropriate factors are selected as part of the design. Using inappropriate factors adds expenses to the research.

2. Design #4 requires a larger number of subjects than Design #1.

(continued)

Figure 2.1 (continued).

Design	Flow Diagram	Advantages	Disadvantages

Design #4 (cont.)

Discussion: As with Design #1, E and C groups are formed in Design #4, but a further division of relevant categories is distinguished, for instance, by sex. This additional factor permits study of the interaction of the experimental variable and a second factor (sex), as well as with control groups likewise distinguished by sex. Thus, comparisons can be made directly by male versus female O_1/O_2 and O_5/O_6 versus O_3/O_4 and O_7/O_8. It can be made by experimental versus control groups O_1/O_2 and O_3/O_4 versus O_5/O_6 and O_7/O_8. But the major comparison would probably be the interaction of the experimental status and sex compared with control status and sex, O_1/O_2 versus O_3/O_4 versus sex, O_1/O_2 versus O_3/O_4 versus O_5/O_6 versus O_7/O_8.

Disadvantages (Design #4):

3. See the disadvantages for Design #1.

Design #5:
Group Time-Series Design

Discussion: Given a sufficient amount of pre-test information that indicates "all plausible patterns of variation" are present (Cook and Campbell 1976, p. 275)—that is, that there is a stable pattern of typical behaviors of the group E, then some intervention X is introduced, while measurements are continued through the post-intervention period. A

Flow Diagram (Design #5):

Time
$$1 \quad 2 \quad 3 \cdots t_x \quad t_{x+1} \quad t_{x+2} \quad t_{x+3}$$

? ─ E : $O_1 \quad O_2 \quad O_3 \quad X \quad O_4 \quad O_5 \quad O_6$

Variations: one might randomly allocate an E group and a C group from a common sample, and conduct a group time-series design on both simultaneously:

E : $O_1 \quad O_2 \quad O_3 \quad X \quad O_4 \quad O_5 \quad O_6$

C : $O_1 \quad O_2 \quad O_3 \quad C \quad O_4 \quad O_5 \quad O_6$

S R R

Advantages (Design #5):

1. An approximate form of evaluation may be obtained, even when no control group is available.

2. This before/after design with one group "controls" completely on the equivalence of the "compared" group, unlike any other group design that depends on random assignment for comparability.

3. The sequential data collection permits closer monitoring of the experimental events than group designs usually permit.

Disadvantages (Design #5):

1. The population or sample from which this group is drawn is not known—this is the meaning of the "?"—thus limiting generalizability.

2. It is not clear how much pre-testing is needed to establish a stable baseline period.

3. This design is open to alternative explanations for its results, the effects of history, maturation, etc. (See Campbell and Stanley, 1963; Technical Note 4.6.)

discontinuity between the typical pattern of events in the pre-test (baseline) situation and the pattern of events emerging over a similar time period in the post-intervention may be visible (through changes in level, direction, and degree of slope of the data curve). Or, various statistical analyses may indicate a significant difference between these two time periods.

Design #6:
Nonequivalent Experimental/Control Group, Pre-test/Post-test Design

Discussion: The samples represent "naturally assembled collectives" (Campbell and Stanley, 1963, p. 47) such as classrooms of the same grade level that are presumed to be similar, but the population characteristics are unknown (strictly speaking). The actual [E] and [C] groups are randomly assigned. The basic difference between this Design #6 and Design #1 is that the latter is drawn from a known population (possibly even randomly drawn from that known population), while the former is not. This means that in Design #6, the [E] and [C] groups are nonequivalent strictly speaking, even though they are manifestly similar on some dimensions. The pre-test O_1 and O_3 describe the extent of that comparability on the measures obtained. The more similar they are, the more this design approximates Design #1. The dashed line indicates the nonequivalence of [E] and [C] groups.

This would be a variation of Design #1 in a time-series form. Other time-series designs are possible (see Bloom and Fischer, 1982).

$$\text{Time}$$
$$1 \quad 2 \quad 3$$
$$? \; S\text{-}R \to [E] : O_1 \; X \; O_2$$
$$- - - -$$
$$? \; S\text{-}R \to [C] : O_3 \; C \; O_4$$

Variation: It would be possible to construct a time-series design with nonequivalent groups that would provide more detailed information on their comparability over time:

$$\text{Time}$$
$$1 \quad 2 \quad 3 \ldots t_x \quad t_{x+1} \; t_{x+2} \; t_{x+3}$$
$$[E]: \; O_1 \; O_2 \; O_3 \; X \; O_4 \; O_5 \; O_6$$
$$- - - -$$
$$[C]: \; O_7 \; O_8 \; O_9 \; C \; O_{10} \; O_{11} \; O_{12}$$

4. This design requires that a time series of measurements are possible and are nonreactive on the variables in question.

1. By taking advantage of whatever naturally similar groups are available for research, we probably expand the volume of research over what it would have been, had rigorous randomization rules been upheld.

2. Design #6 is better than the nonexperimental designs (such as the one group pre-test/post-test design—see Campbell and Stanley, 1963) because it provides a reasonable empirical context against which to compare the comparability of the [E] and the [C] groups.

3. This design does control for some alternative explanations such as history, testing, etc. (See Campbell and Stanley, 1963.)

1. The major disadvantage is that the [E] and [C] groups may not be equivalent on important characteristics known or unknown to the experimenter, even if they are comparable on pre-test scores. This will affect internal validity.

2. Interaction effects of the [E] and [C] groups with maturation and selection are more likely to occur when the groups are not formed by random assignment from a common population.

(*continued*)

Figure 2.1 (continued).

Design	Flow Diagram	Advantages	Disadvantages
Design #7: **Cross-over Design**		1. This design gives a second testing of the experimental intervention, and even the removal of that intervention from a previously successful treatment, in order to test the lasting effects of the service under more nearly natural circumstances.	1. This design is more complicated to carry out because of the longer time period involved, but generally people understand the principle of the waiting list.

Discussion: The first three time periods of this design are like Design #1: O_1 X O_2

O_3 C O_4

Then, for both ethical and experimental reasons, the control group receives the experimental intervention (which presumably has been shown to have been positively effective with the experimental group). There are several variations of the cross-over design: The experimental group may also be crossed over in the sense of having the experimental intervention removed and replaced by C, or the standard community treatment. (This presumes that the intervention can be removed—interventions composed of educational training cannot be removed.) Or, the [E] group may continue to receive the experimental condition along with the [C] group at time 4.

Several new comparisons can now be made. 1) The sequential effect of X on two equivalent groups. If O_1-O_2 and O_4-O_6 differences are of the same magnitude, we can logically assume more support for the inference that X is the causal factor. 2) The changes between O_2 and O_5 represent the probable learned (or stable) effects of X. 3) O_5 and O_6 should approach comparability once again (as they had in O_1 and O_3), unless there are carryover effects from the earlier stages of the design.

Flow Diagram:

Time
1 2 3 4 5

E: O_1 X_1 O_2 C_2 O_5

C: O_3 C_1 O_4 X_2 O_6

Advantages:

2. In addition, this design satisfies the ethical consideration of not withholding a proven successful intervention from a group who would benefit from it. This approach is sometimes referred to as a *waiting list approach* on grounds that not everyone can be served all at once, and so some experimental understanding may be gained from this necessary limitation.

Disadvantages:

2. But in addition, there may be differences between final outcomes O_5 and O_6 because of the effects of events in time (history or maturation).

CHAPTER 3

Ideas and Observations: The Great Cycle of Research

Overview

In this chapter, I want to present some impressions of the moments of insight and the years of toil that went into the Benjamin Rose Institute Protective Services Project, a great cycle that moved between ideas and observations. Occasionally the movement was back and forth, each process trying to stimulate and to raise the other, but without much success. At other times, the movement was a spiral, a dialectic in which the questions we had posed led to answers that produced new questions of a higher order. And there were some tailspins, when the observations simply didn't make any sense in connection with the ideas with which we were working. Fortunately we were engaged with many of the steps of the research process simultaneously—an approach necessary to carrying out a large-scale project on a reasonable time schedule—and so the moments of excitement and of depression didn't all come at the same time.

It is possible to step back from this experience and generalize to a broader view of these great cycles in any research process. This topic will be developed in the last part of the chapter.

Narrative Section

Prior Research: The Community Service Society Project and the Terrifying Idea
The Relocation Shock Hypothesis: Ideas and Observations
Pauses in the Great Cycle of Ideas and Observations: Decision Making
Cycles of the Research Process: Overview Through a Glass Darkly

Technical Notes Section

The Narrative

PRIOR RESEARCH: THE COMMUNITY SERVICE
SOCIETY PROJECT AND THE TERRIFYING IDEA

In spite of all the events that were interacting in the configural background of the Benjamin Rose Institute Protective Services Project as described in Chapter 2, I suggested there that it was the principal researcher who ultimately selected the combination of ideas and observations that became the concrete study. In this chapter, I would like to examine this crystallizing process more closely. I believe that it was a kind of dialectic in which the principal investigator engaged both her past and her present experiences in creating a future.

Margaret Blenkner and her colleagues had recently completed a major study at the Community Service Society of New York (Blenkner, Jahn, and Wasser, 1964). In this study, older applicants to a social services agency were randomly assigned among different programs that varied in length and intensity of service. A nonapplicant group of older persons was selected from people identified in an area probability sample in the same area of New York City. Research interviews independent of the service programs were conducted at the beginning of the service and at a six-month follow-up. If the broad outlines of this Community Service Society project and the later BRI project sound familiar, it is because they were. The New York study employed a powerful research design and sampling methodology, as compared with most comparable social work (then and since). Not everything was repeated in the BRI study, although we did try. We did explore the possibility of using area probability samples to locate older persons in need of protective services. This process would have been extremely expensive and might not have generated the numbers of participants that we ultimately needed for such a project. However, such a sample would have made the question of generalizability of our research much cleaner. It was, as often occurs in research planning, a trade-off between the ideal and the feasible.

The aim of the Community Service Society project was to test whether the combined services of social workers and public health nurses in a short-term or a long-term contact would be significantly superior to the standard treatment program, in which these helping professionals usually worked separately using extended contacts. It turned out that there were no major differences in the outcomes from long-term or short-term services, and hence that it would be preferable—in terms of efficiency as well as effectiveness—to use short-term intervention programs for older persons with either type of professional helping separately.* This finding, by the way, was important in the building of an empirical basis for short-term therapy, a movement that has mushroomed considerably from the 1960s to today (see Germain, 1983; Maluccio, 1981; Reid and Shyne, 1969; Barton, 1971).

---

* Technical Note 3.1 (p. 85) presents the important question of *ethical concerns* in the entire research process. I earlier pointed out that sociocultural values represent the largest context in which research takes place. Ethical issues are the major dimension of this context. I have offered some suggested guidelines for your consideration.

Incidental to these findings was a statistically nonsignificant piece of information whose implications were perhaps more important for the elderly than the major findings that were statistically significant. It was a dreadful observation and led to a terrifying idea: the observation was that there was a higher death rate among clients in the service program who had been relocated from their unpleasant and inadequate homes in the community to some institution whose resources were undoubtedly far superior to the home situation. The number of persons involved was small, and so any statistical statement did not have much strength. But this finding gave rise to an idea that was terrible in its implications. Did the helping professionals unwittingly take part in the premature death of their clients by relocating elderly persons, even to an environment that was superior on any conceivable standard of safety, sanitation, and decency?

Whenever a set of data points to a humanly important outcome, particularly when that outcome is untoward and deadly, then the sensitive researcher pays careful attention. One such set of data becomes the stimulus to double-check the original figures to make sure that there are no simple errors of addition or subtraction. Another check is made on the "pluses" and "minuses" because it is very easy to reverse these, and thus to obtain a completely opposite meaning from the results. In dealing with large numbers of figures and signs, it is very easy for a human error to occur. Even computers are not strictly immune from processing or printing errors, although their programmers are responsible for almost all of the errors that come through this channel. In the New York data, even when the researchers went back to the raw information from the schedules, it was clear that there was no simple error of calculation. The service clients did, in fact, die off in higher proportions than would have been expected on actuarial data alone and than did the control clients, although not at a statistically significant level.

The next step is to report the finding, even in its most tentative form, as an hypothesis to be tested in future research or in a reanalysis of the existing data from other studies. Because of the dramatic implications of this New York finding, Margaret Blenkner gave the hypothesis a label, the *relocation shock* or the *transplantation shock hypothesis.*

Dr. Blenkner reviewed the extant literature and found a number of like findings on the negative effects of relocation on older persons.* For example, Aldrich and Mendkoff (1963) reported that a deleterious side effect of a fire in one wing of a nursing home, in which no one was injured, but that required the relocation of the elderly patients to another wing of the same home. There was an unusually high death rate in the three to six months following the fire that could not be explained in terms of the death rates of persons at that institution. (See Chapter 12 for a discussion of this literature. I should also add that there were dissenting reports that later emerged; these are also discussed in Chapter 12. I will discuss these events near the end of the book, so as not to get ahead of my story. Likewise, I will discuss some alternative ideas that were published later, which might have been employd with these data. But rather than showing "textbook hindsight," I would rather continue the experience of research as we lived it.)

---

* Technical Note 3.2 (p. 87) takes us into the world of information science to examine a precision information-retrieval system called the *Social Sciences Citation Index,* which can, in principle, connect you with *any* published information in the social and behavioral sciences from 1960 onward.

The relocation shock hypothesis began its scientific existence as Margaret Blenkner and her colleagues in New York (Blenkner, Jahn, and Wasser, 1964) expressed it in the form of a discrete hypothesis and its corollary:

> *Hypothesis:* There is a negative association between placement and survival among older persons which prevails even when physical condition is held constant.

> *Corollary:* If service to infirm or incapacitated older persons is primarily directed toward securing the necessary care in settings other than the person's own home, the survival rate of the clientele will be lower than that of a service which provides the necessary care in the client's own home, or of a program that makes no attempt to provide any personal care.

The corollary is necessary because to test the hypothesis directly, one would have to place some old people at random in institutions and compare their mortality rate with that of others who were not so placed. Although, in fact, many older persons are stuck into institutions, ethical practitioners and researchers cannot do that for the sake of a research study, especially one that suspects that doing so might be harmful to the elderly. And so the logical alternative is to prevent or delay such events from occurring by means of some experimental program, and then to compare the mortality rates of this group with the natural experiences of a control group, some of whom will be placed in institutions by practitioners in the community acting as they usually do. This is exactly the tack taken in the BRI Protective Services Project.

THE RELOCATION SHOCK HYPOTHESIS: IDEAS AND OBSERVATIONS

In this section, I will illustrate some of the cyclic happenings that went into the testing of the Relocation Shock Hypothesis as a concrete example of a general process involving ideas and observations, and the creative interaction between them.* The task was to tease out the answers to this complex question concerning the possible association of the removal of an older person to a safer and more healthful environment—and the premature death of that person.

The hypothesis seems so simple, just twenty-one words that all seem straightforward and clear. Where's the complexity? For the scientific investigator, the complexity comes in trying to clarify all of the logical and conceptual meanings of the "simple" words while looking for unambiguous operational definitions of these terms (see Technical Note 1.1, p. 19). It turns out that even simple words have a way of taking on various meanings, only some of which may be intended by the speaker.

Let's look more closely at this clarification process of the Relocation Hypothesis. The first content term is *placement*. (The prior terms, such as *negative association*, are methodological terms that are part of the common scientific language—mean-

---

* Technical Note 3.3 (p. 90) describes *creativity* in the research process. Except for those rare total replications of a prior research project, every new study involves some degree of creativity, some unique combination of existing ideas that offers the promise of producing new information. I believe that the real challenge of research is to stimulate creative thinking.

ing that as one variable increases, the other decreases—and should present no problems.) *Placement* refers to the placing of a person in some protected setting; it is commonly used in such diverse areas as foster child care, occupational work with the mentally retarded, and various forms of institutionalization. Common to these diverse settings is the assumption that some person is unable to carry out adequate self-care, lacks a family willing and able to do so, and thus needs assistance from third parties, possibly including institutionalized care.

If this is a reasonable meaning of *placement* with reference to an elderly person, then a host of questions emerges. For instance, how willing is the elderly person to accept this placement? Remember Miss Edel, who locked her door against intruders who might—and did—"shanghai" her to some institutional setting. We'll meet other protective participants who literally begged to be taken to an institution, at least sometimes. Is there a difference between willing and unwilling placement?

In a dissertation study by Ferrari (1964), a group of older residents of several small homes for the aged were required to move to a single large home that had a much more pleasant physical setup. Ferrari found that those older persons who expressed their unwillingness to relocate, for whatever reason, were more likely to die than those who expressed willingness to move. The relocation was inevitable as the smaller homes were being closed down. The older persons all had social workers who discussed the move with them, and yet the fatal difference between willing and unwilling relocated persons appeared.

Another question is What is a "new environment"? For a person who is mentally confused about time, place, and person, a relocation to a new physical setting may be as unrecognized as was the old place. Or is it? Let me speculate about some ideas—some rather far-out ideas, to be sure—that may have a bearing on this question. There is a marvelous section in Kenneth Grahame's *The Wind and the Willows* (a delightful children's book that has long entertained youngsters and their parents) where the principal characters, a rat and a mole, are making their way back to Rat's fine hideaway when they pass a place that Mole had made into his home long ago. Mole knows this because the senses of smell and other animal senses tell him that he is near home, security, and the familiar. This information is not like the Mole's seeing a signpost telling him that this is where he built his home. It is, in the words of the novelist, a more primitive form of communication that calls in an unheard language to which the animal responds as a whole. Home. Refuge against the bitter winds and the dangers all about. Home.

As a matter of fact, Mole's wish to return to his home is mirrored in every survey of the housing preferences of older persons, a wish to be in one's own home and living neither with relatives nor in an institution (Shanas, 1962). What I am driving at is a question about whether there might be something in our animal nature that makes the experience of returning home or being at home somehow reassuring and pleasurable. Some mentally unclear persons might not know what day it is or the name of the President of the United States, but they might know the location of the light switch or the bathroom. This minimal information, which perhaps gets embedded in one's animal senses as well as in one's mind, may be reassuring in an otherwise confusing world.

Speaking of moles and rats, there is the gruesome but fascinating study by Richter (1959) in which rats were placed in a vessel of water from which there was no hope of escape. Ordinarily the rats would swim for dozens of hours before collapsing and drowning, but when a rat's whiskers were cut off, it would die within minutes. This observation about death and the change in circumstances (this time affecting the animal's sense of touch and perhaps other senses of which we know nothing) is provocative. Remove the sense of contact with the environment, and the animal rapidly gives up struggling and drowns. With these sense organs present, the animal struggles on for days, even though there are no differences in the objective conditions of the environment.

I am embarrassed to frame a logical question in such research: What is the nature of the rat's "hope"? This question clearly anthropomorphizes the situation, and yet it is clear that the presence or absence of the organ of touch that serves so many informational functions for animals of which we know so little is highly important in survival situations. Staying alive. Fighting against the unknown but presumed malevolent forces of nature. Is it like "animalizing" humans, particularly mentally confused older adults living in veritable rats' nests, to suggest that they have some nonverbal or noncognitive link with their environment that in some way provides them with a sense of place, of security, and of hope?

There are many other conceptual questions that are stimulated by a close inspection of the terms of the hypothesis: Are some "home" settings more institution-like than some institutions? (You'll see an example of an institution-like home in Chapter 7, in which we follow an actual interview with a client who might possibly have been in such a situation.) What does it mean to survive? Is survival living with pain and confusion or being a burden to one's loved ones? Is there such a thing as a "good death" that brings a dignified release from unsolvable problems? And so on. Many ideas are stimulated by a consideration of the terms of the hypothesis and its implications.

Note that these ideas have been stimulated by the observations* of others, such as Ferrari and Richter. These data have been translated in our creative imagination into some *ideas* related to our own research. Some of the translations may be rather far-out, whereas others seem closer to the context of the present research. In both cases, the researchers' observations were about single events: "This is what I did and this is what happened."

But note further that the ideas we considered, stemming from these specific research observations, were not fettered to the *raw events.* Rather, we find portions of the observed events that are curious. These selected portions are picked out, often exaggerated and abstracted, so that the original events become visible only after effort. They have become instances of classes of events that the ideas name. These ideas have become *concepts*—the abstracted and generalized classes of events that are removed from time and space bonds, and that exist under the rules of logic and imagination. With these concepts, we can connect our thinking with that of other researchers, theorists, or practitioners who have published their related concepts by means of information retrieval procedures (I'll say more about these procedures in Technical Note 3.2). We can push these same concepts around in our imagination, linking them with other terms and

---

* Technical Note 3.4 (p. 92) is on the philosophical and scientific topic of *empiricism,* the doctrine or perspective that what we know initially comes from the physical environment, even though we may embroider on these sensate ideas. This perspective underlies much—but not all of—modern biosocial science.

thereby expanding the meanings they suggest. The general name for a set of concepts is a *proposition*. Such sets of concepts can guide research (these would be called *hypotheses*); they can be tested empirically* (these would be called *predictions*); or they can be used to get our logical system of ideas moving by our assuming that certain things are as we have described them to be (these are *assumptions* or *postulates*). When sets of propositions are combined, they may form *theories*, those broad networks of ideas that describe, explain, and predict events in the real world.

The great cycle of research moves between observations (one's own or those of others—either can be used) and ideas or concepts because each influences the formation of the other. Does it surprise you that ideas influence "reality"? In fact, it is a common assumption among theorists, from Max Weber to Jean Piaget. The cognitive psychologist Piaget suggested that the mental schema that we form take an active part in creating what we see, just as the environment takes an active part in obliging us to see what is there. What we "see" becomes a dynamic compromise between these two aspects of our mental life. The sociologist Weber noted the association of the beginnings of ascetic Protestantism and the rise of capitalism. In his theory, the ideas that certain people are the elect of God and that signs of this grace are likely to appear in the material rewards that people accumulate, gave rise to the entrepreneurial behaviors of early capitalism.

Ideas and observations; observations and ideas. Not only is there an interaction, but you can see that there may be a synergistic or growth-producing quality about that interaction. One small observation might be the basis of a large idea that covers a broad range of other events. One specific idea may lead to new ways of observing multitudes of different events.

On the other hand, some observations may simply be of unlikely occurrences that do not lead to worthwhile general ideas. Or an idea may be misapplied to a concrete situation in which superficial similarities are misleading. How can one tell whether the idea–observation interchange will be fruitful or misleading? One way is by an empirical test: seeing what happens in a given case. Another way is by logical analysis: What logical ideas might follow from such a hypothetical situation as is suggested by the idea–observation interchange?

The relationship between observations and ideas is more involved than simple interactions. The more bits of observations one has, the more materials there are for forming ideas that incorporate these bits. But obviously, the more pieces there are of a puzzle, the harder it is to put the puzzle together. Sometimes there are pieces to other puzzles mixed in, and one must sort out what observations go together to formulate an idea.

On the other hand, the firmer an idea is, the more resistant it is to the facts of our observations. Some observations may be disregarded because they don't fit into our preconceptions. This is clearly an unfortunate state of affairs because one has lost the single most significant way of obtaining corrective feedback. But one might prematurely drop an idea, especially an idea that is incompletely formed, because of an observation that is contrary to the idea.

---

* Technical Note 3.5 (p. 93) examines more closely the connection of empirical *observation* and the *measurements* constructed from these observed events. Note that measurement is a conceptual process applied to concrete happenings, once again illustrating the close connection between ideas and the observation of things.

Between these two positions in the functioning of ideas and observations is the working truth: there may be many developments in the collection of observations as well as developments in the proliferation of ideas. Sometimes the process is forward-moving; sometimes it is not. From my experience, I would suggest that if you keep in mind the cycle itself, it will be self-correcting: too many observations will force the creation of some superordinate idea just to keep things manageable. Likewise, too many ideas will collapse of their own hollowness; there must be observations to support them—not necessarily all of them, but at least some of the principal props of the theory that one is using to guide one's practice or research.

PAUSES IN THE GREAT CYCLE OF IDEAS AND OBSERVATIONS: DECISION MAKING

At various times in the course of the project, we were obliged to stop playing ping-pong with ideas and observations and make a decision that would result in a concrete action. In this section, I want to focus on decision making in the context of the research process. Decisions, large and small, were a continual part of our activities so that it became a special task to record these decisions so as to document why we did what we did, as well as to record the actions themselves.

Decisions can occur in an instant, such as when I replied to one of the interviewer's questions interpreting an item to be asked of a participant. I had been involved in a long process in developing the questionnaire itself, and I thought I knew what was intended by each item as well as by its placement and wording, so I could report that interpretation to the interviewer. But realistically I probably didn't remember the intention for each of the many items. In short, I probably created new questions, which may not have been altogether bad, as the reinterpretation probably came after more experience than we had had when the item was first developed. But most important, any such interpretation was to be written down so that the same answer would be given to other interviewers. At least, interpretations were supposed to be written down, but again, in fact, there were many interpretations given in contexts where it wasn't possible to record the discussion. This kind of *small decision making on the run* adds up to a contribution to the *error factors* that appear in every research study. The instruments aren't used in exactly the same way with every participant, so that part of the variation in answers comes from the different ways the question is asked, as well as from what comes out of differences in the responses themselves.

Big decisions are usually made in the context of more information and more consideration of the alternatives and implications. For example, the working definition of being in need of protective care emerged after many months of reviewing the literature, talking with BRI social workers about their experiences with what they thought were protective cases, and making some educated guesses about the implications of one or another decision for the working definition. Should physical disability be included as a criterion of being in need of protective care, or should only mental status be used? If mental status only, then should life-long retarded status qualify a person for protective services in old age, or

77

only relatively recent changes in mental status? If relatively recent changes in mental status were to be the focus for the protective client, then what if these were drug-related or caused by transient nutritional factors? And so on. Many implications had to be considered before we came to a decision that involved which clients were to be admitted to the study.

I regret to inform you that there were occasions when big decisions were made on the spur of the moment, and when little points seemed to take an agonizingly large amount of time to decide. The reason I can be so emphatic about this is hindsight. Sometimes we simply didn't think a decision through to its full ramifications. For example, I now believe that we were hasty in defining a *collateral* for the participants in the study as the person who was most likely to be turned to for assistance in time of need. This collateral might not be willing or able to respond to the need or might not act in the best interests of the older person. But because we defined the term collateral rather loosely (we didn't have much experience in pretests to ground our decision very well), we ran into a number of cases where a more effective helper was discovered in the course of our interviews, or where an ineffectual or possibly malevolent person was the official collateral. I am not sure, even now, how to define collateral with clearer boundaries that would avoid the problems I have mentioned, but I now see the problems better. The act of making a decision is now, as it was then, a compromise. What we get in simplicity, we lose in validity; choosing a collateral had to be done quickly, usually based on what the participant told us, so that perhaps not all of these problems could be avoided, given the procedures we followed.

The flow of information, observations as well as ideas, eventually reached a point where a decision was made—or was required to be made whether or not we were ready. Information from the older participants in the study, from their collaterals, from the scientific and practice literature, and from our own imaginations eventually formed the kind of closure that is the heart of decision making: For this time, at this place, the pieces of the puzzle seem to have fallen into an order that requires this or that decision. It is a time to risk. It is a time to act in accordance with the guidelines of a theory while testing the results in the participants' world to see whether events conform to predictions.

Decisions imply testing. A *practice theory* generates a logical prediction that is a description of some future events, presuming that certain interventive steps are taken. For example, here is Miss Edel, who is hostile and suspicious, and who is not able to take care of herself in the manner indicated by community standards. A practice theory might state that a person with these characteristics would benefit from placement in a more protected setting. The decision is that the social worker acts so as to convince Miss Edel to move, even over her strenuous objections, because a mentally confused person cannot understand the gravity of her situation in endangering herself or others. Then, over the next few months, the results of that decision become visible. Miss Edel is much cleaner than before; she is receiving much better food and lots of attention. But Miss Edel dies, apparently prematurely. This was not predicted by the practice theory, or rather, it was a risk factor presumed to be minimal. It may be an unanticipated consequence of the intervention. Although Miss Edel died, it is very difficult to link a given set of factors in her situation with her death. What the Protective Services Project did was to find a *pattern* among similar events, which characterized the relationships among survival, contentment, mental status, and the like. But because of the unexpectedly high proportions of unanticipated deaths among experimental participants, we had to examine the factors related to mortality with great care.

If there is a causal relationship, it can be determined only in a probabilistic fashion with a group of persons as in the experimental research design, not with any one individual. *Causation* * is a logical concept and must be discussed in terms of inferences from a body of evidence. We never see causation as such; we observe only a set of events related to one another in a particular way. From this observation, we form the idea—the concept—of causation. Once we have some evidence that a given pattern of events is caused (at a certain level of probability), then we can use this information as the basis of action. If mentally confused persons cannot take relocation without a high risk of premature mortality, then we had better figure out alternative means of aiding them. Even once a causal relationship has been established, it is not fixed. It may be related to certain contextual factors that have to be present, so that when the causal statement is applied to a new group of persons, it may prove less satisfactory than before because of the absence of these contextual factors, which are hard to sort out.

In the same fashion, innumerable smaller decisions are made and tested, and the outcome are used in the development of new ideas and observations and decisions. A *practice tactic* might state that the practitioner needs to be low-key but assertive in trying to aid the mentally confused elderly person to eat properly. High-pressure tactics could make the person resistant; encouragements that are too weak will be disregarded. Therefore, mid-level pressure, in the context of an established rapport (if possible), is the best tactical prediction for getting a protective client to eat properly. If this hypothetical statement of a practice tactic were enunciated and followed, then the practitioner would observe the minute-to-minute effects of this plan of action. If it proved successful—or more nearly successful than a prior plan of action—then it would be continued. If more problems arose than solutions attained, then the practice might be discontinued. (Not discarded, because the tactic might be more appropriate at another stage in the helping relationship.)

CYCLES OF THE RESEARCH PROCESS: OVERVIEW THROUGH A GLASS DARKLY

"In this section, I present an overview of the entire research process in clear outline form, which means that I am falsifying the unclear process to make it more logical than it really is."

That's not a very positive way to begin. Let me try again: "In this section, I present a tentative, sketchy overview of the entire research process that reflects the subjective and personal factors that influence decisions every intuitive step

---

* Technical Note 3.6 (p. 96) further develops the concept of *causality*. In particular, it presents the common rules for making causal inferences based on some set of observations. Although these rules seem quite simple, they form the basis of modern biosocial sciences.

of the way." Unfortunately, that is no better an introduction because it intentionally minimizes the strong rational element in scientific method.

One more try: "In this section, I will try to present both the rational and the subjective elements that interact during the entire research process. I mean that I will present an outline of the expected steps that research in general has found to be most helpful in solving problems. I also mean that I will discuss the place of professional values and personal interests as they are involved in the research process. Overall I want to sketch a flow diagram of the major ingredients in the research process so that readers will be able to identify these separate pieces when they are discussed in the later chapters."

With an objective like this, you can tell that this is going to be a complicated section. But that is what has to be done. Let's begin with a home-grown version of a Zen puzzle:

> How will you recognize some piece of new knowledge when, by definition, you don't know it in the first place?

To answer this philosophical trick question, you must break out of the context of inquiry in which it is framed. It *is* impossible to know something that you don't known, but, in fact, you know a lot about the unknown idea. For example, you know enough to ask the question. That means that you know some of the terms that define the context in which the answer will appear. You probably know something about related facts because these would have prompted your framing the question in the first place. And you most certainly have a solid grip on a portion of the rest of the universe of knowledge, including the steps for logical thinking and problem solving. (More of this in a moment.) So it would be quite a surprise to do research and turn up some new knowledge that violated all of these other pieces of what you know.

And yet, for the truly big breakthroughs of understanding, great theorists and researchers of the past did violate what was "known" in favor of some singular observations or insights that eventually led to a reorganization of the larger body of facts—what everybody has eventually come to "know." (Think of Einstein or Galileo.) What people of genius appear to have is both the capacity to know the basic scientific information and methodology *and* the ability to disbelieve in order to seek more encompassing answers (cf. Rothenberg, 1979). On the scale of this textbook, we will try to provide both exploration of the basic scientific methods of research and the ability to remain open to innovations—the breaking of some traditional methods in order to arrive at a more effective solution or a more pressing question.

Thus I really don't want to present a nice crisp overview of research because many readers will inappropriately latch onto it as the "truth" or the "right way"—or worse, the "only way"—to do research. However, it is traditional to present such an overview, and so I present a variation of that marvelous map of the Paris Métro system, some dozen criss-crossing subway lines that manage, somehow or other, to move vast numbers of people wherever they want to go (Figure 3.1, p. 83). This is the closest approximation to a diagram that will do justice to the research process. A user of the Métro chooses a given line by identifying what destination he or she is seeking—the ultimate destination, even though the rider may stop at some prior point. At certain junctures, a rider may switch lines in order to get to a destination not served by the first line. These lines may be at different levels and places, so that the person making the transfer walks up or down and some distance from the original line, ever moving toward the ultimate destination. There are all kinds of interesting sights along the way, some hazards, and a number of transportation props (such as the beeps that signal the closing of the doors or the frequent little maps of where you are now and where you can get to from here).

It is my hope that this diagram will be basically unintelligible to you now, even though I think it is essentially correct. I don't want you to hang onto one diagram as if it reflects the complete story of what is a multiple configuration of events. I hope you will come back to this diagram before reading each of the following chapters in order to find where the new section fits into the whole flow of research events. Over time, I hope this diagram will begin to make more sense. And by the end of the book, I hope it will be comprehensible enough to make you disregard it entirely—in favor of a model of the research process that you think better fits your own experience.

I strongly believe that there is little that is mysterious about research because so much of it occurs in the living of our everyday lives. We wonder about things and people, especially if we are in an exotic foreign capital. We formulate hunches based on our past experiences about how to do things and go places, even if our mastery of the French language consists only of polite phrases. We cautiously or incautiously act on these hunches and record the results (in our memory or on postcards to the folks at home) as the basis for further actions. Any problem-solving is akin to research.

But it is important to make a fundamental distinction about how we solve problems. On the one hand, we engage in *substantive problem-solving;* that is, we arrive at solutions for specific concrete problems, like where to buy the bread and cheese that is to be our lunch while touring in Paris. On the other hand, we also perform *procedural* or *methodological problem-solving;* that is, we develop the tools, skills, and methods for solving substantive problems. (For instance, we brush up on our French so as to be able to converse enough to get bread and cheese or the right Métro line. The language skills are procedural; they can be used for any substantive purpose.)

Procedural skills are content-free; substantive skills are focused on particular content. Research, in the narrow sense, belongs to the methodological problem-solving variety. We use research methods to solve substantive problems in order to gain the demonstrable leverage that these procedures provide. We can analyze data from the past or data as they will be collected in the future.* Although research methods aren't the only way to obtain knowledge or results, they have worked remarkably in the past—for good as well as for evil. And we can expect them to continue to solve problems—and to create new ones by their very success. (Think of the social implications of the great advances in genetics or nuclear physics, to say nothing of the impact of such practice theories as psychoanalysis or behavior modification.)

Now is the time to begin to describe the research process. But it is too late,

---

* Technical Note 3.7 (p. 98) takes a formal look at this matter of time in the research context. We can design *retrospective* as well as *prospective studies,* using certain methodological rules, and in either case, we may generate a clear basis for making inferences of causality.

because we are already in the middle of the discussion. There is no single begin-ning to research. It is like getting on board a spinning merry-go-round. You grab hold of a moving awareness about some problem or potential in the human condition that interests you; this is the substantive concern, such as our interests in older persons with protective care problems. At the same time, you grab hold of another moving awareness of the procedures for resolving the substantive questions you have; this would be like choosing to use an experimental–control-group design.

How do you like riding two merry-go-rounds at the same time? This is another of those Zen puzzles that point out the sharp reality that we live simultaneously in multiple worlds, play multiple roles, and seek multiple objectives.

One of these worlds is the realm of *facts,* those objects and events that force themselves into our consciousness and remain there stubbornly, regardless of our wishes or opinions. Another world is the domain of *values,* those emotionally tinged views of objects and events that influence our actions toward them. There is also a third world of *ideas,* by which we move back and forth in our awareness and dealings with facts and values. Ideas take into account facts and values; but ideas also modify facts and values by selecting which are to be considered.

To confuse matters further, you should recognize that the facts, values, and ideas that you hold aren't yours alone. In fact, you have been pocketing them from the ideas and actions of others all of your life. You may have been giving them a distinctive twist that makes these ideas uniquely yours, but for the most part, you follow rather tight conventions, such as the way you talk, the content of your ideas, and the possibilities for combining them. These are largely socially determined. The researcher uses the basic procedures of scientific method to express and to clarify his or her unique curiosity. Beginning researchers follow the scientific methods rather closely if they are wise because these are the proven methods for discovery in substantive areas. I believe that the more seasoned researcher learns that scientific method is not monolithic, that it is unclear about specifics, which require some choice on the part of the user. Moreover, I think some of the pleasure of being a scientist comes from these unclear points in the scientific process, where one sets out on one's own, so to speak, to explore new territory. That's why the Paris métro map may not be such a bad diagram for this purpose.

How to read the schematic diagram (Figure 3.1): Like the diagram of the Paris métro, the schematic diagram of the process *vérité* in research looks forbidding at first, but a little familiarity with it will quickly lead to dread, although it is an effective guide to getting where you want to go.

First, note that each of the lines has two ends, both marked with the same number. These correspond to the two directions of the same Métro line, depend-ing on which way you want to travel. In this research diagram, the two directions tend to be large-scale or small-scale foci of the same theme. For example, Line 5 goes from destination question "What is your overall research design?" to "What particular methods can be used to operationalize this variable?"

Second, note that there are many "stops" along the path or continuum between the two end points. These represent related questions on the same theme. Differ-ent chapters in this book present these related questions; they are not shown here.

Third, the intersections where two or more lines of thought meet represent

82

Figure 3.1 Schematic diagram of the *process vérité* in research (with apologies to the Paris *métro*).

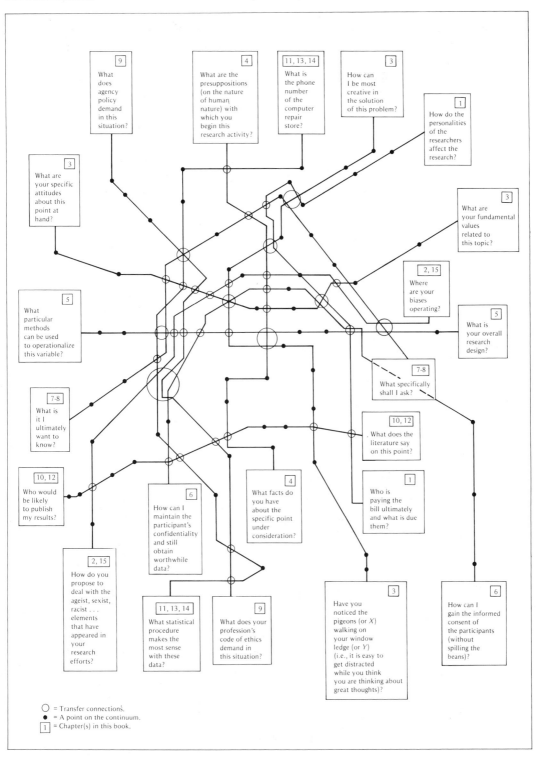

83

transfer connections, where the researcher can shift thoughts, so to speak, to another line of reasoning. Sometimes it takes one or two such shifts to get to different points in the research process.

Fourth, there is no actual beginning point in the research process. It depends on where you are when you start and where you want to get to at the end. I believe that eventually a researcher will have to travel over all of these lines of reasoning in the real world of research. Therefore no line of thought is ultimately more important than any other; you won't have the full experience of research until you have traveled on all of them.

Fifth, sometimes the long way is the shortest path between two points, but don't depend on it. There is probably a better way of going, of which experience will inform you—usually after the fact. As far as possible, I have tried to indicate the chapter where a given line of reasoning is discussed in this book, but as is typical of research, it didn't work out neatly, as some topics appear in several places.

If this diagram does not make the research process immediately clear, systematic, and memorable, don't worry. It may, or may not, grow on you.

Technical Notes

3.1 ETHICS IN RESEARCH

I want to begin the Technical Notes in this chapter with a discussion of ethics in research in order to emphasize the point that ethical decisions are a part of every aspect of the research process, even before the more visible portions of research begin.

Research is an activity that takes place in a social context and thus inevitably has implications for the people involved. These implications are value-tinged; that is, they are ethical or moral concerns because one person's choices of action impinge on the behaviors of another, whether or not the second party agrees. Some of these choices are more serious than others, of course, but all involve choices affecting human behavior and thereby invoke ethical considerations.

Broad ideological perspectives influence what we study and how we approach the task. Why do you suppose research on home aide services began in America only in the mid-1960s, when knowledge of this intervention concept had long been known in Europe? This delay may have had something to do with the fact that such services are not easily provided commercially; thus the delay may have reflected a dominant ideology in the country at large. It may also have been related to the relative status that applied research on the aged or the poor held among funders, reflecting another set of priorities at work in America. Indeed, it may have been affected by the policies and values of the helping professions themselves, which stress highly trained service workers rather than minimally trained ones providing specific services. These are speculations that force us to look sharply at the value context in which all research takes place, a context that is so pervasive, so invisible, and so influential.

Not only are there these broad value contexts; some middle-level values are also involved, such as the perspectives of the cultural groups involved in the BRI project. Benjamin Rose Institute itself had a reputation as an old establishment-oriented agency where few minority-group members were served during the early years of this century. But with the concerted efforts of successive executive directors and boards, the scope of the clientele has broadened to its current levels, where it serves all persons of certain ages and health statuses.

Likewise, there are always idiosyncratic preferences, unique to you and me as individuals, that find their way into what we do as researchers or practitioners. Indeed, personal expressions of values by clients affect the progress of the service program as well. Ordinarily we assume that helping professionals can control their personal attitudes sufficiently to deliver the needed services, but there is ample evidence that such attitudes or values may distort or qualify professional actions (Bloom and Farrar, 1972). So it is incumbent on the helping professional to state some framework for ethical action in contexts where subtle choices may have a powerful impact on the freedom of others.

To this end, I would like to offer two sets of propositions that are counterbalanced; that is, one set is intended to act as a check-and-balance on the other set, although both sets are to be honored as a working approximation of fully ethical behavior in scientific practice or research. The first set of propositions is from the individual perspective:

1. Act (do research or practice) so as to increase the free choice of the participants in your actions. For example, enable your clients to make self-determining choices among a complete set of feasible options.
2. Act so as to increase the fulfillment of whatever potentials your clients have. For instance, seek ways to obtain what a client's strengths permit, as well as to reduce or correct a client's weaknesses.

The second set of propositions concerns a social perspective:

3. Act so as to enable all persons to have the same free choices. This is a provision for equality and justice. For example, all persons should have opportunities for an equal hearing before the law; however, collective action may be necessary to fulfill this claim on justice and equality.
4. Act so as to enable all persons to have equivalent access to public resources. This is a provision of social utilities: basic-human-need fulfillment solely because of one's membership in the society. For instance, collective action is often needed to make health, education, and welfare equivalent across the segments in a community, as well as across communities and regions.

I believe that each of these four ethical directives is valid, but that the set of them is best viewed in a dynamic equilibrium. Each is contingent on the others. Freedom of choice is contingent on a given person's behavior not interfering with the rights of another. Likewise, fulfillment of one's potential should not be undertaken at the expense of the limited resources, so that others are deprived of equivalent support.

Helping professionals, as well as the clients whom they serve, may be viewed as passing through a series of stages regarding moral judgments (cf. Kohlberg, 1969; Tapp and Kohlberg, 1977). Let's review these stages by combining both moral and legal reasoning. The beginning stage is termed the *preconventional level*, at which a person makes a moral or legal judgment depending on the apparent consequences of the act: an act is bad if it leads to punishment by some authority. Good acts are those that lead to some desired reward.

The second level is termed the *conventional level*. Laws and norms are accepted without question, and what is good or bad depends on fulfilling the letter of the law. Justice therefore depends on the will of the majority, and the rights of the individual are subsumed in the norms of the group.

The third postulated level of moral and legal reasoning is termed the *postconventional level*. The distinguishing features of this level involve an awareness of the rights and obligations of the individual and an awareness of the social system of which he or she is a part. Injustices may be challenged and changed through the will of the majority, but regardless, individuals may base their actions on their own views of ethical principles, recognizing the price that they may pay in doing so. (See also Tapp, Gunnar, and Keating, 1983.)

There are several important implications of this theoretical perspective, which suggests that people move through this sequence of moral and legal reasoning to whatever level they are able to attain. Only a small proportion of people ever reach the postconventional level; the conventional level is most common among adults. However, persons who make life commitments to the helping professions, which are not notoriously famous for either financial remuneration or social status, probably have reached the principled judgment level of the postconventional perspective. Assuming this, we can therefore hypothesize that the clients of helping professionals are likely to be at the same or a lower level of moral and legal reasoning; thus clients and professionals may come into *conflict* on the interpretation of acts involving the clients. This conflict may put the helping professional in a difficult bind, where the goals of the client are respected as far as is ethically possible, but where the moral code of the community is equally respected as the working frame of reference for services—unless grounds are found for seeking a change in these working rules (cf. Colett, 1982).

The first step in resolving these complex problems of conflicts of values is awareness of their existence (Tymchuk, 1981). It would be an interesting study to test whether students in the helping professions could be aided in making higher-level moral and legal judgments through the values clarification approach that several writers have suggested (Tymchuk, 1981; Kohlberg, 1969). It would be doubly interesting to see whether training clients in higher levels of moral and legal reasoning might aid them in their day-to-day choices in relating to family members, coworkers, and neighbors (cf. Heitler, 1976).

The major point of this Technical Note is that not only do workers have responsibilities to individual clients and to society at large, but they have to filter these values through their own perspectives and through those of the helping professions that they represent. The clearer it is what is involved, the more likely it is that ethical and responsible decisions will be reached.

3.2 INFORMATION RETRIEVAL

In looking over the broad range of background materials required to construct a research project that builds on this prior knowledge, you may have wondered— as we did—how one finds all of the relevant studies and theoretical or practice papers bearing on the topic. I'll tell you how we did it in the mid-1960s—by laboriously searching individual journals that were thought to be relevant.

Dr. Blenkner subscribed to a large number of scientific and professional journals, as did the BRI library, and these were regularly circulated among the staff. We were expected to read these journals, selectively, of course. Relevant articles or references were pointed out to us, and I often had the job of tracing down an original in the local university or city libraries. Dr. Blenkner's network of colleagues around the country also supplied us with papers and references, and so we thought we had reasonably good information on which to base our work. It is axiomatic in research that one's explorations are limited by the extent of one's knowledge and one's imagination in obtaining knowledge. To put it crudely, we are what we know. And I will candidly say now that I don't think we really knew as much as we thought we did, by contemporary standards of information retrieval.

Much of this Technical Note could not have been written at the time of the Protective Services Project, as innovations in retrieval are very recent. Let me sketch briefly the scope of one information-retrieval tool that is probably the most powerful device easily available today. The *Social Sciences Citation Index* (*SSCI*) is a four-part information-retrieval tool that literally enables the scientific practitioner and researcher to have access to almost every piece of literature on any topic published since about 1960. (The *SSCI* actually began its work in the 1970s but went back to index the previous decade's literature as well.) This amazing claim is accomplished by an intricate system in which each significant item in about fifteen hundred social and behavioral science journals is listed by title, along with titles taken selectively from about twenty-four hundred journals in collateral fields like medicine.

One part of the *SSCI*, the *Permuterm Index*, pairs each term in a title with every other term in that title, allowing the information searcher to find the given reference through multiple entry points—a basic principle of information retrieval. This paired key word–secondary term is a familiar retrieval strategy in many other information tools as well, although with variations in each one, such as in *Psychological Abstracts, Social Work Research and Abstracts, Sociological Abstracts,* and the more than one thousand other such secondary sources for the primary journal literature.

Another part of the *SSCI*, the *Source Index*, contains the full bibliographical citations for the period of time covered. The SSCI has two preliminary paperback documents that cover the first and second thirds of the year, as well as a final hardcover document that includes the information for the entire year. Unlike other bibliographic tools, the *Source Index* lists all of the citations used by a given author for his or her article. A third part of the *SSCI*, the *Citation Index*, lists brief citations of these cited papers or books, together with the names of other persons who have cited these same papers or books in the given time period. In this way, a network of persons may be identified who have a given citation in common, and who may be presumed to be working on related topics. Thus a large number of references may be generated that lead to people doing work on the same or a similar topic area. The benefits for the time-pressured student, researcher, or helping professional are incalculable. The fourth part of the *SSCI* is a *Corporate Index* that lists the items published in the time period covered by a given document by geographical and institutional locations.

Before you rush out to purchase one of these marvelous devices and start to use it immediately, let me warn you that they are expensive (over $1,000 for a year's worth of all the information in the social and behavioral sciences). But more to the point, the *SSCI* is complicated, and one has to learn how to use it and practice the skills before one is proficient enough to benefit. My students who have mastered these skills report that this is one of the most exhilarating experiences that they have had in graduate school, although not one of the easiest.

There are several search strategies for using the *SSCI* in its most effective way, which means finding as many citations as possible that appear to be highly relevant to your search topic. First, if only the topic is known, such as "protective services for older persons living in the community," then one would go to the *Permuterm Index* in search of one of these key terms in combination with another secondary term, such as *protective* and *services* or *protective* and *aged.* There are usually many secondary terms under a given key term. For example, using the *Permuterm Index* of the year 1981 (covering January to April of that year), I located some thirty-eight secondary terms under the key term *protective.* Moreover, there were three items with the secondary term *service* or *services,* thus providing three immediate citations to be considered. But before leaving the *Permuterm,* I also scanned the other secondary terms to find synonyms or antonyms or terms at different levels of abstraction that might be relevant. For example, I found the following secondary terms that might be relevant: *approach, challenge, custody, diseases, effective, emergency, experiment, family, hospitalization, patient,* and *prevention.* If the first set didn't provide any good leads when I found the full citation of these pairs in the *Source Index,* I could go back to these other combinations—or, more likely, look at other *SSCI*s for different time periods for more likely "hits."

If you know a central person in a given field, then you might begin to see whether that person has written anything in the current time period by looking in the *Source Index.* Had you not known that Margaret Blenkner died in 1972, you could have looked for her writing in 1981 and, of course, would not have found any in the *Source Index.* But if you looked to see whether others writing in 1981 were still referring to her work, you would have seen (in the *Citation Index* of that period) that ten people had referred to one or another of her papers between January and April of 1981. Of these, eight referred to some aspect of the Protective Services Project. Now you have eight other citations to look up in the *Source Index* to see what connections these current papers have with her earlier work.

You may be wondering whether the Benjamin Rose Institute was publishing any research on this topic in early 1981, and by consulting the *Corporate Index* under Ohio, and then Cleveland, and then looking for the Benjamin Rose Institute, you would have found none. However, looking under Case Western Reserve University, and under specific departments, such as social work or the center on aging, you would have found some items listed. Assuming that these schools or centers share your interests in dealing with protective services, you might have yet other leads on relevant information.

Let's follow some of these leads and see what emerges. First, of the three references to the pair of terms *protective* and *service* or *services,* we find one reference to protective work with children, another to emergency work with the mentally ill, and one to protective work with the elderly. Only the latter is clearly relevant, and on looking up the full citation, we note that the auther, W. G. Bell, has cited two of M. Blenkner's papers in his paper, a national study on public guardianship and the elderly.

Indeed, going to the *Citation Index,* we find Bell's name twice among the list of those who have cited Dr. Blenkner during this period of time. It would probably be fruitful to read Bell's paper or to explore his references as a way to build up an information network on current users of Blenkner's research. Another author who has cited Dr. Blenkner during this time is C. C. Miller, whose paper is on the primary prevention of child mistreatment. For some reason, Miller has referred to Blenkner's work as relevant to child protective services, thus forging a link between different clientele and their relation to protective work.

Looking at another likely source of information, the *Permuterm* entry on "Protective" and "Services," we find the author M. Jones, whose paper does not cite Margaret Blenkner but still looks very interesting. Its title is "Effective Practice with Families in Protective and Preventive Services—What Works." It turns out that one of the coauthors of this paper is a former colleague of Dr. Blenkner's in New York, another possible link in the network of ideas—although one that I recognize not everyone would connect. This underlines another basic point about information retrieval: the more you know about a given domain and the workers in it, the more information begins to interconnect.

To emphasize the main point of this Technical Note, observe that I located a dozen or more possibly relevant references in just a matter of minutes of searching back and forth through a set of documents for one third of one year. Probably some of these came from journals that Dr. Blenkner did not have access to, but that were relevant. By looking over several years' worth of *SSCI*s, we probably could have accumulated several hundred relevant studies, papers, and criticisms—in fact, possibly every one of them that is in print.

If knowledge is power, then we have come a giant step toward gaining the kind of power we need to be optimally effective in designing our research (always assuming that we use the knowledge wisely—a separate question entirely). But recognize that it is knowledge about knowledge that has provided this power: knowledge about information retrieval procedures.

3.3 CREATIVITY IN THE RESEARCH PROCESS

How I envy those clever people who are in the right place at the right time with the right techniques that produce the right data. Reading some of the classic research projects generates not only interest in the important findings that are reported but utterly unrepentant envy of how the investigators arranged just a few pieces of social happenings so as to tease some significant understanding out of the complex of human behavior. For example, Solomon Asch had a group of students indicate which of three differing lines (A, B, and C) another line (X) was most nearly like. A simple perceptual task, except that seven of the eight students in each group were accomplices of the investigator, who gave incorrect answers on planned occasions in order to see what the one true subject would do in the face of this group pressure.

But what an interesting way to re-create in the laboratory the kinds of group pressures that people face everyday. Asch varied the conditions of the social pressure by having one or more of the confederates give the correct answer to see what affect it would have on group pressure, and so on. In laboratories, one can vary the conditions in this fashion. And although we might now be concerned with the impact of this deception on the true subjects, we still have to admire a creative project for its time (Asch, 1950).

How is creativity generated in the construction of a research project? Or, rephrased, what determines the degree of creativeness that any research project manifests?

The second form of the question is probably the more nearly accurate because every research project that is not a total replication of earlier work is likely to be innovative in one aspect or another, to a large or small degree. The first form of the question addresses the generating of creativity in the service of research. It is this question that I want to address in this Technical Note. First, some definitions.

Creativity in general involves behaviors that produce an innovative and socially

90

useful or valued outcome. Thus creativity has a personal side (the creator) and a social side (the audience that defines and rewards the creator's products). Both have to be considered in the generating of creativity.

Moreover, there is some evidence that creativity is a normally distributed attribute—like events portrayed by the normal curve—and although only a relative few are in the extremely creative class, there are probably a large number who are highly gifted (Nicholls, 1972). Among the many people who obtain a college degree are a sizable proportion who are likely to be in this highly gifted group, even though intelligence in itself is not a good predictor of creativity (Getzels and Jackson, 1962). This finding makes probable the conclusion that many persons who have professional, scientific, or technical backgrounds and who are engaged in research work are likely to have the potential for creative work.

So what determines whether this statistical likelihood will, in fact, be translated into actuality? Pelz and Andrews (1966) and Pelz (1972) have studied creative productions in scientific organizations and have concluded that two major factors are required, each of which contains some specific elements. The major factors are, briefly put, *challenge* and *security*. Although these may sound like contradictory forces, in fact they work together in an interesting fashion. First, on the individual side, a person must have some basic knowledge, talents, and abiding curiosity, which make up part of the challenge, a self-challenge. But in addition, there must be some social pressure or demand, possibly some competition, that builds up the challenge. Second, there must be some secure sense of self, some comfortableness with being different from others, which is often the lot of creative people. On the social side, there must be the security of a job position in which no clear products may be forthcoming for some time, as well as supplying an admiring and rewarding audience when advances are made. Thus both security and challenge, within oneself and from the social environment, are needed for creative work.

Individual researchers can try to achieve these personal aspects of creativity, and they can influence (or choose) organizational environments that provide the collective aspects. Let's look more closely at the personal side, as this is the one that individuals may seek to influence on their own. I believe that the key to learning and using creative modes of problem solving (broadly conceived) is to begin early and to gain continuous practice in trying out innovative solutions (cf. Adams, 1974). These solutions involve both the ideas (head work) and the observations (hand work) in the cycle of research that I tried to describe in the Narrative section of this chapter. First, the thoughts and intuitions try to place the central elements of the problem in context, which means imagining what consequences might follow from various combinations of events. Second, tentative decisions are made to subject one combination to a test to see whether it works as predicted. If it does, fine; you have the solution. If it doesn't, and it usually won't, then what have you learned from this miniexperiment and how next might these or other elements be recombined for another imaginative project?

Scientific creativity is not 100 percent logic, intelligence, or reason. But neither is it 100 percent intuition, emotion, or feeling. It may be closer to Edison's comment about his own work: 90 percent perspiration and 10 percent inspiration.

But this insightful hypothesis doesn't really tell us how to generate creative solutions except to say, "Keep working away at a problem and keep trying different approaches to its solution."

Another hypothesis worthy of note here is that the greater the number of options at one's disposal, the more likely one is to find a successful solution. This is the basis for brainstorming (Osborn, 1963), either by oneself or with a group of individuals sharing—but not censoring—ideas. This is also the basis for some current work in training youngsters adaptive social-interaction skills, by helping them to imagine other ways of doing something and other consequences of any given action (Spivack and Shure, 1974). The point is that generating ideas that make a creative solution more probable is not a mysterious process for the Einsteins alone. It is literally something that each of us can engage in, can practice, and can become more proficient in by the very act of trying and of recognizing progress toward innovative solutions.

3.4 EMPIRICISM

The previous Technical Notes for this chapter were mainly concerned with the idea side of the ideas and observations cycle, the theme of this portion of the book. Now I would like to turn to the observations side in this and the next several Technical Notes.

I would like to begin with an observation about observations, and that is that most people are relatively unperceptive about their environments, internal and external. It is very easy to be seduced into an habitual relationship with the physical environment. When is the last time you looked up and carefully examined the clouds or the stars? Perhaps only when it was threatening rain or when you had to start for home—self-serving purposes but not for the sake of observation itself. Likewise, when did you have your last heart-to-heart discussion with yourself on the state of the You-ion, or the nature of your relationship to your closest friends or relatives? Habit is an aid to performing our everyday tasks, but it can also dull life considerably by reducing everything to a thoughtless and affectless routine. And so it is very important to consider the nature of empirical observations and the information that these observations provide, not only because they supply the foundation of scientific efforts and helping practices, but because they also have implications for us personally. (I call your attention to the literature on practitioner burnout as a case in point; see Maslach and Jackson, 1981; Edelwich and Brodsky, 1980).

John Locke (1939) began his landmark philosophical essay concerning human understanding with this query: "Let us then suppose the mind to be, as we say, white paper, void of all characters, without any ideas; how comes it to be furnished? . . . Whence has it all the materials of reason and knowledge? To this I answer, in one word, from experience" (p. 248). This essay introduces a major characteristic of modern science, its *empirical* basis: all knowledge arises from experience, either one's own or the experiences others share with us.

However, the contemporary scientific position does not deny the existence of mental processes whose categories seem innately present (a theory espoused by writers from Immanuel Kant to Noam Chomsky). Moreover, experience appears to be required to get even these innate categories or processes to work on behalf of their owners. And so, one way or another, experience—observations of and interactions with one's physical and social environments—seems to be not only the royal road to science and scientific practice, but really the only road.

Contemporary science, as well as the world at large, has a healthy respect for the empirical position. The citizens of Missouri have as their state motto: Show me! But we forget that this respect for empiricism was earned the hard way. Galileo tried to get the religious establishment of his age to look through his telescope to verify for themselves the planetary notions he espoused. Not everyone wants to look at the empirical evidence and to give up the more comfortable nest of ideas and assumptions in which they dwell. Ask your friend the smoker about empirical evidence on smoking, your associate who forever eats fast foods about the empirical evidence on nutrition, or possibly your honored instructors about their sedentary life.

We all live in our own world of ideas to some degree of comfort—or tolerable discomfort. Empirical evidence is usually discomforting. It is tough to obtain and challenging to understand, and it is difficult to make appropriate responses to it because these often require us to change. We pay lip service to the value of science, including the empirical procedures that are its hallmark, but most of us ignore this knowledge base in favor of creature comforts. I am not moralizing. I am pointing out the obstacles to the researcher at every step of the process of doing research. For the researcher's own discomfort, for the discomfort of the agency colleagues, for the discomfort of the participants and the taxpayers who get involved in the study, directly or indirectly, empirical research is a pain.

But this self-imposed pain, this often exquisite discomfort, is part of the great human adventure in science in which you are now taking part, albeit at an introductory level. Once you accept the challenge of the Missourians ("Show me!") and the response of the Galileos ("Look here!") you will have achieved a significant step in your own development and perhaps as a contributor to social development.

3.5 OBSERVATION AND MEASUREMENT

We are constantly observing portions of the world around us, scanning for events and objects that are meaningful to us, and then reacting appropriately. The researcher's *observations* are similiar to this common phenomenon but are more orderly and systematic so that the observations can be, in principle, repeated exactly by another person. Therefore what is observed, how, when, where, and by whom, is carefully noted as the basis for informing others about a given scientific observation.*

There are several ingredients in *scientific observation* worth noting. First, the observer is trained to use standard methods of taking in information, processing it according to rules or classifications, and reporting the findings. In some situations, the observer is simply a human instrument for transmitting information to others, who do the classification and the interpretation.

* Keller's (1983) sensitive biography of geneticist Barbara McClintock emphasizes the important role of careful observation in the work of this Nobel-prize winning scientist.

Second, observation may be direct, as when a given person perceives and records another's behavior; or it may be indirect, such as when a mailed questionnaire is returned and coded by someone "observing" a participant's answers.

Third, either information may be produced by the participant and brought very near to the end of the interpretation process by that participant, or the information may be filtered through another observer, who hears the participant's answers and then makes marks on questionnaires—it is these marks of the observer that are the ultimate data for analysis.

Fourth, information may be unitary or multiple with regard to a given topic. That is, one can look at one aspect of a topic area as an indicator of the whole, or one may look at several aspects of that topic and use some rule about handling multiple observations in order to come up with an aggregated view of that topic.

There are many other related aspects of observation, but these are sufficient to alert the reader to the kinds of issues that emerge in considering when an observation is to become the basis of a scientific statement or whether it is part of everyday life. Both kinds of observations are serious business in the sense that important decisions are made on the basis of both. But it is the rigor and the repeatability of the scientific observation that ultimately distinguishes it from the more casual one.

Measurement is a related process; in fact, some consider it a part of observation. Let's agree that *measurement* is the process of assigning symbols to objects or happenings according to rules. Then we have to consider what types of rules are used to assign symbols to such objects or happenings. The following four major sets of rules are commonly discussed in the literature:

Nominal data are symbols assigned arbitrarily to objects, such as the numerals on a basketball player's shirt; or the psychiatric system of diagnostic categories like "schizophrenic" or "manic-depressive"; or the symbols ♂ and ♀ referring, respectively, to male and female in the biological literature. These are strictly descriptive categories used to identify and to categorize events as belonging to or not belonging to the categories. It is possible to assign numbers that represent groupings of discrete though presumably related categories as does the *Diagnostic and Statistical Manual of Mental Disorders* (DSM-III) (see Technical Note 4.5, p. 120), but strictly speaking these "numbers" are simply separate categories. What one does to apply a nominal scale is to locate a new event that fits exactly the description of the named category.

Ordinal data are symbols indicating order on a given attribute in some given group of objects or happenings. For example, grades of A, B, and C are assigned in a classroom to indicate the general order among a set of scores on a test. The grade of A is better than the grade of B in this order, but it is difficult to say how much better. Moreover, a grade of A in one class might be only a B in another, so that the comparison is made within a defined sample of events. We can make assumptions about the numeric value of a grade of A or B when we compute a grade-point average across classes, but this is risky business, strictly speaking. The "easy A" and the "tough B" grades do not reflect the reality of what you know to be the case, but that is the fault of the inappropriate use of numbers with ordinal data. The operations one would take in using an ordinal scale consist of locating two or more events belonging to the same category of events and then indicating on some scale that one has a greater magnitude than the other on this scale. This order is then labeled with some recognized symbols.

Interval data are symbols (often numbers as commonly understood) indicating the intervals between the points on a scale. A score of 115 IQ points is one mental measurement unit higher than a score of 114, just as 100 is 1 point higher than 99. Whether that same 1 IQ point holds the same meaning for scores near the extremes of the scale is questionable. The assumptions of interval data are that the intervals are even and consistent, but that the zero point and the units of measurement used are arbitrary. The operations used in interval data are truly quantitative. Each of the characteristics of the earlier types of data is repeated here—discrete categories, ordered relationships—but an addition is the maintenance of the relative differences between the objects measured; that is, the intervals are maintained in any mathematical analysis.

Interval data are often used as if they were ratio data, the highest level of measurement categories. *Ratio data* are symbols, now acting as true numbers, indicating both even intervals and known ratios on a scale because of the presence of an absolute zero point. The ratio of any two points is independent of the measurement units themselves. For example, if one person has $1 and another person has $10, then the latter has ten times as much as the former. But this is exactly the same ratio of difference as when one person has $10,000 and another has $100,000—because all of these comparisons are made against a known zero point. With IQ scores, there really is no clear zero point, just some assumed region of very low performance. The operations used with ratio scales, as with interval scales, are fully quantitative but in addition, the ratios are maintained even when the numbers involved are multiplied by a positive number. (For a more detailed discussion, see Siegel, 1956.)

Note that this discussion of data refers to quantification, not psychological attribution. If one were speaking of the psychological concept of *relative deprivation,* we could not use ratios to express what the people *felt* who were on the short end of a 1-to-10 ratio or a $10,000-to-$100,000 ratio. In general, it is very difficult to construct a true ratio scale for social and behavioral events because there are few absolute beginning points or zero equivalents in the human domain. Therefore I suggest combining the interval and the ratio data, as in Table 3.1.

For each of these types of scales, there are statistical procedures that are appropriate in the sense of using whatever information is available to the optimal level. That is, each statistical procedure makes assumptions about the kinds of events that can be properly used with its operations. Some levels of data meet the assumptions for one statistical procedure but not for another. For example, Siegal (1956) pointed out that with a one-sample case, if one has data that are at the nominal level of measurement, then the appropriate statistical procedures to use would include the binomial test, whereas if one had data at the ordinal level of measurement, then one might use a Kolmogorov–Smirnov one-sample test. These particular tests make an optimal use of the available information. One could use a weaker test, but it would waste available information and so would not be the statistical test of choice. Seigel (1956) and the authors of other books about statistics have discussed these procedures in detail.

Researchers may occasionally use more powerful statistics than the quality of their data supports. Numbers can be produced in such a circumstance, but what the numbers *mean* is another question. If you "add" one apple and one

Table 3.1 Levels of Measurement.

Definition of Levels	Measurement Characteristics
Nominal Level: Objects or events are distinguished and classified. Examples: males, females; marital status—married, widowed, divorced, separated, never married. These are qualitative distinctions and represent the lowest but most basic level of measurement.	*Categorizing:* Once distinctive and homogeneous classes are identified, any object or event of the specified type may be counted as an instance of that category. Example: a class of 13 males and 17 females. It makes no sense to attach numbers to the categories, "male" and "female" other than to distinguish them in coding.
Ordinal Level: Objects or events bear an ordered relationship to one another, such as "greater than" or "less than." This is the minimal quantitative distinction. Examples: answers on a questionnaire—"generally happy," "about even happy and unhappy," "generally unhappy"; socioeconomic status levels—upper, middle, and lower class.	*Comparing:* Objects and events are identified (building on nominal-level characteristics) and rank-ordered relative to one another on some attribute—without indication of the magnitude of the differences. Example: "generally happy" is more than "about even happy and unhappy" on the attribute happiness, but the comparison tells us nothing about how much more one is than the other.
Interval and Ratio Levels: Objects or events have the properties of the number system, such as equal intervals between ranks (interval level) and an absolute zero or origin point (ratio level). Examples: Calendar time, A.D. 1985 (arbitrary beginning point—interval level); height, weight, age (data with an absolute zero or origin point—ratio level). These are the highest levels of measurement. For practical purposes, there are few distinctions between interval and ratio levels.	*Measuring:* Objects and events are identified (nominal level), ordered (ordinal level) in ranks of equal intervals (interval level), and analyzed by means of the number system. We perform the measurement operations on the assumption that the data are isomorphic with the number system. Example: We ascertain how much income clients have and then compare individuals by the number of dollars they possess. One person may be twice as wealthy as another. Each income interval is an equal distance ($1 more or less) from the adjacent ones (. . . $1001, $1002, $1003 . . .) and there is an absolute beginning point ($0) with which to compare different persons' income or the ratios of their income. (This quantitative comparison is to be distinguished from the subjective comparisons people make, as indicated by the term *relative depreciation.*)

orange, the summary number (two) does not reflect the events. (See Table 3.1 for an overview of the levels of measurement.)

3.6 CAUSALITY

There is an unspoken assumption operating throughout the scientific enterprise, and it involves causality. The reason that we go through all of these efforts is to produce information that will provide the basis for making causal judgments. When the research involves an applied topic, such as was true of the BRI Protective Services Project, then the implication is that we will take our hard-earned causal information and put it to work in the service of others, like the participants in our study. Thus *causality* is an assumption operating in almost all scientific work. We assume that things are as they are because they were caused by certain prior events operating in predictable and knowable ways—even though we may not currently know what these ways were.

If you stop to think about these assumptions, you realize just how far we have moved from the mystic beliefs of our not-so-distant ancestors. (Knock wood!) Moreover, these assumptions run counter to very contemporary beliefs in fate, divine intention, or whatever. I mention these everyday mysticisms to emphasize what assumptions we make when doing scientific research—and perhaps how inconsistent we may be in our personal and scientific lives.

People are naive scientists, according to psychologists Kelley (1955) and Heider (1958), that is, ordinary people act as if they were following the scientific method in sorting information, making hypotheses, and benefiting from feedback from these activities in their future actions. We all see countless instances of causation, one thing making another happen. But the strict philosophical analysis of David Hume showed that all we really experience is the relationship between two or more events. We never see causation as such. We must *infer* it from the available observations.

How do we infer causality? How do we know that the marital disputes of the parents are making the teenage daughter act out at school? Or that the young child will demand that the parents buy X Brand cereal because he saw it advertised on TV? How do we know that a lifetime of smoking will very likely reduce the number of years of life of a person approaching late adulthood? If we did know these causal relationships for sure, it would be a relatively easy matter to devise ways of breaking the causal chain, presumably for the better, if there were still time to do so.

Philosopher John Stuart Mill and scientist Robert Koch contributed the general perspective that most scientists take regarding the *rules for making causal inferences.* Let me summarize these briefly as follows:

1. *Constant and concomitant variation:* The presence (or absence) of a target condition varies with the presence (or absence) of the presumed causal factor.
2. *Level of exposure and strength of association:* The greater the level of exposure to the predicted causal factor, the greater the magnitude of the target condition. Likewise, the higher the level of the statistical association between two events, the stronger the basis for inferring causality, other things being equal. (No direction of causality is implied at this point.)
3. *Constancy of exposure:* Whenever the predicted causal factor is studied in regard to the target condition, they are found to be related, regardless of the different populations or circumstances under consideration.
4. *Temporal relationship:* An asymmetrical relationship between events is assumed in matters of causation, so that one event appears before the other in all cases. The one appearing first is presumed to cause the other, and not the other way around.
5. *Compatibility with existing evidence:* Any new causal statement should fit with what is currently known about such phenomena.

97

Taking any one of these rules or postulates alone would not be an adequate basis for making a causal inference. It is the *set* of them that is presumed to provide an adequate basis for making a causal inference. Note that I am speaking of inferences, not certainties. We are continually discovering that two events never operate in isolation, and that it may, in fact, be the effect of a third factor that explains the observed outcome. (See Susser, 1973, for a discussion of the logic of multiple causation, which involves different systems and levels of relationship, and some procedures for teasing out causal relationships.)

An interesting and significant example of causal inference is found in discussions of smoking and lung cancer (see Mausner and Bahn, 1974). The separate factors are noted from large numbers of studies. People who smoke large numbers of cigarettes a day and do so consistently over long periods of time are likely to be overrepresented among persons who die of lung cancer. From what we know of cancer, as produced by carcinogenic substances found in cigarette smoke and other places, it makes conceptual sense to assert this causal link. There is considerable experimental evidence that the predicted outcomes have been produced in laboratory animals. There is evidence that, when people stop smoking for good, their observed mortality rates eventually drop to those of nonsmokers (provided there is enough time for this to occur). Another portion of evidence concerns the differential mortality rate for males (who took up smoking in the early part of this century) and females (who started smoking en masse only recently) (cf. Grannis, 1970; Waldron, 1976). And no one presumes that cancer causes people to smoke—to illustrate the order of events involved.

But still some people do not accept these aggregated empirical relationships as a causal relationship. They point out that smoking may lead to outcomes other than lung cancer, such as coronary heart disease, peripheral vascular disease, tuberculosis, cancer of the mouth and bladder, and so forth. These are also empirical relationships, but there was no implication that smoking causes only lung cancer. In addition, some people get lung cancer who do not smoke. This is true, but in such cases, it is likely for other causes to be detected: pollutants from the workplace and from the environment or other causes. Even some inconsistencies have appeared in research, as in the early study that showed that inhalation did not increase the risk of lung cancer. Susser (1973) pointed out that such evidence may be related to the difficulty of obtaining objective reports on vaguely defined aspects of the smoking process. In general, it is a long and difficult battle to sort out all of the possible connections of one event, smoking cigarettes, and another event, lung cancer. However, there are sets of approaches that, in combination, move our understanding of a causal inference to the point where logical action can be taken to remediate the situation. As the example of smoking illustrates, there are many more aspects than logic alone governing collective and individual behavior toward smoking, including economic, political, and cultural factors.

3.7 RETROSPECTIVE AND PROSPECTIVE STUDIES

In this Technical Note, I want to continue part of the discussion begun under the topic of causation (Technical Note 3.6). One of the dimensions in making a judgment about causation concerns time, when one factor occurs before or after another. Time is important when one is trying to understand the process or etiology of a disease or a disability, as these events occur over time. There are two major approaches to this study of time: the retrospective and the prospective methods.

In the *retrospective* method, a group of persons is identified at the present time as having or not having some specific condition, such as lung cancer. Then the past experiences and characteristics of these people are examined for any subset of factors that may be related to the presence or absence of the condition. To continue the illustration about lung cancer and smoking, if we began with a large number of persons who currently have lung cancer and another large group who do not have it, we can determine through questioning whether smoking occurred in one group but not in the other, and to what degree (cf. Mausner and Bahn, 1974).

In a *prospective* study, a group of persons who are currently without a given target condition, such as lung cancer, is identified. Then the experiences and characteristics of these people are examined, and the changes in their health and other conditions are noted over a period of time (sometimes running for many years) so that the researcher may discover whether any subset of these factors emerges as a predictor of the future health condition. For instance, if we were to follow a large group of persons who do not smoke at the beginning of the project, we would very likely find that some portion of them have taken up smoking by the end of the project. Following the entire group for several decades will yield differential mortality rates, especially in connection with lung cancer.

As Mausner and Bahn (1974) pointed out, the critical difference between the two approaches is not time itself but how the groups are selected at the beginning. In the retrospective study, two groups are selected that differ mainly in the presence or absence of the target condition (lung cancer, in this case), but that are as similar as possible in other ways. In the prospective study, a single group of persons is followed for their exposure to the predicted experiences that constitute the presumed cause of the condition (such as cigarette smoking as linked to lung cancer). This single group should be as similar as possible on other major distinguishing factors.

In either approach, if it is found that people with the target condition (lung cancer) have in common the specific experience (cigarette smoking), whereas those who do not have the condition also have not, by and large, had that experience, then one has the basis for an inference of causality: cigarette smoking is one probable cause of lung cancer. (Review Technical Note 3.6 to see how the retrospective and prospective methods use the five criteria for causality.)

Each approach has advantages and disadvantages. Retrospective studies are relatively less expensive because smaller numbers of participants may be involved, and the results may be obtained more quickly because the researcher doesn't have to keep track of the sample for as long. However, the data from the past may be incomplete, biased, and dependent on the quality of the selecting process. (See the Technical Note on randomization and matching, 1.7, p. 32).

Prospective studies provide information on the relative risk of the identified experience over time, whereas the researcher has to reconstruct such information from the reports of the participants in a retrospective study. The prospective study is free of the biases inherent in the selection process for the retrospective study because all participants are presumed to be free of the target condition.

However, prospective studies have serious disadvantages connected with the logistics of the research itself. It is expensive to form a large number of participants in a long-term study, where attrition (loss due to death, movement away from the research center, refusal, and so on) is likely. Also, the choice of instruments and variables made at the beginning of a study may lock the researcher into tools that are limited (according to later studies).

But in effect, we must either go back in time with retrospective analysis, take a current slice of life in a single cross-sectional project, or move ahead with the sample of participants in order to attempt to understand the connection between sets of events. Or we can use combinations of these approaches.

CHAPTER 4

The Development of a Conceptual Road Map: Three Tries

Overview

The process of research involves a flowing back and forth between concepts that guide practice and experience that shapes concepts. In this chapter, we will focus on the conceptual side by getting at this abstract topic in three different ways. The interactive and inductive way involved us in building up the bits of ideas into concepts, then propositions, and finally a small theory related to this protective project. Another way of conceptualizing the process is from a psychological perspective, and yet another is from the sociological point of view. Each adds some insights into the continuous task of conceptualizing and testing out ideas in experience. The chapter ends with a listing of the specific concepts used in the BRI Protective Project. We will use this list frequently from here on.

Narrative Section

Introduction
First Try: Conceptualizing from an Inductive and Interactive Approach
Second Try: Conceptualizing from a Psychological Perspective
Third Try: Conceptualizing from a Sociological Perspective
The Conceptual Package Used in the BRI Protective Study
Summary and Generalizations

Technical Notes Section

4.1 Philosophy of Scientific Practice: Concepts, Constructs, Constants, and Variables
4.2 Philosophy of Scientific Practice: Assumed and Operating Propositions
4.3 Philosophy of Scientific Practice: Theories and Empirical Laws
4.4 Explanation and Control
4.5 *Diagnostic and Statistical Manual of Mental Disorders* (DSM-III)
4.6 Classical Research Designs and Threats to Their Validity and Generalizability

The Narrative

INTRODUCTION

The task of this chapter is to introduce a formal process of building conceptual networks to guide the research effort. To do this, I will try to construct a sort of programmed text in which my part is to frame some questions in a purposive sequence, and the reader's part is to respond to these questions, while keeping an eye on the kind of question being asked as well. This approach differs from the Socratic art of questioning in that the response is not built into the query itself; it will require imaginative thinking. I will respond after the reader has a chance to answer, so we can compare notes on where we are in the process.

FIRST TRY: CONCEPTUALIZING FROM AN INDUCTIVE AND INTERACTIVE APPROACH

Let's start in this way: Recall the brief description of Mrs. Caraway, the seventy-year-old widow who had become estranged from her three children because of her abuse and neglect of them when they were young. There is no way to soften the fact that her children described her as a despicable individual. She was in constant trouble with her neighbors; it seemed transparently clear that she was the cause of the many disputes. And inspite of her serious diabetic condition, she ate candy by the bagful as if it were the only thing that gave her any pleasure. This also depleted her already marginal financial situation. She appeared not to care a damn, nor did anyone else, except the bill collectors. At them (and other, random passersby), she would shake her wooden club menacingly, and the problems would become compounded. Although she was well known to several social and health agencies, no one could quite decide who was to bell this cat. And so the situation continued to grow worse.

The beginning of conceptualizing is both easy and complex at the same time. The easy part is to ask this question: What appears to be the main or dominating feature of this situation (a specimen of older persons in need of protective services)? Jot down your first dominant or comprehensive impression:

1. _____

Now, let's compare notes. There are lots of details presented, but the question asks for a summary impression, the big picture. Some people respond that they see a *hostile* person who doesn't seem to be able to *control* her life in many significant ways. Let's take this as one comprehensive impression and check it out: Pick several very different instances of Mrs. Caraway's situation to see whether they are clearly linked to this summary characterization.

2. _____

_____

What details caught your attention? For hostility, you might have pointed to the very old examples of her abuse and neglect of her children, or more recently, you might have observed threatening behavior (with her club) and her (unexplained) conflicts with her neighbors. With regard to being out of control of her life, you may have noted her life-threatening eating of sweets, given her diabetic condition. But note that some people even consider her hostile behavior—including all of the examples listed above—another indication of being out of control.

What have we done so far? We have reduced a lot of details to fit within several categories, and possibly even into one category: being out of control. This is an inductive process, looking at specific instances and finding some more inclusive idea common to them all. However, what we end up with is an arbitrary construction—we never see "out-of-control-ness" directly expressed in so many words. Rather, we see specific behaviors. But it makes sense to us to use the more inclusive idea, "being out of control," to summarize what we have seen as being common to diverse behaviors. Note that applying an arbitrary and more comprehensive label is risky. It clearly begins a mental set of what to look for. It also begins to close out other behaviors that we might have looked at. Approach any inductive effort or conceptualizing with caution.

In addition to simply summarizing, this inclusive term can be useful in uncovering new instances in Mrs. Caraway's behavior, if the term is meaningful. We formulate these abstract terms and continue to use them only as long as they are useful to us as accurate summarizers, and only as long as they lead us to new instances of behavior as well. What other instances of "being out of control" would you look for in Mrs. Caraway's case?

3. _____

_____

Because I can't respond to your written suggestions, at least let me offer some of the ideas that others have had for this question: People have guessed that Mrs. Caraway was overweight, smoked too much, and maybe consumed alcohol too much as well. Others thought about her being in debt, being in trouble with utility payments, and getting into arguments with strangers in stores and other public settings. As it happens, most of these guesses were true to some degree (there was no evidence that she drank to excess), but the more important point is that once we had the idea—being out of control—we could imagine other instances where that dominant characteristic might be exhibited. A person doesn't have to be out of control in every aspect of life to fit that category. We make a judgment as to how many defining characteristics are necessary to place a person in that category.

This process of arbitrarily constructing a general class of events from some

103

specific set of instances is termed *concept formation*. The new abstract and general-ized term, or *concept*, is different from any specific instance, but it shares some essential common features with all of them.* The concept is neither true nor false, simply fruitful or not fruitful for the purposes intended, namely, describing, summarizing, and suggesting new instances.

What I find particularly fascinating about this abstract discussion of how concepts are formed is that the process isn't particularly strange or unfamiliar; we do it all of the time in our everyday lives. For example, we meet a new person and are attracted to her by her striking physical appearance. We observe how she acts in this social context, and we listen to what she says about her experiences, her ideas, and her values. We discover that we share many of these attributes, and at some point, we realize that we would like to have this person as a friend. The concept *friend* was formed in other circumstances, from our own experiences as well as from the experiences of others (transmitted through poetry and drama, for example). Having the concept in mind, we came to apply it when some critical number of attributes in a new person emerged to fit the general pattern. In a similar way, we know what *hostility* is and come to attach it to specific persons because of some critical number of attributes or defining characteristics. The scientist tries to be more precise in specifying how many of what types of attributes are needed to connect the conceptual label *hostility* to a particular person. But the process of concept formation and connec-tion is essentially the same.

I had earlier mentioned that the process of conceptualizing is both easy and complex at the same time. The easy part was described above: our rather natural tendency to find commonalities among a set of events and to give that set a label. The complex part comes in when several people observe the same set of events and find different major features, which, of course, get different labels, perhaps because they begin with different values and assumptions. There is no external guarantee that the common label we find will be the "right" one, on which all can agree. Rather, concepts are formed from many perspectives, and we can judge their worth only by the fruitfulness of their usage. Let me ask you to take another look at the description of Mrs. Caraway, and to see whether you can infer another set of psychological or psychiatric terms that could characterize her situation:

4. _____

Some other responses I have had from this case illustration include labels of pathology, such as paranoia. This term has had an extensive career of being defined by therapists and scientists, and of being redefined and redefined again. Do you get a bit uneasy with all this redefinition? Don't. It is actually part of the process of scientific defintion, a continual readjustment to make sure that the perception of the majority are accurately represented in the term. (See Techni-cal Note 4.5, p. 120, on the *Diagnostic and Statistical Manual of Mental Disorders*).

* Technical Note 4.1 (p. 115) deals with a set of related conceptual terms: *concepts, constructs, constants,* and *variables*. These terms are the building blocks of conceptual and empirical analyses and thus introduce the technical discussion that is called *philosophy of science*. Because these terms serve applied purposes as well, I call the enterprise the *philosophy of scientific practice*.

One has to be open to new information that extends or contracts the original definition to include the new instances, or to correct inaccuracies in the old one.

On the other hand, I get very uneasy when people, other than those who are presumably highly trained in diagnostic procedures, use such powerful and dangerous terms as *paranoia* or *psychotic* because these labels may literally become life sentences in contexts (cf. Szasz, 1961) where they are misapplied. In spite of the eloquent defense for the use of diagnostic labels by leaders of the psychiatric establishment (cf. Spitzer, 1975), I am concerned about their use by less-well-trained persons who may be in positions of authority. It is the least-trained, not the best-trained, persons in such contexts who become the most grave threat to civil liberties and to an effective and humane helping practice. (See Rosenhan, 1973; Spitzer, 1975.)

The major point that I want to emphasize in this exercise is that concepts are easily formed but that they may not be well or wisely formed, and thus, they may not be fruitful guides to action. When a term is constructed and seems logically sound and consistent with the known facts, it becomes the basis for testing: Does it in fact perform its functions (description, summarization, and location of new instances) appropriately? Another function of a concept is to be capable of being linked with other concepts to form propositions (such as hypotheses or predictive statements).* It is as if concepts have to have coupling devices built into them, so that larger, more comprehensive statements that describe, summarize, and predict can be formed.

Let's try this. With what other concepts would you relate "not being in control"? Let me give some hints about what might be appropriate linking concepts. First, they have to be in the same ballpark. The originating concept, "not being in control," refers to an individual. Other linking concepts have to be related or relatable to individual behaviors. The originating concept can be in several kinds of relationships to other concepts, such as causing some, being caused by others, or having some mutually interdependent relationship. (We don't ordinarily form propositions with unrelated or unrelatable terms.) Now, with what concepts do you think "not being in control" could be related in Mrs. Caraway's case?

5. _____

When I ask students this question, I generally get a wide array of possible connecting concepts, suggesting that there are fewer clues to what are the predominant features of the case to which we should pay attention. Some typical responses include connecting hostility with being out of control—although in this case, students often disagree about whether hostility led to being out of control, whether it is the other way around, or whether they are interactive.

But there are other possible solutions to this question of linking "being out

* Technical Note 4.2 (p. 116) introduces the several types of *propositions,* that is, sets of concepts that serve special functions beyond the meanings of the terms individually. Propositions make some statement of how the world works; at least, propositions get the scientific process started in thinking about how some portion of the world works. Some propositions describe assumptions; others indicate ideas to be tested.

of control" to another concept to form a proposition that can be tested for its accuracy in predicting or describing some new state of affairs. Think about the first concept, "being out of control," and ask yourself what it implies. What logically completes, or is related to, the first concept?

6. _____

You might have made several observations. For one, someone else probably has to provide control. For another, there is probably some cause or causes for being out of control; it isn't something that occurs by accident, especially if there are instances that run throughout much of the person's life. Any number of inferences might be made along these lines.

Each of these instances, thus far, has involved someone or some others viewed in reference to Mrs. Caraway, as victim, as antagonist, as whatever. This may be an important observation because if she had a good relationship with her now-adult children, they might have provided some needed supports and controls for Mrs. Caraway's behavior, and a need for protective service might never have arisen. She has no one available, at least who is willing to serve in that capacity, to provide support.

If we look at these two concepts ("being out of control" of her actions, which are unsocial and dangerous to herself, and "not having a supportive other who is able or willing to compensate for her limitations," what relationships can be seen? This is a very important question because for the first time in this discussion we have combined two concepts (as contrasted to combining various attributes), and now we are able to generate totally new information that may provide some insight into the concrete situation from which it was derived. Let's see how this process can be developed.

Let's draw a graph in which the vertical line represents degrees of "being out of control," and the horizontal line represents degrees of "having support from the environment." Now the two concepts have been linked so that each is the context of the other. When you look for some degree of being out of control on the graph, you can also look to see what degree of lack of support is also present. Common sense would suggest that if enough support were available to compensate for limited amounts of self-control, there would be no need for protective services. Likewise, if you found a high degree of self-control combined with a very low degree of social and environmental support, you might predict a fragile situation where the person is currently "making it" on the basis of his or her own resources, but where, if those reserves should falter or fail, there would be little to fall back on, to compensate. (See Figure 4.1.)

Linking these two concepts together in such a graph produces a qualitatively different conceptual tool, one that is capable of generating new information. This is a kind of logic machine; we might even grace it with the name of *theory*. *
It frames logical combinations of the concepts and directs us to see what implications there are, should instances of these logical combinations occur in real life. I have mentioned two logical combinations: high environmental support combined with low self-control, and low environmental support combined with

---

* Technical Note 4.3 (p. 117) introduces the general topic of the nature of *theories* and *empirical laws*. This completes our introduction discussion of the philosophy of scientific practice.

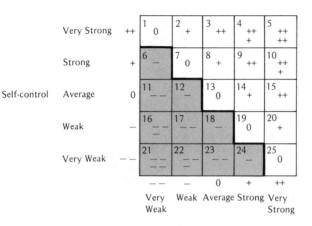

Figure 4.1 The logical combinations of degrees of self-control and environmental support used in defining "need of protective care" (shaded area).

high self-control. But there are many other combinations, composed of the degrees of self-control and of environmental support.

By systematically asking what combinations of self-control and environmental support are necessary for one to be in need of protective services, we can create a new entity, a conceptual description of when being in need of protective services exists. In Figure 4.1, the concept *being in need of protective services,* would be indicated by the portion of the graph that is shaded. Let me describe how this new entity was generated. First, we have to assign some meaning to the degrees of being in self-control and of having environmental support. For simplicity, I have chosen a 5-point scale representing different degrees. I then assigned weights to each degree using a balanced scale, two positive degrees and two negative degrees, with a neutral degree in between. (These are indicated by the ++, +, 0, −, − − symbols.) Then I combined the weightings for each particular cell. For example, Cell 21, formed by the intersection of the two − − weights, has a combined value of − − − −. Cell 1, formed by the intersection of ++ and − −, has a combined value of 0. And so on.

The final stroke is to draw a line separating the portion of the graph that contains minus signs (representing the imbalance that suggests being in need of protective services) from the zero or plus signs (representing at least marginal if not positive strengths in the person–environment context). Now we can say that, given these definitions and assumptions, being in need of protective service is explained by this line on the graph. This explanation then becomes the basis for making plans to influence or control the situation.*

There is a great deal riding on the values given the two dimensions, that is, what degrees of self-control and support are "minus" or "zero" or "plus." I have no bias or value preference as to what the psychological factor, *self-control,* is "worth," any more than I have for the social–environmental factor, *support.* So I chose to given them equal weights and equal balance. This is a conceptual choice, but as I indicate in the following sections of this chapter, it is influenced

---

* Technical Note 4.4 (p. 119) elaborates on the meaning of the terms *explanation* and *control* because these are basic concepts in the service of the helping professions. We cannot hope to influence or control problems until we understand a critical portion of the system of elements involved.

by values and one's intellectual orientation to problem solutions. The general point here is that the graph and mathematics in general are value-free, and it is we who bring values to bear on our decision making by setting up the rules by which mathematical outcomes are generated.

Do not imagine that we have created a miracle by simply attaching numbers to ideas. The degree of precision is artificial. For example, there are several points where the algebraic sum is 1 minus point—in Cells 6, 12, 18, and 24. But the meaning of 1 negative point for each of these combinations seems qualitatively different. The logical machine may be too simplistic for this more complicated task of sorting out the differences among needs when one needs protective service. However, we can make new conceptual rules that attempt to be equal to the human tasks we face; this simple logical machine is merely an introduction to this enterprise.

SECOND TRY: CONCEPTUALIZING FROM A PSYCHOLOGICAL PERSPECTIVE

Keep in mind that what we are doing is forming some conceptual guidelines that will direct both our research and our practice. Whatever we create, we must live with. Once we have a set of concepts interwoven as a theory, and we begin to collect data from the research and practice that it directs, we compare these data with the predictions from that theory. Concepts, empirical findings, and practice experiences—all are intrinsically linked together, each supporting and influencing the others.

In this section, let's look at some specific psychological concepts to see what we can develop into a guiding theory. I will retell Mrs. Caraway's story—not changing any significant facts, but reorienting them as they are required to serve another purpose.

Mrs. Caraway, at age seventy-four, was experiencing some physiological changes that are common to older persons: a slowing down of her energy level; a hardening of her bones, which gave greater risk of fracture; and a slight decrease in her hearing ability. But like most older persons, she accommodated to these changes—at least to the extent that she was aware of them. Her level of functioning wasn't very different from what it had been in her sixties. She shook a mean club then, just as she was shaking threatening clubs at age seventy-four. In that sense, she was among the lucky elderly, as sometimes physiological changes can produce profound deficits that also limit functioning.

But in terms of psychological functioning, it was very clear that Mrs. Caraway was having considerable difficulties.* She wasn't clear about who were old neighbors and who were the bill collectors. Her indiscriminate behavior was a threat to these people, but it was also a threat to her in that if some stranger didn't take kindly to her waving a stick at him, he might return the violence. In addition,

---

* Technical Note 4.5 (p. 120) briefly introduces the issues of diagnostic categories, their strengths and limitations, and the enormous collective effort that went into the construction of the most recent—and yet still fallible—*Diagnostic and Statistical Manual of Mental Disorders* (DSM-III).

her eating behavior was clearly self-destructive, in light of her medical condition. She appeared to be aware that she had diabetes and that eating candy was highly risky, but she still ate it with abandon. The stereotype of older persons scrimping by, always saving for a rainy day, must be totally rejected in Mrs. Caraway's hedonic behavior. There was, in short, ample reason to question the way in which Mrs. Caraway was leading her life.

I want to make a short digression that will become a major topic of discussion in later chapters. A cartoon in the *New Yorker* showed a middle-aged matron answering the door of her swanky apartment with a cigarette in one hand and a martini glass in the other. Before her were several men, some dressed in conspicuous doctors' uniforms. The caption read something like this: "Mrs. Jones, we have reason to believe that you are not taking good enough care of yourself."

There is an ethical question posed at this point, both in the cartoon and in Mrs. Caraway's life: Ought some professional helper to go in and straighten out Mrs. Jones's smoking and drinking behavior, or Mrs. Caraway's hostile actions toward others and possible self-destructive acts toward herself? Perhaps Mrs. Jones enjoyed smoking and drinking; perhaps Mrs. Caraway enjoyed a lively confrontation to spice up an otherwise dull day. Neither Mrs. Jones nor Mrs. Caraway had actively committed a crime at the time of their contact with "helping professionals." And although the predictive evidence is strong that smoking and drinking, or threatening people and eating large quantities of sugar, were "bad" for the parties involved, still it seems like a value judgment that we, as outsiders, are imposing on the lives of these individuals. Have people the right to kill themselves in polite ways like overeating, drinking, and smoking? (I would like to have the answer to this question right away, please, as some of my highly educated friends and colleagues are doing this very thing. And they are not in need of protective services; at least, I don't think they are. What are my duties toward them?)

Psychologically speaking, we can view Mrs. Caraway's situation by noting that her degree of mental disorganization was not counterbalanced by her capacities for self-control or adaptation. We have elsewhere argued that this complex set of forces may describe "normal" aging (Bloom and Nielson, 1971). The more nearly balanced the forces of cognitive disorganization and the adaptive mechanisms of self-control are, the more nearly is the aging person growing old within normal limits. When the cognitive disorganization exceeds adaptive ability, then we find a candidate for protective care.

This psychological view points the way to more specific concepts—the dimensions of this psychological inner space, so to speak. I'll return to these other components, as they became the specific variables of the research project. On the other hand, when adaptive ability exceeds cognitive disorganization, then we have instances of psychologically superior people. Such people are making efficient use of their level of energy, their talents, and their time; and they are likely to be enjoying their lives. As Breslow (1968) described them:

> The healthy older person has not received sufficient attention. All of us know such persons—those reaching the upper reaches of life in fabulous health, enjoying almost every hour of everyday, accomplishing a great deal—living a full, vigorous life into the seventies and eighties and sometimes even into the nineties. (p. 97)

109

Let's consider further the dysfunctional balance between cognitive disorganization and adaptive capabilities. Note first that the process of coming to need protective services is wholly involuntary and is largely a product of cognitive events that can be set off by internal changes (such as arteriosclerosis) or by external ones (such as changes in social relationships that produce stress). Second, it should be clear that at times an older persons who is becoming mentally unclear may be completely unaware of this deteriorating cognitive change, especially in its later stages. The ordinary adaptation to the normal decrements of aging eventually fail to be sufficiently corrective, and attempts to conceal these decrements become in themselves maladaptive. (If you refuse to let people into your apartment because you want to disguise the fact that you are forgetful, you may not have anyone present to remind you to turn off the burner under the soup pot until it is too late.) And finally, there are no public markers of these inner changes. No one holds a bar mitzvah for you when you become mentally confused, indicating your new status as being in need of protective care. And there you are left, often alone, against a world that is indeed becoming increasingly aloof or hostile toward you.

Does this grim scenario regarding the power of psychological variables make you want to change the weightings of the logical machine that we constructed a few pages back? Perhaps you might want to give more weight to the psychological factor, *self-control,* and to leave environmental support as it is. Let's see what would happen: Figure 4.2 represents such a redefinition of weightings. When the psychological factor is weighted more heavily (becomes more important in your mental equation) than the environmental, we can see that the line separating the needful from the nonneedful incorporates a larger number of instances than in Figure 4.1. Indeed, there are fifteen cases that would fit this definition of being in need of protective services, as contrasted with ten instances in Figure 4.1. This is what happens when we give priority—as we are fully entitled to do—to one or another element in our theoretical map. In so doing, we are directed toward emphasizing that variable more strongly in our preventive or interventive service program. We have to live with the consequences of our conceptual decisions as they direct our practice.

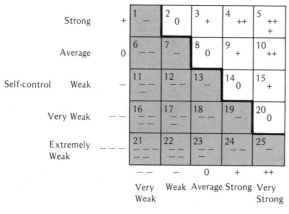

Figure 4.2 The logical combinations of degrees of self-control and environmental support used in defining "need of protective care" (shaded area)—emphasizing the psychological factor of self-control.

THIRD TRY: CONCEPTUALIZING FROM A SOCIOLOGICAL PERSPECTIVE

By now, you should have seen through my strategy in generating a logical prediction machine, that is to say, a small theory about being in need of protective care. I simply identify two relevant concepts, then vary the strength of each, then graph the results as an operational definition of this theory. In this section, I would like you to try your hand at theory construction by thinking about the sociological dimension, *environmental support.* Let's say, for example, that some wise bureaucrat has decided that people in Mrs. Caraway's category are getting entirely too much public welfare and cuts her income by one third, thus precipitating a shift in what Mrs. Caraway has to spend on various essentials and nonessentials. The "social environment" has become distinctively less supportive. But more than that, this little illustration shows how vulnerable people like Mrs. Caraway are to fiscal changes made in far-off places. Regardless of how psychologically in control Mrs. Caraway is, the social facts are real and powerful.

Does this illustration make you want to readjust the weighting in our logical prediction machine? I hope so—if only for the experience of playing with a theory. In Figure 4.3, I present one new set of weightings, emphasizing the sociological dimension relative to the psychological one, and I ask you to fill in the cells and to determine what the effect is of this maneuver.

I hope you have examined Figure 4.3 carefully and have worked out the algebraic weightings of the cells so as to be able to draw a new line linking the "minuses," that is to say, all those combinations of conditions that indicate that a person is in need of protective services. If so, I think you will find only eight such cells, reflecting the power that environmental support is presumed to have in affecting the "need for protective services." Note that this is a value assumption: if people had enough social and physical environmental supports, even if they were confused, they would still have enough to enable them to cope effectively. Such an assumption leads directly to a practice model: Supply people with sufficient social and environmental supports so as to enable them to cope effectively.

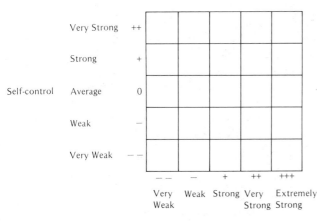

Figure 4.3 The logical combinations of degrees of self-control and environmental support used in defining "need of protective care"— emphasizing the sociological factor, *environmental support.* The reader is to fill in the algebraic weighting of the cells in order to determine the area in "need of protective care."

Looking back at Figures 4.1, 4.2, and 4.3, we next have to ask which theory is best? Which theory most nearly describes what "being in need of protective services" is really like? I would like to tell you the correct answer—but I don't think there is one in the usual sense of the word. Each theory clearly expresses assumptions in its weightings, reflecting some conceptual orientation toward the world—specifically the world of protective needs. One theory has a clear practice implication, whereas another perhaps is more helpful in our thinking about some of the possible factors operating on the need for protective care. These may be trade-offs, depending on what it is important to you to know. But the ultimate test of any theory is in what predictions may be derived from it, and in whether these receive empirical confirmation that enables you to understand the phenomenon more clearly, to control its practical manifestations, and to make further explorations of related topics. These criteria of the comparative worth of theories requires that they be put to the test of research, practice, and further theory construction.*

THE CONCEPTUAL PACKAGE USED IN THE BRI PROTECTIVE STUDY

We have explored three artifical theories, little logical machines used to generate predictions about what people are likely to be in need of protective services. The purpose of that part of this chapter was theory construction. Next I want to turn to what was actually developed for the BRI project. In some ways, we used the conceptual dimensions of the preceding examples. But in another way, we had to look at more specific ingredients of self-control and environmental support in order to be clearer about what interventions to attempt.

For example, one aspect of self-control might be a person's cognitive functioning. However, it was clear from the literature that there are many ways to look at this topic. We selected two measurement tools, one for *intelligence* per se, and the other for what is called *mental status,* meaning degree of mental clarity or functioning with regard to persons, place, and time. We recognized that we could not affect a person's general intelligence, but there was some evidence that mental status might be aided with suitable interventions, from good nutrition to visual reminders of the time of the day or the day of the week. Thus some aspects of cognitive functioning we saw as stable features, whereas others might be influenced (through intervention) to help in effective functioning. In this way, we attempted to specify the particular aspects of self-control and environmental supports that we thought were most important in the present context.

Table 4.1 presents the set of variables that we used in the Protective Project. Some of the factors will look familiar, even though the labels are somewhat different. *Personal competence* is the broadest term we could think of, related to the bio-social factors in need for protective services. Self-control, the term used

---

* Technical Note 4.6 (p. 123) continues the discussion of the *classical research designs* that can be used to test which hypothesis derived from which theory leads to positive outcomes. We now have to consider *alternative explanations* of how such outcomes could have come to be, because there may be causes of the results other than the experimental interventions. Another important topic is whether the results of one project may be legitimately *generalized* to other similar samples.

Table 4.1   Components of "Being in Need of Protective Services"

Being in need of protective services involves:

I. Personal Competence
   A. Cognitive functioning
      1. Intelligence
      2. Mental status (confusion as to person, time, and place)
      3. Anomie
   B. Affective funtioning
      1. Contentment
      2. Signs and symptoms of affective or behavioral disorders
   C. Physical and behavioral functioning
      1. Survival and mortality
      2. Morbidity (not measured in this study)
      3. Physical functioning activities
         a. Activities of daily living (lower level of physical functioning)
         b. Physical functioning (higher level of physical functioning)
II. Environmental Protection
   A. Physical environmental protection
      1. Physical environmental characteristics
      2. Community versus institutional residence
   B. Social environmental protection
      1. Interested parties
      2. Concrete assistance
   C. Collateral stress

in the prior illustrations, might be considered one aspect of personal competence. As I will be discussing these variables at many points in the remainder of the book, I will only briefly introduce you to these terms here.

The two main factors, as in our examples above, are psychological and sociological in nature. We then divided personal competence into three subfactors, reflecting the general literature regarding what is important in a person's functioning. I have tried to indicate briefly in Table 4.1 the nature of these variables, if the label isn't self-explanatory. Note that some subfactors have further subdivisions. For example, physical functioning was further subdivided into some very basic functions (called "activities of daily living," like eating, toileting, and bathing), along with another set of physical functions that were of a higher level (such as walking, and working). Together, these provided a continuum of physical functioning. We had to focus on this degree of detail because of the nature of our participants. We applied the same rationale to our emphasis on the details of "cognitive functioning."

Environmental protection includes both the physical environment, such as the part one's home plays in providing safety and sanitary living conditions, and also the social environment, that is, how others affect and are affected by an older person in need of protective services. In some cases we recognized that we might not be able to compensate for a participant's severe mentational deficits, but we could reduce the worrisome burden that this problem caused that participant's relatives. Such an act would be a socially valued objective in its own right; we called this a reduction in collateral stress.

SUMMARY AND GENERALIZATIONS

1. It is possible to begin from any set of observed events and to generalize to some concept that abstracts the essential features of these events. It is possible to combine such concepts into propositions so that they assume or assert something about a portion of the world. It is possible to form logical machines (theories) that generate new ideas. Some of these new ideas may be put into the form of hypotheses (or predictions) suitable for testing whether the theory is a good guide to that part of the real world. It is possible to benefit from empirical research of this sort to modify the theory so as to make it a more fruitful guide, not just in research, but in practice as well. It is possible for the researcher to do all these things, but it is equally useful for a scientific practitioner to perform these steps as well, as part of the process of professional helping.

2. Conceptual mappings may be made from many perspectives, starting with specific events or starting from broad abstractions. What is important is the weaving back and forth between observing and conceptualizing, each directing the other to look a little more sharply at a portion of the universe, and each correcting the other in the process. But once you form a theory and are guided by it, be careful, because it has strong implications for that part of reality at which you will look and on which you will act. It is very easy, with a slight change of some conceptual weightings, to come up with quite different views of reality and what ought to be done about it.

3. Any research project is thus a compromise among the many forces acting on it: conceptual and empirical, and also practical and valuational. It is through your awareness of these pressures that the most useful package of research and of practice can be put together.

Technical Notes

4.1 PHILOSOPHY OF SCIENTIFIC PRACTICE: CONCEPTS, CONSTRUCTS, CONSTANTS, AND VARIABLES

Molière, the great French dramatist, created a character in his play, *The Bourgeois Gentleman,* who is universal. It seems that this fellow has come into some money and is trying to pick up culture quickly by hiring a tutor in language. Beginning at the beginning, the tutor divides all language into poetry or prose. The bourgeois gentleman suddenly gets the revelation that as he hasn't been using any poetry, then he has been speaking prose all his life and never knew it. Thousands of people have laughed at that line in the play, not realizing that they are in a roughly comparable position in speaking in concepts, propositions, and possibly theories all their lives without a suitable recognition of this noble state of affairs.

So it is that we must also begin at the beginning and make some vital distinctions among the basic building blocks in science.

Concepts are the classes of abstracted and generalized ideas that we hold about our experiences. Let's go over this definition from a process point of view. First, we experience one event or happening, then another, and another. From these many experiences, we *abstract* common elements, and then we *generalize* on these commonalities to an abstract class of ideas that is apart from any single instance of the concept. The abstract idea or concept exists in our minds, reflecting experiences that we (or others who have told us about theirs) have had, and is expressed through symbols such as language and numbers.

As Jean Piaget expressed it, we develop schemata about experiences over our entire lifetime, and these generalized ideas help us to adapt to new experiences based on the old. I think it would be correct to say that we generally think in terms of these abstract categories, except in moments of high individual excitement or terror, when the specific elements of nature force their way past the veneer of our civilized way of experiencing things.

Just look at how we talk: "Aren't these New Hampshire fall leaves beautiful?" "I wonder whether there will even be a social security program by the time I retire." "Pass the catsup, please." Except for the logical connectives (which are concepts in their own right), all of the action and object terms refer to broad classes of ideas, even though in the case of "I" there may be only one member in that class. "I" am the product of my entire developmental experiences, the feedback from others, the assertive acts on my own, and the physical environmental response to my actions. To talk is to use common categories of experience so as to be understood.

Scientific concepts are different from the concepts emerging from everyday experience in that they are presumably developed with greater clarity and rigor. These stem from the need to use such concepts with precision, to report exactly what happened, and to permit others to repeat the process for themselves if they wish. It is this reflective rationality that distinguishes scientific usage from lay language, although I believe this distinction to be a matter of degree rather than kind.

The term *construct* is sometimes used interchangeably with the term *concept*, but I would recommend that constructs be viewed as concepts of a higher level of generality. Instead of being generated out of experiences, as concepts are, constructs may be viewed as emerging from commonalities among concepts. However, be prepared to find different usages in the literature.

The term *variable* is important because it links the empirical with the theoretical realm. A variable is a marker of some concept in that it indicates a range of empirical characteristics that that concept can theoretically take. For example, the variable *depression* can take on degrees of magnitude, reflecting in the empirical world what the concept *depression* intends to represent in the theoretical domain. Note that the word *depression* can be used as either a variable or a concept; hence, the possibility of confusion if you don't keep the context of a word's usage clear.

A *constant* is an empirical indicator of a concept that is held steady for purposes of some experimental or statistical manipulation. By holding the variable of age constant for a given analysis, the researcher can remove that factor from his or her consideration of what may be influencing the object of his or her analysis: All persons involved in a given analysis are of the same age—which is being held constant—and so differences among them must be attributed to other causes.

4.2 PHILOSOPHY OF SCIENTIFIC PRACTICE: ASSUMED AND OPERATING PROPOSITIONS

In the previous Technical Note, I discussed that basic unitary abstraction, the *concept*. In the present Technical Note, I want to discuss several ways in which concepts can be linked together in logical sentences. The set of concepts would then constitute a *proposition*. Propositions are the forms we use so as to put concepts to work, because a concept alone cannot be tested for its veracity as a guide to some portion of the universe. Rather, it is when we combine concepts that we can begin to make some statements about the world that are suitable for testing. Let's see how this new attribute belonging to sets of concepts (a proposition) comes about.

First, let's make a distinction between two forms of propositions. I would call one subgroup the *assumed propositions* because it is with these that we get the business of science off the ground. We assume that certain relationships are maintained between two or more conceptual portions of the world, and then we go on to form other propositions (to be discussed later in the category of operating propositions) to conduct the actual scientific investigation. *Postulates* are one form that these assumed propositions may take, in which we provision-ally consider something to be the case so as to formulate premises in a logical argument that can later be tested. *Axioms* are seen as self-evidently true and are at the moment capable of neither proof nor disproof.

I would suggest that values may be another form of assumed proposition, although there isn't much agreement about values in the literature. A *value* propo-sition asserts that certain linked concepts describe a preferred or a nonpreferred state of affairs, which then organizes the direction that an intervention takes. For example, we assume that people prefer to be independent in maintaining their own households as long as possible, and we go on from there to plan service programs accordingly. I would suggest that this assumption reflects a value statement, possibly one that is based on surveys of relevant persons, but a preference statement nonetheless.

There is no problem when some propositions are assumed, as long as these assumptions are spelled out for everyone to see. But by their very nature, some of these are so deeply buried or so omnipresent that they are invisible directives on the way we conduct our research (or anything else). To the extent that we are not aware of these assumptions, we do not have control over our own rational choices. It would also be possible to connect these personal value assumptions to the collective ideologies that we hold as a people or as a culture, which may be equally invisible to us, and again, to that extent, which may act as a limitation on what we might have chosen to do had all the options been open to us. And although these distinctions may seem to border on nitpicking, they have important implications in practice, as we shall see.

The other type of propositions may be termed operating propositions; that is, these are the scientific sentences that are used in directing actual research. The major step in forming such *operating propositions* is that we move toward putting our hunches on how two or more portions of the universe are linked to an empirical test. That is, from the conceptual world that specifies what should happen between two concepts, we can move to the empirical world to see whether this prediction appears in the variables used to indicate the conceptual relationship.

I would suggest the term *hypothesis* for the proposition that is derived from a theory (to be discussed in the following Technical Note). It is a theoretical statement involving logical relationships between concepts. When variables are used in place of concepts, the relationship can be termed a *prediction*, which can be tested for its empirical truth or falsity. Do the events that are indicated by the variables relate, in fact, to each other as predicted? If so, then the prediction is *empirically true*, and the conceptual hypothesis from which the prediction is derived has received *confirmation*. Should the empirical evidence not support the prediction, it would be proved *false*, and the hypothesis would receive *disconfirmation*.

As usual, these terms are often used interchangeably, so keep an eye on the context of what you are reading to distinguish the empirical or the theoretical domains in regard to propositions, as they differ in their functions accordingly.

4.3 PHILOSOPHY OF SCIENTIFIC PRACTICE: THEORIES AND EMPIRICAL LAWS

As you can see from the two preceding Technical Notes, we are building the conceptual and the empirical network, from concepts and variables at the *unitary* level, to hypotheses and predictions at the *comparative* level, to theories and empirical laws at the *systemic* level.

A *theory* is a system of propositions concerning some portion of the universe. The systems element is most important. First, it specifies that some network of conceptual elements is interrelated. For example, one systemic network is the Syllogism: A (a given propositon) implies B (another proposition), B implies C, and therefore A implies C. Second, it requires that the interrelationships between or among propositions be such that a change in one part has implications for the other parts. This idea is important because when it comes time to use a theory to guide practice in the real world, the theory suggests points at which intervention or prevention may take place so as to change some other elements in the real world in a way parallel to the changes implied in the logical universe of theory.

A theory, then, is a parsimonious way of *understanding, explaining, predicting,* and potentially *controlling* some portion of reality.

Once formed, a theory has an internal development. New propositions should be capable of being derived from the logical network, thus expanding on the parts of reality to which the theory is applicable. As hypotheses derived from the theory are stated in variable form as predictions and are subjected to empirical testing, some may gain objective confirmation. Others may not; reconsideration may be required of both the predictions and the hypotheses from which they are derived—each may need other factors to help clarify what is a more fruitful view of reality.

As the supportive evidence mounts, these statements become *empirical generalizations,* that is, empirical evidence from a variety of sources related to the one prediction. When there is a great deal of support, such statements may achieve the status of *scientific laws.* However, it is rare for there to be such uniformity of agreement among qualified observers that it establishes scientific laws, especially in the social and behavioral sciences. For example, the learning theorists assembled an extraordinary amount of laboratory research and clinical investigations showing that positive reinforcement of a behavior made it more likely that that behavior would be repeated. More recent research on the cognitive conditions surrounding reinforcement situations has shown that even this powerful empirical generalization needs qualification or, to put it another way, that it has not yet been stated in such a way as to constitute an empirical law held without exception in the scientific community. However, once accepted, such laws would take a considerable effort to "repeal." But overturning a scientific law is not impossible; remember Copernicus, Kepler, and Galileo.

Sometimes a theory can be stated in a few short sentences, such as Albert Ellis's theoretical model of rational-emotive therapy. (This *A-B-C-D* model might be conveyed briefly as looking at an unpleasant state of affairs, the *C*onsequence, and finding an apparent cause in an *A*ntecedent event, whereas it is really an intervening event, the irrational *B*elief system operating, that, in fact, causes the *C*onsequence. Solution: *D*ispute the irrational *B*elief system and replace it with a rational one.) Other theories are very complex and require books to expound (such as Freudian theory). To the extent that it is difficult to state a theory clearly, it is also difficult to derive clear hypotheses from which exact empirical tests may be derived. Any theory that does not permit disconfirmation is not a theory, but an ideology. However, being brief and concise does not necessarily make a theory fruitful. Successfulness of a theory depends on the empirical results that stem from using it. Practice theories have been notoriously difficult to test, or rather, it is difficult to get others to accept the results as confirming or disconfirming the theory from which they were derived. (See the critical discussions of Fischer, 1976; 1978; 1980; Parloff, 1979, 1980; Reid and Hanrahan, 1982; Mullen and Dumpson, 1972; Wood, 1978; Luborsky, Singer, and Luborsky, 1976; Meltzoff and Kornreich, 1970; Bergin, 1966; Smith, Glass, and Miller, 1980; Garfield, 1983.)

One way or the other, theories are here to stay in the sciences and in the applied sciences. We may not love them, but we can't do without them. The best approach seems to be trying to use them clearly, to bring their hypotheses to a form where we can test the predictions, and then to modify the theories according to what portions receive continuing confirmation. Or taking the empirical route, we can assemble those empirical generalizations that offer entry points for prevention or intervention (Fischer, 1978). This approach may lack the intellectual need for a system of coherent ideas, but it does provide a cafeteria of reasonably workable techniques.

4.4 EXPLANATION AND CONTROL

I would like to tie up the previous several Technical Notes dealing with matters from both the theoretical and the empirical domains by discussing the concepts of *explanation* and *control*. Let's begin with an example about snakes, a topic chosen solely to make my point simple and clear.

Mrs. Caraway was very fearful of snakes. The interviewer didn't bring up snakes, but Mrs. Caraway did, even though talking about them made her feel nervous. How was one to explain her antipathy to snakes? And what was one to do about it?

One possibility comes to mind regarding her antipathy. Maybe she had been frightened by a snake some time earlier and the memory still remained lively to that day, whenever some words or events reminded her of her encounter with the snake. Or another approach is to assume that snakes meant something symbolically for her that generated anxiety. Whenever she thought about snakes, her thoughts wiggled some unconscious connection that raised a cloud of anxiety.

These are two explanations about the presence of some behavioral characteristic in a given individual. *Explanations* in general are attempts to specify the sequence of events that describe fully the conditions under which the given events vary, including how they come to begin and how they continue to exhibit their presence. With this description, we can say that we understand the phenomenon, such as Mrs. Caraway's anxiety about snakes. It has not been said that an explanation is truthful, just that it describes a sequence of events offering a theoretical perspective on a real event. Explanations belong to the conceptual realm.

Control is a different matter, one that belongs to the observable world. *Control* involves taking a conceptual picture and acting on it so as to produce changes in events in the real world. If one can act according to a plan and obtain the results that one expected according to that plan, then one can assert that he or she has control over the events in question. For example, if one followed the learning explanation of Mrs. Caraway's reaction to snakes, then it might follow that one could help her to unlearn that connection and relearn others, perhaps through systematic desensitization. The relief likely to follow would thereby completely eliminate the problem, with no underlying problems remaining and no substitution of symptoms to other objects. Such success in controlling the problem would provide some confirmation of that theoretical explanation and would lead one to repeat that technique (systematic desensitization) and that theoretical model (a learning approach) in similar situations.

Likewise, had one pursued a psychodynamic approach in helping Mrs. Caraway to deal with the unconscious associations that generated the anxiety by facing realistically the effects of id and superego demands on ego, and if these had resulted in a successful resolution of the problem, then this, too, would have constituted an instance of control based on the use of a theoretical explanation.

In this example, it appears possible that there can be two or more very different explanations for the same phenomenon, and that each may lead to a set of actions that lead to control (successful resolution) of that problem. Although having two different explanations and approaches for controlling outcomes may disturb those who believe that there is only one cause for one effect, it is probably more realistic to believe that there may be an array of possible theoretical explanations of any given phenomenon and that there are also a number of ways of achieving a successful resolution of a problem or achievement of some desired potential. It may be a question of efficiency; that is, the choice of an optimal solution may be based on costs as well as effects. It may also be a question of which solution fits better the larger sociocultural context of the client.

The major point of this Technical Note is to link, once again, the conceptual and the empirical, this time to the practice theories and techniques of the helping professional. Research findings are a major partner in this process, aiding professionals to make their initial selection of techniques for control based on the body of evidence for theoretical explanations.

4.5 *DIAGNOSTIC AND STATISTICAL MANUAL OF MENTAL DISORDERS* (DSM-III)

Practitioners have long been well aware of the nature of concepts, propositions, and theories and have tried to make use of them in their work. But major problems have ensued. Practitioner X would observe a number of clients identified as belonging to the same class of problems and would form concepts about them on what she thought were the major features. But Practitioner Y would observe another set of clients presumably of the same type as Practitioner X's and form another set of concepts about them, as would Practitioner Z, and so on. Unfortunately, these conceptualizations didn't always agree—to put the matter in its very best light. This is understandable, as different people in different situations are likely to exhibit some different characteristics, even though they may be suffering from the same general class of disorder. But people and circumstances always differ. Is there no way to form a clear and systematic way of classifying human behavior so as to advance the social and behavioral sciences, as well as the helping professions?

The challenge is extraordinarily complex. Classification systems are the first step toward a strong science. The periodic table of elements was one such major step that had some self-validating properties, for example, the gaps in the pattern of atomic weights that suggested the existence of then-unknown elements. But it appears that, to date, we have no such classification system in the social and behavioral sciences. Here, classification systems tend to be agreements among experts on how events are to be labeled for certain purposes. Thus these classification systems may change over time and may contain portions that are unreliable in their use as well as invalid in their meaning (see Technical Note 4.6). Yet the search goes on to find some common language about that moving, multilevel complexity that is human behavior.

As a case in point, let's examine the DSM-III, the friendly shorthand name for the third edition of the *Diagnostic and Statistical Manual of Mental Disorders* (1980); another revision by the American Psychiatric Association is currently in the works. Earlier efforts had established a list of nomenclature that could be used for *diagnostic* purposes (that is, for giving a label to the configuration of problem behaviors that different persons manifested in different contexts), as well as for *statistical* accounting (that is, how many of what types of problems were being encountered in what contexts, information that would be very useful in planning and management).

By the mid-1970s, a committee (headed by Dr. Robert Spitzer) began to develop a new philosophy of a DSM and a new definition of terms, partly in response to the growth of the psychiatric literature, as well as because of pressure from various groups. For instance, some groups and individuals objected to calling homosexuality a mental illness. The final product was a result of many field tests with patients, by multiple raters from diverse theoretical backgrounds, working cooperatively because of the obvious value of having a common language. The authors of the DSM-III claim to having achieved acceptable reliability, greater than had been reached using the DSM-II. However, there is still dispute about its reliability (see, for example, Albee, 1983).

Nonetheless, let's examine what went into constructing this new tool of classification. A new perspective added in the DSM-III was the multiaxial evaluation, in which a given case was to be assessed on five axes or dimensions. The first is the presenting clinical syndromes as well as codes for conditions that are not attributable to a mental disorder but are the focus of current attention or treatment. The second axis deals with personality disorders and specific developmental disorders. These two axes comprise the entire classification of mental disorders.

The third axis involves physical disorders or conditions, and the fourth indicates the severity of psychosocial stressors. The fifth axis permits the clinician to judge the highest level of adaptive functioning by the client in the past year, so as to get a sense of what level of rehabilitation is likely to be achieved.

The DSM-III is a descriptive tool, atheoretical with regard to the etiology of the identified conditions (except in those few cases where etiology is well established). Even so, the disorders are grouped together on the basis of shared clinical features. The diagnostic criteria presented in the manual include the essential features of the disorder, the associated features, the age at onset, the course of the disorder, the nature of the impairment, the complications that can arise, the predisposing factors, the prevalence of the disorder, the sex ratio found with regard to this disorder, familial patterns, and differential diagnoses.

It is also important to note what is not in the DSM-III. There are no theories of etiology, management, or treatment of the disorders; nor does this classification include disturbed dyadic, family, or other interpersonal relationships, except as part of the stressors acting on a given client. There is little information on cultural or social variations, or on the clinicians themselves as part of the classification phenomemon. No cross-cultural evidence is presented on the use of this tool.

Clearly, an enormous effort was expended in developing this psychiatric classification tool. And yet each new advance brings new criticisms—and new revisions. Let me illustrate with a widely publicized event that took place a half dozen or so years before the publication of the DSM-III; it represents the perennial debate between those who assert that diagnosis deals with characteristics of the client and those who suggest that diagnosis involves the whole contextual arrangement including the observers themselves.

As part of an experiment designed by Rosenhan (1973), eight normal people who had never had symptoms of serious psychiatric disorders made appointments at a dozen psychiatric facilities with the presenting complaint that they heard voices that said "empty," "hollow," and "thud." The eight—including three psychologists and a psychology graduate student, a psychiatrist, a pediatrician, a painter, and a housewife—were admitted to the various types of psychiatric facilities and stayed on the average 19 days (with a range of 7 to 52 days). During this time, they did not receive much psychiatric help and spent most of their time publicly taking notes about what was happening. To use the author's phrase, they were being "sane in insane places," and it was Rosenhan's contention that the medical staffs failed to detect them.

The eight were admitted with the label of *schizophrenia* (except one, who was labeled *manic-depressive*). Once inside, they acted sanely, that is, with an absence of any signs of serious mental disturbance. The only people who noticed their strange behavior were other patients, whom Rosenhan assumes were insane. These patients said, "You're not crazy. You're a journalist or a professor. You're checking up on the hospital" (Rosenhan, 1973, p. 252).

Eventually, all of these fake patients were discharged with the same diagnostic label, "schizophrenia, in remission" (or "manic-depressive, in remission") (Spitzer, 1975, p. 442). This diagnosis means that on discharge, there were no current signs or overt symptoms of the identified psychiatric problem.

Moreover, there was a related experiment that involved informing the staff at a research and teaching hospital that at some time in the following three months one or more pseudopatients would try to gain admittance. In fact, none (as far as Rosenhan knew) did so—and yet 10 percent of admissions were suspected as being fake by two or more staff members. Rosenhan (1973, p. 179) concluded that any diagnostic process that lends itself so easily to these kinds of errors cannot be very reliable. The publicity that attended this interesting experiment was more heated than most that is published in the technical literature.

For present purposes, I want to report the response of Robert Spitzer (who later went on to head the revision leading to the DSM-III). He began by asking how one detects fake patients. Even if these people are lying, all the admitting medical staff has to go on is the person's word. A person who feigns a psychiatric symptom deserves some label because this isn't ordinary behavior, even if it is research behavior. Rosenhan suggested that the proper label should have been "hallucination of unknown origin," not "schizophrenia," as the former can occur in the absence of the latter, and the latter can occur with or without the former.

Spitzer (1975, p. 449) noted that the purposes of diagnostic labels are to enable helping professionals communicate effectively among themselves, to comprehend the pathological processes involved in the psychiatric illness, and to work toward control of these disorders. And although he recognized then (1975), as I suspect he would now, that our understanding of these complex entities called *schizophrenia* or whatever is limited, still he suggested that the category system of psychiatric diagnoses performed moderately effectively, at least in communications among helping professionals. For example, Spitzer found it gratifying that all of the fake patients were released "in remission" because he pointed out that such an asymptomatic state was most unusual in serious psychoses. Spitzer interpreted this finding to mean that diagnoses were rationally applied to the patient and were not unduly influenced by the settings in which they were made. Such diagnoses may not help us to understand the processes themselves, but it does offer some help in the control of many mental disorders. This element of control is based on knowing the likely course of events and on taking suitable action for a given phase (Spitzer, 1975, p. 449).

Interestingly, Rosenhan's suggestion for more specificity of classification, rather than using global labels, seems to have been incorporated into the revision of the DSM for which Spitzer provided so much leadership. Whether the underlying questions were ever answered, or whether the value of diagnostic category systems was ever demonstrated, is still a matter of opinion.

4.6 CLASSICAL RESEARCH DESIGNS AND THREATS TO THEIR VALIDITY AND GENERALIZABILITY

In an earlier Technical Note (1.3, p. 23), I discussed some aspects of experimental and control groups, particularly how they are arranged in the course of a research study so as to give information about the impact of the experimental intervention. In this Technical Note, I would like to expand on that discussion to point out the logic underlying classical research designs with groups of subjects. This note will link with other Technical Notes, such as the ones on causality (3.6, p. 96), validity (5.13, p. 148), and the ethics of research (3.1, p. 85).

Research designs are planned or observed arrangements of events that permit the researcher to make judgments about the nature of those events, for example, which are related to which, and possibly, whether any are causally related. Often these judgments involve the use of statistics, so that part of the planning involves generating data that will be capable of being used by appropriate mathematical operations (see Technical Note 3.5, p. 93, on observation and measurement). Thus research designs may supply descriptive, correlational, or causal information, depending on the purposes and resources of the researcher.

Why go through so much trouble to design a research study? Because any understanding depends fundamentally on the conditions in which something becomes known. For example, say that you are in a hikers' lodge in the forest during a rainstorm and you see a bolt of lightning strike a tree. Soon after, a limb breaks off and falls to the ground. "Ah, ha!" you say. "The lightning

123

broke the limb." But later, when the rain stops, you examine the limb and discover that it was practically hollow with decay, and now you wonder whether the high winds of the storm caused it to break. You also see claw marks on the tree and speculate that a bear climbing on the branch may have broken it. You don't really know because there are reasonable alternative explanations for a given event and you have little way of reconstructing the situation so as to figure out whether it was this or that or some other factor that caused the limb to break. Mere preception doesn't supply the knowledge without the context in which that perception occurred. Research designs simply specify the context in which we make our observations.

Specifically, the contexts of research are logical arrangements that enable us to say that one factor or group of factors that were manipulated in given ways at specified times were or were not likely to have been causal ingredients in the observed change in another factor or factors. Campbell and Stanley (1963) and Cook and Campbell (1979) have provided a helpful overview of these logical arrangements:

But first, remember that research work involves a process or a flow of events, so that although the notations appear to indicate discrete steps, in fact they flow into one another. Several major types of activities can be indicated. One is the planned observation or measurement of some event. Such observations may vary from a casual observation in the open environment to observations in a highly rigorous laboratory situation in which every conceivable function is "wired" for measurement. In addition, observations may vary from one-time affairs, such as a massive survey questionnaire asked on one occasion with a large number of subjects, to the continuous monitorings of the heart rate of a stroke victim. Simple or complex, discrete or continuous, these are the major subtypes of observations used in research.

The other major type of activity in research is the experimental or service component, in which the researcher or the service staff introduces something new into the participants' lives in order to learn what will happen. Actually, the researcher has a very good idea about what will happen. These ideas are formally stated in predictions (Technical Note 4.2, p. 116) as derived from the conceptual overview of the situation. Moreover, the researcher cannot go around doing things to just anybody for curiosity's sake; safety and privacy procedures are carefully spelled out (see Technical Note 6.10, p. 179, on review committees for research involving human subjects).

The experimental or service component can also vary on whether it is simple or complex, and whether it is a one-time affair or is a continuous series of services. Moreover, there are questions of timing, such as when the experimental variable is to be introduced into the research context. These types of factors have to be considered as the researcher plans his or her design, for each has implications for what knowledge may be obtained at what cost.

Now we are ready to combine observations and experimental or service components in a variety of ways that constitute creating research designs. I have already suggested one arrangement, the basic experimental–control-group design used in the BRI Protective Services Project (Technical Note 1.3, p. 23), in which an identified population was randomly sampled so as to form two groups whose members had an equal chance of appearing on either the experimental or the control side. But there is no limit to the number of experimental or control groups that may be used, nor to the order in which observations are made on them.

For example, another common type of experimental–control-group design is termed the *Solomon Four-Group Design* (see Technical Note 2.9, p. 63), in which the effects of pretreatment interviewing itself as a causal factor are studied. There are two experimental and two control groups; only one of each is interviewed before the experimental intervention is made, and all four are interviewed thereafter. The researcher can sort out the effects of interviewing itself and the experimental intervention itself, by comparing the scores of combinations of the four groups at different times. If the two experimental groups differ after intervention (when random selection would presumably have made them comparable to begin with), then perhaps the pretreatment interviews have had an effect on the outcome. This inference would be strengthened if the same pattern were true for the two control groups as well, in which the pretreatment-interviewed group is much different from the other control. However, if both experimental groups are much different from both control groups, but each pair does not differ much between themselves, then this outcome would argue logically for an effect of the intervention, not the pretreatment interviews. There are many other designs that are more complicated and more specialized in their use, but these will serve to introduce the topic. (See Campbell and Stanley, 1963, and Cook and Campbell, 1976, for a further discussion.)

What each of these possible designs attempts to do is to eliminate *alternative explanations* of why the results appear as they do. Campbell and Stanley (1963) presented classes of alternative explanations that research designs could logically avoid. Let me summarize their discussion briefly:

CAMPBELL AND STANLEY'S LIST OF THREATS TO INTERNAL VALIDITY:

1. *History:* Did any other event occur during the time of the research process that may be responsible for the particular outcome?
2. *Maturation:* Did any maturation occur in the participants during the time of the research project that would itself have made them different from when they began?
3. *Testing or reactivity:* Did the effects of the pretreatment observation or testing influence the participants' attitudes or behaviors as measured in the final observation period?
4. *Instrumentation:* Did changes in the instruments used to measure the participants have any impact on the differences in outcome?
5. *Statistical regression:* Did participants begin their measurement period in the study at a time of crisis? (It is likely in the normal course of events that a crisis would become resolved and their scores would be less extreme on a second measurement.) Any person making an extreme score will likely produce a less extreme one—more toward the mean of all scores—on a second testing.
6. *Multiple interventions interfering with interpretations:* If several interventions are used at different times, it is difficult to know what effects the order of presentation or prior exposure have on the eventual outcomes.

In contrast to "pre-experimental designs," like a clinical case study that provides no logical basis for making causal inferences, or "quasi-experimental designs," such as the single-subject or time-series designs that provide approximations of causal information, the "true experimental designs" described by Campbell and Stanley meet the logical objections of these threats to internal validity. For example, because random samples are drawn and observed during the same time period, it is unlikely that differential effects of history or maturation would affect the outcomes; each effect is equally likely to influence the experimental as well as the control groups. Thus experimental designs increase our confidence that the evidence we have obtained occurred because of the special treatment conditions, and not because of extraneous effects that happened differentially to the experimental and the control groups.

However, it is difficult to attain external validity or generalizability with classical research designs, although different designs resolve these doubts to a greater or lesser degree. Although the implications of generalizability are discussed in other Technical Notes (2.4, p. 53, and 4.4, p. 119), I wanted to list the main threats to generalizability discussed by Campbell and Stanley at this time. The underlying issue is whether what we discover about one sample of persons will be usable in connection with other groups of persons in other studies.

Campbell and Stanley's list of *threats to generalizability* include these:

1. *Different independent or intervention variables:* Any new intervention applied by different workers to different clients will very likely differ from the original study, thus producing dissimilar results.
2. *Different dependent variables:* There may be differences in how outcome variables are conceptualized or operationalized, thus reducing the likelihood of identical results.
3. *Different measurement effects:* If the measures used are different, differences in outcome may be expected.
4. *Interaction effects:* If different historical or contextual events are occurring in a second study, these may affect the outcome of the research, accounting for some differences.

It is clear that these are difficult threats to overcome, and thus that they limit the generalizability of results from one study to the next. The major point of this note is the underlying logic of designs, the arrangements that attempt to partial out alternative explanations to the results that we obtain. Each design has to be made not in the abstract, but in connection with the realities of the participants involved, and these introduce limits on the complexity of the designs. As usual, research is a compromise between what is desirable and what is feasible.

CHAPTER 5

"You Have Asked Me All of Your Questions, but You Still Don't Know the Real Me"

Overview

This chapter discusses the development of the research instruments we used in the BRI Protective Project. It also describes the major types of instruments: the questionnaire, so frequently used in survey research; the standardized scale or measure; various kinds of projective tests, including analogues and simulations; ethnomethodology and other qualitative approachs to measurement; and a consideration of unobtrusive and nonreactive measures. The chapter also deals with several major attributes of instruments: their validity, reliability, utility, and adaptability.

These topics are all somewhat technical in nature, and so I have combined the Narrative with the Technical Notes format. This begins my long-term objective of introducing readers to the ordinary scientific literature, where narrative and technical materials are blended.

Technical Narrative Section

The Technical Narrative

INTRODUCTION

>"You have asked me all of your questions, but you still don't know the
>real me," she said.

"What do you mean?" I asked the elderly women with whom I had spent
the past hour engaged in a *pretest* of our interview questionnaire.

"I mean that even though I answered your questions as accurately as I could,
I don't think that those answers describe the person that I really am, my thoughts
and feelings about important things, you know, things like my purpose in life,
my life accomplishments, my family," she replied.

The late afternoon sun cast harsh shadows across the polished floor of her
room at the Margaret Wagner House, the Benjamin Rose Institute's multifunction
home for the aged and nursing home. The dinner hour was approaching, and
nurses' aides were moving down the hall readying the residents for the coming
mealtime, so I knew that I couldn't stay to discuss this point much longer.

"Well, what sorts of questions should I be asking so that I can have a description of the person you really are?" I asked.

"I can't say exactly, and I certainly can't speak for others, but if you wanted
to learn about my life, I think you have to let me speak about it in my own
words—not always in your questions. Maybe you have to encourage me, yes,
I know you have to do that, because I probably wouldn't have said even this
much unless we had had some time to get to know each other a bit. It's a
matter of trust. Now I know you are really serious about learning about older
people and I can respect that. But you have to wait until I'm ready to say
things that are important to me." She stopped talking and we looked at each
other for a few seconds.

I knew she was right. I had inherited a large collection of questions borrowed
from other studies; some of them had dealt with seriously mentally ill people
and the questions were hard to ask because they were "crazy" questions, that
is, questions that sort of assumed that the respondent was possibly deranged.
And when the respondent wasn't deranged or mentally confused, the questions
sounded to me—and so probably I made them sound to the respondent—like
harsh and phony questions that I had to get through because they were on
the questionnaire.

But this was a pretest of the questionnaire, and so I had expected to make
changes. However, I wasn't prepared to have an eighty-year-old woman tell
me how to construct an interview instrument. I take it as a sign of my growing
sensitivity to the elderly—and of the pressure that my boss, Margaret Blenkner,
was applying ever so subtly—that I was able to listen and to profit from this
wise advice. As Shakespeare says (in King Henry IV, Part I): Anyone can call
the gods; the question is, will the gods answer? In terms of the research situation,
any one can ask a set of questions on a questionnaire. But the real issue is
whether the answers that you, the interviewer, receive are any good? Do they

describe the person as he or she really is? Do they provide any useful information on which you can compare other like persons so as to arrive at some useful conclusions for the helping professions?

I thanked this lady for a very helpful conversation. She was a sharp and rather critical person, but she had generously agreed to be interviewed (her social worker from the Rose Institute had asked her), and I was grateful for such carefully considered feedback. (I think this may have been the only client whom I received such volunteered information from, except for another client, an elderly gentleman who kept on saying of every question, "That's a damn fool question." Even he may have been right, simply indiscriminate in telling me that all of the items were worthless. We should listen to what the interviewee says, both the content and comments about the method of asking questions themselves—but we must also retain our own sense of perspective. I knew from prior research that some ideas, even the "damn fool ones," were useful for certain purposes that were not apparent to the respondent.)

I went home and pondered that interview, more than the other interviews that I had had with more docile respondents. And the next day I charged into Dr. Blenkner's office ready to tear the questionnaire in half and start again. As usual, she listened carefully to what I was saying because part of the purpose of my conducting these pretest interviews was to get a sense of whether they were doing what we had intended them to do. I had had enough experience in research interviewing to recognize when I was getting a valid interview—or at least I thought so. And now I was quite convinced that I wasn't getting enough of the individual respondent, even though I was obtaining the standardized measures and answers to questions that had been used in other studies. I recognized the value of being able to compare our study with these others and of using common questions asked of participants in the various research projects. But we couldn't sacrifice obtaining meaningful answers just to get reliable ones (see Technical Notes 5.13, p. 148, and 5.14, p. 152).

Dr. Blenkner said that she agreed in principle about obtaining meaningful information. But what did I have in mind to cut out of the questionnaire? I pulled out a few questions that seemed to be particularly hard to ask: I noted that except for people living in a named institution, like the Institute's nursing home, the Margaret Wagner House, the question, "What is the name of this place?" which was borrowed from a standardized measuring tool (The Mental Status Questionnaire, Kahn, Pollack, and Goldfarb, 1961) sounded as if the interviewer was crazy. She agreed and then asked what would I suggest to take its place, as the use of a measure of mental status was essential to a study of protective services.

Hem, hem, haw. Well, that's another question. Yes, I agreed that we did need to make use of the general scale, *adapting* it to fit the needs of this population. But how were we to adapt it so that it still obtained the essential information while being sensitive to the diverse characteristics of the elderly protective-care participants? We explored the underlying point of the original question: to learn whether the respondent was mentally clear about the place where he or she was living. How were we to get at alertness to place by questioning a diverse set of people in all kinds of situations? The question had to be reasonable, to fit within the regular schedule, and to provide good data. What kind of place question could be asked all of the participants, who lived in everything from single-occupancy hotel rooms to spacious old houses in the green-belted suburbs? What was common about place questions, and yet specific enough to serve as a source of objective data?

The answer to our search seems so obvious—in retrospect. But I assure you that it took a considerable period of time and pretesting before we arrived at the solution, and a good solution at that. At the end of the interview, after the interviewer had put away his pencil and questionnaire, he simply asked for some directions to the main intersection nearest to the respondent's home. Some orderly response, like "First turn right, then turn left," was sufficient to demonstrate knowledge of place for our revised and much more flexible version of the Mental Status Questionnaire. An answer like "I don't know" told us more about the respondent than the question seemed to ask. But we could say, "Well, I'm sure I can find my way, but thanks anyway," and it was a natural response to a reasonable question. Once outside, the interviewer could then record this last interchange in the appropriate place on the questionnaire.

DEVELOPMENT OF THE RESEARCH INSTRUMENTS

Many pretest interviews were made, each with a somewhat different question-naire.* We cut and pasted new items onto the old questionnaire, scratched out some words, wrote in new ones, and tried some new arrangements in the order in which we asked our questions. All of these changes were being made in the hope that what we were asking would be clear and important. We didn't want to intrude or waste the participants' time obtaining answers to questions that had no place in our developing understanding of the factors related to protective services.

On the other hand, we knew that we didn't have a complete picture of what life was like for these elderly people, and so we tried some frankly experimental questions. We had some theoretical basis for asking the question, but these were "long shots," of which some paid off, whereas others fell flat. (I'll return to these long-shot questions shortly.)

My point is that researchers developing interview questionnaires face some contradictory pressures, to ask everything under the sun in hopes that some of the questions will be the "right" ones, as well as to ask as few questions as possible so as not to offend the participant or to wear out this elderly person in the process. Thus we wanted to make our questions as *reliable* as possible (a goal aided by having large numbers of items for each factor under study), while making the instrument as *valid* as possible (by having just those items that tapped what we were seeking to ask, and no other questions that might confound, tire, or annoy the participants). If these sound to you like contradictory pressures, you are correct. But these are realistic pressures—both scope and precision are needed.

---

* I will indicate by this subtle means that the Narrative you are about to read is, at the same time, a Technical Note on the *development of research instruments* (5.1). There really is no difference between good scientific writing and what we have been calling "Narratives" and "Technical Notes." It is all in the eye of the adequately prepared beholder.

We worked out our own guidelines for the development of these research instruments. First, we knew that we must have a *conceptual or empirically-based reason for every item.* This is a sequential principle; that is, at first, it was necessary to explore with a larger number of items that may not remain in the final form of the questionnaire. But each of these items was selected as potentially useful and was subject to an item analysis (see Technical Note 6.9, p. 179) to ascertain how important it actually was in its overall contribution to our knowledge. Second, we recognized that *there were trade-offs between a good sensible question that needed to be asked and one that was palatable to the elderly persons in our study,* some of whom had limited education, limited cognitive clarity, and limited patience. We always opted in favor of the participants out of an ethical responsibility to do no harm in the course of our questioning. But we tried to obtain information in ways that are called nonobtrusive or nonreactive (Webb et al., 1981). That is, if we could not ask a question directly, we tried to figure out ways of looking for reasonable indicators of the answers. For example, if we needed to know about how safe a person was in his or her home—a rather complex question— we built in places in the questionnaire where we directed the research interviewer to look at or for safety features (or the lack thereof) during the course of the conversation. The interviewer might simply look around for slippery throw rugs, exposed lamp cords, and the like and then make some brief notes on the interview form that would later be transferred to a research interviewer's rating form, where the same items would reappear, but as formal questions. This is not always a satisfactory solution, but at least it is a systematic way to obtain information that might not otherwise be obtainable. (More on nonobtrusive measures later in this chapter.)

Third, we developed *short sets of questions representing all of the major variables under study.* That is, in addition to a lengthy list of fifteen to twenty items that related to a given topic like the person's capacities in physical functioning, we also identified the five best predictor items in that longer list that would be asked as a *short form* or brief form, when we suspected that we would not be able to ask all of the long-form items. This approach proved to be very useful because we could often get many of these items—on the way out the door!—when it would have been impossible to sit down for an hour or so in order to obtain answers on the longer version of the questionnaire. In the analysis of these data, the five-item short form correlated with the ten-item or long form at about the .90 level on all variables on which scores were available (Blenkner et al., 1974, p. 119). So important did these short-form versions of our questionnaire become that we remodeled the format of the questionnaire to make them more usable. As mentioned elsewhere, we had color-coded the interview questionnaires so as to be able to distinguish easily the initial session from the follow-up sessions. We stapled firm cardboard covers on the questionnaires to make them look professional. We had the usual identifying information—no names— on the cover, as a statement of our pledge to keep these interviews confidential. However, we soon learned of the value of printing all of the short-form questions on that one back cover—all five major variables, as I will describe below. (See Figure 5.1.) We also marked the short-form items within the questionnaire itself, in case the interviewer was able to ask more items, because, occasionally, when a participant began to feel comfortable with the interviewer, he or she permitted a whole interview to be conducted.

Figure 5.1   Illustration of summary of short-form items on the cover of the one-year questionnaire.

---

1 Year   P _____   Case # _____   Date _____   RI # _____

C2.   Has your health been a worry for you in past month? y   n   –
C13.   Would you say you have been happy or unhappy during the past month? vu   u   m   h   vh   –
C29.   In general, how satisfied are you with your present arrangements for housecleaning, cooking, laundry, & shopping (in this place)? s   partly s   dis-s
C80.   Would you agree/disagree with those people who say "things keep getting worse for me as I grow older"? a   d   –
C82.   On the whole, how satisfied would you say you are with your way of life today? vunsat.   us   m   s   vs   –
C7.   How are your spirits/general mood? ok   high   low   erratic
C61.   How do you feel about this neighborhood as a place to live: good place, not so good, what? vbad   b   m   g   vg
C63.   If you had your choice, would you prefer to live here or in some other place, or what? diff.   same with modif.   same
C79.   Is your income adequate or inadequate? vinadeq.   i   m   a   va   –
C83.   What are you worried about for the future? What do you hope will not happen to you? 0w   1w   2ws   3/perva.   ws   –

CA24. (noninst. P only) Who takes care of housecleaning here? self   1/2   full dom.   rel/fri-in/out house
CA28. (noninst. P only) Who takes care of laundry here? self   1/2   full dom.   rel/fri-in/out house
CA30. During past month, did you get any help/advice from organizations in community, like church, hospital, or social agency? y   n   –
CA32. Does a nurse come to visit you? y   n   –

Service only: Did P like AIG caseworker? vm   m   s   l   vl   –
CA59. How often do you get help in keeping your money matters straight, like help in budgeting, planning, etc? none/less than needed/when needed/often/other

Pf19. Would you say you are able to walk up and down a flight of stairs? y   n   –
Pf20. Are you able to walk 1/2 mile (8 blocks)? y   n   –
Pf22. (m) Are you able to work at a full-time job? (w) Are you able to do the ordinary house work? y   n   –
Pf23. Are you able to do work around the house like washing the inside windows? y   n   –
Pf58. Do you need any help in getting places, like shopping, church, visiting? y   n   –

SS6.   Did you feel dizzy or faint in past month? y   n   –
SS8.   Were there times when you felt extremely angry? y   n   –
SS10. Did you feel afraid for no particular reason in past month? y   n   –
SS12. Did you get very tearful (or have crying spells)? y   n   –
SS81. During the past year, did you ever feel so badly that you thought life wasn't worth living? y   n   –

IP46. Is there anyone you can depend on for advice, or whom you can confide in about personal troubles? Who?
       0   1   2   3+_____
IP47. Is there anyone who gets in touch with you if they don't see or hear from you as often as usual? Who?   0   1
       2   3+_____
IP50. Who could you turn to for help in an emergency? Do you have somebody's name and telephone number by your phone (or in wallet/purse)? Who?   0   1   2   3+_____
IP53. How many of your close relatives live in the Cleveland area (include suburbs)?   0   1   2   3+
IP54. How often do you see them? not at all/several times mo/once a week/several times wk

MSQ4. Recognize RI–immed/reminding/later/no/NR/RI/ don't know

      C = Contentment items.
     CA = Concrete assistance items.
      P = Participant.
     Pf = Physical functioning items.
     SS = Signs and symptoms of affective and behavioral disorder items.
     IP = Interested party items.
    MSQ = Mental status questionnaire item.

Abbreviated answers: y = yes; n = no; – = other answers; a = agree; d = disagree; us = unsatisfied; vm = very much; etc. (See Chapter 7 questionnaire items.)

OPERATIONALIZING THE VARIABLES

In Chapter 4, I discussed the overall conceptual framework that was evolved for this study, the theoretical map that guided our selection of some things to study and that excluded other things. In this section, I want to consider the operationalization of these concepts. One of the major steps in the social sciences came as the need for some clear statement of key ideas was recognized. If we could not speak clearly about out major terms, then how could we communicate them to others, let alone seek to study them? But how should we make our wiggly language hold still long enough to obtain this clarity of meaning? The philosopher of science Rudolph Carnap (1953) provided one important suggestion. Each of our major terms should be *operationalizable;* that is, we should state the operations that one would go through so that the same could be observed on a second occasion or by a second observer.* For example, you might ask people the following questions in a prescribed interview context

> *Has your health been a worry to you in the past month?* (Yes, no, some other answer)
>
> *Would you say that you have been happy or unhappy during the past month?* (Very happy, happy, mixed, unhappy, very unhappy, some other answer)
>
> *In general, how satisfied are you with your present arrangements for house cleaning, cooking, laundry, and shopping (in this place)?* (Satisfied, partly satisfied, dissatisfied, some other answer)
>
> *Would you agree or disagree with those people who say "Things keep getting worse for me as I grow older"?* (Agree, disagree, other answer)
>
> *On the whole, how satisfied would you say you are with your way of life today?* (Very unsatisfied, unsatisfied, mixed, satisfied, very satisfied, other answer)

The answers would constitute the operationalized meaning on the short form of the variable called *contentment.* In fact, these items are embedded in the context of the rest of the interview schedule, but these questions could be asked just as they were presented above in the short-form version, if necessary.

There are great advantages to having such an operational definition of a variable under consideration. When we say, "Contentment," you will know exactly what we mean (or, more precisely, when we say, "The short-form version of contentment," because that is what these five items constitute). Moreover, if you want to repeat the research, or a portion of it—thus testing whether what we reported also happens to the people in your sample—you can do so, at least within the limits of interviewing. Obviously, you won't be able to duplicate exactly the field demonstration that we conducted because of the differences in participants, interviewers, and the social-physical contexts. But on the essential variables—such as contentment—you and anyone else can repeat the core questions to find out how different people respond. This clarity of operational definitions makes a social science potentially replicable and generalizable; we are able to build on the research of others, rather than reinventing the wheel or the questionnaire on every occasion.

* This discussion of *operationalization of the variables* constitutes Technical Note 5.2.

On the other hand, there are some problems with operational definitions. It just so happens that there are many other sets of questions—including some with a few of the exact same items as well as some different ones—that go under the labels of *contentment, happiness, life satisfaction,* and so on (see Lawton, 1977). Which is the correct definition of *contentment?* The answer is that they are all the correct definitions of *contentment*—that is, each measures a different though related version of contentment. Each has the exact meaning of just the set of items that it includes—and no other meaning. A more important question is Which of these several operational definitions of the core concept of contentment is the best one to use? To answer that question takes you beyond simply the items in the operational set of questions to questions of validity, reliability, adaptability, and utility, which will be discussed later in this chapter. It is enough at this point to recognize that merely creating a set of questions and giving it a label, "Yankee Doodle," does not constitute a satisfactory operational definition of a concept. One must test the set of questions against some known criterion for that concept.

For example, how else might one judge whether five statements were a reasonable indicator of a complex psychosocial state called *contentment?* One might compare such items with a family member's rating of the participant as contented or discontented. One might have some other professional person who knows the participant well make a judgment about his or her contentment. Or one might correlate the answers to these questions with a host of behavioral indicators, such as "smiles frequently and appropriately," "is adapting to life stresses in apparently successful way," and "is involved in activities that suggest purpose and meaning to life." There have been many ways to link a set of operations to the concept that they are supposed to embody, but every one is fallible and incomplete. Their success depends on the system of other research events that gives meaning to the whole. That is, there should be some internal consistency within the participant's own answers, between the responses of participants and other observers, and within the cluster of events that makes up the participant's life. In developing the questionnaire, we used all of these methods for improving the validity of our questions.

TYPES OF RESEARCH INSTRUMENTS

In the following section, I present an overview of the types of instruments that can be used in field studies such as the Benjamin Rose Institute Protective Services Project. But first, let me prepare you for what may be a surprise: there is an amazing array of types of instruments. Why should this be? It did not happen by accident; rather, there are very good reasons for approaching a given body of information from a variety of different angles. Each question or exploration of a participant's behavior is selected from a huge number of potential questions or ways to explore. Moreover, any specific piece of the participant's behavior is also a tiny sample of a vast number of like—or unlike, but related—behaviors. Therefore, even if you asked five or twenty-five or even five hundred questions, you would only begin to tap the portion of a person's whole life that is represented by the concept.

Because questions are simply samples of participants' behavior, it is also true that how one approaches a given set of behaviors determines the answers that one obtains. For example, if you ask questions in the form, "How do you feel about this, about that, about other things?" you will get answers in the form of feelings. Fine, this may be just what you are looking for. But life is filled with more than feelings about this, that, and the other. And so you might ask questions about "What have you done recently in connection with this, that, and the other?"—and you will receive information that presents a related but different perspective on the core questions. Feelings, thoughts, actions, and reactions—these are artificial divisions of human behavior, but they do appear to tap different perspectives that may be important to different helping professionals.

In addition, you might ask questions directly, for example, "Do you feel excessively warm at this moment, or are you cold, or are you about average in temperature?" But for some types of information, it might be better to use a standardized device—like a thermometer or its social equivalents. What is a *social thermometer?* It is like the physical device, a construction of elements whose use provides relatively constant information across a variety of participants. But instead of glass and mercury, the social scientist uses various devices to attain a standardized measurement. "Normal" is any score at or above a given number, based on tests with large samples of persons with known characteristics. This standardized measurement device provides normative information, comparing the individual with large numbers of others. This is quite a different approach from simply asking the participant individualized questions. Clearly, gains and losses are involved. One loses the uniquely individual answers of a participant in order to gain a comparative perspective on the adaptiveness of the person's way of behaving.

Virginia Woolf once noted that biographers who have studied the lives of their subjects in great depth may know a handful of the personality variations that each exhibits, whereas in fact, each individual is several thousand personalities over a lifetime. Granting literary license, the point that she was making is important for researchers as well. We grasp only a tiny, time-limited segment of a complex life when we ask research questions for an hour or less, four times a year. If we can mix the ways in which we view a participant, we can hope to capture more nearly the full roundness of a human life. An impressionistic package of observations connected by means of a conceptual perspective that gives the separate pieces meaning is about as close as we can get to knowing something important about a person without having to devote a biographer's energies to that one subject. And by applying the same configuration of questions to a number of persons, we profit by the comparisons that we can make among them, a point to which we will return when discussing the analysis of data.

Now let's look at some types of research instruments. The following discussion involves Technical Notes blended into a Narrative form. There is little need for the distinction now that you are involved in the experience of this research project. The Narrative will become increasingly composed of technical ingredients—or, what amounts to the same thing, the technical details may become increasingly real, as if they, too, are part of a story. (However, I will continue to number these notes for ease of reference.)

The Questionnaire

The *questionnaire** is a set of topics to be explored in which the researcher directly or indirectly communicates with the participant. The *direct* way involves a research interviewer's stating the question and providing any additional, but standardized, information about the question if necessary, as she or he has been trained to do by the researcher. The *indirect* way is to give the participant a self-instructional group of questions and to ask him or her to read them, to perform the tasks as instructed (like circling the most nearly correct answer), and then to return the document to the researcher through the mail or by other means.

There are advantages to each method. Obviously, in the direct questioning method, the research interviewer can determine whether the participant understands the question and is answering with usable information. Direct questioning also permits the interviewer to observe that the research experience isn't damaging to the participant. However, merely asking questions may be intrusive to some people and may produce some "experimental effects" apart from any direct service provided. This was clearly the case when some participants in the experimental group commented to their social workers that another person—the research interviewer—was coming to see them and to help them. This apparent misinterpretation of the interviewer's role reflected the confusion of some of the elderly participants in the study, but it may have been a natural effect of some pleasant person's coming periodically to inquire how they were feeling and how life was treating them. True, this interviewer didn't actually give them any medicine or money, but just being important enough to be interviewed may be a special kind of medicine for some, a social value that money can't buy, a point which I want to expand on in a technical footnote, 5.4.**

---

* This discussion of the *questionnaire* constitutes Technical Note 5.3.

** For purposes of identification, let's call this footnote Technical Note 5.4. I want to discuss an interesting topic, the *placebo effect* in research and practice. Some writers have suggested that the placebo has been the most powerful therapeutic ingredient throughout history, up to the time when specific drugs were identified as having specific effects, beginning largely in the nineteenth and twentieth centuries (Shapiro and Morris, 1978). In general, chemical placebos may be defined as substances that produce visible effects in humans without there being a chemical basis for these effects. For example, sugar pills may be given to persons suffering from some psychosomatic condition under the guise of being powerful medications. If the subjects respond (usually in the desired direction), even though there is nothing in the pill that could cause the results, then we can speak of a *chemical placebo*.

It is more difficult to speak of *social placebos* because we don't have a scientific basis like a chemical analysis to discover what are inert social interactions. The laying on of hands for a sick true believer appears, in some cases, to have desirable psychosocial effects; this result is documented, not speculative (Kleinman, 1978). Negative symbolic messages, such as voodoo curses, have also been documented as having the desired harmful effects on true believers. The true-believer aspect is the critical ingredient. Does the client believe that this worker, with whatever skills, diplomas, and status symbols are present, has the wherewithal to bring about a positive change? Believing may make it so—in those cases where mental acts may have created the problem in the first place. Sometimes psychological malfunctioning is caused by a person's own mental actions; at other times, there are physical and/or social ingredients on which believing may not have any impact.

Thus it seems in our present state of ignorance on the workings of human behavior that some

(*continued*)

Questionnaires can also be of an open-ended or closed-ended type. *Open-ended questions* provide the stimulus but not the boundaries for participants to respond. "How are you feeling?" is one example. The interviewer would record verbatim what the participant responds and then leave it to others (the people involved in coding and scoring the data; see Chapter 6) to interpret. At other times, the interviewer is directed to make a rating after hearing the participant respond. This would be a piece of information in its own right, and also a guide to the coder.

The *closed-ended form* is a stimulus with a bounded set of alternative responses. "Would you say that you are happy or unhappy these days?" is a kind of question that provides its own alternatives. However, even the interviewer's providing the alternatives doesn't mean that the participant will accept the alternatives. Indeed, the participant may simply hear the spirit of the question and proceed to give a long address on happiness, leaving the interviewer several options. First, the interviewer may simply repeat the question, seeking to get one answer from the alternatives listed. Or the interviewer may rephrase the question—thus changing it—so as to prompt the participant to respond within the options given: "But can you tell me wh 'her what you have just said means that you are happy or unhappy these days?" Or the interviewer may take the liberty (with or without sanction from the researcher) to make an interpretation from the vantage point of being on the spot with the participant and judging whether the flow of words, gestures, and context means "happy" or "unhappy." There is no one right way; what is important is knowing what the interviewer has done to obtain the data that are returned to the coders for analysis. This is so because, ultimately, what the researcher has to analyze is the little marks on paper made by the interviewer, and these may be quite a different thing from the communications made by the participant. Readers of the reported research should be informed about the structure of the interview questionnaire, so that they can make up their minds on how strong and valid the reported information is.

Surveys employing questionnaires have constituted one of the major forms of information gathering in the social sciences and the applied social sciences.* In essence, some standard set of questions is presented to some sample of persons, one or more times. The data are analyzed for their *descriptive* purposes, possibly as *exploratory* of some significant issue, and on occasion, they may be used as the basis for formulating some *explanatory* reasons for it. The point is that one may survey people in different ways for different purposes. Let's look at these differences.

---

portion can be influenced by the client's believing in the helping person's ability to help. Depending on what other factors are present, this belief may or may not be enough to influence changes in human thoughts, feelings, and behaviors. Likewise, not believing that a given helping professional will be able to help may add the significant factor in defeating an otherwise potentially effective action.

In research, we have talked about designs that try to eliminate the effect of an initial interview because that itself might have a placebo effect on subsequent behavior (Technical Note 2.9, p. 63). In the service variable, we sometimes try to have an equivalent placebo effect—such as giving a control group "attention" by the researchers—so as to equalize this effect on the overall outcome of the study. Thus placebo effects are everywhere in research and practice. We haven't by any means learned all there is to be known about these fascinating experiences.

* This discussion of *Surveys* constitutes Technical Note 5.5

An ordinary survey usually involves some defined sample who receive a one-time standardized questionnaire. From their answers, a composite description is made of how these people respond to such-and-such stimuli. Depending on the number of persons involved, how carefully (i.e., how randomly and by what stratification procedures) they were selected, and what questions were asked, it may be possible for the researchers to go beyond descriptions of responses to exploratory ideas of what dynamics might be working in connection with the research topic. This is an hypothesis-generating use of survey data. For instance, if a number of people tend to respond in one way to a given item, then the researcher may begin to speculate on what common forces might be influencing this patterned response. If enough related questions of the right sort have been asked, it may be further possible to make some explanatory guesses about why the events occurred as they did. It is quite difficult to collect enough information to provide the bases for inferring the causes of given outcomes. However, a powerful set of explanatory statements provides the grounds for the experimental research usually needed in studying cause–effect relationships.

When a sample is reinterviewed, one or more times, then a new form of survey research is present. A *panel study* involves reinterviews within the same original sample; *cohort studies* involve reinterviewing persons from the original population—but not the original sample. Each form of survey has strengths and weaknesses. It is clearly more expensive and more difficult to conduct a panel study (even simply to find the original persons, who may have moved), but information obtained from the same persons over time may provide a powerful basis for examining trends and possible explanations of events. (See also Technical Note 2.2, p. 49.)

Single-system designs (Bloom and Fischer, 1982) are something like panel surveys made with one client (or client group) over time. The number of reinterviews may be frequent, as when a practitioner sees a client in a hospital daily for many months, recording standardized observations on each occasion using some standardized observational tool. (See Chapter 13.)

The Standardized Scale or Measure

Standardization of measures * means that some researcher has undertaken the task of generating a set of items and testing them against samples of people whose characteristics on the topic of study are already known; for example, people hospitalized with a diagnosis of depression may be used to develop a depression scale (Zung, 1965). Their scores should be more extreme than those of a group of persons coming to an outpatient clinic with a diagnosis of depression—at least this second group is able to function in the community whereas the first group cannot. However, the outpatient depressives should score more extremely on depression than a group of patients coming to the clinic for some medical problem. And these, in turn, should be somewhat more extreme than their neighbors, who are troubled by neither medical nor psychological problems. By such means, a scale is tested with numbers of persons in each of these identified groups. If a set of items, in fact, produces results like those expected (hospitalized

* This discussion of *standardized scales or measures* constitutes Technical Note 5.6.

depressives being more extreme than outpatient depressives, who are more extreme than outpatients troubled with medical difficulties, who are more extreme than persons in the community with neither medical nor psychological problems), then the scale is deemed indicative of these distinctive groups and may be used in new samples to identify a score that is like the average score of the known groups. This procedure does not guarantee that the individual will, in fact, be like the group within whose range he or she has scored, but this is the prediction, other things being equal. (See Technical Note 6.8, p. 177, on the null hypothesis.)

Sometimes new tests are standardized against a known test. For example, many brief intelligence tests are given along with a well-known long-form IQ test in the hope that there will be some correlation between them. If this turns out to be the case, then the brief form of the intelligence test—which may be more suitable to the characteristics of the given sample—will be used as an approximation of the longer one.

In the Protective Project, we used a brief intelligence test called the Kent E-G-Y (1946), a test originally developed to be used with children, but later adapted by Katz and Crook (1962), who established norms for the elderly. This brief test asks questions about commonplace knowledge: "Can you tell me the names of some large cities?" "What kinds of materials are houses made of?" "At what time of day is your shadow the shortest?" Points are given for the number of correct answers (up to a specified amount—for example, four cities earn 4 points, and one noontime answer earns 1 point).

When I began my work with protective service clients, I had some misgivings about asking such asinine questions, until I conducted a pretest interview with Dr. XX, a retired professor of psychology who was living at a private mental hospital. I thoroughly enjoyed the interview, as Dr. XX was very knowledgeable, answered the Kent E-G-Y questions as fast as I could ask them, and threw in some additional comments that reflected her creative and witty mind. I wondered why she was at this mental hospital until I got to another section of the questionnaire that asked about her family and her living place. Here Dr. XX began to talk about living with her sister at home—totally off-the-wall answers given with as much precision and wit as the intelligence test answers. Questions that may seem strange and intrusive or foolish to us may in fact be seen that way by some participants as well, but not necessarily. The reason that these questions are included is that they have a job to do, and as we cannot know in advance what cognitive, affective, or behavioral deficits our participants may have, it is well to include measures that tap these dimensions. Even if sticky questions are mildly discomforting *for us* to ask, we must live with them if they provide valid and significant information.

On the other hand, if I had it to do over again, I think I would suggest one approach for Dr. Blenkner's scrutiny: rank-ordering each set of questions and beginning with the hardest one, so that if a person was able to answer that question, the interviewer would have the option of eliminating the others. This approach assumes an ordered set of questions; procedures exist for generating such a set of items. This process is called *scalogram analysis,* or *Guttman scaling* after its originator (Guttman, 1946). In any case, this would have been a good compromise between asking childish or crazy questions of people who were functioning well on the dimension of intelligence, and failing to pick up vital information about the extent of the deficits of the participants in our study.

140

This is like a short form of a standardized scale. But note that this is an empirical issue: the choice of the ordered set of questions requires a thorough analysis of the pretest data.

Projective Tests

What kind of question can be asked when the participant may not know the answer himself or herself? Perhaps the answer exists but is locked in the hidden recesses of the mind, unavailable to conscious awareness. Projective tests* assume that it is possible to discover these deeply repressed feelings and ideas. The theory of the projective test assumes that unconscious stimuli can be discovered through disguised conscious behaviors, if one has the key to their interpretation. This key is psychoanalytic theory—provided one accepts its tenets as valid (Silverman, 1976).

The Protective Services Project used a type of projective test in an unconventional way. It was a story problem about a protective service situation. What was interesting was the number of persons for whom this story had close parallels. The story goes like this:

> Mildred Thomas, a widow close to seventy-eight, is now living alone in a dilapidated house. She had been able to keep it up fairly well until recently, but the health department has declared the house a firetrap and beyond repair. Yet Mrs. Thomas refuses to move. What's more, she has been extremely suspicious of other people lately and says she "hears voices." Her only living relative is a daughter who lives in another city and who does not seem to be close to her mother. The daughter does not accept the seriousness of the situation and denies reports of her mother's illness. A neighbor, who is also an old friend of the family, is concerned about Mrs. Thomas. What should the neighbor do?

It is interesting to note that the participants in the project who exhibited paranoid behaviors could discuss Mrs. Thomas's paranoia as a maladaptive behavior but could not see similar patterns in their own lives. The projective part of this question is in the classes of answers that the participants suggested. Some suggested legal-social interventions, something they would not tolerate in their own situation. Other's suggested letting the old neighbor help out, a wishful—and perhaps impractical—suggestion that would at least enable Mrs. Thomas to remain in her own home, an aspiration widely shared by the elderly. And still others suggested that the daughter be brought into the situation and be made to help out. What we saw, in effect, was a problem-solving strategy suggested by the participant that might be, by inference, the same strategy that he or she would accept for him or herself in a similar set of circumstances.

How good a predictor are projective questions? Anastasi (1968) has suggested that little evidence exists of their validity or utility, but this fact has not stopped the flood of attempts in using them. We recognized the chancy nature of this question but felt that identifying a problem-solving approach might be insightful in showing how people of very limited resources managed to maintain themselves in the community.

---

* This discussion of *projective tests* constitutes Technical Note 5.7.

Analogues. Analogues are contrived events that simulate some other complex event, which is difficult to study directly.* For example, in training interviewers to work with older persons in need of protective services, we found it useful to present some role-playing enactments in which one person (experienced in working with this type of clientele) played a protective participant to another person's enactment of the interviewer. The other trainees watched and critiqued the overall performance. Analogues are contrived in the sense of emphasizing certain features—such as the suspiciousness of some project participants—while in effect ignoring a host of other characteristics. (Some of these other characteristics might later be the subject of role plays.)

Analogues can be developed through paper-and-pencil materials, audiovisual tools, or playacting. In all cases, the point is to present some specific event or behavior to the participant, rather than the real-life event of which the former is an analogue, in order to study the participant's reaction. This reaction is presumed to be like the one that might be given in the real-life situation.

I have described the use of the analogue in training interviewers, but I also want to mention that other researchers have used it as a data collection device as well. In a sense, the story project described above as a projective device was one version of an analogue measure. More familiar analogues would be functional vision tests, such as the one we gave older persons in another Benjamin Rose Institute study that involved three sizes of newspaper print. This was an analogue of the various sizes of print that persons might find in their everyday world. Certain visual problems restricted people to only the largest print, whereas others were able to read all sizes of print on the test card. We assumed that passing this analogue measure meant that they were able to read the full range of print available to them in magazines and newspapers and on posters.

Simulations. Simulations are also contrived stimuli that elicit reactions.** But simulations are often used in the sense of games, relatively elaborate systems of rules about a pretend context in which participants have certain roles to play that can be evaluated. For instance, we used an embedded-figures test for another elderly population, but we put this test in a game context. This test was like the children's game of "find the face in the clouds," and the participants were asked to play along with this game. They were given small cardboard cutouts of various shapes (a triangle "tent" and a square-plus-triangle "house"). Then they were given some practice experiences in placing these models on the pieces of the same shape on larger pictures. The pictures were graded for normative difficulty in locating the embedded figure; that is, it was determined in developing this instrument that in some pictures, it was easy to locate the embedded test figure, whereas in others, it was more difficult. These norms were then used to determine the degree of "field dependence" operating in the participant (Witkins, et al., 1954; Karp, 1966). *Field dependence* refers to the degree of influence that an environment has on how a person perceives things in it. A dependent person is strongly influenced by the environmental surround, and if the test figure is embedded in a strongly dominating environment, the person may not be able to locate

---

* This discussion of *analogues* constitutes Technical Note 5.8.
** This discussion of *simulation* constitutes Technical Note 5.9.

it. A *field-independent* person appears to operate on his or her own inner directedness in regard to locating test figures embedded in a complex picture. This psychological attribute is correlated with other interesting factors, which make the test useful as a basis for more important predictions. For instance, we used the field-dependence variable as a predictor of whether a person would survive relocation to a new nursing home, reasoning that a person tied to (dependent on) a familiar place would be more stressed in a relocation than a person not as dependent.

Ethnomethodology and Other Qualitative Approaches to Measurement

Ethnomethodology is an approach to studying the processes of people's ordinary everyday actions within the context in which they occur.* This contextual microanalysis seeks to identify the patterns or norms by which commonplace communications are understood and shared among a group of intimates.

My wife and I are reading in the den. The wood-burning stove is lit and we are deeply absorbed in our books. My wife looks up and says, "What did you say?" I reply that I didn't say anything. She continues, "I thought you were upset or worried." I ask what made her think that, and she replies that she heard me whistle or groan or something. I say that I thought that was the wood stove making noises because of the green wood I put in. She thinks about that for a moment and goes back to her book. I think about it for a moment and remember my cavalier comment about Miss Edel's hearing voices from her stove. Did she say that she heard conversations or just some stray words or whistles or groans? I realize how important context is for the meaning of words, and how much we assume about that context—without always checking its meaning fully.

We talked about that little interchange later, and we came to realize a sort of rule of the house that appears to go like this: When we are both working (reading or whatever else takes concentration), the one who wants to say something will make some sort of noise, like a whistle, whose meaning is "Wow, listen to this!" If the other person can interrupt his or her train of thought, he or she will respond to that signal by looking up or saying something, an indication that the other person should go on. Without that response, the first person will continue to read silently unless the message is very important, in which case it is delivered whether the other wants it or not. On the other hand, if the other is in the middle of composing a complex sentence, he or she will actually say something to the effect of "Hold it a minute" in order to go on working on the sentence in silence.

We speculated that this might be like other ways in which people precommunicate to others, in order to "get the floor," so to speak. Then we wondered whether people who violate this rule of precommunication get labeled as crude or unmannerly or whatever. We began to watch our words and nonverbal communiqués more closely to see what patterns were present and whether these patterns were generalizable to other contexts.

If this little bit of microsocial analysis is more than you want to know about

---

* This discussion on *ethnomethodology* and related techniques constitutes Technical Note 5.10.

143

a commonplace process of communication, then ethnomethodology isn't for you. But if you are interested in how these rules of ordinary discourse are formed and how they operate generally across married couples or people dating, for example, then ethnomethodology might be just your ticket.

There is a growing literature in ethnomethodology as theorists begin to show in-depth concern about forms of everyday behavior (such as Goffman's classic works, 1959, 1962, 1963a, 1963b, 1971), and as researchers explore these events with new perspectives, new tools, and new ways of presenting findings (see, for example, Bailey's 1978 summary on ethnomethodology, as well as the research of Garfinkel, 1974). The importance of this approach for helping professionals who are conducting research may be summarized as follows:

1. The emphasis of ethnomethodology (as contrasted with large surveys or control-group designs) is on a process, usually viewed within a relatively short time span and definitely within a given context. This is precisely the situation in which clinical research occurs.
2. The analytic methods tend to be more holistic and qualitative than objective in the usual research sense. The ethnomethodologist seeks to understand the meaning of the process that he or she is witnessing (the method is like Weber's *Verstanen*) and does this with as much concern for order and accuracy as the most rigorous laboratory scientist.
3. The validity of the ethnomethodologist's findings are immediately present and are relatively close to the content in question, even though the norms are abstract. It is like getting an insight into a conversation into which one has walked halfway through: the rule or pattern of what is being discussed becomes clear.
4. The emphasis is on an analysis of communication behaviors, verbal and nonverbal, within the context of the relevant primary and secondary groups. This emphasis is also very close to practice conditions. It can be maintained over time and thus might be related to time-series designs (see Chapter 13). The relationship to classical research might be one that suggests vital hypotheses to be tested for basic knowledge. However, in relation to practice, ethnomethodology might be used in an evaluation of how well the intervention has been progressing in the eyes of relevant persons.

Unobtrusive and Nonreactive Measures

There is a charming scene in the marvelous musical *Fiddler on the Roof,* concerning life among the Jews in czarist Russia. The village rabbi is, or should be, the chief leader, helping people to resolve the disputes that inevitably arise. On one occasion, a group of persons comes to him and complains that such-and-such is creating a problem, and the old rabbi says, "You're right." Then the opposing group presents its case before him, and he responds, "You're right." But then both groups crowd around the rabbi and insist that his judicial decisions are contradictory, and he says, "You're right." Such is the power of obtrusive and reactive questioning.*

Only somewhat less blatant is much of research interviewing. Consider. A total stranger comes to your home, introduces himself or herself with various

---

* This discussion of *unobtrusive and nonreactive measures* constitutes Technical Note 5.11.

statements indicating how legitimate and important this interview is, and how its results will influence the fate of people perhaps very much like you—with care taken to emphasize that there is no reward for giving this interview. Now the answers that you give will be anonymously combined with many others to produce research reports that may influence decision makers in our society.

How can you resist such blandishments? In fact, only a small number of persons in our study actually refused to be interviewed at all. (See Chapter 10 for a discussion of refusals.) But a more important question, raised by Webb and his colleagues (1966, 1981), is whether the answers obtained through this frontal attack on the interviewee were truly valid. Or did the interviewee say what he or she believed the interviewer wanted to hear? Is this possible? As the old village rabbi said, "You're right"—it is possible and thus puts a great deal of conventional questionnaire data under a cloud of doubt. Such interviews might produce data that is *reactive,* that is, influenced by the very act of asking questions. It might take the form of a "guinea-pig effect," in which the participants feel that they must do their best or present themselves in the best possible light. Or the participants may take a perceived role—after all, they are told that they represent many other persons in the community who are not being asked these same questions. Likewise, participants may get into what is called a *response set* of always giving the same kind of expected (conventional) answers. (Some college sophomores get into an idiot-response set, giving socially impolite answers just to be annoying.) Other times people may give *acquiescent* answers— socially polite responses, whether they mean them or not.

In any of these types of situations, the data one obtains clearly do not reflect the truth of these people's lives, and to that extent, the research has not been effective. Is there no way around these communication dilemmas? Fortunately, there are a number of ways. First, some general observations. As it is practically impossible to avoid reactive questions, be aware of the problem and add other forms of observation and information collection that can augment and validate the questionnaire data. As much as possible, try to reduce the extent of the pressure of being questioned by emphasizing that there are no right answers, and that all that is wanted is an honest statement of how these topics appear to the interviewee. Some standard scales are hard to fake, and perhaps these can be used as part of the interview.

But the main emphasis of Webb and his colleagues is on unobtrusive and nonreactive measures. What are these and how are they to be employed? Webb and his colleagues discuss four broad types: archival records, behavioral products, physical traces, and simple observations. Let's discuss each in turn.

Archival Records. There are many forms of records, from a person's keeping a diary or a calendar to institutional forms. Bureaucratic organizations, especially professional helping agencies, are built on mountains of records, and so it is likely that some of these existing records—collected for a different purpose from that of the research in progress—will be useful in reflecting patterned behaviors without the current participant's knowing that the information is being used in this fashion. (Of course, there is the problem that when the information was collected in the first place, it might have been reactively biased. However, this problem is speculative, and some records are less likely to be strongly biased regardless.) For example, in the Protective Service Project, we made a routine

145

check with the social service exchange to find out whether a given participant was known to other social agencies. And at the conclusion of the study, we went back to the referring agencies to see what their records showed, particularly for the control participants, about what services these people had recevied. It would have been possible to compare the participants' answers about what services they had received at various phases in the life of the project, and with what the records of the referring agencies showed. With participants whose central problems were related to cognitive clarity and control, we might expect considerable discrepancy between the two reports.

I am not saying that unobtrusive and nonreactive measures are "true" and all others false. Rather, they supply different information. Agency records, fallibly supplied and maintained, are one source of data, and a person's memory, motivations, and manipulations are another. Each presents information from which researchers reconstruct a whole picture. If you infer that researchers' reconstructions are not necessarily any more true than archival records or reactive statements by participants, "You're right." But the "truth" is a rigid abstraction; *truths* as seen and lived by many involved persons are probably closer to what the purpose of research is about: reflecting life and giving insight into its workings, including its contradictions.

Behavioral Products. This form of nonobtrusive measure relates to the products of behavior, rather than to the behaviors themselves. How much does a person smoke? Count the cigarette butts that remain, assuming that the participant is the one who has smoked them. How neat and organized is a person? Look around you at her or his home or apartment. Clearly, you don't have to be present to see a person smoke or clean her or his home, but you do have to make some assumptions about who was involved in these actions.

Physical Traces. This form of nonobtrusive measure involves either the wearing down or the building up of physical evidence of the person's behavior. For example, one might observe a worn spot in front of the television set and learn thereby how the individual spends a considerable portion of his or her time. An instance of accretion or adding on will always remain with me from when I first entered the home—or better, the den—of a hoarder. Piles of items were stacked every which way. One such hoarder was compulsively neat, and so the piles were neat, when they weren't falling over by shear weight and height. Another hoarder was a total slob and there was no order at all to her hoarding. There was no need to ask questions about these people's tendencies to "save for a rainy day."

Simple Observations. This final method of nonobtrusive measure entails using one's interviewing time to look around at the participant's environment to take note of other events of interest. We used this approach extensively (as described in Chapter 8) in noting matters related to safety, sanitation, and decency in the home environment. It would be possible to have candid cameras* working in

---

* We did use a camera in one instance. We photographed the interior of the house of a hoarder, which might have to be used as evidence in a court if this person resisted guardianship. We recorded not merely the accumulated filth of years, the evidence of a dozen dogs and cats kept inside all the time, and the decaying body of one poor beast, but also the signs of fire damage. This photographing was done after the participant had been taken to a health care facility under emergency medical

(continued)

some settings to record certain types of behaviors nonobtrusively, but this procedure raises other questions in regard to confidentiality and honesty in dealing with research participants, a point discussed in Technical Note 3.1 (p. 85).

In general, these methods, which are used to obtain data where the very asking of the question does not influence the information obtained, are ingenious—but limited. They make important assumptions that are not tested in practice. They are quite indirect and therefore require further assumptions that such measures are, in fact, related to the topics in question. But they can make an important contribution to the total research package. This is the major point that Webb and his colleagues made. When these methods are used in combination with conventional questionnaire information, the overall picture of the life of the participant is probably more accurate than when any one method is used alone.

Document Studies: Content Analysis

At various times, it may be possible to study some set of documents, speeches, books, or journals in order to locate some underlying pattern within these types of communication. The process by which the underlying meaning is ascertained is called *content analysis.* * It involves identifying some set of documents, establishing a procedure that indicates what types of meanings are represented by what parts of the documents, and then proceeding to categorize the documents according to the typology. The results indicate how many of each category of communication are represented in these documents. If different sets of documents are analyzed over a period of years, the results represent the changes of patterns over time.

In the Protective Services Project, we did not do any formal content analysis, as there were no sets of documents common to all of the participants in the study. However, we might have used content analysis techniques to locate some meaningful patterns in the protective test question, the story of Mrs. Thomas, the widow who was experiencing some problems in everyday life. In this story problem, there were several resources mentioned: a daughter, a neighbor, the police, social agencies, and the elderly woman herself. If these resources represents a set of mutually exclusive and exhaustive possibilities for actors involved in the situation—perhaps with the addition of "other helping actor—specify" and "no one seen as taking positive action"—then we could categorize the participant's response to the question in terms of who was seen as the dominant actor in correcting Mrs. Thomas's situation.

In addition, we might indicate another parallel typology. Did the kind of action represented in the participant's response indicate a "hopeful" or a "hopeless" attitude? (These terms would be operationally defined, perhaps with a sampling of actual examples from the participants.) In such a case, we would be able to have a complex analysis—both who was the dominant actor and what was the dominant attitude regarding a possible solution. These are indepen-

---

conditions—but not with her permission. These were difficult ethical and legal issues in the no-man's land that protective services for the elderly occupied in the mid-1960s. They remain vexing problems today.

* This discussion of *content analysis* constitutes Technical Note 5.12.

dent dimensions, but when combined, they begin to provide important insights into the responder's view of protective situations. We might infer further that if participants viewed this projective situation in one way, then they would be likely to view their own related situation in a similar way. However, such an inference is risky, as people may be able to see more problems and solutions in the affairs of others than in their own lives.

VALIDITY

There is nothing mysterious about validity,* for it is something that we undertake to check on frequently in the course of a day. Consider the following conversation:

> "What did he mean by that?"
> "On the face of it, I'd say that he meant no harm."
> "But look at what else he's doing now; I'll bet it will lead to no good."
> "Well, it would certainly be consistent with his personality if he did."
> "You can say that again."

This bit of nonsense dialogue can, with excessive sympathy on the part of the reader, be interpreted as an outline on validity. Let's see how:

"What did he mean by that?" This is the basic question regarding *validity:* What is the relationship between an action and the intention of its actor? When used in connection with tests and measures—as in a research book of this nature—the question becomes *What does the test measure?* A *test,* you will recall, is simply a set of structured activities intended to reflect some underlying pattern of attitudes, beliefs, or actions. How do we know that the set of structured activities that we construct (i.e., the test or scale), in fact, measures or relates to what we have indicated by the title of the measure? For example, here is a "contentment scale" that is composed of a set of questions. How do we know it measures "contentment"? The concept *contentment* exists in one realm, and the events of everyday life exist in another. If people use language in a shared manner, then presumably there will be some relationship between the concepts (words) that we use and what we commonly agree the words refer to.

Unfortunately, you know that people do not always use the same words in the same way, so it is difficult in ordinary affairs to find examples of perfect correlations between stated intentions and actual behavior (cf. Fishbein and Ajzen, 1976). Likewise, in research, people may use concepts like contentment in different ways. And so the meaning of one scale is not discerned without some effort, and the set of activities that determines whether a scale accurately measures what it purports to measure is termed *validity.*

Face Validity

Continuing with the dialogue at the beginning of this section—"I'd say on the face of it, that he meant no harm"—we have one way in which people commonly

---

* This discussion of *validity* and the several ways in which it is defined constitutes Technical Note 5.13.

consider the truth in the connection of words (concepts) and the events of everyday life to which they refer. They make a judgment based on the events in question. In the research context, if one sees questions that appear to ask about happiness, satisfaction, and the like, then one might make a judgment that the set of them can fairly be said to deal with contentment because we use the word *contentment* in ordinary language to refer to or represent feelings like these.

Problems arise when someone rightly points out that "I don't use the notion of immediate satisfactions to refer to long-term contentment, because the former can vary greatly whereas the latter stays on about the same level." And then we are involved in a word game that makes us wonder whether people in everyday life really do have as much uniformity in shared meaning as the dictionary would suggest. There is a sense of a range of common usage—not a specific meaning for a given world. This same variability in judgment plagues the researcher as well because we can't be certain that there is a commonsense obvious meaning to words that people commonly disagree on.

Thus selecting items for a test or scale on the basis of their face validity is a risky business. With good judgment (or good guesses), one can construct a good measure. With poor luck, items that seem to be related to the variable being measured may, in fact, turn out not to be related. Moreover, it may turn out that items that lack face validity are empirically related to the concept in question. An item may have just another pretty face (validity) without leading to a deeper relationship.

Criterion Validity

Let's continue to examine that bit of dialogue at the beginning of this section. The next speaker says, "But look at what else he is doing now; I'll bet it will lead to no good." In a sense, what this speaker is talking about concerns looking at a given behavior in terms of, first, what else is happening now and, second, what will happen in the future. These same types of tests of validity are distinguished in research. When one predicts, from a given current behavior, what else is happening now, this is an instance of *concurrent validity*. When one predicts, from that same current behavior, what will happen in the future, this is an example of *predictive validity*. In each case, one's current test or scale is being compared to something else that is presumed to be a known entity. Thus, if one's test or scale is clearly linked (statistically associated) with the other known event, then it provides a kind of validity to one's measure as well. This other event, in either its concurrent or its future form, is taken as the criterion with which one compares his or her new measure.

This form of validation is empirically based, but it, too, assumes that there is a known criterion with which the new test or measure can be compared. Researchers tend to use other "established" measures as the criterion, a procedure that can lead to an infinite regression: What was the first incontrovertibly true measure with which all of the others have been compared?

Concurrent validity involves comparing the new test or scale with a currently known test or situation. If the correlation is high, then the new measure is said to have high concurrent validity. *Predictive validity* involves comparing the new test or scale with some future test or situation. Again, if the correlation is high, then the new measure is said to have high predictive validity; knowing a person's score on the new test will predict to his or her score on the future test.

Construct Validity

Once more, the dialogue: "Well, it certainly would be consistent with his personality if he did." What this speaker is expressing—or rather, assuming—is a conceptual notion about the person in question. *Personality* means to the speaker a set of consistent actions expected of this person, and so the new behavior currently under discussion is, in effect, derived from the larger network of ideas (i.e., the person's personality). The new behavior is theoretically likely because it fits in with the personality construct.

In a similar way, researchers hold theories about certain events that include predictions or derivations from the conceptual relationships within the theory. In looking at events in the real world, the researcher conceives of some concrete happening as being an instance of what the theory predicts, and then the researcher determines by observation whether that happening turned out as the theory predicted it would. If the happening occurs, then the measure is said to have high construct validity.

One interesting variation on construct validity comes from the writings of Campbell and Fiske (1959), who described a complex method of predicting both what will occur and what will not occur in the same set of events. This interrelated set of predictions makes the validation stronger than predicting only one outcome. A measure of this type is said to have high validity if it correlates highly with those events that it is theoretically supposed to, and if it correlates to a low degree with those events of which it is theoretically supposed to be independent.

Before turning to the last line of the immortal dialogue at the beginning of this section, I want to raise the question of which form of validity to use in research. What should you look for in reading about the work of others, and what kinds of validity tests should you perform in your own work? There is no uniform answer. Clearly, there are strengths and limitations in each method, and none of them give certainty. They differ in the degree of difficulty in obtaining the measure, in the assumptions that one makes in using them, and in the time involved (concurrent versus future). Presumably, if all types of validity tests were used and the answers were uniformly favorable, then this result would provide the most confidence that the test or scale is measuring what it purports to be measuring. But whether you prefer an empirical (criterion) or a conceptual (construct) form of validation, or one based on the apparent content of the items as judged to be relevant to the topic at hand, that is up to you. (See Table 5.1.)

Now, that last line of dialogue: "You can say that again." This statement takes us to another area of assessment of measuring instruments: reliability. You can see that this sentence, "You can say that again," is of a different order—emphasizing procedures of knowing—from the preceding ones dealing with validity, which emphasize the substance of what is known. However, validity and reliability, are related. Let's first look at the distinctive characteristics of reliability and then compare it with validity.

Table 5.1 Validity: An Overview of Types and Measurements.

Type	Definition	Appropriate Use	Means of Measurement
Content Validity (or Face Validity)	The extent to which the measured object or event appears to be representative of, or related to, the concept being measured. Some distinguish content validity (representative of) from face validity (related to).	This type of validity is used as a first approximation and a rapid assessment and can be used with every measurement.	By researcher judgment: One compares the operational definition of the concept to the measurement operations to discover how many aspects of the concept are included or excluded (or different concepts included) in the measurement process. Ultimately, the decision is subjective and depends on how the terms are defined.
Criterion of Empirically Predictive Validity			By empirical comparison: This approach to validation uses correlational measures. One correlates a given test or score with another either concurrently or in the future. If the correlation is high, the measure can be said to have high criterion validation.
a. Concurrent Validity	The extent to which one variable can empirically predict another variable concurrently	This type of validity is used when the accuracy of specific outcome predictions are to be tested. It is also used to compare a new test or scale with a known older one.	
b. Predictive Validity	The extent to which one variable can empirically predict another variable at some future time.		
Construct Validity	The extent to which a measure is related to the conceptual framework of which it is a part.	This type of validity is used when one is interested in the meaning of a measurement procedure in the context of the theory that one is using to guide one's research or practice.	By a combined logical and empirical process: First, a conceptual network is identified of which the variable is a part. (The measured variable is a proxy for the concept that is an ingredient in the conceptual network or theory.) The hypotheses are derived from that theory and are put to an empirical test. If the hypothesis is supported empirically, this suggests that the concepts used to make up that hypothesis were good guides to reality. This empirical and logical link is the basis for providing construct validation.

151

RELIABILITY

Reliability * refers to the consistency and the stability of the tests or scales that a researcher uses, or to the consistency between observers. Let's look at intertest reliability first. A reliable test is one that gives the same results when used with the same person at two different times. This definition is clear in principle, but in practice, there are two problems. First, the second administration of the test can't be too far from the first, or else the person could have changed naturally. Second, the second administration of the test can't be too close to the first, or else the person may remember his or her first answer or become suspicious and possibly uncooperative ("What's this wise guy trying to do to me by repeating the same items that I answered on the other page?").

As an approximation of consistent and stable performance on a test or scale, the researcher can perform some statistical operations that indicate comparisons, such as the correlation of a test with itself upon a second administration, or the correlation of a test divided into two equal parts, or having two separate forms. In another Benjamin Rose Institute study, we used an embedded-figures test to measure field independence or dependence (Witkins, et. al., 1954). The form of this test involved a number of pictures containing the outline of a certain figure (like a triangle) embedded in a complex one (like a scene of a house). The participant had to find where the outline of the figure was in the picture. As there was a large number of figures and because it took time and effort to give this test, we decided to divide the pictures in half by the relative difficulty that people had in locating the outline of the figure. In this way, we selected what we thought were two equal forms. We tested this assumption by giving the whole test to some pretest persons and then statistically determining whether both forms of the test yielded equivalent information. This was another type of reliability test.

Another type of reliability results when two or more observers judging the same phenomenon agree on what they observe. This is called *interobserver reliability* and can be very important in evaluation in the helping professions when objective tests and scales may not be used. The basic issue is still whether the instruments of observation and measurement (in this case, the helping professionals) are consistent and stable in the observing, scoring, or judging of a given event. Sometimes a supervisor is used as the comparative observer; at other times, a peer is used. In both cases, the issue is the proportion of agreement on what was seen.

When two observers looking at the same phenomenon—or two halves of a single test or two administrations of the same scale—show a high positive correlation indicating agreement, then the procedures that they are using may be said to have high reliability. Convention in these matters suggests that a positive correlation of .80 or better is reasonable, but it depends in part on the test or scale being assessed and the content of its assessment. In exploratory studies, one might accept somewhat less agreement, but in studies using standard tools, one should expect higher levels of agreement. (See Table 5.2.) When we trans-

---

* This discussion of *reliability* and the ways in which it is defined constitutes Technical Note 5.14.

Table 5.2 Reliability: An Overview of Types and Measures.

Type	Definition	Appropriate Use	Means of Measurement
Reliability of tests			
a. Test-Retest	A test-retest reliability coefficient is obtained by administering the same test on two different times.	This form of reliability is used in assessing the stability of a measure over time.	When repeated measures of a test or scale are taken, the correlation between scores indicates the stability of the test. (Obviously, when some intervention is added to the situation, the test will change if it is a valid measure of the treated condition.) After the treatment is over (and assuming the client doesn't keep changing as a result), the repeated testing of that scale should show a new stability.
b. Parallel or Alternative Forms	A parallel-form reliability coefficient is obtained from two similar tests given in same time period.	This form of reliability is also used to assess the relative equivalence of two measures.	As above, a correlation measures reliability. The higher the correlation, the stronger the indications of parallel-form reliability, that is, that the two constructed forms are responded to in similar ways in spite of the differences in question content.
c. Internal Consistency or Split-Half	Internal consistency is obtained by dividing one test on some basis and comparing its halves.	This form of reliability is also used to assess the relative equivalence of two measures.	Frequently some simple procedure is conducted, like taking odd and even items as belonging to the split halves. Then a correlation coefficient is taken to indicate the internal consistency. (See also the Kuder–Richardson formulas (in Cronbach, 1960, p. 141) for other approaches to the measurement of internal consistency.)
d. Standard Errors of Measurement	The standard errors of measurement of the person's actual scores are used to indicate "true" scores versus the "error" components of a score.	This approach is used in interpreting individuals' scores directly.	Test theory suggests that there is a "true" score on any test or scale representing the average of many tests of the phenomenon under study; there is also an "error" score representing the fluctuations that occur in any test situation. A standard error of measurement estimates the error component and thus, by some statistical procedures, what portion of the test score is due to what the individual truly knows about that content (Cronbach, 1960, pp. 129–130)
Reliability of Observers (Interobserver reliability)	This form of reliability is a determination of whether two (or more) observers are seeing, scoring, measuring, or judging a given phenomenon in the same or a similar way.	This type of reliability is vital whenever a personal judgment will be made for a significant decision.	Interobserver reliability ratings may be made either with or without one observer's knowing that another is looking at the same phenomena and will be making the same judgments. Then the ratings and judgments are compared, either by the percentage of agreement or the range of agreement (for example, on a five-step scale, how many agreements are exact or one step away?)

153

ferred information from the questionnaire to coding sheets, we had to check ourselves for accuracy (see Chapter 6). By having two coders transfer the same set of date—and then compare answers—we were using another form of inter-observer reliability check. The same norms of accuracy are applicable here.

Comparing Validity and Reliability

Intuitively, there should be some relationship between whether a test or a scale measures what it purports to measure, and whether that same test or scale produces consistent results every time it is used. The actual logic is somewhat complicated and not necessary for understanding this important point: if a measure is unreliable, then there is no way it can be valid. However, if a measure is valid, it may not necessarily be highly reliable. It is obviously preferable that a test or scale always (i.e., reliably) provide information about exactly what it is supposed to be providing (i.e., validity).

UTILITY AND ADAPTABILITY

Validity and reliability are the traditional research dimensions of assessing a measure. But for helping professionals, there are other dimensions as well. The *utility* * of a measure is one of these. In the applied social sciences, it is clearly necessary that a measure be useful. That is, the information it provides should be helpful in the various phases of helping: the assessment of a problem, the monitoring of the intervention process, and the evaluation of outcomes.

Whether an instrument will be useful is often judged on the basis of a sample of experiences. Is the measure easy to use? Do the participants accept the measure, or does it cause problems in its very administration? Can the instrument be modified to be made more acceptable to the participants without significant changes, being made in the quality of the information obtained?

One usually answers these questions by being aware of the questions in the context of pretesting. Researchers don't often make formal tests of these questions—although such tests would be possible. Rather, they attempt to be sensitive to the nuances of the test situation in making decisions on whether to continue to use a test that has been shown to have an acceptable level of validity and reliability—on the basis of whether it has been useful in and adaptive to the context of the research itself.

I want to introduce another aspect of adaptability here, even though I will develop the topic more fully in Chapters 7 and 8. For a questionnaire to be adaptive to the context, it must communicate—in several senses of the term, as we discovered.

First, in culturally diverse Cleveland, we discovered that we had to use language interpreters at times. This is an interesting situation where the interviewers become teachers of interpreters, trying to convey to them the nuances of what the questions mean and trying to extract from them the nuances of the answers. We used official interpreters on occasion, as well as the adult children of the

* This discussion of *utility* and *adaptability* constitutes Technical Note 5.15.

protective participant—which was doubly tricky. However, if we were to obtain answers, we had to resort to these basic communication means.

Second, we discovered that many of the participants had various difficulties that made asking questions somewhat hazardous—both in sending the messages to the participants and receiving the answers back from them (see Bloom, Duchon, Frires, Hanson, Hurd, and South, 1971). These difficulties included limitations in hearing, vision, language function, mobility, balance, pain, fatigue, emotionality, and mentation. For each of these conditions, we tried to devise ways of recognizing the problems and of coping with them. For example, with hearing difficulties, the interviewers were directed to speak in a normal voice, and to sit in a clear light so they could be easily seen. If the older person wore glasses, he or she was encouraged to put them on because seeing tends to facilitate hearing. In such simple, yet over looked, ways, we tried to adapt the interview to fit the capabilities of the participant.

SUMMARY AND GENERALIZATIONS

1. The development of adequate research instruments is a never-ending task. The researcher simply must come to an arbitrary determination that a given set of instruments, duly selected, pretested, and adapted with reference to the participants in the study, is the best that he or she can do at this moment. Recognize the responsibilities that this statement carries when you are doing longitudinal research.

2. After you have gone through all of the scientific procedures to make clear operational definitions of your major research variables, sit back and reflect on the commonsense evaluation of these tools. Do they really make sense? Do they really measure what you mean them to measure? Do you really believe that interviewers who are human can deliver these questions in an intelligible manner to participants who are equally human?

3. A clear question isn't necessarily a good question, in the sense of supplying you with the information that you think you need. Do you have enough evidence from the literature or from your pretest experiences so that the question is expressed in the best manner? For example, would it be better as part of a standardized scale? Or would it be more sensitive as a projective question? In the second case, what do you propose to do with the sensitive reply that you get to make it fit into your less-than-sensitive categories of responses? Are the questions you are asking too intrusive? Are there other ways of obtaining the same information that are nonreactive?

CHAPTER 6

The Research Project Begins—Ready or Not

Overview

This chapter presents a glimpse of the flurry of activities at the beginning of a large-scale community project, as well as some of the continuing frenzy that existed throughout in order to keep it running smoothly. This chapter also discusses the topic of confidentiality in research, with its many manifestations and implications.

Technical Narrative Section

Technical Notes Section

The Technical Narrative

INTRODUCTION

Remember when you were in the high-school play? First, you practiced your lines privately and then you talked them through with the others. Next, you walked around the stage, script in hand, trying to get a feeling for how the words were to be spoken onstage. Meanwhile, the scenery and costumes were being made and tried out. The rehearsals got longer and longer, and finally the dress rehearsal came, when you thought everything was supposed to be ready—only to discover that one prop was missing or the costume didn't fit, and no one had ordered the handbills, and . . . Then it was opening night, and the play had to begin, ready or not.

I didn't want to upset you by reminding you of those marvelously nerve-racking days of yesteryear, but it is as good a metaphor of what happens in research as one can imagine. The individual pieces of constructing a research project are separately made and then brought together for various rehearsals and critiques. The pretrials supply the information, not always welcomed, that one thing or another doesn't fit well and has to be revised. But inevitably the opening night comes and we have to be ready. This chapter describes some of the organized frenzy that exists when a project begins.

ASSOCIATES IN GERONTOLOGY (AIG): PUBLIC TITLES AND PRIVATE FUNCTIONS

The story of the beginning of the Protective Project has its practical side in the formation of a dummy research entity labeled Associates in Gerontology.* This unimaginative title was Margaret Blenkner's brainchild; others had suggested an acronym that spelled *AGE,* but she wanted something as unrememberable and vague as possible, yet with a scientific flourish. The point was to have a public identity, separate from the very-well-known Benjamin Rose Institute, that gave service to the elderly, as the control group would not be receiving any service for at least a year from BRI. And so AIG was born.

This foundling organization was housed in spartan accommodations just around the corner from the more grandly accoutered Institute offices. The glass panel door, with *Associates in Gerontology* neatly painted on it, opened directly to the hall and elevators, a position that meant that we had various strangers wander in asking for directions. The main secretarial area held three desks with phones. Off to the side were two "formal" rooms kept more-or-less free of the clutter of mountains of interviewing forms and other papers that became

---

* Discussion of the *public identities of this research organization* constitutes Technical Note 6.1, even though it appears in the Narrative Section. I am continuing the blending of the technical with the narrative.

the hallmark of the research office. These were to be used for in-office interviews, should that contingency occur. (In fact, there were a few such interviews held there, with collaterals who worked downtown and who found that option more suitable than a home visit. And even a few participants found their way to these offices, usually in a state of outrage about being interviewed. For these people, the interviewing supervisor would put on his coat and tie, so as to look legitimately "professional," and come over from the Institute offices, where he usually worked, in order to try to calm down the participants and clarify the nature of scientific research to some upset older persons. Needless to say, they were only slightly pacified, but enough, apparently, to prevent the court or police actions that were threatened.)

The back rooms of the AIG office were filled with tables and shelves holding the interviewing materials for the coming visits, as well as the work space for the coders who translated the completed interview forms into forms suitable to being fed into a computer. Interviewers also worked back here, translating their scrawls into legible forms so that the interviewing supervisor would "pass" them over to the coders. This review process also gave the opportunity to the supervisor to make sure that all questions had been answered, or to note that a participant had refused to answer a question. Everything had to be accounted for on the schedules as on the computers.

Later, these rooms also housed the growing number of publications and progress reports emanating from the project. Margaret Blenkner was always in high demand to make presentations at gerontological and other conferences, in this country and abroad. Cartons upon cartons of paper of many colors were brought into the office, only to reappear in printed form indicating what interview series and for what interviewee each was intended. Color coding was a very useful innovation that Dr. Blenkner brought to AIG; it was used both in the filing and in the interviewing process, as an aid to matching up the continuing flow of documents as well as possible. At any one time, some participants might be having their initial interviews, whereas others were on their three-month, six-month, or one-year interviews, or possibly, the terminal interview (in cases where a participant died, the collateral was interviewed within two weeks of the funeral). Participant as well as collateral interviews were being conducted, and completed forms were being brought back to the office, logged in by the secretaries, checked by the supervisor, and filed by the clerk for eventual coding by the coders. Order was absolutely necessary.

Soon, large flowcharts appeared to prevent anyone from getting lost amid all of the paper. We never did "lose" any participant interview because the date of a follow-up was overlooked—thanks to the conscientiousness of the data control clerk, a young secretary who had received training and who also brought to the job a good sense of hard work and dedication. This is not simply a bit of praise for the secretaries; it is rather a statement of fundamental principle: a research project runs smoothly to the degree that the secretarial staff participates with high involvement in the entire process. I should also note that there was no turnover in seven years among the secretarial staff in AIG, a major benefit that made us able to find files and mislaid papers, as well as to produce the needed materials. Again, this is not a random bit of picturesque description; it is another fundamental axiom: to prevent needed documents from getting lost and to be able to have them appear at the right time and in the right place, it is essential that the secretarial crew share the values of scrupulosity and meticulousness, mixed with a generous dose of compulsivity. You also have to have a lot of fun and games to keep things going smoothly over the long dull periods of routine work.

A principal secretary was employed in the Institute research office, where she handled the great volume of Dr. Blenkner's typing, filing, finding, fetching, and jollying. Dr. Blenkner kept everyone very busy almost all of the time and made considerable demands on their energies and abilities. Occasionally, there were minor squabbles among the secretaries about overwork, preferential assignments (as if any were preferred!), and so on. And the principal secretary had to sort out the problems and jolly the boss a bit, because she tended to overreact to the stupidities of others.

I look back in wonder at the lucky balance of personalities and tasks that Margaret Blenkner assembled for the Protective Project. A fine degree of camaraderie evolved over the seven years of the Blenkner reign, again, one of those principles of the organization of research that doesn't get enough mention in classical texts. Don't try to do research unless you have an organization that supports it, informally (socially and humanly) as well as formally.

COLLECTING AND HANDLING DATA

Interviewers in the Protective Services Project completed their assignments within the time intervals specified for each type of interview, such as five days for the initial interview and ten days for the one-year interview.* Because the interviewers had several types of interviews or reinterviews with a number of participants in each month, they were able to attempt some economies of timing and driving by seeing participants in the same part of the city on the same day. However, the participants were no ordinary citizens, and often as not, they were not at home or did not wish to see the interviewer at that time. And so return calls were made. (The rule for counting a participant as "not available" for a given interview was three tries.)

But eventually the interviews were completed on large majority of the participants and collaterals, and the information was brought back to the office, where it was logged in and combined with others of its type for analysis. The first step was to transfer the information from the questionnaires to some other form where the data could be easily handled. It would be highly desirable to go directly from the interview schedule to data analysis because the more in-between transfers there are, the more opportunities there would be to make errors in transferring. But usually there had to be several intervening steps in the sheer handling process itself.

Code sheets were made up for each variable.** These consisted of a brief labeling of the items on a given scale, what the interview schedule had indicated a given participant had answered for this question, and also what the *scoring*

---

* This discussion of *collecting and handling research data* constitutes Technical Note 6.2.
** See Technical Notes 6.6 (*Codes and Scores*), 6.7 (*The Code Book: An Overview*), and 6.9 (*Item Analysis*) for more details.

was for that item. (The latter point means that we indicated what were positive, negative, or not ascertainable scores for that given question. For instance, if a *Likert-type response* was available for a given contentment item—"strongly agree," "agree," "mixed," "disagree," "strongly disagree"—then which of these answers indicated contentment and which discontent? These determinations were made empirically. Suppose that one analysis showed that only "strongly agree" and "agree" represented a positive score on this contentment item, while the others were correlated with how discontented people had responded in our pretests. These other responses would be indicated as negative or unfavorable in the scoring.

After a set of schedules was coded and scored in this fashion, all were totaled at one time. (This little bit of mass production in data handling is useful, if tedious.) Now the coding sheets were completed as far as they went. Reliability checks were regularly made because the routineness of the task made clerical errors likely. However, the forms that we developed tended to be structured enough so that few such errors were made. (See Technical Note 5.14, p. 152).

This description of the hand transfer of questionnaire information to machine-digestible data may seem somewhat medieval, like some monk transcribing a page of a manuscript in fancy script and gilt-edged curlicues. I would like to be able to tell you that there are vastly improved and more rapid ways of performing this necessary task, but there still are not. Various researchers have experimented with machine-readable questionnaire forms, or even with punching holes in computer cards, but the bulk of questionnaires still requires some transition process using human coders.

From these coding sheets, we then transferred the data to computer cards, having designed the layout of the eighty columns to suit our needs. It is helpful to put all of one type of variable on one card if the researcher had accessible some simple counter–sorter equipment, as we had. In the world of large-scale computers and tape disks that hold nearly continuous and infinite series of data, it is less important to make layout plans. However, one still needs an address system to know what data are located in what place on the computer disk, so as to obtain computer-generated analyses of the data.

The next step is often removed from the direct handling by the researcher. The data on computer cards or disks are processed by the appropriate personnel and equipment. The researcher specifies what he or she wishes to obtain from the computer printouts. By stages, the researcher asks for some of the larger trends to see if any of the major hypotheses appear to be supported. As a trend becomes clear—if, for instance, the scores of the experimental group are clearly superior to those of the control group—then the researcher requests additional runs from the computer on other combinations of factors that may be related to the trend. Likewise, when the trend is negative, it may be equally important to assess what factors are contributing to this state of affairs. In this way, the data are processed in stages. First, one set of relationships (or nonrelationships) is empirically considered, and then another set. Statistically, it is known that by chance alone, a few significant correlations should appear, so that the findings have to be fairly strong and numerous before a trend appears to be supported.*

* For a discussion-review of basic *statistics* for nonmathematicians, see Technical Note 6.5.

Anomalies in the data often provoke looking at new combinations of findings in new ways. If some unlikely trend emerges, then what factors can be located to account for this strange pattern? For example, in the pretests for the Protective Services Project, we discovered a strange situation where the most disoriented persons seemed to have the greatest number of persons in the picture, even though they still needed protective services. This finding made no sense until we distinguished between merely being in the picture ("interested parties") and actually providing some help ("concrete assistance"). Then the anomaly disappeared. Very few highly disoriented people were receiving any effective aid.

Fortunately or not, computers are able to print out large numbers of correlations between variables very easily. So it is possible to compare almost every variable with every other variable—whether or not it makes any theoretical or practical sense to do so. This activity generates huge mountains of computer printouts for a given run and allows the data grubber—like Margaret Blenkner—the sheer delight of having all kinds of correlations available as items are tested or new, empirically-based hunches emerge.* (It also reduces the creative process of thinking up relevant linkages and produces countless papers by new doctoral students stricken with Midas' computer printout touch. See Chapter 14.)

CONFIDENTIALITY, CONSENT, AND CONFIDENCE

In order for researchers to gain the confidence of interviewees and other participants in a project—and thereby to obtain truthful and complete information—there has to be a guarantee of confidentiality and all that it implies.** This section summarizes the larger issues surrounding the ethics of research and emphasizes several topics of specific concern to researchers in the helping professions.

Consider *1984,* the great anti-utopian novel by George Orwell, much discussed in the current press not only for the coincidence of calendar dates, but because of some chilling similarities in our present life to what Orwell predicted in 1948, when the book was published. The novel begins with the clock striking thirteen, as Winston is climbing the seven flights of stairs to his flat. At each level he hears the same "fruity voice" discussing pig-iron production. Entering his own room, he hears the same message from his telescreen, a device that cannot be turned off, as it both transmits (propaganda) and receives information (i.e., it spies on the viewer) simultaneously. And no one can ever tell when the Thought Police are watching YOU. And this frightening prospect is expanded into a view of a whole society spying on its citizens, keeping them in subjugation, for its own inscrutable ends: War is peace, freedom is slavery, ignorance is strength—the slogans of the ruling party.

I have just returned from some grocery shopping and a stop at the bank, where I was watched by remote-control cameras and one-way mirrors. But like Winston in *1984,* I am used to this and thought nothing of it. I read today's newspapers, filled with "Newspeak": Country A was building more destructive weapons and weapon carriers in order to defend the peace, and Country B

---

* See Technical Note 6.8 for a discussion of the *null hypothesis.*
** This discussion of *confidentiality* constitutes Technical Note 6.3.

was going to do likewise, but a little more than Country A. But I am used to this and thought nothing of it. A city truck drives by spraying some chemical into the air to kill insects, and I wonder about the bees my friends keep, or about the birds that feed on insects, or about the people that take delight in the flowers and wildlife. But I am used to this and think nothing of it. And yet, each of these events, large and small, represents an erosion of my confidence in the rationality of the institutions that influence everyday life.

In a parallel way, if researchers were to threaten the survival of participants, if interviewers were to damage the living spaces of interviewees, it would be blatantly unethical to conduct this business. Indeed, for these reasons, scientists have been obliged to clarify the value issues surrounding the production of research as well as its consumption.*

Confidentiality and *consent* are the twin pillars of a trusted science. Without a guarantee of participants' confidentiality with regard to the personal information that they share with the interviewer (and through him or her, with the world of others who may eventually read about the project), one must be suspicious of the quality of the information provided. Although Winston works in the Ministry of Truth, he is suspicious of the quality of information supplied him and everyone on the telescreen; such suspicion is the ultimate sin in *1984*.

Confidentiality means keeping in confidence (secret) the specific information that a given individual provides. Confidentiality is different from preparing reports on the *aggregated information* that comes from all of the participants in a study—with no one of them mentioned individually by name (or by other identifying signs). The research interviewer has the obligation, on behalf of the entire research project, to make this distinction clear to the interviewee. What the participant tells the interviewer will never be identified as being said by a specific individual; however, the answers will be combined with the answers of many others who also are volunteering to participate in the project. The responses will be treated statistically, and mean scores and the like will be presented in the written reports.

Should the participant trust this total stranger who is asking him or her personal information? Many people do and think nothing of it. But many other people do think about this and are suspicious. What can the researcher do to generate well-deserved confidence from a participant? We can look at this issue in several stages:

Stage 1: Building Confidence into the Research Project and the Design. At the very outset, the researchers can intend to create an ethical project whose goals and means are designed to augment information that may be beneficial to the persons involved, or perhaps to others like them if the actual participants cannot be directly aided. No harm should be perpetrated on these participants that is not avoidable and/or greatly balanced by the likely social utility of the information obtained from them in the process. This is an important proviso. Pain (psychological, more likely than physical) may stem from a research interview, but this harm of participants may be permissible if the overall utility of the information will be of important social benefit. For example, in our project, we knew that many older persons in need of protective care would find interviews

---

* See Technical Note 6.10 for another perspective on the *protection of human subjects*.

oppressive and threatening, and thus constituting psychological pain and conceivably even physical stress. But we sought information that would potentially be of great value in serving such persons, so that in our own minds, we were doing ethical research, even recognizing the pain that it might cause.

During this stage of research development, it was necessary to share the plans of the project with other researchers for an independent consideration of our ethical analysis. Government grants require such an independent check to prevent identifiable plans that would likely be in violations of the rights of human subjects. In addition, the proposed project is reviewed by many others in a social welfare organization. Various persons and groups at the Benjamin Rose Institute considered the research plan, mainly because the reputation of the Institute was at stake, and its strong values of humane service had to be honored, even through its research division—perhaps especially through its research wing. Instances of the purposive violation of the rights of human subjects are perhaps more common in medical settings, but psychosocial studies have had their share of inappropriate projects.

Stage 2: Building Confidence into the Interviewing Process. There are a number of steps whereby confidence can be well earned in the interviewing context. First, one should gain the *informed consent* of the interviewees regarding the nature of their participation. Informal consent involves a reasonable disclosure of the nature of the study, what is to be expected in the interview, and what will happen to the information afterward. For example, in the Protective Services Project, even though it involved persons who were presumed to be mentally confused to some degree, each interviewer was instructed to clearly identify himself or herself by name, and to hand the interviewee a pamphlet printed in large-sized type that repeated the basic message of our seeking information about older persons in the Cleveland area in order to provide information that might, one day, be helpful in aiding the elderly. The interviewers also left a small name card with the agency name, address, and phone number on it.

But how much information is to be given in order to comply with the letter and the spirit of informed consent? Such a quantity is hard to state in the abstract, but as a general rule of thumb, I would suggest that enough information should be provided to allow the participant to make an informed decision on whether to continue the interview or not: (1) Is the purpose of the overall study socially important? (2) Is my part in the study in any way harmful to me—not only physically harmful, but also socially and psychologically? (Will I be embarrassed by the questions or the answers that I am likely to give? Will my privacy be invaded? Will the information I give be used in any way against me—for instance, will any social services that I would have received be influenced by my answers?) (3) Will I gain anything of importance from being in this study, such as the satisfaction of having helped others, financial compensation for my time, or actual services?

Another rule of thumb of the "Researcher, interview thyself" variety goes like this: What if someone asked you to participate as a subject in your own study? Would you be willing to do it? What if someone asked your aging parent or grandparent? Or your best friend (who knows everything there is to know about you)? If you can honestly say yes to these questions, then chances are that the study is ethically adequate to be continued.

However, this is a difficult business. One person's meeting with an interviewer is another person's poison. It is difficult to make judgments when there is a fine line between the ethical and the questionable. It is better to err on the side of good ethical practice, and not to use a given item or a given approach if it is potentially problematic.

There will always be some person who finds participation objectionable. For this person, there should always be a way out of having to take the test or to answer the question. This, too, should be part of informed consent: if at any time one wishes to stop an interview or participation in a study, that person should be allowed to do so, with no prejudice to any services that he or she may be receiving.

Another way of building confidence into the interview situation is to make the language used in the questionnaire easy to understand. This clarity has two functions. First, it enables people to decide whether the question itself is to be answered at all, and how it is to be answered. Such clarity could be threatening for some protective participants because they might be asked about areas of their incompetences, which they believe, perhaps rightly, may get them institutionalized. It was difficult to guess the entire range of topics on which some people might feel threatened, and so we chose to ask basic questions—on food, shelter, and friends—as simply and directly as possible. No doubt we lost interviews or had them cut short because even these questions were perceived as threatening by some.

The second aspect of the language used in questionnaires concerns the fact that some questions are asked as the basis for inferences about other topics, not for their own sake. For example, we didn't need to find out who was currently the president of the United States. This item was part of a set of questions from which we inferred the mental status of the participant. We did not tell people that some of our questions were used as a basis for such inferences because we thought this declaration would be very threatening, particularly if we had to go on to explain our interest in mental status. We believed that this degree of explanation was going beyond the meaning of informed consent. It would have created the very stresses that we wanted to avoid in interviewing these elderly people. Yet, by not telling them all of what we were going to do with our questions, we were deceiving them.

It is difficult to walk the narrow line between asking meaningful questions and making a full disclosure of their function in the interview. This is where outside review committees can offer their greatest service, both to science and to society. I would offer the advanced monitoring rule that if you have strong doubts yourself of the value of a question or an approach, then trust your doubts and stop.

Sometimes it may be possible to offer pure anonymity to the respondent. This degree of anonymity usually occurs in one-shot studies where what is important is the pattern of answers among a number of individuals, where it is not particularly important to identify any one person in the study itself. However, even such anonymity has its risks. For example, a faculty person responded to an anonymous questionnaire during a university reaccreditation that asked for critical assessments of the top administration of the university. As the questionnaire was anonymous, he felt free to say what he thought—

highly negative—until he came to the end of the questionnaire, where it asked for a few simple demographic facts: age, sex, race, school, and professorial level. Given the limited numbers of persons involved, these questions were tantamount to asking him to sign his name. Remember, if twenty dichotomous questions are answered like sex, race (white or nonwhite), and age (under forty or forty or over), then it is possible to identify one unique individual out of a million individuals sharing some of these characteristics.

Anonymity is, of course, impossible in panel-type studies, where the same individuals are reinterviewed over time so that earlier answers can be compared to later ones. Researchers have to know which individuals are responding at each stage. Yet even panel studies do not require the name of the specific individual; a code identification will do as well for the purpose.

When principles come into conflict—when not wanting to create needless or avoidable anxiety in the participants conflicts with not wanting to deceive them about the types of questions involved or the uses to which their answers will be put—then we have a new *level* of problem in research ethics. Any specific conflict in ethical principles has to be resolved in favor of the least harmful option balanced against the most socially useful option. What we have done is to raise the level of the principles involved from specific ones (creating anxiety versus deception) to more general ones (personal harm versus social benefit). This raised level should make the case more easy to decide, but it may not. Personal harm and social benefit are still on different scales, and the decision depends on whether one puts the individual ahead of the society or the other way around. Thus, ultimately, one's ideology (or the dominant ideology of one's subculture) determines the decision. Rationalizations follow. It is, unfortunately, possible to rationalize just about every decision. In science, the only protection is that many eyes may assess a given set of designs, instruments, results, and interpretations; weak rationales may be criticized soundly. In addition, a researcher who cannot back up his or her work—or has been caught red-handed cheating—can be drummed out of the profession and may face legal action as well.

Here is another point regarding confidence within the interview situation. What if the participant asks the interviewer for specific information about the question asked or the research in general? For instance, what if Mrs. Caraway had asked the interviewer whether he was trying to find out whether she was crazy in order to get her locked up? Responses to these kinds of questions have to be clear and honest, lest the participant detect deceptive hedging, for which a refusal to cooperate would be in order. It is easy to say that the intention of the question and the study is not to get a participant locked up. But what about the larger picture? It may be that information resulting from the study will suggest that older persons in need of protective services should be "locked up" for their own good. (The results didn't turn out that way, fortunately.) The facts of the matter are that no one knew how the study was going to turn out, and its intention was explicitly to learn about how older persons live in the community (albeit older persons in need of protective services—a point that was not shared with the participants). Therefore, in this case, the suspiciousness may have derived from the person's condition or from prior experiences with "interviewers." But just how much is the participant supposed to believe on faith alone? It may ultimately come down to a personal trust of the interviewer. This is, unfortunately, a very weak basis, and we turn next to the third major stage of building confidence.

Stage 3: Building Confidence Within the Profession Based on the Handling of Information and Data. The threat of collegial reaction to one's scientific work is always present, wonderfully concentrating the mind on earning confidence and the reputation for being an honorable scientist. Here, too, the process of gaining external review and critique is risky. Letting fellow researchers be critics may be like letting the foxes guard the chicken coop. Someone's buddy may be appointed to a review-of-human-subjects committee at some level, as the buddy would have to be knowledgeable in the common research area in order to make an informed judgment about how adequate the procedures are in that context. Of course, cronyism is possible, and so is the less-than-impartial judgment that may emanate from that condition. But to a large extent, such proceedings are a matter of public record. Reviewers are exposing themselves to risk by partial judgments just as much as are researchers conducting investigations without these safeguards. And so a human system of checks and balances is once more instituted in the pursuit of honest science and honest practice. This system is fallible, but certainly the very public nature of the review probably screens out the grosser risks.

There is another side to this story. Review boards may be too scrupulous, and may squelch projects involving human subjects under conditions that justify the risk. Although it is better to err in favor of the safety of human subjects, still it may be a loss to society not to have information from this study. Review boards that I have been on have sometimes made concrete suggestions whereby researchers may modify the project to conform to guidelines on the ethical use of subjects in research. These suggestions are not always received with gladness and joy because they require modifications of plans imposed by "outsiders." That's too bad (that it makes the researchers angry), but overall the system of review works reasonably well (for human subjects, if not for humane researchers).

One footnote: When human-subject review committees first became required (in response to some abuses in various fields of medical and social research), some people thought the deathknell of the sciences had been sounded. In fact, there was little pause in the overall flow of research. Rather, projects became more sophisticated, attacking previous issues in new ways that showed ingenuity and greater openness. Today, few complain about the principle of review, although particular renderings may upset individual researchers who have a high investment in the "one right way" to do a given piece of research.

Research in the helping professions was always under the cloud of suspicion for the reasons that interviewing might upset the participant, intrude on privacy, and so forth. So these review committees were seen as the natural allies of an anti-research orientation among practitioners. In fact, just the reverse occurred. These regulations were imposed not to reduce research on the clients of helping professionals, but to make the research more humane and efficient. To the extent that review committees can add to this process, they will aid clients, researchers, and practitioners.

BIASED, INSPITE OF OURSELVES

Biases, or preferences that reflect distorted or incomplete reasoning, are all too common in every walk of life, including research.* In doing scientific research, we assume that each step of the way is clearly and carefully analyzed to remove bias. But we can never reason completely or view anything other than through the lens of our own experience. So the best thing we can do is to recognize the biases that exist, to remove the most blatant and harmful ones, and to warn future readers of our perspective so that they can correct for these biases, if necessary.

Prejudices may be defined as preconceived judgments based on selective values. (This definition is not traditional; I am making the comparison between a bias that has to do with distorted reasoning and a prejudice that has to do with personal values that are expressed in ways detrimental to others, in order to make the contrast clear and to illustrate several problems in research.) Thus, one's values, facts, or reasoning processes may all be implicated in adding problems for ethical research.

The next major point is that bias or prejudice may take place at every stage of the research process: How we pick our problems for study, and what we ignore; how we select theories or hypotheses; what methods we use to select our samples; how we interview participants; and how we choose to interpret the findings and report these interpretations—all of these are open invitations to let our biases and prejudices hold sway. Why, then, is research worth a damn? Because we have the potential for compensating for these biases and prejudices. Science is cumulative in the sense that one person's report becomes the beginning point for the next person's work. People don't always share the same biases and prejudices, and so there tends to be a blending of these preferences. When a large number of varied biases and prejudices are represented in a given research topic, it is unlikely that any will be dominant. This multiplicity of views may be a rough operational definition of "objective" research. In principle, because any qualified scientist can repeat the previous study, the biases can be corrected. Even if large numbers of persons are operating under the same value or ideological banner, there are other banners and other ways in which scientists with other ideologies can replicate research that may correct for value differences.

SUMMARY AND GENERALIZATIONS

1. It is easy to start a project—you just keep starting. It is more difficult to finish starting, to have everything done on time in the right place. Make a generous calculation of the amount of time it will take to get to the starting line—then double it.

---

* This discusson of *bias* and *prejudice* in the research context constitutes Technical Note 6.4.

2. Keeping track of the project during its operation is also easy. Simply find a meticulous and compulsive person who will do secretarial duties cheerfully year in and year out. It will also help if you have large flowsheets keeping track of where everything is supposed to be, and when and why. Just don't forget to look at the charts regularly.

3. Handling data is also easy, depending on the system you use. If the handling is all done mechanically, so that the raw information is immediately and accurately transferred into coded and scored information, which is then stored in computers with infinite memories and only slightly less infinite patience with your finite memory, then the task is very easy. Anything less than full automation is difficult. The more a human hand touches data at any stage, the more likely it is to attract errors like flies to honey. But don't spend all your time worrying about handling data; give your critics something to think about, too.

4. Accept the fact that, to someone else's way of thinking, you have "isms." Your socialization as a young person in this society has left you with many rewards, and some burdens as well. Be aware of your biases; they will emerge at every stage of the research process.

5. Perhaps most important, value your participants' privacy and confidentiality. Do nothing that jeopardizes their human and civil rights, for even if you succeed in obtaining scientific information at the expense of these rights, you have gained nothing and humanity is the loser. Any research must have an overwhelming social benefit to be tolerated at all, so use your portion of this social toleration of research wisely.

Technical Notes

6.5 STATISTICS: A LITERARY OVERVIEW FOR NONMATHEMATICIANS

Statistics is one branch of mathematics, the great universal language of scientific understanding. Statistics (as well as mathematics in general) also scares the hell out of some people, possibly for good reasons, but mainly because people scare themselves needlessly. In any case, rest easily, I do not propose to present a textbook on statistics. However, it is necessary to understand the ideas involved so that one can be a more effective reader and interpreter of the statistics that one inevitably comes across in any professional or scientific literature.

One of the best approaches to statistics for nonmathematically-oriented persons is the literary approach. That is, by using a language natural to the student that is roughly equivalent to what statisticians are trying to do, it is often possible to communicate some very basic ideas about statistics. At least, that is my strategy. In Figure 6.1 (pages 170–173), I have expressed some basic questions that are really statistical questions in a literary form. They are sensible questions, questions that you have probably asked about things around you, without recognizing that you were indeed speaking in that great universal language, or one dialect of it.

There are many other questions like these, literary forms of basic statistics, but I think these will be sufficient to get across an important truth—that you are quite capable of understanding that set of logical rules applied to numbers called statistics. Once you have learned these basic statistics—and many readers have already taken a statistics course—then you can go on to learn how to generate new information using these various tools. Now, on to the statistics for nonmathematicians.

6.6 CODES AND SCORES

This Technical Note has to do with how raw *data* (participants' replies to interview questions) are transformed into usable information in connection with a given study. As will be illustrated in Chapter 7, the actual interview schedule allows space for the interviewer to record direct statements by the participant and/or observer-supplied indications of the participant's agreement with one or another of the limited choices available: "agree," "disagree," and so on. Even at this stage, there is a distinction between codes and scores. The term *codes* refers to the division of responses into mutually exclusive and exhaustive categories. Such categories are arbitrary. One can permit the participant either to agree or to disagree (a two-category choice) or to agree strongly, to agree slightly, to disagree slightly, or to disagree strongly (a four category choice); or one can permit the participant to talk about his or her feelings and beliefs with regard to this same topic. The interviewer would then try to record verbatim what and how the participant communicated. Someone else will have to interpret what these remarks mean, a situation which raises the interesting question:

Figure 6.1 Statistics: A literary overview for nonmathematicians.

Literary Questions About Mathematical Topics (or, were you asking mathematical questions all your life without knowing it?)	Measurement Strategies	Formulas (or cookbook: how-to-do-something to answer the literary question)
1. What is it?	1. Qualitative approach: Categorize the object or event as belonging to a given class or set of like things.	1. Look carefully at the object or event for its major characteristics, and then mentally place it within the category of things that has that major characteristic as its classification definition.
2. How much of it is there?	2. Quantitative approach: Attach numbers to the specific instances of the thing and then use the number system properties (such as 1 + 1 = 2) to represent the things counted.	2. The major mathematical step is to link numbers to things and then play around with the numbers (rather than push people around) in order to answer questions (like how many are there of this thing? Which person has more of it? etc.). After we have used the number system to answer the numerical question, we then re-apply the answer to the things themselves.
3. What is typical about all of these things we have observed?	3. We are seeking ways to indicate the central features or typical pattern among a set of events or objects. One way to do this is to indicate the average member of that set of things.	3. There are several ways to indicate averages, which vary depending on the type of things one is analyzing. With nominal data we could look for the most frequently occurring observation—the mode. With ordinal data, we might look for the midpoint in an ordered set of data—the median. With interval or ratio levels of measurement, we would use the mean score in which one would take the sum (Σ) of the observations (x) and divide by the number of observations (n). Here is the formula: $$\text{Mean or } \bar{x} = \frac{\Sigma x}{n}$$
4. What is the range of observations, from the biggest to the smallest?	4. Now we are seeking the boundaries around our set of observations. This is called the range, from the biggest to the smallest scores.	4. The procedure for finding the range among a set of observations is simply to subtract the smallest observation from the biggest. This doesn't tell us anything about how many instances there are at any place in between, but it gives us a quick picture of the data.
5. What variation from the typical is typical?	5. Each instance we observe will be above, below, or at the typical (mean) score. What we are looking for is a way to summarize these differences of each score from the mean (or typical) of that set of scores. This is called deviations from the mean. Different groups could have the same mean but differ in how	5. There are several ways to measure the deviations from the mean. I will describe only the *standard deviation* because it is likely to be most useful and most used. The formula for standard deviations tells us exactly what steps to perform in what order to obtain this useful characteristic—how much variation from the typical is typical. Take an example of 5 test scores listed below whose mean score is 5.0 (see #3 above for formula):

Col. 1	Col. 2	Col. 3	Col. 4	Col. 5	Col. 6
Scores on a test:	Differences between each score and the mean:	Square each answer from col. 2:	Sum scores from col. 3:	Divide this sum by number of observations:	Take square root of the answer from col. 5:
9	$9 - 5 = 4$	$4^2 = 16$	40		
7	$7 - 5 = 2$	$2^2 = 4$		$5\overline{)40}$ $\dfrac{8}{}$	$\sqrt{8} = 2.83$
5	$5 - 5 = 0$	$0^2 = 0$			
3	$3 - 5 = -2$	$-2^2 = 4$			
1	$1 - 5 = -4$	$-4^2 = 16$			
$\Sigma = 25$					
$n = 5$					
$\overline{x} = 5.0$					

The general formula for a standard deviation is SD or $\sigma = \sqrt{\dfrac{\Sigma(x-\overline{x})^2}{n}}$

---

tightly (small deviations) or loosely (big deviations) their members were spread out from that mean score.

6. What do I do with all the facts I have about this thing? What do I do with all these numbers?

6. Since we can't make much sense of large bunches of numbers, we have to reduce them by creating a small number of suitable categories and then indicate by numbers or pictures how many are in each category.

6. There are many ways to reduce masses of numbers to manageable size. One can make *pictorial representations*, like how much of the pie goes to this purpose, and how much of it goes to some other purposes. Or, one can make a *frequency distribution*, a set of mutually exclusive and exhaustive categories that indicates how many actual things are in each category. A *cross-classification table* tells even more; it is a set of interrelated categories that indicates numbers of things viewed jointly. For example, a frequency distribution indicates the number of men and women in a certain class; a cross-classification table would indicate men and women by age groupings in that class.

Frequency Distribution	
Males	Females
13	17

Cross-classification Table		
Age	Males	Females
<18	4	6
18-21	8	8
>21	1	3

7. How do things co-vary? How is one thing related to another?

7. Often, things do not appear together by accident. The first step in understanding how they are related is to ask whether they vary in concommitant ways, or whether they are independent of one another.

7. Again, there are various ways to respond to the question about concommitant changes or independence between two sets of things. First, one could make a cross-classified picture (scattergram) of the joint occurrences of two sets of things, like age and grades. (Do older students get better grades, or do younger ones, or doesn't age make any difference?) I'll present 3 scattergrams of these three possibilities.

(*continued*)

Figure 6.1 (continued).

Literary Questions About Mathematical Topics (or, were you asking mathematical questions all your life without knowing it?)	Measurement Strategies	Formulas (or cookbook: how-to-do-something to answer the literary question)

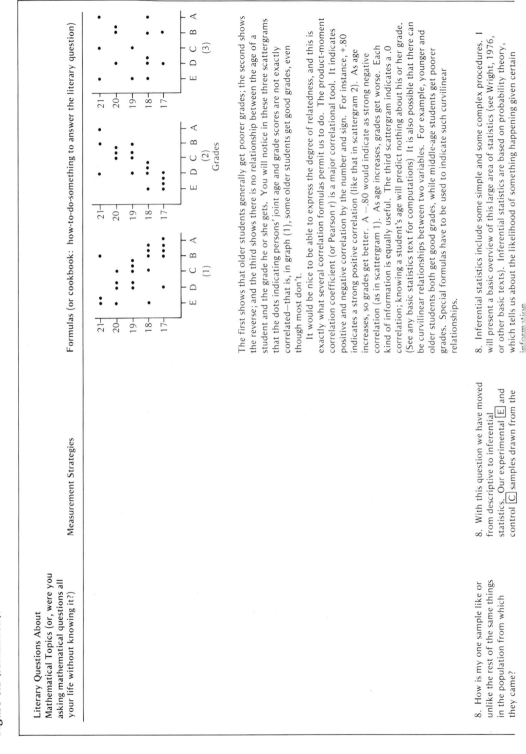

The first shows that older students generally get poorer grades; the second shows the reverse; and the third shows there is no relationship between the age of a student and the grade he or she gets. You will notice in these three scattergrams that the dots indicating persons' joint age and grade scores are not exactly correlated—that is, in graph (1), some older students get good grades, even though most don't.

It would be nice to be able to express the degree of relatedness, and this is exactly what several correlation formulas permit us to do. The product-moment correlation coefficient (or Pearson r) is a major correlational tool. It indicates positive and negative correlation by the number and sign. For instance, +.80 indicates a strong positive correlation (like that in scattergram 2). As age increases, so grades get better. A −.80 would indicate as strong negative correlation (as in scattergram 1). As age increases, grades get worse. Each kind of information is equally useful. The third scattergram indicates a .0 correlation; knowing a student's age will predict nothing about his or her grade. (See any basic statistics text for computations.) It is also possible that there can be curvilinear relationships between two variables. For example, younger and older students both get good grades, while middle-age students get poorer grades. Special formulas have to be used to indicate such curvilinear relationships.

---

8. How is my one sample like or unlike the rest of the same things in the population from which they came?

8. With this question we have moved from descriptive to inferential statistics. Our experimental E and control C samples drawn from the

8. Inferential statistics include some simple and some complex procedures. I will present a basic overview of this large area of statistics (see Wright, 1976, or other basic texts). Inferential statistics are based on probability theory, which tells us about the likelihood of something happening given certain

172

same population are likely to be somewhat different because there are more factors influencing them than the few we have selected for study. Could the post-intervention differences between $\boxed{E}$ and $\boxed{C}$ have happened by chance because they are still parts of the same broad population, or are the differences so great that the groups are no longer part of the same population? (We would then presume that the intervention caused these differences.)

The strategy in inferential statistics is to estimate from the available data on the samples at hand to some population characteristics so as to infer whether the intervention results are like what might be expected from other random samples from the typical portions of that population. If the results are still like typical samples from that population, then the $\boxed{E}$ and $\boxed{C}$ groups don't differ statistically, and the intervention is not effective. If the E group can no longer be seen as a typical member of that population, then this is statistically significant and the intervention is effective.

Things distribute themselves in nature similar to theoretical curves. One important probability curve is the Gaussian distribution, better known as the normal frequency distribution or the normal curve. The percentages of areas under the curve are clearly known and thus becomes the frame of reference against which samples can be compared. Below is a normal curve:

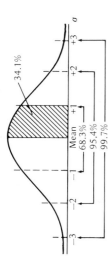

The area from the mean to $+1\sigma$ accounts for 34.1% of the area under the normal curve. $\pm 1\sigma$ to $-\sigma$ (or $\pm\sigma$) accounts for 68.3%, and so on.

A researcher would set a level of significance that represented what would be the typical zone of the normal curve. If 95% of the area under the curve is considered typical, then the .05 level of significance indicates what the experimental group must exceed in order to be statistically significant, by falling outside of that typical middle range. The figures below indicate two ways in which this could occur. (Note that $\pm 2\sigma = 95.44\%$; $\pm 1.96\sigma = 95.\%$)

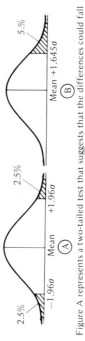

Figure A represents a two-tailed test that suggests that the differences could fall in either tail of the curve (and so the 5% is divided between them). Figure B is a one-tailed or directed test that suggests that the differences will fall only in one end of the curve. (Most treatment tests are one-tailed--we expect clients to improve.) The null hypothesis is that there will be no significant differences between E and C since they are part of the same population even after intervention. The alternative research hypothesis indicates that E will fall in that 5% critical region, which could not have happened by chance alone except less than one time in twenty (the .05 level of statistical significance). We infer that the intervention was the cause of this change.

There are other important distributions, especially with small samples, such as the t test and the chi-square distribution. (See Wright, 1976.)

To whom do these data belong—the participant, the interviewer, or the final interpreter of the coding? We may be building a knowledge base on what some interpreter thinks the world looks like to various groups of persons, and not on what these people themselves actually think!

Scores are the ways codes are to be interpreted within the context of the study itself: which categories of answers are presumed to be positive or favorable, and which are thought to be negative or unfavorable with reference to the objectives of the study itself. These, too, are arbitrary, as different studies may have different objectives for which the same answers may be interpreted in different ways. For example, in many studies, if a participant would not answer a question, the researchers might be stymied and might count this nonanswer as lost information. In the Protective Services Project, we tried to use all information as it related to assessing mental status or social protectiveness. So, for example, if a participant couldn't think of a single person who offered concrete assistance or even refused to answer this question, this response would be *coded* as whatever answer the participant made, but it would be *scored* as unfavorable, that is, as evidence that there were no persons present to provide concrete assistance for the participant. This rule for scoring "no information" assumes that a reasonable question (set within a body of reasonable questions) can be interpreted favorably or unfavorably within the context of the whole interview. This extended interpretation by the researcher is necessary when participants cannot or will not cooperate. It is clearly risky; all inferences are. But when the same risks are present for both experimental and control participants, the risk is at least equal for both, and readers are forewarned. In this way, more of the potential information deriving from a participant–interviewer contact can be squeezed out with the same degree of effort.

6.7 THE CODE BOOK: AN OVERVIEW

A *code book* is a vital part of the research process. It contains the procedural key by which data collected in the study are prepared for various forms of analysis (such as counting and tabulations by categories). The objective is to specify how each item is to be used in the analysis. (The principle of questionnaire construction urges the curiosity-struck investigator to some restraint, because every item must be used somewhere within the network of ideas of the analysis.) Every question must have an identified place, even though it may require some content-analysis procedure (see Technical Note 5.12, p. 147) before the coder is able to impose a number on the response that can then be handled in further analysis by computers. Let's look at an example of a typical code-book page to identify the ingredients.

As shown in Table 6.1, this hypothetical code book page (modeled after the one used in the BRI Protective Services Project) has seven components. The item number as it appeared on the questionnaire is given first. Because of the number and types of interviews to be conducted in the study, some other identifying information was also given: *P/I- #1* stands for participant, initial interview, first item on the questionnaire. Some information from the questionnaire appeared on the cover sheet, such as the participant's identification number, and therefore did not have an item number as such.

Table 6.1 Hypothetical Code Book (participant interview schedule, initial interview).

Item Number on the Questionnaire	IBM Card Number and Column Location	Question (and Short Tag Name)	Code: Translation of Participant's Answers to a Standard Numerical Category	Score: Evaluation of the Code on a Given Scale	Scale of Which the Item Is One Component	Interview Form Used: Long (L) or Short (S) Form
—	IBM card I, Columns 1, 2, 3	Participant identification number	001 through 164	—	—	1 = L 5 = S
—	I-4	Research interviewer identification number	1 = Mary G 2 = Dale H 3 = Joan D	(not relevant)	—	1 = L 5 = S
P/I* = #1	I-8	Have you lived in Cleveland a long time? (*time in Cleveland*)	1 = less than 1 year 2 = 1–4 years 3 = 5–9 years 4 = 10–24 years 5 = 25 years or more; or born in Cleveland 7 = P doesn't know 9 = not asked	—	—	1 = L
P/I = #3	I-10, 11, 12	How old are you? (*age*)	Code actual statement of age in number of years, or 000 = don't know 999 = not asked for some reason	1 = accurate age, verified from some other source. (If none available, use correspondence between birth date, Question 4, and the age given.) 0 = not accurate according to our best information	MSQ (Mental status questionnaire—short form)	1 = L 5 = S
P/I = #14	I-25	In general, would you say your health is now good, fair, or poor (probe for degree) (*perceived health*)	1 = very poor 2 = poor ("not very good," etc.) 3 = fair (speaks of chronic condition that limits functioning slightly) 4 = good 5 = very good 6 = inappropriate response 7 = no response; don't know 9 = not asked	1 = codes 4 or 5 0 = codes 1, 2, 3, 6, 7 9 = code 9	S and S (Signs and symptoms scale—long form)	1 = L

P/I. = Participant initial interview.

175

Likewise, there were many items to be scored, and not all fit on one computer card. So we indicated the card or deck number in roman numerals, and the location on the computer card in terms of specific columns from the eighty columns available. A set of columns (or a field) may be used, such as the participants' identification numbers, mutually exclusive and continuous numbers from the first case (001) to the last (164). The set of columns contains the identifying information for this case. For example, Mrs. Edwards was Case Number 055, the fifty-fifth consecutive case admitted to the project.

Other questions have just a one-column answer, such as Question 1: "Have you lived in Cleveland a long time?" Both the full question and a brief tag name are given, so that this item can be discussed in the text more easily. The codes used in the answers take what the participant said and interpret it as fitting one of a series of mutually exclusive and exhaustive categories. For instance, Code 1 stands for having lived in Cleveland less than 1 year. Code 2 stands for living in Cleveland for between 1 year and 4 years and 363 days (that is, just short of 5 years). The next code then starts at 5 years and runs to 9 years and 363 days. Note that the number of years in each of these codes is arbitrary; some codes might represent even intervals, whereas we made these codes represent census divisions so that we could compare our answers with those of the U.S. Census if we wished to. Even so, we combined some age periods for our own convenience; we didn't want that much detail for this item, and so we condensed answers accordingly. Indeed, observe that, functionally speaking, having lived for twenty-five or more years in Cleveland was made equivalent to having been born there. We knew that these two events weren't strictly equivalent, but in terms of our judgment, these were essentially the same thing.

Another code, 7, reported the participant response that the person didn't know the answer to this question. Not knowing how long one has lived in a city might have been an item for the memory part of the mental status questionnaire, but the originators of that scale did not use this item, so we simply noted this fact and did not score it, that is, did not place an evaluation on the fact that the participant did not know a simple memory item. Code 7 is to be distinguished from Code 9, which tells us that the question wasn't asked for some reason. Not every item has a score; such items are likely to be purely descriptive, such as "time in Cleve.," the tag name we used for the length of time the participant had lived in Cleveland.

Question 3, "How old are you?," is coded in terms of the actual statement that the participant made in response to this item, within the limits of a three-column field. The code 000 was used for a "don't know" answer, and 999 was used for when the question wasn't asked for some reason. We tried to be consistent in our use of 9's as representing the instances when the question wasn't asked for some reason. In some cases, not asking a question might be construed (evaluated) as bad, when the participant was alert enough mentally to be asked the question, or as neutral, when the participant was ill or not at home to answer any questions. We don't know what the context was, and so we simply leave the code as 9 and choose not to score it one way or the other.

The fun starts when we try to score an answer. In the case of *Age* (the tag name for "How old are you?"), we had to have a verified age either from some other source, such as from social security records or perhaps from a collateral of the participant, or failing that, from a correspondence between the *Age* answer and the following one on birth date. We assumed that if a person gave an age answer of seventy-three, and then responded that her birth date was June 25, 1890 (which would have been seventy-three years ago in the year of the interview), then that was reasonable internal evidence of the accuracy of the age. In this way, we verified the answer to Question 3 against the best available information before giving a score: 1 for an accurate answer, 0 for an inaccurate one. The scoring of this item took much extra effort because it linked information from other sources, such as casework records and calls to social security. Eventually, after a determination was made, a score of 1 or 0 was given. The scale, of which this was one item was the mental status questionnaire, or MSQ for short. This item appears on both the long and the short forms of the interview schedules, and the specific form is indicated by a 1 for the long form or a 5 for the short form.

Similar reasoning was used in the last example in the code book in Table 6.1 (*Perceived Health*). Here the coded answers also included some typical responses that emerged in pretesting or in early interviews. These anchoring illustrations simply helped to make the information more comparable and consistent across interviewers. These illustrations may not be full enumerations; it depends on how much need there is to identify typical responses, otherwise, the respondents appeared to use our guided phrases ("good," "fair," or "poor") and then the degree that we obtained from probes such as "Poor or very poor?"

The most critical part of this code book was the formation of the scores for various codes. With Item 14 (*Perceived Health*), there were five essential codes (from "very poor" to "very good"), plus a code for inappropriate responses, like that of one lady who said, "I'm dead." Because this item belongs to the "signs and symptoms of affective or behavioral disorder scale," a code of 7 ("no response" or a "don't know" response) was coded as indicating a sign of affective or behavioral disorder. Thus only two codes, "good" and "very good," were scored as positive responses on this scale. The others, 1, 2, 3, 6, and 7, were all scored as negative responses in the context of what this item was seeking information about. Code 9 ("not asked") was an indeterminable response, evaluated neither positively or negatively. The overall principle is to find the meaning of the coded answers in the context of what the study is seeking to discover so that as much meaningful information as possible can be obtained, even when inappropriate responses are given. (See Technical Note 6.9, p. 179, on item analysis).

6.8 NULL HYPOTHESIS

The *null hypothesis* is a paradoxical creation of probability theory combined with historical scientific research. The null hypothesis states that there will be no statistical difference between two or more groups (such as a sample and the population from which it is drawn) with regard to a given variable, or that there will be no statistically significant relationship found between these variables. The null hypothesis is set up in order to be rejected in favor of some alternative hypothesis. The null, in effect, predicts that the findings will fall in the typical range of the normal curve, what one might expect by chance alone.

Often the null hypothesis is linked with given alternative hypotheses, those that the researcher expects to occur. When helping professionals are evaluating their impact on client behavior, the practitioners fully expect that the predicted "no difference between the experimental and the control groups" will not occur. Rather, they expect that positive outcomes will occur in the treatment group (to which they are contributing the planned service); this is the alternative hypothesis that they might formulate.

But the null hypothesis is useful in reminding the researcher, especially the helping professional doing evaluative research, that the probability curve has two tails, and that it is possible to reject the null hypothesis because events are better or worse than the null predicted. The negative changes reflect deterioration, what Stuart (1970) called an "iatrogenic effect," as the would-be helping professional, in fact, creates new and unexpected problems for the client.

Positive changes are another matter. If one rejects the null hypothesis because the data differ in the desired direction, one is tempted to assert that the alternative hypothesis is correct—because the outcomes were what one really expected and what one, in fact, acted to produce. But all one has done is to reject the null in favor of another hypothesis; one has not proved that this alternative is true. In fact, philosophically, it is very difficult to prove the truth of anything; it is possible merely to prove that first one thing is not the case, and then another is not the case. One merely approximates what is believed to be true by disproving false states of affairs (cf. Popper, 1959). These are subtle philosophical arguments, not critical to an understanding of research as such, but they are very close to the heart of the matter. Science provides not a royal road to truth, but only to approximations of it.

In practical terms, we summarize these complex considerations about the null hypothesis by referring to a level of significance such as the .05 level. The .05 means we accept the risk of rejecting the null hypothesis (5 percent of the time) when in fact it is true. This statement is termed a *Type I error,* an error of scientific judgment that occurs when one rejects a null hypothesis when it is in fact true. On the average, a .05 level would mean that we would be wrong in our decision about one time in twenty. If we can accept this risk, then we can use the .05 level as the basis for testing the null hypothesis. In matters of life and death, perhaps the researcher is not willing to accept a one in twenty chance of being wrong. In such a case, the researcher can simply set the level of significance higher, say at .01. This means that the chances for a random error occurring is one in 100.

This sounds very nice, but setting the Type I error at this level has a price. We are now in danger of committing a *Type II error,* accepting a null hypothesis when it is false. Depending on the content of what one is studying, the researcher has to balance off each risk against the other. These types of errors are inversely related for a given sample size, which makes the choice all the more complicated. Most workers are concerned about Type I errors, in part because the mathematics are easier to calculate. But in fact, both are important. This dilemma of the two types of errors is illustrated in Technical Note 11.5 (p. 289).

6.9 ITEM ANALYSIS

An *item analysis* is used in the development of a measuring instrument in order to include specific items that perform what they are intended to do in a given scale. One performs an item analysis in any of several ways: First, one can compare a given item with a known external standard. For example, a given item on depression should be responded to in one way by a group of hospitalized depressives; in another way by a group of hospitalized persons recovering from hip fracture; and in yet a third way by a comparable age group of persons living in the community. Those most depressed (the hospitalized depression group) should respond to the new item with more agreement (more members of the group expressing a greater intensity of depression) than the other hospitalized group, which, in turn, should be more depressed than the community group, other things being equal.

In the BRI study, we had few opportunities to test the items on our questionnaires in this external fashion; we weren't working with groups whose known attitudes were distinct enough to provide this comparison. So we used internal comparisons, the correlation between a score on a given item and the overall score on that scale. Assuming that the items derived from other studies of depression did, in fact, measure depression in one fashion or another, then the total score of this group of items would be a more stable indicator of depression than any one item, especially more stable than any new item that we were experimenting with as being more appropriate for this particular population. This procedure is, frankly, a supporting of one's questionnaire choices by one's own bootstraps. It is a weak way of identifying the validity or the reliability of the items in the scale, but when nothing else is possible, then this is one approximate method. (Also see Technical Note 5.6, p. 139, on the standardization of measurement instruments. Item analysis is frequently used in that process.)

6.10 PROTECTION OF HUMAN SUBJECTS

This Technical Note presents an excerpted version of the federal regulations (45 CFR 46) concerning the *protection of human subjects,* revised as of March 8, 1983. I am including these regulations in some detail so that you can see the extent of the protections participants in research have.

There are four subparts to this federal regulation: A) basic Health and Human Services policy for the protection of human research subjects; B) additional protections related to research involving fetuses, pregnant women, and human in vitro fertilization; C) protections pertaining to research involving prisoners as subjects; and D) additional protections for children involved as subjects of research.

The critical element is the *institutional review board* (IRB), a group of persons who are specially selected to consider proposals and to review the research periodically for a given institution. A large university or agency sets up such an IRB according to procedural rules established by the Department of Health

179

and Human Services. Then the IRB is empowered to ensure that the organization is complying with the general guidelines.

Having served on institutional review boards, I can tell you that participation is a labor of love—there are no rewards, and occasionally, a researcher will get angry at what he or she thinks is too much scrupulousness on the part of the IRB. However, the IRB is established to protect human subjects—and the reputation of the institution and its researchers—so when the system works well, it serves a very useful purpose. And so far as I know, the process is working reasonably well.

Excerpts from the Code of Federal Regulations 45 CFR 46, on the Protection of Human Subjects

§46.101   To What Do These Regulations Apply?

(a) Except as provided in paragraph (b) of this section, this subpart applies to all research involving human subjects conducted by the Department of Health and Human Services or funded in whole or in part by a Department grant, contract, cooperative agreement or fellowship. . . .

(b) Research activities in which the only involvement of human subjects will be in one or more of the following categories and are *exempt* [emphasis added] from these regulations. . . .

> (1) Research conducted in established or commonly accepted educational settings, involving normal educational practices. . . . (2) Research involving the use of educational tests (cognitive, diagnostic, aptitude, achievement), if information taken from these sources is recorded in such a manner that subjects cannot be identified, directly or through identifiers linked to the subjects. (3) Research involving survey or interview procedure, except where all of the following conditions exist: (i) responses are recorded in such a manner that the human subjects can be identified . . . , (ii) the subject's responses, if they became known outside the research, could reasonably place the subject at risk of criminal or civil liability or be damaging to the subject's financial standing or employability, and (iii) the research deals with sensitive aspects of the subject's own behavior, such as illegal conduct, drug use, sexual behavior, or use of alcohol. All research involving survey or interview procedure is exempt, without exception, when the respondents are elected or appointed public officials or candidates for public office. (4) Research involving the observation (including observation by participants) of public behavior, except . . . (the same three subpoints in #3 above). (5) Research involving the collection or study of existing data, documents, records, pathological specimens, or diagnostic specimens, if these sources are publicly available or if the information is recorded by the investigator in such a manner that subjects cannot be identified. . . .

(c) The Secretary [of the Department of Health and Human Services] has final authority to determine whether a particular activity is covered by these regulations. . . .

Reprinted from Code of Federal Regulations, Title 45 Public Welfare, Department of Health and Human Services, National Institutes of Health, and Office for Protection from Research Risks. Part 46—Protection of Human Subjects revised as of March 8, 1983. Government Printing Office, 1983.

§46.103   Assurances

. . . (b) The Department will conduct or fund research only if the institution [conducting or seeking funding for research] has an assurance approved as provided in this section, and only if the institution has certified to the Secretary that the research has been reviewed and approved by an IRB [an Institutional Review Board] provided for in the assurance, and will be subject to continuing review by the IRB. This assurance shall at a minimum include: (1) A statement of principles governing the institution in the discharge of its responsibilities for protecting the rights and welfare of human subjects of research conducted at or sponsored by the institution, regardless of source of funding. . . . (3) A list of the IRB members identified by name; earned degrees; representative capacity; indications of experience such as board certifications, licenses, etc. sufficient to describe each member's chief anticipated contributions to IRB deliberations. . . . (4) Written procedures which the IRB will follow (i) for conducting its initial and continuing review of research and for reporting its findings and actions to the investigator and the institution. . . .

§ 46.107   IRB Membership

(a) Each IRB shall have at least five members, with varying backgrounds to promote complete and adequate review of research activities commonly conducted by the institution. The IRB shall be sufficiently qualified through the experience and expertise of its members, and the diversity of the members' backgrounds including consideration of the racial and cultural backgrounds of members and sensitivity to such issues as community attitudes, to promote respect for its advice and counsel in safeguarding the rights and welfare of human subjects. . . . (b) No IRB may consist entirely of men or entirely of women, or entirely of members of one profession. (c) Each IRB shall include at least one member whose primary concerns are in nonscientific areas; for example: lawyers, ethicists, members of the clergy. (d) Each IRB shall include at least one member who is not otherwise affiliated with the institution and who is not of the immediate family of a person who is affiliated with the institution. (e) No IRB may have a member participating in the IRB's initial or continuing review of any project in which the member has a conflicting interest. . . .

§ 46.109   IRB Review of Research

(a) An IRB shall review and have authority to approve, require modification in (to secure approval), or disapprove all research activities covered by these regulations. . . .

§46.111   Criteria for IRB Approval of Research

(a) In order to approve research covered by these regulations the IRB shall determine that all of the following requirements are satisfied:

(1) Risks to subjects are minimized: (i) By using procedures which are consistent with sound research design and which do not unnecessarily expose subjects to risk, and (ii) whenever appropriate, by using procedures already performed on the subjects for diagnostic or treatment purposes.
(2) Risks to subjects are reasonable in relation to anticipated benefits, if any, to subjects, and the importance of the knowledge that may reasonably be expected to result. . . . (3) Selection of subjects is equitable. . . . (4) Informed consent will be sought from each prospective subject or the subject's legally authorized representative, in accordance with, and to the extent required by §46.116. . . . (6) Where appropriate, the research plan makes adequate provision for monitoring the data collected to insure the safety of subjects. (7) Where appropriate, there are adequate provisions to protect the privacy of subjects and to maintain the

confidentiality of data. (8) Where some or all of the subjects are likely to be vulnerable to coercion or undue influence, such as persons with acute or severe physical or mental illness, or persons who are economically or educationally disadvantaged, appropriate additional safeguards have been included in the study to protect the rights and welfare of these subjects. . . .

§46.116 General Requirements for Informed Consent

. . . An investigator shall seek [informed consent] only under circumstances that provide the prospective subject or the representative sufficient opportunity to consider whether or not to participate and that minimize the possibility of coercion or undue influence. . . . (a) Basic elements of informed consent. . . . The following information shall be provided to each subject:

(1) A statement that the study involves research, an explanation of the purposes of the research and the expected duration of the subject's participation, a description of the procedures to be followed, and identification of any procedures which are experimental. (2) A description of any reasonably foreseeable risks or discomforts to the subject; (3) A description of any benefits to the subject or to others which may reasonably be expected from the research; (4) A disclosure of appropriate alternative procedures or courses of treatment, if any, that might be advantageous to the subject; (5) A statement describing the extent, if any, to which confidentiality of records identifying the subject will be maintained; (6) For research involving more than minimal risk, an explanation as to whether any compensation and an explanation as to whether any medical treatments are available if injury occurs and, if so, what they consist of, and where further information may be obtained; (7) An explanation of whom to contact for answers to pertinent questions about the research and research subjects' rights, and whom to contact in the event of a research-related injury to the subject; and (8) A statement that participation is voluntary, refusal to participate will involve no penalty or loss of benefits to which the subject is otherwise entitled, and the subject may discontinue participation at any time without penalty or loss of benefits to which the subject is otherwise entitled. . . .

§46.117 Documentation of Informed Consent

(a) . . . Informed consent shall be documented by the use of a written consent form approved by the IRB and signed by the subject or the subject's legally authorized representative. A copy shall be given to the person signing the form. . . .

CHAPTER 7

One Participant's Responses to the Initial Research Interview

Overview

This chapter contains the initial research interview with one participant in the BRI Protective Services Project. It describes more fully what life is like for such an elderly person, but at the same time, this chapter illustrates the ways in which abstract theories are translated into concrete questions so as to provide standardized and objective information about the participant. By adding observations about the context in which the questions were asked and how the responses were made, I also hope to show that not all standardized and objective questions come out that way.

Chapter 8 continues an examination of interviews—with the participant in follow-up contacts, with her collateral (the next-door neighbor who was helping the participant), and with the referring agency worker—as well as the observations made by the interviewer and the ratings made by the social worker on this case. This kaleidoscope of bits of information approximates the life of one elderly woman in need of protective services. This process, repeated with individual variations with the other 163 participants, produced the data that were used for the final analysis of the study.

Technical Narrative Section

In this chapter, I am continuing the blending of a Narrative with Technical Notes, but with a difference. This chapter contains a large excerpt from a disguised interview, along with observations about the questions, the answers, and whatever else requires comments. Only two Technical Notes are presented, in contrast to the many such notes in earlier chapters. This time, the reader must submerge himself or herself in the flow of the conversation reported here so as to capture the experience of research indicated by the Technical Notes.

This is not an ordinary conversation—at least on the part of the interviewer. It is highly structured and directed, even though there was much freedom to adapt to the immediate circumstances. And yet, by the end, there emerges some sense of wholeness—I hope—that the questions provoke but do not create. We, the audience, create the sense of what life is like for the participant. As researchers, we then have to translate this sense into sensible data and sensitive interpretations. This translation is no easy matter—perhaps it is the most difficult task in the entire research process.

Introduction
The Initial Participant Research Interview (Technical Note 7.1)
Strategies for the Organization of the Questionnaire (7.2)

The Technical Narrative

INTRODUCTION

There is no better way to convey a sense of the questions we asked than to report one participant's responses (suitably disguised to protect confidentiality) to a full set of interview and observer-rating schedules. In the following pages, I present the world according to Mrs. Alma Edwards. You may not recognize this world exactly, because it appears with the distortions generated by a transient confusional condition. But what you must understand is that this is her perception of her world, as best as we can obtain it from a finite set of questions. It is not "Truth," but her truth as we interpret it.

Is such "truth" of any value? We know it contains errors of fact and fantasy. Of what use is such a perception of reality? The answer is clear: We live our lives according to selected truths and illusions. It is unfortunate that we cannot always tell one from the other, especially as states of confusion come upon us. But regardless, it is with these perceptions of reality that we live our lives. If we, as helping professionals, are to influence the lives of our clients, then we must understand their lives. And this requires that we enter their world by communicating with them, even if such questions and observations are not always reliable or valid.

THE INITIAL PARTICIPANT RESEARCH INTERVIEW

It is a cool fall day as the research interviewer drives up to a small house in a working-class neighborhood.* A Ford automobile factory is nearby—he can hear the noises and smell the fumes. It is an old neighborhood; the houses are separated by makeshift fences. Some of the lawns are well-cared for; clumps of chrysanthemums bloom. A few of the homes are in obvious need of refurbishing. Mrs. Edwards lives in a white clapboard cottage somewhat yellowed by age and inattention. The interviewer rings the bell and waits several minutes until Mrs. Edwards shuffles to the door. She opens it immediately and invites the interviewer in without really understanding his explanation: "I am Martin Bloom, from Associates in Gerontology. We are conducting a study of the attitudes and activities of older persons in the Greater Cleveland area. We are interested in learning how people are getting along in everyday matters, what are some of the problems they are facing, and what are some of the things that are making them happy nowadays." Nor does she pay much attention to the interviewer's card, which has the name, address, and phone number of Associates in Gerontology. Mrs. Edwards doesn't even look at the simple large-type brochure describing the project and the agency, although other participants are very suspicious of

---

* This long section illustrates an actual *interview;* along with some commentary. The section constitutes Technical Note 7.1.

the interviewers ("What are you selling?") and have called the Better Business Bureau (with whom we were listed as a research group) or the police (we made contact with the Cleveland police and sent letters to the twenty some communities in the vicinity explaining our project).

"Come in, dearie. The neighbors are rubbernecking," Mrs. Edwards says as she both holds onto the interviewer and pulls him into her house toward the kitchen, which is warmer than the other rooms. She walks slowly and unsteadily in floppy house slippers. Her wool skirt is wrinkled and dirty, but her bright blue sweater seems new. Her white hair is somewhat disheveled but appears clean. Mrs. Edwards talks volubly and almost nonstop. She sits down at the table and then immediately gets up to go to the couch in the other room to lie down: "I feel sick, miserable." It is a natural lead into the interview, even though it doesn't conform to the order of the interview schedule. [For Items 1–13, see pp. 189–190].

The interviewer said, "I'd like to ask you some questions about your health":

14. *In general, would you say your health is now good, fair, or poor? (probe for degree).* Mrs. Edwards replied that her health was very poor. There was no need to probe further; she supplied the degree.

15. *During the past month, did any health problems, sickness, or ailment keep you from carrying on the things you usually do around the house?* Mrs. Edwards answered yes and proceeded to give several illustrations, such as being too tired to take in the plants before an early frost killed them. She would happily have gone on in this vein, but the interviewer took advantage of a brief pause to continue the questioning.

16. *Were you in bed most of the time for a day or more during the past month (because of any health problem)?* Mrs. Edwards thought a moment and replied no. Had she said yes, then the interviewer was prompted in Question #17 to ask a related question, *About how many days did your health problem keep you in bed last month?* But since Mrs. Edwards did not have such a health problem, the interviewer was directed to skip over the next question. This kind of direction to the interviewer is typical; it presents a logical follow-up question where relevant, or it appropriately shortens the questionnaire by eliminating an unnecessary question.

18. *Were you kept in the house but in a chair most of the time?* Mrs. Edwards said no.

19. *Were you kept in the house but still able to get around?* She responded vigorously yes and proceeded to talk about what she wasn't able to do anymore. In so doing, she, in effect, answered the next several questions, which were sequentially graded items about *getting outside, climbing stairs, walking about eight ordinary blocks, doing ordinary housework,* and *doing heavy housework.* So the interviewer circled answers to these questions without asking them—indicating by his initials what he had done. (The four italized items belong to the short form of the Physical Functioning Scale, see Table 4.1 for a list of the variables used in the Protective Services Project.)

25. (Observe if possible:) *Does anyone help you in walking (on a level area)?* The interviewer had already experienced first hand how Mrs. Edwards had taken advantage of his assistance in walking, even though she could manage with considerable effort to walk on her own, using the furniture

along the way as an aid. The interviewer was directed to code the most typical mode.

The interviewer then asked a series of questions that were manifestly related to health, but that, in fact, represented some other facets of mental functioning as well. (See Table 4.1, p. 113.)

26. *In the past month or so, did you tire more easily than you used to a year ago?* Mrs. Edwards replied that this was so. The interviewer then probed further: *Did this happen only a few times or often?* And Mrs. Edwards observed that this happened often.

27. *Did your health worry you in the past month or so?* Yes, Mrs. Edwards replied, it worried her very frequently—thus anticipating the interviewer's probe for degree of worry. [This is an item on the short form of the Contentment Scale, see Table 4.1.)

28. *Are you concerned about a long-term disabling illness?* To this question, Mrs. Edwards replied with her current problems, and even when the interviewer tried to clarify by repeating the question, Mrs. Edwards was so focused on her current problems that she didn't ever answer that question. This reaction was recorded as an "Other" reply, and the interviewer noted her preoccupation with her here-and-now problems.

Other questions in this series included items on waking up tired and exhausted in the mornings, being bothered by feeling weak all over, *feeling dizzy or faint,* being made irritable and impatient by things, *feeling afraid for no particular reason, feeling extremely angry, having crying spells,* or losing or misplacing things—all questions referring to events in the past month. (The italicized items belong to the short form of the Scale of Signs and Symptoms of Affective and Behavioral Disorders; see Table 4.1.) Mrs. Edwards replied that most of these happened to her often, except for being tired on arising or feeling extremely angry.

The questions continued:

37. *How is your memory? Would you say that you were able to remember as well as you used to a year ago?* Mrs. Edwards said, in effect, that her memory was fine and that there had been no change in the past year.

38. *And how are your spirits? Have you felt blue or like you were floating on air or how has your general mood been lately?* This question set Mrs. Edwards off on a tearful recitation of her problems, and the interviewer had to try gently to bring her back to the question specifically—rather than to the specific medical concerns that she had presented earlier. She said that she was in low spirits all or much of the time.

39. *Did you find yourself having thoughts about death in the past few months?* To this question, Mrs. Edwards replied that she had thought about death a few times, but she spoke primarily about the death of some relatives in recent months. This answer supplied the answers to the next question:

40. *When you thought about death, what did you think about?* And so the interviewer made the appropriate notes for this question, even though it had been answered previously.

41. *Have you made your own funeral plans?* Mrs. Edwards replied yes. There was no sense of morbidness in her reply.

The interviewer then went on to another set of questions, again nominally related to the health topic, but extended into other variables thought to be important in the everyday functioning of older persons:

42. *Do you need any help in matters of health, like help in reminding you when to take medicine drops or pills, or giving you injections, or making doctor's appointments for you?* Mrs. Edwards thought that she really could use some help in these kinds of medical matters.

43. *Who could you turn to for help in an emergency? Do you have somebody's name and telephone number by your phone? (or in your purse?) Who is that?* Mrs. Edwards reported that she could "ask school children passing by for help in an emergency." (This is an item on the short form of the Interested-Parties Scale: see Table 4.1.)

44. *Who is your doctor? (the family or regular general practitioner?) Or do you go to a health clinic? Where?* On these questions, Mrs. Edwards was somewhat vague but eventually said that she had no regular doctor or clinic.

45. *When is the last time you saw a doctor?* Mrs. Edwards was even more vague. She couldn't say when it was.

The next group of questions asks about specific behavior or events:

46. *How has your appetite been in the past month or so?* Not so good, according to Mrs. Edwards. A probe of the frequency was noted as "happening often."

47. *Were you bothered in the past month by not being able to go to the toilet regularly?* No problem for Mrs. Edwards.

48. *Some people need help to manage getting around and doing routine things. Does anyone help you to get in or out of the bath tub?* No help needed. Likewise, with a set of related questions 49–55, Mrs. Edwards said that she didn't need help in getting dressed, going to the toilet, getting in and out of bed or chairs, or feeding herself. Nor did she have to go to the toilet frequently at night or have toileting accidents. (These items belong to the Index of Activities of Daily Living, an index that precisely measured degrees of lower level physical functioning [Katz et al., 1963]; see Table 4.1.)

After some forty questions on health, there was a change to items about the contentment and satisfaction that the participant was experiencing. The interviewer simply continued the questions without any transition statement:

56. *What are some of the things you are most satisfied about nowadays?* The interviewer was directed to record the number of mentioned satisfactions as well as their content. Mrs. Edwards couldn't think of anything that she was satisfied about these days.

57. *During the past month or so, would you say that you have been happy or unhappy?* The interviewer was further instructed to probe for degree of either happiness or unhappiness. Mrs. Edwards reported that she was unhappy, but a probe did not change the degree. (This is an item from the Contentment Scale.)

58. Depending on the answer to Question 57, the interviewer was instructed to ask for examples: *What are some of the things that you are not too happy*

about these days? What would you say are the main problems in your life lately? Mrs. Edwards began a long rambling recitation of her problems, including health, the neighbors, loneliness, and some others that were less clear. The interviewer interpreted these answers to mean pervasive unhappiness, based on the number and range of things mentioned.

59. *How do you think things will be six months from now—do you think things will be happier for you than they are now, about the same as they are now, or less happy?* Mrs. Edwards predicted a worsening scenario.

60. *What are you worried about for the future? What do you hope will not happen to you?* To this question, Mrs. Edwards had many answers. She hoped her health wouldn't worsen; she was concerned about the cold weather and her keeping warm; and she mentioned something about the neighbors as being worrisome to her. This mention of neighbors was a natural lead to the next set of questions, which the interviewer introduced as follows:

61. *Let's talk a bit about other people, now, about your friends and relatives.*

    Is there anyone on whom you can depend for advice, or whom you can confide in, about your personal troubles? Who is that? The interviewer was instructed to specify who this person was, what relationship he or she was to the participant, and an address if possible. Mrs. Edwards said she had no one to depend on. (This item and the one following are from the short form of the Interested Parties Scale.)

62. *Is there anyone who gets in touch with you if they don't see or hear from you as often as usual? Who is that?* Again, the interviewer was directed to obtain names, relationships, and addresses. Mrs. Edwards mentioned a Mrs. Young next door who wasn't as bad as some neighbors because she showed a real interest in her. Mrs. Young helped with her shopping, and she brought over food sometimes, or just chatted.

These questions also gave the interviewer the opportunity to go back to the opening questions on the interview schedule that had been skipped when the interviewer moved directly into health questions following Mrs. Edwards's lead:

1. *Have you lived in the Cleveland area for a long time?* "Yes, all my life," Mrs. Edwards replied.

2. *Where were you born?* "In Cleveland."

3. *How old are you?* Mrs. Edwards wasn't too sure. She thought she was about eighty-three or maybe eighty-seven. (This item and the following one belong to the Mental Status Questionnaire, see Table 4.1.)

4. *And when were you born? Could you please give me your complete birth date?* Mrs. Edwards knew her birthday was on September 11, but she couldn't remember what year it was, except that "it was a long time ago, dearie."

She didn't know the answers to the next two questions, where her mother and father were born, but she was able to respond to another question:

7. *What nationality do you consider yourself?* The interviewer was directed to probe for ethnic group if it was not clear from the previous comments. Mrs. Edwards said her roots were German.

8. *Are you now single, married, widowed, divorced, or separated?* Mrs. Edwards reported that she was widowed. In fact, she proceeded to tell about her

husband, who had died a very long time ago, and about her son, who was currently living with her, and about a daughter, who had died about six years before of cancer. These comments answered the next two questions on the number of children the participant had and which of these lived in the Cleveland area.

By observation, the interviewer recorded the answers for questions 11 and 12, the race and sex of the client—Mrs. Edwards was white—and asked the last demographic question:

13. *What is the last grade of school you finished?* Mrs. Edwards couldn't remember.

These responses by Mrs. Edwards and some observations by the interviewer further answered the next questions (63 and 64) on who was living with Mrs. Edwards (just her son) and whether she had a telephone (the interviewer observed one in the kitchen). So the interviewer continued asking this next set of items:

65. *Do you talk with friends or relatives by phone very often?* Mrs. Edwards said she talked to no friends or relatives, thus obviating the need to ask the next question about who these people might be. Instead, the interviewer was directed to skip that item and go on to the next:

67. *How many close relatives—brothers and sisters, children, grandchildren, nieces and nephews, and their spouses—live within walking distance of you?* Except for her son who was currently living with Mrs. Edwards, there were no living relatives. Her daughter had never married. The interviewer skipped the next question about how often she saw them and what their relationship was to her.

70. *How many close relatives live in the Cleveland area?* (including suburbs) Mrs. Edwards mentioned some nieces, Millie Rawlings and Anne Duval, and a brother, Andrew, who was in a nursing home. These names and information on where the relatives lived would be collected in Question 72.

71. *How often do you see them?* Mrs. Edwards said that she almost never saw them, and the interviewer interpreted this according to the categories on the interview schedule: "not at all this month." (This item and the one following are from the short form of the Interested Parties Scale.)

73. *How many close relatives do you have who live outside the Cleveland area?* Mrs. Edwards reported that she had none living outside this area, so the interviewer skipped the next few questions, which ask about numbers, names and addresses, and frequency of contact.

76. *Do you have a special friend whom you feel very close to, like a member of the family?* It turned out that Mrs. Edwards did have a confidante, her old friend Violet McGraw, who was very ill and in a nursing home. Thus Mrs. Edwards hadn't seen her for many months.

The next questions concerned the people whom Mrs. Edwards wrote to. Arthritis had prevented her from writing at all, but even so, she had never written to anyone even when she could move her hands easily. Another set of questions concerned assistance she had received from agencies and organizations:

81. *During the past year did you receive any help or advice from organizations in the community—such as your church or hospital or social agency?* Mrs. Edwards wasn't

sure, but she thought not. (This item and the one following in italics [*nurse*] are from the short form of the Concrete Assistance Scale; see Table 4.1.)

The interviewer then asked a series of questions related to specific kinds of visitors, such as whether a *nurse,* a worker in public assistance for the aged, a social worker, or other helping person had visited her. Mrs. Edwards said no, no one like that ever came.

87. *If you had to get help from your relatives (children), friends, or neighbors—if you suddenly became sick—who would be the first person you would ask?* Mrs. Edwards said there was no one she could ask in such a circumstance.

The interviewer continued to get at this same question from another direction by asking whether she had any pets or plants, and if so, whom she would ask to take care of them if she had to be out-of-town for a week or so? Mrs. Edwards said she had no plants or pets, even though the interviewer could see some small pots of ivy or violets in the kitchen.

Then the interviewer introduced some new topics without explanation:

90. *Do you find that you are less interested lately in your personal appearance and table manners and things like that?* Mrs. Edwards said no.
91. *Which of these two statements is more important to you?:*
    a. *Trying to have peace of mind, or*
    b. *Trying to live by the golden rule*
    Mrs. Edwards thought a moment and replied, peace of mind.
92. *Which of these two statements is more important to you?:*
    a. *Trying to keep healthy, or*
    b. *Trying to be useful*
    Mrs. Edwards answered that both were important to her and she didn't know how to answer. This reply meant that the next question on value orientation, which compared the two "winners" from the previous two questions, couldn't be asked.

The next set of questions concerned financial and legal matters:

94. *Do you need any help in keeping your money matters straight, like helping you to budget, or plan what to buy, or paying bills or debts?* Mrs. Edwards allowed as how she did need this sort of help.
95. *How often do you get help in keeping your money matters straight? Regularly or once in a while or what?* This question set Mrs. Edwards off onto a private discourse about a dishonest lawyer and other matters not clearly related to the question. The interviewer circled the "other" answer and tried to capture some of these comments, although they didn't make any sense, especially when the interviewer went over the schedule later to make it easier for others to read. However, these random comments were the essence of what Mrs. Edwards had said. (This is another concrete assistance item.)
96. *Who helps you out in these money matters?* The interviewer was supposed to get the name and relationship of the helping person, but the best he was able to manage was the information that her attorney helped her in these matters.

191

97. *Do you need any help with legal matters, like taxes or lawsuits or wills?* Mrs. Edwards answered yes, but on the follow-up question, how often that happened, and who that person was, she was rather vague. The interviewer did not press the question when she seemed uncomfortable about either the topic or not knowing the answers.

The next set of questions mixed observations, which were noted on the interview schedule, with regular questions. Question 100 was on the type of housing unit. The alternatives ranged from a private house (such as Mrs. Edwards's), to apartments and rooms in various settings (hotels, apartments, clubs, boarding houses, foster homes, and so on), as well as various institutional settings, which were included to be used on follow-up interviews although all participants were living in the community to begin with. Let me illustrate how we mixed observational with direct question formats:

NB: Living space
Furnishings
Stairs/floors/rugs

101. *Who takes care of housecleaning here?* Mrs. Edwards indicated that she herself did, as contrasted with domestics, friends, or relatives. (This is a concrete assistance item)

102. *Who takes care of the shopping?* Mrs. Edwards mentioned that her neighbor, Mrs. Young, did this for her.

NB: Inaccessibility to shopping/visiting
Energy required for upkeep

103. *Who takes care of the cooking?* Mrs. Edwards replied that she did most of it. Her son had been doing some since he returned home. (The interviewer didn't take this natural opportunity to explore this situation, a mistake in the sense that the occasion arose when the client herself had mentioned the son and might have been willing to say more about what he was doing there and why.)

NB: Observe cooking/refrigeration
Observe plumbing/washing/washing facilities.

The *NB*s were prompts to the interviewer to look around and, in some cases, to ask to see where the participant cooked, laundered, and so on. These observations were eventually recorded on the interviewer's rating scales about the participant and the environment.

Answers to some of these questions are not without their pathos, as when asked the ordinary question

104. *Who takes care of the laundry?* Mrs. Edwards replied that she couldn't do it by herself anymore and so she wore clothes until they were torn and dirty, and then she threw them away. (This is another concrete assistance item.) After some other prompts to observe lighting and ventilation; litter and junk; and heating and cooling, the interviewer asked:

105. *In general, how satisfied are you with your present arrangements for housecleaning, cooking, laundry, and shopping? Are you satisfied, partially satisfied, or dissatisfied?* Mrs. Edwards replied that she was dissatisfied. (This is an item from the Contentment Scale.) Then the interviewer was directed by this answer to ask:

106. *Which aspects are you not satisfied with?* Her answer was somewhat confusing. She said she was dissatisfied with the neighbors. The interviewer tried to find out what she meant, and it appeared that she was referring to the lack of help she received from them in laundry—but also in general, not being helpful, and also being noisy. The interviewer recorded this free-floating jumble of observations, without comment.

The next set of questions focused on Mrs. Edwards's living situation, how long she had lived in this house and whether it had various facilities (like a complete bathroom, hot running water, a handrail on the stairs, and concealed wiring), together with notes for the interviewer to observe signs of deterioration in the house (holes, cracks, worn steps, and so on). Blended with these questions were others:

114. *How do you feel about this neighborhood as a place to live? In general, would you say that it is a good place to live, or not so good, or what?* It didn't take much probing for the interviewer to discover that Mrs. Edwards thought the neighborhood was very bad. She added comments about how the neighbors were trying to get rid of her, and how they did some terrible things to her—unspecified.

115. *Do you need any help in getting places, such as getting to church or to some shopping place, or getting out to visit friends?* Mrs. Edwards admitted to needing help but stated that, although a minister—she couldn't remember his name—called on occasion, she never got any help, thus anticipating the next questions: how often she got help and from whom. (This is a physical functioning item; see Table 4.1.)

118. *Has there been any change lately in the way you get along with neighbors or friends or relatives, or the way they act toward you?* This was a question that prompted a long monologue by Mrs. Edwards on how the neighbors were all very nasty to her, and how she didn't know any of them because the old ones had all died or moved away. Of course, that new neighbor, Mrs. Young, seemed pretty nice because she brought things to Mrs. Edwards, but at times Mrs. Edwards wasn't really sure about Mrs. Young either. These comments more than answered the next question, about what Mrs. Edwards had noticed by way of changes.

120. *How do you get along with your son (who lives with you)? Do you get along well or not so well or what?* At this question, Mrs. Edwards burst into tears and the interviewer wasn't sure what had happened. In between sobs, she reported how her son had been treating her against her will, such as pouring burning substances down her throat to cure her cough. Mrs. Edwards begged the interviewer to help her escape. Her son, Jonas, had been let out of the insane asylum, but he was still crazy, she said. Mrs. Edwards was clutching the interviewer, still sobbing, when she heard a car door slam. "It's him," she announced, and blew her nose as she tried to disguise the fact that she'd been crying.

Jonas Edwards wandered in. He was a thin, small man in his sixties, wearing soiled work clothes. He was suspicious of the interviewer and asked many questions about the interview and what his mother had said. He told her that he didn't like people asking questions, prying into their business, but Mrs. Edwards said it was just like visiting with the neighbors: not much of importance had been said, but she was enjoying the visit and wanted the interviewer to stay. Jonas was wavering about throwing the interviewer out or leaving himself. And for no apparent reason, he suddenly walked out and drove off.

The interviewer was undecided what to do next. The rules of the interview called for no intervention except in the case of a crisis. He decided that this was a critical situation, but not a life-threatening crisis, and went on with the questions. As it happened, the next question was most appropriate to this tense situation:

121. *If you had your choice, would you prefer to live here or in some other place or what?* Contrary to what the interviewer expected or what the participant had said just minutes before, Mrs. Edwards stated that she wanted to stay right where she was, and that she was satisfied with her arrangements. Without calling the contradiction into question, the interviewer went on:

122. *Now I would like to tell you about a real-life situation and I would like to get your opinion about it.*

Mildred Thomas, a widow close to seventy-eight, is presently living alone in a dilapidated house. She had been able to keep it up fairly well until recently, but the health department has declared the house a firetrap and beyond repair. Yet Mrs. Thomas refuses to move. What's more, she has been extremely suspicious of other people lately and says she "hears voices." Her only close living relative is a daughter who lives in another city and who does not seem to be close to her mother. The daughter does not accept the seriousness of the situation, and denies reports of her mother's illness. A neighbor, who is also an old friend of the family, is concerned about Mrs. Thomas. What should the neighbor do? Mrs. Edwards became engrossed in this story problem and asked for more details. The interviewer simply repeated the relevant parts of the story or said he didn't know, if the question went beyond the given information. Mrs. Edwards said that it made her sad to see how some children treated their parents, and that she thought the police should make the daughter pay more attention to the mother. Maybe the daughter was sick and that was the reason she didn't help. The neighbor was definitely to continue helping Mrs. Thomas with everything, and that would make everything come out all right.

123. *Have you had any accidents of any kind in the past few months—things like leaving the stove on or the water running or cutting yourself, or maybe falling or bumping into things—anything at all like that in the past few months?* Mrs. Edwards said no, but talked about being afraid of fire. Her sweater sleeve had caught on fire some time ago; she wasn't exactly certain when it was. So, even though the participant gave a no answer, her discussion suggested a yes answer, and this is how the interviewer reported the information.

124. *Have you lost any money or checks in the past year?* Mrs. Edwards reported that she thought someone had stolen some of her money recently, but she couldn't be sure.

125. *During the past year, did you ever feel so bad that you thought life wasn't worth living?* Mrs. Edwards admitted that she had felt this way.

126. *Have you at any time in your whole life felt so bad that you thought of suicide?* Mrs.

Edwards paused a few seconds and said no. The interviewer did not press for more explanation.

Then Mrs. Edwards was asked about whether she was a member of any church (yes—at least she used to be) or clubs, lodges, or other organizations (no). She reported her religious preference as Lutheran.

Next, the interviewer asked whether Mrs. Edwards usually wore glasses, as she wasn't wearing any at the moment. She said that she had glasses somewhere, and the interviewer asked her to put them on so as to read a card that he handed to her. It contained some simple sentences printed in three different sizes of type—a rough indicator of visual ability. Mrs. Edwards finally found her glasses after a short excursion to the kitchen. She put them on and looked at the card with the three sizes of print, but she put the card down, saying that she wasn't able to see anything clearly enough to read.

The interviewer then asked about her hearing, and she reported—and demonstrated—that her hearing was adequate.

Next, the interviewer introduced a set of ten questions:

Let me ask you some questions like those they ask people on quiz programs.

The interviewer was directed to discontinue these questions after four continuous failures. (These next eight items are from the Kent E-G-Y Intelligence Test; see Table 4.1.)

134. *First, can you tell me the names of some large cities?* Mrs. Edwards repeated the question several times and then said, "Like Cleveland?" The interviewer replied yes, and she then proceeded to list three other large cities without hesitation. She received four out of four points on this question.

135. *What kinds of materials are houses made of?* Mrs. Edwards laughed at this question and listed four materials, thus obtaining the highest number of points on this item.

136. *Tell me the names of some fishes.* Mrs. Edwards struggled with this one but was able to come up with four types of fish and the full four points.

137. *What is sand used for?* Mrs. Edwards said something about cement and earned two out of a possible four points, according to the scoring directions for this measuring device.

138. *What metal is attracted by a magnet?* Mrs. Edwards said gold, and this was a wrong answer.

139. *At what time of day is your shadow the shortest?* Mrs. Edwards didn't know the answer to this question.

140. *If the flag floats to the south, what direction is the wind coming from?* Again, Mrs. Edwards couldn't answer this question.

141. *How many stripes are there in the American flag?* Mrs. Edwards said forty-eight. The interviewer repeated the question, thinking that perhaps she hadn't heard it clearly, but when she repeated her answer of forty-eight, he decided to discontinue this sequence of ten questions because she had made four continuous errors.

However, the interviewer went on to ask other questions of the same sort, even though they were not in the set of intelligence questions:

144. *Do you remember who were the two major candidates in the last national presidential*

election? Mrs. Edwards didn't understand the question, and so the interviewer was directed to add: *Who were the Republican and the Democratic candidates for president?* With this restatement, Mrs. Edwards was able to identify one candidate, "the one who died." (The assassination of President Kennedy had taken place a few weeks before.) (This item and the next one are from the Mental Status Questionnaire; see Table 4.1.)

145. *Can you give me the full date today?* Mrs. Edwards was unable to give any information about the day's date—day, month, or year. But she did comment that this was a long interview. The interviewer asked if she was too tired to continue, and Mrs. Edwards said no, but she hoped it wasn't too much longer. The interviewer said it wasn't, but that if she was getting tired, he could come by another time. No, said Mrs. Edwards, she really liked to talk, but the questions were getting awfully hard. The interviewer said the next questions would be easier.

146. *When you think back over your whole life, which of these has been more important to you? Trying to have some enjoyment in life or trying to lead an upright life?* Mrs. Edwards replied with a laugh, enjoyment.

147. *And which of these has been more important to you over your whole life? Trying to get a steady and secure income or trying to be a success in life?* Mrs. Edwards said economic security.

148. *Now which of these has been more important to you over your whole life, enjoyment or economic security?* Mrs. Edwards had trouble with this and wouldn't make a choice. She said that she didn't know.

I now realize that while we thought we were asking paired sets of *value* questions, in effect we were testing people's *cognitive capacities* to compare pairs of ideas. The answers may have told us more about mental confusion then about values. At the time of this research, we noted that few participants answered and of those that did, few showed any apparent pattern, and so the data were not analyzed further.

The interviewer then turned to a series of demographic questions about what kinds of work she had done during most of her life ("housewife"), as well as the kind of work her husband had done ("foreman at a furniture factory"). Then questions were asked about how adequate or inadequate her income was ("inadequate") and the major sources of that income. Mrs. Edwards thought most of her income came from social security, but she wasn't sure. She didn't think she had any other source of money. She was asked about having a bank account—she had one now—and was asked to pick an amount of money from a list on a card that was the amount nearest to the amount she spent on food each week. (The interviewer read the amounts to Mrs. Edwards.) This was something she couldn't do or wouldn't do. Likewise, when asked about the amount of her total income the previous month, she was unable to answer. The interviewer noted her overall pattern of responding to any question on money matters, but no specific question was asked on this topic.

In the last part of the interview, Mrs. Edwards was asked whether she would agree or disagree with some opinions that had been expressed by various people:

165. *Once your mind is made up, don't let anything change it.* Mrs. Edwards disagreed with this. But she agreed with all of the following statements, which are a sample of those asked:

166. *One drink is one too many.*
167. *These days a person doesn't really know whom he can count on.* (This, and the next four items, belong to the Anomie Scale, a measure used to describe the sample; see Table 4.1.)
168. *Most public officials are not really interested in the problems of the average man.*
169. *Nowadays, a person has to live pretty much for today and let tomorrow take care of itself.*
170. *In spite of what some people say, the lot of the average man is getting worse, not better.*
171. *It's hardly fair to bring children into the world with the way things look for the future.*

You may have noticed that these questions were expressed in the colloquial language of the day, including some grammatical infelicities. Those were intentional. We thought we would communicate better by so doing.

172. *Behind your back people say all kinds of things about you.*
173. *More older people use alcohol to lighten their spirits than people think.*
174. *Always be on guard with people.*
175. *Things just keep getting worse for me as I get older.* (A contentment item embedded in this set of questions.)

Another group of items completed the interview. These dealt with some attitudinal questions of which the following were the most important:

180. *As you get older, would you say things seem to be better or worse than you thought they would be?* Mrs. Edwards said that things were much worse than she had thought they were going to be.
181. *On the whole, how satisfied would you say you are with your way of life today?* Mrs. Edwards said with a sigh that she was very unsatisfied. (Another contentment item.)
182. *This is the end of the interview. How did you like it?* Mrs. Edwards seemed confused about the fact that this had been an interview. She had liked chatting with the interviewer. Was he going to come back soon? The interviewer replied that he had enjoyed talking with her, too, and that he would like to return in about three months. This statement didn't seem to register with Mrs. Edwards, who said, "Why wait so long?"
183. *I would like to thank you for your cooperation. Can you tell me how to get to (the nearest main cross-street)?* Mrs. Edwards was able to give accurate directions to the large road just a block from her house. (This is our substitute for the final item in the Mental Status Questionnaire.)

STRATEGIES FOR THE ORGANIZATION OF THE QUESTIONNAIRE

One hundred and eighty-three questions can be asked in any one of many billion possible combinations. What determined the one that we eventually chose? Or more generally, how should one go about organizing a questionnaire for scientific research?*

* This discussion on *strategies for organizing questionnaires* constitutes Technical Note 7.2.

197

Several major suggestions are found in the literature, picturesquely described as the funnel approach or the pyramid approach, depending on whether one starts from broad questions and zeros in on specifics later in the interview, or whether one starts with specific questions and gets into the broad queries later. These metaphoric suggestions may be useful on simple questionnaires, or within any given section of a complex one, but there are many other considerations that are perhaps of greater weight than the breadth or the narrowness of the questions.

Another general organizational issue is the hotness or the coolness of the questions. If you expect one question or one type of question to be hot to handle (that is, either the participant is likely to have some reservations in responding to it, or the interviewer will have difficulty asking the question), then it seems reasonable to put this question later in the interview, when some degree of rapport has been attained and both participant and interviewer are at ease. Then it is a good idea to embed the question among other neutral ones and to ask it matter-of-factly.

Another dimension concerns facts versus opinions. If the questions require factual answers (for example, what is your birth date? How many friends have you seen in the past week?), then these might seem to be easier questions to answer than those that require opinions or judgments that reflect the respondent's knowledge or character. On the other hand, for persons having cognitive deficits such as forgetfulness, factual questions may themselves produce some discomfort: "I know I am supposed to know my birth date, but I just don't remember; does this mean I am senile?" And so, if one is constructing a questionnaire related to the likely abilities and deficits of the responders, then it might be easier to make some broad judgments on which there are no right or wrong answers, simply opinions. The point is probably to get the interviewee into the questionnaire fully before challenging him or her with any types of questions that may be difficult or embarrassing. One cannot say in advance whether facts or opinions are easy or difficult without knowing the nature of the interviewees.

The same is true of several possible dimensions, such as personal versus impersonal types of questions; present time versus either past or future; and long versus short questions.

All questions should be as brief and as clear as possible. Brevity may require consideration of the level of language used. Unless you are surveying presidents of universities, I recommend that you simplify your level of language to the point of rock-bottom simplicity. Simplification means challenging any word more than three letters long to see if there isn't a simpler, clearer, more expressive way of communicating the question. Moreover, words have multiple meanings. The constructor of effective questionnaires must be as certain as possible that the words that he or she has chosen have the same meaning perceived by the responders. The closest researchers can come to approximating this state of certainty is to conduct pre-tests of the questionnaire with people like the intended participants of the real study.

Another issue is whether to have one long questionnaire as a series of questions, or whether to break it up into modules either by interviewing the responder at different times, or in some other way presenting the questionnaire as different sets of questions. If one breaks up a long questionnaire into modules of manageable size, it may seem less burdensome to the responder. Psychological breathing spaces are created; people feel as if they have accomplished something when they have completed a given section.

On the other hand, we discovered an essential tool for interviewing the mentally and socially frail elderly, and that is to have a short form of the questions arranged separately so that it is convenient to ask just a handful of items rather than the whole questionnaire—and preferably to avoid having to search through many pages to find these short-form items.

As discussed previously, short-form items are empirically selected as the best predictors of the longer and more reliable forms of the scales. But brevity is always preferred over length if the data obtained on the short form are a reasonable approximation of those attained on the long form. This correlation of a short form with the long form requires a pretesting that shows how few items you can get away with and still have some faith in the reliability of your questions.

So what is the upshot of this discussion? How should one arrange questions to get at the information that one seeks while doing as little harm as possible to the responders? My suggestion is unfortunately not very scientific, but I think practical experience supports it. This suggestion is to make a good story line and sustain it until a body of internally self-sufficient and self-supporting information is obtained. I suggest creating a cluster of questions that hang together on some superficial basis, such as putting together all the questions about how the interviewee is getting along in her or his home. In fact, such a story line of questions may include items on a variety of topics—this mix of topics is no problem, as the computer will sort out where your questions are located and combine relevant items for a given scale. What is important is that your interviewee feel that something sensible is being asked in some comprehensible manner. And so, if you can label the modules, such as "questions about how you are getting along at home" or "about your friends," or whatever, and then proceed to ask whatever questions fit, it makes answering easier. Indeed, sometimes the participant volunteers answers from the module in advance of questions as often happened with the Protective Services Project items.

In order to tell a good story, you have to select most wisely the opening portions of the interview because these will make or break whatever follows. Literally, the participant may break off an interview because something offends, however unintentional the offense may have been on the part of the researcher. Because of this risk, I recommended to interviewers that they ignore the questionnaire itself in favor of gaining some working rapport, particularly with resistant participants. In practice, rapport-building would mean trying to find something of immediate interest to begin the conversation. For instance, if invited to come in to ask questions, during the process of walking to a sitting area and opening his or her briefcase the interviewer might make some light conversation, such as "I hope you have been able to get outside to enjoy this beautiful weather we are having." This comment may provoke a response about the participant's health, which means that the interviewer can move first to the section on health. Then, while waiting for another remark on family or background, the interviewer can return to the questions skipped earlier.

Doesn't this change of the order of the questions violate the sacred laws of research interviewing: ask the questions, only the questions, and just the questions in the order prescribed, so help you? Yes, it does. So if your clientele

199

permit you to follow that sacred order, do so. But if it is a choice of getting an interview by modifying the order of items to suit the immediate situation, or getting no information at all, then I would recommend flexibility in asking the questions over purity. The order of asking and responding to questions has an effect, no doubt, but that is less serious a challenge to the validity of the answers than not having any answers at all.

This flexibility in moving modules of questions around does not extend to changing questions *within* a module—except in using short-form items as discussed above, in which case these items are definitely torn from the fabric of their context. We know this violates a rule of interviewing, but the weight of the decision is almost entirely on the side of getting information versus not getting it. It is important that the questions be asked in exactly the form that they were designed in, in order to present a common stimulus on which answers from different respondents are to be compared.

After you have constructed a questionnaire, try to step back and look at the larger features of its design. You may discover that you have moved in a funnel-like or a pyramid-like fashion. But you may also discover that you have several sets of modules that are practically interrelated and that flow relatively smoothly in pretests with persons very similar to the future participants in your study.

There are no sacred laws of interview construction, but common sense and a good deal of preliminary experience will help to eliminate the major faults and may help to polish some of the more sensitive and sensible decisions about arrangement. Ultimately, we ask ourselves whether or not what we ask, how we ask it, and the order of the questions, in fact, contribute to the knowledge we seek—given the nature of our participants. If we can feel comfortable with the answers to the questions on obtaining sensitive information, then the chances are that the organization of the items will take care of itself. Don't be afraid to innovate, but have a good reason for doing something in an unusual way if the traditional way would serve equally well.

CHAPTER 8

957 Days: Follow-up Interviews and Other Data Gathering Efforts

Overview

This chapter continues to explore the life situation of one participant in the BRI Protective Services Project. After the initial research interview of the participant (Chapter 7), there were several other follow-up interviews spread over the remaining year (at three months, six months, and twelve months from the anniversary date). In addition, interviews were conducted with a collateral, that is, a person who knew the participant well.

The research interviewer provided observations and made judgments about the participant's behavior and situation after each interview. The social worker, on the experimental cases only, made retrospective ratings of the participant during the one year of service. If the participant died during this year, a terminal interview was conducted with the collateral.

After the project year, an interview was held with the person who originally referred the case to BRI for an independent look at events during this period of time. In all, fourteen or fifteen contacts were made during the one year, all seeking to understand the stream of events, feelings, and ideas that constituted the life of this one participant. Again, I will use the Technical Narrative format.

Technical Narrative Section

Introduction
The Initial Collateral Interview (Technical Note 8.1)
The Third-Month Follow-up Interview: A Look at the Observer's Ratings (8.2)
The Six-Month Follow-up Interview: Questions on Relocation (8.3)
The One-Year Participant Interview: On Comparative Questions (8.4)

The Terminal Interview With the Collateral (8.5)
Referrral Agency Follow-up Interview at the End of the Project Year: Identifying
    the Service Experiences of Control Participants (8.6)
Clinical Rating Scales (8.7)
Two-Year Through Five-Year Follow-up Reviews (8.8)

The Technical Narrative

INTRODUCTION

In about an hour and a half, the interviewer asked the participant some 183 items, as well as making numerous observations that would be recorded on a research interviewer's rating form (see pages 183–200). We received structured impressions from sets of questions that composed the variables in our study. And we obtained many observations on how Mrs. Edwards uniquely viewed the world. In her case in particular, we observed a major discrepancy: she proclaimed how miserable she was and how much she wanted to receive proper care in some other location (especially to get away from the rough ministrations of her son, whom she saw as inflicting more pain than help), but she also denied these statements and stated that she wanted to remain just as she was (although this latter statement may have been in part out of fear of her son's reactions). So what had we really learned from this interview?

THE INITIAL COLLATERAL INTERVIEW

One approach to checking the accuracy of the participant's view of her world is to obtain some judgments from a person close to the participant on a parallel set of questions. Presumably, we might be able to locate a *collateral,* * that is, a close relative or friend who knew the situation of the participant, regardless of his or her ability or desire to make constructive changes in that situation. Recall that a number of questions asked of the participant could have led to the indication that some one knew about his or her situation. Mrs. Edwards, for example, indicated that her neighbor, a Mrs. Young, knew about her and was helping in various ways. This was a good lead, but it was, in Mrs. Edwards's case, augmented by the fact that the referring agency—the health department of the city—had indicated that Mrs. Young was a dependable person whom the city public-health nurse could ask for assistance as needed.

How well can a neighbor or a friend know what life is like for an elderly person showing signs of confusion? How valid is the information derived from such a source? Clearly, the quality of the information depends on the specific collateral and how closely he or she is to the participant. Mrs. Young was a *natural helping person:* she provided friendly assistance to several elderly people on the block for the enjoyment of being helpful, with no thought of reward and without any professional training (cf. Collins and Pancoast, 1976). She was, according to the observation of the research interviewer, an intelligent and kindly woman who was concerned especially about Mrs. Edwards's health. So she visited frequently, bringing a bit of food one time and some flowers another, as well

---

* This discussion of the *initial collateral interview* constitutes Technical Note 8.1.

as doing the shopping. She was a careful observer and, more than many collaterals, turned out to offer some insight into Mrs. Edwards's situation.

Instead of repeating the entire questionnaire, which followed the order of the participant interview, except for changes of wording to indicate an external observer's views, I'll select a few illustrative questions parallel to those asked of Mrs. Edwards. In addition, there were questions asked in order to characterize the collateral person. For example, the interview began with careful explanations of how the collateral had been selected (for instance, Mrs. Edwards had mentioned Mrs. Young's helpfulness on many occasions) and what the purpose of the interview was (a study of the attitudes and activities of older persons in the Greater Cleveland area, conducted by Associates in Gerontology). (Again cards and brochures were left with the collaterals.) Then Mrs. Young was asked

1. *First, can you tell me what is your relationship to Mrs. Edwards?* (or an alternative form: *Am I correct in saying that you are Mrs. Edwards's closest friend and neighbor?*) Mrs. Young replied that she didn't know if Mrs. Edwards had any other friend, so she supposed that she was her closest friend.
2. *How long have you known Mrs. Edwards?* (or, in the case of relatives, interviewers asked how long they had known the participant well). Mrs. Young answered, "for about fifteen years."

Then the questions turned on health concerns, paralleling the ones asked of Mrs. Edwards. Some interesting differences emerged. For example:

6. *During the past month, did any health problem or ailment keep Mrs. Edwards from doing the things she usually does around the house?* Mrs. Edwards had said yes to this item, whereas Mrs. Young said that she didn't know. The house was clean, but she (Mrs. Young) never saw Mrs. Edwards or anyone else cleaning it. But it did get done, so Mrs. Edwards must be doing it.

Mrs. Young confirmed the set of questions about Mrs. Edwards's limitations in getting around, but she added the observation that Mrs. Edwards used a broom to steady herself in walking around the house. She added information that Mrs. Edwards had not given, such as the fact of a hospitalization about two years before. Mrs. Young thought that Mrs. Edwards had been failing in her health since that time, but especially in the past few months. This observation confirmed the range of problems that Mrs. Edwards had mentioned in her interview.

Concerning memory, Mrs. Young marveled at Mrs. Edwards's memory, especially about stories from her childhood. However, Mrs. Edwards had asked Mrs. Young to help her find some lost items; she couldn't remember where she had put them, and Mrs. Young doubted whether she had ever had them in the first place. This information confirmed a suspicion that the interviewer had about Mrs. Edwards's mental state, which was expressed in the interviewer's rating forms. These ratings were, by instruction, the product of all the information available to the interviewer: what the participant and the collateral said and the interviewer's own observations. It also came out that Mrs. Young had called the city doctor for Mrs. Edwards two weeks before, and that he had come out and had given her some medicine. The information further appeared to confirm Mrs. Edwards's short-term memory loss.

The interview then turned to questions about Mrs. Edwards's contentment

204

and her sources of concern. Mrs. Young thought that the major problem was money. For example, Mrs. Edwards used to have a hairdresser come in to fix her hair, but she couldn't do that anymore because almost all of her money that month had gone to pay the taxes, and there was little left over for food, especially when her son had returned home unexpectedly, and without contributing to the household finances.

The interviewer asked some questions that led to a discussion about the son, and Mrs. Young was very guarded in her answers. She hadn't known about him until he showed up one day. There was a mystery about him, and she surmised that perhaps he was an adopted son and had been away in prison or in a mental hospital, but Mrs. Edwards had not said much about him. The interviewer did not ask directly about whether he was in any way abusing his mother; this was not a question on the schedule, although, in retrospect, it should have been a part of the questionnaire. The distinction between research and practice had to be maintained if we were to obtain standardized information, even though the interviewers—most of them having had some clinical experience—might have liked to pursue these interesting leads.

The predominant focus of Mrs. Young's comments was Mrs. Edwards's need of some help to maintain herself in her home. Mrs. Young said she came in every day and did some cooking or shopping—this was more frequently then Mrs. Edwards or the referring agency had reported—but she had her own family and several aged aunts to look after as well, and the demands that Mrs. Edwards was making were becoming burdensome for Mrs. Young, even though she wanted to help. This comment on burdensomeness led nicely into a set of distinctive questions asked of the collateral that became a major variable: *collateral stress* (see Table 4.1). Let's see how Mrs. Young responded to these items:

58. *Have you found that helping Mrs. Edwards has been a physical strain on you?* Mrs. Young admitted that it had been some strain, and that she was not feeling very well herself at the moment.

62. *Have you found that helping Mrs. Edwards with financial matters has ever constituted a financial burden for you?* Mrs. Young clarified that she never spent any of her own money on Mrs. Edwards's food, and that her neighbor was very careful to pay her.

66. *Have you ever found that helping Mrs. Edwards has caused a fuss or arguments in your family, or about family matters?* Mrs. Young said that her husband didn't really mind, but he couldn't understand how Mrs. Edwards could be so dependent on Mrs. Young and at the same time complain to other neighbors (so the reports had it) that the Young's catalpa tree leaves cluttered up her yard. The interviewer probed for the degree of family argument caused, and Mrs. Young said that it was really minimal.

70. *Have you ever found that helping Mrs. Edwards has presented problems in your own social life, such as getting together with your own friends or leading your own life?* Mrs. Young paused and said that she hadn't thought about it in that way, but that, yes, she had had to make a number of changes in what she might prefer to do in order to help Mrs. Edwards.

126. *Have you found that helping Mrs. Edwards has ever caused you to become depressed or very unhappy, or that you just couldn't put her problems out of your mind?* Mrs. Young didn't think this had ever occurred.

205

148. *Have you found that helping Mrs. Edwards has ever caused you to lose sleep or have other difficulties in eating, or other health problems?* Heavens, no, replied Mrs. Young.

In general, the information provided by the collateral paralleled quite closely the information that the participant had given, thus giving us greater confidence in the elderly person's responses.

THE THIRD-MONTH FOLLOW-UP INTERVIEW: A LOOK AT THE OBSERVER'S RATINGS

As described in Chapter 6, after the participant was first interviewed by the research team member, he or she was randomly assigned to an experimental or control group. The referring agency was informed of this assignment so that, in the case of the control subjects, the agency could continue to provide whatever service it ordinarily provided and, in the case of the experimental subjects, some agreement was reached about the provision of services for the duration of one year—the length of time that each participant was in the study. In some cases, such as income-maintenance agencies, the financial support of the elderly person continued. In the case of social service agencies, ordinarily the Associates in Gerontology worker took over the direction of the case. At the end of the project year, the research interviewer questioned the referring agency about what services they had provided, or what they knew other agencies had provided.*

It would have been ideal to have a continual flow of information about each participant in the study, as in a single-system design, but it would have been prohibitively expensive to obtain that amount of information on 164 subjects. So a research design was constructed that included a reinterview of the participants and the collaterals at three additional points in time: three months, six months, and one year after the first interview. (However, it was later decided that going back to the collaterals that frequently might be counterproductive, and so the decision was made to have only six-month and one-year reinterviews of the collaterals. The exception to this rule was when a participant in the study died between the initial interview and the three-month follow-up; in such cases, the collateral was seen in a terminal interview, which is further described on page 214.)

In general, the three-month and six-month follow-up interviews were much more brief than the initial and one-year interviews. The main purpose was to obtain information on survival and relocation, especially institutionalization. Short-form sets of questions were used in the three-month and six-month follow-ups, and some validity and reliability checks were also made with these interim follow-ups. If demographic information had not been obtained in the initial interview, the interviewers were instructed to try again to obtain it.

In the three-month interview and thereafter, we put all of the short-form items on the major variables together on a single page. This arrangement enabled the interviewer to focus on relating to the participant rather than flipping through the pages of a questionnaire. For each follow-up interview, a new training session

---

* This discussion of the *observer's ratings* constitutes Technical Note 8.2.

was held, as it had been before the initial interview. However, there was no turnover of interviewers, and so over the year, they became quite conversant with the questions, including the variations in the follow-up series. Figure 5.1 presents the summary page of short-form items.

The follow-up interview was somewhat different from the initial interview. Ten days before the follow-up interview was due, an intent-to-interview form was sent to the social worker involved in the experimental cases, providing her or him with the opportunity to indicate whether an interview was contraindicated. This option was exercised fewer than a half-dozen times during the two years of the project. When a participant was identified as not approachable for an interview, the interviewing supervisor met with the service director to discuss the case and to reach a decision. Failing to agree, they would present the case to the project director, who had the final decision. I must report that Dr. Blenkner gave the service director a very hard time trying to justify the research contraindication, but she uniformly agreed not to send the interviewer in when there was any substantial evidence. It was a workable system, and fortunately, the service workers were comfortable with the research interviewers' ability not to overtax the participants with questions.

Five days before the scheduled interview date, the referring agency was called to check on the most current address of the participant—especially the control participants, with whom we had no direct contact for months at a time. (We did have a "death watch" assignment, in which someone went over the obituaries in the local newspapers to spot any references to people in our project.) At the same time, we asked the referring agencies for some basic information about whether they had been actively involved in that case in the interim period.

One or two days before the follow-up interview was due, the research interviewer called the project social worker on the experimental cases in order to clear a time for the proposed interview when the social worker was not planning to see the participant at the same time. This is a very important point that bears clarifying. The basic rule was to separate research from service, so that the research interviews would be as comparable as possible for the experimental and the control groups. But for reasons of efficiency, it was decided that interviewers could make contact with social workers for the following reasons: (1) to clear a time for a follow-up interview—no discussion of the case was to take place; (2) to use the master address file in the AIG office, as a way of providing central and up-to-date information about all participants; no information other than address and phone number was available; (3) to hear the decision on cases in which the social workers had recommended that no research interview take place; only the outcome of the process was given to interviewers; and (4) to handle emergency situations if an interviewer discovered that the participant was in a dangerous condition; even here, the interviewer was to contact the interviewing supervisor, who notified the service worker on the case. Thus, to the best of our ability, and at the price of some frustrated workers and interviewers who wanted to clarify why they had or had not done something with regard to a given situation, we kept the research portion separated from the service component. Only Dr. Blenkner got full reports from both sides. She occasionally grinned like a cheshire cat because she knew both sides of a story, but she was absolutely silent. (At least, she never told me about the service side of cases unless it related to one of the conditions listed above.)

207

The office staff gave each interviewer a five-week calendar of events at the beginning of each month so that plans might be made for conducting the follow-ups. Special instructions were occasionally given, such as asking the interviewer to get additional demographic information. These instructions were indicated on the *observer schedule* for the participant. I would like to illustrate what this schedule looked like, so that when data from it are being discussed, the reader will have a sense of its organization. The three-month observer schedule was typical. It began with a statement of purpose:

> The purpose of this schedule is to provide the Research Interviewer (RI) with the opportunity to make judgments about the participant and the general interview situation, and to record special information and instructions for reference when reinterviewing.

The interview identification was given on the face sheet, along with the time of the interview. Notes were made on the follow-up preparation given to the participant by the interviewer. For example, in the case of Mrs. Edwards, the interviewer said he would be back to visit again in three months, to which Mrs. Edwards replied, "Why wait so long?" Notes were also made on the best time to see this participant and the best approach to take. Because Mrs. Edwards was open—too open—to visitors, the interviewer noted that there would very likely be no problem. (In fact, Mrs. Edwards did not remember the interviewer's initial visit when he returned in three months.) Also on the face sheet was an indication of the demographic information that the interviewer had not obtained the last time and so was directed to try again to get. This page was filled in after the first interview and was given to the interviewer with others five weeks before the reinterview was due, so that she or he could plan the follow-up appropriately.

The main body of the observer's rating schedule followed. The three-month schedule described here is much like all the other observer rating forms. First, a thumbnail sketch of the participant was given—an individualizing description of the person physically, psychologically, and socially. This sketch could include such matters as the person's physical appearance, dress, grooming, and facial expression. Also, the participant's gait, physical handicaps, mannerisms, and gestures might be described, so as to capture the overall impression of this individual. For example, for Mrs. Edwards's three-month interview, the interviewer wrote the following observations—in sentence fragments:

> Gray hair covered with net. Pallid. Dresed neatly in plain bathrobe (at 10:30 in the morning), with sweater under robe. She wore socks and floppy bedroom slippers. Looked clean and neat. Walks slowly, usually grasping for support. Complained of dizziness and weakness that were making it difficult for her to get around. Spoke with firmness, and in a complaining manner. No sense of humor about her. Complained about neighbors—"hillbillies"—and is preoccupied with her problems. Said her niece had "let her down" and that her son had gone away again.

The observer schedule also asked for a statement about the rapport of the interviewer with the participant. For Mrs. Edwards, the interviewer noted that his rapport had been fair. Mrs. Edwards had expressed suspicion about the questions that the interviewer was asking and had complained that many people came to ask questions, but no one came to help.

The overall reliability of the answers was noted as fair. This included how well the participant understood the questions and cooperated in answering. Another question asked about other distractions arising during the interview that might invalidate the information obtained. None were present, unlike at the initial interview. There were no other people present, nor was there a language problem.

Next, the interviewer was asked to describe the physical environment, including the setting in which the interview had taken place and a description of the neighborhood. This was a global description, because later on, there was a set of specific questions on the safety, sanitation, and decency of the dwelling. The description was not much changed from the first interview time (described at the beginning of Chapter 7).

The next long section was on ratings of the participant's living conditions. For such items as plumbing, washing, and bathing facilities; cooking and refrigeration; living space; furnishings; stairs and floors and rugs; lighting and ventilation; heating and cooking facilities; and the presence of litter, the interviewer was to rate the degree of safety, sanitation, and decency from very positive to very negative, and if negative, the interviewer was to indicate what aspects made it so. In Mrs. Edwards's case, all of these facilities were considered safe by the interviewer except for the cooking and refrigeration question, which he recorded as "unsafe" and indicated why: Mrs. Edwards did not have a working refrigerator. She also had a space heater, but it was considered safe by the interviewer, assuming that she could use it properly (an assumption made in regard to any electrical equipment she had in her home).

Another item inquired about the upkeep of the residence, in terms of the energy required of the participant. The interviewer admitted that he did not know who did the housework. Mrs. Edwards said that she did it but shouldn't. (In fact, it turned out that the social worker and the project staff had been doing it.) Another item concerned the accessibility of other persons to the participant, or the participant's accessibility to them. This item was marked unsafe on the grounds that Mrs. Edwards would require an automobile ride to get to the doctor's office; a domestic would have to take a bus ride and probably a transfer to get to her home.

The next set of questions contained a checklist of items on the inside and outside structural features. No problems were noted, except for the unusual location of the house, almost in the rear of the neighbor's house. The neighborhood was not pleasant because of the noise and fumes from the nearby factories. But there were no obvious problems in the house itself. Thus the overall rating of the house was "sound" (as contrasted with "dilapidated," "deteriorating," or "other"). The definitions were provided from reports in other studies so that the participants' homes in this study could be compared to those in other locations (cf. Beyer, 1961).

The most important part of the observer schedule was a set of questions related directly to the major variables of the study. The interviewers were asked to use observations and knowledge from other sources, as well as what the participant said, in making judgments on the following questions (notice the short operational definitions built into each item):

48. *Contentment-happiness-comfort. Rate the participant's general feeling of satisfaction with what he has, including physical health, physical comfort, finances, interpersonal relations, and so on (as compared to what he wants) in his present life. Also look for a state of ease in mind about significant life matters, and general pleasure in life. Do not rate on the basis of the participant's physical capacity.*

The interviewer could select a point on a 5-point (Likert-type) scale from "very discontented" through "mixed" to "very contented," or "other" or "don't know." Similar questions were asked about concrete assistance; interested parties; mental functioning (orientation); physical functioning; and signs and symptoms of affective and behavioral disorders. Each had a scale with anchoring points related to its own content, such as mental functioning (orientation):

1. Very disoriented and confused.
2. Disoriented and confused.
3. Mixed.
4. Clear.
5. Very clear.
6. Other (specify).
9. Don't know.

If "other" was specified, the interviewer attempted to describe why he or she had chosen that answer. For example, although what the participant said was clear, it didn't make any sense because she was talking about people who it seemed were no longer alive. But not knowing the full details of a participant's life, the interviewer couldn't make a judgment.

THE SIX-MONTH FOLLOW-UP INTERVIEW: QUESTIONS ON RELOCATION

Six months after her admission to the Protective Services Project, Mrs. Edwards had another interview with the same person who had called on her twice before.* Mrs. Edwards didn't remember the interviewer from before but allowed him into the house. A woman identified as "my housekeeper" was talking with Mrs. Edwards, obtaining a shopping list from her. They finished this discussion and the housekeeper left; Mrs. Edwards turned to the interviewer and made a racist remark ("You have to talk very slowly to those people"—the housekeeper was black). The interviewer decided this was not the time to discuss racism and turned directly to the questionnaire. The interviewer's personal values have to be controlled in the interviewing context.

The six-month interview is like the three-month one, beginning with health questions. Mrs. Edwards complained of being terrible this morning. Her right hand and arm were paralyzed. (During the interview, Mrs. Edwards sat down at her kitchen table and proceeded to eat with her right hand and arm.) She

---

* This discussion of *questions on relocation* constitutes Technical Note 8.3.

was teary-eyed as she talked of the recent deaths of some relatives and friends, but she couldn't remember their names.

Mrs. Edwards indicated that she was very dizzy, almost every day. But in response to the question about whether she was healthy enough to go outdoors for a long walk, she answered in the affirmative—with her "nurse" helping her because she got dizzy suddenly. (The interviewer presumed that this "nurse" was also the housekeeper, and knowing that this was a service case, he further presumed that this person was actually a home aide employed by the AIG.)

I won't repeat the whole interview, as no new questions were asked. Mrs. Edwards seemed more confused or forgetful than before. She knew that she was receiving some help from some agency in the community, but she couldn't remember its name. She thought she was receiving regular visits from a nurse, but she wasn't sure that the person was really a nurse—and she didn't like her anyway because she was too sassy to Mrs. Edwards, always nagging her to do this and do that. Then she leaned over and said, confidentially, that the nurse purposely spilled water on Mrs. Edwards. The interviewer decided not to follow up on that remark either.

The interviewer skipped over some new questions about relocations that might have occurred between the three- and six-month follow-up interviews, as Mrs. Edwards was obviously in the same residence as before. But let me review this set of questions because there were many moves among the other participants in the study:

36. *Have you been living here all the time for the past three months? or have you been on a visit or at a hospital or anything like that?*
37. (If moved, ask) *Where did you go?*
38. *Was it a short visit, or did you plan to move permanently, or what?*
39. *Has anyone else come to live with you here?*
40. (If at a new address, ask) *How long have you lived here?*
41. *Where were you before you came here?* (This question and its probe were an attempt to get all of the steps of the relocation prior to the present residence.)
42. *How did you come to move here? Why did you move from your other home?*

Several questions asked about the name and location of this current residence, items that were associated with the person's cognitive orientation rather than with the relocation itself.

43. (If the participant is in an institution or other than his or her own home, ask) *How long will you be staying here?*
44. *Did you have a choice about coming here?* (This issue of choice has turned out to be very important in the literature on relocation shock.)
45. *Who was involved in your move here?* (The answers to this question involved a long list of possible helpers: relatives, friends, and helping professionals.)
47. *How do you like this new place as compared to the last place you lived at?*

Then the interview continued, repeating the same questions asked in earlier interviews. A six-month observer-rating schedule was completed after this interview that was very similar to the three-month one described above.

211

THE ONE-YEAR PARTICIPANT INTERVIEW: ON COMPARATIVE QUESTIONS

In some ways, the most critical interview of all was the final one because the initial sample had been randomly assigned to experimental and control groups, an assignment that should have made their initial interviews statistically comparable. The final interview came after the experimental group had received a planfully intensive service program, whereas the control group had received whatever services the community ordinarily offered, which generally were not very many.

The one-year participant interview was in many ways like the earlier ones.* It began with questions about current health:

> 1. *How is your health now, in general?* Mrs. Edwards reported that she had fallen yesterday and was very sick today. She had called her pastor this morning, but he hadn't called back yet.

But a new form of question was also asked, a comparative question that attempted to allow the participant an opinion on the very issues that the researchers were going to make judgments on, based on comparing answers on identical questions in the initial and final interviews. So Mrs. Edwards was asked:

> 3. *In the past month, did you tire more easily than you used to a year ago?* This question took Mrs. Edwards by surprise, and the best answer she could give was "I think so."

The interviewer expressed his opinion, in a marginal note, that this seemed to be an answer given simply because the question was asked; it may not have been an answer on which Mrs. Edwards felt firm and clear. Indeed, the next question, on whether the participant recognized the interviewer at any time during the interview as having been there before (a new mental status item), indicated that Mrs. Edwards did not remember clearly, and thus it offered some support to the question of whether such comparative responses are valid (although the answer was recorded as given and was processed). How many other participants were as vague or uncertain in their comparative responses is a matter of conjecture; they may simply have been giving an opinion *now* about how the past compared with the present. In this event, the answers were not comparative at all; they were simply responses to a different kind of current attitude question and in this guise were fully valid.

> 5. *How is your memory now as compared with October of last year when I first met you? Would you say that you can remember better now than you used to a year ago, or as well as you used to, or less well? or what?* To this question, Mrs. Edwards replied that her memory was better. However, the interviewer reported that she said in passing that she certainly hoped this was the case. Again, the comparative questions may not have accurately tested the comparison so much as the *current attitude* about the comparative issue.

---

* This discussion on the *final interview* (the one-year interview) constitutes Technical Note 8.4.

I will skip now to the another comparative question, passing familiar items about the participant's state of health and mind and the like (questions we discussed on the initial interview schedule):

14. *Looking back to October a year ago when I first saw you, would you say that you are more happy or less happy now than you were then?* Mrs. Edwards had no trouble indicating that she was less happy and could enumerate the reasons: particularly because of the deaths of relatives and friends that had occurred in this time period.

Was this a true comparative response or simply another attitude about happiness? It is impossible to say with certainty, and so with concerns like these, the research staff decided to treat the comparative questions as descriptions, not as true comparisons in the sense of providing validation for the statistically compared responses that the computer was able to generate.

Another set of questions was new in the final interview schedule and reflected the researcher's attempt to get direct information from participants regarding what services they had received in the past year. Some questions were asked about nurses and social workers, and what they had done that had been helpful to the participant—or things they had done that had made matters worse. And in the experimental cases only, the participant was asked whether he or she liked the social worker. Mrs. Edwards said that she did not get any nursing care, but she did recognize that a social worker saw her regularly. She could not name the organization that the social worker was from. This social worker was described as helping a great deal, specifically in taking Mrs. Edwards to the doctor. Mrs. Edwards was then asked:

40. *Do you like your caseworker?* She replied, "I like them all."

This answer suggests that she was unable to distinguish among the various service workers who were on the service team: the social worker, the director of home aides, the home aide assigned to work with Mrs. Edwards, and an assistant to the social worker who occasionally walked with Mrs. Edwards and drove her to the doctor's office.

On the many questions concerning what help Mrs. Edwards got around the house or in the community, she mentioned the names of the social worker and of her pastor. She did not mention the name of the helpful neighbor whom we knew from the reports of the home aide to be a frequent and helpful visitor, compared with the pastor. But such was the perception of the participant in the study. Whether the answer was "true" or not was not the point; it was the client's response to the standard question, and it was that response that became part of the data, not the various inferences that the interviewer and the researchers back at the office made from the whole body of responses. These other inconsistencies were picked up, to some degree, in other ways, but I wanted to call this situation clearly to the attention of the readers, lest they think that the printed word is the final word.

Again, relocation items were asked, but as Mrs. Edwards had not moved, they were not relevant, and the interviewer skipped over them. The final interview did call for asking once again the intelligence test questions and the questions on orientation to person, time, and place. Interestingly, Mrs. Edwards answered nearly as well one year later as she had the first time. The street directions she gave to the interviewer likewise remained accurate.

At the conclusion of the interview, the interviewer told Mrs. Edwards that he would not be coming to see her anymore, and that he wished her well in the future. Mrs. Edwards, who didn't really remember that he had been there before, was taken by this announcement and burst into tears. The interviewer expressed sadness at leaving and at being the cause of her tears, but Mrs. Edwards noted that she had lost "fourteen dear friends" lately and was crying because so many of her friends were leaving her. The interviewer remained with her until she had stopped crying, and then he left.

THE TERMINAL INTERVIEW WITH THE COLLATERAL

For persons of the age range of the participants in this project, death was always a possibility—indeed, a predictable expectation. When a death occurred, the research interviewer was notified to conduct a terminal interview with that participant's collateral* after a respectable period of time (about two weeks). We didn't want to intrude on the mourning process, if, in fact, the collateral was someone closely attached to the participant; many were not. But we did want to ask some important questions about the participant's last month of life and about the nature of his or her death while the details were still relatively fresh in the mind of the collateral.

The interviewers approached this task with some trepidation, groundless as it turned out. People were quite willing to share their memories of the deceased and to report whatever they could about that person's life and death. The questions were the familiar ones, items on contentment, concrete assistance, and the like (including collateral stress), rephrased to fit the conditions of the participant's death.

Some new items involved the collateral's feelings about whether everything was done that could have been done to aid the participant in making his or her life easier. This question led to others about who was assisting, including helping professionals of all sorts. Some exploratory items were asked about the collateral's reaction to the participant's death, where it might best have taken place (home or elsewhere), and what the dying person might have wanted from his or her friends and relatives at this time. As always, the interviewer concluded by thanking the collateral for his or her contributions to this study.

REFERRAL AGENCY FOLLOW-UP INTERVIEW AT END OF PROJECT YEAR: IDENTIFYING THE SERVICE EXPERIENCES OF CONTROL PARTICIPANTS

As described previously, all participants in the Protective Services Project were referred by thirteen participating agencies that typically served the aged in one capacity or another. The plan was to have the research team work with persons randomly selected for the experimental program for one year. Then these persons

---

* This discussion of *terminal interviews* constitutes Technical Note 8.5.

were to be transferred to the regular staff of the Benjamin Rose Institute to provide a continuity of services. Persons who fell into the control group would stay with the referring agency and whatever service it offered.* It was important to learn about the extent to which services were offered to the experimental and the control participants by the referring agencies and other health and welfare units during the experimental year because these services could be a confounding factor. If a control participant received extensive services from other agencies in Cleveland, then the enriched program offered by the research project team would not be distinctively different, and hence one would not be able to say what had caused the results in the study. (See also Chapter 9.)

So it was necessary to go back to the referring agency and to inquire what, if anything, it had done for the client during the project year, and whether it knew of any services that other agencies had provided. Let me illustrate this referral-agency follow-up interview with a discussion that the research interviewer had with the city health nurse who had referred Mrs. Edwards's case originally.

The cover sheet of this schedule listed the participant's name, the date of her registration in the project, and information on the referring person and agency, including whether that agency was actively involved in the case at the third-month, sixth-month, and one-year intervals. In Mrs. Edwards's case, the city health department was active throughout the year. Here is the first question asked about what the agency actually did for the participant:

> 33. *According to our records, this case was registered in the AIG project on 10–26–64. What disposition did your agency make on this case after it was registered with AIG? Was the case closed at any time, or was your agency active part or all of the project year?* The city nurse, Mrs. Razandi, who had referred the case, told the interviewer that Mrs. Edwards occasionally called the city doctor herself and received some advice, but that no in-person contacts had been made. Also, the nurse herself had not seen Mrs. Edwards except at two times near the beginning of the project, when she accompanied the team social worker to acquaint the participant with her new worker. Thus, although the case remained officially open, little service had actually been provided. The nurse indicated that she had seen Mrs. Edwards after the conclusion of the project year to get reacquainted and to check out her medical needs.

The interview schedule also asked how many other agencies were named by the referral person during this part of the discussion. No other agencies were named. This same point was then covered directly in the next question:

> 37. *Did you or any other member of your agency refer the participant for service to agencies other than AIG during the one year period of registration in the AIG project?* The city nurse said no. Had she said yes, the interviewer would have probed which agencies were involved.

The interview schedule listed the thirteen cooperating agencies—as they were the most likely to be providing services to the elderly—and had space for others as well. The probe would have asked: *What is the primary service of this agency?*—

* This discussion of the *referral agency follow-up interview* constitutes Technical Note 8.6.

if the function were not obvious. The next question explored the details of the services that the referring agency had offered:

Did you or a member of your staff provide, or did your agency pay for, any of the following services for the participant during the one year of registration in the AIG project?

41. *Counseling or casework?* The city nurse had not offered these services to Mrs. Edwards, although she was qualified to provide these.

42., 43., 44. *Medical services?* The city nurse indicated that the city physician had talked with Mrs. Edwards by phone two times, although he had never examined or treated her in-person, nor had the agency received medical consultation from some other agency. The interviewer indicated that the two phone calls to the doctor were contacts with a physician on the grounds that some aid was given for symptomatic relief.

45., 46., 47. *Psychiatric services?* The city nurse noted that none had been offered to Mrs. Edwards.

48., 49. *Legal services?* There had been a sanitary violation during the year, in which Mrs. Edwards had let some garbage accumulate in the back yard. A neighbor had called the city nurse, who had referred the case to the city prosecutor, and so the nurse may have had indirect contact with Mrs. Edwards at that point. The interviewer interpreted this as a provision of legal services in that the nurse had been instrumental in the prosecutor's being advised.

The next group of questions concerned financial services of several types. *Had the city nurse or members of her agency provided or paid for:*

50. *Advising or helping the participant to utilize the financial resources he has or that are available to him?* The response was no, but the interviewer was directed to clarify what this meant because some services may have been offered but not actually delivered because of the participant's reactions. In the case of Mrs. Edwards, aid on financial resources had not ever been offered.

51., 52., 53., and 54. These questions asked whether the agency had offered specific kinds of financial aid: social security, public assistance, or other financial aid. None of these were services provided by the agency, so the questions were marked "not relevant."

The next group of questions concerned guardianship:

55. *To your knowledge, does Mrs. Edwards have a guardian?* The city nurse said no, and the interviewer was directed to skip the next related questions regarding who paid for the provision of guardianship, and who that guardian was.

Next, the interviewer asked about *representative payees,* that is, persons who could receive Mrs. Edwards's social security check on her behalf. Although the city nurse knew that Mrs. Edwards was getting social security, she did not know of any representative payee, nor did her agency have anything to do with this arrangement.

The interviewer than asked whether the participant had received homemaker or home aide services provided by, or paid for by, the referring agency. The answer was no.

Another group of questions in this section concerned nursing services. Here, the city nurse indicated that Mrs. Edwards had received direct professional nursing services and evaluation by a nurse of the care needed by the participant. (No nursing consultation was needed, of course, by the city nurse.)

A long set of questions on relocation was asked:

> *Did you or a member of your staff provide, or did your agency pay for, any of the following services for the participant during the one year of registration in the AIG project?*

66. *Arrangements and other services related to admission to a general hospital or a rehabilitation hospital?* The answer was no, thus making unnecessary questions about whether the participant had retained or given up her dwelling and possessions when in the hospital.

68., 69., 70., 71., 72., and 73. These questions asked about relocation to mental hospitals, other specialized medical facilities (like contagious disease hospitals), nursing homes, homes for the aged, boarding or foster homes, or simply a change of residence in the community. The answers were that services related to such relocations had not been offered to Mrs. Edwards during the project year.

A final question in this series asked: *Are there any other services the participant gets, which you or your staff provides, or which your agency pays for?* There were no other such services.

Next, the interviewer asked about the impact of the project on the participant and on the referring agency:

75. *In your opinion, what has been the effect on the participant, and her situation, of the casework and ancillary services provided by AIG?* The interviewer recorded the highest point on the 7-step scale: "extremely positive" (unconditionally and exceedingly beneficial). Her verbatim comments were recorded as well, to the effect that Mrs. Edwards was in better health than before; she was much more tidy and now she trusted some professional helping person, whereas before she had not. The city nurse also noted improvements in her emotional health.

77. *In your opinion, what has been the effect on you and your agency's work with the participant because of the casework and ancillary services provided by AIG?* To this question, the city nurse answered that there were positive effects (the second highest rating on the 7-point scale, indicating predominantly and substantially helpful effects, or effects that facilitated the agency's work). Her verbatim comments included the fact that AIG had alleviated work for the city nurse because she had received fewer calls from neighbors than she had in the past.

In order to study the effect of having interviewers asking questions on periodic occasions, we included the following item:

79. *In your opinion, what has been the effect on you, and your agency's work with the participant, of the AIG research interviewer?* The city nurse answered that

217

there had been no significant effect, positive or negative, because of the research interviews. (This answer fell at the midpoint on the 7-point scale.)

And with that question, the referral agency follow-up interview was concluded.

CLINICAL RATING SCALES

The project social workers were involved in making clinical judgments about the experimental participants at various times. In particular, at the end of the project year, the workers were asked to make ratings on seven scales for both the registration period and for the closing one year later.* The rationale for this plan was that the workers needed to have as much information available to them as possible when making their clinical judgments. These ratings could also be used as one test of the validity of the outcome scores obtained from the research interviews. We assumed that the kind of intensive and extensive knowledge that a worker came to have about a participant over a year's time was perhaps the best standard with which to compare the structured questionnaires of the interviewing staff. If the consistency was high, then there was more confidence that the information obtained on the control participants, for whom we had no social worker ratings, was also relatively valid.

The clinical scales were developed by Dr. Blenkner, working with her practice staff and associates. Test cases were developed from agency case records, and the project social workers were trained in using the scales to a level of interjudge reliability that was deemed acceptable. That is, the workers eventually learned to use these scales on test cases in such a way that they all arrived at highly similar judgments. Then, they used these scales and the anchoring definitions that evolved to rate their own individual cases. A manual was developed to clarify the meanings of the terms (Meyer and Blenkner, 1966).

Each scale was divided into eleven intervals, from extremely low to extremely high, as indicated below:

1. Physical competence:

1 2	3 4	5 6 7	8 9	10 11	12
Extremely low	Poor	Average	Good	Extremely high	Insufficient information

The social worker rated Mrs. Edwards as 4, the higher end of the poor range.

The other scales were similarly defined. I list them here and add the rating that the social worker gave to the initial status of Mrs. Edwards at the time she entered the project:

2. Mental competence (rating of 4).
3. Signs and symptoms of affective and behavioral disorders (rating of 4).

* This discussion of *clinical rating scales* constitutes Technical Note 8.7.

4. Environmental protection: social (rating of 4).
5. Environmental protection: physical (7, in the moderate range on high side).
6. Contentment (3, the low side of the low range).
7. Need for protective services (4, the low side of high need range). Note that the meaning of this item was scored in the same way as the other items. Thus, the "extremely low" category referred to functioning at a very low level that required protective services.

For the one-year rating, the social worker gave the following (I have arranged the two sets of ratings together for ease of comparison):

	RATING FOR INITIAL TIME	RATING FOR ONE-YEAR TIME
1. Physical competence	4	2
2. Mental competence	4	2
3. Signs and symptoms	4	2
4. Environmental protection: social	4	7
5. Environmental protection: physical	7	7
6. Contentment	3	2
7. Need for protective services	4	2

These scores indicate that the worker believed that the participant had got worse on physical and mental competence, as well as showing more signs of affective or behavioral disorders. Environmental protection (the social dimension) had improved, whereas the physical environment had remained about the same as far as protectiveness was concerned. Contentment had decreased, and the level of functioning deteriorated, thus calling for more protective services.

Having read the preceding descriptions of the research interviewer's schedules, the reader is in a position to judge whether there was any comparability between the social worker's views and the data emerging from the research instruments.

In addition, the social workers rated the collaterals on the degree of stress that they were under, as well as on their adequacy as protectors of the participant. These judgments were made for both the initial and the one-year periods. An 11-point scale was again used for physical, social, financial, family, psychological, and general stress. The adequacy of the collateral as a protector also involved an 11-point scale, plus a determination of the source of inadequacy—whether it was predominantly in the personality or in the circumstances of the collateral, or both.

TWO-YEAR THROUGH FIVE-YEAR FOLLOW-UP REVIEWS

It was very important to follow the progress of the participants in the project, both experimental and control, for a number of years after the project ended, so as to determine the immediate and delayed reactions. Interviewers spoke with the referral agency staff to obtain some basic information about survival, relocation, and the agency services being provided. I will present these follow-up reviews for Mrs. Edwards.*

The two-year follow-up inquired about the type of residence in which Mrs. Edwards was living at the time of her second anniversary of being admitted to the project; her residence was a nursing home. No details were provided here about what had caused this relocation; what was learned was only that the move had occurred between the ending of the project and the second-anniversary date. This was a permanent institutionalization. The referral agency was not active in the case any longer, as the nursing home gave full service. The Benjamin Rose Institute had been active, at least until the institutionalization occurred.

Essentially, this information told us that Mrs. Edwards was still alive but was living permanently in an institution. This concern with relocation is the focus of these brief follow-ups.

The three-year follow-up (like the four-year and fifth-year follow-ups) reviewed residential status, relocations during this time period, and related matters. It was with this follow-up inquiry that we learned that Mrs. Edwards had died at the nursing home. We were given no information about the cause of death or related matters.

Because of her death, some other questions were asked, in particular, the number of days she had survived since her registration in the project; Mrs. Edwards had survived 957 days. Also, we asked the number of days she had been permanently institutionalized before death: 562 days. The number of relocations was zero, after she had moved into the nursing home. These became important pieces of information in the overall study, as we shall see.

The four-year and five-year follow-ups were completed by office staff at the institute, who indicated that this participant had previously died.

Thus ended the data collection phase for one individual over a six-year period (the project year plus a five-year follow up). This large amount of information had to be categorized, reduced to a manageable size, and combined with the data on the other 163 individuals in the project, so that we could begin to describe what had happened.

* This discussion of *long-term follow-up reviews* constitutes Technical Note 8.8.

CHAPTER 9

The Analysis of Practice

Overview

This chapter provides a small window on the practices employed with an elderly client needing protective services. The purpose of this chapter is not to describe practice as such, but to consider the complex question of analyzing what services have been given by whom to the participant under what conditions and with what effect. In this way we can begin to link practice with measures of the effectiveness and efficiency of that practice. Two approaches are illustrated from the BRI Project, one quantitative and the other qualitative.

Technical Narrative Section

Introduction
A Social Worker's Case Record (Technical Note 9.1)
Categorical Recording of the Services Rendered (9.2)
Toward an Adequate Content Analysis of Practice (9.3)
A Practice–Wisdom Approach to Describing Services to Protective Clients (9.4)
Summary

The Technical Narrative

INTRODUCTION

One of the hidden benefits of working on a community-based research and demonstration project is that researchers and practitioners have to talk with each other. This is no small achievement. The literature is littered with laments by each party, saying that communication is nearly impossible with the other. In particular, researchers lambaste practitioners for their fuzzy, incomplete, and irregular presentations of the service component in a study. What is it that practitioners do that is to be evaluated?

However, close quarters mean that the realities of practice become clearer to researchers. In this chapter, I present a disguised set of perceptions and reflections about this service component as it related to one elderly gentleman who was a participant in our project, Mr. John Landis Emery. You will recall from being introduced to Mr. Emery (Chapter 1) that he was a seventy-six-year-old retired lawyer who was having difficulty in preparing suitable food for himself and keeping his apartment in livable condition. He was also very hard of hearing, which made communication difficult. Never wealthy, he apparently had retired from law practice to write novels that never were published. His life revolved around his writings. However, it was a precarious life, in part because of some serious medical conditions and in large measure because he forgot to take medication—or perhaps, because his limited financial resources caused him to stretch out the medicines he took; thus their effectiveness was diluted.

In the first section of this chapter, I present some disguised excerpts from the social worker's record of her observations about Mr. Emery. In the next section, I illustrate some of the information storage systems that evolved in the project to capture some aspects of this experimental practice. In the final section, I consider the larger issues of evaluating something as complex and protean as practice in a community setting.

A SOCIAL WORKER'S CASE RECORD ON MR. EMERY

The folder that contains the social worker's case record* was about three quarters of an inch thick. It began with a face sheet containing the basic information, including emergency numbers. Mr. Emery had been referred by the Metropolitan Housing Project; Mrs. Kohlberg was the project manager. He was divorced and had been living alone for most of his adult life. His present phone number and address, the amount of his rent, and the name of his landlord were given, as was the name of a person to be called in case of an emergency. There was also information on his religion and church affiliation, his former occupation,

---

* This discussion and presentation of *a case record* constitutes Technical Note 9.1.

and his educational background. Other spaces provided for information on the family: the name of his spouse and the names of his and his spouse's parents, and of their children. For Mr. Emery, much of this information was blank; we never learned much about this part of his background.

The face sheet continued with space for the names, relationships, and ages of other people in the household or interested relatives and friends—and whether they might be able to assume any responsibility for the participant. Mr. Emery had a nephew (Henry Rothman) and an old friend (David Siedel) listed in these spaces.

The face sheet ended with a list of other active agencies (none, in this case) and with a report from the social service exchange in Cleveland that indicated where Mr. Emery had been registered for service in previous times. He had received visiting-nurses care on one occasion, as well as being listed as living in the city's metropolitan housing project. All of these questions and answers are compactly squeezed onto a single sheet of paper so that once you know where to look for a given item, the mountain of bureaucratic information doesn't look so horrendous.

There next appeared an AIG project-registration form, which identified the participant, his location, and possible problems for research interviewers—such as deafness and some suspected confusion. A responsible party (or collateral) was also tentatively identified by the referral agency.

Now, let me present some brief disguised excerpts from this record, to give a flavor of what goes into service with the elderly protective individual:

> *Referral:* Mr. Emery was referred to the AIG project on 11–13–64, by Mrs. Kohlberg, manager of the metropolitan housing project. He had been a refined gentleman, well functioning although in a weak financial situation, when he first came to the housing project. But gradually, Mrs. Kohlberg noticed some signs of deterioration in his behavior. His appearance was decidedly less neat, and his apartment looked to be in great need of cleaning and tending. His deafness presented a barrier to his communicating with neighbors, and he was consequently alone a great deal of the time. He typed on an ancient manual machine, talking his words out loud as he typed, whether any one was present or not. Mrs. Kohlberg viewed him as rigidly independent at a time in his life when he was no longer able to care for himself and his property in a safe and sanitary manner.

> *Home Visit, 11–14–64:* Mrs. Kohlberg arranged to meet me at the office and to escort me to Mr. Emery's apartment, a small third-floor efficiency off a dark and dirty corridor in one of the cluster of buildings that makes up this old metropolitan housing complex. We knocked loudly on the door for several minutes before Mr. Emery answered it. He was dressed in a bathrobe and underwear—it was 11:30 A.M.—and had not shaved for a considerable period of time. He looked somewhat confused, trying to comprehend what we were doing there. Mrs. Kohlberg spoke very loudly, putting her face directly in front of his, and repeating her short sentences frequently. He answered that he understood and invited us into his apartment. He apologized for the mess, saying he hadn't the energy to do much cleaning these days.

> Papers were everywhere. It looked as if the breeze had blown his typed manuscript pages all about. He had been trying to put them back in order when we came in, but the opened door merely set up new breezes that added to the disorder. The little kitchenette was also a mess, with dirty dishes standing

on the counter and in the sink. A teapot was whistling—Mr. Emery didn't hear it. I called Mr. Emery's attention to it and turned off the burner. The pot looked as if it had been burned on previous occasions.

Mr. Emery cleared away a place for us to sit down. I could see all around the apartment from where I was sitting. The living room had several pieces of old furniture around the edges; a big table was placed in the center of the room and served as Mr. Emery's work space. Boxes, presumably of his other manuscripts, were nearby. There were no other books in sight. The living-room walls were bare except for some newspaper clippings taped up. On the bedroom walls were some pornographic photos, by the bed. There were some family photos on the dresser, as well. Mr. Emery had piles of clothing around the bedroom. Everything looked as if it were in a state of continuing chaos and disintegration.

Mrs. Kohlberg introduced me as a social worker from the Benjamin Rose Institute who would be able to help him with his problems. I quickly modified this statement, saying that I was from AIG and was interested in learning more from him about what he saw his problems to be, and then we could work together in solving them. Mrs. Kohlberg excused herself, and Mr. Emery and I continued to discuss his situation. It was slow going. I would lean over and shout some short message into Mr. Emery's ear, and he would repeat what I had said—or what he had heard me to say, which wasn't always the same thing. Then he would reflect on the question and answer it in his deep, sonorous voice. His careful answers suggested that he was in no way mentally confused.

There was a knock on the door, which Mr. Emery did not hear. I called his attention to it and opened the door to let in a neighbor and friend, David Siedel. He had overheard our conversation and wanted to know what the problem was. I introduced myself and Mr. Emery succinctly summarized what we had been talking about, adding off-handedly that Mr. Siedel knew more about him than he did, and that I should go to talk with Siedel sometime. I followed up on this suggestion, saying that I would like to talk more with Mr. Siedel sometime soon if that would be possible. But I hinted broadly that I wanted to finish my conversation with Mr. Emery, and Mr. Siedel said that he would be home all day—he had just wanted to make sure that there was no trouble with his friend, Mr. Emery.

After Mr. Siedel left, I commented that it must be reassuring to have such a thoughtful friend as Mr. Siedel nearby. Mr. Emery agreed but felt a little pressured by Siedel, who was always pushing him to do this, do that, when he really couldn't do anything much anymore. But Mr. Siedel was an old friend, and he (Mr. Emery) was being as patient as he could be. Siedel had problems, too, but never told Emery about them.

Social Work Services and Plans: After hearing about Mr. Emery's views on his current status and what problems he saw, I suggested that we continue our discussions after I had been able to look more carefully into the matters that he had mentioned. He raised some question about his veteran's benefits and some missing social-security checks that I would have to look into. But he also told me about his medical condition, and I wanted to consult with the clinic doctors about this—he agreed to permit me to talk with the doctors on his behalf.

I had some immediate concerns that I expressed to Mr. Emery. First, I was worried that he wasn't getting enough to eat, a circumstance that might contribute to his general weakness. I noticed that he didn't have a refrigerator and asked about this. He felt that one was not needed; he kept food in pans of cold water when he had to, and the electricity would be too expensive for him. He also commented that it "didn't really matter" whether he had good food or not, at his age. I said that we would talk further about that, but I was also concerned about his medical condition and felt that he might benefit from an updated examination. His response was vague; I felt that he was purposely evading the topic.

Impressions: My first impression was that Mr. Emery was malnourished. The symptoms I observed were dryness, itching, and scaling of the skin; broken, split fingernails; pain in the legs; and a general feeling of weakness and malaise. These could be due to vitamin deficiency and malnutrition. Also, Mr. Emery's deteriorated grooming might be related to malnutrition, which is known to hasten mental deterioration, and perhaps to his general lack of interest in such matters.

On the other hand, Mr. Emery appeared alert and oriented. He was certainly task-oriented, spending considerable time and energy on his writings. He had some supportive friends at the housing project and seemed reasonably content with his diminished life circumstances. Reminder: Clarify again with Mrs. Kohlberg the differences between BRI and AIG.

Collateral Interview, 11–15–64: David Siedel lived next door to Mr. Emery. Mr. Siedel was a widower who had lived in the housing project for over ten years and had known Mr. Emery for all of this time. Mr. Siedel was a joker. Everything was turned into a humorous remark, which made short visits very amusing, but I wondered whether in the long run, it would get wearing on the listener. And as Mr. Emery had hinted, Mr. Siedel was also very clear on what everyone ought to do about any situation. Some of his opinions were sensible, whereas others appeared idiosyncratic and rigid. However, it was clear that Mr. Siedel had taken a big-brother approach to Mr. Emery and had tried to watch out for his better interests, as far as Mr. Emery would let him. This amounted to some aid in shopping, an occasional evening together, and some rare walks (when Mr. Emery felt stronger).

Mr. Siedel was interested in the fact that Mr. Emery was going to receive some social-work services and wanted to know about the agency and the reason that Mr. Emery had been picked for these services. He was satisfied with my explanation and then went on to talk freely about his memory of Mr. Emery over the past ten years, and how in the last year or two, Mr. Emery had taken a turn for the worse—inspite of Mr. Siedel's efforts to prevent it. Mr. Siedel commented that Mr. Emery had always been a friendly person but had taken more interest in others (when he could hear them better) and had enjoyed more vigorous activities than lately, when his health had all but confined him to his apartment.

Mr. Siedel reported what he knew about Mr. Emery's background but could not add more to what the referring agency had already provided. Mr. Emery was reticent about his earlier life and, inspite of their good relationship, had not shared any of it with Mr. Siedel. In turn, Mr. Siedel did not talk much about himself with Mr. Emery (but broadly hinted that he, too, had serious problems and had experienced grave troubles in his life. I did not follow up on these leads, but perhaps I should do so, if Mr. Siedel proves to be of continuing aid to Mr. Emery).

Currently Mr. Siedel looks in on Mr. Emery at least once a day. He tries to suggest how to make Mr. Emery's little supply of money stretch further, but he admits not having much effect on how Mr. Emery spends his money. Mr. Siedel is worried about his friend, but for all his humor and his forceful, if not aggressive, manner, he feels stymied. Mr. Siedel raised one point that I had noticed but could not put my finger on, namely, the fact that Mr. Emery seemed to be anxious about something. Mr. Siedel couldn't figure out what it was; there were plenty of worrisome things in Mr. Emery's life, but this appeared to be apart from them. We agreed that Mr. Siedel would call me if anything untoward occurred, and that we would talk further on how I could be of aid in his efforts to help Mr. Emery.

Impressions of the Collateral: Mr. Siedel was a well-meaning, but somewhat ineffective, elderly friend of the participant. He made strong statements that Mr. Emery had enough sense to disregard, for the most part. Mr. Siedel's strongest contribution was his clear friendliness toward Mr. Emery, even in the recently diminishing communication between them because of Mr. Emery's hearing troubles.

Visit, 11–21–64: I knocked loudly and was lucky to catch Mr. Emery's attention right away. He recognized me, invited me in, and immediately sat down on his chair (sitting on a pile of papers). He wasn't feeling well and was upset about this. He looked very ill, and I persuaded him that it would be appropriate to have a doctor see him. I went back to the office and made a call to Dr. Sam Minor, who fortunately agreed to see him later that afternoon.

Dr. Minor's Examination, 11–21–64: I drove Mr. Emery to Dr. Minor's office and spoke with the doctor after the exam while Mr. Emery was getting dressed. Dr. Minor said that he couldn't get much of a medical history, either because Mr. Emery didn't know or because he was refusing to talk about it. Mr. Emery did discuss his eating habits, and Dr. Minor confirmed that he was suffering from malnutrition. However, he had also discovered several masses in Mr. Emery's stomach that Dr. Minor could not account for, and as a possible source of cancer, this condition might be another explanation for Mr. Emery's general weakness. Dr. Minor said that Mr. Emery must get more nutritious foods immediately, as his dehydrated condition was serious. He suggested placing Mr. Emery in a nursing home, recognizing that that would very likely mean his losing his apartment in the housing project. On the other hand, without rapidly improved nutrition, Mr. Emery was in serious danger because of his overall weakened condition.

I was greatly concerned about Dr. Minor's predictions of the course of Mr. Emery's malnutrition and began considering alternatives to nursing-home placement with Dr. Minor, who agreed that it wouldn't be necessary to institutionalize Mr. Emery if he got a better-balanced diet immediately.

Grocery Shopping with Mr. Emery, 11–21–64: On the way home, I stopped at the grocery store with Mr. Emery and asked him what his favorite foods were. He said he couldn't afford any foods now, and I said that I was going to get some for him. He was concerned about being indebted to me, and I explained that my agency had small amounts of funds for emergency purposes, which I considered his not having enough food in the house to be. Finally, he conceded and mentioned some fast-food products that I tactfully rejected as not being as nutritious as others he might like to try. I left him in the car—he felt too weak to walk around—and did some fast shopping by myself. I tried to imagine what foods he had been used to, which were also nutritious and inexpensive.

When we arrived at his apartment, I realized my mistake in purchasing foods that also needed to be refrigerated: he did not have a refrigerator. So I helped cook a supper and asked Mr. Siedel if I could store some of the perishable foods at his apartment. This solved the problem temporarily, but it was clear that Mr. Emery's nutrition was linked to having some basic equipment.

Telephone Conference with Public Assistance, 11–21–64: Returning to the office, I called Miss Mitchell at Public Assistance, who was Mr. Emery's worker. I explained to her his needs, Dr. Minor's medical judgment, and my observations. We explored briefly what options were available to Mr. Emery under Public Assistance or, failing that, through private charity or my agency. Miss Mitchell agreed to reevaluate his Public Assistance benefits and would check on whether it was possible to purchase a small or secondhand refrigerator. She suggested that this might take some time and that I might also wish to consult other possible sources to see whether more rapid progress might be made. I asked her to begin the process through Public Assistance and told her that I would explore other options and get back to her.

Conference with Miss Cole, Director of Services, AIG Project, 11–22–64: I discussed these financial matters with Miss Cole the next day, and we decided that Mr. Emery's medical needs constituted exactly what was intended by the discretionary funds we had available. So I called Miss Mitchell back and told her that I was going to purchase a refrigerator immediately. She was pleased and reported that she had already processed a reevaluation of his monthly assistance on the basis of Dr. Minor's statements (which will have to be verified formally, for state records).

Conference with Mrs. Grimm, Director of Home Aides, AIG Project, 11–23–64: Mrs. Grimm knew of several places that sold reconditioned refrigerators that had limited guarantees, but that were reasonably reliable. One in particular also delivered the item. We agreed that she would purchase the refrigerator and that I would call her from the housing office where Mr. Emery lived, to confirm the time for delivery.

Visit, 11–23–64: I discussed with Mr. Emery the purchase of the refrigerator as a part of Dr. Minor's recommendations for his basic health, and so that he might feel better once again. Mr. Emery was predictably concerned about the cost of the electricity, but he seemed to accept my role as helping him to get such equipment. I was somewhat bothered by this sense of growing dependency on me, but in the medical emergency, I decided to get the malnutrition looked after first.

I called to arrange for the delivery of the refrigerator and asked Mrs. Grimm to come over to meet Mr. Emery, as I was also planning with her to have a home aide come in at least once a week to prepare foods, as well as to do some cleaning.

CATEGORICAL RECORDING OF SERVICES RENDERED

However interesting it is to read a worker's account of a case, the researcher must reduce this volume of impressions, facts, and hunches to a more manageable form so as to make the information serve the larger purposes of the demonstration project, namely, ascertaining whether the experimental service made any difference in the lives of the older persons in need of protective services.* Because a large number of persons were in the experimental group, the method of reducing firsthand impressions to objective information became even more difficult. Categories had to be employed that were potentially useful for any type of client by any of the social workers and research interviewers. Although much of the

* The following discussion and examples of *categorical recording* constitute Technical Note 9.2.

richness of the real experience is lost when counts of categorical happenings are made, at least one can go back and read illustrations of the categories for a sense of what really happened—and still be able to count these happenings across diverse participants so as to determine whether, overall, the project was successful in achieving its objectives.

What categories should be used? How should they be defined so as to capture as fully as possible the service efforts that were actually expended? For example, suppose we had a category entitled "meeting with participant at home." This category makes sense across all kinds of participants in all kinds of homes and suggests the efforts made to drive to the home of the participant, to get to the door and into the home (this may not be easy, if you recall my experience with Miss Edel, reported in Chapter 1), and then to hold a meaningful conversation with the participant (also not always easy, such as when the worker had to shout her words to the deaf Mr. Emery). However, inspite of these variations, the similarities are more important, so the category "meeting with participant at home" has meaning.

Some sample records were used as the basis for developing a range of categories that were further examined for their logical breadth and completeness. Usually, an "other" category completed the list as a catchall, and if it became too large, another analysis was made of it, for other relevant categories.

It should be clear that forming categories in this fashion is arbitrary, but hopefully true to the events from which they emerge. It is also possible to form purely theoretical categories, and these can be useful in testing hypotheses. But in an exploratory study, where there are few theories to guide the researcher, a pragmatic content analysis will do quite well as a point of departure. (See Technical Note 5.12, p. 147.)

The essential ingredients of the category system include the following: Who does what, when, to whom, under what conditions, and with what effect? This familiar journalistic formula is helpful in an analysis of the events of everyday life, including service activities on behalf of an older person in need of protective services. I will use abbreviations to simplify the effort—it takes effort to keep this recording accurate and up-to-date. I'll return to this point later.

P = participant	SW = social worker
C = collateral	HAS = home aide supervisor
R = referring agency worker	HA = home aide
	MD = medical doctor
	RN = staff nurse
	SWS = social work supervisor
	RI = research interviewer
	RIS = research interviewing supervisor

The following list represents a disguised categorical case summary of services rendered. The original ran to about ten pages, about 250 entries, for the one-year period in which service was provided. I give only a small portion of this categorical service summary, to illustrate the potential richness of this form of content analysis, as well as the frustrations and limitations of this approach. I summarize the preceding section, which reported the case in some detail, so that the reader can compare the categorical analysis with the raw data (the case record):

DATE	SERVICES RENDERED

11–10–64: P referred to AIG by Mrs. Kohlberg (The social worker was not informed of the research interviewer's contact on 11–11–64.)

11–14: SW made home visit to P, with Mrs. Kohlberg, who introduced SW. SW also met C, who came to P's door.

11–15: SW made home visit to C.

11–21: SW made home visit to P and found him very ill.

11–21: SW contacted Dr. Minor, asking him to examine P. Doctor agreed.

11–21: SW drove P to MD and discussed P's condition in private with MD.

11–21: SW shopped for P.

11–21: SW called Public Assistance worker regarding increased funds for food; raised question about purchase of refrigerator.

11–22: SW met with SWS at AIG about financial arrangements for P.

11–22: SW met with HAS at AIG about purchase of refrigerator, and about planning for home aid services in the near future.

11–22: SW met with P, regarding food and refrigerator.

11–22: SW called HAS at secondhand store regarding purchase of refrigerator and its immediate delivery. HAS was to come to see P at this same time, to discuss the home service with him.

(At this point, the listing of service categories extended beyond the case recording excerpted above.)

11–23: HAS met with P, prepared foods for next several days.

11–24: SW met with P, checked on use of prepared meals and on refrigerator.

11–24: SW discussed home aide for P with HAS at AIG office.

11–24: SW dictation.

11–26: SW and HAS introduced HA to P. Plans call for three mornings a week until food situation stablizes. SW discussed return visit to MD later this week with P.

11–29: SW escorted P to MD. MD informed SW that P's deafness is not correctable by medical means. P was less dehydrated but still needs careful attention to nutrition. P refused to give history that might be related to masses in stomach; MD still concerned about possible cancer.

11–30: HA bought groceries for P; prepared meals for two days at a time; encouraged P to eat.

12–2: SW met with P. Apartment looking much better, thanks to HA. P reported feeling stronger but looked depressed. Not working on his novel. Unclear why.

12–4: SW met with C, regarding P's depressed state. C added nothing.

12–9: HAS reported to SW that HA routine had been established and was working according to plans. HA reported P still depressed, not writing. C reported to be visiting regularly. (HA is buying groceries on regular basis; this will not be further reported in this listing.)

12–11: Call from Public Assistance, problems with bills for extra food. SW clarified situation.

SERVICES RENDERED (*continued*)

12–15: HAS directed HA, with SW approval, to involve P more in his own food preparation.

12–17: Fire department called because of small fire in P's apartment because of food burning on stove. P not aware of problem until much smoke in kitchen. C called fire department. P very upset. SW called and met with P; Discussed safety with P.

12–18: HA met with SW and HAS at AIG office to discuss safety in P's apartment; devised a system of lights to remind P when food is cooking.

12–23: SW drove P around city to look at Christmas lights. P talked about his childhood memories. SW gave P small Christmas gift. P insisted on having "tea" at his apartment and gave SW a reading from his latest novel as his Christmas present to her. The chapter was about a man who was dying and gave SW an opportunity to discuss P's concerns and fears about his health.

12–27: P received notice of Public Assistance grant increase.

1–3: SW phoned social security office regarding P's checks. He believes that not all of his monthly checks have arrived. Social security will check on this.

1–8: HAS reported HA routine going well. P is preparing more of his own meals, suggesting that he is stronger. HAS recommended cutting HA to two days a week.

1–15: Social security called back; all checks are accounted for.

1–15: SW met with P; reported social security findings; discussed ways of keeping track of finances.

1–17: HA resigned; HAS met with P to prepare him for new HA. HAS shopped for groceries for P.

1–19: New HA introduced; arrangements were made for twice-a-week service.

1–28: SW met P at apartment; discussed health and fears about dependency and institutionalization. P felt better but was still weak compared to level of strength of past few years.

2–15: HA reported P ill: dizzy and weak.

2–15: Project RN met P and substantiated HA's report; called SW.

2–15: SW met P; made MD appointment; took P to MD, who prescribes medication.

2–16: SW met P at apartment. P was in bed. C was bringing him his food prepared by HA the day before. P was very upset.

2–17: HA was sent in by HAS a day early; will come in daily for duration of P's illness. Medication was reducing dizziness.

2–19: SW checked with HA on P's progress. All going well. P discussed feelings of fear with HA.

2–25: SW determined P is reasonably well; HA back on twice-a-week schedule. HA renewed medication.

3–11: SW dictation.

3–13: HA reported another small fire at apartment. P put it out by himself. He forgot to turn off burner again.

DATE	SERVICES RENDERED (*continued*)
3–15:	SW met P; Discussed funeral arrangements and wishes. P less fearful of illness when in a satisfactory state. P pleased with meals, but worried about money. P had forgotten the increased grant from Public Assistance.
4–2:	SW met P at apartment. P was writing again but had stomach pains; agreed to see MD again for tests.
4–2:	SW made appointment for P with MD.
4–10:	SW took P to MD. Tests taken; will report findings in several days.
4–14:	MD called SW. Tumors present but benign. Some evidence of diabetes requiring further workup. Appointment set.
4–16:	HAS met with SW at AIG office to review past months of HA service plans. Agreed on maintaining HA services at present level, until further medical tests are conducted. HA very helpful in discussing fears with P.
4–24:	HAS took P to MD for further testing (SW had emergency on another case).
4–25:	MD called SW; reported mild diabetes condition and recommended dietary control for the time being, and some medication. SW discussed medical situation with HAS and made plans on changes in food purchases and P's taking medication on regular basis.
4–26:	SW met with P to discuss MD's findings and plans. HA involved in this discussion. SW purchased medication (tablets) and discussed with P how many to take after meals.
4–28:	HA called HAS, reporting that she didn't think P was taking his medication regularly or consistently.
4–29:	HAS met with SW on medication routine. P's forgetfulness may be part of the problem, or fears associated with an illness like diabetes may also be at work. HAS purchased a five-day medical dispenser (device with compartments marked for five days' worth of medicine) and taught HA how to use it with P.
5–15:	SW met with P. Medical routine stablized. P feeling much better, writing more. SW explored possibility of P's giving "readings" to local public-library book club. P ambivalent. Will think about it.
5–19:	SW dictation, six-month summary.

TOWARD AN ADEQUATE CONTENT ANALYSIS OF PRACTICE

This six-month segment of a brief listing of events is sufficient to represent the flow of crises and routines, of significant interactions and everyday happenings of which everyone's life is composed.* Knowing the detailed fragment from the case record for the first few days provides a further clue to the enormous potential richness to be found in the records, and to the difficulty in extracting information from them in any way that would be comparable across clients.

---

* This discussion of the *content analysis of practice* constitutes Technical Note 9.3.

Thus a category system, like the one presented in the preceding section, is one compromise in seeking to evaluate the service component of a demonstration project.

Some simple analyses can be made. For example, how often did the social worker see the participant? I count nineteen times during this six-month segment. Obviously the quality of these contacts differed greatly, depending on the circumstances involved, but is not easily observed by a simple count. Adding a weighting or qualifier to the listing might help. How many times did the social worker contact the participant to provide social or personal support, or to explore underlying and nonverbalized feelings? It might be possible to make such a count, assuming that this type of information was put into the categories in the first place. (These types of social information clearly appear in some places, but whether they were consciously and regularly added is not known.) One of the problems of content analysis is that one cannot be certain of the adequacy of the original information, particularly when the listing was made at intervals, during which definitions or interpretations of events might change. One could go back to the original case recordings, but even here, there is no guarantee that the records are complete with regard to the categories being currently analyzed.

Another problem is that service plans change. It is clear, for instance, that there was a switch in policy in trying to deal with Mr. Emery's apparent depression by getting him to take more control over his own life. This excessive helping is a common error of helpers of all types: not letting clients do for themselves all that they are capable of doing. Once the error is recognized, the helpers can try to balance out the provision of services with the need for the client to maintain control. But in evaluating the listing of services, it is unclear how to count these changes of policy. The sheer number of contacts goes down—for therapeutic purposes. However, numerical averages do not indicate these kinds of changes in service plans.

Yet another concern is how to count the weight of assistance. The social worker is the most highly paid professional on the project. It is less costly to have home aides do some of the things that social workers can do, like prepare meals and shop. Indeed, because home aides can spend more time with the participants, they may be able to do these services more ably. However, aides cannot make the kinds of clinical judgments that social workers can; but when trained to do so, aides can act as the early-warning system for the professionally trained members of the team. Thus, overall, the team approach makes sense in terms of costs and benefits. But when one is trying to evaluate the relative proportioning of team member contributions, it is unclear what the total service component is. Needs change: Mr. Emery needed daily home aide service when ill, and only twice a week when not. Averages disguise these changes in service needs over time.

What, then, is the answer to describing adequately what the service component is in a large demonstration project? There is no perfect answer. However, there are some logical alternatives to be explored. For one, consider identifying the patterns of service by the quarters of the service year. For Mr. Emery, the first quarter involved a medical emergency, with consequent flurries of activities by many members of the service team. In the second quarter, although there was another spell of illness, it was not as serious as before. A routine service pattern was used successfully. And so on. It would be possible to identify some basic patterns of service across different participants in the project, and thereby to describe the project in holistic units rather than in averages.

A PRACTICE–WISDOM APPROACH TO DESCRIBING SERVICES TO PROTECTIVE CLIENTS

There are, of course, many other ways to go about the task of sorting through the practice experiences of the four social workers (and the ancillary service personnel who were involved with these participants). (See Chapter 10.) I want to describe one of these because it reflects another side of Margaret Blenkner, the rugged empiricist. It involved employing a sensitive and experienced social worker to read the service records and to formulate practice strategies from them.*

Being an outsider to the everyday routines, this practice consultant could bring a fresh perspective to the task. She could (and did) ask some questions that would penetrate the "traditions" that had arisen unobtrusively in the course of the project. And she could find connections across the diverse efforts of the four social workers, each with her own style of practice.

But even though Dr. Blenkner convinced her former colleague from the New York study, Edna Wasser, to take on this practice consultant role, it was still a very difficult task for anyone. There were intensive reading periods when the case recordings from the project social workers were sent to Mrs. Wasser; these periods were followed by periods of intense discussion among the social workers, Mrs. Wasser, and Dr. Blenkner, too. The consultant wrote several drafts of her thinking, and each was soundly scrutinized for its ability to capture the essence of the practice with protective clients. Edna Wasser was an enormously talented gerontological social worker who had written many important papers and monographs on this subject (for example, see Wasser, 1961, 1966a, 1966b, 1974). But it was very difficult to convince any two people, especially if one of them was Margaret Blenkner, that a given statement represented the essence of protective practice. And so, after a great deal of effort, the major presentation of the Protective Services Project in *Social Casework* (Blenkner, et. al., 1971) also contained a paper by Mrs. Wasser on the practice component. I will summarize that paper briefly to highlight a transferable model of practice, developed through the imaginative reconstruction of a sensitive gerontological social worker, Edna Wasser. Compare this with the possible content analyses or other quantatitive methods described previously.

Where does one begin in working with the elderly protective client? First, the social worker has to enter the situation, whether or not the elderly person invites her or him in. This uninvited intervention is justified by the assumption that the self-endangering or other-endangering behavior of persons in need of protective services are not "free choices" in any sense of the phrase. Thus *not*

---

* This discussion of *how to describe qualitatively the services to protective clients* constitutes Technical Note 9.4.

to intervene in such situations constitutes social neglect. The social worker must get into and stay in the situation, as long as these efforts do not constitute a clear danger to the older person.

Second, the social worker has to acquaint the protective person, who may never have had any other such contact with professional helpers, with the possibilities of helping services by introducing whatever is needed, whether the client requests it or not. In Mrs. Wasser's fine phrasing, "The worker presumes that the client develops a taste for service by tasting it." (Wasser, 1971, p. 516.) These services can range from the tangible (doing the dishes) to the intangible (talking about fears and hopes).

The third step appears to be a routinization stage in which social work as the core service is mixed, as needed, with the array of ancillary services, including financial aid, home aide services, medical care, psychiatric examination, legal consultation, fiduciary and guardianship services, and placement services. However, how this mix is to be brought about depends on one's theory of protective needs.

The predominant conceptual map that Mrs. Wasser described is that of the protective client's sense of self in the context of the supportiveness of the social environment. These terms are very similar to the personal and environmental variables around which the conceptualization of the protective person was constructed for this project. This conception made it necessary, as she wrote, "to balance interventions intended for the very survival of the client against the negative impact these can have on the client's sense of self" and, ultimately, on the client's life as well (Wasser, 1971, p. 518).

The tasks required to maintain oneself in the community are minimal, but the social worker finds himself or herself in the position of having to judge whether they are being performed adequately: A person has to go to bed at night; get up in the morning; toilet and cleanse herself or himself; eat some food, however simple; take medicines as needed; care for the home with at least some minimum of safety, sanitation, and decency; and keep track of and spend money according to her or his needs (Wasser, 1971, p. 518). This list contains many value judgments that a reader might question, if not challenge. But this is exactly what *practice wisdom* generates: a sense of the minimally necessary behaviors viewed from the perspective of a gatekeeper between the individual who is to continue living in the community and some institutional network that presumes to provide for one or more of these behaviors.

Perhaps the critical dimensions of the practice model, the ones that vary most dramatically from the established practice of that time, are contained in the theme of *social treatment* rather than *psychotherapy*. In effect, the practice strategy concludes that it is more productive to enlist environmental supports to aid the protective participant, so as to restructure the situation to compensate for the older person's deficits, than to seek to change the person's personality structure, ideas, feelings, and certain behaviors directly. (See Glenwick and Jason, 1982, for a more recent version of this position applied to a wide spectrum of targets and clientele.)

One must contrast the supportive environment approach with the prevalent psychoanalytic or neopsychoanalytic therapies of that time, which sought to change the individual rather than the environment. Even more recent modes of helping, stressing as they do the interaction between the individual and the social environment, do not go as far as the protective strategy evolved from the BRI study. As I read it, the BRI strategy was to emphasize the supportive environment strongly, as well as seeking to gain the older person's cognitive-affective acquiescence to—or minimally, contentment with—the social worker's interventions.

As Mrs. Wasser described this mode of helping, the social worker is like a case manager or balance wheel in the intermeshing of the social environmental services provided by the various activated disciplines, as well as a provider of services herself or himself. But, in what must have been verging on heresy in the late 1960s, Edna Wasser, the quintessential psychoanalytically-trained social worker, advocated "inquiry into the use of behavior modification techniques" (Wasser, 1971, p. 522), apparently because these seemed to meet the environmental change needs while maintaining minimal psychological rapport. Likewise, Mrs. Wasser urged consideration of cognitive and social methods of analysis, thus moving the helping professional further away from sole reliance on the affective methods of the psychodynamic school in connection with work with the elderly protective-services case.

The last point of the interventive model for work with the elderly protective is institutional placement, but Mrs. Wasser was cautious about actually connecting it with the practice model. She noted that in one field of service after another, helping professionals had given up the institutional solution to problems in favor of a less awesome and less comprehensive solution. Perhaps, she noted, it was time for protective services for the frail elderly to consider seriously other options in the continuum of care (Wasser, 1971, pp. 520–521).

In retrospect, Wasser's was a watershed paper on the state of social work practice because at about this time there was a general disaffection with psychodynamic methods and a shifting to the exploration of alternatives or supplements. Fischer's (1976) critical analysis of evaluative research, including the BRI Protective Services Project, concerns studies that used psychodynamic methods. A more recent paper by Reid and Hanrahan (1982) covers the next generation of evaluative research and reports largely successful results, with the note that more diverse and more behaviorally-oriented methods were generally employed. (Other commentators in psychology and related fields have likewise reviewed the same territory and have given conflicting interpretations: Bergin, 1966; Gurman, 1973; Luborsky, Singer, and Luborsky, 1976; Meltzoff and Kornreich, 1970; Smith, Glass, and Miller, 1980; Mullen, Dumpson, and others, 1972; Geismar, 1972; Wood, 1978.) Garfield (1983) termed this consideration of the research on the effectiveness of psychotherapy a "perennial controversy."

The main point for consideration now is whether a literary statement of practice like that by Mrs. Wasser advances our knowledge any further than the quantitative approaches suggested above. This is a moot point, insofar as Margaret Blenkner never lived to complete a full quantitative analysis of practice, although she spoke of doing so. Perhaps it is enough to say that this early study (the BRI project) raised some questions, which still remain to be answered, about how research is to grasp the subtle workings of the helping practitioner sufficiently to be able to transfer this knowledge to others with some degree of verisimilitude. The recent literature, as illustrated by the *Handbook of Clinical Social Work* (Rosenblatt and Waldfogel, 1983), continues to explore these same issues.

SUMMARY

1. Describing the intervention variable in a complex demonstration project is perhaps the most difficult task of the evaluator. Many crude indicators can be given separately: How many of what general types of worker or ancillary interventions were made, under what conditions, toward what persons or things, with what effects? But when one seeks ways of combining these aspects into a single intervention variable that is explicable to others seeking to replicate the study, the complexity of the task emerges in its full glory.

2. Two general approaches to the BRI project are illustrated in this chapter, and their strengths and limitations are noted. The quantitative method involved trying to sort into systematic, objective, and useful categories all of the relevant behaviors and events that took place during the project year. Some brief illustrations of raw materials—a case record and the categorical analysis of it—were presented to illustrate this approach. It was so complex that the BRI staff completed only some sketchy outlines of it, more for illustrative purposes than for a true scientific evaluation.

3. The second general approach was a qualitative analysis made by an outside consultant, who had available to her all of the case records plus long discussions with the social workers. Trying to distill into principles of practice with protective persons a vast body of records and conversations was difficult enough; attempting to get agreement among the involved social workers and Margaret Blenkner was another task in itself.

4. Yet, for all the difficulty in describing practice, one can see outlines of the patterns of protective services emerging from these discussions. At least, there is now sufficient information to begin to frame better questions for the next study on services to the mentally fragile aged.

CHAPTER 10

What Happened?
Presentation of Results

Overview

Finally, here I present the outcome of the Protective Services Project. And what a surprise it was! I have included as a Technical Note the complete original report as it appeared in a major social-work journal, and I have made a number of observations to help explain what goes into writing a summary report like this.

Technical Narrative Section

Introduction
Usable Data (Technical Note 10.1)
The Hypotheses (10.2)
How Results Are Presented (10.3)
The Construction of a Table Summarizing the Research Data
Comparisons Among the Three Research Perspectives: The Participant Interview, the Research Interviewer's Observations, and the Social Worker's Ratings (10.4)
Comparisons on Services Received in Experimental and Control Groups (10.5)
The General Format for Presenting Published Research Report (10.6)
Published Report (10.7)
       Margaret Blenkner et al.: "A Research and Demonstration Project of Protective Services" (1971).

The Technical Narrative

INTRODUCTION

After the year of preparation and the several years of implementing the demonstration project, we eagerly ask, "What happened?" Was the experimental service program effective? Had we learned which tactics worked well with these elderly protective clients?

Unfortunately, it isn't quite that easy to answer the question of what had happened in the project and as a result of the service program. It took us many months to sift through the information and to make a final report. Knowing this would be the case, we had been developing progress reports so that the final writing would not overwhelm us—or the readers. After all, consider the scope of the task.

USABLE DATA

There were about 90,000 separate pieces of information formally asked of or about the participants.* Most came from the participants themselves, another large portion came from the collaterals, and the research interviewers contributed the next largest number of items, followed by the social workers in the project, as well as a smaller number of questions asked of the original referring agency. This information was obtained for each participant (except that the control participants lacked a BRI social worker) over four points during the full year that each participant was enrolled in the project. Only death could remove a participant from the roster. Indeed, one of the first facts to be presented is the number of research interviews obtained (either long-form or short-form) over the cycles of interviews with the participants surviving at each of these points in time. Table 10.1. presents this information.

There were surprisingly high percentages of at least short-form data from this group of hard-to-communicate-with elderly protectives (Blenkner, Bloom, Nielsen, and Weber, 1974, p. 118). This overall level of usable data is quite adequate for purposes of research, although missing data are a problem. One can see whether the missing data are spread about equally between experimental and control groups (as they were in the BRI study), in which case one might infer that there was no systematic bias favoring one or the other group. Or possibly, one might assign the group's average score on a given item to approximate a missing score. But anything one does with missing data is risky, and as you will see in the following chapter, even experts disagree on what is the best way to handle missing data. Dr. Blenkner's resolution was simply to call attention to the data we had and to the fact that some data were missing, but as a reasonable amount of information was present, she went ahead with the data analysis.

* This discussion of *usable data* constitutes Technical Note 10.1.

238

Table 10.1 Research Interviews Obtained on Experimental and Control Participants over the Four Interview Periods (percentages based on number of survivors at each period).

Research Interview Obtained (short or long form)	Research Interviews							
	Initial		3-Month		6-Month		1-Year	
	Exp.	Control	Exp.	Control	Exp.	Control	Exp.	Control
Yes	88%	87%	81%	82%	81%	78%	88%	93%
No	12	13	19	18	19	22	12	7
Number of Survivors	76	88	67	83	64	76	57	72

Data collected from collaterals were not at as high a level, probably because the collaterals were not strongly involved in the participants or lacked the energy or the time to meet with the interviewers. There were no known collaterals for some truly isolated participants.

In Table 10.2, the usable data are itemized by specific variable. In this table, one can see that not all of the variables are represented at equal levels, probably because of the relative ease of collecting answers to some questions and not to others: it was apparently most difficult to obtain answers on a person's mental functioning, whereas answers on physical functioning seemed to be the easiest to collect. When the operationalization of a variable required a comparison between initial and one-year scores on the same item, there was great risk that one or the other score might not be available in order to provide the change score. So it was with mental functioning, in particular, as only 49 percent of the surviving participants in the experimental group met the requirement of having answered both the initial and the one-year questions. The bulk of other change scores ran between 61 and 75 percent data obtained. Whether even this amount is adequate for analysis is subject to debate, but as Dr. Blenkner detected no systematic bias in these data, she went ahead with the analysis, having presented these facts for the attention of the reader.

Thus the essential task of presentation of research was the reduction of this mountain of available questionnaire data into manageable piles of information. To do this, we returned to the hypotheses framed *before* any data were collected; the essence of scientific research is to call the shots in advance and give the data a fair chance to confirm or disconfirm those hypotheses. Let's review these hypotheses, as they became an outline of how information was presented on the major variables.

THE HYPOTHESES

Three major hypotheses* were framed:

1. It is hypothesized that the group scores (averages or percentages) of the service participants will be more favorable than those of the controls at successive follow-up periods on

---

* This discussion of *hypotheses* in the context of the BRI study constitutes Technical Note 10.2.

239

Table 10.2 Usable Data on Criterion Variables: Initial, One-Year, Change Scores (percentage of surviving participants).

Criterion Variables	Initial Interview					One-Year Interview					Changes (between initial and one-year)				
	Interview Scores[a]		Ratings			Interview Scores[a]		Ratings			Interview Scores[a]		Ratings		
			Observer		SWer			Observer		SWer			Observer		SWer
	E%	C%	E%	C%	E%	E%	C%	E%	C%	E%	E%	C%	E%	C%	E%
Competence															
Mental functioning (MSQ, MFO, MC)[b]	62	63	88	85	92	72	76	89	94	91	49	58	79	79	91
Physical functioning (PFQ, PFO, PC)	83	81	98	96	96	86	83	89	93	93	72	72	—	—	93
Physical environment (PE, EPP)	82	81	c	c	95	70	64	c	c	93	58	62	c	c	93
Protection															
Concrete assistance (CA, CAO, EPS)	78	83	87	86	95	82	85	91	93	93	67	75	79	81	93
Interested parties (IP, IPO)	79	82	86	86	—	81	83	91	94	—	65	74	77	81	—
Affect and Behavior															
Contentment (Con, ConO, ConC)	74	77	86	85	92	84	94	88	94	94	67	75	75	81	93
Signs and symptoms (S&S, SSO, SSC)	72	73	88	85	96	82	81	89	94	91	61	67	79	81	91
Effect on Others															
Collateral stress	79	78	76	77	—	—	—	63	53	63	d	d	—	—	—
Comparative collateral stress	—	—	—	—	—	65	61	—	—	—	d	d	—	—	—
No. of surviving participants	76	88	76	88	76	57	72	57	72	57	57	72	57	72	57

SOURCE: Blenkner, et al., 1974, Table 4–2, pp. 101–102.

[a] Short-form interview scores are used on all variables, except MSQ and physical environment.

[b] These abbreviations refer to the same criterion variable, but with data collected from two or three sources: the participant interview schedule, the research interviewer's observer rating (0), and in some cases the social worker's ratings (c) of the cases—in this order.

[c] No interviewer ratings were made; data from participant interview was used directly.

[d] No change score obtained; use comparative collateral stress score as indicated.

   a. Length and rate of survival,
   b. Contentment,
   c. Behavioral and affective signs, and
   d. Induced collateral stress.
2. It is further hypothesized that scores on
   a. Functional competence, and
   b. Environmental protection
among the service group will equal or better those of the controls.
3. The demonstrated service will be considered successful if the combined probability of the two events,
   a. Survival rates favoring the service group, and
   b. Average contentment scores of the survivors favoring the service group,
is significant at the .05 level, irrespective of the findings on the other variables; it will be considered unsuccessful if the results do not significantly favor the service group when these two variables are combined. (Blenkner, 1963)

Let's examine these hypotheses with regard to their form and function. An hypothesis is a proposition linking two concepts (or variables—the empirical forms that concepts may take). The link may be simply one of *association*; X is related to Y. But the potentially more useful hypotheses are those that suggest that a *causal* relationship exists, that X causes Y (or, perhaps more correctly, contributes to the manifestation that Y takes, as there may be other causal factors as well). A researcher as well as a practitioner may believe the X causes Y and may put his or her belief to the test by formulating an hypothesis.

The form of the hypothesis permits a test to occur because each variable is stated in *operational* form, and the *relationship between the variables* is such that it permits one either to accept or to reject the hypothesis on the basis of the outcome. To the extent that concepts or hypotheses are not clear on these two characteristics, it becomes difficult to conduct the research or to interpret the findings. Ambiguous or controversial value terms are often the causes of this difficulty, a problem found frequently in the practice literature.

With regard to the BRI hypotheses, I have previously discussed how we attempted to operationalize the variables. One may disagree with us on whether our efforts were adequate, but at least, the operational statements were clearly presented. The more interesting question concerns the way the variables were related. If you look for the *if—then* arrangement in hypotheses, you will be able to sort out what was being linked to what. The first hypothesis says, in effect, *if* you look at the group score of the service (or experimental) participants on the variable "length of survival," *then* it will be bigger than the comparable score of the control participants. The implication is that this difference will be due to the planned treatment because the research design permits this logical inference when an experimental factor is associated with different outcomes in two groups originally shown to be comparable. The scores on length of survival were carefully defined. The relationship statement was carefully constructed: *if* the experimental group has a larger average score than the control group on this variable, *then* we can accept the hypothesis as being supported. *If* the scores are not as hypothesized, *then* we can take these facts as evidence that the hypothesis has been disproved.

Note the subtle language difference in the preceding two statements. Discon-

241

firming evidence offers disproof, but confirming evidence simply offers support for, not proof of, the hypothesis. This linguistic usage stems from the probabilistic way in which hypotheses are constructed. We know only approximately what is confirmed; there are other unknown contributors to this outcome. But we are clear about what is disconfirmed.

Hypotheses can be quite complex in their statement, as when a joint occurrence is required before a positive outcome or confirmation is accepted. By stating the *statistical significance* at the .05 level, Dr. Blenkner followed a long tradition in the social sciences. However, it is a tradition that is controversial, as there are no external reasons for selecting this level of probablility over others. It is simply a compromise between the kinds of errors one can make in including or excluding a finding as happening by chance alone. (See discussion of Type I and Type II errors, p. 178.)

In addition to statistical significance, I want to emphasize that there is another consideration, often termed *practical or clinical significance.* This term refers to the social or personal meaning of a given set of findings. Researchers pay special attention to findings that even hint at a connection between a service program and mortality because the social meaning is so enormous. Thus, even when there are no strong statistical correlations between a service program and death, the mere presence of this relationship appropriately raises social concern. The statistics tell us that the findings could have happened by chance alone, but the practical import is to demand a thorough reconsideration to make sure that the service program did not, in fact, contribute to the untoward outcome. It is difficult to maintain an olympian scientific perspective when human lives are at stake. Watch for this mortality issue when the critical reviews of the project are presented in the following chapter.

HOW RESULTS ARE PRESENTED

The task of this chapter is to illustrate the presentation of results* by explicating the available data relevant to these hypotheses. One might expect this to be an easy task—just take the hypothesis and see what the data said. Unfortunately, data mumble. Or else they shout irrelevant facts and conflicting opinions. (Uncannily human.) So we must approach the data with tact and resolve: never believe one datum until other data dealing with the same topic are considered for consistency of results; never believe you are successful unless you have given equal efforts to disproving your apparent success (and vice versa, in cases where you apparently have not been successful); never believe that there is only one way to perceive the truth on a given question.

Let me give a brief example of this delicate approach to the data, by referring to the first hypothesis, that the experimental or service group would have group scores more favorable than the controls on length and rate of survival. That seems straightforward. Let's simply look to see which group had the greater number of persons surviving at the end of the project year. Or rather, since

---

* This discussion and the following one on the *presentation of results* constitute Technical Note 10.3.

there were more participants in the control group to begin with than experimental participants (88 to 76 to be exact), we shouldn't look at the number but at the *proportion* of survivors. For example, it would have taken 44 deaths in the control group to reach 50 percent, whereas it would have taken 38 persons in the service group to achieve a 50 percent survival rate. So we have to be very clear, whenever we discuss percentages, to indicate what specific group of persons we are referring to.

Moreover, we know that men and women have different expectations of mortality; men die at younger ages than women. So that means that if we have different proportions of males and females in our experimental and control groups, we have to adjust the survival rates based on these *sex-linked expectations.* (One might even argue—with Grannis (1970), and Waldron (1976)—that it is smoking behavior, not gender itself, that generates these differences in the survival of males and females. However, we did not collect information on smoking behavior over the lifetime of each participant in order to make this correction.)

Yet another factor in survival is the *age* at which one is considering mortality predictions. It stands to reason that older persons are more likely to die than younger ones, all things being equal. It happened that, by random allocation of participants into experimental and control groups, the average age of the groups was different by a margin that could not have happened by chance alone, except less than 5 times in 100. Thus, all of the mortality data—and the data on the other major variables as well—had to be adjusted for this age differential. The average age of the experimental participants was 78.0, whereas the average age for the controls was 75.8. This became a major point of contention in the later analysis and interpretation of the data, so we will return to this point shortly.

I could go on to point out that three other factors—*living arrangements, institutional status,* and *level of physical functioning*—may influence mortality expectations, and we wanted to make sure that the experimental- and control-group samples were adjusted for these known characteristics as well. In short, we could continue to clarify the mortality expectations of the participants on these five basic categories of variables, attempting with each to sharpen what we expected to happen based on the known characteristics of the groups to which the participants belong. This became an intricate juggling act because some factors may add years and other factors may subtract them from the prediction. Wouldn't you expect a young (i.e., between age sixty and age seventy-four) white female to live the longest? As a matter of fact, this would be an accurate prediction at birth: such an individual would be expected to have the longest life span as compared to white males or nonwhites, male or female. But an interesting change occurs in life tables in that, at age seventy, both nonwhite and white females have the same expectation of years of life, namely, 14.4 years more. (This same change occurs among males at age sixty-five, when for the first time, nonwhite and white males have the same predicted number of years left in their expected life, 13.7.) From there on, nonwhite females and males are expected to *outlive* their white peers. (See National Center for Health Statistics, presented in Bloom, 1980, p. 470.) Getting a simple answer to an hypothesis is really rather complicated. Moreover, there is ample room to argue that this or that combination of qualifications is the best one to use in providing the answer. And unfortunately, there is nothing explicit in the scientific method that specifies this combi-

243

nation. Therefore some of the arguments and conflicts among scientists are honest differences of opinion on what is to be included in any calculation, although the calculation procedures can be fully verified by reanalysis.

Let's take another example of a white male aged sixty-nine and a black female aged eighty. It just so happens that actuarially these two individuals have about the same remaining life expectation, close to eleven years of life, even though one is "young" (between sixty and seventy-four) and white, and the other is "old" (over seventy-five) and black. Thus, every answer to an hypothesis requires a careful specification of what factors are involved in providing the answer—or, more correctly, the answers. Convention, reified by textbooks, attempts to build up a series of expectations about what is the most reasonable way to handle any set of data. But expect differences, because there is no one dominant convention or textbook, and even when there is general agreement for a time, the best guess is that that agreement will be challenged when a new perspective on scientific practice is born. If you think science is monolithic and unchanging, you're in for a big surprise. What does not change (much) is the expectation of being able to be methodical so as to increase the objectivity (i.e., the intersubject agreement) about some specified body of observations.

Now, let's see how these all-important survival data were presented in the final report:

> Differences in survival rates between experimental service cases and controls, while not statistically significant, consistently favored the controls during the first year. At each follow-up period a slightly higher proportion of control than service participants was found alive. At 3 months, 94 percent of the controls compared with 88% of the service participants had survived; at 6 months, the figures were 86 percent vs. 84 percent; and at one year they were 82 percent vs. 75 percent. (Blenkner, Bloom, Nielsen, and Weber, 1974, p. 130)

The report goes on to make some observations about the implications of these findings for interpreting other data (a point to which we will return in the discussion of the other variables), before it concludes with the following grim statement:

> In general, taking into account the survival criterion as well as the functional competence measures, it is reasonable to conclude that the experimental treatment variable was of no use in preventing or slowing deterioration in the service group as compare with the controls and that the overall trend in protective cases, with or without intensive protective service, is downward. In addition, one should be willing to at least entertain the hypothesis that intensive service of the sort supplied in the project with its reliance on custodial case as indicated by the institutionalized rate may accelerate the decline. (Blenkner, Bloom, Nielsen, and Weber, 1974, p. 133)

There it is. These are the core findings that launched many controversies on a sea of printers' ink and, beyond that, in the policies and practices of many social service agencies and programs. Because of the seriousness of the implications of these findings, we will devote Chapter 11 to the critical response. But it is necessary to anticipate the overall outcome in order to keep the specific findings in perspective. Recall that Hypothesis 3 stated that both the survival and the contentment had to be significant in order for the demonstration service

244

to be considered successful, regardless of the outcome on the other variables. A priority among variables had been identified, reflecting the conceptual framework and some value assumptions. Some may question the propriety of the value assumptions that gave survival such a strong weight in the overall project (see Dunkle, Poulshock, Silverstone, and Deimling, 1983), and that is a matter to be considered in accepting the findings as stated. But what cannot be undone is the scientific act of stating the priority in the first place, based on conceptual and practical grounds. This statement of the project goals is what Dr. Blenkner constructed, and it is up to the reader to decide whether these grounds are sufficient ones on which to build a case for—or against—the type of practice exemplified by the service program in the Protective Project.

THE CONSTRUCTION OF A TABLE SUMMARIZING THE RESEARCH DATA

In discussing the construction of tables to convey technical information in an intelligible fashion, I will refer to a table in the most accessible of the reports on the BRI study, which appeared in *Social Casework* (1971). In that paper (reproduced at the end of this chapter) Table 3 presents the overall findings on the major variables of the Protective Project (not including survival and mortality, factors discussed in the text of the paper before the table). In its highly condensed form, the table summarizes massive amounts of information and requires considerable study to understand. However, it is also a masterful way of presenting the major trends of a complex study; Margaret Blenkner captured the significant patterns from the participant interviews, the research interviewers' ratings, and the clinical ratings of the social workers (on the experimental cases only). Moreover, she did this while providing information on the direction and the significance of the changes between admission into the program and one year later. That's a lot of information, but it can be seen better because it is in one table; it also becomes possible to see connections or inconsistencies among the sources of information being used.

It might be helpful to see how such a table is constructed. I will review the steps in the construction of many other tables that went into this summary Table 3. Mr. Emery (see the description in Chapter 9) contributed his responses to the standard questionnaire items, such as those dealing with a variable we called "concrete assistance." His responses to the following short-form items were all scored as unfavorable, that is, as not having concrete assistance when it was needed (the question numbers refer to items in the initial participant interview form—see Chapter 7): (83) no nurse was seeing him regularly; (95) he was getting no help in keeping his money matters straight; and (101 and 104) he received no aid in laundry or housecleaning—and his apartment looked it. He did receive a favorable score on one item of concrete assistance (81), because an organization (public welfare) did help him. His total score would be a 1, representing the total number of favorable scores on concrete assistance.

Mr. Emery's scores on this one variable were combined with others, and a mean score was obtained. As mentioned earlier, five major categories of analysis were used with each variable: age, sex, whether the person lived alone or with someone, whether the person was in an institutional or a noninstitutional setting, and physical-functioning status. So, for example, the concrete assistance data from all 164 cases were divided into age groups: under 75 years and 75 and over. The mean score overall on concrete assistance was 1.52 out of a possible range of a low of 0 to a high of 5. Mr. Emery was 76 years old, so his responses were also analyzed in the age category for the 75-or-over group, whose mean was 1.70, in contrast to the 1.16 of the participants under 75 years of age. The older participants had a higher mean score on this one factor than did the younger ones, although all were very low indeed on receiving concrete assistance, as would be expected in a sample of persons in need of protective services (Blenkner et al., 1974, p. 74). There may or may not have been significant differences when the five categories were used to analyze each finding, but it was necessary to check so that differences between the experimental and the control participants could be seen in finer detail. This procedure was also a means of controlling for differences that appeared in the course of the random assignment to the experimental and the control groups.

The same procedure was used again with the data collected from Mr. Emery and all the surviving participants at one year after admission to the program. Using mean scores disguises the fact that a reduced number of persons was involved in the one-year data, so one must read any table as involving survivors. Moreover, when the death rate is higher for one group (as it was in our study), the group means of the survivors are likely to be higher than the group means of the survivors of the other group because the sicker people had probably died. Thus, Dr. Blenkner decided to use change scores, rather than simply gross comparisons between the initial and the one-year data. The changes for one individual, such as Mr. Emery, were compared for the initial and the one-year interviews. There are problems with this decision, as some people weren't interviewed initially, although they may have been at one year, and vice versa. In short, we lost some information by not being able to use one or the other set of interview data. But we gained something more important: a stronger measure of change.

Using change scores, as indicated above, meant that we had to have a new convention in presenting data. For example, Mr. Emery was interviewed at one year and responded to the concrete assistance items differently. He was now receiving assistance with his housecleaning and laundry, as well as getting aid from public welfare. So his total (favorable) score was 3. This is a *change* from his initial score of +2. It would have been possible for matters to get worse; Mr. Emery might have lost his public assistance for some reason; the result would have been a concrete assistance score of 0, representing a change from his initial status of −1. [0 (1 year score) minus +1 (initial score) equals −1.]

The mean change score for experimental participants was a gain of +1.6, whereas the controls gained +0.4. One can ask the question: How significant are differences of this magnitude? That is, how likely are changes of this order to occur by chance alone? Statistical procedures were used that take into account the various factors influencing chance with this many persons on a scale of so many degrees, and it was found that the experimental group's change was highly unlikely to have occurred by chance alone. In statistical language, it would not be expected to happen by chance except less than 1 time in 1,000. Likewise, the control-group change was statistically significant, but at a lower level: 1

chance in 20, or 5 chances in 100. (This would be expressed as $p < .05$, meaning that the probability of two events' occurring as they did could not have happened by chance alone except less than 5 times in 100.) The two events, scored by one person at two different times, were thus statistically rare, and we had to explore possible explanations of why they occurred as they did. One immediate possibility was that the experimental service program contributed to the desired change, a point to which I will return shortly. There were other possibilities, but the experimental–control-group design with randomized allocation of persons to the two groups tended to control for some of these alternative possibilities (see Technical Note 4.6, p. 123). Still, individual differences may have been at work, which is why the data were routinely reanalyzed in relation to the five categorical variables: age, sex, living status, institutional status, and physical functioning.

The next step in analysis might be to compare the differences between the experimental and the control groups. Let's look first at this comparison on the initial interview. (See Table 10.3.) The control group mean score (1.5) on having concrete assistance was higher than the experimental group mean score (1.2) by a small amount (−0.3), one that was not statistically significant. However, by one year, a change had occurred. Now the experimental group had a higher mean (2.8) than the control group (2.1), and the difference between these means (0.8) was statistically significant. (As shown in Table 10.3, such a difference between these two events could not have happened by chance alone except less than 2 times in 100.)

One more step. If we take these two change scores, the mean difference between the experimental and the control groups initially (−0.3) and at one year (0.8), there was also a difference (1.1). Here, the change was favorable to the experimental group; the mean difference was statistically significant at the .001 level.

Now we are ready to look at Table 3 of the Blenkner et al., article (p. 266) and understand where it indicates in the first column ("Service group," "Interview scores") and in the fourth row ("Protection," "Concrete Assistance") where there appears the following: "up[d]." Up indicates the direction of the change on this variable (concrete assistance) for this source of information ("Interview scores with experimental or service participants"). Up is reflected in the positive change score in Table 10.3. The d represents the degree of the significance of the change. As indicated at the bottom of Table 3, $d = p < .001$. This is just what I described above when I pointed to the mean difference of +1.6, a positive change comparing the initial to the one-year scores for the experimental participants. Up is a lot simpler and clearer—once you know where that up comes from.

Exactly the same thing is meant by up in the "Control" column, "Interview scores," on this same variable, "Concrete Assistance." Up represents a positive change (0.4) over the course of the project year. The a indicates that the change was at the $p < .05$ level.

Finally, we can look at the last pair of columns headed, "Program favored" and "Significance of difference" on this variable, "Concrete Assistance." For the interview source of data, we see "Service" which means that if we look at this variable, "Concrete Assistance," over a year's time for the mean differences between the experimental and the control participants, the overall result favors

247

Table 10.3 Interview Scores of One-Year Survivors: Initial, One-Year, and Change Scores with Differences Between Treatment Groups.

Criterion Variables[a] (5 items in each, except as noted below)	Mean Scores						Mean Differences[b] Between Service and Control Groups		
	Service			Control					
	Initial	One-Year	Change[c]	Initial	One-Year	Change[c]	Initial	One-Year	Change[c]
Competence Mental functioning (MSQ) (9 items)	5.1	4.4	-1.1^{***}	5.2	4.5	-0.3	-0.1	-0.1	-0.8
Physical functioning (PFQ)	2.5	2.1	-0.2	2.7	2.7	-0.1	-0.2	-0.5	-0.1
Physical environment (PE) (10 items)	7.3	8.4	0.8	7.1	7.5	0.4	0.2	0.8^{*}	0.4
Protection Concrete assistance (CA)	1.2	2.8	1.6^{****}	1.5	2.1	0.4^{*}	-0.3	0.8^{**}	1.1^{****}
Interested parties (IP)	2.5	2.6	0.0	2.4	2.9	0.4	0.0	-0.3	-0.3
Affect and Behavior Contentment (Con)	2.7	2.9	0.3	2.6	2.6	0.2	0.1	0.2	0.2
Signs and symptoms (S&S)	3.0	3.3	0.4	3.0	3.1	0.1	0.0	0.1	0.2
Effect on Others Collateral stress (Coll) (6 items)	4.2	—	—	4.0	—	—	0.2	—	—
Comparative collateral stress (CCS) (6 items)	—	1.9	—	—	0.9	—	—	1.0^{***}	—

SOURCE: Blenkner, et al., 1974, Table 4-6, pp. 111–112.

Significance on two-tailed tests: * $p < .05$; ** $p < .02$; *** $p < .01$; **** $p < .001$.

[a] All variables are scored so that a high score is a favorable score, and a negative change is unfavorable.

[b] A minus (—) favors the controls.

[c] A change score is the one-year score minus the initial score of the individual, with means calculated for all survivors in the E or C group. A minus sign indicates a downward or unfavorable trend.

the service group. The statistical significance of this result is at the $p < .001$ level. This is what is indicated by the "1.1****" in Table 10.3.

All of this work went into each of the terms and letters appearing in Table 3 of the article. This is what is meant when we say tables condense information to a manageable size. We didn't say that it wouldn't take work to understand how to manage it, only that it would be manageable. A few other notes will help you to understand Table 3. For the "Physical Environment" variable, the observer rating was made as part of the participant interview, so we see the information source as coming from both the interview and the observer's ratings. The symbol *n.d.* means no data were obtained for this particular cell entry. Observer ratings of participants' physical functioning were not obtained because the observers were asking standardized questions that were likely to be better than observer judgments. The symbol *n.s.* means that the changes observed were not statistically significant, although the trend of the data is given by a notation, such as "Service, n.s." This means that there were no statistically significant differences between the experimental and the control groups, but that whatever differences did exist favored the service group. There you have it.

COMPARISONS AMONG THE THREE RESEARCH PERSPECTIVES: THE PARTICIPANT INTERVIEW, THE RESEARCH INTERVIEWER'S OBSERVATIONS, AND THE SOCIAL WORKER'S RATINGS

Rashomon, the poetic film by the renowned Japanese filmmaker Akira Kurosawa, involves the telling of the same tale of love and murder from the different perspectives of the three parties involved. It challenges the viewer to decide which interpretation is right, because each contains internal evidence of its veracity and represents the perspective of an involved party. The film also provokes the viewer into comparing the several versions, as each goes over what are presumably the same events. The overall effect of the film is one of profound insight into not merely the human condition, but the social condition as well.

Strangely enough, the very techniques used so artistically by Kurosawa are present in many research studies. For example, in the Protective Services Project, the older person in need of protective services expressed his or her views, albeit indirectly, on the standardized questionnaire. In addition, the research interviewer made some standardized observations based on this interview as well as on that of the collateral. Independently of these, the social worker, who had contact only with the service cases, made her own ratings on standardized forms. Thus, through the workings of three sources of data on one life situation, we have a *Rashomon*-like situation: What correspondences were there among the three perspectives? Which was most truly accurate?*

In place of the dreamlike cinematographics of *Rashomon,* I have to offer only a humble table (Table 10.4). However, I believe we can discover some interesting comparisons and challenges even here. Let's begin by looking at the table because

---

* This discussion on the *comparability of the research data obtained from different sources* constitutes Technical Note 10.4.

Table 10.4 Correlations Among Measures (data from initial interview status).

| Criterion Variables | | Participant Interview Scores Compared with Research Interviewer Observations | | | | | | P. Interview Scores Compared with Social Worker Ratings | | Research Interviewer Observations Compared with Social Workers Ratings | |
| | | Experimental | | Control | | Total Sample | | Experimental | | Experimental | |
		n	r	n	r	n	r	n	r	n	r
Competence	Mental functioning (MSQ, MFO, MC)[a]	47	.46***	54	.42***	101	.44***	45	.45***	61	.50***
	Physical functioning (PFQ, PFO, PC)[a]	63	.62***	71	.66***	134	.64***	60	.49***	65	.53***
	Physical environment (PE, EPP)[a]	—	—	—	—	—	—	60	.61***	—	—
Protection	Concrete assistance (CA, CAO, EPS)[a]	57	.51***	73	.45***	130	.47***	55	.24	62	.37***
	Interested parties (IP, IPO, EPS)[a]	59	.23	71	.31***	131	.28***	56	.18	61	.25
Affect and Behavior	Contentment (Con, ConO, ConC)[a]	56	.67***	67	.61***	123	.65***	52	.30*	60	.46***
	Signs and symptoms (S&S, SSO, SSC)[a]	55	.21	63	.41***	118	.33***	52	.25	64	.49***
Effect on Others	Collateral stress (Coll, CollO, CollC)[a]	58	.69***	65	.43***	123	.57***	43	.31*[b]	42	.38[b]

SOURCE: Blenkner, et al., 1974, Table 4–3, p. 124.

[a] The abbreviations stand for the measurement instrument used by the participant (e.g., MSQ), the research interviewer (e.g., MFO), and the social worker (e.g., MC), respectively, except on the physical environment variable, where only the participant and social worker data are compared. The meaning of the correlations in this table has been made uniform, even when this required reverse scoring of the CAO and the IPO measures, where low scores are favorable.

[b] Collateral is not always the same person in both measures.

* p < .05; *** p < .01

it is another densely packed arrangement of facts. First, the title indicates that the table covers correlations among measures. This title is somewhat misleading, although technically accurate, because correlations compare only two sets of things at a time. If P stands for the participant's interview data, R for the research interviewer's observations, and W for the social worker's ratings, then we can expect to find the following correlations presented: P-I, P-W, I-W. (These are presented in the three main columns in Table 10.4.)

In addition, these various comparisons can be made for both experimental (that is to say, service) and control groups—except no social worker ratings were made for the control participants. So Table 10.4 contains secondary columns on service and control subsamples, as well as a total sample when appropriate.

In the generation of correlations, we have to know how many persons were involved when the scores of two perspectives were compared. So each of the subcolumns is further broken down into n (= number of persons involved in the comparison) and r (= Pearsonian correlation coefficient, the most common form of correlation—see Technical Note 6.5, p. 169). All of these data are based on the participants' situation at their entrance into the project, because this was the only time that the researcher interviewers' ratings were made without knowledge of whether the older person would go into the experimental or the control group. Nor did the interviewer know at that time what final set of items would be used for any given measure. Of course, by design, the interviewer's observations were influenced by what the participant had told him or her in the interview, but these observations were not limited to these statements. The interviewer was instructed to use direct observations and good judgment, as well as information supplied by the collateral, in making these final observational ratings.

Looking at the body of Table 10.4, we can see that most of the correlations are not actually high as such (the highest is only .69), but the majority of them reach statistical significance (29 times out of a possible 36). The possible reasons for the low correlation are many, including the fact that the measurement scales themselves were not reliable instruments. But also, the way we defined each variable may have been somewhat different for each of the three perspectives. We asked the participants facts that we thought they could be reasonably expected to know and to tell us; the research interviewers made judgments based on broadly behavioral grounds, as we had a diverse group of interviewers who could not all be expected to use the same frame of reference; and the social workers understandably were using a clinical perspective.

The table tells us that there was considerable agreement among all three perspectives on mental and physical functioning and levels of contentment. Of these, physical functioning was the highest in terms of agreement among the three perspectives, perhaps because it was the clearest and most objectively visible aspect of the participant's life. The lowest levels of agreement were on the psychopathology aspect (the signs and symptoms of affective and behavioral disorders) and what we termed "interested parties" (those persons who were present in the participant's life but who were not doing anything to assist matters).

Looking at specific pairs of perspectives tells us another story. The research interviewers' ratings are uniformly significant in comparison with the total participants' initial interview scores, as might be expected because they both used much of the same information in making their judgments. However, the interviewers were not uniformly successful because on two variables (signs and symptoms, and interested parties) in the experimental group, they did not significantly correlate with the participants. The reasons for these differences are not clear. We simply don't know why the interviewers showed moderate but statistically significant correlations with the control group and not with the experimental group. No doubt, there is some explanation, but it often occurs in the life of the researcher that she or he finds data that defy reasonable explanation. This was one such occasion.

In contrast to the uniform agreement between the participants' interviews and the interviewers' observations, look at the few agreements between the social workers' ratings (on service cases only) when correlated with the participants' initial interviews. Five out of eight comparisons are statistically significant—but be careful of the significance on the variable of collateral stress, as the social worker and the research interviewer did not always choose the same person as the collateral. The nonsignificant correlations on three variables suggest that the social workers and the participants were not looking at the same facts or were interpreting them differently. This difference might be expected; the participants may have been, in effect, viewing their life situation in ways that were adequate (to keep them from being institutionalized, which almost all abhorred), whereas the clinical perspective might have been to be aware of personal difficulties and lack of social supports. Whatever the reason, the facts are that the lowest proportion of agreements among rating scales were to be found between the social workers and the participants' interview data.

The social workers and the research interviewers showed high levels of significant correlations on relevant variables. (The interviewers did not make observational judgments on the physical environment because they rated the physical setting in such detailed terms that an overall observation would have added little.) This pattern suggests that even though the clinical perspective of the social workers differed greatly from the research perspective of the interviewers, they still viewed behaviors and events in the participants' lives with reasonable levels of agreement.

And so the overall answer to the first *Rashomon*-like question regarding multiple perspectives on one happening is that all three perspectives seem to have been reasonably similar, given errors in the reliability of the measures used, but the fewest number of agreements (and of statistically significant correlations) is to be found between the social worker and the participants' initial interview data, where about half of the variables are significantly related.

The second *Rashomon*-like question (Who was telling the truth?) is much more difficult to answer. One response is that everyone was telling the truth from his or her own perspective, and if these truths differed, it was merely because the perceptions differed. Truth is not a fixed aspect of reality but a social construction. A second response is that everyone was not telling the truth to some degree, probably because of some systematic biases in their perspectives on the nature of the problem. In this view, truth is a fixed aspect of reality, which we know only approximately, but it is "out there" if we can only reach it. (This is not to say, by the way, that anyone was lying; such purposive changing of the facts of nature probably played a very small part in this study, even granting that the participants were fearful of being uprooted and institutionalized by "helping professionals." I, at least, was continually struck by the brutal honesty of many of the answers that the participants gave us, when they could. I also believe that the participants gave "information" whether they knew it to be true or not, simply to be civil when someone asked them a direct question. As I mentioned in Chapter 7, it is hard to deal with such social acquiescence, other than to help the respondent not to feel that pressure.)

Ultimately, which perspective was true or most nearly true depends on your own view of truth. For obvious reasons, I cannot legislate that. But do ask yourself what view of truth you hold: Is it an independently existing condition "out there," which we come to know only approximately, or is it an arbitrary construction whose common agreement we can approximate only to a limited degree? As you define these presuppositions of research, so you influence how you collect and interpret information.

COMPARISONS ON SERVICES RECEIVED IN EXPERIMENTAL AND CONTROL GROUPS

In a demonstration project, one of the critical factors is the experimental intervention. This is the point where the research-independent variable meets the practice demonstration services. It also provides us another opportunity to examine how research data are presented.

With regard to the BRI project, you will recall that the referring agencies were asked to provide whatever services they had been giving to the control participants, and to refer these cases to other service providers as needed (except that the Benjamin Rose Institute would not take them for the duration of the project). In some cases, the referring agencies, like public housing and public assistance, continued their services to the experimental participants as well.

Now the question arises, how similar or different was the experience of services between the experimental and control groups?* If there was to be a treatment effect, then that experimental variable should have been strong and clean. Unfortunately, in community studies, it is not always possible to keep services separate. But let's examine what happened in the Protective Project.

In Table 10.5, nine categories of services are distinguished, and the rank order and percentage of use are indicated for experimental and control participants. These data were gathered from interviews with professionals at the referring agency as well as with the AIG social workers. The similarity in the rank order of most of the categories is the most obvious feature of that table. The percentages of use differ considerably. Note first that the proportion of experimental participants reported as receiving a given type of service is higher in all cases than the proportion of controls, reflecting the strength of the treatment variable. Even when a rank order of categories is similar for both experimental and control groups, the percentage of its use may differ. For example, medical treatment, evaluation, or consultation was ranked high in both experimental and control groups, but the percentage of persons getting this type of service varied considerably.

Likewise, the lowest five categories are similar for both groups with the excep-

---

* This discussion of the *comparison of services received by experimental and control groups* constitutes Technical Note 10.5.

Table 10.5 Services During the Demonstration Year, Comparing AIG with Community Services, as Reported by AIG and Referral Agency Workers.

	Rank Order		Percentage Receiving Service	
Type of Service	AIG Experimental Service	Controls (Community Service)	AIG	Controls
Counseling/casework	1	2	82%	60%
Medical treatment, evaluation, consultation	2	3	78	44
Financial assistance, advice	3	1	75	69
Home aide/homemaker	4	7	50	9
Nursing care, evaluation, consultation	5	4	47	33
Placement	6	5	43	25
Psychiatric evaluation, treatment, consultation	7	8	38	8
Legal services, consultation	8	6	34	11
Guardianship	9	9	16	2

SOURCE: Blenkner, et al., 1974, Table 3–3, p. 91.

tion of home aide or homemaker services. This is the one major exception to ranking (and correspondingly, to the percentage of use of this service). This use of home aide service reflects not only the state of affairs in Cleveland but throughout the United States as well; it also reflects a state of mind in using such services. However, Dr. Blenkner was quick to recognize the implications of this service in combination with a professionally-led team; later research studies and service programs at the Benjamin Rose Institute reflected this interest.

I call your attention to the figures regarding placement. The experimental program exceeded the control group on their use of this service. This point became the basis of considerable discussion of the outcome, as you will read in the paper produced at the end of this chapter. Thus simple lists of rank orders or percentages of use may conceal some powerful factors that both verify the strength of the experimental variables and offer some explanation of why the outcomes appear as they do. But tables always require careful reading.

THE GENERAL FORMAT FOR PRESENTING PUBLISHED RESEARCH REPORTS*

1. A report of research, particularly one presented in a professional journal, typically has a number of basic features. First, there is some statement of the problem being addressed, possibly including the background for the researchers'

* This discussion of the major parts of *format for presenting published research reports* constitutes Technical Note 10.6.

interest in it, or perhaps including a statement of current theories and research—and the points missing or in conflict in them. In addition, for applied social sciences, there is often a statement of need, justifying the research and demonstration efforts. There may also be a discussion of current practice methods with the population at risk and of their shortcomings. The hypotheses to be studied in this project are often presented.

2. The second major category is a methodological section, with two major parts: one deals specifically with the research, and the other deals with the intervention being evaluated in that research. Included in the research methodology are such topics as an examination of the population from which the sample was drawn and the methods used in constructing the sample (for purposes of future generalizations from the data). The research design is also discussed, so that readers can establish what alternative sources of influence may account for the results, as well as the power of the study to be generalized to other samples.

3. The service or treatment design calls for equally careful specification, so that persons seeking to replicate the project will know as clearly as possible what was involved and how it was carried out.

4. Then the findings are presented, as related to the guiding questions (hypotheses) of the study, or in descriptive form. The researcher has to sharply reduce the innumerable pieces of information to some intelligible form that presents the major trends (and tests of hypotheses) as clearly and accurately as possible.

5. The report concludes with the implications of these data, in light of the nature of the problem and the specific hypotheses that guided the study. This is also the place where the researcher can suggest leads to new research that may answer questions raised in the course of the present study.

6. Having described the general outline, I can only say that every writer varies it to suit his or her own needs, but you will very likely find most of these topics covered in one way or another in most scientific reports.

PUBLISHED REPORT

A Research and Demonstration Project of Protective Services*

Margaret Blenkner, Martin Bloom, and Margaret Neilsen

Some of the data pertaining to factors predictive of institutionalization or survival suggest that changes may be introduced in lives least able to bear them.

American society and American social work are not comfortable about the aged in their midst, and they should not be. In comparison with the elderly living in other advanced

From *Social Casework*, 8 (October 1971), 483–499. Reprinted with permission from Family Service America, New York.

   * *Editorial Note:* This presentation of the entire published paper reporting the BRI Protective Services Project constitutes Technical Note 10.7.

industrial societies, the old people of the United States live in greater relative poverty and are offered social services that are deplorably underdeveloped, especially community-delivered services.[1]

Of particular cause for concern are the mentally impaired aged living within the communities outside of institutional walls. These are the old people whose memory, orientation, and judgment appear so faulty or whose perception of reality is so distorted that one questions their ability to perform effectively the simple acts of day-to-day living. These are persons who cannot manage their finances without spending too little money or overspending, who cannot negotiate with others to secure their necessities or to protect themselves from exploitation, who cannot maintain their persons and their habitats so as not to offend or endanger others, and who cannot control their emotions so as not to erupt in abusive or—more rarely—in violent attacks on others.

Members of several professions—social work, law, and medicine in particular—have become increasingly concerned about the protection of such persons, especially those who have no relatives or friends able and willing to look after them and those whose relatives and friends either cannot give the required time and energy or are doing what they do poorly and improperly. The problem is most acute in the large metropolitan areas, where the old person without close friends or family ties is easily lost from sight unless his condition or behavior warrants a sensational news story—and by the time the news story appears, it is usually too late to do much to help him.

Even where the will to care for "protectives" exists, highly complicated social and legal aspects are entangled in the conflicting concern for individual rights and public duty.[2] Historically, community concern for this group found its expression in legal provisions to protect property holdings from dissipation, but there was little emphasis on the protection of the person. Commitment to a mental hospital was used as a last resort, but few professional services—short of the drastic step of commitment—were available.

By the early 1960s, it was clear to almost everyone that better solutions to the problem must be found. Three long-term demographic trends occurring simultaneously made the need imperative. These trends were (1) a shift in living patterns from the three- to the two-generation household, (2) the tendency for couples with young children to move to the suburbs and leave their aged relatives in the city, and (3) the marked lengthening of the average life span.

In carrying out its responsibilities for administering the public assistance and social insurance provisions of the Social Security Act, the federal government had become acutely aware of the problem and the lack of services to meet it. In 1962 the Social Security Administration made a grant to the Benjamin Rose Institute (BRI) of Cleveland—one of the few agencies at that time providing extensive protective service to old people—to plan a research and demonstration project on the problem. This grant was followed by a series of grants from the Welfare Administration and later from the Social and Rehabilitation Service. With additional grants from the A. M. McGregor Home of Cleveland, the institute was enabled to carry out the controlled demonstration and the five-year follow-up reported on in this article.[3]

Prevalence

There have been many definitions of the need for protective service, but explicit or implied in all of them are two components: defective mental functioning and defective social resources. How many persons are there in the United States who have these two problems in combination? To answer this question requires assembling facts on mental illness among

1 Ethel Shanas et al., *Old People in Three Industrial Societies* (New York: Atherton Press, 1968).
2 The word *protectives* is used in the articles in this series to denote persons in need of protective service.
3 Social Security Administration Research Grant No. 072, Welfare Administration and Social and Rehabilitation Service Research Grant No. 175, and National Institute of General Medical Science Grant No. GM-12302, Department of Health, Education, and Welfare, Washington, D.C.

the older population and facts on the existence and adequacy of what one might call "protecting others" among the friends, relatives, and agents of that population. No really solid epidemiological data are available, however, and the best one can do is make an educated guess based on data from various samples of older persons studied in recent years in several different urban areas.

As might be expected, the prevalence of mental impairment is much greater among the institutionalized than among the noninstitutionalized aged, although it is not inconsiderable among the latter. Various isolated studies indicate that the prevalence of mental impairment may be as high as one half among the institutional and one sixth among the noninstitutional populations. For example, Alvin I. Goldfarb's studies of selected New York institutions show that chronic brain syndrome characterized from one half to four fifths of the elderly inmates of the various sites studied, depending on the nature of the institutions. The institutions included philanthropic homes for the aged, proprietary nursing homes, and state mental hospitals.[4] Goldfarb's New York findings, which were based on direct psychiatric examinations, correspond well with data released by the National Center for Health Statistics, which indicate that 50 percent of the residents of institutions for the chronically ill and aged were reported by the administrators of these institutions to be mentally confused most or part of the time.[5]

Fewer than 5 percent of the older population are in institutions of any sort, however, so that even a rate as high as 50 percent mentally impaired accounts for no more than 2 to 3 percent of the total older population. One must, therefore, look to the noninstitutionalized elderly residing in their own homes or in the homes of relatives for the great majority of brain damaged or mentally disturbed people who require the protective services provided by the organized welfare and health agencies of the nation.[6]

One of the earliest studies relating to mental illness among the aged was done in Syracuse in 1960 for the Research Unit of the New York State Department of Mental Hygiene.[7] This study attempted to determine the number of persons aged sixty-five and over who would be judged as "certifiable" to a state mental hospital. Data from the survey indicated that 7 percent of the enumerated population, which included institutionalized as well as noninstitutionalized persons, met the definition of "certifiable." Five percent lived in their own homes, and 2 percent lived in institutions of one sort or another. Using less stringent criteria than those used by the Syracuse study, which selected the most severely disturbed or deteriorated individuals, other studies have indicated still higher prevalence rates for mental disorder among the noninstitutionalized aged in urban areas.

Margaret Blenkner estimates that among the noninstitutionalized population sixty years of age and over in New York City, somewhere between 14 percent and 16 percent are mentally impaired. This estimate is based on unpublished data accumulated during 1957 at the Community Service Society of New York from an area probability sample of older residents of Manhattan, the Bronx, and Queens.[8] This 14-to-16-percent figure corresponds

4 Alvin I. Goldfarb, "Prevalence of Psychiatric Disorders in Metropolitan Old Age and Nursing Homes," *Journal of the American Geriatrics Society,* 10:78–84 (January 1962).
5 U.S., Department of Health, Education, and Welfare, National Center for Health Statistics, *Characteristics of Residents in Institutions for the Aged and Chronically Ill, United States, April–June 1963,* Public Health Service Publication No. 1000, Series 12, No. 2 (Washington, D.C.: Government Printing Office, September 1965).
6 One should not assume, however, that the institutionalized aged do not need protection. More than 80 percent are in proprietary nursing homes, and the circumstances of many are grim and in some instances scandalous. Perusal of the files of the daily newspapers in any major city over the last ten years will attest to this statement.
7 New York State, Department of Mental Hygiene, Mental Health Research Unit, *A Mental Health Survey of Older People* (Utica, N.Y.: State Hospital Press, 1960).
8 Community Service Society, Institute of Welfare Research, "Demographic Data on Protective Cases Among a Sample of Older Applicant and Non-Applicants," unpublished (New York: Community Service Society, 1962).

257

well with the 17 percent of a sample of residents of a large New York City housing project found to show definite signs of chronic brain syndrome.[9] It also approximates the 16 percent with "low psychiatric status" whom Marjorie Fiske Lowenthal found among a sample of elderly San Francisco residents.[10] Because no two studies used the same definitions or criteria, the results are not strictly comparable. Nevertheless, it is probably safe to say that at least a modicum of mental impairment or behavior disturbance or both characterizes approximately 15 to 20 percent of the urban aged in the United States today. A reservoir is thus formed of three to four million potential candidates for protective service should their normal social resources fail them.

How large is the number of older citizens who, at any given time, need some form of continuing supervision and assistance from a community agency because they are mentally incompetent or only marginally competent and lack the usual protecting others, such as capable and responsible relatives or friends? To answer this question there are really no data available, but the writers estimate that between 7 and 10 percent of the urban population over sixty years of age may come under this rubric, depending on how strictly or loosely one construes the word *protective*. This estimate is based on observations made during the past fifteen years at the Community Service Society of New York and at the Benjamin Rose Institute of Cleveland, where the writers studied data collected on older persons who had *not applied* for service. Among older persons who apply or on whose behalf an application is made to these or similar voluntary casework agencies, the need for protective service may run as high as 25 to 30 percent. James J. Burr cites data indicating that 10 percent of the adult caseload of public welfare agencies—consisting largely of recipients of old age assistance—are in need of protection.[11] Ruth Weber reports that 8 percent of a sample of 752 public housing tenants over sixty years of age were classified as needing protective service by the housing staff who knew them well.[12]

An estimate of 7 percent would put the number of mentally impaired older persons in need of protective service in the United States today at about one and one-half million. A more conservative estimate of 5 percent would put the number at approximately one million.

Past Action

The protective is an extremely difficult client to serve. Every case has legal and psychiatric ramifications as well as social and medical ones. With rare exceptions no agency, either public or private, has been able or willing to assume responsibility for the problem in any community.[13] There has been, however, general agreement regarding the need for aid and the fact that social work is the logical profession to assume primary responsibility.

Among the national agencies that have been in the forefront of the push to define the problem and to demonstrate approaches to its solution have been the National Council on Aging, the American Public Welfare Association, the Family Service Association of Amer-

9 State of New York, Department of Mental Hygiene, "Early Brain Damage in the Aged: A Community and Clinical Study," prepared for the Office of the Consultant on Service for the Aged by Mayer Fisch, Siroon Shahinian, and Alvin Goldfarb, mimeographed (Albany: Department of Mental Hygiene, 1962).

10 Marjorie Fiske Lowenthal, Paul I. Berkman, and Associates, *Aging and Mental Disorders in San Francisco: A Social Psychiatric Study* (San Francisco: Jossey-Bass, 1967).

11 James J. Burr. "Program Goals and the Specialist's Function in Public Welfare," in *Planning Welfare Services for Older People: Papers Presented at the Training Institute for Public Welfare Specialists on Aging, Cleveland, Ohio, June 13–24, 1965* (Washington, D.C.: U.S. Department of Health, Education, and Welfare, 1966), pp. 5–12.

12 Ruth Weber, "Protective Service for Older People" (paper presented at the Annual Conference of the National Association of Housing and Redevelopment Officials, North Central Regional Council, Columbus, Ohio, May 1964).

13 The United Charities of Chicago and the Benjamin Rose Institute of Cleveland are outstanding examples of the exceptional agency that has long served this clientele.

ica, and—within the Department of Health, Education, and Welfare—the Welfare Administration and its successor, the Social and Rehabilitation Service, the Social Security Administration, and the Public Health Service. The Veterans Administration, with an aging clientele, has also become increasingly interested in the problem. Several books that are landmarks in the developing conceptualization of what is involved in protective service were published by the National Council on Aging.[14] Under a grant from the National Institute of Mental Health, the council also stimulated a series of demonstrations in various settings across the country extending protective service to older people.

Further evidence of the growing recognition of the need for adult protective services was indicated by their inclusion among those services prescribed for recipients and potential recipients of public assistance under the 1962 Amendments to the Social Security Act. Continuing interest at the federal level was indicated in 1967 when, under the demonstration grants progrm of the Social and Rehabilitation Service, the Administration on Aging began its National Protective Services Project in three rural Colorado counties and in the city of Washington, D.C. The Benjamin Rose Institute's Protective Service Project, on which this report is based, is unique among protective service demonstrations in the rigor of its design and in the length of time the population sample was followed.

Population Studied

The BRI project concentrated on the noninstitutionalized older person who was likely to come to the attention of welfare and health agencies that offered individual services as differentiated from group services. The BRI research department secured a sample of 164 protectives from thirteen participating agencies over a twelve-month period from June 1964 through May 1965. It defined the sort of person it was seeking as "a person 60 years of age or over . . . whose behavior indicates that he is mentally incapable of adequately caring for himself and his interests without serious consequences to himself and others and has no relative or other private individual able and willing to assume the kind and degree of support and supervision required to control the situation."

The referring agencies were of the following four main types: (1) economic maintenance, represented by the county welfare department, the county old-age-assistance office, and a social security office; (2) housing, represented by the local housing-authority apartment complex having the highest concentration of older residents; (3) health, represented by the public-health nursing division of the city health department, the visiting nurse association, the social service department of the city hospital, and a chronic illness center; and (4) counseling, referral, and information, represented by the three family service agencies, a community information center, and a psychiatric unit within the probate court.

Before the sample was selected, a survey of caseloads in the participating agencies was undertaken to provide some basis for assigning referral quotas so that the intake volume could be controlled. The survey indicated that as many as two hundred persons in need of protective service might be identified by the thirteen participating agencies in any one month.

The economic maintenance agencies ranked first in the number of cases identified, followed by housing, health, and the counseling, referral, and information agencies. These findings,

14 Virginia Lehmann and Geneva Mathiasen, eds., *Guardianship and Protective Services for Older People* (Albany, N.Y.: National Council on the Aging Press, 1963); Rebecca Eckstein and Ella Lindey, eds., *Seminar on Protective Services for Older People: Proceedings of a Seminar Held at Arden House, Harriman, New York, March 10–15, 1963* (New York: National Council on the Aging, 1964); Ella Lindey, ed., *A Crucial Issue of Social Work Practice: Protective Services for Older People* (New York: National Council on the Aging, 1965); Gertrude H. Hall, ed., *The Law and the Impaired Older Person: Protection or Punishment* (New York: National Council on the Aging, 1966); and Gertrude H. Hall and Geneva Mathiasen, eds., *Overcoming Barriers to Protective Services for the Aged: Report of a National Institute on Protective Services, Savoy-Field Hotel, Houston, Texas, January 16–18, 1968* (New York: National Council on the Aging, 1968).

of course, reflect the relative proportion of older persons in the community who are known to the various types of agencies. In was clear that the family service agencies—the agencies with the greatest concentration of casework expertise, as represented by the highest proportion of staff with graduate training and supervised experience—were the least likely of all the participating agencies to encounter the older person in need of protective service. (The relative infrequency with which the family service agency encounters the protective client might not hold true in other communities. Cleveland has the unique advantage of having the Benjamin Rose Institute, which may drain off many of the applications that in other communities are made to family agencies.)

Another point of interest was the finding that the health agencies reported a wider variety of case sources than did other agencies. This finding indicates the extent to which the general public thinks of the health agency as a logical source of help for the person needing protective service.

An analysis of the demographic characteristics of the persons identified in the preliminary survey and of the 164 persons who constituted the demonstration phase sample suggests that those old people likely to be identified as needing protective services by the types of agencies cooperating in the sampling procedure are predominantly over seventy-five years of age, female, white, native-born, and nonmarried (widowed, divorced, separated, or never married). They have grammar-school educations only, reside in their own homes, and live on social security, old age assistance, or both, with incomes rarely more than $150 and often less than $100 a month. (See Table 1.)

In comparison to the general older population of the community but with age differences controlled, the following groups are underrepresented in the protective sample: men, non-whites, the foreign-born, and married persons. Overrepresented are women, native-born whites, and divorced, separated, or never married persons. Whether these departures from the general population represent likelihood of need for protective service or likelihood of identification cannot really be determined by the data, but it seems logical to hypothesize that advanced age and nonmarried status are predictors of need, whereas sex, color, and nativity may be primarily predictors of identification.

A recital of demographic characteristics captures neither the flavor of the personalities and behaviors exhibited in the sample nor the full range of pathology, frustration, and pathos with which the soical workers and research interviewers dealt during the study. Some of these persons represented one generation in a multigenerational chain of pathology, reaching back to their parents and grandparents and proceeding forward in their children and grandchildren, but many had demonstrated average or even above average competence most of their lives. Some were rootless, always isolated "loners," but others had simply outlived what had once been strong and numerous family and neighborhood ties. Most showed signs of chronic brain syndrome, but a few seemed to represent purely affective psychoses or long-standing and severe neuroses. Some, from such history as was obtainable, appeared to be mental retardates who had always operated at a marginal level. Nearly all showed the ravages of physical disease and disability in addition to their mental infirmities, and, by definition, none had families or friends adequate or willing to take on the full load of stress and responsibility involved in protective care. In almost all instances they were nonvoluntary clients. They had not sought help themselves from the referring agencies, and they were fearful and threatened by any approach from persons representing the power and authority of society. They suspected, often with good reason, that this power and authority would be used to curtail what little freedom of action and choice they still had.

The cases were randomly allocated to two groups as they were referred: (1) the experimental or demonstration service group, $N = 76$, and (2) the control or standard treatment group, $N = 88$. Persons in the experimental group were served in the project for one year; those in the control group were left with the referring agency to be served (or not served) in the normal fashion of the agency. All will be referred to in the remainder of this article as participants.

260

Table 1 Characteristics of BRI Protective Sample from Initial Interview Data

Characteristic	Percentage
Age	[95%][a]
60–74	37
75 and over	63
Median, 78 years	
Range, 60–102 years	
Sex	[100%]
Male	31
Female	69
Color	[100%]
White	91
Nonwhite	9
Nativity	[72%]
Native-born	72
Foreigh-born	28
Marital status	[92%]
Married	15
Widowed	59
Divorced, separated	9
Never married	17
Education	[73%]
Non formal schooling	7
Grammar school only	57
Some high school	20
Some college	8
Other	8
Type residence	[89%]
Private house	36
Apartment, public housing	24
Apartment, other	24
Room	15
Other	1
Major income source	[81%]
Social security	47
Old age assistance	34
Pensions, dividends, rents	7
Other income	7
Withdrawals from savings	3
No income	3
Monthly income	[70%]
Less than $50	11
$50–74	15
$75–99	22
$100–149	38
$150–199	8
$200 and over	5
Median, $102	

[a] Figures in brackets are the percentage of total sample on whom data were available for the particular characteristic. The number of the total sample was 164.

All participants—both experimental and control—were interviewed by research staff during the demonstration year in the following pattern: (1) a long, detailed initial interview was held within five days of registration and before any contact was made by the project service staff; (2) short follow-up interviews were held after three months and six months; and (3) a longer, more detailed follow-up interview was held after one year. Research interviews were also held with collaterals (generally the closest or most active relative or friend of the participant) at the time of registration and at six-month and at one-year follow-up periods.[15]

Staff members of the original referring agencies were also interviewed after one year in order to provide additional follow-up information regarding events during the participants' demonstration period. (Many of the persons in the experimental group were active with the referring agencies during their research year because the services offered by these agencies, such as public assistance, public housing, and visiting nurse services, would not otherwise have been available.)

At the end of the participants' demonstration year, direct research interviewing and service from the project staff were discontinued. Surviving participants in the experimental group who continued to require service were transferred to the regular BRI social work program. Follow-up of the remaining experimental participants and of the control participants has been continued through research contacts with the various social and health agencies maintaining service contacts with them.

The purpose of the follow-up contact was to determine three facts about the participants: have they survived, have they relocated, and, if so, where? In the case of the few persons not maintaining service contact with BRI or with one of the participating agencies, direct research follow-up has been carried out with either the participant or a collateral to determine current circumstances. As of this writing, minimal data have been gathered over a five-year follow-up period for every participant in the experimental and control groups.

Service Design

Because the research design called for standard treatment rather than for no treatment for the controls, it was reasoned that the demonstrated service had to be a strong variable if statistically significant differences between the control and the experimental service groups were to be anticipated at the conclusion of the demonstration. That is, the demonstration project would have to provide considerably greater service of a more varied nature than was ordinarily available in the community to older persons in need of protective service.

Social casework was seen as the core service, and an experienced, fully trained staff was secured for the project. Two caseworkers were selected from the regular BRI staff and two were recruited from outside. All held master's degrees in social work and one had an additional third year of graduate social work training; all had more than fifteen years of experience. Two were medical social workers, one had an extensive background in child welfare, and another had an extensive background in family casework.

One overriding directive governed the caseworker's activities: *Do, or get others to do whatever is necessary to meet the needs of the situation.* Upon registration, each participant was assigned to a caseworker, who then undertook to direct the course of whatever service or activity was required to meet his needs for the next twelve months. Cases were kept open and active throughout the year if at all possible, the only acceptable reason for closure being death. Because there was no casework staff turnover during the project, each participant was served by the same caseworker throughout his demonstration year.

15 The research interviewing process and schedules used are fully described in two previously issued documents. See Martin Bloom, "The Initial Research Interview: BRI Protective Services Project," mimeographed (Cleveland: Benjamin Rose Institute, 1964); and Martin Bloom and Margaret Blenkner, "The Follow-up Interviews: BRI Protective Service Project," mimeographed (Cleveland: Benjamin Rose Institute, 1966).

From the beginning it was recognized that although building relationships of trust and mutual respect between client and worker was an important aspect of the caseworker's job, such relationships were not enough. These clients would need much in the way of concrete assistance in meeting the daily demands of life, and the caseworker would often need to draw on the knowledge and skills of professions other than his own. With this practical thought in mind, funds were budgeted to provide—through the project or by purchase from outside sources—the following ancillary or supportive services: financial assistance, medical evaluation, psychiatric consultation, legal consultation, fiduciary and guardianship services, home aide and other home help services, nursing consultation and evaluation, and placement in a protective setting. Because the workers were under no compulsion to use a particular service, the statistics to be cited reflect the needs of the participants as the service staff saw them. Nursing consultation was required for all the persons receiving home aide service.

It was decided that the treatment of choice for the older protective was a form of social therapy rather than psychotherapy.[16] In the latter, emphasis is placed on the therapeutic interaction within the worker–client dyad, through which the client is expected to learn to feel and think differently and to develop his own inner controls. Such an approach requires a highly motivated, voluntary client capable of good verbal communication who is rarely found among protectives. Therefore, instead of intervening largely through verbal interaction, it was considered particularly necessary to enlist environmental supports to reach the client, restructuring the situation to compensate for the older person's deficiencies. It was hoped that this approach would lead to less disordered behavior and decreasing anxiety because the person could then cope with the simplified and supportive situation. At this stage the client might be able to make some use of a therapeutic relationship, and built-in protections within the person's familiar abode might make unnecessary the trauma of institutionalization.

The number of casework interviews held with the participants and collaterals during the participants' demonstration year provides a measure of the intensity of service. The average number of participant interviews was 18.0, the range being 0–54. The average number of collateral interviews was 13.9, the range being 0–41. Altogether, counting both participant and collateral interviews, 2,421 personal casework interviews were held for seventy-six participants, an average of 31.8 per participant.

The greatest number of casework interviews with a particular participant in any one month was ten; the greatest number for the collateral for a particular participant was fourteen. With little variation, the caseworkers averaged slightly more than two interviews per working day during the first year.[17]

Comparison of Demonstration and Community Services

It will be recalled that the referring agencies were asked to provide the participants falling in the control group with the same services they usually offered. To understand these services in terms comparable to those used in the experimental sample, workers in the referring agencies were interviewed regarding the control participants following the conclusion of the demonstration period. The project caseworkers were also interviewed regarding the service sample participants at the same time.

Following their original registration in the project, about two thirds of the control group (64 percent) and a not too dissimilar proportion (70 percent) of the service sample remained active with the referring agency for at least thirty days. Services for almost half (47 percent)

16 Ruth Weber, "Definition, Case Identification, and Sample Characteristics of Older Persons," in Lindey, *Crucial Issue in Social Work Practice,* pp. 3–9.
17 The first year's figures are given here because they are the most applicable to what might be anticipated in nonresearch practice. After the first year of the project, intake was closed and workers spent proportionately more time on such research-engendered tasks as judging the status of their clients on the clinical rating scales and dictating transfer of closing summaries of cases.

263

of the surviving controls and for nearly as many of the survivors in the experimental sample (40 percent) were still provided after one year. This continuation of service, however, was primarily a reflection of the public housing and public assistance that continued to be supplied to control and service participants alike during the course of the demonstration. In addition, it was reported that almost one half of the controls and only one eighth of the experimental sample had been referred to some other community agency for services.

Concerning the breakdown by type of service as indicated in Table 2, it is interesting to note that in all instances the proportion of participants reported to have received a given type of service is considerably higher among the sample served by the project. The rank order of most services does not, however, differ greatly. In fact, it is only in respect to the use of home aide and homemaker services that there is an appreciable difference. The service is ranked fourth for the project and seventh for the community services. The percentage differences for this category are gross: 50 percent of the project clients and only 9 percent of the control clients utilized this service. These figures reflect the development of home aide services in Cleveland at the time of the demonstration. The services have improved somewhat, but, as in nearly all American communities—even the most advanced on the social welfare front—they are still vastly underdeveloped.

The similarity of the ranked positions of both the project and community agency services testifies to a constancy of need. The fact that the percentages of clients receiving the various services are much higher for those served by the project testifies to the comparative strength of the experimental variable. The difference in the amounts of services received was also revealed in the follow-up measures of "environmental protection" and "concrete assistance" described and discussed later in this article.

Findings from the Demonstration

To assess change and to evaluate the impact and effectiveness of the experimental service, four aspects of the participants' lives and situations were measured during the demonstration year: competence, environmental protection, affect, and effect on others. Measures to tap each of these aspects were developed or adapted from data obtained from three major sources: (1) participant (or collateral) responses to highly structured research interviews, (2) observer ratings by the research interviewer, and (3) clinical ratings by the caseworkers for the service sample only.[18]

Multiple measures of mental functioning, physical functioning, physical environment, concrete assistance, interested parties, contentment, signs and symptoms of disturbance, and collateral stress were derived from all three sources. These measures yielded quantified scores that could be treated statistically. Two additional measures—survival and institutionalization—complete the list of variables on which conclusions regarding outcome are based. In the "competence–protection–affect–effect" rubric of this analysis, death is viewed as the ultimate deterioration in competence and institutionalization as the ultimate attempt at protection or control.

Each measure used has advantages and limitations. The interview scores were obtained on the least number of participants, ranging from a high of four fifths on the physical functioning questionnaire (PFQ) to a low of three fifths on the mental status questionnaire (MSQ). Observer ratings, on the other hand, were obtained on nine tenths of the participants for all variables except collateral stress; for the latter, ratings were obtained on fewer than four fifths of the participants because many of the protectives simply had no personal collateral

18 For observer rating scales, see Bloom, "Initial Research Interview"; and Bloom and Blenkner, "Follow-up Interviews." For clinical rating scales, see Rose Mayer, Ruth Weber, and Margaret Blenkner, "The BRI Clinical Rating Scales: A Manual, mimeographed" (Cleveland: Benjamin Rose Institute, 1966). See also, Martin Bloom and Margaret Blenkner, "Assessing Functioning of Older Persons Living in the Community," *The Gerontologist,* Part 1, 10:31–37 (Spring 1970).

Table 2 Comparison of Project and Community Services During Demonstration Year as Reported by Project and Referral Agency Workers

	Rank		Percentage	
Type of Service	Service (Project)	Control (Community)	Service ($N = 76$)	Control ($N = 88$)
Counseling, casework	1	2	82%	60%
Medical treatment, evaluation, consultation	2	3	78	44
Financial assistance, advice	3	1	75	69
Home aide, homemaker	4	7	50	9
Nursing care, evaluation, consultation	5	4	47	33
Placement	6	5	43	25
Psychiatric evaluation, treatment, consultation	7	8	38	8
Legal services, consultation	8	6	34	11
Guardianship	9	9	16	2

who could be interviewed. The clinical ratings made by project caseworkers were obtained for all service participants, but no comparable ratings were available for the controls.

When one assembles the data from all three sources—interview responses, observer ratings, and caseworker judgments—they are found, in the main, to be strikingly similar in regard to the changes that occurred during the demonstration year.[19] Table 3 shows the direction and significance of the changes that occurred in the various areas. It also shows which program (service versus control) makes the superior showing on each variable, and it indicates whether the obtained change differences are sufficiently great to be statistically significant.

Competence

The trend was downward for both physical and mental competence on all available measures in both programs. Differences, such as they were, favored the control group but were not statistically significant.

In regard to death—the ultimate deterioration in competence—the rate at the end of the demonstration year was 25 percent for the service participants and only 18 percent for the control participants–a discouraging but not significant difference. It is clear that the demonstrated treatment did not prevent or retard deterioration.

Protection

In the area of protection, there were clear differences, particularly in regard to the variable of concrete assistance. The trend was *upward* in both samples, probably reflecting the initial crisis state of most of the participants. There was, however, a significant shift toward greater protection in the experimental group that far exceeded the shift found for the control group. The differences between the two programs can be considered significant.

The difference in institutionalization rates during the demonstration year—34 percent among the service participants and 20 percent among the controls—was consistent with

19 Differences in initial status of the two subsamples were slight in most criterion variables, being of the order that one would expect by chance in 30 to 80 percent of similarly chosen samples. For the important age variable, however, in which the service cases were on the average about two years older than the controls, the difference approached significance. For this reason, age was controlled in all criterion analyses, but in none did it prove to be the explanatory variable insofar as differences between service an control cases were concerned. Space does not permit presentation of all the data obtained. For more details, see Margaret Blenkner et al., "Protective Services for Older People: Final Report."

Table 3 Change over Demonstration Year Showing Direction, Significance of Difference Between Service and Control Participants

	Variable	Direction and Significance of Change					Program Favored and Significance of Difference	
		Service			Control			
		Interview Scores	Observer Ratings	Clinical Casework Ratings	Interview Scores	Observer Ratings	Interview Scores	Observer Ratings
Competence	Mental functioning	down[c]	down[c]	down, n.s.	down, n.s.	down, n.s.	Control, n.s.	Control, n.s.
	Physical functioning	down, n.s.	(n.d.)	no change	down, n.s.	(n.d.)	Control, n.s.	(n.d.)
Protection	Physical environment	up[b]				up[a]	Service[a]	Service[a]
	Concrete assistance	up[d]	up[d]		up[a]	no change	Service[d]	Service[d]
	Interested parties	no change	up, n.s.		up, n.s.	no change	Service, n.s.	Service, n.s.
	Environmental protectoin—social			up[d]				
Affect	Contentment	up, n.s.	up, n.s.	up[a]	up, n.s.	up, n.s.	Service, n.s.	Service, n.s.
	Signs and symptoms	less, n.s.	less, n.s.	less, n.s.	less, n.s.	no change	Service, n.s.	Service, n.s.
Effect	Collateral stress		less[d]	less[a]		less, n.s.		Service[a]
	Comparative collateral stress	less			less		Service[c]	

Note: Based on change in mean scores (one-year score minus initial score) except for last variable, comparative collateral stress, which is based on collateral's judgment of change in stress.

Significance: [a]$p < .05$; [b]$p < .02$; [c]$p < .01$; [d]$p < .001$, two-tailed test.

266

the other findings on protection. Thus, in the area of protection, all measures favored the experimental program, and the measures of protection, as well as the data presented previously about services, indicate that the experimental variable was a strong one, an important fact to establish.

Affect

The trend in regard to affect was positive but not significant. Both samples showed some increases in contentment and some decreases in symptoms of emotional disturbance or behavioral disorder. These changes, however, possibly reflected the initial crisis state. Service participants displayed more positive change than did control participants, but not to a significant degree.

Effect on Others

In both sample groups, collateral stress diminished during the demonstration year. This change was brought about largely by the institutionalization of participants. The change was significant, however, only within the experimental group, with the difference between the two programs significantly favoring the experimental program.

In summary, the demonstrated protective service did relieve stress among collaterals. For the participant himself, however, there was no significant impact with respect to increased competence or slowed deterioration and greater contentment or lessened disturbance. Furthermore, although he was more "protected," the participant was no less likely to die when given protective services than when left to the usual and limited services of the community. In fact, the findings on functional competence together with those on death and institutionalization force consideration of the hypothesis that intensive service with intensive service with a heavy reliance on institutional care may actually accelerate decline. It is this disturbing thought that caused the project staff to continue at least minimal follow-up on all surviving participants, both experimental and control, beyond the demonstration year.

Findings from the Follow-up Study

The higher death and institutionalization rates observed in the experimental sample did not come as a complete surprise to the investigators. Based on previous research at the Community Service Society of New York, Blenkner had theorized in the original BRI project proposal that because hopelessness could literally kill and because institutionalization generated feelings of hopelessness, whichever group (demonstration or control) had the higher placement rate would also have the higher death rate.[20]

Survival and death are rarely, if ever, used as criteria of outcome in welfare research. Death does, however, head the list in the field of health,[21] and in sociological or psychological research, it is studied as a phenomenon but not as an outcome. Nevertheless, in demonstrations and experiments in the care of the old—among whom death is a fact of life—survival must necessarily be viewed as an end result and as an outcome variable. Every service, every program, every helping act that is strong enough to have a real effect on the course of events may also be strong enough to be stressful, noxious, or even lethal to

20 See Margaret Blenkner, Julius Jahn, and Edna Wasser, "Serving the Aging: An Experiment in Social Work and Public Health Nursing," mimeographed (New York: Community Service Society, March 1964); and Margaret Blenkner, "Demonstration for Protective Service for Older Adults: Project Plan" (Cleveland: Benjamin Rose Institute, 1963).

21 Paul J. Samazaro and John W. Williamson, "End Results of Patient Care: A Provisional Classification Based on Reports by Internists," *Medical Care* 6:123–20 (March–April 1968). The authors list six D's as criteria for assessing the end results of patient care: death, disease, disability, discomfort, dissatisfaction, and disruption.

some, no matter how beneficent the intent. Medicine learned this stance long ago. Social work, as it matures and moves toward a scientifically based status, must also adopt it.

Transfer, at the end of their demonstration year, of the great majority (79 percent) of surviving service participants to the regular program of the Benjamin Rose Institute allowed continued study of service effect on the factors of relocation, institutionalization, and survival. Data have now been collected for five years but have been intensively analyzed for only four years (for some variables only three) at the time of this writing. Because only three control participants became BRI clients within the first four years following the demonstration, like attenuation of service effect has come about through this factor. All cases, whether active with BRI or not, have been followed, and the original randomization has been maintained.

Institutionalization

The primary finding with regard to institutionalization is that service increases its likelihood. Despite the availability of an ancillary home aide service program, it appears that the well-trained social worker who is assigned responsibility for the welfare of older people has a strong tendency to move them into "protective settings." Persistently and consistently, institutionalization rates have been higher for demonstration participants than for controls. By the end of the fifth year from time of registration, more than three fifths (61 percent) of the demonstration participants and fewer than one half (47 percent) of the control participants had been institutionalized. Males in particular contributed to the difference, and it was at first suspected that the fact that all the project caseworkers were female might have some bearing on the subject. A check of caseloads in the regular BRI program indicated, however, that whether the worker and client are of the same sex or of different sexes and whether the worker is male or female, the man who is seen by a social agency in his old age is likely to be institutionalized.

The males in this sample of protectives offer dramatic confirmation of Lowenthal's "social visibility theory." Lowenthal and others suggest that older persons "suffering from serious psychogenic disorders and exhibiting bizarre behavior" may nevertheless remain in the community "because they are capable of minimal self-maintenance and are socially submerged. Were they to . . . come to the attention of a concerned friend or relative or an official decision-maker of some sort, they might well become hospitalized."[22] This result, in effect, is what seems to have happened to many persons in the experimental sample, first in the demonstration and later in the regular BRI program.

Survival

The greater number of deaths among protectives as compared to the general older population and the particular abnormality of rates among institutionalized protectives may be noted in Table 4 in the discrepancies between the expected and observed survival rates. The observed rates are those actually found among the protectives in the study during a four-year experience period; the expected probabilities are for computer-simulated populations of the same age, sex, race, and geographic structure derived from standard life tables.[23] Thus, whereas the expected survival rate in the simulated populations at the end of the first year was over 90 percent (.903 for the service group and .917 for the control group), only 75 percent of the service participants and 82 percent of the control participants actually survived. By the fourth year, expected survival rates had dropped below 70 percent (.671 for the service group and .696 for the control group), but actual survival rates were much lower—37 percent for the service participants and 48 percent for control participants.

22 Lowenthal et al., *Aging and Mental Disorder*, p. 255.
23 The writers wish to express their gratitude to Dr. Thomas Downs, Associate Professor of Biometry, School of Public Health, University of Texas at Houston, and Dr. Julio N. Berrettoni, Chairman, Department of Statistic, School of Management, Case Western Reserve University, for their assistance and advice in analyzing the survival data. Appreciation is also due to the Department of Biometry, School of Medicine, Case Western Reserve University, for access to its computer facilities.

Table 4 Expected and Observed Survival Rates[a] from Time of Registration for Institutionalized and Noninstitutionalized Protectives

| Year After Registration | All Participants | | | | Institutionalized | | | | Noninstitutionalized | | | |
| | Service | | Control | | Service | | Control | | Service | | Control | |
	Exp Rate	Obs Rate	Exp Rate	Obs Rate	Exp Rate	Obs Rate	Exp Rate	Obs Rate	Exp Rate	Obs Rate	Exp Rate	Obs Rate
One	.903	.750	.917	.818	.892	.738	.900	.853	.919	.765	.928	.796
Two	.818	.605	.838	.750	.795	.548	.803	.794	.848	.677	.862	.722
Three	.739	.474	.762	.649	.706	.381	.714	.559	.779	.588	.797	.704
Four	.671	.369	.696	.477	.633	.310	.639	.324	.715	.441	.735	.574
Number	76		88		42		34		34		54	

[a] Expected probability of surviving to end of year, based on general population of the same age, sex, race, and geographic structure at each year. See U.S., National Center for Health Statistics, *United States Life Tables 1959–61*, Public Health Service Publication No. 1252, Vol. 1, No. 1 (Washington, D.C.: Department of Health, Education, and Welfare, 1964).

Among the institutionalized protectives, the expected survival rates were approximately the same for both groups—approximately 90 percent for the first year and 63 percent by the fourth year. Nevertheless, the observed rates were considerably lower for the service participants than for those in the control group. In the fourth year, however, both subsample observed rates dropped to between 31 and 32 percent, approximating one half the expected survival rate of "normal" populations of the same age, sex, race, and geographic structure.

For the noninstitutionalized protectives, the fourth year expectation was between 71 and 73 percent, but the observed rates were only 44 percent for the service group and 57 percent for the control group. In all instances the discrepancy between the expected and observed rates was greater for the service group than for the control group.[24]

Of additional interest is survival from the time of institutionalization for those so classified within three years of registration.[25] Table 5 shows the data by quarters so that the very rapid drop-off in survival during the first year can be easily compared to what would be expected in a general population of the same age, sex, race, and geographic structure. This drop-off is especially precipitate among the service cases, in which only 78 percent survived the first quarter despite the fact that the expected rate was 97 percent. In the control group, 88 percent survived the first quarter.

The "half-life" of the service participants after institutionalization—the point at which only half the group survives—was little more than one year. That of the control group was more than two years.

It should be noted that institutionalization is not a random event. The best predictor of

24 In addition to this biostatistical type of analysis, the survival data were also subjected to a "quality control" approach using a Weibull analysis. Based on a three-year experience period, Julio N. Berrettoni and Blenkner describe the conclusion from this approach as follows: "The statistical analysis reveals that the service group inspite of all its directed and intensive protective services has lower mean life and higher mortality rates than the control group. Also, it seems that noninstitutionalized participants live longer on the average than those placed in protective surroundings. . . . There isn't any age interaction because the mean life of control differs from that of service by the same positive amount regardless of age groups." Julio N. Berrettoni and Margaret Blenkner, "Reliability Analysis of an Experiment to Prolong Human Life" (paper presented at the Twenty-third Annual Technical Conference, American Society for Quality Control, Los Angeles, California, May 5, 1969), p. 2.

25 There is a year's time lag for the life tables based on time of institutionalization; hence, survival data for those institutionalized within four years will not be available until the five-year follow-up data are analyzed.

269

Table 5 Expected and Observed Probability of Survival of Participants Institutionalized Within Three Years After Registration[a]

| Quarter After Institutionalization | All Participants | | | | Participants Seventy-five and Over Only | | | |
| | Service | | Control | | Service | | Control | |
	Exp	Obs	Exp	Obs	Exp	Obs	Exp	Obs
One	.969	.783	.971	.880	.963	.718	.963	.829
Two	.939	.732	.949	.849	.926	.686	.934	.784
Three	.910	.575	.928	.753	.892	.523	.907	.646
Four	.882	.520	.906	.687	.857	.488	.878	.600
Five	.855	.462	.884	.687	.825	.413	.848	.600
Six	.829	.462	.862	.648	.793	.413	.817	.543
Seven	.803	.425	.842	.559	.764	.369	.788	.470
Eight	.780	.387	.821	.510	.736	.323	.756	.385
Nine	.760	.348	.806	.453	.712	.277	.733	.275
Ten	.739	.307	.792	.453	.686	.226	.703	.275
Eleven	.724	.307	.780	.453	.665	.226	.675	.275
Twelve	.710	.204	.768	.453	.648	.075	.000	.000
Number institutionalized within three years	42		34		32		24	

[a] Expected probability of surviving to end of quarter, based on general population of the same age, sex, race, and geographic structure at each quarter. See U.S. National Center for Health Statistics, *United States Life Tables, 1964.*

institutionalization among service cases was the caseworker's initial clinical rating of the need for protective service, followed by the participant's initial score or rating on the contentment variable. On the three methods available to measure contentment—interview score, observer rating, and caseworker rating—the difference in means among the service participants institutionalized and not institutionalized within four years of registration in the project was significant at the .05 level or beyond. In addition, the initial ratings of the observer and caseworker on the "signs and symptoms" index distinguished significantly among service cases. Their interview scores were not distinctive. Unfavorable showings for both contentment and signs and symptoms were predictive of institutionalization.

Among controls, on the other hand, only age and initial mental status—both from the MSQ score and from observer ratings—distinguished significantly among those who were not subsequently institutionalized; advanced age and low MSQ score were predictive of institutionalization. The same direction was observable among service participants but not to a significant degree.

Despite higher institutionalization rates, the very old protectives—those already seventy-five years of age or over when registered in the project—did not follow the same pattern with regard to higher death rates during the demonstration year as did the service group as a whole. Because there was a good match between this group of experimental and control participants,[26] one may speculate on three theories to explain this finding: (1) the inroads of advancing age alone are sufficient to override other effects; (2) the very old are more resigned and ready for the loss of independence and control that goes with institu-

26 The initial means between the subsamples of protectives seventy-five years of age and over were as follows: age, 81 and 82; MSQ, 4.4 and 4.2; PFQ, 3.1 and 4.1; sex distribution 31 percent male and 69 percent female and 34 percent male and 66 percent female. In each case, the first figure is for the service group and the second figure is for the control group.

tionalization; or (3) the service staff was better able to counteract the negative effects of institutionalization in the very old. If the third possibility were accurate, the improvement would have been reflected in the survival experience following institutionalization as shown by the data on the right-hand side of Table 5. In Table 5, one notices that there is a precipitate drop during the first year that is greater for service participants over seventy-five than for the controls; the half-life after institutionalization of the control group was almost nine months longer than that of the service participants. Thus, even among the very old, there seems to have been a negative service-effect that appeared in the second and third years following registration but began to dissipate in the fourth year. Whether the change in the fourth year was the result of shifts in BRI service strategy made because of suggestions that the negative effects reported in the research might be attributable to the excessive use of institutionalization or simply to a "catching-up" effect in the control sample is impossible to determine from the data on hand.

Taken separately, the best predictor of survival among both samples was age, followed by mental and physical status. The mean MSQ scores at the initial interview distinguished between survivors and nonsurvivors in the service sample at the .01 level and among controls at the .001 level over a four-year period. The mean PFQ scores distinguished at the .01 and .08 levels, respectively. The mean age distinguished at the .001 level in both samples.

Because of its importance, care was taken throughout the analyses to control the age factor beyond the original randomization. Use was made of such statistical means as examining separately participants over and under seventy-five years of age and sometimes at finer age groupings and the construction of expected survival rates by computer simulation. In no instance did the data indicate that age was a sufficient explanation for differences found between the service and control groups.

Discussion and Conclusions

In measuring the success of efforts to help people, outcome variables may be expressed in relation to ultimate or operational goals. The ultimate goals are those things one wishes to have happen for his client, such as survival, contentment, and relief of collateral stress. The operational goals are those things one strives to do or bring about that one assumes will promote the ultimate goals, such as concrete assistance in home management and personal care and decent, safe, and sanitary housing. Strictly speaking, operational goals should be conceived as measures of effort and not as effect, because the effect is only assumed.

In this study, operational goals were in large measure achieved. The two variables on which truly noticeable and statistically significant differences in mean scores occurred were clearly operational goal variables—concrete assistance and physical environment. Much of the service gain on these two variables must be attributed to the relatively high institutionalization rate among the service participants, although a part of it was also due to the introduction of home aide and other ancillary services. With regard to ultimate goals, however, only that pertaining to the relief of collateral stress reflected a positive service effect.

Taking the findings as a whole, it is difficult to avoid the conclusion that (1) participants in the experimental service program were institutionalized earlier than they would otherwise have been and that (2) this earlier institutionalization did not—contrary to intent—prove protective of the older persons although it did relieve collaterals and community agents. That the services provided, first through the project and subsequently through the regular program of the Benjamin Rose Institute, might have had a deleterious effect on some participants is a hypothesis that should be entertained in future research. It is possible, of course, that what occurred was a rare statistical event in which two random samples from the same population were, in truth, very different to begin with on variables that were not measured or controlled. Studies such as this one, which have potentially grave import for practice, should always be, but never are, replicated.

In describing this study, the writers reported the survival data in detail. The data were subjected to far more analysis than they would probably have undergone had the findings run the opposite way, that is, had they favored the experimental program. To reiterate, studies of the effectiveness of programs and services to the old must set survival as an outcome criterion with the hope that the accumulated data will eventually determine some definitive practice goals.

It does no good to speak of "shorter lives but merrier ones" or of a "good death." There was no evidence in this study nor in any other known to the writers that those who died were happier than those who survived, nor that the cause or place of death differed significantly among service and control participants. All well-controlled studies of services for the noninstitutionalized aged of which the writers have personal knowledge indicate a negative, although not necessarily significant, association between intensive service and survival.[27]

These are discouraging facts that should not deter us from further attempts to help. We should, however, question our present prescriptions and strategies of treatment. Is our dosage too strong, our intervention too overwhelming, our takeover too final? Some of the data pertaining to factors predictive of institutionalization or survival suggest that we are prone to introduce the greatest changes in lives least able to bear them.

27 See Blenkner, Jahn, and Wasser, "Serving the Aging"; Amasa Ford et al., "Results of Long Term Home Nursing: The Influence of Disability," *Journal of Chronic Diseases* 15:785–794 (1962); and Harry Posman et al., "Continuity in Care for Impaired Older Persons," mimeographed (New York: Community Service Society, 1964).

CHAPTER 11

Critical Reactions

Overview

This chapter is very technical. It consists largely of articles and reports critiquing the original Protective Services Project, or else critiquing the critics of it. I recommend that you read these papers first, to get the main theme of their criticisms, and second (to the extent your statistical knowledge permits) to understand their specific arguments. You will very likely get the main ideas and then see how these ideas, and the statistical techniques they involve, are batted back and forth in scientific dialogues. This dialogue is a very special part of the scientific process, one that adds to its continuing vitality. I again use a technical narrative to present these critical papers.

Technical Narrative Section

Introduction
What Others Said We Found: The Diffusion of Information (Technical Note 11.1)
Published Reports
> Raymond Berger and Irving Piliavin: "The Effect of Casework: A Research Note" (1976). (11.2)
> Joel Fischer and Walter W. Hudson: "An Effect of Casework? Back to the Drawing Board" (1976). (11.3)
> Raymond M. Berger and Irving Piliavin: "A Rejoinder" (1976). (11.4)
> Dennis Wagner and Michael J. Osmalov: "The Impact of Social Casework on the Elderly: A Reappraisal of the Controversy Surrounding the Benjamin Rose Institute's Protective Services Study" (1978). (11.5)
> Ruth E. Dunkle, S. Walter Poulshock, Barbara Silverstone, and Gary T. Deimling: "Protective Services Reanalyzed: Does Casework Help or Harm? (1983). (11.6)
Summary and Generalizations

The Technical Narrative

INTRODUCTION

This is a chapter that standard research books usually omit, as if the research process stops at the end of the presentation of results. In real life, this is often the beginning of another great cycle of research, the reactions of one's scientific colleagues, who point out the strengths and weaknesses of one's research—mostly the weaknesses—not out of any particular malice, but because vigorous pointing out of errors or misinterpretations are required to stimulate critical discussion and further research. Let me explain. Once a study has been published in the professional literature, it may be drawn on by practitioners as a source of guidance in their work. However, the time required to read a report, to locate problems in it, to write up a statement about those problems, and to get them printed in the same journal as the original article may be many months. Meanwhile, the original study may begin to influence the practices of professionals exposed to it. So, when a rebuttal or criticism of the original study comes off the presses, it has to be clear and strong in order to attract the attention both of scientists (who may assess the validity of the criticisms) and of practitioners (who may wish to modify their interventions based on the original study).

Margaret Blenkner was very good at criticitizing others, as I mentioned before, and so her own writings were prime targets. However, rather than being stung by less-than-complimentary statements, she was energized by criticism. There was for her, as for any truly good scientist, a kind of cooperative agreement among fellow scientists on moving forward the boundaries of our knowledge by using correct methods and designs sensitively and appropriately. She loved a good scientific fight.

It is therefore sad that Margaret Blenkner died just before some of the excitement erupted over the findings of the Protective Services Project. She was as surprised as anyone by the findings, and she checked and rechecked what was found countless times—I can testify to that, as I was involved in many of those reanalyses. She talked and talked about the design, as if she were reliving the decisions that she had made in its formation, and she speculated whether there were other approaches that could have been used. Yes, no doubt she uncovered a preferable method there and a different strategy there, but it is my recollection that overall she found the original design and analysis to be a reasonable and defensible handling of the problem and the data.

Thus what she (and her colleagues) reported (in the paper reproduced in Chapter 10) was her honest opinion. It was the truth, the whole truth, and nothing but the truth. (Well, not the whole truth, as there were space limits, so a later report, Blenkner et al., 1974, represents the final report of the Protective Service Project. There were also yearly progress reports that presented additional information. The article appearing in Chapter 10 is a comprehensive summary and the most commonly available statement on the project.)

Because I didn't have much to do with the final phase of the publishing, I can say that I recognize and admire Dr. Blenkner's determination to tell the story accurately, without disguising the warts or wrinkles, even when they appeared on her own face (and those of her friends and colleagues). I further admire the agency for having the guts to permit this material to be published. Lesser agencies would have tried to protect their image. In all, this was a prime example of honest reporting in the scientific practice arena. Whether it was an accurate, valid report is another question, to which we now turn.

WHAT OTHERS SAID WE FOUND: THE DIFFUSION OF INFORMATION

Consider this statement, which summarizes the seven years of effort expended on the BRI Protective Services Project:

> Nursing home replacement can lead to the funeral parlor earlier than otherwise might have been expected. (Johnson and Williamson, 1980, p. 28)

As a brief summary of the project, it certainly captures the ironic tenor of the results and states them in a catchy if oversimplifed way. The same authors elsewhere expanded on the nature of the sample, to the effect that elderly individuals who were institutionalized died sooner than an equally handicapped but noninstitutionalized control group. The problem with this brief summary is that a reader might not know the characteristics of the sample on which this generalization was made. Moreover, it is not clear that this is the textbook authors' summary, not the original researchers'.

Compare these statements with Margaret Blenkner's carefully worded conclusion on the outcome, that "one should be willing to entertain the hypothesis" that intensive services such as were given in the Protective Services Project "may have accelerated the decline" that appeared to occur in the elderly protective (Blenkner et al., 1971, p. 498). Not as jazzy, but this was the real conclusion of the study.

Other writers looked more closely at the study, and in fact, some even replicated the data analysis.* Dr. Blenkner had graciously and appropriately shared copies of the original data and all of the documents for analyzing them with several researchers who had requested them for teaching purposes. These researchers eventually did some reanalyses that resulted in full-blown reports, some of which are reproduced in this chapter. This is an important point: Scientific findings are supposed to be replicable in order that independent observers may make their own observations about the data. If they agree, their agreement lends extra support to the original conclusions. If they disagree, then the reasons for the disagreement must be made clear. Some of these reasons may be factual, such as the application of accepted methods of mathematical handling; others may be more judgmental, such as choices of which variables are chosen as measures of ultimate outcomes of the study. Everything and anything is subject to review. This is the essence of a viable science.

---

* This general introduction to how others interpreted the facts in the Protective Services Project indicates a much-neglected aspect of research, namely how *information—or misinformation—is disseminated.* Technical Note 11.1.

275

I can't tell exactly what Dr. Blenkner would have said or done had she lived to respond to these reactions, but I do know that she would have enjoyed the scientific enterprise of seeing her work soundly, roundly, and professionally critiqued. As you read the papers reported in this chapter, both those that are critical of the original study and those that defend its scientific virtues, your task is not to determine truth as such, for honest, well-meaning, and talented researchers disagree on facts and interpretations. Rather, your task is to try to answer the following questions: How do these various critical reactions modify the main thrust of the findings? What variables appear to be dependable? Which questionable? To whom do the findings clearly apply, if anyone? And to whom are they applied only with weak assumptions? Most important, where should we go next to find out a closer approximation of the impact of social casework on persons in need of protective services?

I would also like to raise some specific questions for consideration while you are reading the critical materials:

1. How much violence to the rules of research methods and statistical analysis is permissible in a research context such as this one?
2. How much effort should be exerted to disprove negative results, as contrasted with the effort exerted to disprove positive results?
3. What weight is to be assigned disagreements on value-based choices, as contrasted with decisions made on the basis of standard procedures?
4. What is the relatively naive practitioner to make of all these disagreements? What can the helping professional do with this entire set of documents (original articles, criticisms, and rebuttals)?
5. If you had an elderly friend or relative in need of protective services, based on all of this information what would you choose to do on this elderly person's behalf?

We'll return to these questions later in the chapter.

PUBLISHED REPORTS

The Effect of Casework: A Research Note*

Raymond Berger and Irving Piliavin

In a review of eleven controlled studies, Fischer concluded that social casework services—defined broadly as the services provided by professional caseworkers—yielded no greater improvement among a variety of client populations than did no intervention at all.[1] One of the studies reviewed by Fischer was the Protective Services Project for Older Persons,

Reprinted with permission, from *Social Work*, 21:3 (May 1976), 205–208. Copyright © 1976 by the National Association of Social Workers, Inc., New York.

Editorial Note: This "research note," which appeared in a major social work journal, constitutes Technical Note 11.2. It is one form that *criticism* can take.

276

a longitudinal study directed by Blenkner under the auspices of the Benjamin Rose Institute in Cleveland, Ohio.[2] According to Fischer, the results of this study suggested that the special, enriched services of the institute in fact worked against the clients, since the mortality rate of the clients who received the special services was higher than that of the control clients. Three years after the beginning of the program, 47.4 percent of the special service clients were still alive compared to 64.9 percent of the controls.[3] The implication that social services can have debilitating effects is obviously a matter of concern.

This research note presents a more elaborate statistical analysis of the original data than that carried out by the researchers of the Rose Institute study. Such analysis indicates that the apparently negative effects of the institute program are attributable to factors other than the special services program itself.

Participants in the Rose Institute study were 164 elderly persons who were in need of protective services and who had come to the attention of various community agencies. Seventy-six persons were randomly assigned to an experimental group and received intensive casework and other services for a period of one year. Eighty-eight persons were assigned to a control group and received only those incidental services normally provided by community agencies. The effects of service were evaluated by a variety of variables that measured mental and physical competence, environmental protection, affect, and effect on family and close friends.

Analyses reported by the researchers revealed few differences between experimentals and controls other than that the experimentals were less likely to survive and more likely to be institutionalized than were the controls. Although institutionalization was related to poor survival for both groups, it did not account for the different survival rates between experimentals and controls. Statistical tests were not reported but experimentals among both institutionalized and noninstitutionalized participants were said to be less likely to survive than the controls. The reason for the poorer survival rate among experimentals remained something of a mystery.

In reviewing the analytic procedures utilized in the Rose Institute study, the authors found two possible explanations for the findings reported by Blenkner and her colleagues. The first concerns the influence of important covariates of survival. Although the original investigators found that pretest data on age, physical functioning, and mental status of participants were linked to survival (see Table 1), these variables played only a limited role in the analysis of experimental and control survival rates.[4] This was unfortunate, since these variables indicated that the experimentals were more debilitated than the controls.

The second possible explanation for Blenkner's findings involves the substantial number of cases with missing pretest data. The overall comparison of control and experimental death rates included individuals for whom information on physical functioning and mental

Table 1 Correlations of Age, Mental Status, and Physical Functioning with the Number of Years of Survival at Three Years Among Rose Institute Study Participants[a]

	r [b, c]	p	n
Age	−.335	<.001	164
Mental status	.333	<.001	102
Physical functioning	.280	<.001	134

[a] Number of years of survival was coded 0, 1, 2, or 3 as recorded at three years. All other variables were measured at the inception of the study.

[b] Advanced age, low mental status, and low physical functioning were associated with low survival rates.

[c] Replacement with means procedure was employed to estimate missing data for the mental status and physical functioning variables.

status was lacking. Admittedly, the percentage of such individuals was about the same for experimentals and controls, but it is possible that the health status of nonassessed experimentals was worse than that of nonassessed controls. Unfortunately, there is no way of directly confirming this possibility since the original Rose Institute study provides very little information on the procedures by which diagnostic information on participants was obtained at the inception of the experiment. However, there are data—the variables just discussed—suggesting that the assessed experimentals were older and less well at the outset of the project. If the nonassessed participants were similarly distributed, experimentals would be more likely to die in the course of the project even in the absence of any project effects.

Covariates of Survival

The data that suggested greater debilitation among experimentals are shown in Tables 2 and 3. These tables present selected cross-tabulations of the project participants' age and mental status and of their age and physical functioning. The last two attributes were measured by instruments developed during the Rose Institute study.[5] The Rose Institute investigators found that whereas the experiments were somewhat older than the controls, they were no worse off in terms of average mental or physical functioning. The distributions in Tables 2 and 3 suggest otherwise. In particular, they indicate that the experimental group contained not only more older individuals but those who had extreme mental and physical deterioration scores. The degree to which these distribution differences may have accounted for the negative consequences attributed to Rose Institute services was tested by two regression models* whose results are presented in Table 4.[6] The first model examines three-year survival status as a simple function of a dummy variable** indicating experimental group membership.[7] The second model may be depicted as follows:

$$Y = a + \sum_{i=1}^{6} b_4 X_4$$

where Y is survival status at the end of three years, X_1 is a dummy variable given the value 1 for experimentals and 0 otherwise, X_2 denotes age in years, X_3 equals mental status score (0–9), X_4 represents physical functioning score (0–5), X_5 is a dummy variable

---

Editorial Note: I do not wish to detract from the critical discussion, which clearly demands a reasonably sophisticated level of statistical knowledge if you are to appreciate the fine points of the debate to come. However, I offer a few clarifications, if only to further your understanding and enjoyment of the criticism.

The regression models that Berger and Piliavin discuss come from a method of describing the association between two variables, as well as predicting other sets of possible values of the variables. Think of a simple scattergram in which the values of some variables, X, are presented in relationship to the values of another variable, Y. If all of the values from an empirical study of these two variables fell on a single straight line—called a *regression line*—then it would be possible to describe fully the relationship between X and Y, and moreover, it would be possible to predict new values of X, given a knowledge of the values of Y.

However, most of the time, variables are related not simply on a straight line, but in some complex clustering—as we discussed Technical Note 6.5 in relationship to correlations between variables. Regression models are ways of summarizing the best-fitting line among a set of empirical values, assuming that one variable is the independent variable, and the other the dependent variable. This is to say that we are predicting the values of the dependent variable, given the values of the independent variable. (For further information, see Babbie, 1979; Grinnell, 1981; and other standard statistics books. Also Berger and Piliavin, footnote 6.)

** *Editorial Note:* The use of a *dummy variable* is simply a procedure by which variables composed of three or more values or categories (such as upper class, middle class, and lower class) are dichotomized into two classes for purposes of statistical analysis (e.g., lower class versus any other class designation). The researcher can choose to compare any or all of the values for categories in a variable by such a procedure. (See Berger and Piliavin, footnote 7.)

Table 2 Distribution of Rose Institute Study Participants by Age and Mental Status (percentage)

	Experimentals ($n = 47$)				Controls ($n = 55$)		
	Mental Status[a]				Mental Status		
Age	0–2	3–9	Total	Age	0–2	3–9	Total
75 and under	4	30	34	75 and under	9	33	42
Over 75	28	38	66	Over 75	13	45	58
Total	32	68	100	Total	22	78	100

[a] Poor mental status is indicated by a low score (0–2).

Table 3 Distribution of Rose Institute Study Participants by Age and Physical Functioning (percentage)

	Experimentals ($n = 63$)				Controls ($n = 71$)		
	Physical Functioning[a]				Physical Functioning		
Age	0–1	2–5	Total	Age	0–1	2–5	Total
75 and under	13	24	37	75 and under	8	32	40
Over 75	32	32	64	Over 75	24	35	59
Total	45	56	101	Total	32	67	99

[a] Poor physical functioning is indicated by a low score (0–1).

Table 4 A. Estimated Effect of Experimental Group Membership on Three-Year Survival Status of Rose Institute Study Participants[a] (Model I, $n = 164$)

Variable	β	Significance Level of β[b]
Experimental group membership	−.387	.0456
$R^2 = .02$		

B. Estimated Effects of Experimental Group Membership and Selected Personal Characteristics on Three-Year Survival Status of Rose Institute Study Participants[a] (Model II, $n = 164$)

Variable	β	Significance Level of β[b]
Experimental group membership	−.283	.110
Age	−.281	.026
Mental status	.163	.007
Physical functioning	.061	.391
Mental status × age	.084	.832
Physical functioning × age	−.491	.132
$R^2 = .23$		

[a] Means substituted for missing data. Number of years of survival was coded 0, 1, 2, or 3 as recorded at three years. Advanced age, low mental status, and low physical functioning were associated with low survival rates.

[b] Traditionally, an effect is considered significant at .05 or less.

279

that equals 1 for individuals over seventy-five years old with severe mental deterioration scores (0–2) and 0 otherwise, and X_6 is a dummy variable that is set at 1 for individuals over seventy-five having extreme physical deterioration (0,1) and at 0 otherwise. Group means were assigned to the individual independent variable scores when data were missing. Although experimental group membership has a significant effect in the first model, this is not true in the second model. This reduction in experimental group influence and the significant age and mental status effects in the second model support the hypothesis that the original Rose Institute study findings were the consequence of initial group differences in survival-related characteristics.

Missing Pretest Data

The second possible explanation for the higher frequency of death among the Rose Institute study participants concerns the rate of survival among the nonassessed participants. Although the authors do not have direct information that the nonassessed experimentals were less well than the nonassessed controls, the issue can be examined indirectly by studying the survival status of only those participants whose mental status and physical functioning were assessed. Again, two regression models were run, one examining only the effect of experimental group membership and the other studying the influence of this factor along with the marginal effects of age, physical functioning, mental status, and their interactions. The results presented in Table 5 are quite clear. No significant experimental group effects are found even in the simple regression model.

Conclusions

When those participants for whom data on survival-related characteristics were missing are omitted from the analysis, there are no significant experimental group effects evident

Table 5 A. Estimated Effect of Experimental Group Membership on Three-Year Survival Status of Rose Institute Study Participants[a] (Model II, $n = 101$)

Variable	β	Significance Level of β[b]
Experimental group membership	−.265	.2731

B. Estimated Effects of Experimental Group Membership and Selected Personal Characteristics on Three-Year Survival Status of Rose Institute Study Participants[a] (Model IV, $n = 101$)

Variable	β	Significance Level of β[b]
Experimental group membership	−.116	.583
Age	−.247	.092
Physical funcitoning	−.017	.831
Mental status	.173	.003
Deteriorated mental status × age	−.020	.958
Deteriorated physical functioning × age	−.708	.065

[a] Analysis limited to participants for whom full data are available.
[b] Traditionally, an effect is considered significant at .05 or less.

in the Rose Institute study. When these particpants are included and control for the effects of survival-related characteristics is maintained, the authors again find no significant experimental effects. Clearly the nonassessed experimentals were more likely to die than the nonassessed controls, although the reasons for this are not provided by the data.

There were differences in the initial health status of assessed experimentals and controls and it must be assumed that they were due to chance factors—factors that might affect nonparticipants in the same way. Although this is not a satisfying explanation of an undeniably unsatisfying situation, it is nevertheless difficult to attribute the higher death rate of the nonassessed experimentals to the Rose Institute services project.

The authors wish to point out that the original Rose Institute study finding that experimental group members were more likely to be institutionalized is not explained away by the analyses represented in Tables 4 and 5. That is, controlling for survival-related characteristics does not mitigate the strong effect of experimental group membership on the tendency to be institutionalized.[8] Perhaps, as the original researchers suggested, social workers simply believed nursing home placements provided better assurance of care than did impoverished life in the community.

The foregoing analysis has not, alas, revealed social casework services to be beneficial. It has, however, substantially ruled out the more disquieting conclusion that they are harmful. The analysis also provides a case example of the maxim that randomization, particularly in small samples, is no guarantee of equivalence among controls and experimentals. Finally, the analysis illustrates the utility of multivariate techniques, given the proper circumstances for their use.

Notes and References

1. Joel Fischer, "Is Casework Effective? A Review," *Social Work,* 18 (January 1973), pp. 5–20.
2. *See* Margaret Blenkner, Martin Bloom, and Margaret Nielsen, "A Research and Demonstration Project of Protective Services, *Social Casework,* 52 (October 1971) pp. 483–499; and Blenkner et al., *Final Report: Protective Services for Older People* (Cleveland, Ohio: Benjamin Rose Institute, 1974).
3. Blenkner, Bloom, and Nielsen, op. cit.
4. Blenkner et al., op. cit., p. 143
5. Martin Bloom, "The Initial Interview" (Cleveland: Benjamin Rose Institute, 1964). (Mimeographed.)
6. A regression model is a linear combination of variables, called independent variables or predictors, that best accounts for the observed variation in some dependent or predicted variable. The general form of the equation can be written thus:
$$Y = X_a + b_1 X_1 + b_2 X_2 + \cdots + b_n X_n$$

   or

$$Y = X_a + \sum_{i=1}^{n} b_1 X_1$$

   where Y is the dependent variable and the X_1 are the independent variables.
7. A dummy or binary variable is one which can take on only two values: 1 when the indicated characteristic is present, and 0 when it is not. The coefficient b_1 of the dummy variables X_1 represents the effect on the depedent variable of having the particular characteristic in question. An extensive discussion of the uses to which dummy variables can be put may be found in Jerry L. L. Miller and Maynard L. Erickson, "On Dummy Variable Regression Analysis." *Sociological Methods and Research,* 2 (May 1974), pp. 409–431.
8. These analyses are available from the authors.

An Effect of Casework? Back to the Drawing Board*

Joel Fischer and Walter W. Hudson

An article by Raymond Berger and Irving Piliavin ("The Effect of Casework: A Research Note," May 1976 issue of *Social Work*) consists of a reanalysis of some data from the Protective Services Project for Older Persons. The stated reason for the reanalysis was to bring "elaborate statistical analysis" to bear on a particularly thorny problem—the possibility that social work services can have a debilitating effect on clients. Such a conclusion seemed warranted in view of the findings described by Berger and Piliavin as follows: "Three years after the beginning of the program, 47.4 percent of the special service clients were still alive compared to 64.9 percent of the controls.[1] Table 1 indicates that the difference between the groups—which favors the controls—is statistically significant.

Table 1 Frequency Distribution of Project Participants: Experimental–Control-Group Membership by Survival Status

	Experimental	Control
Survived	36	57
Deceased	40	31

Source: Berger and Piliavin, p. 205.

Chi square = 4.35, $df = 1$, $p < .05$.

Certainly, it is welcome and refreshing to find social work journals publishing research notes that use such sophisticated statistical techniques as multiple-regression procedures. However, enthusiasm must be tempered in this instance because, in the opinion of the authors, Berger and Piliavin have made some critical mistakes in their understanding and use of the raw data that have made the use of these sophisticated procedures open to question.

Berger and Piliavin raise two issues that might account for the significantly greater number of deaths in the experimental group. One issue is that on important covariates of survival, despite random assignment, the experimentals were more aged and more debilitated than the controls. The second issue is that since there are several cases in both groups for which pretest data were missing, "it is possible that the health status of nonassessed experiments was worse than that of nonassessed controls."[2] However, it is important to note that in each case the groups were randomly assigned and that the percentage of cases with missing data was about the same for both groups.

Central to the Berger and Piliavin argument is the thesis that the experimental and control

Reprinted with permission, from *Social Work*, 21:5 (September 1976), 347–349. Copyright © 1976 by the National Association of Social Workers, Inc., New York.

* *Editorial Note:* This *response* to the preceding research note constitutes Technical Note 11.3. The vehicle is a "points and viewpoints" portion of a professional journal. This "viewpoint" offers a critique of the previous critical paper.

1 Raymond Berger and Irving Piliavin, "The Effect of Casework: A Research Note," *Social Work*, 21 (May 1976), p. 205.
2 Ibid.

groups were initially different. Berger and Piliavin present two tables showing percentage distributions and state that "the experimental group contained not only more older individuals but those who had extreme mental and physical deterioration scores."[3] However, for some unexplained reason, Berger and Piliavin either do not test these differences statistically, or do not report the results of the tests they did conduct. Because of this omission in reporting data that are crucial to their thesis, the present authors have reanalyzed the data.

In essence, these analyses completely refute the Berger and Piliavin argument. In no instances were they any statistically significant differences between the experimental and control groups. Using the percentage data provided by Berger and Piliavin, a series of chi squares reveal that there were no significant differences between the experimental and control groups on the survival covariates of age, mental status, and physical functioning. (See Tables 2–5.) Thus, even though age, mental status, and physical functioning were linked with the clients' years of survival, there were no differences between the experimental and control groups on these dimensions. This means that Berger and Piliavin's conclusion that the original findings of higher mortality in the experimental group "were the consequence of initial group differences in survival-related characteristics" was not justified by the data they presented.[4] (In fact, as Tables 3 and 4 show, there were actually more people who were older in the *control* group.) This, of course, does not mean that if the missing pretest data were considered, there would be no initial group differences in survival-related characteristics or that the missing data do not account for some unexplained variance regarding survival rates. What it does mean, however, is that the data presented by Berger and Piliavin were incorrectly used and that the unknown effects of the missing pretest data must remain just that—unknown.

Table 2 Frequency Distribution of Project Participants: Experimental–Control-Group Membership by Mental Status

	Experimental	Control
Poor (0–2)	15	12
Good (3–9)	32	43

Source: Berger and Piliavin, Table 2.

Chi square = 0.86, $df = 1$, $p > .05$, N.S.

Table 3 Frequency Distribution of Project Participants: Experimental–Control-Group Membership by Age

	Experimental	Control
75 and under	16	23
Over 75	31	32

Source: Berger and Piliavin, Table 2.

Chi square = 0.36, $df = 1$, $p > .05$, N.S.

Table 4 Frequency Distribution of Project Participants: Experimental–Control-Group Membership by Age

	Experimental	Control
75 and under	23	28
Over 75	40	42

Source: Berger and Piliavin, Table 3.

Chi square = 0.05, $df = 1$, $p > .05$, N.S.

Table 5 Frequency Distribution of Project Participants: Experimental–Control-Group Membership by Physical Functioning

	Experimental	Control
Poor (0–1)	28	23
Good (2–5)	35	48

Source: Berger and Piliavin, Table 3.

Chi square = 1.58, $df = 1$, $p > .05$, N.S.

3 Ibid., p. 206.
4 Ibid.

Missing Data

Although there is no statistical support to justify Berger and Piliavin's reanalysis of the data, they cling to the thread of the missing data as one explanation for the observed difference between the experimental and control groups in survival rates. They apparently did this because they were convinced that the experimental and control groups were not equated with respect to the survival-related covariates of age, mental status, and physical functioning. Thus they conclude with the admonition that "randomization, particularly in small samples, is not guarantee of equivalence among controls and experimentals."[5] This is a flimsy argument for two reasons. Berger and Piliavin appear to have forgotten their elementary statistical theory; it simply is not true that randomization is *particularly* weak in small-sample research. On the contrary, smaller samples tend to favor the null hypothesis—that is, they make it more difficult to obtain significant differences between groups. In addition, the data that Berger and Piliavin report are in contradiction to their claim that the experimental and control groups were not equivalent. Indeed, within the limits of chance variation, their data clearly show that the experimental and control groups *were* equivalent with respect to the three covariates that concerned them: none of the differences were statistically significant.

Berger and Piliavin conclude as follows:

> When those participants for whom data on survival-related characteristics were missing are omitted from the analysis, there are no significant experimental group effects evident in the Rose Institute study.[6]

They apparently drew this conclusion by comparing one regression model having $n = 164$, which showed a significant difference in survival status between experimental and control groups, with another regression model having $n = 101$ that showed no significant difference between groups. (See their Tables 4A and 5A.) The fact is that the error term for the first model has 162 degrees of freedom, whereas the second has only 99. That reduction alone may be enough to account for the difference between the two models, especially since the β of the first model is only marginally significant. One of the elementary truths of statistical theory is that smaller samples favor the null hypothesis. By eliminating all the persons for whom any covariate data were missing, Berger and Piliavin have reduced the size of the original study samples by 38.4 percent. A third regression model containing all the covariates and with $n = 101$ obviously has the same weakness. (See their Table 5B.)[7]

In their Table 4B, Berger and Piliavin present one regression model that is of interest. With $n = 164$, that model indicates that there is no significant difference between the experimental and control groups with respect to survival status after the effects of age, mental status, and physical functioning have been accounted for. Unfortunately, the problem of missing data is a serious problem in this model as well. It is clear that one or more values for age, mental status, and physical functioning were missing for 63 persons. This means that the missing values represent between 12.8 percent and 38.4 percent of all the covariate data. However, Berger and Piliavin fail to shed any further light on this issue.

Researchers must always confront the potential hazard of losing important data. When that happens to a small degree, group means can be used to estimate the missing values.

5 Ibid., p. 208.

6 Ibid., p. 207.

7 Berger and Piliavin's disregard for loss of degrees of freedom is also exhibited by leaving three nonsignificant covariates in their model of Table 4B and four in their model of Table 5B. A better procedure would have been to first test the covariates step by step. After retaining the significant covariates, the experimental variable could then be tested to determine whether it made an additional significant contribution to the explained variance.

However, when it becomes necessary to estimate a large percentage of the data that are crucial to an analysis (in this case up to 38.4 percent), this practice is not only dangerous but there is a high risk of producing an incorrect conclusion.[8]

Even if the significant effects of age and mental status as predictors of survival rates are accurate, this does not mean—as Berger and Piliavin still argue—that the original findings of higher mortality rate in the experimental group "were the consequence of initial group differences in survival-related characteristics."[9] Tables 2–5 in this rebuttal demonstrate that there *were* no differences between the groups on these survival-related dimensions.

Berger and Piliavin's conclusion, "Clearly the nonassessed experimentals were more likely to die than the nonassessed controls," is not justified by their analyses.[10] Furthermore, since it is already known that experimentals had a higher death rate than controls, their "conclusion" becomes a tautology. Presumably, what Berger and Piliavin meant was that because of an unintended sampling bias, nonassessed experimentals at the pretest stage included a high proportion of individuals who were more likely to die than were the nonassessed controls. (That is, nonassessed experimentals were older and more debilitated physically and mentally.) It has already been demonstrated that the likelihood of this error in sampling is remote and that the statistical "evidence" presented by Berger and Piliavin seems flawed. However, given the fact that these pretest data are missing, even a direct statistical test comparing survival rates between nonassessed experimental and nonassessed controls would be irrelevant because the data already show that experimentals were more likely to die than controls. Thus, it could not be demonstrated that differences in survival are due to differences in initial status.

Alternative Tests

Perhaps a more appropriate argument for Berger and Piliavin would have been that nonassessed experimentals were more likely to die than assessed experimentals—although for sampling reasons described earlier this too is unlikely. Berger and Piliavin might then have used a direct test to compare nonassessed and assessed experimentals (and, of course, tested nonassessed and assessed controls as well). For example, they could have included a second dummy variable in their simple regression model (their Table 4A). Such a model would be written as follows:

$$y = a + b_1 X_1 + B_2 X_2 + e$$

In this case, y = survival status, X_1 is coded as 1 for experimental group membership and as 0 for control group membership, and X_2 is coded as 1 for assessed individuals and as 0 for nonassessed individuals. (This model is nothing more than a two-way analysis of variance; in the event the subclass $N's$ are disproportionate, they should use a nonorthogonal procedure such as the one recommended by Bock.)[11] Or they might have used two simple chi-square tables (one for the experimental and one for the control group) comparing

8 The analyses of the Berger and Piliavin data in Tables 2–5 on these pages indicate that the experimental and control groups are equivalent with respect to the covariates. Therefore, inclusion of the covariates in their model (their Table 4B) should have only one effect—reduction of the error term. This would mean that the β of their simple model (their Table 4A), which showed a statistically significant effect of experimental group membership on survival, should not change in model 4B (where it was lower and not significant), and that its partial F-ratio should increase as a result of the reduced error term. Thus, the statistical test should provide stringer support for group differences in survival status rather than weaker support as described by Berger and Piliavin.

9 Berger and Piliavin, op. cit., p. 206.

10 Ibid., p. 207.

11 R. Darrell Bock, *Multivariate Statistical Methods in Behavioral Research* (New York: McGraw-Hill Book Co., 1975).

285

assessment status (assessed versus nonassessed and survival status, or a single chi-square table adding to these dimensions experimental-control group membership. In this last case, the procedures recommended by Goodman could be used to partition out the source of any effect.[12]

Although in all these instances a significant finding might bring some indirect evidence to bear on the Berger and Piliavin thesis, it still would not "prove" that the differences were due to differences in initial status. Once again, because the data on initial status are missing, it would be impossible to rule out the effects of other variables—for example, differential patterns (rate, intensity, and the like) of professional services.

To what can the greater amount of deaths in the experimental group be attributed? Since the experimental and control groups were equivalent on the crucial covariates of survival, and in the absence of clear evidence about the missing data, one possible answer is that the experimental group was exposed to something that the control group was not. The only phenomenon meeting that criterion is professional casework services.

Conclusion

This reanalysis of the data from the Berger and Piliavin article raises once again the disturbing possibility that professional casework services may be related to client deterioration. Although the use of sophisticated statistical techniques in the social work literature is encouraging, such sophisticated analyses should not be undertaken at the expense of forgetting more basic lessons in quantitative analysis. In this instance, the lapse appeared to stem from the claim that differences existed between experimental and control groups on the basis of distributions. A simple statistical test, however, would have revealed that there were no significant differences. Thus, what the Berger and Piliavin article best illustrates is that the use of sophisticated statistical procedures cannot produce findings for researchers that are not contained in the data.

12 See Leo A. Goodman, "A Modified Multiple Regression Approach to the Analysis of Dichotomous Variables," American Sociological Review, 37 (1972), pp.28–46; and Leo A. Goodman, "A General Model for the Analysis of Surveys," American Journal of Sociology, 77 (1972), pp. 1035–1086.

A Rejoinder*

Raymond M. Berger and Irving Piliavin

The critique by Fischer and Hudson, "An Effect of Casework? Back to the Drawing Board," argues that our reanalysis of the Protective Services Project for Older Persons that appeared in the May 1976 issue of Social Work is methodologically flawed. They contend, as did the original researchers, that the only reasonable explanation of the findings is that provision of services was associated with diminished survival.

In the opinion of the present authors, however, there are a number of misconceptions and inaccuracies in the Fischer and Hudson critique. When these are considered, our original conclusion—that differential survival rates in the service and control groups may be due to initial group differences on survival-related characteristics—appears to be reasonable.

Fischer and Hudson argue that since the experimental and control groups did not differ

Reprinted with permission, from Social Work, 21:5 (September 1976), 349, 396–397. Copyright © 1976 by the National Association of Social Workers, Inc., New York.

* Editoral Note: This rejoinder to the preceeding "viewpoint" constitutes Technical Note 11.4. It is a third way the critical debate on research findings can be conducted.

significantly on the survival-related covariates of age, mental status, and physical functioning, the observed differences between the groups cannot be accounted for by the differences in these variables. In fact, the present authors were aware that these differences were not significant by chi-square analysis.[1] However, the question of whether these differences were statistically significant is irrelevant. The findings on all three covariates were consistent; that is, the experimental group, proportionately, had participants who were older and of poorer mental status and physical functioning than did the control group. Taken in combination, the effects of these initial differences over a three-year interval could reasonably lead to a significant difference in survival rates.

Small-Sample Research

Fischer and Hudson do not accept the present authors' contention that small-sample research can result in lack of equivalence of experimental and control groups. They state: "it simply is not true that randomization is particularly weak in small-sample research." In fact, lack of equivalence of groups created by random assignment is *always* a concern in small-sample research. For instance, in a discussion of the random assignment of underachieving children to experimental and control groups. Kerlinger noted:

> [The investigator] wishes to have the two groups equal in other independent variables that may have a possible effect on achievement. One way he can do this is to assign the children to both groups at random. . . . He can now assume that the groups are approximately equal in all possible independent variables. The larger the groups, the safer the assumption. Just as there is no guarantee, however, of not drawing a deviant sample . . . there is no guarantee that the groups *are* equal or even approximately equal in all possible independent variables.[2]

In confirmation of this, Hays observed:

> . . . Given some sample it will always be true that factors other than the ones manipulated by the experimenter will contribute to the observed differences between subjects in the particular situation. If it should happen that some extraneous factor operates unevenly over several treatment groups or over different subjects, this can create spurious differences, or mask true effects in the data.[3]

Fischer and Hudson challenge the analyses presented in Tables 4 and 5 of our article and the conclusions drawn from them.[4] Specifically, they argue that Tables 4 and 5 are not comparable because of the loss of degrees of freedom in going from Table 4 (based on all participants) to Table 5 (based on assessed participants only).[5] Fischer and Hudson are correct in noting that a loss of degrees of freedom favors nonsignificance. However, the argument presented by us in that article—that the findings of the original Rose Institute study concerning greater mortality among experimentals may be invalid—rests on the following point: In both Table 4B and Table 5B, when the effects of survival-related characteristics are controlled, the difference in survival rates between groups is not significant. In addition,

1 The chi-square analysis performed by Fischer and Hudson in Tables 1–5 represents the weakest statistical test—the one least likely to lead to significance.
2 Fred N. Kerlinger, *Foundations of Behavioral Research* (New York: Holt, Rinehart & Winston, 1973), p. 123.
3 William L. Hays, *Statistics for the Social Sciences* (New York: Holt, Rinehart & Winston, 1973), p. 562.
4 Berger and Piliavin, "The Effect of Casework: A Research Note," *Social Work,* 21 (May 1976), p. 207.
5 Assessed participants ($n = 101$) included those who were assessed on both mental status and physical functioning at pretest. All participants had complete data on the remaining variables—age, group membership, and survival.

a comparison of Tables 4B and 5B does not involve a substantial loss in degrees of freedom because the substitution of means for missing data method (Table 4B) computes an error term that is based only on the count of data actually present.[6]

Fischer and Hudson argue further: "The unknown effects of the missing pretest data must remain just that—unknown." They imply that the present authors claim to have determined definitively the effects of the missing data. In fact, although we suggested a possible relationship between the missing data and survival, we are in agreement with Fischer and Hudson regarding the unknown effects of the missing data. In the conclusion of the article we observed: "Clearly the nonassessed experimentals were more likely to die than the nonassessed controls, although the reasons for this are not provided by the data."[7]

Fischer and Hudson claim that Table 4B is of dubious validity because of the large amount of missing data. They are correct in noting that analyses for which substantial amounts of data are missing would be of questionable validity. However, in our analyses we examined in two models the effects of group membership and of the covariates on survival. The first model (Table 4B) involved the estimation of missing data values; the second model (Table 5B) did not. In both cases, once the effects of the covariates on survival were accounted for, survival status was not significantly related to group membership.

The present authors believe that the issue of missing data must be kept within a realistic perspective. A unbiquitous problem in social work research, the question of missing data is certainly pertinent to the original Rose Institute study. This does not mean, however, that analyses should necessarily be abandoned, particularly when crucial questions of research are involved. The present authors' reanalysis of the study exemplifies one solution to the problem by performing comparative analyses and analyses that attempt to answer questions indirectly.

A major thrust of the Fischer and Hudson critique seems to be based on the assumption that the present authors claim to have proved that initial group differences accounted for the difference in survival rates between experimental and control groups. For instance, Fischer and Hudson stated:

> Even if the significant effects of age and mental status as predictors of survival rates are accurate, this does not mean—as Berger and Piliavin argue—that the original findings of higher mortality rate in the experimental group "were the consequence of initial group differences in survival-related characteristics."

Fischer and Hudson are correct in all respects except in their assumption that the present authors followed that argument. The complete quotation from our article read as follows:

> This reduction in experimental group influence [as a result of controlling for effects of the covariates (Table 4B)] and the significant age and mental status effects in the second model support the hypothesis that the original Rose Institute study findings were the consequence of initital group differences in survival-related characteristics.[8]

Although Fischer and Hudson do not challenge the use of covariates in the analysis, it is important to note that the kind of analysis performed by the present authors has an important place in the evaluation of research data. When there is sound theoretical reason (as there is in this case) to believe that important covariates are substantially related to the dependent variable, the use of covariates reduces error variance and thus permits more sensitive tests of significance.

The Fischer and Hudson critique of our reanalysis of the Protective Services Project for Older Persons raised once again "the disturbing possibility that professional casework services

6 The computer programs used in the data analysis are available from the Madison Academic Computing Center—The University of Wisconsin, DSTAT 2 and REGAN 2.

7 Berger and Piliavin, op. cit., p. 207.

8 Ibid., p. 206.

may be related to client deterioration." This conclusion was based on a criticism of the methodology used by the present authors in their reanalysis. Specifically, Fischer and Hudson argued that the experimental and control groups were equivalent on initial survival-related characteristics and that there were no clear data regarding the effects of missing data on survival status. The present authors attempted to show that initial group differences in survival-related characteristics do, in fact, constitute a plausible alternative hypothesis to the contention that provision of casework services was related to increased mortality.

The Impact of Social Casework on the Elderly: A Reappraisal of the Controversy Surrounding the Benjamin Rose Institute's Protective Services Study*

Dennis Wagner and Michael J. Osmalov

Abstract

In 1971, Blenkner, Bloom, and Nielson reported disturbing findings from the Benjamin Rose Institute's Protective Service Demonstration Project. These findings (in part) suggested that debilitated older persons who had received intensive protective casework services evidenced a higher mortality rate and shorter longevity as a result.

Berger and Piliavan (1976a) reanalyzed the BRI data, using multiple-regression analysis, and concluded that the higher mortality rate and shorter longevity of the experimental group were not effected by the receipt of these casework services. Instead, Berger and Piliavin suggested that preexisting, mortality-related health differences between experimental- and control-group members accounted for the disturbing outcome. It is argued here that Berger and Piliavin's rejection of the original findings was in error because (1) they subjected their statistical results to an inappropriate test of significance, and (2) more important, they failed to consider the *substantive* significance of the results of their analysis. Furthermore, it is argued that Berger and Piliavin did not establish that the groups were not equivalent at pretest. A guideline intended to prevent possibly dangerous misinterpretations in future reanalyses is offered, and a method by which possible group nonequivalencies may be detected and controlled is suggested.

Introduction

In 1964, the Benjamin Rose Institute (BRI) initiated a mjaor research and demonstration project designed to evaluate the impact of intensive protective services on a noninstitutionalized aged population. The major finding of the BRI study was that the provision of such protective services appeared to be life-shortening (Blenkner, Bloom, and Nielsen, 1971). This disturbing but important finding was later disputed by Berger and Piliavin (1976a). They claimed that their multivariate statistical reanalysis of the BRI data "substantially ruled out the . . . conclusion that [social casework services] are harmful" [pp. 276–281 in this book], ascribing observed differences in mortality to predemonstration health differences between subjects. This refutation of the original major finding was then opened to question by Fischer and Hudson's limited, secondary analysis of the BRI data (1976). Thus, the

Used with permission from the authors.

* *Editorial Note:* This paper constitutes Technical Note 11.5. The authors were, at the time of its writing, doctoral students in the same department as the people whom they were critiquing, one of whom was a senior professor. One must admire their courage. The paper has not been published previously.

289

major BRI finding—that intensive protective services may have actually shortened the lives of older persons seemingly in need of protection—has been subjected to considerable controversy. Although we acknowledge Berger and Piliavin's contribution in utilizing multiple regression to examine the BRI data, we argue that the results of their reanalysis do *not* meaningfully contradict the major finding of the original researchers.

Background

The BRI project was undertaken to determine the effect of intensive protective services on the lives of persons at least sixty years of age whose behavior indicated that they were "mentally incapable of adequately caring for [themselves] . . . without serious consequences" and who had "no relative(s) or other private individual(s) able and willing to assume the kind and degree of support and supervision required to control the situation." Such persons were referred to BRI by thirteen agencies of four types (economic maintenance; housing; health; and counseling, referral, and information) from June 1964 through May 1965. Upon referral, subjects were randomly allocated to either the demonstration service (experimental) group ($N = 76$) or the standard treatment (control) group ($N = 88$). Members of the experimental group were to be offered intensive protective services for a period of one year; controls were left under the auspices of the referring agency "to be served (or not served) in the normal fashion of the agency." At the end of the one-year demonstration period, surviving experimentals who continued to require service were transferred to the regular BRI Social Work Program (Blenkner, et al., 1971, pp. 255–272 in this book).

Pretest data on both experimental- and control-group members were gathered within five days of subjects' registration in the project and before contact had been made by the project service staff. Pretest data were obtained from structured responses to BRI-developed instruments, observer ratings of various dimensions of subjects' behavior, and interviews with subjects' collaterals. Follow-up data were gathered after three months, six months, and one year of subjects' entrance in the project (Blenkner, et al., 1971, pp. 255–272 in this book). In addition, data on postparticipation relocation and survival were gathered for a ten-year period.

Description of BRI Protective Services

The central service intervention offered to BRI experimental-sample members was social casework provided by professionals who were instructed to "do, or get others to do, whatever is necessary to meet the needs of the situation" while "building and maintaining relationships of trust and mutual respect" (Blenkner, et al., 1971, pp. 255–272 in this book). Caseworkers also had at their disposal an array of client supportive services including (1) medical evaluation and treatment; (2) financial assistance for special needs; (3) psychiatric outpatient consultation; (4) legal consultation; (5) fiduciary and guardianship services; (6) public-health nursing consultation; (7) social service aides providing visiting, escort, shopping, and transportation services; (8) home aide services (made available only to certain members of the experimental group) including housekeeping, food preparation, and other activities that were intended to allow recipients to remain in their own homes; and (9) placement services for relocating those incapable of remaining in their own homes to suitable institutions.

Prior to the beginning of the demonstration period, BRI researchers hypothesized that the provision of intensive protective services would cause the experimental group to demonstrate in comparison with the control group: (1) greater length and rate of survival; (2) greater contentment; (3) fewer behavioral and affective symptoms; and (4) greater functional competence. For the BRI project to be considered successful, the experimental group had to demonstrate both a significantly greater survival rate and greater average contentment scores than controls, irrespective of findings on the other dependent variables (Blenkner, Wasser, and Bloom, 1967, p. 52).

290

In addition, Blenkner had theorized that:

> because hopelessness could literally kill and because institutionalization generated feelings of hopelessness, whichever group (demonstration or control) had the higher placement rate would also have the higher death rate. (Blenkner, et al., 1971, p. 267 in this book.)

BRI Findings on Institutionalization

It bears reiteration that, at the time of registration, none of the 164 BRI subjects were residing in institutions. By the end of the five years following subjects' registration in the BRI demonstration, 61 percent of the original experimental group had been institutionalized, as compared to 47 percent of the controls (see Table 1). Blenkner, et al., 1971 noted that, throughout the demonstration and its follow-up period, experimentals experienced a higher rate of institutionalization than did controls.

Table 1 Cummulative Percentage of BRI Subjects Institutionalized, from Time of Registration

Years After Registration	Experimental Group	Control Group
One year	34%	20%
Two years	49	34
Three years	55	39
Four years	59	48
	$N = 76$	$N = 88$

Note: Adapted from Blenkner (1969, p. 5), Table 1.

BRI Findings on Survival

By the end of the third year of subjects' participation in the BRI demonstration, more experimental group members had died (53 percent) than controls (35 percent). By the end of the fourth year, the difference in survival between the groups had abated somewhat (63 percent of the experimentals had died, as compared to 52 percent of the controls) (see Table 2).

Table 2 Cummulative Percentage of BRI Subjects not Surviving, from Time of Registration

Years After Registration	All Subjects		Institutionalized		Noninstitutionalized	
	Exp.	Con.	Exp.	Con.	Exp.	Con.
One year	25%	18%	42%	28%	16%	16%
Two years	40	25	51	23	28	26
Three years	53	35	62	44	41	30
Four years	63	52	69	67	55	39
$N =$	76	88	42	34	34	54

Note: Adapted from Blenkner (1969, pp. 5–10), Tables 2 and 3.

291

Of the BRI subjects who had become institutionalized, the difference between the two groups in the proportion of those who died was marked (62 percent of the experimentals, against 44 percent of the controls) by the end of three years from registration. By the end of the fourth year, however, this discrepancy had disappeared (69 percent of institutionalized experimentals had died, as compared to 67 percent of the institutionalized controls) (see Table 2).

Of the BRI subjects who had not been institutionalized, 41 percent of the experimentals, as compared to 30 percent of the controls, had died by the end of the third year. By the end of the fourth year, 55 percent of the noninstitutionalized experimentals had died, as compared to 39 percent of the noninstitutionalized controls (see Table 2).

BRI Conclusions Regarding Survival and Institutionalization

BRI-affiliated researchers concluded that "the service [experimental] group in spite of all its directed and intensive protective services [had] lower mean life and higher mortality rates than the control groups" (Berrettoni and Blenkner, 1969, p. 2, cited in Blenkner, et al., 1971, p. 269 in this book). This conclusion was based on data accrued by the end of three years following subjects' registration. It was noted that, in both the experimental and control samples, the most efficacious predictor of survival was age, followed by subjects' predemonstration mental status, indicated by MSQ score, and level of physical functioning, indicated by PFQ score[1] (Blenkner, et al., 1971, p. 271 in this book).

BRI-affiliated researchers tentatively concluded that the provision of intensive protective services to experimentals may also have caused them to be institutionalized earlier than controls. Since noninstitutionalized subjects tended to live longer than those institutionalized (Berrettoni and Blenkner, 1969, p. 2, cited in Blenkner, et al., 1971, pp. 268–270 in this book), it appeared that earlier institutionalization had not proven to be protective (Blenkner, et al., 1971, pp. 268–270 in this book).

When the BRI findings regarding institutionalization and death rates are considered jointly, they appear to provide support for Blenkner's prediction that the group with the higher institutionalization rate would also have the higher death rate. Thus an overview of the findings of BRI-affiliated researchers suggests strongly a causal model in which exposure of debilitated elderly persons to intensive services leads to earlier institutionalization which leads to earlier death. To date, the validity of this causal model has not been adequately tested.

Blenkner, et al. (1971) also proposed a rival hypothesis that could explain the apparently service-induced difference in survival and placement rates between the experimental and control groups. The rival hypothesis suggests that these differences between the groups in survival and placement rates might not have been service induced, but instead might have reflected "a rare statistical event in which two random samples from the same population [were] in truth very different on crucial variables . . . not measured or controlled" (1971, pp. 271–272 in this book). The issue raised by this proposed rival hypothesis is that the experimental and control groups evidenced significant predemonstration differences from each other on survival- and institutionalization-related dimensions. That the groups were in fact nonequivalent became the central argument in Berger and Piliavin's rejection (1976a) of Blenkner, et al.'s (1971) conclusions regarding the effect of intervention on subjects' longevity.

Description of the Berger-Piliavin Reanalysis

Berger and Piliavin estimated two simple regression models (1976a, pp. 279–280 in this book, Tables 4A and 5A) and two multiple-regression models (1976a, Tables 4B and 5B), which described in years the effects of various independent variables on subjects' postregistration length of survival. The independent variables included in the multiple-regression models were mental status, as indicated by subjects' scores on the MSQ instrument; level of physical functioning, as indicated by subjects' scores on the PFQ instrument; age; and whether or not subjects were members of the experimental group (i.e., whether or not subjects had the opportunity of receiving intensive protective services). Two additional independent variables represented the respective interactions between advanced age and low PFQ scores and advanced age and low MSQ scores. The dependent variable was subjects' postregistration length of survival in years. The four regression models are reproduced here in Tables 3–1, 3–2, 4–1, and 4–2.

In each of the two multiple regressions, presented here in Tables 3–2 and 4–2, the coefficient calculated for experimental-group membership represents (in years) that fraction of subjects' postregistration longevity accounted for by subjects' belonging to the experimental group, *after* the effects on longevity of subjects' age, predemonstration mental status (MSQ scores), predemonstration physical status (PFQ scores), and various interactions were statistically removed. The removal of the effects of these other variables on longevity is quite important, given the concern that predemonstration, survival-related differences between

Table 3–1 Estimated Effect of Experimental-Group Membership on Three-Year[a] Longevity of 101[b] BRI Demonstration Subjects

Variable	β[c] Estimated Coefficient	Significance Level of β (two-tailed)
Experimental group membership[d]	−.265	.2731

Note: Adapted from Berger and Piliavin (1976a, p. 280 in this book), Table 5A.

[a] Longevity is coded 0, 1, 2, or 3 as recorded at the end of the first three years following participants' registration.
[b] Sixty-three subjects were excluded from this analysis.
[c] Coefficients estimated here are unstandardized; they may be interpreted as a fraction of one year of life.
[d] Coded 0 for controls, 1 for experimentals.

Table 3–2 Estimated Effect of Experimental-Group Membership and Selected Personal Characteristics on Three-Year[a] Longevity of 101[b] BRI Subjects

Variable	β[c] Estimated Coefficient	Significance Level of β (two-tailed)
Experimental group membership[d]	−.116	.583
Age[e]	−.247	.092
Physical functioning (PFQ)[f]	−.017	.831
Mental status (MSQ)[g]	.173	.003
Deteriorated mental status × age[h]	−.020	.958
Deteriorated physical functioning × age[i]	−.708	.065

Note: Adapted from Berger and Piliavin (1976a, p. 280 in this book), Table 5B.

[a] Longevity is coded 0, 1, 2, or 3 as recorded at the end of the first three years following participants' registration.
[b] Sixty-three subjects were excluded from this analysis.
[c] Coefficients estimated here are unstandardized; they may be interpreted as a function of one year of life.
[d] Coded 0 for controls, 1 for experimentals.
[e] Age in years.
[f] PFQ coded 0 (low) through 9 (high).
[g] MSQ coded 0 (low) through 5 (high).
[h] Interaction of low MSQ (0–2) with age over seventy-five years. Coded 1 for subjects over 75 with low MSQ, and 0 for all others.
[i] Interaction of low PFQ (0 or 1) with age over seventy-five years. Coding similar to h above (see Berger and Piliavin, 1976a, p. 279 in this book, for variable codes).

293

Table 4–1 Estimated Effect on Experimental-Group Membership on Three-Year[a] Longevity of BRI Demonstration Subjects (N = 164)

Variable	β[b] Estimated Coefficient	Significance Level of β (two-tailed)
Experimental group membership[c]	−.387	.0456

Note: Adapted from Berger and Piliavin (1976a, p. 279 in this book), Table 4B.

[a] Longevity is coded 0, 1, 2, or 3 as recorded at the end of the first three years following participants' registration.
[b] Coefficients estimated here are unstandardized; they may be interpreted as a fraction of one year of life.
[c] Coded 0 for controls, 1 for experimentals.

Table 4–2 Estimated Effects of Experimental-Group Membership and Selected Personal Characteristics Three-Year[a] Longevity of BRI Demonstration Subjects (N = 164)

Variable	β[b] Estimated Coefficient	Significance Level (two-tailed)
Experimental group membership[c]	−.283	
Age[d]	−.281	
Physical functioning (PFQ)[e]	.061	
Mental status (MSQ)[f]	.163	
Deteriorated mental status × age[g]	.084	
Deteriorated physical status × age[h]	−.491	

Note: Adapted from Berger and Piliavin (1976a, p. 279 in this book), Table 4B.

[a] Longevity is coded 0, 1, 2, or 3 as recorded at the end of the first three years following participants' registration.
[b] Coefficients estimated here are unstandardized; they may be interpreted as a fraction of one year of life.
[c] Coded 0 for controls, 1 for experimentals.
[d] Age in years.
[e] PFQ coded 0 (low) through 9 (high).
[f] MSQ coded 0 (low) through 5 (high).
[g] Interaction of low MSQ (0–2) with age over seventy-five. Coded 1 for subjects over seventy-five with low MSQ, and 0 all others.
[h] Interaction of low PFQ (0 or 1) with age over 75 years, similar to h above (see Berger and Piliavin, 1976a, p. 279 in book, for variable codes).

experimentals and controls might have accounted to a significant extent for their differences in postregistration longevity. By statistically removing the effects of age, MSQ scores, PFQ scores, and their interactions on subjects' longevity, predemonstration differences between the two groups on these variables are controlled out. Therefore, the unstandardized coefficient for experimental group membership (in Tables 3–2 and 4–2) represents the unique result, expressed as a fractional part of one year of life, of subjects' exposure to intensive protective services.

The Berger and Piliavin simple regression represented in Table 3–1 yielded a coefficient for experimental-group membership of −.265 of one year. After removing possible effects of age, PFQ scores, MSQ scores, and their interactions, the coefficient for experimental-group membership dropped to −.116 (Table 3–2), indicating a life-shortening effect of approximately 42 days.[2] It must be noted, however, that both the simple and the multiple regressions described here were based on a selection of only 101 (62 percent) of the 164 BRI subjects. Berger and Piliavin eliminated all data obtained on 63 population members from these two regressions because these subjects' MSQ and/or PFQ scores had not been determined by BRI interviewers. Data available on the 63 subjects' age, group membership (experimental or control), and length of survival were thereby ignored. It is quite unlikely that chance factors caused 63 subjects to fail to respond to their interviewers (see Footnote 1). Thus the 101 remaining subjects do not constitute a random sample of the entire BRI demonstration population. For this reason, the results of the two regressions calculated on the nonrandom subpopulation of 101 (Tables 3–1, 3–2) reflect sampling bias and may not be valid estimates from which to draw inferences about the effects of the BRI demonstration services.[3]

Berger and Piliavin's other two regressions (Tables 4–1 and 4–2) were performed on data from *all* 164 BRI subjects. Where data on as many as 63 subjects' MSQ and/or PFQ scores were absent, Berger and Piliavin used group means on these variables to estimate their scores.[4] The simple regression represented in Table 4–1 yielded a coefficient for experimental group membership of −.387. Removal of the effects of age, MSQ scores, PFQ scores, and their interactions reduced the effect of belonging to the experimental group to −.283 of one year's longevity. Given the configuration of Berger and Piliavin's regression model, this coefficient indicates that experimental-group membership *by itself* reduced subjects' longevity by approximately 103 days (−.283 × 365 days = 103 days).

Although the experimental effect which they estimated is both negative and large (103 days of life), Berger and Piliavin rejected the findings of the original BRI researchers and concluded that "the foregoing analysis has not, alas, revealed social casework services to be beneficial. It has, however, substantially ruled out the more disquieting possibility that they are harmful" (1976a, p. 281 in this book).

Reconsidering the Berger–Piliavin Findings

1. The Effect of Experimental-Group Membership on Longevity

We believe that Berger and Piliavin's conclusion that there was no experimental effect on longevity may not be warranted, for two reasons: (1) they utilized a two-tailed test of significance when a one-tailed test was indicated, and (2) they neglected to interpret the substantive meaning of the −.283 coefficient they estimated.

There is a sound reason for challenging Berger and Piliavin's choice of the two-tailed test and the conclusion they reached through its application. The original BRI researchers had presented fairly conclusive evidence that experimental subjects demonstrated a substantially lower three-year survival rate than controls (see Table 1). Given knowledge of this well-documented relationship, the selection of a test which provides for discovery of a strong positive result is difficult to justify in a secondary analysis. In this case, a one-tailed, or directional test should have been employed (see, for example, Blalock, 1972, p. 164; Wonnacott and Wonnacott, 1970, pp. 64–67).

The structure of the two-tailed, .05-level significance test utilized by Berger and Piliavin and the conclusion that it leads researchers to draw about the −.283 experimental effect coefficient (estimated in Table 4–2) are presented graphically in Figure 4–1.

The critical decision regions illustrated in Figure 4–1 are bounded by the coefficients of ±.339, which correspond to experimental effects on survival of ±124 days. Thus, when the estimated experimental-group coefficient falls between these particular decision limits, the researcher may conclude that there was no statistically significant experimental effect at the .05 level.

When, instead, the one-tailed test is used (see Figure 4–2), the −.283 coefficient Berger and Piliavin estimated is statistically significant at the .055 level, easily within rounding error of their .05 criterion. (One-tailed significance may be calculated by dividing obtained two-tailed levels by a factor of two: .110/2 = .055).

Thus the use of the one-tailed test instead of the inappropriate two-tailed test might have led Berger and Piliavin to conclude that the experimental effect on survival was indeed negative. It would appear that only a minor error in test specification may have caused Berger and Piliavin to reject rather than reaffirm the major conclusion of the original BRI researchers.[5]

Perhaps more important, in relying solely on a test of statistical significance as a basis for drawing conclusions, Berger and Piliavin failed to consider the substantive significance of their estimated coefficient.

295

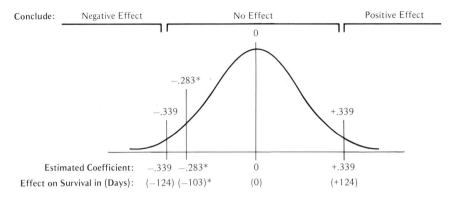

Note: Critical regions are calculated by multiplying the standard deviation (SD) of the estimated coefficient by the critical t value for a .05 two-tailed test:

$$\pm .339 = .173 \times \pm 1.96$$

Figure 4.1 Two-tailed .05-significance test for the experimental-group coefficient estimated in Table 4–2 ($\beta = -.283$, $SD = .173$, $N = 164$).

Statistical significance is a probability assessment of inferential error made against a criterion that the researcher may determine prior to the test; it is not a measure of a relationship's strength, or of its practical importance. The confusion of statistical significance with substantive significance must be carefully avoided (Gold, 1969; see also, for example, Duggan and Dean, 1968; Selvin, 1957). The magnitude and direction of experimental effects may be assessed independently of statistical significance and constitute important evidence for research conclusions in their own right (Frideres and Taylor, 1972, pp. 461–469).

As noted earlier, the −.283 coefficient constitutes an estimate that the experimental effect was negative and in the magnitude of 103 days. We submit that this is a substantively significant finding.

By way of illustration, if we assume that the estimated experimental-group coefficient had indicated a life-shortening effect of 85 days, it would not have been significant at the .05 level, either one- or two-tailed. Nevertheless, such a finding would remain seriously disturbing and critically important. The same could be said of a life-shortening effect of, for example, 30 days, significant (one-tailed) at the .32 level. The striking point illustrated here is that despite the sample estimate indicating that large and substantively important life-shortening effects had occurred, Berger and Piliavin's reliance on a purely statistical test of significance led them to the conclusion that the experiment had no life-shortening effects.

We are, of course, not suggesting that tests of significance serve no useful purpose. However, when applied to instances where length of human life appears in the relationship under test, use of the .05 significance level (or any other arbitrarily set level) as the sole criterion for assessment may lead to potentially dangerous conclusions.

2. Inferences Regarding Human Life

The purpose of the BRI experimental intervention was to prolong human life. Any evidence of an opposite impact can be considered to indicate an unacceptable result. Conclusions regarding the experimental effect on length of human life must be drawn from a decision rule which minimizes the probability of committing what is commonly termed *Type II error,* or mistakenly inferring that the intervention had no effect when in fact it did have an effect (see, for example, Blalock, 1972, pp. 159–162). Minimizing the probability of commit-

296

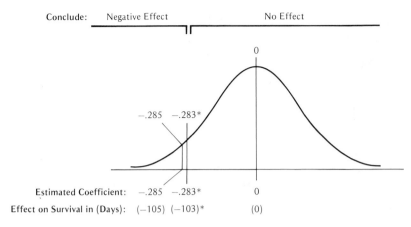

Conclude: Negative Effect   No Effect

            −.285   −.283*

Estimated Coefficient: −.285   −.283*   0

Effect on Survival in (Days):   (−105)   (−103)*   (0)

Note: Critical region calculated by multiplying the standard
deviation (SD) of the estimated coefficient by the
critical t value for a .05 one-tailed test:

$$-.285 = .173 \times -1.65$$

Figure 4.2 One-tailed .05-significance test for the experimental-group coefficient estimated in Table 4–2 ($\beta = -.283$, $SD = .173$, $N = 164$).

ting this type of error is especially critical in situations where the effect that might not be detected could be life-shortening. Thus an appropriate decision rule may be stated very simply: If a statistic indicates a negative experimental effect on longevity, it is unsafe to conclude that there was no effect, irrespective of the results of significance testing. In subsequent statistical reanalyses of the BRI demonstration data, only the estimation of a positive coefficient should be regarded as a meaningful and safe contradiction of the evidence established by BRI researchers that the experimental effect was life-shortening.

3. The Effect of Experimental-Group Membership on Institutionalization

Berger and Piliavin did confirm the BRI conclusion that experimental-group membership was strongly related to earlier institutionalization, although they did not present results from statistical tests. Because they concluded that experimental-group membership had no effect on survival, it is unlikely that they considered Blenkner's hypothesis (noted above) that earlier institutionalization caused earlier death.

4. The Question of Nonequivalence

Berger and Piliavin's reanalysis does raise again Blenkner, et al.'s (1971) suggestions that predemonstration differences between experimental and control groups may have accounted for the lower rate of survival later observed in the experimental group (1971). We do not believe, however, that Berger and Piliavin have demonstrated that the groups were not equivalent. In fact, it may not be possible to test this proposition directly.

Any meaningful support for the rival hypothesis of nonequivalence must be inferred from a test that establishes both that the groups were not equivalent at registration and that they were not equivalent in a way that caused experimentals to die at a higher rate than controls. Similarly, a nonequivalence hypothesis that explained the difference between groups' institutionalization rates could be supported only by meeting analogous test objectives.

These two objectives can be met only by the discovery of a variable or variables that (1) were measured prior to the application of experimental services; (2) had a meaningful different distribution in the experimental group than in the control group; and (3) were related to institutionalization and/or survival in such a way that the already observed relationships between experimental-group membership and earlier institutionalization, and/or between experimental-group membership and earlier death, would disappear when controlling the variable(s). Berger and Piliavin's regressions did not meet this set of conditions because the negative relationship between experimental-group membership and survival did not disappear. Perhaps more important, the distribution within the groups of two of the test variables Berger and Piliavin selected—mental status and physical functioning—remains unknown because of the inability of BRI interviewers to obtain MSQ or PFQ scores on a sizable (38 percent and 18 percent, respectively) nonrandom subpopulation of subjects. It is not possible to settle claims that the groups were equivalent or not equivalent when the variables on which these claims are based contain no observations on a sizable number of subjects.[6]

It is not apparent that Blenkner, et al.'s (1971) hypothesis of nonequivalence has ever been adequately tested. Given that this rival hypothesis is plausible, conclusions regarding the effect of BRI's experimental intervention may be disputed. This issue may be settled only by determining the extent to which randomization succeeded or failed at predemonstration to equalize the groups on survival- and institutionalization-related dimensions. If the groups were essentially equivalent, the observed negative relationships between experimental-group membership and institutionalizations are real. If, on the other hand, the groups were not equivalent, and the variables which demonstrate this are located and controlled, the observed negative effect of casework intervention may disappear. We believe this question must be considered open to the extent that reasonable doubts about equivalence remain. However, until these doubts are firmly established, it is not safe to reject the original conclusions reached by Blenkner, et al. (1971).

We would like to propose a method for examining the question of group equivalence. The 164 demonstration subjects were referred to BRI by thirteen agencies of four types (economic maintenance; housing; health; and counseling, referral, and information). It seems not unreasonable to presume that a subject referred from a health agency probably was in worse health than a subject referred from an economic maintenance agency. The most direct test of unintended bias resulting from the allocation of subjects to groups is to examine the pattern of allocation itself. If it could be demonstrated that (1) subjects referred from, for example, health agencies had an unusually high death and/or institutionalization rate, and (2) that subjects referred from these same agencies tended to be allocated to one of the two groups, then it would be reasonable to assume that the results of the experiment at least partially reflected bias. Should such a discovery be made, a variable indicating referral source could be entered into a regression equation and thus controlled. The coefficient for experimental-group membership should then reflect a relatively bias-free estimate of the experimental effects on survival/institutionalization.

Summary

Berger and Piliavin concluded that the receipt of intensive protective services did not shorten longevity. This conclusion was based on the failure of their regression coefficients for experimental-group membership to reach significance at the two-tailed .05 level. An attempt has been made in this paper to demonstrate that these decision rules were inappropriate. Given the particular structure of the regression models which Berger and Piliavin estimated, it appears that the inference which may be most judiciously drawn is that experimental-group membership probably had a negative effect on longevity. Thus we believe that the evidence offered by Berger and Piliavin does not meaningfully contradict the conclusions reached by BRI-affiliated researchers. There may be, however, other variables not yet considered which may alter the estimate of experimental effect.

As noted, BRI-affiliated researchers concluded that those who were offered intensive protective services experienced institutionalization, and that those who were institutionalized had shorter longevity. The inference that has been drawn from these conclusions is that exposure to services accelerated institutionalization which caused earlier death. Even if one readily accepts the BRI conclusions, it must be recognized that the validity of this proposal causal chain has yet to be tested.

When the results of an important experiment remain in doubt, it is considered to be sound practice to replicate that experiment. Given the tentative conclusions that have been drawn from the BRI study, replication could very well prove to be a costly course of action. As Blenkner (1967) suggested, the importance of analyzing the results of "natural experiments" analogous to the BRI protective-services study cannot be overestimated. In addition, further reanalysis of the BRI data may prove useful in resolving the important and disturbing questions that remain unanswered. Since the BRI protective-services study addressed issues crucial to planners and practitioners, such reanalysis is essential.

Footnotes

1. *MSQ* and *PFQ* refer to the mental status questionnaire and the physical functioning questionnaire instruments used in the BRI initial research interview. These instruments were very carefully developed by BRI (see Bloom, 1964). A large number of respondents failed to complete the MSQ and PFQ instruments, ostensibly because they grew tired, did not wish to divulge personal information, or refused to submit to an interview. The interview itself was quite long—sixty to ninety minutes. Twelve percent of the 164 subjects refused the interview (Bloom and Blenkner, 1966, pp. 3–10).

2. An unstandardized coefficient of +.500 for the effect of experimental-group membership calculated from such a multiple regression would have indicated that belonging to the experimental group resulted in increased longevity of approximately one-half year. Conversely, a calculated coefficient of −.500 for the effect of experimental-group membership would have indicated that belonging to the experimental group was life-shortening by approximately one-half year. A coefficient of .000 would have indicated that belonging to the experimental group had approximately no effect on subjects' longevity. Fractions of years are converted to days when multiplied by 365.

3. See Cohen and Cohen (1975, pp. 267–269), for a discussion of the problem inherent in the exclusion of subjects (and all observations available on them) from analysis on the basis of missing data on selected variables. See also Mackelprang (1970, 494–495).

4. Replacement with group means reflected Berger and Piliavin's assumption that, since experimental group members whose physical (PFQ) and/or mental status (MSQ) were assessed appeared to be more debilitated than assessed controls, nonassessed experimentals would have evidenced similar differences from nonassessed controls (see Berger and Piliavin, 1976a, pp. 276–281, in this book). As noted previously in text, it is unlikely that those whose PFQ and/or MSQ scores could not be assessed by BRI interviewers constituted a random sample of BRI demonstration subjects, or that nonassessed experimentals or controls constituted a random sample of their respective groups. Thus, the assumption upon which replacement by group means was based may be incorrect.

    It may have been a better procedure to replace missing values by substituting the grand mean of the variables in which observations were missing. The grand mean is a neutral value; as such it leaves the coefficients unbiased by assumptions about the missing observations. (See Cohen and Cohen, 1975, pp. 282–287; also Hiatovsky, 1968, pp. 67–82).

5. The original BRI researchers did, in fact, specify a one-tailed .05 test of the no-effect null hypothesis, against the alternative that service *increased* longevity. It is ironic to note that BRI researchers might have concluded that protective service increased longevity, had they observed an experimental effect this large (−.283, see Table 4–2) of the *opposite* sign. (See Blenkner, Wasser, and Bloom, 1967, p. 52.)

6. Fischer and Hudson (1976) engaged Berger and Piliavin (1976a) in a dispute as to whether the groups were equivalent. Fischer and Hudson claimed that, since chi-square tests of

299

group differences on single variables were not statistically significant, the groups were equivalent. Berger and Piliavin responded that these tests were irrelevant in that differences in multivariate combinations of age and physical and mental status could lead to differences in survival rates (1976b; pp. 276–281 in this book). Berger and Piliavin are correct in their statement, but neither single nor multivariate distributions can be determined for variables with nonrandom missing data (i.e., mental status and physical status).

References

Berger, R. M., and Piliavin, I. "The effect of casework on the aging: a research note." *Social Work,* 21 (1976), 205–208. (a)

Berger, R. M., and Piliavin, I. "A rejoinder by Berger and Piliavin." *Social Work,* 21 (1976), 349, 396–397. (b)

Blalock, H. M., Jr. *Social Statistics.* New York: McGraw-Hill, 1972.

Blenkner, M. *Demonstration of Protective Service for Older Adults: Project Plan.* Cleveland: Benjamin Rose Institute, 1963.

Blenkner, M. "Methodological problems in evaluating service demonstrations." Paper presented at the 6th International Gerontological Congress, Copenhagen, August 1963.

Blenkner, M. "Environmental change and the aging individual." *Gerontologist,* 7: 2 (Part I), (1967), 101–105.

Blenkner, M. "Service and survival." Paper presented at the 8th International Congress of Gerontology, Washington, D.C., August 1969.

Blenkner, M., Bloom, M., and Nielson, M. "A research and demonstration project for protective services." *Social Casework* 52 (October 1971), 483–499.

Blenkner, M., Bloom, M., and Weber, R. *Protective Services for Older People: Final Report on the Planning Phase of a Research and Demonstration Project.* Cleveland: Benjamin Rose Institute, 1967.

Blenkner, M., Wasser, E., and Bloom, M. *Protective Services for Older People: Progress Report 1966–1967.* Cleveland: Benjamin Rose Institute, 1967.

Bloom, M. *The Benjamin Rose Institute Protective Service Project: The Initial Research Interview.* Cleveland: Benjamin Rose Institute, 1964.

Bloom, M., and Blenkner, M. *The Benjamin Rose Institute Protective Service Project: The Follow-up Interview.* Cleveland: Benjamin Rose Institute, 1966.

Cohen, J., and Cohen, P. *Applied Multiple Regression/Correlation Analysis for the Behavioral Sciences.* Hillsdale, N.J.: Lawrence Erlbaum, 1975.

Draper, N. R., and Smith, H. *Applied Regression Analysis.* New York: Wiley, 1966.

Duggan, T. J., and Dean, C. W. "Common misinterpretations of significance levels in sociology journals." *The American Sociologist,* 3 (February 1968), 45–46.

Fischer, J., and Hudson, W. "An effect of casework? Back to the drawing board." *Social Work,* 21 (September 1976), 347–349.

Frideres, J., and Taylor, K. W. "Issues versus controversies: Substantive and statistical significance." *American Sociological Review,* 37 (August 1972), 464–472.

Gold, D. "Statistical tests and substantive significance." *The American Sociologist,* 4910 (February 1969), 42–46.

Haitovsky, Y. "Missing data in regression analysis." *Journal of the Royal Statistical Society,* 30 (1968), 67–92.

Mackelprang, A. J. "Missing data in factor analysis and multiple regression." *Midwest Journal of Political Science,* 14 (August 1970), 494–504.

Selvin, H. C. "A critique of tests of significance in survey research." *American Sociological Review,* 22 (October 1957), 519–522.

Wonnacott, R. J., and Wonnacott, T. H. *Econometrics.* New York: Wiley, 1970.

Protective Services Reanalyzed: Does Casework Help or Harm?*

Ruth E. Dunkle, S. Walter Poulshock, Barbara Silverstone, and
Gary T. Deimling

In the early 1960s, Margaret Blenkner and her associates at The Benjamin Rose Institute (BRI) in Cleveland, Ohio, designed and implemented a major evaluation research effort which addressed the issue of the effectiveness of protective services for older persons. The stated aim of the project was to "develop, carry out, and analyze a program of protective services for non-institutionalized older adults in such a way that its effectiveness, utility, and cost may be determined and the results incorporated in new or ongoing programs of practice, teaching, and research in the field of social work with aging."[1]

The conception of the project was notable. The interest in protective services for older persons and the innovative nature of the project's experimental design were unique at that particular time. These features, however, were overshadowed by the controversial nature of the project's findings, which concluded that the "demonstrated protective service . . . did not prevent or slow deterioration among elderly clients but did increase the likelihood of their institutionalization."[2] Moreover, mortality rates for the experimental group were found to be higher than for a control group not receiving special services.

Subsequent interpretations of these findings by the professional community ranged from indictments of casework practice—epitomized by the slogan "casework kills"—to expressed concern about the research methodology. Several independent analyses of the original data were undertaken to determine if these findings were indeed the result of differential services or rather the end product of a flawed methodology. However, these efforts did not satisfactorily explain the underlying causes of the controversial findings. The lack of conclusive results encouraged BRI to mount its own reanalysis during the period 1978–1979. Conclusions based on this reanalysis indicate that basic design problems in the original project vitiate the study's major findings.[3] Therefore the study by Blenkner and her associates should not be cited as evidence of the negative effects of casework practice.

The Original Study

The subject of the original BRI project, entitled "Protective Services for Older Persons," defined the older protective as "a person 60 years of age or over whose behavior indicates that he is mentally incapable of adequately caring for himself and his interests without serious consequences to himself and others and has no relative or other private individual

From *Social Casework*, 64:4 (April 1983), 195–199. Reprinted with permission from Family Service America, New York.

* This paper constitutes Technical Note 11.6. It is most unusual to have any group, let alone another generation of researchers at the same institution, go through the effort to reanalyze data. But here is such an instance. The paper presents a *summary interpretation* for distribution in a *professional journal*. The authors also have technical reports of their analysis on which this paper is based. This approach constitutes yet another way to present a critique of a research report.

1 Margaret Blenkner, Martin Bloom, and Margaret Nielsen, *Final Report: Protective Services for Older People* (Cleveland: The Benjamin Rose Institute, 1974), p. 6.
2 Ibid., p. 181.
3 Ruth E. Dunkle, "Protective Services for Older People: A Reanalysis of the Benjamin Rose Institute Study," mimeographed (Cleveland: The Benjamin Rose Institute, 1981).

able and willing to assume the kind and degree of support and supervision required to control the situation."[4]

The research design chosen for the original project was the Pretest–Posttest Control Group Design.[5] All subjects in both the experimental and control groups were interviewed initially and at the end of the demonstration year. A sample of 164 protectives from thirteen participating agencies was secured over a twelve-month period. Seventy-six subjects were randomly assigned to the experimental group and were provided a wide range of services: medical, legal, homemaker-home aide, psychiatric, financial assistance, placement in a protective setting if the need arose, and casework services from specially trained social workers who played a central role in coordination and planning. The social workers were instructed to "do, or get others to do, whatever is necessary to meet the needs of the situation."[6] The remaining eighty-eight persons in the study were assigned to a control group and all of them received assistance ordinarily available in the community.

It was hypothesized by Blenkner and her associates that the experimental group scores would be more favorable at the end of the demonstration year than those of the control subjects on the following variables: measures of mental and physical functioning (competence), contentment, behavioral signs and symptoms, protection in terms of the physical environment and concrete assistance, and stress on collaterals (i.e., neighbors). Two additional measures—survival and institutionalization—completed the list of variables on which conclusions regarding outcome were based.

As previously mentioned, results showed that the experimental group did not do as well as expected in all the areas identified. Most importantly, the experimental group had higher mortality as well as institutional rates than the control group after one year. These findings on mortality and institutionalization rates, together with the fact that the experimental group members demonstrated no improvement on any of the outcome variables, led Blenkner and her associates to the following carefully stated conclusion: "The helper would do well to adhere to the principle of minimal intervention, introducing change slowly and only in the amount necessary to make the clients more comfortable and more acceptable to his neighbors."[7]

Prior Reanalyses

Several researchers attempted to explain these results by investigating possible methodological errors in the original analyses.[8] Critics of the study's methodology placed emphasis on the following:

1. Basic differences between the experimental and control groups on survival-related characteristics at pretest (lack of equivalence) made differences between the two groups at the end of the project year difficult, if not impossible, to interpret.
2. The effects of substantial missing data in the original study created a situation in which the results were obtained from only a subgroup of cases for which there was complete data, thus introducing a systematic bias.

4 Margaret Blenkner, Martin Bloom, and Margaret Nielsen, "A Research and Demonstration Project of Protective Services," *Social Casework 52* (October 1971): 487–89.
5 Donald T. Campbell and Julian C. Stanley, *Experimental and Quasi-experimental Designs for Research* (Chicago: Rand McNally, 1963).
6 Blenkner, Bloom, and Nielsen, *Final Report,* p. 12.
7 Ibid., p. 157.
8 Raymond Berger and Irving Piliavin, "The Effect of Casework: A Research Note," *Social Work* 21 (May 1976): 205–8; Joel Fischer and Walter W. Hudson, "An Effect of Casework: Back to the Drawing Board," *Social Work* 21 (September 1976): 347–49; and Dennis Wagner and Michael J. Osmalov, "The Impact of Social Casework on the Elderly: A Reappraisal of the Controversy Surrounding The Benjamin Rose Institute's Protective Services Study," dissertation proposal, mimeographed (Madison: University of Wisconsin, 1978).

3. The possibility that certain inferential statistical techniques, if used in a different manner, would have led to a completely different interpretation of the data.

Despite these extensive reanalyses and the related criticism of the Blenkner study, the original findings continue to be utilized by critics of casework practice as evidence of its inefficacy.

The BRI Reanalysis

The BRI staff undertook an examination and recording of the raw data to minimize the impact of any inaccuracies or omissions on the original data set. During the process of reanalysis, it became apparent that flaws in the original design, rather than issues related to specific methods or statistics, or the incompleteness of the data, were the greatest threats to the validity of Blenkner's findings:

1. The creation of *two* nonequivalent experimental groups in the original design that were collapsed in the original analysis.
2. The inability to detail the differences between the services provided to the two experimental groups and the control group, thus potentially invalidating the assumed distinction between groups.
3. The nonrandom assignment of caseworkers to the two experimental groups.
4. The unwarranted emphasis on the rates of mortality and institutionalization as indicators of program impact.

Two Experimental Groups

The first design issue to surface in the reanalysis, and potentially the most confounding one, centered on the fact that, despite the original design of dividing the experimental group into two subsamples—Group A and Group B—on the basis of availability of financial assistance, twelve of the thirty-eight subjects in Group A did receive financial assistance whereas only Group B was to receive this assistance. Perhaps it is this deviation from the original design that accounted for the merging of the two experimental subsamples in the original analysis. Nevertheless, the facts that two experimental samples did exist and that they were treated differently than indicated in the original design raise doubt about the equivalence of the three groups, and certainly raise questions about the validity of the original findings.

In addition to the design implications, the division of the sample into two subsamples raises a statistical issue as well. With the two subsamples, the size of the group is reduced to half ($N = 38$ for each). Conclusions based on statistically significant findings are affected inasmuch as the determination of statistical significance can be a function of sample size. Obtained substantive differences between the experimental and control groups were reduced in terms of their statistical significance.

The second design issue is related to the distinction between the services given to the control group and those provided the experimental groups. While the type and number of services utilized by the control group were known, the actual amount of various service types was not. Moreover, the consistency of service delivery provided to control group participants across agencies was also unknown. In contrast to the control group, subjects in both experimental groups received social casework as provided by staff specifically hired for the demonstration project. The project caseworkers were mandated to "go where the client is and do, or get others to do, whatever is necessary." Unfortunately, it is not known how this statement was interpreted and translated into specific services by the caseworkers. As a result of the lack of documentation of service quantity and quality, it was not possible to use multivariate procedures to control for the effects of service in the reanalysis. The distinction between the experimental groups and the control group on this critical variable remains an assumption.

303

Caseworker Assignment

The third issue is the nonrandom assignment of caseworkers in the original investigation. Four specially trained social workers were hired for the demonstration project and assigned to the two treatment groups. Moreover, these caseworkers were not "blind" to the design of the study and were aware of which group of participants they were serving. Blenkner and her associates recognized that these problems could have introduced systematic bias. This issue and the lack of detailed documentation of service delivery make it impossible to separate the effects of different levels and patterns of service delivery from group assignment and make accurate interpretation of the results highly questionable.

Choice of Outcome Measures

The final design question raised during the reanalysis is related to the emphasis placed in the original analysis on mortality and institutionalization rates as indicators of program impact.

Institutionalization was considered an outcome measure directly resulting from deterioration. However, it is equally possible that placement occurred as a result of financial problems, lack of informal supports, or caseworker pressure. In situations where financial assistance is readily available, such as in experimental Group B in the original study, relocation into a nursing home could be a realistic benefit to the participant by providing safer housing, for example. Unfortunately, there were no records of service goals which could provide the context in which institutionalization was considered as a program outcome. As a result of the number of possible interpretations and the lack of contextual information in each case, the assumption cannot be made that institutionalization was the result of deterioration or that placement was premature.

Similarly, the use of client survival (mortality rates) as a central indicator of service efficacy is problematic. In a frail elderly population, where the likelihood of dying in any given year is a strong one, death can result from a variety of causes, including accidents or acute illness as well as general deterioration. Moreover, since a number of participants entered the program in advanced stages of physical deterioration, the success or failure of the service program should not have been evaluated by as gross a measure as the death rate.

Furthermore, the results of the reanalysis did not provide conclusive evidence that the protective services were related to positive or negative changes in participant competency (mental or physical functioning) nor were they significantly related to rates of death and institutionalization. The results do suggest that an important portion of the differences found by Blenkner and her associates between the control group and the single experimental group (A and B combined) could be attributed to substantial differences between Group B (financial assistance available) and the control group, and virtually no differences between Group A (limited financial assistance) and the control group. More significantly, the previously discussed issues of design so confound the efficacy of the original study that no hard and fast conclusions can safely be drawn.

Insights and Questions

Contributions by Blenkner and Associates

In spite of the inconclusiveness of their findings, Blenkner and her colleagues raised the level of consciousness in regard to the importance of evaluation research and draw attention to the plight of the severely impaired elderly in need of protective services. Their insights into the complexity of the protective's situation, as reflected in the study and follow-up reports, raised important questions for the field to pursue.

While the analytic findings of the study are inconclusive, its descriptive features cannot be disputed. Deterioration was a fact of life for most of the frail elderly clients in the study in spite of social services and medical care. Blenkner and her colleagues appropriately raised questions about services, programs, and practices which in the guise of helping may possibly hinder adaptation of frail elderly clients. The translation of these "questions" by other persons into conclusions about casework practice did a great disservice to the social work field.

Implications for the Social Work Profession

A strong working alliance between research and social work practice has yet to be realized. Researchers are frustrated by the lack of specificity and explicit goals in social work practice that makes measurement difficult, if not impossible. Practitioners are suspicious of the "inhuman" aspects of measuring service, aggregate measures that obscure individual differences, and sweeping generalizations made on the basis of unreplicated studies. Blenkner and her associates sought to bridge the gap between research and practice and inadvertently may have widened it due to the heated controversy which ensued.

One implication for the profession arising from these analyses is the need to correct the ambiguity which characterizes social work practice. Unless practitioners clearly specify their goals and activities on behalf of their clients, research studies will continue to miss their mark. The outcome measures of treatment defined by the researcher will hold little meaning for the practitioner. Or worse, evaluation research studies will not be conducted and professional credibility will suffer further.

A consequence of these analyses for the profession is that important hypotheses were generated that still need to be tested within the context of clinical practice. The descriptive findings of the original study suggested that an abundance of health and social services may not necessarily be helpful to very frail elderly clients. The reanalysis also suggested that service goals which are unrealistic and unspecific can create an unfavorable climate for both client and worker.

The corollary to these hypotheses is that specific, attainable goals for social work practice with the frail elderly will result in effective practice. It follows that variables used to measure the attainment of these goals must be realistic for this type of population.

Sound clinical judgment supports such a hypothesis. Goals for the frail elderly must be highly individualized and attainable, ones that are clearly specified and understood and accepted by the client, if possible. This being the case, the chances of success are far greater for both the client and the worker and the sense of achievement may lead to more ambitious goals. An "overload" situation can frighten and weaken the frail elderly, who feel more in control of their lives if help is carefully measured. A professional approach calls for strategies that are based upon accurately appraised needs of the individual client and subsequent service plans that can be tested and evaluated.

Continuing Needs

This article has addressed issues of concern surrounding the controversial findings of the protective services research conducted by Margaret Blenkner and her colleagues in the 1960s and the subsequent reanalysis of these findings by The Benjamin Rose Institute in 1978–1979.

Interpretations of the original study fostered the attitude that casework practice produced negative effects on clients who received an "abundance" of service. In rebuttal, independent studies were undertaken prior to the institute's reanalysis. These studies focused on the possibility of methodological error in the original analysis, the introduction of systematic bias because of missing data, and on the use of certain inferential statistical techniques; the findings, however, proved inconclusive.

The institute's reanalysis clearly suggested that flaws in the original design, rather than in methodology or other related issues, were the underlying cause of the controversial findings. These flaws included the merger in the analysis of the two nonequivalent experimental groups which had been created in the original design; the inability to document and,

305

therefore, to differentiate between services provided to the control group and the experimental groups; the nonrandom assignment of caseworkers to the two experimental groups; and the questionable use of mortality and institutionalization rates as decisive indicators of program impact.

The BRI reanalysis reinforced the belief that these factors contaminated the original research to the extent that conclusive inferences could not be drawn. This evidence notwithstanding, it is felt that the original study made a significant contribution by focusing on the plight of those in need of protective services and raised significant clinical and research questions.

Clearly, important hypotheses emerged that still need to be tested. Of central concern is the degree and type of intervention from which protective service clients can truly benefit. The study further suggests the need for greater specificity of clinical goals so that outcomes may be studied and validated with precision by researchers. It holds implications for social work practice in terms of the need for individualized and attainable goals to achieve successful outcomes. Most significantly, it demonstrates the need to bridge the gap between research and service in order to develop a coherent approach, not only to the delivery of protective services but to all aspects of care of the frail elderly.

SUMMARY AND GENERALIZATIONS

1. Is anything left standing after teams of experts examine the study from every possible angle? Even when other teams of experts try to put the pieces back together again? The first conclusion that emerges from this chapter is that every study, even those very carefully designed by persons well versed in the scientific process, is thoroughly subject to criticism—for good reasons. As a member of the original team, I can only exclaim in amazement, "Good heavens, did we do that?!" And we did. It is a humbling experience to have the obvious pointed out to one in such powerful terms.

2. A second conclusion emerges after some reflection: At the time the critical and criticized decisions were made (or slipped by), what were we thinking of? I believe that the research team, especially Margaret Blenkner, was aware of the risks we were taking in making one or another decision. But in context of what we knew at that time, each decision seemed to be made for correct reasons, in the sense of being both scientifically and practically correct. It is hard to relive these past years, but one experience of research comes through very consistently: to the extent that we were aware of the issues and their implications, we thought we were making the optimal decisions, and given this perception, we have no guilt, no recriminations. Except, as Samuel Johnson was said to have replied when asked why he had misdefined a word in his quintessential dictionary, "Pure ignorance, madam, pure ignorance."

3. A third conclusion: The critics themselves make mistakes. It is fully possible that critics have missed a point because of their own misreading of the existing documents, or their (understandable) ignorance of the scientific and political-social facts of the moment when the research decision was made. Critics often have a style of writing that succinctly cuts to the heart of an issue. However, this style tends to exaggerate certain aspects of situations. (I have tried to address—not explain away—most of the criticisms raised by these writers in the course of developing the other chapters. You will probably be able to go back and find facts or contexts that account for the decisions that critics find so

incorrect.) In short, give critics the same critical scrutiny that you would give the original article that they are critiquing.

4. A fourth conclusion: I have discussed these different interpretations of the critics and the countercritics with yet other researchers not directly involved in the controversy. How can it be that these knowledgeable and well-intentioned scientists can disagree? The emerging consensus I have found is that each team starts off with a set of assumptions and a portion of knowledge about the data and then selects the statistical procedures that seem best to reveal how comparable or noncomparable the groups are, or how significant or nonsignificant the findings are. Each statistic produces its own conclusion. And just as the assumptions and knowledge differ, so do the interpretations based on the different statistical procedures differ. These unstated presuppositions and value judgments subtly shape how investigators select data, work with them, and then interpret the outcomes. (In a parallel vein, I recommend for your consideration Stephan Jay Gould's *Mismeasure of Man,* 1981, a fascinating detective work on how these subtle but powerful presuppositions and values have worked in influencing research on human intelligence.)

5. Finally, the fifth conclusion in answer to the basic question: Who's right? I thought you'd never ask. My answer won't satisfy you, perhaps, but I think it is a fundamental statement about truth in science. Everyone is right, to the extent that his or her data are accurate and the procedures have been correctly used. The interpretations, although differing, reflect the truth of the current state of our understanding, namely, differing interpretations. Science demands not certainty, but only certain procedures, the sum of which represents the nearest approximation to what is true about that portion of reality. This is half the truth.

The other half is that everyone is wrong, in spite of using accurate data and the procedures correctly. Interpretations are always just that: interpretations. They are the frosting of inferences on the cake of fact. They call for further testing to reveal whether such inferences lead the next observer to a predictable end point. By submitting one's darlings (hypotheses) to the rigors of another research design and further statistical analysis, one can have more faith in their usefulness. But by being prepared for being proved wrong, we won't be so surprised when something occurs that is other than we had predicted. And why not? We manipulate a handful of variables, assume others are randomly present, and ignore the many thousands of other possible influences that enter into any situation. The miracle is that we are finding as much usable information as we are.

The experience of research is to feel oneself a part of this process: the pleasure of discovery and contribution, the pain of critical correction, the excitement of data and ideas falling into place, and the dismay on discovering that one's solutions have raised new, perplexing questions. Don't expect ultimate truths; don't settle for less than the best immediate empirical answers that you can obtain in response to the most comprehensive network of ideas you can create.

CHAPTER **12**

The Tides of Research, the U.S. Supreme Court, and Other Matters

Overview

This chapter summarizes some forty years of research on topics related to the major themes of this book. The aquatic allusion in the chapter title refers to progressive variations in the main themes over time, as first one idea is put forth in the research literature, which meets some confirming and some disconfirming evidence, after which some new idea surfaces to capture the attention of researchers for a time. Overall we can sense a general movement in the literature, although, as with the tides, it sometimes seems as if we have not moved at all.

Technical Narrative Section

Introduction
Review of the Literature (Technical Note 12.1)
Research and the U.S. Supreme Court: The Question of Evidence (12.2)
Testing Conceptual Ideas in the Community Arena (12.3)
Dr. Blenkner's Later Research at the Benjamin Rose Institute (12.4)
Meta-analysis: A New Method of Comparing Studies (12.5)
Summary and Generalizations

The Technical Narrative

INTRODUCTION

I have a midwesterner's fascination for water, which probably stems from having seen so little of it in my formative years. In any case, I am fascinated by waves breaking on a shore. I see the water come rolling in and the beautiful whitecaps foaming and bubbling, then break apart, as the wave hits the sand and rocks. I know better. I know that moving water is a partial illusion, for it is a wave of force that moves through a given region of water, raising it momentarily, then dropping it again as the force wave moves on to raise the next region of water. I don't really understand the principles of physics involved, but I do know that I prefer my illusions, especially at sunrise or sunset.

This theme of the tides is the dominant metaphor of this chapter: the illusion of change or permanence in research. It depends on what you look at, and how you look at it, whether relocation stress is a mystery (circa 1971) or a myth (circa 1981).

In contrast to the rest of the book, which has focused in depth on one study, this chapter looks at the sea of research of which the BRI Protective Services Project was one small item. I will try to point out the waves moving through this sea. And the illusions.

REVIEW OF THE LITERATURE

Let's begin (arbitrarily) in the 1940s and 1950s, when there were a few sporadic reports* on detrimental effects on older persons entering institutions. Table 12.1 lists a selected portion of this literature review. The names of the authors and the dates of publication are presented, categorized by the predominant findings regarding mortality:

1. Negative effects of relocation indicated (i.e., high mortality rates for relocated elderly).
2. No difference in mortality rates between a group of moved persons as compared with like nonmoved persons, or actuarial norms.
3. Positive effects of relocation indicated (i.e., lower-than-expected mortality rates for relocated elderly)—at least for some identified portion of a sample. Other portions may have shown no change or even negative effects of relocation.

It is not easy to list authors in these categories because all the studies involved different clients and types of relocations, made voluntarily or involuntarily, with

---

* This discussion of the *review of the literature* pertinent to the research topic constitutes Technical Note 12.1. Note that reviews of the literature are frequently incorporated into proposals and final reports of research.

Table 12.1 Review of Selected Studies Presenting Data on the Relation of Relocation of the Elderly and Mortality Rates.

Time	Negative Effects of Relocation Indicated	No Differences in Mortality Rates from Usual	Positive Effects for Some/All of Relocated Elderly (possibly mixed with negative effects for others)
1940s	Camargo and Preston, 1945		
1950s	Roth, 1955		
	Kay, et al., 1956		
	Whittier and Williams, 1956		
1960s	Aleksandrowicz, 1961	Lieberman, 1961	Carp, 1968
	Aldrich and Mendkoff, 1963	Miller and Lieberman, 1965[2]	
	Aldrich, 1964	Goldfarb, et al., 1966	
	Ferrari, 1963	Novick, 1967	
	Blenkner, et al., 1967	Stotsky, 1967	
	Jasnau, 1967		
1970s	Killian, 1970	Lawton and Jaffe, 1970	Markus, et al., 1970
	Bournstom and Tars, 1974	Lieberman, 1974	Nielsen, et al., 1972
	Pablo, 1977	Markson and Cumming, 1974	Pino, et al., 1978
		Brody, Kleban and Morris, 1974[3]	
		Silverstone and Kirschner, 1974[4]	
		Wittels and Botwinick, 1974[5]	
		Zweig and Csank, 1975	
		Gutman and Herbert, 1976	
		Kowalski, 1978	
		Borup, 1979, 1980, 1981, 1983	
1980s	Wells and McDonald, 1981[1]		

[1] Borup (1981) reported personal communication with Wells and McDonald indicating that these authors disclaimed having proof that relocation per se caused the observed high death rates.

[2] These authors also noted sizable serious physical illness and some deteriorated psychological status among relocated persons.

[3] These authors reported negative short-term effects that returned to baseline conditions by four to eight months.

[4] These authors reported no appreciable change in the death rate or the rate of physical deterioration, but there was a significantly greater number of cases of emotional and mental problems than would normally have occurred.

[5] These authors note that not only was there no difference in the mortality rates in a negative direction, but there may have been a decrease in risk of mortality (which might have shifted this study to my positive results column, had the authors made a stronger statement).

different degrees of environmental changes, and so forth. Some authors focused predominantly on mortality rates, whereas others were more concerned about morbidity (or disease) rates, attitudes, and behaviors, among other targets of observation. Comparing my list with lists of others will show some different interpretations, but the major purpose of Table 12.1 is to show the range of studies that have resulted in different patterns of findings. The synthesizing explanation that would make sense of these findings may not yet have emerged. See what you think.

One set of authors posed the question: "What happens to patients who are hospitalized for the first time when over sixty-five?" (Camargo and Preston, 1945). The answer was that there were very high mortality rates associated with being institutionalized. These findings were reported from hospital records but did not sort out the many possible factors that might have been responsible for these findings. (For example, people are often very sick when they enter hospitals, and it may be that they would have died wherever they had been.)

Further evidence began to accumulate as other researchers focused on specific aspects of being an older person admitted to some institution. For example, Kay, Norris, and Post (1956) sought to locate indicators of early death and early recovery among older persons experiencing psychiatric disorders. They found, as did others, that persons in states of *extreme confusion and disorder* were most at risk for early or premature death. This finding seemed to support a commonsense position, and so the findings were not strongly challenged.

At the start of the next decade, Goffman (1960, 1961) began his series of fascinating reports about life in institutions and the various detrimental effects that his microscopic observations revealed. There was also a series of clinical reports (such as Aleksandrowicz, 1961) and research papers (for example, by Aldrich and Mendkoff, 1963) that gave further confirmation to the idea of the negative effects of institutions on the lives of their residents, but now, these reports discussed relocation within institutions. Aleksandrowicz (1961) reported on the aftermath of a fire that sacked a geriatric ward in a state mental hospital. No one was injured in the actual fire, but it required that the patients be relocated rapidly. However, the death rates in the several months immediately following the fire were unusually high. Aldrich and Mendkoff (1963) followed a group of patients who were relocated when one chronic-disease facility was closed down. They employed more powerful comparative tools to study the mortality figures than had been employed before. Aldrich and Mendkoff calculated the annual survival rates for patients in each age decade for each year of residence in the facility for the past ten years. From these data, they then computed anticipated death rates for the given year of the relocation, corrected for the age of each patient. With this frame of reference, they could compare what they observed to occur after the relocation with what would have been expected from projections from the prior ten years, had the relocation not taken place. Their findings showed a significantly higher death rate for the three months immediately following the relocation, but not in the next nine months. Another provocative point that they mentioned is that patients who responded to the news of relocation with either anxiety, philosophical resignation, or anger where more likely to survive than those who were depressed or who used more primitive defense mechanisms like denial. The pattern of reaction suggests that there is something in how the individual responds to the news of relocation that may be involved in his or her survival.

A different approach was employed by other investigators to gain more control over the factors involved in relocation. For example, Lieberman (1961) compared persons on a *waiting list* for admission into a nursing home with those already in the nursing home on several variables including mortality. Kasl (1972) pointed out that because the waiting period was about six months, it would be appropriate to double the death rate in order to make it comparable to the rate of patients already in the nursing home. When this correction of Lieberman's data was performed, there was no appreciable difference between waiting-list and resident death rates. Waiting-list methodology corrects for one problem (self-selection,

311

in which the most disabled tend to go to institutions for aid), but it admits another (the fact that waiting itself is stressful, a new variable added to the situation).

The next piece of evidence emerged as a by-product of other research in a dissertation by Ferrari (1963), in which older persons were involved in a transfer from several small nursing homes to one larger, more modern facility. Ferrari noted that there was an unusually high death rate among a small group of persons who were *involuntarily relocated.* She speculated whether there might be some connection between a voluntary or involuntary transfer and premature death, a theme that will be taken up in subsequent research, especially when the mental and physical health status of these persons is more clearly documented.

Jasnau (1967) further refined this discussion. His report concerns two groups of nonpsychotic geriatric patients who were transferred from mental hospitals to nursing homes. One group was treated individually with regard to the move. Social workers assessed the nursing homes in advance, took photos of the facilities, and involved their clients in discussions of the transfer. Staff was also involved in the transfer preparations. No individual was made to move against her or his will. The death rate at the end of the first year for this group was very low in contrast to that for the second group of persons from the same hospitals, who were involved in a mass transfer where no advance preparation was possible; in the case of the mass-transfer group, the death rate was very high when compared to the death rates for the prior year. Jasnau credited the planning arrangements with the differential outcome. But the point to note is that his findings indicate that relocation need not be detrimental to all persons in all circumstances. Moreover, Novick (1967) reported another well-planned relocation that resulted in death rates *lower* than those of the previous year. Is it possible that relocation can be positively enhancing?

One important study by Carp (1968) reported positive effects in the relocation of 190 relatively healthy elderly persons living in the community. This involved a voluntary relocation to a new apartment complex. Because space was limited, a control group consisted of persons who were not immediately able to get into the attractive building. Carp reported a 95 percent survival rate twelve to fifteen months after the relocation took place. From this, she inferred that relocation, under these circumstances, was positively enhancing for these elderly.

Dr. Blenkner's reports of the BRI Protective Services Project were issued in waves from 1967 onward to the major published report in 1971 and the final report (Blenkner, Bloom, Nielsen, and Weber, 1974). This book contains much of this information. Let's continue this survey of the literature that followed reports of the BRI Protective Services Project.

There was a great profusion of studies in the 1970s that dealt with one or another aspect of this theme of relocation to institutions and survival. For example, the research of Bourestom and Tars (1974) continued a part of the detrimental effects theme of the prior decade. These authors distinguished *radical involuntary relocation* from more *moderate* but still *involuntary relocation* and found that when the physical environment was radically changed, and when there were major changes in the persons who provided care and in the care routine itself, then patients entering a relocated nursing home faired much worse than when the changes were more moderate. Bourestom and Tars began to specify what aspects

312

of the physical and social environments were related to the outcome measures, whereas Jasnau (1967) had focused on the planning efforts themselves.

Another important conceptual and empirical development was going on at this time. Holmes and Rahe (1967) and their colleagues were developing an instrument to measure various forms of *stress,* whose total weighted scores would predict untoward physical or psychological events in the following year. For example, Rahe (1969) conducted a prospective study of sailors going on sea duty for a six-month period. By assessing the stresses that these people had experienced in the year prior to shipping out, the investigator predicted those who would be most likely to have physical or psychological problems in the next half year. The results supported the predictions. What is important to note is that stress can result from any of a variety of circumstance; the weighted sum of these stresses predicts future problems. The work of Holmes and Rahe was extremely influential in the 1970s and continues to stimulate research and theory building today.

Another aspect of this orientation is the contribution of Hollister (1976), who coined the term *strens* as a concept parallel to *stress.* The term *strens* refers to *growth-promoting experiences,* as *stress* refers to growth-inhibiting ones. A certain amount of stimulation is not only helpful but mandatory for human growth, as indicated in studies of infants and young children, as well as elderly persons, in institutional settings. The conceptual and empirical questions relate to how much stimulation, of what type, and under what circumstances is optimally useful for given individuals. These kinds of issues were explored, under one flag or another, during the 1970s and into the 1980s.

For example, Markson and Cumming (1974) reported on the mass transfer of chronic psychiatric patients, including some elderly, whose hospitals were being closed for budgetary reasons. These persons were relatively physically well patients, and there was no evidence of any markedly deleterious effect on them, including the subgroup of persons sixty-five years or older. There are many other studies of this nature, reporting no statistically significant harmful effects of relocation. These studies often lacked control groups, as did the Markson and Cumming study. But there was great consistency in outcome: relocation did not necessarily produce unexpectedly fatal outcomes.

Lieberman (1974) wrote a thought-provoking review of his and his colleagues' four studies involving various types of elderly—some were mentally and physically comparable to elderly living in the community, whereas others were or had been mentally ill; some of the studies involved persons facing forced relocation, whereas others had volunteered for a much-welcomed transfer; some moves were made en masse, whereas others were individually handled. The findings showed a strong consistency:

> No matter what the condition of the individual, the nature of the environment, or the degree of sophisticated preparation, relocation entails a higher than acceptable risk to the large majority of those being moved. (p. 495)

But Lieberman railed against the "near idiocies [of] the overpreoccupation with death rates" in contrast to a more useful object of study: the physiological, behavioral, and psychological status of a person before and after relocation. From his four studies, he noted that the percentage of the aged showing marked

313

decline behaviorally, physically (including death), socially, or psychologically ranged from a low of 48 percent to a high of 56 percent (p. 495).

Lieberman hypothesized that relocation is risky because it requires new learning for adaptive purposes that some individuals are not able to attain (pp. 497, 499). Therefore he looked at the characteristics of the four environments to see which were facilitative. He offered the observation that *facilitative environments* are those that foster relatively high degrees of autonomy among their residents, those that personalize residents (or patients), and those that foster a sense of integrated community (p. 500). I don't believe that these suggestive ideas have yet received the attention that they deserve among practitioners.

Research by Pino, Rosica, and Carter (1978) began to tease out several of the factors that had appeared in prior studies. These authors distinguished four groups of nursing-home patients: (1) relocated patients (RP) who had moved from either homes or hospitals to a nursing home; (2) prepared transfered patients (PTP), who moved to new buildings in a nursing home and who had been prepared through counseling and group meetings to discuss the move, and by involvement in the move, such as choosing their rooms; (3) unprepared patients (UP), who were transferred in somewhat the same way as the PTP group, but who were not prepared for the relocation; and (4) a control group (C), which included stationary patients at neighboring institutions.

Pino, Rosica, and Carter reported information not only on survival, but also on various aspects of functioning. First, there was a higher death rate for the unprepared group (UP) and for the relocated group (RP), but neither was statistically significant. However, *prepared transferred patients* (PTP) showed less decline in mental status (measured by the MSO discussed in Chapter 4) and in physical functioning (measured by the ADL, discussed in Chapter 7). The relocated patients declined slightly less than the unprepared patients (UP) on these measures, a finding indicating the magnitude of the stress in a new move as contrasted with a transfer.

Just as a footnote to the earlier discussion, a paper by Kowalski (1978) reported another fire at a home for the aged. To make things more complicated, there was also a bomb threat after the fire, and then a move to the new building. But in contrast to the findings of Aleksandrowicz (1961), there were no unusual mortality figures in the three months following these events.

RESEARCH AND THE U.S. SUPREME COURT: THE QUESTION OF EVIDENCE

The 1980s began with a most unusual event in the relations of the social sciences and society.* It began this way:

> O'Bannon, Secretary of Public Welfare of Pennsylvania *v.* Town Court Nursing Center et al.
>
> Certiorari to the United States Court of Appeals for the Third Circuit
>
> No. 78–1318. Argued November 6, 1979—Decided June 23, 1980
>
> After the Department of Health, Education, and Welfare (HEW) and the Penn-

---

* The discussion of a *U.S. Supreme Court decision involving research evidence* constitutes Technical Note 12.2.

sylvania Department of Public Welfare (DPW) had revoked the authority of Town Court Nursing Center (a nursing home) to provide elderly residents of the home with nursing care at government expense under Medicare and Medicaid provider agreements, the home and several of its patients (respondents) brought suit in Federal District Court, alleging, *inter alia,* that the patients were entitled to an evidentiary hearing on the merits of the relocation before the Medicaid payments were discontinued. . . . (447 U.S. 790)*

Part of the argument that the nursing home was making was that there were a number of studies indicating that removal to another home might cause what they termed "transfer trauma," increasing the possibility of death or serious illness for elderly, infirm patients (p. 784). Here is our relocation shock hypothesis, being considered by the U.S. Supreme Court.

Justice Harry Blackmun wrote a separate opinion, concurring with the majority opinion, but for very different reasons. Let me present some of Justice Blackmun's comments. First, he noted that

> Although the Court assumes that "transfer trauma" exists [he refers the reader to a statement that I have presented at the end of the above paragraph], . . . it goes on to reject the argument. By focusing solely on the "indirectness" of resulting physical and psychological trauma, the Court implies that regardless of the degree of demonstrated risk that widespread illness or even death attends decertification-induced transfers, it is of no moment. I cannot join such a heartless holding. (pp. 802–803)

However, Justice Blackmun still concurred with the decision itself—that the patients at the nursing home could not claim transfer trauma as a reason for stopping the nursing home from being decertified and thus closed down. Here is his reasoning:

> The fact of the matter, however, is that the patients cannot establish that transfer trauma is so substantial a danger as to justify the conclusion that transfer deprives them of life or liberty. Substantial evidence suggests that "transfer trauma" does not exist, and many informed researchers have concluded at least that this danger is unproved.[13] Recognition of a constitutional right plainly cannot rest on such an insubstantial body of research and opinion. It is for this reason, and not for that stated by the Court, that I would reject the patients' claim for a deprivation of life and liberty.

That footnote 13 is important, so let me quote it in its entirety.

> 13.   See Borup, Gallego, and Hefferman, "Relocation and its Effects on Mortality," 19 *The Gerontologist* 135, 136 (1979) (Noting that 6 previous studies found increased mortality rates, while 12 did not: "findings have been ambiguous and appear to be contradictory"); id., at 138 (concluding on basis of new study that "relocation does not increase the probability of mortality"); Bourestom & Tarrs, "Alternations in Life Patterns Following Nursing Home Relocation," 14 *The Gerontologist* 506 (1974); Lieberman, "Relocation Research and Social Policy," 14 *The Gerontologist* 494, 495 (1974).

* Quotations on this Supreme Court decision are taken from the *United States Supreme Court Reports,* 1980, volume 447.

That's it. These pieces of cited evidence appears to be the basis for the decision by Justice Blackmun. We have already looked at the papers by Bourtestom and Tarrs (1974) and by Lieberman (1974), and now we will have to look at Borup's research and reviews of the literature because they deservedly received much attention in the gerontological world as well as in larger society. (There is no report that I know of about what happened to the Town Court Nursing Center and how its patients survived the relocation.)

Late in the 1970s, Borup and his colleagues conducted an investigation of the forced closing of nursing homes in Utah because of tightening up on regulations concerning sprinkler systems and other such things. Borup's concerns continued to focus on mortality but emphasized the health and functioning of relocated persons. Borup and his colleagues reported various analyses from this one study on several occasions, along with a consistent interpretation that the relocation stress hypothesis was a "myth." (See, for example, Borup, 1981, p. 510.)

So it seems that we have traveled a long, hard road from mystery to myth in about one decade. Let's look at Borup's presentations to see how he arrived at this interpretation. In a comprehensive survey of the relocation literature, Borup (1981) reported his assessment of the literature:

1. Relocation does not affect mortality rates (based on the observation that *three quarters* of the twenty-five-plus relocation studies cited in Borup, Gallego, and Hetternan, 1979, and also in Borup, 1983, did not indicate an increase in mortality following relocation).
2. Relocation has a positive effect on hypochondria (although Borup, Gallego, and Heffernan, 1980, pointed out that this finding washed out when relocation and sex status, or relocation and age, were considered). This same finding held true for hygiene functioning of patients.
3. Relocation has a positive effect on the stamina of patients, although this finding, too, has to be qualified. When age groupings are compared, relocation affects positively the middle-aged (under 65 years of age), but not the young-old (65 to 79) or the old-old (80 years or over) (Borup, Gallego, and Heffernan, 1980). These findings on stamina do not apply to female patients at all.
4. Relocation has a positive effect on daily functioning (such things as bathing, dressing, and walking), but in an unexpected way. The functional level of relocated patients remains stable, whereas the nonrelocated patients' functional levels deteriorate between the pre- and posttest times.
5. Relocation has no effect on health status, as measured by the self-reports of patients. Borup, Gallego, and Heffernan (1980) speculated that even though the Utah move would constitute a radical relocation in Bourestom and Tars's (1974) terms, the attitudes of the patients might be very significant to how they reacted. Indeed, over four fifths of the patients interviewed felt positive about the move.

These data are drawn from a single large-scale investigation, using a longitudinal panel design. Because of the closing of some facilities that did not meet Medicaid and Medicare standards, and whereas others remained open that met these standards, Borup and his colleagues had a natural experiment in the making.

He used three independent variables: (1) relocated or not; (2) sex; and (3) age divided into under 65, 65 to 79, and 80 and over.

In fact, Borup used one other independent variable about which critics (such as Horowitz and Schulz, 1983) have been particularly concerned. Borup used only those patients regarded by the administrators of the facilities as *interviewable*. Others in the same institutions were not interviewed because of their inability to communicate or because of the presumed mental and physical stress that interviewing would constitute. Borup, Gallego, and Heffernan (1980, pp. 469–470) reported that in most cases administrators allowed the interviewer to interact with those patients identified as noninterviewable to validate this classification. These interviewers reported that in most cases the judgment of the administrators was correct. The interpretations from their study, therefore, have to be limited to identified and interviewable patients, not a full range of elderly persons such as would be found at long-term care facilities.

Indeed, Horowitz and Schulz (1983) raised the obvious question about skimming off the cream of the elderly in this study of relocation effects: Were not these subjects studied by Borup and colleagues simply the healthier, more mentally able and socially involved persons whom common sense would suggest would be the least likely to be ill effected by a relocation? Borup (1983) responded to the vigorous criticisms that Horowitz and Schulz raised about his research. With regard to the issue of using only interviewable subjects, Borup replied that not being interviewable was not the same as being in ill health:

> As would be expected by those who have contact with institutionalized older persons, the interviewers found many patients who were in relatively good health who had physical and/or psychological problems (i.e., speech impairment, stuttering, hearing loss, confusion, paranoia, depression, etc.). (Borup, 1983, p. 235)

Such a statement did little to remove Horowitz and Schulz's claim that Borup had taken only those in the best of physical and mental health. As earlier research had pointed out, confusion, depression, and even possibly sensory losses may be strongly related to mortality or survival after an elderly person is relocated. Margaret Blenkner had noted in her 1967 review of the relocation literature that the factor of "severe brain dysfunction" had emerged as a clear and unequivocal indicator of high risk (p. 103). And as I will soon report, we conducted another set of studies that supported this contention. Markus, Blenkner, Bloom, and Downs (1970) noted that by six months after transfer from an old to a new nursing home, persons with severe mentational dysfunction (as indicated by scores on the mental status questionnaires—MSO) had significantly higher death rates than other relocated participants.

Moreover, looking at the numbers involved in the Utah study, Borup, Gallego, and Heffernan (1980) reported the data found in Table 12.2.

This table indicates that between 38 and 45 percent of the population at risk was not interviewed, a remarkable reduction in available information. Margaret Blenkner would have attempted to get some basic information on all the persons involved in the relocation. She argued that not being able to provide answers to questions about health and psychological functioning *is* an answer in its own right, if the researcher chooses to use it. Moreover, observer ratings can

317

Table 12.2 The Utah Studies

| | Relocated Subjects | | Nonrelocated Subjects | |
	N	%	N	%
Interviewable	326	61.3	249	55.0
Noninterviewable	206	38.7	204	45.0

be used as parallel information. And so, once again, we have researchers of goodwill differing about basic interpretations; these differences once again reinforce the demand that readers of research follow the details closely in order to obtain information that will be useful to their practice needs. If your client is interviewable in the sense that Borup described, then perhaps his data are relevant to your client. However, if your client is too confused, depressed, or paranoid or perhaps requires the skills of an interpreter (as did some of ours in the BRI Protective Services Project—see Bloom, Frires, Hanson, and South, 1966), then you might wish to think twice about whether the relocation stress is a myth or not.

One last point about compiling numbers from research studies of various types that tend to point in one or another direction on the relocation stress hypothesis. Borup reported that three quarters of the relocation studies do not show an increase in mortality. That still leaves one quarter, and the dilemma facing the practitioner who is seeking guidance from the best available literature on this question with regard to a particular client. If one has a one-in-four chance of erring, as Horowitz and Schluz (1983) argued in a somewhat different regard, then it would be preferable to err on the side of caution, as relocation is admittedly a stress-producing situation for anyone. But as we shall see, there is another side to this argument because, for some elderly, relocation is associated with *stimulation* and *lower-than-expected* mortality rates. The question becomes how to sort out these possibilities.

In Chapter 2, where I described how research begins, I didn't mention one situation that occurs on rare occasions, when the stars and the project funders are in alignment in the firmament above. Late in the 1960s, we were presented with an opportunity to study the transfer of a nursing-home population from an ancient facility in the center of a deteriorating urban area to the nearby beautiful suburbs, where a modern modular-designed building was in the process of construction. The Jewish Orthodox Home for the Aged (JOHA) was directed by very knowledgeable people who had planned every facet of the move with extreme care. They involved the residents in various aspects of the transfer, including tours, even for the confused and the disabled. The families of the residents were involved; many dozens of volunteers are activated; all three shifts of the nursing staff were on hand to greet the new arrivals. Their belongings had been packed in boxes in their presence and were opened in their presence in their new rooms. It was a remarkably well-prepared and smooth operation. Our research with JOHA was labeled the relocation studies.

The research question was whether these careful preparations would reduce the stresses associated with relocation. By good luck, we were able to employ our regular interviewing staff, who had, by then, four or five years' experience with our instruments. We adapted our previous instruments for this new project and added some others that turned out to be quite interesting. Let me describe the history of one of these new additions.

TESTING CONCEPTUAL IDEAS IN THE COMMUNITY ARENA

Part of the theoretical dowry that I brought with me to BRI was some interest in the work of Witkin (1954, 1962) on a perceptual characteristic termed *field dependence/independence.* * Witkin had extended this perceptual concept to represent the polar ways that an individual has of relating to the environment. A *field-dependent person* tends to be highly influenced by the environment in getting his or her bearings. Such a person is likely to have poorly developed analytic abilities and tends to use primitive defense mechanisms in dealing with stress. Witkin also found that a field-dependent person has relatively vague concepts of his or her body and self.

In contrast, the *field-independent person* operates on whatever environment he or she happens to be in, using relatively well-developed analytic abilities, as well as more sophisticated and adaptive defense mechanisms, and holding a clearer sense of self and body. In comparing the field-dependent and the field-independent personality types, it seemed very reasonable to me that relocation would be more difficult for the former. Indeed, this personality characteristic could be used as a differentiating predictor of mortality, thus having an abstract term serve as predictor of a life and death outcome. And so, on an experimental basis, Dr. Blenkner agreed to build in to the participant interview a form of the embedded-figures test (Karp and Konstandt, 1963; Schwartz and Karp, 1967) that could be used with the elderly. This text consisted of showing a participant a small figure (like a triangle) and asking her or him to locate that same shape within a larger, complex picture in which it had been embedded.

Fortunately, at this time, a doctoral student from Case Western Reserve University came to work on the relocation project and very ably extended this perceptual investigation along with several other related ideas (Markus, et al., 1970, 1971; 1972). As in the Aldrich and Mendkoff (1963) study, we wanted to compare the death rates in the six months after the transfer with death rates in similar years. However, statistically, it was necessary for us to look at the previous fifteen years and to calculate the probability of death for persons who had been admitted to the nursing home at different initial ages (this is called *admission age*), and who had lived at the nursing home for different lengths of time (this is called *residency*). These two basic characteristics were analyzed separately for males and females. When the death rates following the transfer for any of these subgroups were either greater or smaller than those in fourteen or fifteen of the fifteen prior years, which were used as a control, then those subgroup rates were considered statistically significant.

* This discussion of the *empirical test of a laboratory concept applied to* a wholly different context—*the natural community* where older persons live—constitutes Technical Note 12.3.

The findings were quite dramatic. In general, the relocation appeared to have a clear negative effect on the male residents; there was also a *negative* effect on those persons—male or female—admitted to the nursing home at a *younger* age. However, equally important, relocation appeared to have a *positive* effect on *female* residents, particularly the *older females* (admission age eighty to eighty-four). The probable reasons for these findings were related to facts about the admissions to the nursing home. When younger aged are admitted, it is usually because of serious illness and incapacitation; perhaps the same is true of males in general. There was general support for the predictiveness of the embedded-figures test: field-independent persons tended to survive relocation in numbers statistically greater than field-dependent persons, but the Mental Status Questionnaire proved an even better predictor, and it required less work. In any case, this transfer was clearly split in outcome: the younger males and females suffered from the transfer, as did the males in general, whereas the older females seemed to thrive after relocation.

DR. BLENKNER'S LATER RESEARCH AT THE BENJAMIN ROSE INSTITUTE

We were among the many people most shocked by our findings. For Margaret Blenkner, in particular, this was another instance in which her well-designed demonstration projects in the community turned up disturbing information. But contrast Dr. Blenkner's approach to the research question with how almost all of the other researchers dealt with this issue: Hers were carefully designed demonstration projects in which hypotheses were formulated in advance and complex but controlled programs were initiated. In contrast, most of the other reports were about accidental events: fires or budgetary changes requiring relocation of geriatric patients, with or without advanced planning. The active independent variables were not under the control of the investigator; they were directed by administrators of agencies. In effect, most of these other studies were exploratory observations of naturally occurring situations, whereas Dr. Blenkner had created the situations that she was having observed.

Margaret Blenkner's response to the findings from the Protective Services Project was to develop another large-scale community demonstration.* I would like to discuss that project in some detail because it grew out of the earlier work but was clearly in the mainstream of research in the early 1970s, which looked for differential effects, rather than a monolithic outcome.

We were not totally surprised by the last pieces of data from the Protective Services Project because we were, of course, doing progress reports all of the time. We had begun to see the major trends of the data, although we wondered whether the tentative negative findings were just the wonderful way the law of chance has of playing with us mortals—first a run of data favoring the controls, then another run of data favoring the experimental participants. We really couldn't be certain of the outcome until the final moment, but we could anticipate trends. And these trends were ominously suggesting that highly trained social

---

* This discussion of a *new research project growing out of an old one* constitutes Technical Note 12.4.

workers with many ancillary services at their disposal weren't able to prevent high mortality rates among a sample of mentally disoriented older persons. If these workers couldn't do it, who could?

Margaret Blenkner made a fundamental decision that gained its meaning only in context of her search for answers to the relocation shock hypothesis. She chose to study institutionalization and survival with a sample of persons different from the Protective Services Project participants. The main point was to prevent institutionalization, and so the need was to find a population of persons who were at high risk—but who were not yet institutionalized. Then some service could be offered to a randomly selected experimental group that would aim at preventing the institutionalization that might occur in the natural course of events.

Dr. Blenkner searched around for possible populations and finally decided to use one with which BRI had close contacts. Several years before the research department began, BRI, in cooperation with the medical system of Western Reserve University (now Case Western Reserve University), had developed and had constructed a small rehabilitation hospital, the Benjamin Rose Hospital (BRH), containing about one hundred beds and supporting facilities. BRH was located in the heart of the medical complex of that University. It served patients suffering from stroke, fractures, arthritis, and other conditions. There were not enough of any one of these diagnosed groups to form a sample, but as all were serious medical conditions that might eventuate in institutionalization in physical care facilities, Dr. Blenkner decided this would do as our population source.

This decision meant a shift from mental disorganization to physical disability. More subtly, there was also a shift in the social class backgrounds of these BRH patients; they were decidedly an economically advantaged group, especially in comparison with the Protective Services Project participants. There was one other vital difference that emerged over the course of this new study, and that was the family support that these participants were able to command. I'll return to this factor of family support because it introduces an entirely new path of research and practice, but first, let's see what we learned in the new study.

The problem we faced was quite clear. People who were being rehabilitated from serious physical problems would be returning to their homes in the community if medically possible. However, given the extent of their medical conditions, it was likely that a sizable proportion of them would be requiring further institutional services within a limited period of time, an experience that was associated with higher rates of mortality compared to non-institutionalized older persons. Our task was to find some service intervention that would prevent or delay that entrance into an institution for an experimental group of participants, while observing what happened to a standard-treatment group that received whatever services the community normally offered, including re-institutionalization.

The experimental service was unusual for a highly professional organization like the Benjamin Rose Institute to consider. As usual, the Institute was willing to be innovative in its search for solutions to difficult problems. The primary intervention method used in this new project was the home aide. We had had some limited experience with home aides in the Protective Services Project, and the social workers had been uniformly delighted with their contributions. These home aides were mature women, generally with a high-school education

321

and often some experiences in helping others. They were intensively trained by staff nurses and social workers, plus outside educators, nutritionists, and others. The home aides were supervised by a team composed of a social worker and a nurse, but these professional persons did not provide any direct service. A home aide supervisor tended to the day-to-day management of these workers.

A home aide would meet her clients when they were still at the hospital, so as to learn about their level of functioning in that setting. On the clients' discharge, the home aide provided an array of services, possibly including (1) health care services, such as helping the participant to exercise, or giving medication under a doctor's orders; (2) personal care, such as functions that were measured by the Index of Activities of Daily Living (bathing, dressing, toileting, and so on); and (3) household help, such as cleaning, cooking, doing laundry, and shopping, which are just as vital to a person's everyday wellbeing as health and personal care (just try to do without them!). In addition, the home aides sometimes provided (5) assistance with leisure activities or (6) escort services, such as taking the participant to the hospital for checkups—and through the red tape that often surrounds them.

It was with the greatest of effort that the professional workers on the team kept their hands off the participants; that was part of the experimental challenge. Although the professionals evaluated and supervised, they did not perform any direct services. This kind of challenge is relevant to other aspects of services to persons in need, as I will discuss shortly.

In general, we used the same types of outcome measures as before, but with more attention to the factors related to relocation. It was also possible to be more specific about the costs of the program for eventual cost–benefit analyses. Also, a similar schedule of interviewing was followed: There was an initial interview in the hospital shortly before discharge, and then again within two weeks after the clients left BRH. Interviews with the participants were held at six months and again at one year. Collateral interviews were held in a fashion similar to that in the Protective Project.

It might be worth noting that the experimental intervention was unique. There were homemakers available in the community—I believe the distinction between home aides and homemakers is in the broader range of services that the aides were trained to perform—but only a few control participants received homemaker services. Margaret Blenkner made one of her classic critical comments about this point:

> It is an ironic commentary on our failure to develop community based services as "social utilities" accessible to all aged, that the 3 controls who did receive such services were each black and poor. (Nielsen, Blenkner, Bloom, and Beggs, 1972, p. 1097)

Overall the Home Aide Project was another classical experimental–control-group design with a panel of participants interviewed four times over the course of the project year. The results were determined primarily from comparisons before service and at the end of the project year, with the other interview periods providing descriptive trend data.

What happened? Was Margaret Blenkner vindicated in her search for a causal link between institutionalization and mortality? The answer is very clear. That answer is: Perhaps. It turned out that some medical conditions were so overwhelming that no amount of home aide service appeared to make a difference. Strokes frequently left these participants with so much brain damage that they were unable to respond to home aide service. But institutionalization rates were low in both the experimental and the control groups primarily because the families involved played an important role in keeping the participant at home as long as possible. Remember that most of these families had ample economic resources, so that they were able to purchase specific services as needed (help with cleaning, personal care, and so on). The experimental participants had an extra bonus, but this didn't seem to be strong enough to make any practical differences.

To summarize the statistical findings, there were no statistically significant differences in mortality rates between the experimental- and the control-group participants. High death rates did occur, as one might expect in persons suffering strokes and other vascular diseases. One quarter of the persons admitted for stroke died within the year after discharge.

The experimental participants spent significantly fewer days in institutions than did the controls. Compared to the controls, the women in the experimental group were also observed to spend significantly fewer days in institutions, as were older persons of both sexes seventy-five years and over). The contentment variable also showed changes favoring the experimental group over the controls. But as mentioned above, the surprising thing was the overall low rate of institutionalization for either group, given their prior condition, age, and the like.

So where do these findings leave us with regard to the project's central mission: to see whether a home aide service could prevent or delay institutionalization so as to reduce the hypothesized fatal effects of relocation? There were no statistically significant differences in mortality, and the other two variables (institutionalization and contentment), which favored the experimental group, had limited impact.

However, we did learn some very important things. The data showed that a home-aide-service program was particularly helpful to older women (aged seventy-five or older) who had conditions other than stroke, and who had some natural helping network in their community living situation. The likelihood of their institutionalization was decreased, their contentment increased, and their survival promoted. Why this particular subgroup was favored is not entirely clear. The answer may relate to the social status of older women as contrasted with that of older men, as well as to how the sexes of the generation studied handled illness and dependency. These sex differences probably also suggest a further look at the natural helping networks that abound in society, which are as silent and omnipresent as the forces that make waves in the oceans and lakes.

As is typical of a good scientist, Margaret Blenkner concluded with a call for more experimentation with similar and different samples, for variations in the amount of services required for a cost-effective program (it was an expensive trial program and could probably have been run more economically), and for further study of the connection of home aide services and the presence or absence of a natural helping network.

Dr. Blenkner proved to be a good forecaster because, starting in the mid-1970s, there began a major series of explorations of natural helping networks (Collins and Pancoast, 1975) and of various forms of self-help groups (see Gartner and Riessman, 1980; Lystadt, 1975). Indeed, I would speculate that a new wave of research and practice developed with regard to helping networks, in part because prior research and practice had exhausted experimentation with conventional concepts used to explain complex questions. And so, like the invisible movement of forces through the water that give rise to changing, visible waves, new topics of research have emerged.* Sometimes they have offered insight into the old questions; sometimes they have simply moved on. I still have my midwesterner's fascination for moving water, but now it is joined by my fascination for the movements in research and practice in the helping professions.

* Not only are there new topics in research, but there are also new ways of analyzing data. I want to call to your attention one method in particular because I think it will be used increasingly in the coming years for comparative evaluation. This is a method called *meta-analysis* (Smith and Glass, 1977; Smith, Glass, and Miller, 1980). The following discussion of meta-analysis constitutes Technical Note 12.5.

Meta-analysis involves calculating the size of the effects of services delivered in different studies in a standardized way. The principle of this standardization is familiar; consider how we use percentages or percentiles. One student scores at a certain high level on a math test at her school, and another student makes another high level score on that same test at his school. Perhaps the school of the first student has more able students than has the other student's school. Thus, although these two students may have different numbers of correct answers, they may be compared by saying that each is in the top 10 percent of his or her class. This reference to percentages offers a standard way to compare different situations.

Meta-analysis is somewhat more complicated. Baker, Swisher, Nadenichek, and Popowicz (1984) present an interesting meta-analysis of 40 primary prevention studies in education reported between 1972 and 1982. These studies where chosen for their rigorous experimental designs. Baker and his colleagues then performed the following operations: they subtracted ". . . the posttest mean of the control condition from the posttest mean of the treatment condition," and then they divided the resulting subtrahend by "the posttest standard deviation of the control condition" based on the assumption that this standard deviation was not affected by the preventive service (Baker, et al., 1984, p. 460). This gives a kind of standard score using the model of the normal curve for a given study's results. Next, they summed the standardized scores of the 40 studies and divided by the number of studies to get an average effect size of this sample.

By this method, they transformed data from different studies into a common language so as to be able to compare the overall impact of preventive programs in education. The ultimate numerical result represents "the number of standard deviations separating effects of the [prevention] and control conditions across the studies that were analyzed" (Baker, et al., 1984, p. 460). These authors report an estimated effect size (expressed as a proportion of a standard deviation) for this sample as .55, which they interpret to mean that a hypothetical person at the mean of the control group would improve on the dependent variables being measured .55 standard deviations above the mean after receiving the preventive services. This person would have gone from the 50th percentile to the 73rd percentile as a result of the preventive services, a "medium" size improvement within the perspective of this approach (compare Cohen, 1969). When Baker and his colleagues included the score from one other study that was extreme in its favorable outcome, the average effect size increased to .91, making it a "large" size improvement, according to Cohen's formulation.

While Baker's results are interesting, their importance to us is in the method, a standardized way to compare results across different studies in a common area. Reference to the *Social Sciences Citation Index* (see Technical Note 3.2, p. 87) under the heading of meta-analysis shows a rapid increase in this type of study after 1980. However, I don't want to leave you with the impression that a perfect solution to comparative evaluation has been attained. Meta-analysis has its critics (see, for example, Garfield, 1983).

324

SUMMARY AND GENERALIZATIONS

1. Once again we rediscovered how illusory reality is. We thought that, this time for sure, we would be able to design a project that would make a piece of social reality stop and stand still for a careful examination and a strong push in the direction in which we wanted it to go. But we were wrong, or partly wrong. At best, we captured only a tiny piece of that reality, enough so that we had some specific words of advice for practitioners who might be willing to base their actions on substantiated research—in addition to fancy theoretical speculations. I tried to raise some challenging questions for the researchers who followed the BRI Protective Services Project on whether the relocation shock hypothesis is a myth or not.

2. If we have learned anything, it is about the topic of research itself, and perhaps about the movement of events in the conducting of research. In awe and humility, we have learned how tough it is to do good research, research that will stand the test of critics and of time. If there is any reward in research—in the broad sense of being a scientific practitioner among an invisible college of peers dealing with the same research problem throughout history—then it is in finding a satisfaction in having contributed to the clarification of a question, even though that question was subsequently revised and transformed, and even though a specific answer is not yet at hand. The search is still on, and that is what science is all about.

CHAPTER 13

Single-System Designs: Immediate Evaluation of One's Practice

Overview

This chapter presents a brief and practical account of an exciting development in do-it-yourself evaluation, the single-system design. Notice that it took several years before the BRI Protective Services Project was made available to helping professionals and other researchers. What if you had a client for whom you wanted objective information on whether significant changes in target problems were occurring? Single-system designs provide this brief, approximate type of evaluation, which any practitioner can use on any type of client or client-system targets. The information is processed regularly (in a time series arrangement), and feedback can be obtained rapidly to indicate whether a significant change has occurred in the client or the client-system between the "before" and the "after" periods, and (under some conditions) whether there is sufficient basis for asserting that the helping professional was responsible for the change.

Technical Narrative Section

Introduction to Single-System Designs (Technical Note 13.1)
Types of Measures Used in Single-System Designs (Table 13.1) (13.2)
Analysis of a Case (13.3)
Single-System Designs (Figure 13.5) (13.4)
Self-test (13.5)
Summary and Conclusions
Coda: Answers to the Self-test

The Technical Narrative

INTRODUCTION TO SINGLE-SYSTEM DESIGNS

Before I kid you into thinking that this chapter, however scintillating, will provide you with all you need to know about single-system designs involving individuals, groups, or organizations, let me drop the gentle hint that a colleague and I wrote a 500-page book on this specific topic (Bloom and Fischer, 1982) and still weren't able to deal with all of the important possibilities of this new and rapidly growing field.

However, I do intend this chapter to provide you with enough of the basics to encourage you to try this type of evaluative research with someone, perhaps yourself (Want to lose those extra pounds? Want to improve your physical fitness?) or your clients (Were you able to help your client to deal more effectively with her depression? Did the family you were working with come up with a resolution to their difficulties with their retarded son's behavior?)—to mention just a few of the many projects my students have done, using this evaluation system to discover whether their clients have achieved their objectives. If this possibility of evaluating every client on every target is of interest, I hope you will consider studying these single-system design methods* in greater depth (cf. Hersen and Barlow, 1974).

The introduction to this topic will take the form of a student's disguised but otherwise real case. The helping professional met with a family whose severely retarded son appeared to be causing the mother considerable anguish. The problems were many: The son, Randy, age nine, had to be helped in each step of life's daily activities, such as laying out his clothes each day in the order in which they had to be put on. But Randy sometimes made mistakes and put things on the wrong part of the body or in the wrong order, frustrating the mother's efforts. Also, Randy appeared to be picking up some sexual and excretory terms from his school peers; his mother was afraid that his thoughts about sex were not developing in appropriate ways. But worst of all, the mother reported yelling at Randy and then feeling unhappy about her poor parenting. She loved Randy and yet felt increasingly frustrated by his behavior and limitations.

The social work student sympathized with the feelings of frustration but asked for more information to get a clearer picture of Randy's behavior and the mother's reactions as well, so that once an intervention was agreed on, the family could assess clearly whether these objectives had been attained. So, initially, the problems identified by the mother were translated into operationally defined behaviors:

1. Randy's inappropriate dressing on rising on school mornings was to be measured by a checklist indicating what proportion of his items of clothing was present in the correct place.

---

* This discussion, introducing *single-system designs* by means of a case illustration, constitutes Technical Note 13.1. The entire chapter presents this one case.

2. Randy was using some "dirty" words and behaviors that he had picked up from some other children, without really knowing what he was doing. The mother was trying to get him to think about more polite approaches to sexuality, and to be more controlled in his verbalizations about it. For the hour before supper each day, she recorded every instance of Randy's relevant actions, verbal and otherwise, indicating what his thoughts were about these topics, and the context in which they occurred; that is, what were the apparent antecedents and consequences of his using inappropriate language or actions in inappropriate places.

3. The mother's feelings of being an ineffective parent were measured on a self-constructed scale, in which the mother identified the highest point (10) as being the best, most effective mother possible, and the lowest point (1) being the worst.

Note that we are dealing here with feelings, thoughts, and behaviors. All can be measured by means of various indicators, so that it can be seen whether these targets of intervention have changed. (See Table 13.1 for types of measures used in single-system designs.*) The three targets chosen represent the essential dimensions of the problem situation, as viewed by the mother. Let's follow the process of using a single-system design.

ANALYSIS OF A CASE**

The social work student asked the mother to keep track of these thoughts, feelings, and behaviors for the next ten days, when they would again meet and discuss what actions to take. When the mother returned, she was very surprised to find that the problem she had thought she had with Randy's not dressing properly had occurred to only a small degree during the baseline period. The social work student suggested that she continue to keep track of this behavior, but that they not engage in any maneuvers that would seek to modify it. Don't oil a wheel if it's not squeaking, but keep your eye on it if you think it is a possible problem.

The mother reported a number of occurrences of Randy's expressing sexual and excretory terms. Each day at the same pre-dinner hour she unobtrusively noted every such term that Randy used; she also tried to identify the social events preceding and following Randy's use of these terms. She tried to respond to those terms as she had done before.

The third factor was the mother's feelings of lack of competence in raising her son. For this factor, she turned in the set of scores she had judged at the same time each day to reflect her feelings of competence.

Rather than using words to describe these three targets for change, the social work student chose to use graphic depictions, as indicated in Figures 13.1, 13.2, and 13.3. Each graph has the same essential parts. Note carefully some basic ways to record the information. The vertical axis indicates the target of intervention, operationally defined so that the intervals on the axis have clear meanings. For example, with Randy's dressing behavior, the numbers indicate the percentage of clothing put on correctly.

---

* This discussion of *types of measures used in single-system evaluation* constitutes Technical Note 13.2.
** This *analysis of a case* constitutes Technical Note 13.3.

Table 13.1   Types of Measures Used in Single-System Evaluation

Types of Measures	Examples
Behavioral Observations: Count actual behaviors that manifest or represent the target behavior. Discrete behaviors can involve frequencies of occurrence; continuous behaviors make use of duration measures.	Discrete behaviors: absences from school; number of cigarettes smoked; proportion of voters registered. Continuous behaviors: specified forms of communication between spouses; length of tantrums.
Rating Scales: Either self-ratings or observer ratings. Self-anchored scales are constructed by client and worker to fit specific client contexts; clients usually collect these data. Observers can also make ratings on observable behaviors.	Degree of anger felt about spouse's nagging behavior; time spent thinking about the obsessive topic; expression of anger toward a child in a family therapy situation.
Standardized Measures: These are rating scales that have been developed and tested with known groups of subjects. Their responses become the norms with which new clients or subjects can be compared. Information on validity and reliability, and other matters concerning administration and interpretation, is usually given.	Zung Depression Scale (and the dozen or more other depression scales); MMPI; and the hundreds of other standardized scales as described in Buros's *Mental Measurement Yearbooks;* Robinson and Shaver's *Measurements of Social Psychological Attitudes;* and Levitt and Reid's "Rapid-Assessment Instruments for Practice."
Client Logs: These are journals kept by clients about events related to some problem. Logs may be structured: Who did what to whom under what conditions? Or they may be open-ended.	Logs are individually tailored to meet client needs, e.g.: Under what conditions does mother get upset with child?
Unobtrusive and Nonreactive Measures: These are various ways of collecting information that don't affect the information collected. Archival records are a prime example. (See Webb et al., 1981.)	Examples would include a worker's observation of a depressed client's posture (slumped, over indicating current depressed state); absences in teacher's notebook; empty beer bottles in garbage pail.

Along the horizontal axis is the time line indicating whatever time units are being used in the observation of the targets. In Figure 13.1, the mother used days as being a relevant unit of time in this case. The first ten days were termed *baseline* to indicate that, as much as possible, the worker was seeking to get a quantitative picture of what the target event really looked like in order to be guided in deciding what method of intervention would be most useful. You will note in Figure 13.1 that Randy was pretty good at dressing almost all of the time, and that the mother's perception of the problem was not the same as this objective measure of it. (The social work student might also have reconstructed from the mother's memory what was typical of Randy's dressing behavior to get some ballpark view of the behavior. But reconstructions from memory are risky and should be used only when necessary or when good archival data are available.)

Next, look at Figure 13.3, on the mother's feeling of competence in parenting. The right half of the graph indicates the targeted event during the period of

329

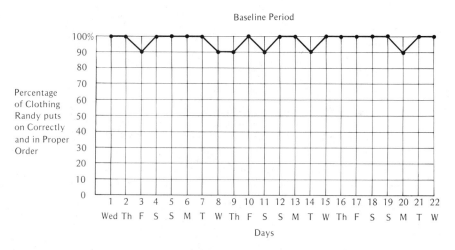

Figure 13.1   Percentage of clothing Randy (a retarded child) puts on correctly and in proper order.

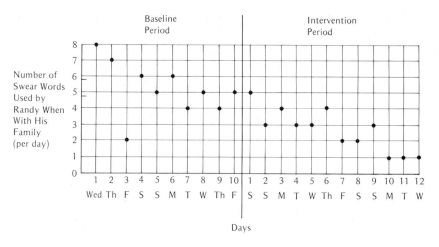

Figure 13.2   Number of swear words Randy uses when with his family (per day).

time when the worker had administered a planned *intervention* meant to change the target in the desired direction. Figure 13.3 shows that the mother's feelings of incompetence or competence had changed to the positive. (By the way, labeling a target with a negative and a positive aspect of the same event helps practitioners to keep a focus on both healthy and pathological functioning in their clients; it is as important to promote strengths as it is to prevent or treat problems.)

   Although you can see that there was some improvement in the mother's feelings about herself, the question is whether there was a *statistically* significant and a *practically* or *socially* significant change in this target. To determine *practical significance* requires that the worker and the client consider the social meaning of the observed changes. Do the differences really make any difference in the people's lives? Does the new behavior fit within the expected ranges of perfor-

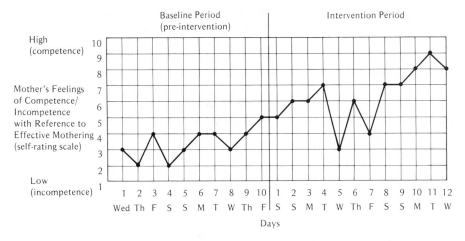

Figure 13.3 Mother's feelings of competence or incompetence with reference to effective mothering (self-rating scale).

mance for any person in similar circumstances? To measure statistical significance requires using some form of analysis, if the visual picture is not thoroughly clear. There are a number of ways of measuring whether there are statistically significant differences between these two sets of data (the "before" and the "after"), some involving elaborate statistical procedures, and others employing some simple approximate approaches using only simple math and reference to a table (see Bloom and Fischer, 1982; Cormier and Cormier, 1979; Fischer, 1978). There are also some complex problems, such as autocorrelation and transformation of data, generality of results, ethical considerations, and all those good things that bedevil any applied research method. However, in this chapter, I would like to present the method that is both the easiest and the safest—at the present time—while suggesting that interested readers pursue the matter in greater depth at some other time.

Here is one analytic procedure termed the *split-middle* or *celeration approach* (Gingrich and Feyerherm, 1979; White, 1977). Essentially, it tries to identify a trend in the baseline data, and then to project that trend into the intervention period, so that one can see whether what really happened is statistically different from what would probably have happened if the baseline trend had continued without the intervention. I'll illustrate the method with reference to Figure 13.4, which is a "worksheet" for data from Figure 13.3. The steps in identifying the trend of the baseline data are these:

1. *Look at the baseline period only.* Take the total number of observations in the baseline period (that would be 10 in Figure 13.4), and divide it in half (which would be 5 in each half). I find it useful to draw a little triangle at the point on the baseline that would exactly balance the two halves and then to draw a construction line perpendicular to that point on the line, as indicated in Figure 13.4. If there were an odd number of observations in the baseline period, say 11, half would be represented by a construction line drawn through Day 6, leaving an equal number on each side, but with the datum from Day 6 removed from this calculation.

331

Figure 13.4 Celeration line analysis applied to the data in Figure 13.3 (see text for discussion).

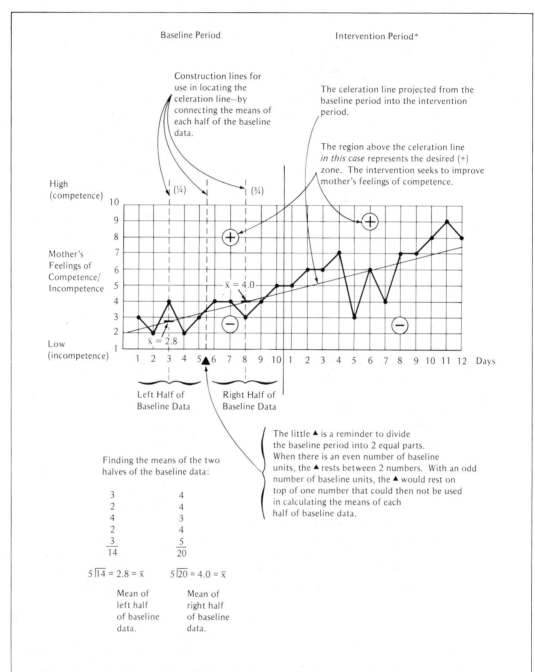

2. Taking each half of the baseline period separately, *add up the scores and divide by the number in each half.* In Figure 13.4, the scores 3, 2, 4, 2, and 3 total 14, which is divided by 5, the number of scores in this half of the baseline period. This gives 2.8. Repeat this process for the other half of baseline: scores 4, 4, 3, 4, and 5 total 20, which is divided by 5, giving 4.0. These are the means or averages, of each half of the baseline.

3. *Indicate these means on the graph itself.* They are put on other construction lines representing one fourth and three quarters of the baseline, as indicated in Figure 13.4. The means are indicated on these construction lines, and then another construction line is drawn connecting the means. This is called the *celeration line.* It may be accelerating (rising) or decelerating (a decending trend). Thus, the celeration line represents the dominant trend of the baseline data. In Figure 13.4, we can see that the line is accelerating, which means, in this case, that the behavior is improving slightly even without intervention. Perhaps even talking about it with a helping professional provides some relief of pressure or some opportunities to think about the problem differently. In any case, there is a slight positive trend, but because an acceptable level of feelings is not likely to emerge very quickly, the worker and the client decide to introduce some mode of treatment to help the improvement along.

4. *The celeration line is projected into the intervention period.* Here the celeration line represents the likely trend of observations if no intervention had taken place. But the celeration line is also an opportunity to make a statistical determination of whether what appears in the intervention period could have happened by chance alone. To make this determination, we have to observe the *baseline proportion of events of some specified type.* In this case, events in the desired portion of the graph, above the celeration line, indicate the more positive feelings of self-compe-tence (each graph may be different, so look at what the target is in order to determine what is the desired portion of the graph). *Proportions are calculated as follows:*

a. Take the number of events in the entire *baseline* period that are in the desired region of the graph, as indicated by the labeling of the target. (In Figure 13.4, this is the region above the celeration line.)
b. Find how many observations were possible in the baseline period. (The number is 10 in Figure 13.4. Read this number on the horizontal line.)
c. Divide the larger number into the smaller one to obtain the proportion of times that events were in the desired region during baseline. In this example 5 is divided by 10, giving .50 as the proportion of events in the desired zone during baseline.

5. *Looking at the intervention period, we note how many observations were possible,* which is to say, how long the intervention period was. In this case, we note that there was a twelve-day intervention period.

6. *Then we have to find the number of events of the same kind during the intervention period.* In this case, this number of events in the desired region of the graph as indicated by the projected celeration line is 10.

7. Finally, *we turn to a table that will tell us whether such a set of events as we have observed could have happened by chance alone or not.* Table 13.2 is carefully constructed. Let's examine it closely before we return to find out whether the intervention

333

Table 13.2 Table Showing the Number of Observations of a Specified Type (e.g., a desired behavior) During the Intervention Period That Are Necessary to Represent a Significant *Increase* at the .05 Level Over the Proportion of Like Observations During the Baseline Period.*

Proportion of Observations in the Baseline Period	Number of Observations in the Intervention Period																												
	4	6	8	10	12	14	16	18	20	24	28	32	36	40	44	48	52	56	60	64	68	72	76	80	84	88	92	96	100
.05	2	2	3	3	3	3	3	4	4	4	4	5	5	5	6	6	6	7	7	7	8	8	8	8	9	9	9	10	10
.10	3	3	3	4	4	4	5	5	5	6	7	7	8	8	9	9	10	10	11	12	12	13	13	14	14	15	15	16	16
1/8	3	3	4	4	5	5	5	6	6	7	8	8	9	10	10	11	12	12	13	14	14	15	15	16	17	17	18	19	19
.15	3	3	4	4	5	5	6	6	7	8	8	9	10	11	11	12	13	14	15	15	16	17	18	18	19	20	21	21	22
1/6	3	4	4	5	5	6	6	7	8	8	9	10	11	12	13	13	14	15	16	17	18	18	19	20	21	22	22	23	24
.20	3	4	5	5	6	6	7	8	9	9	10	11	12	13	14	15	16	17	18	19	20	21	22	23	24	25	26	27	28
.25	4	4	5	6	7	7	8	8	10	11	12	13	14	15	16	17	18	20	21	22	23	24	25	27	29	30	31	32	33
.30	4	5	6	6	7	8	8	9	10	12	13	15	16	18	19	21	22	23	25	26	28	29	30	32	33	35	36	37	39
1/3	4	5	5	6	7	8	9	10	11	14	16	17	19	21	22	24	26	27	29	30	32	33	35	36	38	39	41	41	42
.35	4	4	5	6	7	8	9	9	10	13	15	17	18	20	22	23	25	27	28	30	32	34	35	37	38	39	41	42	44
3/8	4	5	5	6	7	8	9	10	11	14	16	18	19	21	23	25	26	28	30	31	33	35	37	38	40	42	43	45	47
.40	4	5	6	7	8	9	10	11	12	15	17	19	21	23	24	26	28	30	31	33	35	37	38	40	42	44	46	47	49
.45	4	5	6	7	8	9	10	11	12	15	18	20	22	24	26	28	30	32	34	36	38	40	42	44	46	48	50	52	54
.50	—	6	7	8	9	11	12	13	14	17	20	22	24	26	28	31	33	35	37	40	42	44	46	48	51	53	55	57	59
.55	—	6	7	8	10	11	12	14	15	18	21	23	25	28	30	33	35	37	40	43	45	47	50	52	55	57	59	62	64
.60	—	6	8	9	10	12	13	15	16	19	22	25	27	30	33	35	38	41	43	46	48	51	54	56	59	61	64	66	69
5/8	—	—	8	10	11	13	14	16	17	20	23	25	28	31	34	36	39	42	45	47	50	52	55	58	61	63	66	69	71
.65	—	—	8	10	11	13	14	16	18	20	24	26	29	32	35	38	40	43	46	49	52	54	57	60	63	65	68	71	74
2/3	—	—	8	10	12	13	15	17	18	21	24	27	30	32	35	38	41	44	47	50	53	56	58	61	64	67	70	72	75
.70	—	—	—	10	11	13	15	16	18	21	24	28	30	34	37	40	43	46	49	52	55	58	61	64	67	70	73	75	78
.75	—	—	—	—	12	14	15	17	19	22	26	29	32	35	39	42	45	48	51	55	58	61	64	67	70	74	77	80	83
.80	—	—	—	—	—	14	16	17	19	22	25	28	32	35	38	42	45	48	52	55	58	61	65	68	71	74	78	81	84	87
5/6	—	—	—	—	—	—	—	18	20	23	27	30	34	37	41	44	48	51	55	58	61	64	68	71	74	78	81	85	90
.85	—	—	—	—	—	—	—	—	20	24	27	31	34	38	41	45	48	52	55	59	62	65	68	71	74	78	81	85	92
7/8	—	—	—	—	—	—	—	—	—	24	28	32	36	39	43	47	50	54	57	61	65	68	72	76	79	83	86	90	94
.90	—	—	—	—	—	—	—	—	—	—	—	32	36	40	44	47	51	54	58	62	66	69	73	77	80	84	88	91	95
.95	—	—	—	—	—	—	—	—	—	—	—	—	—	—	—	—	—	—	60	64	68	72	76	79	83	87	91	95	99

SOURCE: Reprinted with permission, from Martin Bloom, *Paradox of Helping: Introduction to the Philosophy of Scientific Practice*, New York, John Wiley & Sons, Dec., 1975.

* *Tables of the Cumulative Binomial Probability Distribution*—By the staff of the Harvard Computational Laboratory, Harvard University Press, 1955. This table constructed under the direction of Dr. James Norton, Jr., Indiana University—Purdue University at Indianapolis, 1973.

was significant. The title of Table 13.2 is a set of instructions for using the table. It directs us to find the *proportion* of events of a specified type (such as those in the desired zone) during the baseline period. We have just done this above in step 4. Then the table directs us to find the total *number* of observations possible in the intervention period. We did this as well, in Step 6 above. Now the table says that the number in the cell intersection of a given proportion and a given number represents the number of observations needed to indicate that a statistically significant difference has appeared. If the number we find in the intervention period is at or above the tabled number, then we can assert that a statistically significant difference has occurred in these data at the .05 level. This means that only in 5 times out of 100 would results like these have happened by chance alone. This is one common set of rules that indicates statistical significance. You will often see it expressed as $p < .05$, an abbreviation that means that the two observed events could not have happened by chance alone except less than 5 times in 100. The two events in this case are the "before" and "after" self-reports of feelings of competence.

Now for the climax. Was there a statistically significant improvement in the mother's feelings of competence? In Step 5, we noted that on 10 of the 12 days of intervention, the mother reported feelings at such a level as to be above the celeration line. In Table 13.2, we look at the cell at the intersection of the proportion, .50, and the number of observations, 12. This cell entry is 10. Thus we have reached the number needed to represent a statistically significant difference.

Had we had only 9 observations in the desired region in the intervention period, we would not have had statistical significance, although there would be a strong trend, and it might have been worthwhile to continue the intervention that seemed to be close to statistical significance. Had 11 or 12 observations been in the desired region, these findings would have been even more significant. There are also tables for probability levels .01 and .001 (see Bloom and Fischer, 1982).

What these data mean is that after intervention, the mother reported a statistically significant increase in feelings of competence as compared with the baseline period. Note that with this simple before-and-after design (called an *A-B design* in the literature—see Hersen and Barlow, 1974; Kratochwill, 1978), we cannot say that the intervention caused the change. Other alternative explanations are present—the same ones that we discussed in Technical Note 4.6 (p. 123), citing the work of Campbell and Stanley (1963). However, for this most elementary of single-system designs, we can obtain some vital information that is of great practical significance: the client's problem behavior changed in the desired direction. Other designs, such as multiple-baseline or experimental-reversal designs, reduce the possibility that alternative explanations could have accounted for these results. But these designs require more discussion that this text permits (see Figure 13.5).* However, I want to stress that they are also very simple, approximate ways of testing statistical significance and providing the bases for inferring worker causality.

Thus, by means of a set of simple steps, we can determine for ourselves whether our clients have made statistically significant progress or not. And by

* The tabular discussion of *single-system research designs* constitutes Technical Note 13.4.

Figure 13.5 Single-system designs.

Design	Flow Diagram	Advantages	Disadvantages
Design #1: A-B Design (the basic single system design)		1. This design represents a large advance over case studies without a reference baseline (a kind of own-control group).	1. This simple design is subject to some alternative sources of causation, thus making it a very weak basis for inferring causality of the independent variable, the intervention (B).
		2. The requirement to operationalize both the targets of intervention and the intervention itself oblige the worker to be very clear about the events in this client's situation.	2. Collecting any data (by the clients themselves or by others) is somewhat burdensome; the value of this task must be proven.
		3. The worker may obtain valuable information during the service process, thus may modify the interventions according to observed events, to more nearly attain the goals in the case.	

Flow Diagram for Design #1: Vertical axis labeled (X) Target of Intervention (operationally defined dependent variable) with scale 1–5. Two panels: (A) Baseline and (B) Intervention (independent variable). Data Points plotted over Time Units 1 2 3 4 5 | 1 2 3 4 5.

Discussion: The worker and client identify one target of intervention (X) which is given an operational definition on some scale indicated by the vertical axis. The horizontal line indicates equal time intervals on which measurements are taken of the specific target, both *before* and *during* intervention (and possibly after intervention, in a follow-up period). The before (A) period is called *baseline;* it is the reference point for events after *intervention* (B). Visual and/or statistical analyses are done with these two sets of data, as described in the text.

Variations: Several targets X, Y, and Z... may be used for one client system, each considered separately (different targets and different interventions). This aggregate of A-B designs is termed multiple target design, and offers insight into the concommitant variations among targeted events. (See Bloom and Fischer, 1982.)

Design	Flow Diagram	Advantages	Disadvantages
Design #2: Experimental Replication Design		1. This design permits the worker to demonstrate empirical control over the target of intervention, at least on the logical basis of concommitant variation.	1. It is difficult in many settings to remove an intervention once it has been successful, or if that intervention involves something the client has learned how to do.
		2. This design is frequently used in laboratory research work because it is one of the most powerful of the single-system designs.	2. This design is more complicated to perform; more control must be had over the persons and situations involved.

Flow Diagram for Design #2: Vertical axis labeled (X) Target of Intervention with scale 1–5. Segments labeled A_1, B_1, A_2, B_2 over Time Units 1 2 3 4 5 repeated.

Note: Just as Figure 2.1 presented a number of major variations of group research designs, so there are several variations of single-system designs presented in Figure 13.5. This figure is merely an indication of the tools that are available for the individual helping professional practicing in a field situation away from the fancy technology that much classical group-research entails. My intention in presenting this figure is simply to indicate a few of the major designs to stimulate your interest in pursuing this important topic further (see Bloom and Fischer, 1982).

As in Figure 2.1, I present the name of the design and a flow diagram of its essential features, along with a discussion of what the symbols in the diagram mean. Then I discuss variations on this design, followed by a brief statement of the advantages and the disadvantages associated with the designs. The basic A-B design is the building block for all other designs. It is elaborated on, so as to provide a stronger foundation for inferring causality. But if the reader gains an understanding of the basic design alone, this understanding may prove very helpful in his or her day-to-day practice.

Discussion: This design begins with the basic A-B design in the first two phases, but then adds a return to baseline conditions (A_2) before resuming the same intervention (B_2). The purpose of removing the first intervention (B_1) after it has been shown to be a significant improvement over the initial baseline condition (A_1) is to demonstrate that the intervention itself is the causal ingredient. The logic is that if the problem behavior returns to (or almost to) its initial level at A_2 and then improved in B_2 at it had in B_1, then by reason of this concommitant variation, we can logically infer that the intervention B is causally involved.

Variation: The same logic holds if only an A-B-A design were employed, but it is unadvisable to end a service program without the client's goals having been attained and retained.

Likewise, it is possible to have a B-A-B design, where service begins immediately (as in crisis situations), and then when some successful improvements have been observed, this service is removed (A_1) and the problem reappears. If the service is then reapplied, and the situation improves once again, the basic logic of concommitant variation is indicated.

3. Successful demonstrations of the effectiveness of a technique can add to a worker's repertoire.

3. The length of phases must be about equal, which may be hard to control.

Design #3: Multiple Baseline Design

(X) A_1 | B_1

(Y) A_2 | B_1

(Z) A_3 | B_1

Discussion: This design is a set of interrelated A-B designs in which different targets are dealt with by the same intervention—applied at different points in time. For target X, some baseline A is taken and an intervention B applied until significant improvement occurs. During this time, baseline data have been collected for Y and Z. When X has been shown to improve, then the same intervention is given to Y until it too improves. (This assumes that there is no improvement of Y or Z that occurs when X's intervention is introduced.) And so on, with Z. The logical basis for inferring causality is the changes occurring with and only with the sequential introduction of the same intervention with different problems.

Variations: The multiple baseline design itself can involve three types of comparisons. First, it may be used with one client with two or more problems—this is the usual situation as portrayed earlier. It can also involve two or more clients with a similar problem, thus studying the effects of the same intervention on the several clients. It can also involve two or more situations with the same problem.

1. This is a relatively strong basis for inferring causality, and it doesn't have the drawback of having to remove a successful intervention. This may make it ethically more palitable to service workers.

2. The variations permit comparison of multiple clients, problems, or settings.

3. This design can be used when effects of service are irreversible.

1. It is difficult to arrange life in such neat packages, even though most service workers do work one problem in some sequential fashion.

2. The order of intervention may have something to do with the outcome, independent of the intervention itself.

3. It may be that there is contamination of the service effect. If so, this nullifies the causal implications of this design.

337

using more powerful single-system designs, we can even make inferences about whether we caused these events to occur. By the way, we can also use the same basic procedures to test whether deterioration occurred.

As you are bound to think of some situations to which the steps listed above won't fully apply, let me anticipate them and offer these general guidelines: *Whenever you are faced with a statistical decision, always try to make it more difficult to prove statistically that client events improved.* For example, if you figure a baseline proportion as being .46, use the next higher proportion in Figure 13.5, .50, rather than the next lower one, .45. Why? Because it would have taken only 9 events in the desired region to be significant for the proportion .45 (with 12 observations in the intervention period), whereas it takes 10 for the proportion .50. So it is more difficult to prove statistical significance by taking the next higher proportion when the exact proportion is not shown in Table 13.2.

The same rule applies when the number of observations in the intervention period does not appear in Table 13.2. For example, if there were 11 days, rather than 12 (in Figure 13.4), there is no 11 on the top line of Table 13.2. So the choice is either to use 12, which makes attaining statistical significance more difficult, or 10, which makes it easier. The rule directs us to use the more difficult set of conditions in supporting client improvement. Likewise, if you have to test for deterioration, choose the numbers and proportions in Table 13.2 that make it easier to obtain significant negative results. The reason is that as the method is an approximate one, we are working with crude figures in any case, and we may most wisely use them as if we were not effective in producing client change. Then, when the results still indicate the desired change, we can be a little more confident of these approximate methods.

SELF-TEST

Let's take a self-test* to see if you are following these steps. Evaluate Figure 13.2. Do the data suggest that there are statistically significant changes occurring in Randy's swearing? Let me list the steps that you should be following. Indicate the answers after each—and by the way, check the time; see how long it takes you to determine the statistical significance of the change in this target of intervention. The reason for asking you to do this is to demonstrate how brief and simple this evaluation task is. Despite its approximate nature, for the time and effort expended it may prove to be a useful tool for the helping professional:

1. Locate the baseline on Figure 13.2. That would constitute the first _____ number of days of the time that the worker had contact with the clients. (I provide the answers at the end of this chapter.)
2. Divide the baseline into two equal halves by drawing a construction line on the graph. (I hate to see you mark up as nice a book as this, but go ahead; it's for a good cause.) Where did you draw this construction line? _____
3. Sum the scores of the left half of the baseline (6, 7, 5, 6, and 5). Then divide the sum by the number of scores (which in this case is _____. This number is the mean of the left half of the baseline scores. (The mean is _____.)

* This self-test presents a *programmed exercise* and constitutes Technical Note 13.5.

4. Repeat these steps with the right half of baseline. The mean for the right half is _____.

5. Redivide the baseline with construction lines drawn lightly at the one-quarter and the three-quarter points. Indicate the mean of the left half of the baseline data on the one-quarter construction line. Indicate the mean of the right half of the baseline data on the three-quarter construction line. (I'll have to trust that you did this correctly by using the vertical axis to find where the intervals are located. Just to help you out, I have indicated by small notches on the vertical axis of Figure 13.2 where the means come. You have to put them on the one-quarter and the three-quarter construction lines.

6. Then connect the two means and extend the line into the intervention period. This is the celeration line. Indicate on Figure 13.2 which region represents the desired behavior (from the point of view of the mother, who is the client in this context). (The region above the celeration line is _____.)

7. Figure out the proportion of events in the desired region in baseline. This is _____ out of what total number (_____) of observations occurring in the baseline. Thus the proportion is _____.

8. Count the number of like events in the intervention period (_____) out of a total of how many observations (_____).

9. Looking at Table 13.2, locate the proportion of events in the desired zone (from Step 7).
Then, locate the total number of observations in the intervention period. This number comes from Step 8.
Then locate the cell entry at the intersection of that proportion and that number. What is this cell entry? (_____) Remember that the cell entry means that this number or any larger one represents a statistically significant change in the intervention period as compared with the baseline period.

10. What happened? Was there a statistically significant change? (_____) Notice that you probably could not have predicted this outcome by looking at the data alone. There was a definite decrease in Randy's swearing, but note that the trend before intervention was toward some decrease. So, if you look at the celeration line as a trend of events, you'll find that the intervention had to be even stronger to make a statistically significant change.

Practical significance is independent of statistical significance. What may be meaningful in social terms may or may not be meaningful in statistical terms, and vice versa. Obviously it is preferable to have statistical and practical significance aligned, but this evaluation method provides one path to the assessment of statistical significance. Check your watch again. How long did this evaluation take? Compare this time to the several years it took us to get information about the Protective Services Project. And you did it all by yourself, with a little help from your friends.

SUMMARY AND CONCLUSIONS

Let me make some general observations about single-system designs. Note that the logic in conducting these evaluations of the process and the outcome of practice follows very closely the logic of classical research. The control-group concept is embodied in using the client or client-system as its own control;

that is the "before" part of the data. Randomization is intended to give each member an equal opportunity to fall into an experimental or control group, but with single-system design, there is an exact identification of the two comparison groups because they are, in fact, the same person or social system. Table 13.2 is based on the normal probability distribution curve, as is much of classical research. The simple A-B design illustrated above is threatened by many other possible interpretations of why the results occurred as they did—perhaps Randy's grandparents came to visit during that intervention period and he was too preoccupied with them to think about swearing. But as group designs differ in their power to control alternative explanations of observed events, so, too, do single-system designs.

The differences are overwhelming. You can do the single-system-design evaluations immediately with nearly every client target, if you put your imaginative mind to work. You can get some reasonably objective information back on a day-by-day or a week-by-week basis, so that you have an objective look at the flow of events in the case. You can then take this information while it is hot and use it to modify your intervention, as needed, so as to approximate your objectives of practice as effectively as possible. Sometimes involving the clients in the process of observing their own behaviors, thoughts, or feelings can be very important. For example, the mother was really surprised by Randy's success at dressing; objective looking at "problems" may cut them down to size—or clarify how difficult matters really stand. And finally, you have some objective basis for continuing with or terminating one set of interventions. You can build up a repertoire of successful strategies for later use, and you can document your effectiveness for the powers-that-be. In an age of accountability, that ability is important.

This chapter has presented only the bare essentials for conducting a simple single-system design with a client. Yet, as long as one can identify targeted events (thoughts, feelings, or actions) that can be reliably and validly measured on a regular basis by the client, the worker, or some other person in the situation, the procedures of graphing these events over time can be employed, and an analysis can be generated that provides some crude but objective indicators of the progress and outcome of the case. This simple evaluation procedure is truly worth considering in each and every case situation.

CODA: ANSWERS TO THE SELF-TEST

1. The baseline is the entire period of time between the first contact of the helping professional and the beginning of a planned intervention. In the case of Randy and his mother, the period is 10 days. To be sure, one may argue that merely talking with the mother may be "therapy," but it is not a planned intervention in the sense of having the specific objective of reducing an identified problem. Rapport is necessary to a helping relationship, but don't mistake rapport for planned service directed toward resolving a given problem.

2. There are 10 days in the baseline period, and so you divide the 10 in half in such a way as to have an equal number of days in the two halves of the baseline. With an even number of baseline days, the construction line dividing

it in half falls between two days. In this case, it falls between Days 5 and 6. If there were an odd number of days, such as 11, then the construction line would have to be drawn on top of Day 6. This action means we lose the information in Day 6, as we have to treat each half of baseline equally. We could add Day 6 to both sides, but adding a constant to two sums doesn't change anything. So we simply remove it from the calculations of the means of each half.

3. The left half of baseline was given as 8, 7, 3, 6, and 5. The total is 29. There are 5 scores being added here; 5 is the number of scores and it is used as the divisor of the total: 29 divided by 5 equals 5.8.

4. We repeat this same process for the right side of baseline: The data here are 6, 4, 5, 4, and 5. The total is 24. The number of scores is 5, and 24 divided by 5 equals 4.8.

5. We draw one-quarter and three-quarter construction lines so as to be able to indicate where the means of each half of the baseline go. Usually the mean is a decimal, like our 5.8 and 4.8 in Steps 3 and 4 above. We use the vertical axis in order to note exactly where 5.8 goes. Then we transfer that place to the one-quarter construction line. Likewise, we find where 4.8 goes on the vertical axis and then transfer it to the three-quarter construction line. I put the notches at 5.8 and 4.8 on the vertical line in Figure 13.2. You should have transferred them to the one-quarter and three-quarter construction lines, respectively.

6. When you connect the two means for the halves of baseline, use a ruler or other straight edge. This is very important because a slight error in drawing the line will become a bigger error when you project the celeration line into the intervention period.

Now the question concerns the desired behavior on this given target, which will indicate the desired region above or below the celeration line. This choice is a judgment, usually from the point of view of the client. The mother is the client in this case and feels concerned about what she takes to be improper thoughts on the part of her retarded son. We may or may not agree with this judgment; we may believe that youngsters around this age do begin to learn words that are not appropriate for polite society. But ordinarily children learn where and when to use these terms, and so this retarded child has another lesson to learn in addition to the enrichment of his vocabulary. These decisions on whether to go along with the client on something that the worker doesn't feel is a problem are practice issues; once the worker decides what to do, the single-system design offers a way of evaluating the outcome of the intervention. All this discussion is to rationalize the fact that we will use the region under the celeration line as the desired region in this case.

Note that it is possible for the celeration line to hit the top or the bottom of the graph before the time in the intervention period equals the time in the baseline period. This is an important limitation of the celeration line approach. In such cases, one might either choose an arbitrary criterion of what constitutes "successful" change or guess at the meaning of the intervention period events in a visual analysis. There are other ways to analyze the data in such instances, but I must refer you to other sources for these (see Jayaratne, 1978; Bloom and Fischer, 1982).

7. To figure out the proportion of events in a specified region of the graph during baseline requires us to use all the information generated above. First,

341

look at the constructed celeration line. There is a decreasing trend; that is, it goes from a high of 5.8 to a low of 4.8 in baseline. The projected line continues this decreasing trend into the intervention period. However, looking only at the baseline, and noting that the region under the celeration line is the "desired" zone in this case, we can find four data points in that desired region during the baseline period. These are Days 3, 5, 7, and 9. Note also that day 3 has the one-quarter construction line drawn on top of it, but this fact does *not* remove this datum from the number of events in the desired region. (That is, distinguish this step in using data where a construction line has been drawn from the other construction line used to divide an odd-numbered baseline period where we would lose a day in calculating the means of each half.)

Look next at the total number of days for which observations are available in baseline: 10 days as indicated on the horizontal line. To find the proportion, we use the formula of dividing the number of days of a specified type (in the desired region) by the total number of baseline days in which these particular types of days could occur. That is, 4 desired days divided by the 10 total baseline days. This division gives a proportion of .40.

8. Now we go to the intervention period. First, count the total number of days in this period. In this case, it is 12, a number close to the number of days in the baseline. The reason for having the number of days roughly equal is that the same amount of time is available for random events to occur in the one as in the other.

Next we look on the graph itself and find how many events are in the same desired region as we had identified in the baseline period. The number here is 8.

9. Next we turn to Table 13.2. We locate the proportion (Step 7) that is listed in the left-hand column: .40. Then we locate the number of total observations in the intervention period across the top of the table: 12. Looking at the intersection of .40 and 12, we find the number 9. This means that we need 9 or more events in the desired region to represent a significant increase at the .05 level, given the baseline proportion of like events.

10. What happened? We did not reach the required level for statistical significance. But don't be discouraged. Let me explain why: First, the worker was receiving information from the mother on how much swearing was going on after they instituted some intervention program—perhaps the mother or father had a short, firm discussion with Randy each time he swore, not condemning him, but just explaining that this wasn't the appropriate place to use such language. (The intervention program is a practice decision not discussed here, even though it is very much a part of the evaluation process. See Nelson, 1978.) The data were posted on the graph each day or perhaps each week at the agency. The worker made some quick calculations with the numbers, but also with the practical meaning of the events in order to decide whether the intervention was working at all, was succeeding in resolving the problem completely, or something in between. In this case, it looks as if Randy was learning, before intervention began, that swear words were to be used only in certain places and on certain occasions, and this learning seemed to pick up speed when the parental intervention took place. It was not yet statistically significant, but as *practically* only one or two instances of swearing were occurring near the end of intervention after a steady decline, we can guess that this intervention and

342

Randy's own self-learning were moving in the desired direction. It probably wouldn't be long before the parents would decide to stop the intervention. The worker might be wise to note that there will be occasional eruptions of swearing as Randy continues to learn how and where to speak these emotive words, even if the bulk of the problem is removed.

Thus ongoing evaluation of targeted behavior can be helpful in the making of practice decisions, but it is primarily an aid to practice, not a master of it. At no time should evaluation interfere with necessary practice; but keep in mind that the better the information we have about our practice and its effectiveness, the more effective we are likely to be.

CHAPTER 14

Computers and Statistics

Overview

This chapter describes the historical, contemporary, and future uses of computers, with special reference to the helping professions. It discusses the logical structures of computers, both the micro or personal computers and the giant mainframe computers. Then five applications of microcomputers are illustrated. The chapter concludes with a brief consideration of the use of computers in doing statistics.

Technical Narrative Section

Introduction to the History of Computers (Technical Note 14.1)
The Logical Structure and Functions of Computers (14.2)
Applications of Computers in the Helping Professions (14.3)
Computers and Statistics (14.4)
Summary and Conclusions

The Technical Narrative

INTRODUCTION TO THE HISTORY OF COMPUTERS

Computers are very modern machines that have combined a number of ancient devices into new and powerful tools for communicating information.* Let's review these ancient devices and procedures that have been combined in the modern computer (following Sanders, 1973).

Data, that is, raw facts, must be recorded in some way, such as with the Babylonian cuneiform symbols pressed into clay tablets by means of a stylus, a pointed wedge. It was vital to the development of a society that some means of written communication be developed. These data also had to be classified (sorted into groups) and arranged in some agreed upon fashion to facilitate shared meanings. Language as a written collection of symbols is one such classification system.

Other types of data have to be calculated by means of mathematical operations—yet another form of classification and arrangement of information that dates back to the earliest stages of civilization. Remember how the ancient Egyptians developed trigonometry to deal with land ownership when the Nile flooded its boundaries. Data needed also to be summarized, stored, and they had to be capable of being retrieved when needed. Sometimes stored data had to be reproduced so that they could be circulated to different users at the same time.

All of these functions have been performed separately, by hand for most of history, but increasingly by machines that use mechanical, electromechanical (that is, a combination of mechanics and electricity), and electronic methods. For example, people have counted on their fingers from the beginning of human life: this means, in case you have forgotten, that you represent one thing (like how many years you have lived or how many brothers and sisters you have) with something else (such as the number of fingers you touch). But people quickly ran out of fingers and turned to inventions, such as the abacus, that do the same thing: let one thing (beads on an abacus, for example) represent something else.

The Oxford English Dictionary tells us about the early uses of words. For example, *computer*, or *compute*, appeared as early as 1413 and had a variety of meanings, such as surveying, calculating, reckoning, estimating, taking into consideration, and, most intriguing of all, doing someone out of something by computation. (The latter usage may be a precursor of the term *hacking*.) There are various major advances in the history of computers worth noting, just to get some perspective on these modern inventions.

In 1642, an eighteen-year-old Frenchman, Blaise Pascal, invented a mechanical calculating device in which gears with ten teeth (one for each number, 0 to 9) were intermeshed so that one could add and subtract. When required, the machine would carry over the count to the next gear, as when adding 5 and 5. The unit gear would show 0 and the tens gear would show 1.

---

* This discussion of the *history of computers and computing functions* constitutes Technical Note 14.1.

A more important device was invented by Gottfried Wilhelm Leibnitz (1646–1716). His "stepped reckoner" was supposed to multiply, divide, and do square roots. But Leibnitz's major contribution was that he suggested dividing complex mathematical problems into the smallest possible units that could be easily calculated, albeit in tedious and time-consuming steps. He also used a binary number system (0 or 1 as the basis for composing all other numbers) rather than the usual decimal system with its familiar mathematical symbols that Pascal had painted on his gear.

Sanders (1973) discussed the history of computer development in four stages, beginning with "ancient history" from 1833 to 1937. (I must have been discussing "prehistory" in the paragraphs above.) In 1833, an Englishman, Charles Babbage, started working on his "analytic engine," a machine that was one hundred years in advance of its time and technology. He borrowed features from other machines of the day in order to make a computer. For example, he used punch cards like the kind that were used by Joseph Marie Jacquard to make patterns in loomed fabrics. And he had in mind all of the other significant steps in the logic of computers, as we shall see.

Another phase of this "ancient history" was the push of necessity. Hand calculations were terribly slow. The Bob Cratchits of the day were a maligned lot pushing numbers around by hand forever, like so many office Sisyphuses. The U.S. Census of 1880 took so long to count that the workers finished at just about the time that the next census had to be started. To solve this problem, Herman Hollerith developed a punched standard census card that could be used with an electrical current for calculating totals for the next census. Where there was a hole in the card, an electrical connection was made ("on"), and if there was no hole, no connection was made ("off"). This arrangement was like Leibnitz's binary system, reducing large amounts of raw data to manageable forms through electromechanical means. From there, Hollerith moved on to greater things, including the founding of the firm that became IBM.

Sanders's (1973) "middle ages" include the period between 1937 and 1954, during which the first large-scale electromechanical computer was built: the Mark I, in 1944, product of Harvard people and IBM engineers. Babbage was vindicated at last. At about this same time, a more important development took place at the University of Pennsylvania when the first electronic digital computer was created. This was ENIAC (Electronic Numerical Integrator and Calculator), a thirty-ton monster with many thousands of vacuum tubes that broke down at the rate of one every seven minutes. However, ENIAC could perform hundreds of times faster than the fastest electromechanical devices, and this speed was important in relation to the war effort. (Many non-lethal inventions seem to emerge because of the demands of war, a paradoxical twist in human nature.)

Another significant step in the middle ages of computers was the incorporation of Leibnitz's idea of the binary system, into a working computer, along with some other innovations regarding how instructions as well as data might be stored in a machine for processing. Indeed, not only was this model workable, it was also the first commercially available one: the UNIVAC-1 (*UNIV*ersal *A*utomatic *C*omputer). That was in 1951.

Sanders (1973) continued his history of computers by describing the Victorian period, 1954 to 1964. Several "generations" of computers were developed, with increasing capacities to do more varied work at greater speeds, with decreasing sizes, and with changes in construction materials—from vacuum tubes that required huge spaces and air conditioning to solid-state components like transistors. (Silicon chips were introduced in the late 1960s, and superchips—further miniaturized and empowered—are being announced in tomorrow's newspapers.)

Sanders's (1973) recent period, from 1964 onward, will no doubt be divided into stages as soon as we get some perspective. But what is clear is that developments are happening at such rapid speeds that there has been supertechnological progress into the fifth and sixth generations of computers, whereas human nature is still plodding along in its first and second generations in ethics and self-control.

THE LOGICAL STRUCTURE AND FUNCTIONS OF COMPUTERS

As we have seen, computers are machines made up of bits and pieces of equipment and ideas from all of history. What is new is the way in which these pieces are assembled, which gives computers enormous capacities to do millions of tiny steps of recording, classifying, sorting, calculating, summarizing, storing, retrieving, reproducing, and communicating—all at dazzling speeds and hopefully with great accuracy. Computers do make computer-sized errors, but these are due to human directions; for example, a woman in Salt Lake City wanted to clear up a discrepancy of 29 cents in her charge account at a department store and received a computerized letter of credit for $161 billion (*Washington Post*, November 29, 1983, p. D3). Let's examine the logical structure of computers and the functions that they perform,* recognizing that each brand of computer is structured somewhat differently.

First, consider the basic functions of a computer and the structures that implement them. For example, I am typing on the keys of a microcomputer that is acting as a word processor. My typing can be described as *input* into the system; that is, I am putting in information that will eventually be acted on. The input actually includes a process: taking ideas that I have in my mind and electronically transferring them by my none-too-accurate typing to the central processing unit of the computer. (Fortunately, the word processor enables me to correct my typos easily; would that it would do the same for my ideas.)

The *central processing unit* is the heart of the system, containing several important parts. First, there is a storage area in which several functions occur. Either information that is taken in is held until it is needed for processing, or the intermediate results of processed data are held awaiting further processing, or the final processed data are held until they can be released to the output part of the computer. In addition, the storage area holds programs, that is, instructions that can be used with these data.

The second main part of the central processing unit is the *control section,* which acts on instructions sent from input through the storage section and *executes* the program, that is, translates the general directions from the user into specific actions of the machine.

---

* This discussion of the *logical structure and functions of computers* constitutes Technical Note 14.2.

The third main part of the central processing unit is the *logic-computation element,* which receives data from input through the storage section, then manipulates the data according to instructions from the control section (operating through the storage section), and then returns the processed data to storage. As you might guess, there may be many flows of data back and forth between this logic-computation section and storage.

Finally, the computer has an *output* portion, a device that translates the processed data back into forms that humans will understand, such as printers in word processors, spinning golden words out of the flaxen electronic impulses. Printers also churn out the reams of printouts that doctoral students obtain from batched computer runs or, occasionally, botched computer runs. (I'd better explain the joke: One can use a computer on an *interactive* basis, as I am doing now with my microcomputer and printer; one can also use a computer, especially a large *mainframe* one, at available times, or in *batches.* The mainframe computers take inputs from many users at the same time and turn back their respective outputs in batches, sometimes shortly after the input, and at other times in a matter of days. If a user makes a programming mistake so that the data processing cannot be completed, this time delay can be very costly and frustrating. However, computers always obey the first rule of computer dynamics: Garbage in, garbage out. That's what a botched run is.)

Microcomputers operate on essentially the same logic as the large computers, but there are some terms specific to the small computers that need further clarification. The central processing unit has a fixed, long-term memory component, the *ROM,* which means "Read Only Memory." The central processing unit can read only information that is permanently stored in the ROM. The ROM is programmed or designed to get the central processing unit to perform certain operations on data, to run programs, and to produce output—all in the most basic and primitive way.

But the computer needs a second type of short-term memory called *RAM,* for "Random Access Memory," which enables a user to write specific and more complicated directions for handling a given set of data. The central processing unit not only reads information from the RAM but can write information on the RAM for later use. It is as if you were writing on an electronic blackboard (the RAM), putting up messages, rearranging them, erasing them, and storing the final version of them so that you could print out a hard copy on paper (in contrast to the soft copy that appears on the computer screen). The special problem with the RAM is that it is strictly a temporary memory, and once the electrical power is turned off, everything in the RAM's memory is erased. In electrical storms when the power goes out, even for an instant, all unsaved writing will be erased.

To counteract this possibility, the microcomputer has another storage device by which processed data, either numerical calculations or written text from a word processor, are transferred to *disks.* These are small ($5\frac{1}{4}$-inch or 8-inch) plastic disks covered in iron oxide for the magnetic storing of large amounts of information in binary codes, the patterns of on's and off's that compose letters and numbers. These are called *floppy disks* because they are flexible—and delicate. They are easily remagnetized by coming into contact with other magnetized objects like paper clips or other metal objects. Going through airport metal detectors may also erase your precious files (units of stored information on

348

disks), so take care. There are also hard disks, most of them used in large mainframe computers. New ideas in disks, as in every other feature of computers, come tumbling off the assembly lines seemingly every day.

Information storage involves another set of terms. A *byte* is a unit of memory storage, the space needed to store a single character, number, or letter, or space. A *kilobyte* contains about 1,000 characters. Thus, microcomputers are built with different volumes of kilobytes in the RAM, such as a "64-K capacity." Some portion of this RAM is used to store the particular program being used, and the rest of the space is for writing, editing, calculating, holding data, and so on.

After the central processing unit has done its work of taking in the raw information, processing it into some usable form, and storing it temporarily within its electronic system, the result has to be communicated to the user. In the microcomputer, the results appear on the *screen* of the computer, a cathode ray tube on which patterns of excited electrons sit momentarily (while the viewer may get equally excited). Because the storage on the screen is temporary, it is possible for the user to make further changes in the text or in the calculations before the results are printed. The disk on which the writer's final version of the information is stored obliges by passing the information to the printer, which has been given various directions on how to present the information: spacing, length of lines, and so on. In the not-too-distant future, there will be widespread use of other modes of communicating, including machines and users who can "talk" even at great distances, do the shopping, figure the household budget, and probably to gossip (cf. Toffler, 1980).

APPLICATIONS OF COMPUTERS IN THE HELPING PROFESSIONS

When Newton and Leibnitz corresponded about their current and germinal work in the area of calculus and physics, there was, understandably, widespread interest in what they were telling each other. The seventeenth-century equivalents of carbon paper or reproduction machines were clerics who laboriously copied these learned interchanges multiple times. This learned correspondence led to the founding of scientific societies, the early forerunners of our own professional and scientific associations of today. All because of the need for qualified persons to communicate more effectively.

Computers are no longer new; we've grown quite accustomed to them in the grocery store, the office, and even the home. But we have to remind ourselves that we are experiencing as important a revolution in intellectual and technological development as were the germinal ideas of Newton and Leibnitz in their day. Moreover, we are, historically speaking, at the very beginning phases of this development. We are still experimenting with ways to use this marvelous device in the service of the human race.

There are five major areas in which computers are currently being used in the helping professions (Mutschler, 1984):* research, word processing, data man-

---

* This discussion of *computer applications for the helping professions* constitutes Technical Note 14.3.

agement, database management systems, and decision applications. The bulk of this chapter focuses on research, and so here I will briefly describe the other topics.

Word processing is simply writing by means of a smart typewriter, one that receives a text entered on its keyboard and shown on its video screen for editing, formatting (into paragraphs, footnotes, and headings, all automatically and quickly—including changes in the numbering of footnotes should you change your mind), and storage until the writer desires a hard copy of the text. If you consider how often similar letters are sent to clients, or how service summaries are placed in a common format, or how expensive and time-consuming secretarial services are, then you can appreciate the word-processing function of computers. I must add that there is another, as yet unexplored, aspect: the stimulus to creativity. A writer can rapidly record his or her ideas—more rapidly than on conventional typewriters—modify them, and receive a clean copy immediately, which is a positive reinforcement of the effort expended and a basis for further writing. My prediction is that word-processing skills will become a requirement for professional practice within the decade.

Data management is the third major area served by computers. Mutschler (1984) reviewed the history of this development. Beginning in the 1960s and 1970s, various federal programs paid reimbursements for the costs of social services, provided the necessary documentation was given: who was doing what for whom, when, where, for what reasons, at what costs, and with what results. Other regulations required participation in professional standard-review organizations (PSROs), which also demanded great amounts of specific information on service management. Mutschler suggested that these demands led to the implementation of the computer-assisted management-information system (MIS), which systematically collects information from various organizational documents, accumulates this information in organized data files, and then processes and summarizes selected combinations of these data for various reports.

One interesting example of a data management system involves a computerized information system for the provision of child welfare (cf. Allen and Horniman, 1969; Fanshel, 1976). Imagine the complexities of managing a huge foster-care-services system, with large numbers of children who exhibit a rich diversity of characteristics, placed in various homes and institutions, by different helping professionals, and with a large array of outcomes. Keeping track of all of this information, without losing any child in the process, and doing so in a cost-effective manner, is a gigantic but necessary task. Fanshel's report discusses how the New York City child-welfare agencies cooperated in a data management system that has proved to be not only cost-effective, but humanly effective as well.

The fourth area of computer applications in the helping professions is that of *database management systems* (Mutschler, 1984), which consist of databases—sets of logically related data files—and a set of programs required to store, change, and retrieve information from the databases. In hospital settings, such a database management system might be used to track the progress of patients over the course of treatment, including analysis of client data (including such matters as client background, service episodes, and service evaluation); financial data (involving recorded information on the client's account at the hospital and other cost information); and data on the personnel involved in the case (Mutschler and Hasenfeld, 1983). By interrelating these three sources of information, administrators and practitioners can generate analyses based on the logical linkages among them, in particular, the relationship between program outcome and the costs involved. This type of information leads to a discussion of the last area of computer application in the helping professions.

The fifth area of computer applications in the helping professions is the most recent and the least well developed. It concerns various *decision applications,* in both *administration* and *direct practice* (Mutschler, 1984). Let's look at each of these in turn. For an administrator, information ignored is information lost and means decisions based on a weak knowledge base. But obtaining good current information is difficult, costly, and time-consuming—or at least it has been so, until recently. With computers, it is possible to keep track of large numbers of factors over time—details such as the size of the client population of an agency, the numbers and types of workers, and the various expenses related to both services and personnel. This information may be broken down by types of programs within the organization so that the administrator is able to call up for review up-to-date information broken down in any variety of ways, that is, connecting any specific factors with other factors over time. Moreover, in terms of making future plans, the administrator is potentially able to use the computer's *simulation* abilities: if the numbers of workers or the services to clients are changed, other organizational factors will be affected and will change correspondingly. These complex interrelationships can be shown through a computer simulation (cf. Levin, Hirsch, and Roberts, 1972).

Making administrative decisions on the basis of computer-generated or computer-analyzed data seems reasonable, but it stretches the imagination to think about computer-based decision-making as being related to direct practice. In fact, there are several forms of these efforts. One interesting practice involves clients interacting directly with a computer that asks programmed questions, which the person answers by means of typing in responses. Mutschler (1984) reported that not only do some clients accept this type of interview, but some would rather give sensitive information to the computer than to a therapist. She also noted that with the exception of some clients with manic or antisocial personality disorders, the data provided by clients to computers is about as reliable and valid as those provided directly to clinicians. Computers have the advantage of being more systematic (if they are so programmed) and more complete (if clients respond fully). See Kleinmutz (1969) and Weizenbaum (1976) for an interesting review of early computer work in clinical settings.

Another direct-practice use of computers involves processing client data for use in monitoring client behaviors related to services and the objectives of service. It is also possible to combine these kinds of information with financial information, as discussed above in the administrative handling of client data by computers. The primary change involved in using computer technology in direct practice is to make the objectives of that service explicit and measurable (cf. Seaberg, 1965, 1970; Newkham and Bawcom, 1981; and Mutschler, 1979). Then it is possible to enter into the computer the sequence of measured levels of problem behaviors and strengths related to a condition over time. This information is very similar to the kind of information that is graphed in a single-system design (see Chapter 13). Moreover, as in the project described by Newkham and Bawcom, workers also receive summary reports for each of their clients that facilitate

351

close monitoring, planning, and decision making. Newkham and Bawcom concluded that, based on three years experience, the computer information system enhanced client outcomes and provided for clinical and fiscal accountability.

The possibilities for using the computer in research, practice, and administration seem endless. One enterprising student at my school, Mrs. Pamella Darr, designed an information storage and retrieval system for her reading notes. She types in the basic citation and some other information about the article, such as the categories of topics in the article, the service techniques, and the theoretical orientation. Then she adds a brief abstract to remind her of the main points in the article. The type of program she is using enables her to search her "memory" by using key words from the title, the category system, or the abstract itself, in addition to the name of the author. It takes only an instant to type in the information, and it is never forgotten. Moreover, she can generate a bibliography from the file in alphabetical order.

As can be seen from this discussion, the various uses of the computer in the helping professions blend into one another, and yet, by making the distinctions clear, we can explore the special potentials of these technological contributions to human service programs.

COMPUTERS AND STATISTICS

When I was a doctoral student, I spent more hours than I care to remember pushing buttons on an electric calculator in order to do the computations necessary to perform a statistical analysis on the data from my part-time job. My dissertation required that I enter the inner sanctum of the university computer center, then located in a tiny, decrepit building, and—I can scarcely believe it now—actually wire a board to do a simple statistical analysis on my data. I confess to remembering none of the details now, merely my misery and my ignorance—which may have been one and the same. In any case, with the help of the staff, I made my way through that labyrinth sufficiently well to graduate—only to end up pushing buttons on an electric calculator at the Benjamin Rose Institute for many more years.

Today, life is much easier. Students who have had statistics classes still have to push buttons, but if those buttons are connected with computers, things happen much faster—although I suspect the mystery of how things operate still remains, perhaps amplified. In this section, I briefly review some general statistical ideas in order to connect them with work with microcomputers.*

As discussed in Technical Note 6.5, statistics breaks down into the descriptive and the inferential. *Descriptive statistics* answers the following types of questions: (1) What is it (the targets of your investigation)? (2) What is typical about these targets? (3) How much variation from the typical is typical? (4) How are various targets related to one another? (5) Are any relationships causal in nature? These types of questions can be answered by means of the familiar

---

* This discussion of doing *statistical calculations with personal computers* constitutes Technical Note 14.4.

statistical tools, such as frequency counts, mean scores, standard deviations, correlations, and the multivariate techniques that supply the basis for making causal inferences.

Inferential statistics is more challenging. Taking a broad philosophical perspective, I think it is helpful to think of *inferential statistics* as a form of mathematics that seeks to apply the laws of probability and the rules of logic to the specific set of data that reflect the events in question. The laws of probability involve assumptions about how events would occur in nature, if left to their own devices. Many events would be distributed in a bell-shaped curve around their own mean; this is the familiar normal probability curve, such as the curve of the weight of all persons in Cleveland. Some people would be "light" and others would be "heavy," but the majority would be in between. Assuming that this normal distribution exists with regard to some event or property like weight, we can compare some sample with the total population and ask various questions, such as: Is the sample's weight like the distributions of weights in the city as a whole? How many people can be expected to be "heavy" (i.e., at or above a certain weight)? When we include in the assumption that mental health or mental clarity is also normally distributed, then we begin to see what a powerful tool having this theoretical curve as a frame of reference can be.

There are many ways of performing statistical operations. Each statistical formula expresses some rules that are implied because of the kind of data being used (Stevens, 1951). (See also Technical Note 3.5, pp. 93–95.) Some types of data describe events in a *nominal* fashion; that is, they simply name an event as belonging or not belonging to a given category. For example, a person is placed in either a male or a female category. Or if we are considering "the aged," we have to define categories; for example, ages sixty to seventy-four represent the "young-old," and ages seventy-five and older represent the "old old." These are arbitrary definitions, but they define specific categories.

Other sets of rules describe the *ordinal* relationship of events to one another: greater or lesser, better or worse, and so on. No specific *amount* of difference is implied. The ordinal level includes all of the characteristics of the nominal level; that is, this system of levels of measurement is cumulative. Much of the research in the social and behavioral sciences involves ordinal-level information.

The other, higher levels of measurement, interval and ratio levels, involve measures that operate as does the ordinary number system, where we add and subtract numbers. In the case of ratio measures, we have an absolute zero point that enables us to form ratios between sets of numbers. Because the levels of measurement are cumulative, we can use the lower-level statistics for the higher-level data—but not vice versa; however, if we did, we would lose some of the information that is available to us in these more powerful data. If we use weaker data with more powerful statistics, we are violating the assumptions by which the statistics are calculated, and even though we can get "answers," they have less meaning than they appear to. Indeed, they may have no meaning at all.

Let me propose the following general questions, which may help you to determine which level of measurement and analysis your data most properly belong to. Suppose that you ask your client to rate his feelings of depression using a 5-point scale ranging from very high to very low. What level of data would this response represent?

1. Are the categories that the respondent may use clear and distinct? (These are nominal data, if this is the only question you can answer affirmatively. If you can't answer even this question, then you'd better reconsider your research.)
2. Does a response clearly indicate events that are in an ordered relationship to one another? (Be careful, because semantic scales may not indicate actual relationships.)
3. Does it make any sense to add or subtract the events you are studying? Are the intervals between two events equal? (Again, be careful. Even the familiar letter grades, A, B, C, D, and F, are not equal intervals apart inspite of the "grade-point averages" calculated.)
4. Is there an absolute zero or beginning point to the events under consideration? (Letter grades do not begin at Z, or zero, but weight in pounds does.)

Various writers place the host of types of statistics at one or another level of measurement. For example, see Siegel (1956) for a thorough discussion of types of statistics at the various levels of measurement. What I would like to do now is to illustrate how a basic statistic—let's consider the chi-square test—can be connected with the microcomputer in order to simplify the effort involved in computing the statistic. As you recall from your statistics classes, the chi-square test determines whether two variables are independent. In research, one would frequently like to know whether the observed frequencies with which some objects fall into certain categories could have happened as they did by chance alone. For example, would elderly men or women prefer to live in their own homes or with their adult children? On the face of it, we may not have any idea about how being an elderly male or female is related to wanting to live alone or with others. So we might most reasonably expect that equal proportions of males and females will choose each alternative. The general statistical formula can be expressed as follows:

$$\chi^2 = \sum \frac{(f_o - f_e)^2}{f_e}$$

The χ^2 is simply the name of this statistical procedure, the chi-square test. The f_o means the observed frequency; the f_e means the expected frequency. The summation sign, Σ, means that this product is taken over all categories. In my example of the elderly men and women and their house choices, there are two sets of categories: sex and housing types. So the calculation would proceed as follows: A 2×2 table is constructed so that sex and housing preference are indicated by the two alternatives for each. Then the observed data—let's say that we asked the 164 elderly persons in the Protective Services Project what their preferences were—might look like that in Table 14.1 (these are hypothetical data).

The numbers in parentheses are the expected frequencies (we assume that chance is operating). These numbers are obtained by multiplying the specific row and column marginals together and dividing by the total number. For example, 51 times 137 (with regard to the upper left cell formed by the intersection of these marginals) is 6,987, which is divided by the total number of cases (164), giving 42.6. Next, we subtract each observed frequency from its expected

Table 14.1 Observed Data (hypothetical).

		Sex		
		Male	Female	
Housing Choice	Live in own home	47 (42.6)	90 (94.4)	137
	Live with others	4 (8.4)	23 (18.6)	27
		51	113	$N = 164$

number. For example, $47 - 42.6 = 4.4$; $4 - 8.4 = -4.4$. Then we square these figures: 4.4 squared is 19.36. So is -4.4 squared. Finally, we divide each squared difference $(f_o - f_e)^2$ by the expected frequency (f_e) and add up these numbers. For instance, 19.36 divided by 42.6 $= .454$. The calculations for this chi-square test are shown below:

f_o	f_e	$f_o - f_e$	$(f_o - f_e)^2$	$\dfrac{(f_o - f_e)^2}{f_e}$
47	42.6	4.4	19.36	.454
90	94.4	-4.4	19.36	.205
4	8.4	-4.4	19.36	2.304
23	18.6	4.4	19.36	1.040
				$4.003 = \chi^2$

The number 4.003 isn't the final stop in our analysis. We have to ask about the degrees of freedom that are present in this situation in order to look up the answer on a chi-square table. You recall from your statistics class that degrees of freedom are calculated by this formula: $df =$ (number in row $- 1$) (number in column $- 1$), or $(2 - 1)(2 - 1)$ in this case, which gives 1 df. We enter the table showing critical values of the chi-square in the row marked 1 df and look to see where 4.003 falls. In fact, it falls between the .05 column (3.84) and the .02 column (5.41). The .05 level is commonly taken as a point of statistical significance; lower levels (.02, .01, etc.) may also be used. Something other than chance is operating to produce these results. We don't know what that something is, but this is a beginning point.

Now that wasn't too painful, but with more complicated data and more complex statistical formulas,* the calculation process takes a lot of the enjoyment out of research. With the microcomputer, there is a way to make this task easier. The list of statements in Figure 14.1 is a program for a microcomputer,

---

* For more powerful analyses, or when a person is engaged in research on a full-time basis, it is possible to make use of statistical packages in connection with mainframe computers. A package, such as the most commonly used one, the Statistical Package for the Social Sciences (SPSS) (Nie et al., 1975), permits a researcher to enter his or her data into the computer and instruct it to perform certain statistical operations chosen from a list of available (software) programs.

In some circumstances, it is possible for a researcher to use his or her personal computer and a connecting device (a modem) to communicate with a large mainframe computer. This combination provides the privacy of work in one's own home or office with the power of the large computers.

Figure 14.1 A computer program for computing chi-square test (2 × 2 or larger), using a personal computer.

```
10 REM This program will compute the chi-square statistic for an
        N x K table (at least 2 x 2 size)

20 REM entered by the user in response to the questions asked
        in this program.

30 REM Written by Bard Bloom on 1/3/1984 (more or less voluntarily
        at the request of his father)

40 REM on an IBM PC using Disk Basic.

41 REM This program should run under any reasonable Basic,
        including APPLESOFT.

50 PRINT "What is this collection of data to be called?":

60 INPUT NA$

70 PRINT "How many rows?";

80 INPUT N

90 IF N<2 THEN PRINT "There must be at least two rows." :GOTO 70

100 PRINT "How many columns?"

110 INPUT K

120 IF K<2 THEN PRINT "There must be at least two columns." :GOTO 100

130 DIM X(N,K)

140 FOR I=1 to N

150 PRINT " --- Starting Row ";I;" --- "

160 For J=1 to K

170 PRINT "Observation (";I;",";J;"):";

180 INPUT XX

190 IF XX < 0 THEN PRINT "No Negative Numbers":GOTO 170

200 X(I,J) = XX

210 X(I,J) = XX

220 NEXT J

230 NEXT I

240 REM Print the Data so that the user can be sure it's
        correct.

250 PRINT,

260 For J = 1 TO K

270 PRINT "col";J,

280 NEXT J

290 PRINT

300 FOR I=1 TO N

310 PRINT "row";I;")",

320 FOR J=1 TO K

330 PRINT X(I,J),

340 NEXT J

350 PRINT:  PRINT
    " "

360 NEXT I

370 PRINT "Any corrections (Y for yes)(N for no) ";:INPUT A$:A$=LEFT
        $(A$,1)

380 IF A$<>"Y" AND A$<>"y" GOTO 470

390 PRINT "Row and column number, and correct value:";:INPUT I,J,XX
```

(continued)

Figure 14.1 (*continued*).

```
400 IF I>N THEN PRINT  "There are only ";N;" rows": GOTO 370

410 IF J>K THEN PRINT  "There are only ";K;" columns": GOTO 370

420 IF I<1 OR J<1 THEN PRINT "Rows and columns are numbered 1, 2,...
    ": GOTO 370

430 IF XX<0 THEN PRINT "Frequencies cannot be negative": GOTO 370

440 IF XX<>INT(XX) THEN PRINT "Frequencies must be integers": GOTO
    370

450 X(I,J) = XX

460 GOTO 240 : REM print the data again, showing the revision.

470 REM compute Grand Total

480 GT=0

490 FOR I=1 TO N

500 FOR J=1 TO K

510 GT=GT+X(I,J)

520 NEXT J

530 NEXT I

540 REM Compute row and column sums

550 DIM RS(N), CS(K)

560 FOR I = 1 TO N: RS(I)=0: NEXT I

570 FOR J = 1 TO K: CS(J)=0: NEXT J

580 For I = 1 TO N

590 For J = 1 TO K

600 RS(I) = RS(I) + X(I,J)

610 CS(J) = CS(J) + X(I,J)

620 NEXT J

630 NEXT I

640 DIM E(N,K)

650 FOR I = 1 TO N

660 FOR J = 1 TO K

670 E(I,J) = RS(I) * CS(J) / GT

680 NEXT J

690 NEXT I

700 REM Now, compute the chi square

710 CH = 0

720 FOR I = 1 TO N

730 FOR J = 1 TO K

740 CH = CH + (X(I,J)-E(I,J))*(X(I,J)-E(I,J))  / E(I,J)

750 NEXT J

760 NEXT I

770 DF = (N-1) * (K-1)

780 CC = SQR( CH / (CH + GT) )

790 PRINT " --- "; N; " By "; K; " Chi-Square Analysis of ";
        NA$; " --- "

800 PRINT "Chi Square = "; CH; " with "; DF; "degrees of freedom "

810 PRINT "Contingency Coefficient is "; CC

820 END
```

courtesy of my son, Bard, the computer-science specialist in the family. Once you enter this program in your computer, you can then simply punch in the raw data in a sequence that the program itself asks for, and you have your answer in a trice. The program will compute the chi-square statistic for any size of table, but it must be at least 2 × 2, as in our example. The program is self-explanatory; indeed, Bard has built in some corrections for problems that you might accidently create. Try it and see what you think of the coming generation of statistics classes and research.

A few words of explanation about this computer program for a chi-square analysis. A user would first have to prepare a personal computer to receive this kind of statistical procedure. Unfortunately, there is no standard way to do this among the many brands of personal computers available today. For the IBM PC, one instruction is given on line 40: Use Disk Basic. For the Apple Computer, line 41 indicates the name of the program commonly used for calculations: APPLESOFT. In general, the user must be able to get his or her computer into a Basic language and system that permits him or her to type in numbers and run programs.

The next step is to type in the entire program exactly as shown, with all the funny notations and spacing. If you do all this typing and then find that the program doesn't work, chances are you have made some minor typing or spacing error. Look carefully as you type.

You can probably guess what most of the symbols mean: REM is a reminder; it doesn't influence the program as such, but simply tells you some facts about it. PRINT is an instruction that tells the computer to print whatever is located between the quotation marks, such as line 50, or to print the value of the variable named, as in line 170. INPUT tells the computer to ask the user for input, that is, to add some needed information.

There are also some loops, that is, sets of instructions that direct the user back to an earlier step if some action he or she has taken isn't allowable. For example, on line 90, if you tried to make a chi-square with only one row, you would be told what the rules are, and directed back to step 70.

Some of the statements in the program are strictly for the computer and need not concern us. Indeed, after we have typed the entire program, and have taken the next step to make it operational—namely, to type RUN at the end of the program—we won't see the full set of detailed instructions we have typed in. All we will see are the sequence of printed questions appearing on the screen that ask for information from us. We supply that information, and the computer does the rest, including printing the answer, along with the degrees of freedom involved in the problem.

SUMMARY AND CONCLUSIONS

This chapter has explored the history and potential of the computer in research in the helping professions, as well as considering word processing and various forms of data management for accountability and decision making. It is a difficult chapter for those who have not yet been exposed to microcomputers, and it is a simplistic chapter for those who have. But it is a necessary chapter in the history of research in the helping professions, for as Mutschler (1984) noted, there is no turning back to a precomputer world (unless we get reduced to nuclear rubble, in which case the whole point is moot). We must begin thinking about how to make use of the computer for scientific and humane activities within the human services system.

The most significant observation about computers in the helping professions, as elsewhere, is the enormously rapid pace of developments. Sanders's (1973) "history" of computers places my birth near the end of "ancient history." Charming. But don't laugh because your birth date probably belongs somewhere in his "Victorian era." The point is, of course, that we must change as rapidly as the technology about us, while maintaining the humanistic values of the helping professions. This is a great challenge and a great opportunity.

CHAPTER 15

In the Passing of Time: What Difference Does Research Make?

Overview

This is one chapter you can read without any fear. Your teacher won't ask you any questions on a test from it; I haven't included any foreign language in it. This is a chapter of reminiscences and musings: I raise the question about what difference research makes—particularly to the agency that supported the research in the first place. I returned to Benjamin Rose Institute after a long absence, and I report what I found there—and its relationship to the research that Margaret Blenkner originated.

But in addition, I raise an even more important question: What difference does a vicarious experience of research make to you, in your career? My "answers" are stated as predictions. Time will tell whether they are accurate or not.

Narrative Section

Introduction
Diffusion of Information
And What Difference Does *The Experience of Research* Make to You?

360

The Narrative

INTRODUCTION

After an absence of nearly a decade, I returned to the Benjamin Rose Institute as I began my work on this textbook, at the kind invitation of its director, Dr. Barbara Silverstone. I confess that many memories returned as I took the rapid-transit train from the airport directly to downtown Cleveland. Even more memories were awakened as I entered the lobby of the Rose Building, rode the elevator to the sixth floor, and opened the glass doors to the Institute.

It looked decidedly more humane and in touch with people than when I had last seen the offices. On the entrance walls were big pictures of older persons smiling and coping with the events of everyday life. The formal meeting room of the board of directors looked a lot less forbidding; the fancy tables were gone, and the room looked as if it received frequent and heavy use. In place of the old rackety secretarial pool was a quiet and serene library with its specialized collection on the aged (including all of Margaret Blenkner's papers and publications).

Looking for ghosts, I returned to my old office next to Dr. Blenkner's. Egad! They were veritably empty. I learned that the research department had so greatly expanded that it now occupied separate suites of offices down the hall. I was pleased to be able to meet some of the current research staff, and to learn about the enormous number of completed projects and plans for new projects. I was especially interested in what effects, if any, the Blenkner years had had on the Institute and, in particular, its research arm. Indeed, this is a general question: What happens when research projects are completed? How is knowledge translated from empirical studies (and the theoretical frames of reference from which they are drawn) to practice? What is the role, if any, of the researcher in aiding that translation?

Let me begin with a brief overview of the new Benjamin Rose Institute, under the capable direction of Dr. Silverstone. You may be more familiar with her if you have read her book (coauthored with Helen Kandel) *You and Your Aging Parent,* or if you have seen her on such national television shows as the Mike Wallace show or the Phil Donahue program, because she is an effective communicator on behalf of the aged. (You will also see her work in leadership positions in the Gerontological Society and in various professional publications.) This visibility is far different from the days of old when social workers were simply more quiet and worked through professional channels only. The point is important, because research findings may be transmitted through the mass media as well as through published technical papers and presentations.

Other changes were very visible to me. There were many more men working at the agency, more minority-group members, more non-WASPs, reflecting the values that were permeating the research and service enterprises. I have stressed throughout this book the importance of cultural factors such as these, for the health of a vital research program as well as a vital practice program in a community. I was delighted to observe these changes, and to be informed about more

361

fundamental shifts in agency policy that had occurred in the past few years.

The board and the staff of the Institute had participated in discussions leading to long-range objectives that had shifted from helping older persons in general to providing services for a specific subpopulation of frail and impaired elderly by developing a continuum of care within the network of Institute programs and facilities. Another long-range objective, reflecting the Institute's already long history of contributions, was to exemplify a "model service agency" whose main goal was the delivery of services and training that could be studied for cost-effectiveness and thus could serve as models for wider replication.

DIFFUSION OF INFORMATION

I couldn't help wondering how these changes had come about. Were they in any way connected with Margaret Blenkner's hammering away at traditional social work, even as practiced in its exemplary fashion at the Institute of that day? The populations that she had studied—and had thus brought to the attention of staff, board, and the community at large—were the frail and impaired elderly. (She wasn't alone in this study, of course, but perhaps she had been more conspicuous in making these observations than others.) And also, the effects of her research had stimulated many critical reactions, perhaps modeling a vigorous infusion of research into the practice realm. Of course, the Institute had modeled other activities before; it was among the first to set up senior citizen centers in the late 1930s, I am told. But again, I think it was Margaret Blenkner's highly visible research that had made the potentiality of a model agency an achieveable reality. She was a catalyst of the first magnitude, a fact recognized in 1979, when the Institute officially changed the name of its research department to the Margaret Blenkner Research Center.

Let me mention just a few of the projects of the recent Benjamin Rose Institute. Outposts of the central office have been established to provide neighborhood-based services to the frail and impaired elderly. The first such outpost was at one of the agencies that had referred participants to the Projective Services Project. Another project involves Community Care, providing short-term direct health and social services, as well as referral to community agencies for other aid, including long-term services as needed. This project sounds like one translation of Dr. Blenkner's New York study, where short-term services by a team of public health nurses and social workers had proved to be the method of choice.

The agency had also received federal support for a study of the effects on families of caring for the impaired elderly in their community residences. The results of this study are soon to be published. This project might have arisen from the findings of the Home Aide Study, which cited the presence of a helping natural network as vital in the prevention of institutionalization, although there were doubtless other factors in its development. New staff people are never saddled with old data, but neither do they have to reinvent the wheel.

From its humble beginnings in the Protective Services Project, and from its more fully developed context in the Home Aide Study, the Institute has established a Home Health Aide Department. It occupied the same office as did

Associates in Gerontology—but much renovated and enlarged. The tasks of the new department are fully reminiscent of the Home Aide Study.

Also, the Institute has conducted a study of its community clients using some special instruments to provide insights into their health and well-being. Margaret Blenkner had submitted a proposal to develop standardized instruments to be used with community aged, but that proposal was not approved. I am sure that she would have been delighted to see this new phase in the Institute's self-study. This work is also connected with cost-effectiveness studies, a necessary step in trying to identify programs that should or should not be continued, given the scarcity of resources for serving the aged. Dr. Blenkner was very concerned about cost–benefit considerations, as indicated in many of her writings and presentations; she had attempted some exploratory efforts along these lines, too.

I don't want to give the impression that everything that the Benjamin Rose Institute has done recently has flowed from the germinal work of Margaret Blenkner. The current staff members belong to a new breed of workers and researchers. They seem considerably more talented, informed, and active than were the people of my generation. Maybe I am growing old, but with age comes the capacity to appreciate the fine work being done at the Institute. If there is any reward in doing research, it is in imagining that there is some transformation from the empirical and theoretical ideas of which one was a part, to the exciting, vigorous programs that are in place a decade later.

AND WHAT DIFFERENCE DOES *THE EXPERIENCE OF RESEARCH* MAKE TO YOU?

Imagine that it is a decade after you have finished this class in research. By chance, you come upon your old textbook and remember the very last section of the book, the part that asks you: What difference does *The Experience of Research* make to you in your own life and career? You will probably remember laughing at my predictions—"That will never happen to me!"—but in ten years' time, who knows?

First, I predict that very *few* of you who enter the human service professions will have conducted a large-scale research project, such as the one described in this book. This doesn't mean that you will not have thought about vital questions that could well have been subjected to large-scale research, but only that few of you will actually have carried out such research.

On the other hand, I also predict that *most of you will have participated in one or another type of research project as part of your job.* You may be part of an experimental service team, or even part of the research staff conducting interviews and analyzing the data. But I predict that within the decade, most of you will have gained firsthand experience of group research. The basis of this prediction is that accountability in human services will probably continue to grow, whereas specialized research departments such as BRI may not. Hence collaborative projects are likely to be conducted, and thus more professionals will become involved.

A third prediction is that you will *like* participating in a research project, regardless of your feelings about the research class. You might remember, although doubtless with less clarity than your instructor and I would wish, the love and the passion that go into research, the agony of necessary detail and the ecstasy of discovery, the vast amounts of information that flow to and from the project along with the enormous uncertainties that are a part of every study. And you will remember my prediction that you will like research because it is a nearly universal experience of people who have become deeply involved in an intellectual and empirical exploration.

A fourth prediction: I have no doubt that *almost all of you will have conducted evaluations of your own practice.* I foresee this as an inevitable aspect of the future helping professions. This, too, will be an *experience of research,* one that is very personal to you and your career, yet no less universal, no less scientific.

And the final prediction: About this time (if not sooner), *you will probably be conveying your sense of the experience of research to others* entering the human services. You know how it feels; now it is your turn to try to convey this feeling to others.

And so, in one way or another, I expect you to have a taste of research and evaluation. I only hope your experience with this book has properly whetted your appetite with pleasurable and challenging expectations.

Application Forms for a Public-Health-Service Grant

Form approved
OMB No. 0925-0001

DEPARTMENT OF HEALTH AND HUMAN SERVICES PUBLIC HEALTH SERVICE	LEAVE BLANK		
	TYPE	ACTIVITY	NUMBER
GRANT APPLICATION	REVIEW GROUP		FORMERLY
FOLLOW INSTRUCTIONS CAREFULLY	COUNCIL/BOARD *(Month, year)*		DATE RECEIVED

1. TITLE OF APPLICATION *(Do not exceed 56 typewriter spaces)*

2. RESPONSE TO SPECIFIC PROGRAM ANNOUNCEMENT ☐ NO ☐ YES *(If "YES," state RFA number and/or announcement title)*

3. PRINCIPAL INVESTIGATOR/PROGRAM DIRECTOR

3a. NAME *(Last, first, middle)*	3b. SOCIAL SECURITY NUMBER
3c. POSITION TITLE	3d. MAILING ADDRESS *(Street, city, state, zip code)*
3e. DEPARTMENT, SERVICE, LABORATORY OR EQUIVALENT	
3f. MAJOR SUBDIVISION	3g. TELEPHONE *(Area code, number and extension)*

4. HUMAN SUBJECTS	5. RECOMBINANT DNA
☐ NO ☐ YES { ☐ Exemption # _____ **OR** ☐ Form HHS 596 enclosed	☐ NO ☐ YES

6. DATES OF ENTIRE PROPOSED PROJECT PERIOD	7. DIRECT COSTS REQUESTED FOR FIRST 12-MONTH BUD-GET PERIOD *(from page 4)*	8. DIRECT COSTS REQUESTED FOR ENTIRE PROPOSED PROJECT PERIOD *(from page 5)*
From: Through:	$	$

9. PERFORMANCE SITES *(Organizations and addresses)*	10. INVENTIONS *(Competing continuation application only)*
	☐ NO ☐ YES { ☐ Previously reported **OR** ☐ Not previously reported
	11. APPLICANT ORGANIZATION *(Name, address, and congressional district)*

12. TYPE OF ORGANIZATION	13. ENTITY IDENTIFICATION NUMBER
☐ Public. Specify ☐ Federal ☐ State ☐ Local ☐ Private Nonprofit ☐ For Profit *(General)* ☐ For Profit *(Small Business)*	14. ORGANIZATIONAL COMPONENT TO RECEIVE CREDIT FOR BIOMEDICAL RESEARCH SUPPORT GRANT Code ☐☐ Description
15. OFFICIAL IN BUSINESS OFFICE TO BE NOTIFIED IF AN AWARD IS MADE *(Name, title, address and telephone number.)*	16. OFFICIAL SIGNING FOR APPLICANT ORGANIZATION *(Name, title, address and telephone number)*

17. PRINCIPAL INVESTIGATOR/PROGRAM DIRECTOR ASSURANCE: I agree to accept responsibility for the scientific conduct of the project and to provide the required progress reports if a grant is awarded as a result of this application. Willful provision of false information is a criminal offense *(U.S. Code, Title 18, Section 1001)*.	SIGNATURE OF PERSON NAMED IN 3a *(In ink. "Per" signature not acceptable)*	DATE
18. CERTIFICATION AND ACCEPTANCE: I certify that the statements herein are true and complete to the best of my knowledge, and accept the obligation to comply with Public Health Service terms and conditions if a grant is awarded as the result of this application. A willfully false certification is a criminal offense *(U.S. Code, Title 18, Section 1001)*.	SIGNATURE OF PERSON NAMED IN 16 *(In ink. "Per" signature not acceptable)*	DATE

PHS 398 (Rev. 5/82)

PRINCIPAL INVESTIGATOR/PROGRAM DIRECTOR: _____

ABSTRACT OF RESEARCH PLAN

KEY PROFESSIONAL PERSONNEL ENGAGED ON PROJECT

NAME	POSITION TITLE	DEPARTMENT AND ORGANIZATION

ABSTRACT OF RESEARCH PLAN: State the application's long-term objectives and specific aims, making reference to the health relatedness of the project, and describe concisely the methodology for achieving these goals. Avoid summaries of past accomplishments and the use of the first person. The abstract is meant to serve as a succinct and accurate description of the proposed work when separated from the application. **DO NOT EXCEED THE SPACE PROVIDED.**

VERTEBRATE ANIMALS INVOLVED ☐ NO ☐ YES If "YES," identify by common names and underline primates.

PHS 398 (Rev. 5/82) PAGE 2

TABLE OF CONTENTS

Number pages consecutively at the bottom throughout the application. Do not use suffixes such as 5a, 5b. Type the name of the Principal Investigator/Program Director at the top of each printed page and each continuation page.

SECTION 1.   PAGE NUMBERS

SECTION 3. Appendix *(Six sets) (No page numbering necessary for Appendix)*

Number of publications: _____   Number of manuscripts: _____
Other items *(list)*:

☐ Application Receipt Record, Form PHS 3830
☐ Form HHS 596 if Item 4, page 1, is checked "YES" and no exemptions are designated.

PRINCIPAL INVESTIGATOR/PROGRAM DIRECTOR: _____

DETAILED BUDGET FOR FIRST 12 MONTH BUDGET PERIOD
DIRECT COSTS ONLY

FROM	THROUGH

DOLLAR AMOUNT REQUESTED *(Omit cents)*

PERSONNEL *(Applicant organization only)*		TIME/EFFORT		SALARY	FRINGE BENEFITS	TOTALS
NAME	POSITION TITLE	%	Hours per Week			
	Principal Investigator					
	SUBTOTALS ⟶					

CONSULTANT COSTS

EQUIPMENT *(Itemize)*

SUPPLIES *(Itemize by category)*

TRAVEL	DOMESTIC	
	FOREIGN	
PATIENT CARE COSTS	INPATIENT	
	OUTPATIENT	

ALTERATIONS AND RENOVATIONS *(Itemize by category)*

CONSORTIUM/CONTRACTUAL COSTS

OTHER EXPENSES *(Itemize by category)*

TOTAL DIRECT COSTS *(Also enter on page 1, item 7)* ⟶ $

PHS 398 (Rev. 5/82)   PAGE 4

369

PRINCIPAL INVESTIGATOR/PROGRAM DIRECTOR: _____

BUDGET FOR ENTIRE PROPOSED PROJECT PERIOD
DIRECT COSTS ONLY

BUDGET CATEGORY TOTALS		1st BUDGET PERIOD *(from page 4)*	ADDITIONAL YEARS SUPPORT REQUESTED			
			2nd	3rd	4th	5th
PERSONNEL *(Salary and fringe benefits.)* *(Applicant organization only)*						
CONSULTANT COSTS						
EQUIPMENT						
SUPPLIES						
TRAVEL	DOMESTIC					
	FOREIGN					
PATIENT CARE COSTS	INPATIENT					
	OUTPATIENT					
ALTERATIONS AND RENOVATIONS						
CONSORTIUM/ CONTRACTUAL COSTS						
OTHER EXPENSES						
TOTAL DIRECT COSTS						

TOTAL FOR ENTIRE PROPOSED PROJECT PERIOD *(Also enter on page 1, item 8)* ———▶ | $

JUSTIFICATION (Use continuation pages if necessary): Describe the specific functions of the personnel and consultants. If a recurring annual increase in personnel costs is anticipated, give the percentage. For *all* years, justify any costs for which the need may not be obvious, such as equipment, foreign travel, alterations and renovations, and consortium/contractual costs. For any additional years of support requested, justify any significant increases in any category over the first 12 month budget period. In addition, for COMPETING CONTINUATION applications, justify any significant increases over the current level of support.

PRINCIPAL INVESTIGATOR/PROGRAM DIRECTOR: _____

BIOGRAPHICAL SKETCH

Give the following information for key professional personnel listed on page 2, beginning with the
Principal Investigator/Program Director. Photocopy this page for each person.

NAME	TITLE	BIRTHDATE *(Mo., Day, Yr.)*

EDUCATION *(Begin with baccalaureate or other initial professional education and include postdoctoral training)*

INSTITUTION AND LOCATION	DEGREE *(circle highest degree)*	YEAR CONFERRED	FIELD OF STUDY

RESEARCH AND/OR PROFESSIONAL EXPERIENCE: Concluding with present position, list in chronological order previous employment, experience, and honors. Include present membership on any Federal Government Public Advisory Committee. List, in chronological order, the titles and complete references to all publications during the past three years and to representative earlier publications pertinent to this application. **DO NOT EXCEED TWO PAGES.**

OTHER SUPPORT

(Use continuation pages if necessary)

For each of the professionals named on page 2, list, in three separate groups: (1) active support; (2) applications and proposals pending review or funding; (3) applications and proposals planned or being prepared for submission. Include *all* Federal, non-Federal, and institutional grant and contract support. If none, state "none." For each item give the source of support, identifying number, project title, name of principal investigator/program director, time or percent of effort on the project by professional named, annual direct costs, and entire period of support. (If part of a larger project, provide the titles of both the parent project and the subproject and give the annual direct costs for each.) Describe the contents of each item listed. If any of these overlap, duplicate, or are being replaced or supplemented by the present application, delineate and justify the nature and extent of the scientific and budgetary overlaps or boundaries.

PRINCIPAL INVESTIGATOR/PROGRAM DIRECTOR:
(1) ACTIVE SUPPORT:

PRINCIPAL INVESTIGATOR/PROGRAM DIRECTOR: _____

RESOURCES AND ENVIRONMENT

FACILITIES: Mark the facilities to be used at the applicant organization and briefly indicate their capacities, pertinent capabilities, relative proximity and extent of availability to the project. Use "other" to describe the facilities at any other performance sites listed in Item 9, page 1, and at sites for field studies. Using continuation pages if necessary, include an explanation of any consortium arrangements with other organizations.

☐ Laboratory:

☐ Clinical:

☐ Animal:

☐ Computer:

☐ Office:

☐ Other (_____):

MAJOR EQUIPMENT: List the most important equipment items already available for this project, noting the location and pertinent capabilities of each.

ADDITIONAL INFORMATION: Provide any other information describing the environment for the project. Identify support services such as consultants, secretarial, machine shop, and electronics shop, and the extent to which they will be available to the project.

PHS 398 (Rev. 5/82)   PAGE _____

373

PRINCIPAL INVESTIGATOR/PROGRAM DIRECTOR:_____

CHECKLIST

This is the required last page of the application.
(Check the appropriate boxes and provide the information requested.)

TYPE OF APPLICATION

☐ NEW application *(This application is being submitted to the PHS for the first time.)*

☐ COMPETING CONTINUATION of grant number: _____ .
(This application is to extend a funded grant beyond its current project period.)

☐ SUPPLEMENT to grant number: _____ .
(This application is for additional funds to supplement a currently funded grant.)

☐ REVISION of application number: _____ .
(This application replaces a prior unfunded version of a new, competing continuation or supplemental application.)

☐ Change of Principal Investigator/Program Director.
Name of former Principal Investigator/Program Director: _____ .

ASSURANCES *(See GENERAL INFORMATION section of instructions.)*

a. Civil Rights	b. Handicapped Individuals	c. Sex Discrimination	d. Vertebrate Animals *(If applicable)*	e. Human Subjects *(If applicable)*
☐ Filed ☐ Not filed	☐ Filed ☐ Not filed	☐ Filed ☐ Not filed	☐ Filed ☐ Not filed	☐ Filed ☐ Not filed

INDIRECT COSTS

Indicate the applicant organization's most recent indirect cost rate established with the appropriate DHHS Regional Office. If the applicant organization is in the process of initially developing or renegotiating a rate, or has established a rate with another Federal agency, it should, immediately upon notification that an award will be made, develop a tentative indirect cost rate proposal based on its most recently completed fiscal year in accordance with the principles set forth in the pertinent *DHHS Guide for Establishing Indirect Cost Rates,* and submit it to the appropriate DHHS Regional Office. Indirect costs will not be paid on foreign grants, construction grants, and grants to individuals, and usually not on grants in support of conferences.

☐ DHHS Agreement Dated: _____

_____ % Salary and Wages *or* _____ % Total Direct Costs.

Is this an off-site or other special rate, or is more than one rate involved?   ☐ NO   ☐ YES
(If "YES," explain and provide the basis for the indirect cost calculation.)

☐ DHHS Agreement being negotiated with _____ Regional Office.

☐ No DHHS Agreement, but rate established with _____ Date _____

☐ No Indirect Costs Requested.

PHS 398 (Rev. 5/82)   PAGE _____

PRINCIPAL INVESTIGATOR/PROGRAM DIRECTOR: _____

Detach and clip this page (unnumbered) to the signed original
of the face page of the application. Do not duplicate.

PERSONAL DATA ON
PRINCIPAL INVESTIGATOR/PROGRAM DIRECTOR

The Public Health Service has a continuing commitment to monitoring the operation of its review and award processes to detect—and deal appropriately with—any instances of real or apparent inequities with respect to age, sex, race, or ethnicity of the proposed principal investigator/program director.

To provide the PHS with the information it needs for this important task, the principal investigator/program director is requested to complete the form below and attach a single copy to the signed face page of the application.

Upon receipt and assignment of the application by the PHS, this form will be detached from the application. It will NOT be duplicated and will NOT be a part of the review process. Data will be confidential, and will be maintained in Privacy Act record system 09-25-0036, "Grants: IMPAC (Grant Contract Information)." All analyses conducted on the data will report aggregate statistical findings only and will not identify individuals.

If you decline to provide this information, it will in no way affect consideration of your application.

Your cooperation will be appreciated.

DATE OF BIRTH *(month/day/year)*	SEX
	☐ Female ☐ Male

RACE AND/OR ETHNIC ORIGIN *(check one)*

☐ American Indian or Alaskan Native

☐ Asian or Pacific Islander

☐ Black, not of Hispanic origin

☐ Hispanic

☐ White, not of Hispanic origin

NOTE: The category that most closely reflects the individual's recognition in the community should be used for purposes of reporting mixed racial and/or ethnic origins. Definitions are as follows:

American Indian or Alaskan Native: A person having origins in any of the original peoples of North America, and who maintains cultural identification through tribal affiliation or community recognition.

Asian or Pacific Islander: A person having origins in any of the original peoples of the Far East, Southeast Asia, the Indian subcontinent, or the Pacific Islands. This area includes, for example, China, India, Japan, Korea, the Philippine Islands and Samoa.

Black, not of Hispanic origin: A person having origins in any of the black racial groups of Africa.

Hispanic: A person of Mexican, Puerto Rican, Cuban, Central or South American or other Spanish culture or origin, regardless of race.

White, not of Hispanic origin: A person having origins in any of the original peoples of Europe, North Africa, or the Middle East.

PHS 398 (Rev. 5/82)

List of Technical Notes by Chapter

Chapter 1

1.1 Scientific Definitions
1.2 Demographic Characteristics of the Sample
1.3 Experimental and Control Groups
1.4 Types of Research: Laboratory, Field Studies, Field Experiments, and Field Demonstrations
1.5 Research Designs and Practice Designs
1.6 Goals of Research: Ultimate, Intermediate, and Immediate
1.7 Randomization and Matching

Chapter 2

2.1 Epidemiology
2.2 Longitudinal and Cross-sectional Studies
2.3 Needs Assessments
2.4 Basic and Applied Research
2.5 Research Proposals
2.6 Research and Evaluation
2.7 The BRI Protective Services Proposals
2.8 Population, Sample, and Case
2.9 Group Research Designs: An Overview

Chapter 3

3.1 Ethics in Research
3.2 Information Retrieval

Chapter 7

Chapter 8

Chapter 9

Chapter 10

Chapter 11

Bibliography

Adams, J. L. *Conceptual Blockbusting: A Pleasurable Guide to Better Problem Solving.* New York: W. W. Norton, 1974.

Albee, G. "The argument for primary prevention." In H. A. Marlowe and R. B. Weinberg (eds.). *Primary Prevention: Fact or Fallacy?* Tampa: University of South Florida, 1983.

Aldrich, C. K. "Personality factors and mortality in the relocation of the aged." *The Gerontologist,* 4 (1964), 92–93.

Aldrich, C. K., and Mendkoff, E. "Relocation of the aged and disabled: A mortality study." *Journal of the American Geriatrics Society,* 11 (1963), 185–194.

Alexsandrowicz, D. R. "Fire and its aftermath on a geriatric ward." *Bulletin of the Menninger Clinic,* 25 (1961), 22–33.

Allen, B. R., and Horniman, A. B. *Child Welfare and the Computer: A Project of Potential.* New York: Edwin Gould Foundation for Children, 1969.

Anastasi, A. *Psychological Testing,* 3rd edition. London: Macmillan, 1968.

Asch, S. E. *Social Psychology.* New York: Prentice-Hall, 1950.

Babbie, E. R. *The Practice of Social Research,* 2nd edition. Belmont, Calif.: Wadsworth, 1979.

Bailey, K. D. *Methods of Social Research,* 2nd edition. New York: Free Press, 1982.

Barker, R. G., and Wright, H. F. *One Boy's Day.* New York: Harper & Row, 1951.

Baker, S. B., Swisher, J. D., Nadenichek, P. E., and Popowicz, C. L. "Measured effects of primary prevention strategies," *The Personnel and Guidance Journal,* 62:8 (1984), 459–464.

Barton, H. *Brief Psychotherapies.* New York: Behavioral Publications, 1971.

Bennett, R., and Eisdorfer, C. "The institutional environment and behavior change." In S. Sherwood (ed.). *Long-term Care: A Handbook for Researchers, Planners, and Providers.* New York: Spectrum Publications, Wiley, 1975.

Berger, R., and Piliavin, I. "The effect of casework: A research note." *Social Work* (May 1976), 205–208.

Berger, R., and Piliavin, I. "A rejoinder." *Social Work* (September 1976), 349–351.

Bergin, A. E. "The evaluation of therapeutic outcomes." In A. E. Bergin and S. L. Garfield (eds.). *Handbook of Psychotherapy and Behavior Change.* New York: Wiley, 1971.

Bergin, A. E., and Lambert, M. J. "The evaluation of therapeutic outcomes." In S. L. Garfield and A. E. Bergin (eds.). *Handbook of Psychotherapy and Behavior Change,* 2nd edition. New York: Wiley, 1978.

Beyer, G. H. "Living arrangements, attitudes and preferences of older persons." In C. Tibbitts and W. Donahue (eds.). *Social and Psychological Aspects of Aging.* New York: Columbia University Press, 1962.

Birren, J. E. *Handbook of Aging and the Individual.* Chicago: University of Chicago Press, 1959.

Blackmum, J. "Concurring opinion on O'Bannon *vs.* Town Court, U.S. Supreme Court ruling delivered June 23, 1980." *The United States Law Week,* 48W (1980), 4846–4850.

Blalock, H. M., Jr. *Social Statistics,* 2nd edition. New York: McGraw-Hill, 1972.

Blenkner, M. Demonstration of Protective Services for Older Adults: Project Plans. Cleveland, Ohio, Benjamin Rose Institute, July 1, 1963 (mimeo).

Blenkner, M. "Social work and family relationships in later years with some thoughts on filial maturity." In E. Shanas and G. F. Streib (eds.). *Social Structure and the Family: Generational Relations.* Englewood Cliffs, N.J.: Prentice-Hall, 1965.

Blenkner, M. "Environmental change and the aging individual." *The Gerontologist,* 7 (1967), 101–105.

Blenkner, M., Bloom, M., and Nielsen, M. "A research and demonstration project of protective services." *Social Casework,* 52:8 (1971), 483–499.

Blenkner, M., Bloom, M., Nielsen, M., and Weber, R. Final Report: Protective Services for Older People. Findings from the Benjamin Rose Institute Study. Cleveland: Benjamin Rose Institute, 1974 (mimeo).

Blenkner, M., Bloom, M., and South, V. Protective Services for Older People: Progress Report, 1965–1966. Cleveland: Benjamin Rose Institute, 1966 (mimeo).

Blenkner, M., Bloom, M., and Weber, R. E. Protective Services for Older People: Final Report on the Planning Phase of a Research and Demonstration Project. Cleveland: Benjamin Rose Institute, 1964 (mimeo).

Blenkner, M., Jahn, J., and Wasser, E. Serving the Aging: An Experiment in Social Work and Public Health Nursing. New York: Community Service Society, 1964 (mimeo).

Blenkner, M., Wasser, E., and Bloom, M. Protective Services for Older People: Progress Report, 1966–1967. Cleveland: Benjamin Rose Institute, 1967 (mimeo).

Bloom, M. The Initial Research Interview. Cleveland: Benjamin Rose Institute, 1964 (mimeo).

Bloom, M. *Life Span Development.* New York: Macmillan, 1980.

Bloom, M. *Life Span Development,* 2nd edition. New York: Macmillan, 1985.

Bloom, M., and Blenkner, M. The Follow-up Interviews. Cleveland: Benjamin Rose Institute, 1966 (mimeo).

Bloom, M., and Block, S. R. "Evaluating one's own effectiveness and efficiency." *Social Work,* 22 (1977), 130–136.

Bloom, M., Butch, P., and Walker, D. "Evaluation of single interventions." *Journal of Social Service Research,* 2:3 (1979), 301–310.

Bloom, M., and Chellam, G. Demographic Profile of Cleveland's Older Population: A Fact Book, 1963. Cleveland: Benjamin Rose Institute, 1963 (mimeo).

Bloom, M., Duchon, E., Frires, G., Hanson, H., Hurd, G., and South, V. "Interviewing the ill aged." *The Gerontologist,* 11:4 (Part 1), (1971), 292–299.

Bloom, M., and Farrar, M. "Becoming a professional social worker: Two conceptual models." *Social Work Education Reporter,* 20:2 (1972), 23–26.

Bloom, M., and Fischer, J. *Evaluating Practice: Guidelines for the Accountable Professional.* Englewood Cliffs, N.J.: Prentice-Hall, 1982.

Bloom, M., Frires, G., Hanson, H., and South, V. "The use of interpreters in interviewing: Characteristics, conceptualization, and cautions." *Mental Hygiene,* 50:2 (1966), 214–217.

Bloom, M., and Nielsen, M. "The older person in need of protective services." *Social Casework,* 52:8 (1971), 500–509.

Booth, C. (ed.) *Life and Labour of the People of London.* London: Macmillan & Co., 1892–1897.

Borup, J. H. "Relocation: Attitudes, information network, and problems encountered." *The Gerontologist,* 21 (1981), 501–511.

Borup, J. H. "The effects of varying degrees of interinstitutional environmental change on long-term care patients." *The Gerontologist,* 22 (1982), 409–417.

Borup, J. H. "Relocation mortality research: Assessment, reply, and the need to refocus on the issues." *The Gerontologist,* 23:3 (1983), 235–242.

Borup, J. H., and Gallego, D. "Mortality as affected by interinstitutional relocation: Update and assessment." *The Gerontologist,* 21 (1981), 8–16.

Borup, J. H., Gallego, D., and Heffernan, P. "Relocation and its effect on mortality." *The Gerontologist,* 19 (1979), 135–140.

Borup, J. H., Gallego, D., and Heffernan, P. "Relocation: Its effect on health, functioning, and mortality." *The Gerontologist,* 20 (1980), 468–479.

Bourestom, N., and Pastalan, L. "The effects of relocation on the elderly. A reply to J. H. Borup, D. T. Gallego, and P. G. Heffernan." *The Gerontologist,* 21 (1981), 4–7.

Bourestom, N., and Tars, S. "Alteration in life patterns following nursing home relocation." *The Gerontologist,* 14 (1974), 506–510.

Breslow, L. "The public health problem." In A. Simon and L. J. Epstein (eds.). *Aging in Modern Society.* Washington, D.C.: American Psychriatric Assoc., 1968.

Brody, E., Kleban, M., and Morris, M. "Measuring the impact of change." *The Gerontologist,* 14 (1974), 299–305.

Buros, O. K. (ed.). *The Eighth Mental Measurement Yearbook* (2 vols.). Highland Park, N.J.: Gryphon Press, 1978.

Butler, R. N., and Lewis, M. I. *Aging and Mental Health: Positive Psychosocial and Biomedical Approaches,* 3rd edition. St. Louis: Mosby, 1982.

Camargo, O., and Preston, G. H. "What happens to patients who are hospitalized for the first time when over 65 years of age?" *American Journal of Psychiatry,* 102 (1945), 168–173.

Campbell, D. T., and Fiske, D. W. "Convergent and discriminant validation by the multitrait-multimethod matrix." *Psychological Bulletin,* 56 (1959), 81–105.

Campbell, D. T., and Stanley, J. C. *Experimental and Quasi-Experimental Designs for Research.* Chicago: Rand McNally, 1963.

Carnap, R. "Testability and meaning." In H. Feigl and M. Brodbeck (eds.). *Readings in the Philosophy of Science.* New York: Appleton-Century-Crofts, 1953.

Carp, F. "Effects of improved housing on the lives of older people." In B. Neugarten (ed.). *Middle Age and Aging.* Chicago: University of Chicago Press, 1968.

Code of Federal Regulations, Title 45 Public Welfare. Department of Health and Human Services, National Institutes of Health, and Office for Protection from Research Risks. Part 46—Protection of Human Subjects revised as of March 8, 1983. Washington, D.C.: Government Printing Office, 1983.

Coffman, T. L. "Relocation and survival of institutionalized aged: A reexamination of the evidence." *The Gerontologist,* 21 (1981), 483–500.

Cohen, E. S. "Legal issues in 'transfer trauma' and their impact." *The Gerontologist,* 21 (1981), 520–522.

Cohen, J. *Statistical Power Analysis for the Behavioral Sciences.* New York: Academic Press, 1969.

Colett, I. V. "The case of Lisa H. The role of mental health professionals where the social contract is violated." *International Journal of Social Psychiatry,* 28:4 (1982), 283–285.

Collins, A. H., and Pancoast, D. L. *Natural Helping Networks: A Strategy for Prevention.* Washington, D.C.: National Association of Social Workers, 1976.

Cook, T. D., and Campbell, D. T. "The design and conduct of quasi-experiments and true experiments in field settings." In M. Dunnette (ed.). *Handbook of Industrial and Organizational Psychology.* Chicago: Rand McNally, 1976.

Cook, T. D., and Campbell, D. T. *Quasi-Experimentation: Design and Analysis for Field Settings.* Chicago: Rand McNally, 1979.

Cormier, W. H., and Cormier, L. S. *Interviewing Strategies for Helpers: A Guide to Assessment, Treatment, and Evaluation.* Monterey, Calif.: Brooks/Cole, 1979.

Csank, J. Z., and Zweig, J. P. "Relative mortality of chronically ill geriatric patients with organic brain damage, before and after relocation." *Journal of the American Geriatric Society,* 28 (1980), 76–83.

Davenport, J. A., and Davenport, J., III. "Helping rape victims in rural areas." In S. B. Day (ed.). *Life Stress: A Companion to the Life Sciences,* Vol. 3. New York: Van Nostrand Reinhold, 1982.

Diagnostic and Statistical Manual of Mental Disorders, 3rd edition—DSM-III, Classifications with Annotations by R. L. Spitzer and J. B. W. Williams. Washington, D.C.: American Psychiatric Association, 1980.

Dixon, W. J., and Massey, F. J., Jr. *Introduction to Statistical Analysis,* 3rd edition. New York: McGraw-Hill, 1969.

Dunkle, R. E. Protective Services for Older People: A Reanalysis of the Benjamin Rose Institute Study. Cleveland: Benjamin Rose Institute, 1981 (mimeo).

Dunkle, R. E., Poulshock, W. P., Silverstone, B., and Deimling, G. T. "Protective services reanalyzed: Does casework help or harm?" *Social Casework,* 64:3 (1983), 195–199.

Edelwich, J., and Brodsky, A. *Burn-out: States of Disillusionment in the Helping Professions.* New York: Human Sciences Press, 1980.

Ellis, A. *Reason and Emotion in Psychotherapy.* New York: Lyle Stuart, 1962.

Epstein, R., and Lindley, E. (eds.). *Seminar on Protective Services for Older People: Proceedings of a Seminar Held at Arden House, Harriman, New York, March 10–15, 1963.* New York: National Council on the Aging, 1964.

Eysenck, H. J. "The effects of psychotherapy: An evaluation." *Journal of Counseling Psychology,* 16 (1952), 319–324.

Eysenck, H. J. *The Effects of Psychotherapy.* New York: International Science Press, 1966.

Fanshel, D. "Computerized information systems and foster care: The New York City experience with CWIS." *Children Today,* 44 (1976), 14–18.

Ferrari, N. A. "Freedom of choice." *Social Work,* 8 (1963), 104–106.

Fischer, J. *The Effectiveness of Social Casework.* Springfield, Ill.: Charles C Thomas, 1976.

Fischer, J. "Does anything work?" *Journal of Social Service Research,* 1 (1978), 215–243.

Fischer, J., and Hudson, W. "An effect of casework? Back to the drawing board." *Social Work* (September 1976), 347–349.

Fraser, D. W., and McDade, J. E. "Legionellosis." *Scientific American* 241:4 (1979), 82–101.

Garfield, S. L. "Effectiveness of psychotherapy: The perennial controversy." *Professional Psychology: Research and Practice,* 14:1 (1983), 35–43.

Garfinkel, H. "Studies of the routine grounds of everyday activities." *Social Problems,* 11 (1964), 225–250.

Gartner, A., and Riessman, F. *Help: A Working Guide to Self-Help Groups.* New York: New Viewpoints/Vision Books, 1980.

383

Geismar, L. L. "Thirteen evaluative studies." In E. J. Mullen and J. R. Dumpson (eds.). *Evaluation of Social Intervention.* San Francisco: Jossey-Bass, 1972.

Germain, C. B. "Technological advances." In A. Rosenblatt and D. Waldfogel (eds.). *Handbook of Clinical Social Work.* San Francisco: Jossey-Bass, 1983.

Getzels, J. W., and Jackson, P. W. *Creativity and Intelligence: Explorations with Gifted Students.* New York: Wiley, 1962.

Gil, D. *Unravelling Social Policy.* Cambridge, Mass.: Schenkman, 1973.

Gingerich, W., and Feyerherm, W. "The celeration line technique for assessing client change." *Journal of Social Service Research,* 3:1 (1979), 99–113.

Glenwick, D., and Jason, L. (eds.). *Behavioral Community Psychology: Progress and Prospects.* New York: Praeger, 1980.

Goffman, E. *Asylums: Essays on the Social Situation of Mental Patients and Other Inmates.* Garden City, N.Y.: Doubleday, 1961.

Goffman, E. *Stigma: Notes on the Management of Spoiled Identity.* Englewood Cliffs, N.J.: Prentice-Hall, 1963.

Goffman, E. *Interaction Ritual.* New York: Anchor Books, Doubleday, 1967.

Goldfarb, A. I., Shahinian, S. P., and Turner, H. T. "Death rate in relocated aged residents of nursing homes." *The Gerontologist,* 6 (1966), 30.

Goplerud, E. N. "Unexpected consequences of deinstitutionalization of the mentally disabled elderly." *American Journal of Community Psychology,* 7 (1979), 315–328.

Gould, S. J. *The Mismeasure of Man.* New York: Norton, 1981.

Grahame, K. *Wind in the Willows.* New York: Viking Press, 1983. (Originally published, 1908.)

Grannis, G. F. "Demographic perturbations secondary to cigarette smoking." *Journal of Gerontology,* 25:1 (1970), 55–63.

Grinnell, R. M., Jr. (ed.). *Social Work Research and Evaluation.* Itasca, Ill.: F. E. Peacock, 1981.

Gurman, A. S. "The effects and effectiveness of marital therapy: A review of outcome research." *Family Process,* 12 (1973), 145–170.

Gurman, A. S., and Kniskern, D. "The outcome of family therapy." In A. Gurman and D. Kniskern (eds.), *Handbook of Family Therapy.* New York: Brunner/Mazel, 1981.

Gutman, G. N., and Hebert, C. P. "Mortality rates among relocated extended care patients." *Journal of Gerontology,* 31 (1976), 352–357.

Guttman, L. "A basis for scaling qualitative data." *American Sociological Review,* 9 (1944), 139–150.

Heider, F. *The Psychology of Interpersonal Relations.* New York: Wiley, 1958.

Heitler, J. B. "Preparatory techniques in the initiating expressive psychotherapy with lower-class, unsophisticated patients." *Psychological Bulletin,* 83:2 (1976), 339–352.

Hersen, M., and Barlow, D. H. *Single Case Experimental Designs: Strategies for Studying Behavior Change.* New York: Pergamon, 1976.

Hill, R. *The Strengths of Black Families.* New York: The National Urban League, 1971.

Hilts, P. J. "Probe finds kickbacks on pacemakers." *Washington Post* (September 5, 1982), A1, A18.

Hollister, W. "The concept of strens in education: A challenge to curriculum development." In E. Bower and W. Hollister (eds.). *Behavioral Sciences Foundations in Education.* New York: Wiley, 1967.

Holmes, T. H., and Rahe, R. H. "The social readjustment scale." *Journal of Psychosomatic Research,* 11 (1967), 213–218.

Horowitz, M. J., and Schulz, R. "The relocation controversy: Criticism and commentary on five recent studies." *The Gerontologist,* 23:3 (1983), 229–233.

Hudson, W. W. *The Clinical Measurement Package: A Field Manual.* Homewood, Ill.: Dorsey Press, 1982.

Jasnau, K. F. "Individualized versus mass transfer of nonpsychotic geriatric patients from mental hospitals to nursing homes, with special reference to death rates." *Journal of the American Geriatric Society,* 15 (1967), 280–284.

Jayaratne, S. "Analytic procedures for single-subject designs." *Social Work Research and Abstracts,* 14:4 (1978), 30–40.

Jayaratne, S., and Levy, R. I. *Empirical Clinical Practice.* New York: Columbia University Press, 1979.

Johnson, E. S., and Williamson, J. B. *Growing Old: The Social Problems of Aging.* New York: Holt, Rinehart and Winston, 1980.

Kahn, R. L., Pollack, M., and Goldfarb, A. "Factors related to individual differences in mental status of institutionalized aged." In P. H. Hoch and J. Zubin (eds.). *Psychopathology of Aging.* New York: Grune & Stratton, 1961.

Karp, S. A. "Field dependence and aging." *Research Reports* (Sinai Hospital of Baltimore), 1 (1966), 1–9.

Kasl, S. V. "Physical and mental health effects of involuntary relocation and institutionalization on the elderly: A review." *American Journal of Public Health,* 62 (1972), 377–384.

Kasl, S. V., and Rosenfield, S. "The residential environment and its impact on mental health." In J. E. Birren and R. B. Sloan (eds.). *Handbook of Mental Health and Aging.* Englewood Cliffs, N.J.: Prentice-Hall, 1980.

Katz, L., and Crook, G. H. "Use of the Kent E-G-Y with an aged population." *Journal of Gerontology,* 17:2 (1962), 186–189.

Katz, S., Ford, A. B., Downs, T. D., Adams, M., and Rusby, D. I. *Effects of Continued Care: A Study of Chronic Illness in the Home.* Washington, D.C.: Department of Health, Education, and Welfare, 1972.

Kay, D., Norris, V., and Post, F. "Prognosis in psychiatric disorders of the aged." *Journal of Mental Science,* 102 (1956), 129–140.

Kazdin, A. E., and Wilson, G. T. *Evaluation of Behavior Therapy: Issues, Evidence, and Research Studies.* Cambridge, Mass.: Ballinger, 1978.

Keller, E. F. *A Feeling for the Organism: The Life and Work of Barbara McClintock.* New York: W. H. Freeman, 1983.

Kelly, G. A. *A Theory of Personality: The Psychology of Personal Constructs.* New York: Norton, 1955.

Kelman, H. C., and Warwick, D. P. (eds.). *The Ethics of Social Intervention.* Washington, D.C.: Hemispheric Publishing, 1978.

Kennedy, M. M. "Generalizing from single case studies." *Evaluation Quarterly,* 3:4 (1979), 661–678.

Kent, G. A. *Series of Emergency Scales Manual.* New York: Psychological Corporation, 1946.

Killian, E. C. "Effects of geriatric transfers on mortality rates." *Social Work,* 15 (1970), 19–26.

Kiresuk, T. J., and Garwick, G. "Basic goal attainment scaling procedures." In B. R. Compton and B. Gallaway (eds.). *Social Work Processes,* rev. ed. Homewood, Ill.: Dorsey Press, 1979.

Kleinman, A. "Clinical relevance of anthropological and cross-cultural research: Concepts and strategies." *American Journal of Psychiatry,* 135:4 (1978), 427–431.

Kleinmuntz, B. (ed.). *Clinical Information Processing by Computer.* New York: Holt, Rinehart & Winston, 1969.

Kolberg, L. "Stage and sequence: The cognitive-developmental approach to socialization." In D. A. Goslin (ed.). *Handbook of Socialization Theory and Research.* Chicago: Rand McNally, 1969.

Kowalski, N. C. "Fire at a home for the aged: A study of short-term mortality following disloaction of elderly residents." *Journal of Gerontology,* 33 (1978), 601–602.

385

Kowalski, N. C. "Institutional relocation: Current programs and applied approaches." *The Gerontologist,* 21 (1981), 512–519.

Kratochwill, T. R. (ed.). *Single Subject Research: Strategies for Evaluating Change.* New York: Academic Press, 1978.

Kutner, B., et al. *Five Hundred Over Sixty: A Community Survey of Aging.* New York: Russell Sage Foundation, 1956.

Lawton, M. P. "Morale: What are we measuring?" In C. N. Nydegger (ed.). *Measuring Morale: A Guide to Effective Assessment.* Washington, D.C.: Gerontological Society, Special Publication No. 3, 1977.

Lawton, M. P., and Yaffe, S. "Mortality, morbidity, and voluntary change of residence by older people." *Journal of the American Geriatric Society,* 18 (1970), 823–831.

Lehmann, V., and Mathiasen, G. *Guardianship and Protective Service for Older People.* New York: National Council on the Aging Press, 1963.

Levin, G., Hirsch, G., and Roberts, E. "Narcotics and the community: A systems simulation." *American Journal of Public Health,* 62:6 (1972), 861–873.

Levitt, J. L., and Reid, W. J. "Rapid-assessment instruments for practice." *Social Work Research and Abstracts,* 17 (1981), 13–20.

Lieberman, M. A. "Relationship of mortality rates to entrance to a home for the aged." *Geriatrics,* 16 (1961), 515–519.

Lieberman, M. A. "Relocation research and social policy." *The Gerontologist,* 14 (1974), 494–501.

Locke, J. "An essay concerning human understanding." In E. A. Burtt (ed.). *The English Philosophers from Bacon to Mill.* New York: Modern Library, 1939.

Loether, H. J., and McTavish, D. G. *Descriptive and Inferential Statistics: An Introduction,* 2nd edition. Boston: Allyn & Bacon, 1980.

Luborsky, L., Singer, B., and Luborsky, L. "Comparative studies of psychotherapies: It is true that "Everyone has won and all must have prizes?" *Archives of General Psychiatry,* 32 (1975), 995–1007.

Lystad, M. H. "Violence at home: A review of the literature." *American Journal of Orthopsychiatry,* 45:3 (1975), 328–435.

MacMahon, B., and Pugh, T. F. *Epidemiology: Principles and Methods.* Boston: Little, Brown, 1970.

MacMahon, B., Pugh, T. F., and Ipsen, J. *Epidemiological Methods.* Boston: Little, Brown, 1960.

Maluccio, A. N. *Promoting Competence in Clients: A New/Old Approach to Social Work Practice.* New York: Free Press, 1981.

Markson, E. W., and Cumming, J. H. "A strategy of necessary mass transfer and its impact on patient mortality." *Journal of Gerontology,* 29 (1974), 315–321.

Markus, E., Blenkner, M., Bloom, M., and Downs, T. "Relocation stress and the aged." In H. T. Blumenthal (ed.). *Interdisciplinary Topics in Gerontology.* Basel, Switzerland: S. Karger, 1970.

Markus, E., Blenkner, M., Bloom, M., and Downs, T. "The impact of relocation upon mortality rates of institutionalized aged persons." *Journal of Gerontology,* 26 (1971), 537–541.

Markus, E., Blenkner, M., Bloom, M., and Downs, T. "Some factors and their association with post-relocation mortality among institutionalized aged persons." *Journal of Gerontology,* 27 (1972), 376–382.

Maslach, C., and Jackson, S. E. "The measurement of experienced burnout." *Journal of Occupational Behavior,* 2:2 (1981), 99–113.

Mausner, J. S., and Bahn, A. K. *Epidemiology: An Introductory Text.* Philadelphia: W. B. Saunders, 1974.

Meenaghan, T. M., and Washington, R. O. *Social Policy and Social Welfare: Structure and Applications.* New York: Free Press, 1980.

Meltzoff, J., and Kornreich, M. *Research in Psychotherapy.* New York: Atherton Press, 1970.

Meyer, R., Weber, R., and Blenkner, M. The BRI Clinical Rating Scales: A Manual. Cleveland: Benjamin Rose Institute, 1966 (mimeo).

Miller, D., and Lieberman, M. A. "The relationship of affect state and adaptive capacity to reactions to stress." *Journal of Gerontology,* 20 (1965), 492–497.

Moynihan, D. P. *The Negro Family: The Case for National Action.* Washington, D.C.: Department of Labor, 1965.

Mullen, E. J., and Dumpson, J. R. (eds.). *Evaluation of Social Intervention.* San Francisco: Jossey-Bass, 1972.

Mutschler, E. Computers. *1983–1984 Supplement to the Encyclopedia of Social Work,* 17th edition. Silver Spring, Md.: National Association of Social Workers, 1983.

Mutschler, E., and Hasenfeld, Y. "Computer assisted decision making in social service agencies." Paper presented to the 1983 NASW Professional Symposium, Washington, D.C., 1983.

Nelson, J. C. "Use of communication theory in single-subject research." *Social Work Research and Abstracts,* 14:4 (1978), 12–19.

Newkham, J., and Bawcom, L. "Computerizing an integrated clinical and financial record system in a CMHC: A pilot project." *Administration in Social Work,* 5 (1981), 97–111.

Nicholls, J. G. "Creativity in the person who will never produce anything original and useful: The concept of creativity as a normally distributed trait." *American Psychologist,* 27:8 (1972), 717–727.

Nie, N., Hull, C. H., Jenkins, J. G., Steinbrenner, K., and Bent, D. H. *Statistical Package for the Social Sciences,* 2nd edition. New York: McGraw-Hill, 1979.

Nielsen, M., Blenkner, M., Bloom, M., Downs, T., and Beggs, H. "Older persons after hospitalization: A controlled study of home aide service." *American Journal of Public Health,* 62:8 (1972), 1094–1101.

Novick, L. J. "Easing the stress of moving day." *Hospitals,* 41 (1967), 64, 69–70, 72, 74.

Orgren, E. N., and Linn, M. W. "Male nursing home patients: Relocation and mortality." *Journal of American Geriatric Society,* 19 (1971), 229–239.

Orwell, G. *1984.* New York: Harcourt, Brace & Company, 1949.

Osborn, A. *Applied Imagination.* New York: Scribner's Sons, 1953.

Pablo, R. Y. "Intra-institutional relocation: Its impact on long-term care patients." *The Gerontologist,* 17 (1977), 426–433.

Parloff, M. B. "Psychotherapy and Research: An anaclitic depression." *Psychiatry,* 1980, 43:4, 279–293.

Parloff, M. B., Waskow, I. E., and Wolfe, B. E. "Research or therapist variables in relation to process and outcome." In S. L. Garfield and A. E. Bergin (eds.). *Handbook of Psychotherapy and Behavior Change,* 2nd edition. New York: Wiley, 1978.

Patnaik, B., Lawton, M. P., Kleban, M. M., and Maxwell, R. "Behavioral adaptation to the change in institutional residence." *The Gerontologist,* 18 (1974), 167–172.

Pelz, D. C. "Environments for creative performance within universities." Paper presented at the conference on Cognitive Styles and Creativity in Higher Education, Montreal, November 1972.

Pelz, D. C., and Andrews, F. M. *Scientists in Organizations: Productive Climates for Research and Development.* New York: Wiley, 1966.

387

Piliavin, I. M., Rodin, J., and Piliavin, I. M. "Good samaritanism: An underground phenomenon." *Journal of Personality and Social Psychology,* 32 (1975), 429–438.

Piven, F. F., and Cloward, R. A. *Regulating the Poor: The Function of Public Welfare.* New York: Pantheon, 1971.

Popper, K. R. *The Logic of Scientific Discovery.* London: Hutchinson, 1959.

Rachman, S. J., and Wilson, G. T. *The Effects of Psychological Therapy,* 2nd edition. New York: Pergamon, 1980.

Rahe, R. H. "Life crisis and health change." In P. R. A. May and J. R. Wittenborn (eds.). *Psychotropic Drug Response: Advances in Prediction.* Springfield, Ill.: Charles C Thomas, 1969.

Reid, W. J., and Hanrahan, P. "Recent evaluations of social work: Grounds for optimism." *Social Work,* 27:4 (1982), 328–340.

Reid, W. J., and Shyne, A. *Brief and Extended Casework.* New York: Columbia University Press, 1969.

Richter, C. "The phenomenon of unexplained sudden death in animals and man." In H. Feifel (ed.). *The Meaning of Death.* New York: McGraw-Hill, 1959.

Robinson, J. P., and Shaver, P. R. *Measurements of Social Psychological Attitudes,* rev. ed. Ann Arbor: Institute for Social Research, University of Michigan, 1973.

Rosenblatt, A., and Waldfogel, D. (eds.). *Handbook of Clinical Social Work.* San Francisco: Jossey-Bass, 1983.

Rosenhan, D. L. "On being sane in insane places." *Science,* 179 (1973), 250–258.

Roth, M. "Natural history of mental disorder in old age." *Journal of Mental Science,* 101 (1955), 281–301.

Rothenberg, A. "Einstein's creative thinking and the general theory of relativity: A documented report." *American Journal of Psychiatry,* 136:1 (1979), 38–43.

Rowland, K. F. "Environmental events predicting death for the elderly." *Psychological Bulletin,* 84 (1977), 349–372.

Sanders, D. H. *Computers in Society: An Introduction to Information Processing.* New York: McGraw-Hill, 1973.

Schinke, S. P. "Ethics." In R. M. Grinnell (ed.). *Social Work Research and Evaluation.* Itasca, Ill.: F. E. Peacock, 1981.

Schulz, R., and Brenner, G. "Relocation of the aged: A review and theoretical analysis." *Journal of Gerontology,* 32 (1977), 323–333.

Schwartz, D. W., and Karp, S. A. "Field dependence in a geriatric population." *Perceptual and Motor Skills,* 24 (1967), 495–504.

Seaberg, J. R. "Case recording by code." *Social Work,* 10 (1965), 92–98.

Seaberg, J. R. "Systematized recording: A follow-up." *Social Work,* 15 (1970), 32–41.

Segal, J., Boomer, D. S., and Bouthilet, L. (eds.). *Research in the Service of Mental Health: Report of the Research Task Force of the National Institute of Mental Health.* Rockville, Md. 1975.

Shanas, E. *The Health of Older People: A Social Survey.* Cambridge: Harvard University Press, 1962.

Shapiro, A. K., and Morris, L. A. "The placebo effect in medical and psychological therapies." In S. L. Garfield and A. E. Bergin (eds.). *Handbook of Psychotherapy and Behavior Change,* 2nd edition. New York: Wiley, 1978.

Siegel, S. *Nonparametric Statistics for the Behavioral Sicences.* New York: McGraw-Hill, 1956.

Silverman, L. H. "Psychoanalytic theory: 'Reports of my death are greatly exaggerated.'" *American Psychologist* (September 1976), 621–637.

Silverstone, B. M., and Kirschner, C. "Elderly residents' reaction to enforced relocation during a hospital strike." *The Gerontologist* 14 (1974), 71 (abstract).

Smith, M. L., and Glass, G. V. "Meta-analysis of psychotherapy outcome studies." *American Psychologist,* 32 (1977), 752–760.

Smith, M. L., Glass, G. V., and Miller, T. I. *The Benefits of Psychotherapy.* Baltimore: Johns Hopkins University Press, 1980.

Smith, R. T., and Brand, F. N. "Effects of enforced relocation on life adjustment in a nursing home." *International Journal of Aging and Human Development,* 6 (1975), 249–259.

Spark, M. *Memento Mori.* New York: Putnam, 1982.

Spitzer, R. L. "On pseudoscience in science, logic in remission, and psychiatric diagnosis: A critique of Rosenhan's "On being sane in insane places." *Journal of Abnormal Psychology,* 84:5 (1975), 442–452.

Spivack, G., and Shure, M. B. *The Social Adjustment of Young Children: A Cognitive Approach to Solving Real-Life Problems.* San Francisco: Jossey-Bass, 1974.

Stevens, S. S. "Mathematics, measurement, and psychophysics." In S. S. Stevens (ed.). *Handbook of Experimental Psychology.* New York: Wiley, 1951.

Stevens, S. S. "A metric for the social consensus." *Science,* 151:3710 (1966), 530–541.

Stotsky, B. A. "A controlled study of factors in the successful adjustment of mental patients to nursing homes." *American Journal of Psychiatry,* 123 (1967), 1243–1251.

Stuart, R. B. *Trick or Treatment: How and When Psychotherapy Fails.* Champaign, Ill.: Research Press, 1970.

Susser, M. *Causal Thinking in the Health Sciences: Concepts and Strategies in Epidemiology.* New York: Oxford, 1973.

Szasz, T. S. *The Myth of Mental Illness.* New York: Hoeber-Harper, 1961.

Tapp, J. L., Gunnar, M., and Keating, D. "Socialization: Three ages, three rule systems." In D. Perlman and P. C. Cozby (eds.). *Social Psychology.* New York: Holt, Rinehart and Winston, 1983.

Tapp, J. L., and Kohlberg, L. "Developing senses of law and legal justice." In J. L. Tapp and F. J. Levine (eds.). *Law, Justice, and the Individual in Society: Psychological and Legal Issues.* New York: Holt, Rinehart and Winston, 1977.

Thomas, E. J. "Uses of research methods in interpersonal practice." In N. A. Polansky (ed.). *Social Work Research,* rev. ed. Chicago: University of Chicago Press, 1975.

Thomas, E. J. "Research and service in single-case experimentation: Conflicts and choices." *Social Work Research and Abstracts,* 14 (1978), 20–31.

Tibbitts, C. *Aging in the Modern World: A Book of Readings.* Ann Arbor: University of Michigan Press, 1957.

Toffler, A. *The Third Wave.* Toronto: Bantam Books, 1980.

Toward a Social Report. Washington, D.C.: U.S. Department of Health, Education, and Welfare, 1969.

Tymchuk, A. J. "Ethical decision making and psychological treatment." *Journal of Psychiatric Treatment and Evaluation,* 3 (1981), 507–513.

United States Supreme Court Reports, 447 (1980), 773–804.

Wagner, D., and Osmalov, M. J. The Impact of Social Casework on the Elderly: A Reappraisal of the Controversy Surrounding the Benjamin Rose Institute's Protective Services Study. Madison: School of Social Work, University of Wisconsin-Madison, 1978 (mimeo).

Waldron, I. "Why do women live longer than men?" *Journal of Human Stress,* 2 (Part 1), (1976), 2–13.

Wasser, E. "Responsibility, self-determination, and authority in casework protection of older persons." *Social Casework* (May–June 1961).

Wasser, E. "Protective practice in serving the mentally impaired aged." *Social Casework,* 52:8 (1971), 510–522.

Wasser, E. Protective Casework Practice with Older People. Cleveland: Benjamin Rose Institute, 1974 (mimeo).

389

Watson, C. G., and Buerkle, H. R. "Involuntary transfer as a cause of medical hospitalization in geriatric neuropsychiatric patients." *Journal of the American Geriatric Society,* 24 (1976), 278–282.

Watson, W. H. "A case study of black aging and transplantation shock." In W. H. Watson (ed.). *Stress and Old Age.* New Brunswick, N.J.: Transaction Books, 1980.

Watts, T. D. "Ethnomethodology." In R. M. Grinnell (ed.). *Social Work Research and Evaluation.* Itasca, Ill.: F. E. Peacock, 1981.

Webb, E. J., Campbell, D. T., Schwartz, R. D., and Sechrest, L. *Unobtrusive Measures: Nonreactive Research in the Social Sciences.* Chicago: Rand McNally, 1966.

Webb, E. J., Campbell, D. T., Schwartz, R. D., Sechrest, L., and Grove, J. B. *Nonreactive Measures in the Social Sciences,* 2nd edition. Boston: Houghton-Mifflin, 1981.

Weber, M. *The Methodology of the Social Sciences.* Glencoe, Ill.: Free Press, 1949.

Weber, R. E. Older Persons in Need of Protective Services Encountered by Thirteen Selected Cleveland Agencies in March 1964: A Survey. Cleveland: Benjamin Rose Institute, 1964 (mimeo).

Weiss, C. H. *Evaluation Research: Methods of Assessing Program Effectiveness.* Englewood Cliffs, N.J.: Prentice-Hall, 1972.

Weizenbaum, J. *Computer Power and Human Reason: From Judgment to Calculation.* San Francisco: W. H. Freeman, 1976.

Wells, L., and MacDonald, G. "Interpersonal networks and post-relocation adjustment of the institutionalized elderly." *The Gerontologist,* 21 (1981), 177–183.

White, O. R. "The 'split middle'—A 'quickie' method of trend estimation." Experimental Education Unit, Child Development and Mental Retardation Center, University of Washington, 1974.

White, O. R. "Data-based instruction: Evaluating educational progress." In J. D. Cone and R. P. Hawkins (eds.). *Behavioral Assessments: New Directions in Clinical Psychology.* New York: Brunner/Mazel, 1977.

Whittier, J., and Williams, D. "The coincidence and constancy of mortality figures for aged psychiatric patients admitted to state hospitals." *Journal of Nervous and Mental Diseases,* 124 (1956), 618–620.

Witkin, H. A., Dyke, R. B., Faterson, H. F., Goodenough, D. R., and Karp, S. A. *Psychological Differentiation.* New York: Wiley, 1962.

Witkin, H. A., Lewis, H. B., Hertzman, M., Machover, K., Meissner, P. B., and Wapner, S. *Personality Through Perception.* New York: Harper, 1954.

Wittels, I., and Botwinick, J. "Survival in relocation." *Journal of Gerontology,* 29 (1974), 440–443.

Wood, K. M. "Casework effectiveness: A new look at the research evidence." *Social Work,* 23 (1978), 437–458.

Wright, R. L. D. *Understanding Statistics: An Informal Introduction for the Behavioral Sciences.* Orlando: Harcourt Brace Jovanovich, 1976.

Yawney, B. A., and Slover, D. L. "Relocation of the elderly." *Social Work,* 18 (1973), 86–95.

Zimbalist, S. E. *Historic Themes and Landmarks in Social Welfare Research.* New York: Harper & Row, 1977.

Zung, W. W. K. "A self-rating depression scale." *Archives of General Psychiatry,* 12 (1965), 63–70.

Zweig, J. P., and Csank, J. Z. "Effects of relocation on chronically ill geriatric patients of a medical unit: Mortality rates." *Journal of the American Geriatrics Society,* 23 (1975), 132–136.

Zweig, J. P., and Csank, J. Z. "Mortality fluctuations among chronically ill medical geriatric patients as an indicator of stress before and after relocation." *Journal of the American Geriatrics Society,* 24 (1976), 264–277.

Author Index

393

Subject Index

* Technical Notes (T.N.) are indicated by number and page, and their titles are italicized.

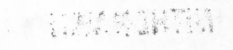